3e

Organizational Change

This book is dedicated to our partners: Heather, Bertha, and Steve.

3e

Organizational Change

AN ACTION–ORIENTED TOOLKIT

Tupper F. Cawsey
Wilfrid Laurier University

Gene Deszca
Wilfrid Laurier University

Cynthia Ingols
Simmons College

Los Angeles | London | New Delhi
Singapore | Washington DC | Boston

Los Angeles | London | New Delhi
Singapore | Washington DC | Boston

FOR INFORMATION:

SAGE Publications, Inc.
2455 Teller Road
Thousand Oaks, California 91320
E-mail: order@sagepub.com

SAGE Publications Ltd.
1 Oliver's Yard
55 City Road
London EC1Y 1SP
United Kingdom

SAGE Publications India Pvt. Ltd.
B 1/I 1 Mohan Cooperative Industrial Area
Mathura Road, New Delhi 110 044
India

SAGE Publications Asia-Pacific Pte. Ltd.
3 Church Street
#10-04 Samsung Hub
Singapore 049483

Acquisitions Editor: Maggie Stanley
Associate Editor: Abbie Rickard
Editorial Assistant: Nicole Mangona
eLearning editor: Katie Bierach
Production Editor: Libby Larson
Copy Editor: Terri Lee Paulsen
Typesetter: C&M Digitals (P) Ltd.
Proofreader: Bonnie Moore
Indexer: Will Ragsdale
Cover Designer: Michael Dubowe
Marketing Manager: Liz Thornton

Printed in the United States of America

Library of Congress Cataloging-in-Publication Data

Cawsey, T. F.
Organizational change : an action-oriented toolkit / Tupper F. Cawsey, Gene Deszca, Cynthia Ingols. — Third edition.

pages cm
Includes index.

ISBN 978-1-4833-5930-4 (pbk. : alk. paper)
1. Organizational change. I. Deszca, Gene. II. Ingols, Cynthia. III. Title.

HD58.8.C39 2016
658.4′06—dc23   2015006458

This book is printed on acid-free paper.

18 19 10 9 8 7 6 5

Brief Contents

Detailed Contents

Preface

Since the publishing of the second edition of this text, the world has continued to churn in very challenging ways. Uneven and shifting global patterns of growth, sluggish Western economies, continuing fallout from the financial crisis, stubbornly high unemployment levels in much of the world, and heightened global uncertainty in matters related to health, safety, and security define the terrain. Their consequences continue to unfold. The massive credit crisis was followed by unprecedented worldwide government stimulus spending, followed by sovereign debt crises, followed by . . . ??? Wars and insurrections in parts of Africa, the Ukraine, and much of the Middle East; deteriorating international relationships involving major powers; fears of global pandemics (Ebola and MERS); and the rise of ISIS and Boko Haram and their unprecedented inhumanity have shaken all organizations, big or small, public or private. They have also made us, your authors, much more aware of the extreme influence of the external environment on the internal workings of an organization. As we point out in our book, even the smallest of firms have to adapt when banks refuse them normal credit, and even the largest and most successful of firms have to learn how to adapt when disruptive technologies or rapid social and political changes alter their realities.

Our models have always included and often started with events external to the organization. We have always argued that change leaders need to scan their environments and be aware of trends and crises in those environments. The events of the past two years have reinforced our sense of this even more. Managers must be sensitive to what happens around them, know how to make sense of this, and then have the skills and abilities that will allow them to both react effectively to the internal and external challenges *and* remain constant in their visions and dreams of how to make their organizations and the world a better place to live.

A corollary of this is that organizations need a response capability that is unprecedented, because we're playing on a global stage of increasing complexity and uncertainty. If you are a bank, you need a capital ratio that would have been unprecedented a few years ago. If you are a major organization, you need to build in flexibility into your structures, policies, and plans. If you are a public sector organization, you need to be sensitive to how capricious granting agencies or funders will be when revenues dry up. In today's world, organizational resilience and adaptability gain new prominence.

Further, we are faced with a continuing reality that change is endemic. All managers are change managers. All good managers are change leaders. The management job involves creating, anticipating, encouraging, engaging others, and responding positively to change. This has been a theme of this book which continues. Change management is for everyone. Change management emerges from the bottom and middle of the organization as much as from the top. It will be those key leaders who are embedded in the organization who will enable the needed adaptation of the organization to its environment. **Middle managers need to be key change leaders.**

In addition to the above, we have used feedback on the second edition to strengthen the pragmatic orientation that we had developed. The major themes of action orientation, analysis tied with doing, the management of a nonlinear world, and the bridging of the "Knowing–Doing" gap continue to be central. At the same time, we have tried to shift to a more user-friendly, action perspective. To make the material more accessible to a diversity of readers, some theoretical material has been altered, some of our models have been clarified and simplified, and some of our language and formatting has been modified.

As we stated in the preface to the first edition, our motivation for this book was to fill a gap we saw in the marketplace. Our challenge was to develop a book that not only gave prescriptive advice, "how-to-do-it lists," but one that also provided up-to-date theory without getting sidetracked by academic theoretical complexities. We hope that we have captured the management experience with change so that our manuscript assists all those who must deal with change, not just senior executives or organizational development specialists. Although there is much in this book for the senior executive and organizational development specialist, our intent was to create a book that would be valuable to a broad cross section of the workforce.

Our personal beliefs form the basis for the book. Even as academics, we have a bias for action. We believe that "doing is healthy." Taking action creates influence and demands responses from others. While we believe in the need for excellent analysis, we know that action itself provides opportunities for feedback and learning that can improve the action. Finally, we have a strong belief in the worth of people. In particular, we believe that one of the greatest sources of improvement is the untapped potential to be found in the people of the organization.

We recognize that this book is not an easy read. It is not meant to be. It is meant as a serious text for those involved in change—that is, all managers! We hope you find it a book that you will want to keep and pull from your shelf in the years ahead, when you need to lead change and you want help thinking it through.

Your authors,

Tupper, Gene, and Cynthia

Acknowledgments

W e would like to acknowledge the many people who have helped to make this book possible. Our students and their reactions to the ideas and materials continue to be a source of inspiration. Cynthia's Leadership and Organizational Change course, spring 2014, included Mshael Alessa, Daniella Comito, Katrice Krumplys, Jill Peterson, and other students who applied the concepts in this book and made a difference through their change projects at Simmons College.

Managers, executives, and frontline employees that we have known have provided insights, case examples, and applications while keeping us focused on what is useful and relevant. Ellen Zane, former CEO of Tufts Medical Center, Boston, is an inspiring change leader; her turnaround story at Tufts Medical Center appeared in the second edition of this book and is published again in this third edition. Cynthia has also been fortunate to work with and learn from Gretchen Fox, founder and former CEO, FOX Relocation Management Corporation. The story of how she changed her small firm appeared in the second edition of the book and the case continues to be available through Harvard Business Publishing (http://hbr.org/product/fox-relocation-management-corp/an/NA0096-PDF-ENG).   Katharine Schmidt, a former student of Gene's and the CEO of Food Banks Canada, is another of the inspiring leaders who opened her organization to us and allowed us to learn from their experience, and share it with you in this edition.

Several colleagues have provided guidance and feedback along the way that have helped us test our logic and develop our thinking and writing. Cynthia would like to especially thank Professor Mary Shapiro, a colleague at the School of Management, Simmons College, who read each chapter thoroughly and gave insightful feedback on the manuscript. Dr. Paul Myers, consultant, Boulder, CO, read Chapters 2 and 3 with a fine-tooth comb and gave us astute criticism, allowing us—paradoxically—to both simplify and add complexity to those chapters.

Our research assistants have provided valuable support. John Schappert and Charles Newell assisted with the search for relevant research articles, reports of change initiatives, and websites of interest.

We owe a HUGE THANKS to Paige Tobie. She searched for articles and web-based materials, participated in our conference calls, made sure ideas and changes didn't get lost, and kept us on track, on time, and working with the right versions

xviii ORGANIZATIONAL CHANGE

of the manuscript. She provided valuable input on drafts of the manuscript from a student/practitioner's perspective, and then read the entire manuscript one last time, catching problematic areas. She did all these tasks while retaining her sense of humor and remaining a pleasure to work with. Thank you so very much, Paige: You have been a wonderful project manager, researcher, and colleague!

As with the last edition, our partners Heather Cawsey, Bertha Welzel, and Steve Spitz tolerated our moods, our myopia to other things that needed doing, and the early mornings and late nights spent on the manuscript. They helped us work our way through ideas and sections that were problematic, and they kept us smiling and grounded when frustration mounted.

Our editors at SAGE have been excellent. They moved the project along and made a difficult process fun (well, most of the time). Thank you, Maggie Stanley, our acquisitions editor, for keeping us on task and on time (or trying to keep us on time . . .). We appreciate your style of gentle nudges. Nicole Mangona, editorial assistant, was constantly on top of the various parts of the book and helped us push through to the end.

Finally, we would like to recognize the reviewers who provided us with valuable feedback on the second edition. Their constructive, positive feedback and their excellent suggestions were valued. We thought carefully about how to incorporate their suggestions into this third edition of the book. Thank you, Jeff Zimmerman, Northern Kentucky University; Lorraine M. Henderson, Nazareth College of Rochester; Ross A. Wirth, Franklin University; Ericka Kimball, Augsburg College; Whitney McIntyre Miller, Northern Kentucky University; Sandra R. Bryant, Tiffin University; John Anthony DiCicco, Curry College; and Paul M. Terry, University of South Florida. In short, our thanks to all who made this book possible.

CHAPTER 1

Changing Organizations in Our Complex World

It is not the strongest of the species that survive, nor the most intelligent, but the most responsive to change.

CHAPTER OVERVIEW

- The chapter defines organizational change as "planned alteration of organizational components to improve the effectiveness of organizations."
- The orientation of this book is to assist change managers or potential change leaders to be more effective in their change activities.
- The social, demographic, technological, political, and economic forces pushing the need for change are outlined.
- Four types of organizational change are discussed: tuning, adapting, reorienting, and re-creating.
- Four change roles found in organizations are described: change initiators, change implementers, change facilitators, and change recipients and stakeholders. The terms *change leader* and *change agent* are used interchangeably and could mean any of the four roles.
- The difficulties in creating successful change are highlighted, and then some of the characteristics of successful change leaders are described.

Organizations fill our world. We place our children into day care, seek out support services for our elderly, and consume information and recreational services supplied by other organizations. We work at for-profit or not-for-profit organizations. We rely on organizations to deliver the services we need: food, water, electricity, and sanitation and look to governmental organizations for a variety of services that we hope will keep us safe, secure, well governed, and successful. We depend on health organizations when we are sick. We use religious organizations to help our spiritual lives. We assume that most of our children's education will be delivered by formal educational organizations. In other words, organizations are everywhere. Organizations are how we get things done. This is not just a human phenomenon—it extends to plants and animals—look at a bee colony, a reef, a lion pride, or an elephant herd and you'll see organizations at work.

And these organizations are changing—some of them declining and failing, while others successfully adapt or evolve, to meet the shifting realities and demands of their environments. What exactly is organizational change? What do we mean when we talk about it?

Defining Organizational Change

When we think of organizational change, we think of major changes: mergers, acquisitions, buyouts, downsizing, restructuring, the launch of new products, and the outsourcing of major organizational activities. We can also think of lesser changes: departmental reorganizations, installations of new technology and incentive systems, shutting particular manufacturing lines, or opening new branches in other parts of the country—fine-tuning changes to improve the efficiency and operations of our organizations.

In this book, when we talk about **organizational change**, we refer to planned alterations of organizational components to improve the effectiveness of the organization. Organizational components are the organizational mission, vision, values, culture, strategy, goals, structure, processes or systems, technology, and people in an organization. When organizations enhance their effectiveness, they increase their ability to generate value for those they serve.*

The reasons for change are often ambiguous. Is the change internally or externally driven? In winter 2014, Tim Hortons (a Canada-based coffee restaurant chain) announced that it was aiming to open 1,000 new stores globally by 2018, joining their network of 3,468 outlets in Canada, 807 in the United States, and 29 in the Persian Gulf. It has also been busy revising its menu to shore up flattening same-store sales, adding Wi-Fi access, undertaking major store remodeling, and making changes to its sustainability and corporate social responsibility initiatives. What is driving these changes? The executives reported that they were undertaking these actions in response to competitive pressures, customer needs, market opportunities, and the desire to align their efforts with their values. For Tim Hortons, the drivers of change are coming from both the internal and external environment. Dunkin' Donuts, a much larger U.S. chain with similarities to Tim Hortons' business model and competitive pressures, seems to be pursuing similar adaptive

---

*Organizational change and organizational development are often seen as very similar. A discussion of the evolution of these concepts can be found in the preface.

responses.[1] It is essential for managers to be sensitive to what is happening inside and outside the organization, and adapt to those changes in the environment.[†]

Note that, by our definition and focus, organizational change is intentional and planned. Someone in the organization has taken an initiative to alter a significant organizational component. This means a shift in something relatively permanent. Usually, something formal or systemic has to be altered. For example, a new customer relations system may be introduced that captures customer satisfaction and reports it to managers; or a new division is created and people are allocated to that division in response to a new organizational vision.

Simply doing more of the same is not an organizational change. For example, increasing existing sales efforts in response to a competitor's activities would not be classified as an organizational change. However, the restructuring of a sales force into two groups (key account managers and general account managers) or the modification of service offerings would be, even though these changes could well be in response to a competitor's activities rather than a more proactive initiative.

Some organizational components, such as structures and systems, are concrete and thus easier to understand when contemplating change. For example, assembly lines can be reordered or have new technologies applied. The change is definable and the end point clear when it is done. Similarly, the alteration of a reward system or job design is concrete and can be documented. The creation of new positions, subunits, or departments is equally obvious. Such organizational changes are tangible and thus may be easier to make happen, because they are easier to understand.

When the change target is more deeply imbedded in the organization and is intangible, the change challenge is magnified. For example, a shift in organizational culture is difficult to engineer. A change leader can plan a change from an authoritarian to a more participative culture, but the initiatives required to bring about the change and the sequencing of those initiatives are trickier to get a hold of than more concrete change initiatives. Simply announcing a new strategy or vision does not mean that anything significant will change since: "You need to get the vision off the walls and into the halls."[2] A more manageable way to think of such a culture change is to identify concrete changes that reinforce the desired culture. If management alters reward systems, shifts decision making downward, and creates participative management committees, then management increases the likelihood that it will create cultural change over time. Sustained behavioral change occurs when people in the organization understand, accept, and act. Through their actions, the new vision or strategy becomes real.[3]

The target of change needs to be considered carefully. Often, managers choose concrete tangible changes because they are easiest to plan for and can be seen. For example, it is relatively easy to focus on pay and give monetary incentives in an attempt to address employee morale. But the root cause of these issues might be

---

[†]While we were completing the final draft of this book, Tim Hortons and Burger King announced their $12.5 billion merger on August 26, 2014, forming the third largest quick-service restaurant in the world. They will maintain these two distinct brands, but take advantage of synergies by leveraging their respective strengths and geographic reach. They announced their global headquarters will be in Canada. For details, see http://www.theglobeandmail.com/report-on-business/burger-king-tim-hortons-ink-merger-deal-for-125-billion/article20203522/.

managerial styles or processes—much more difficult to recognize and address. In addition, intervening through compensation may have unanticipated consequences and actually worsen the problem. An example of this can be found in the story below.

> ## CHANGE AT A SOCIAL SERVICE AGENCY
>
> In a mid-sized social service agency's family services division, turnover rates climbed to more than 20%, causing serious issues with service delivery and quality of service. The manager of the division argued that staff were leaving because of wages. According to him, children's aid societies' wages were higher and staff left to join those organizations. Upon investigation, senior management learned of morale problems arising from the directive, noninclusive management style of the manager. Instead of altering pay rates, which would have caused significant budgetary and equity problems throughout the organization, senior management replaced the manager and moved him to a project role. Within months, turnover rates dropped to less than 10% and the manager decided to leave the agency.[4]

In this example, if the original analysis had been accepted, turnover rates might have declined since staff may have been persuaded to stay for higher wages. But the agency would be facing monetary issues and would have had a festering morale problem.

The Orientation of This Book

The focus, then, of this book is on organizational change as a planned activity designed to improve the organization's effectiveness. Changes that are random (occur simply due to chance) or unplanned are not the types of organizational change that this book will explore, except, insofar, as they serve as the stimulus for planned change initiatives. Similarly, changes that may be planned but do not have a clear link to attempts to improve organizational effectiveness are not considered. That is, changes made solely for personal reasons—for personal gain, for example—fall outside the intended focus of this book.

> There is a story of two stonecutters. The first, when asked what he was doing, responded, "I am shaping this stone to fit in that wall." The second, however, said, "I am helping to build a cathedral."

The jobs of the two stonecutters might be the same, but their perspectives are dramatically different. The personal outcomes of satisfaction and organizational commitment will likely be much higher for the visionary stonecutter than for the "just doing my job" stonecutter. Finally, the differences in satisfaction and commitment may well lead to different organizational results. After all, if you are building a cathedral, you might be more motivated to stay late, to take extra care, to find ways to improve things, and to help others when help is needed.

In other words, the organizational member who has a broader perspective on the value of his or her contributions and on the task at hand is likely to be a more committed and capable contributor. As a result, we take a perspective that encourages change leaders to take a holistic perspective on the change and to be widely inclusive in letting employees know what changes are needed and are happening.

If employees have no sense of the intended vision and see themselves as "just doing a job," it is likely that any organizational change will be difficult to understand, be resisted, and cause personal trauma. On the other hand, if employees "get" the vision of the organization and understand the direction and perspective of where the organization is going and why, they are more likely to embrace their future role—even if that future means they leave the organization.[5]

This book is aimed at those who want to be involved in change and wish to take positive action. We encourage readers to escape from passive, negative change recipient positions and to move to more active and healthy roles—those of change initiators, facilitators, and implementers. Readers may be in middle-manager roles or may be students hoping to enter managerial roles. Or they may be leaders of change within an organization or a subunit. The book is also intended for the informal leaders in organizations who are driving change, sometimes in spite of their bosses. They might believe that their bosses "should" be driving the change but don't see it happening, and so they see it as up to them to make change happen regardless of the action or inaction of their managers.

This book has an action, "how to do it" emphasis. Nothing happens unless we, the people, make it happen. As one wag put it, "The truth is—the cavalry aren't coming!" There will be no cavalry charging over the hill to save us. It is up to us to make the changes needed. At the same time, this "how-to" orientation is paired with a focus on developing a deep understanding of organizations. Without such an understanding, what needs to be changed, and what the critical success factors are, change efforts will be much more difficult. This twin theme, of knowing both how to do it and what to do, underpins the structure of this book and our approach to change. To paraphrase Zig Ziglar: "It's not what happens to you that matters. It's how you respond that makes a difference."[6]

Change capability is a core managerial competence. Without skills in **change management**, individuals cannot operate effectively in today's fluctuating, shifting organizations.[7] Senior management may set the organizational direction, but, in this decentralized organizational world, it is up to managers and employees to shift the organization to accomplish the new goals and objectives. To do this, change-management skills are paramount. In many organizations, those managers are looked to for insights, innovative ideas, and initiatives that will make a positive difference in their firms. Investigate firms such as Google, the Mayo Clinic, Cisco, and others listed among the 100 best to work for here and offshore, and you will find many examples of firms embracing these practices.[8] They do so with a realistic appreciation for the fact that change management is often more difficult than we anticipate. We believe, as do Pfeffer and Sutton, that there is a Knowing–Doing gap.[9] Knowing the concepts and understanding the theory behind organizational change are not enough. This book is designed to provide practicing and prospective managers with the tools they will need to be effective change agents.

Environmental Forces Driving Change Today

Much change starts with shifts in an organization's environment. For example, government legislation dealing with employment law pushes new equity concerns through hiring practices. Globalization means that marketing, research and development, production, and other parts of an organization (e.g., customer service's call centers) can be moved around the world and/or outsourced. International alliances form and reform. These and related factors mean an organization's competition is often global in nature, rather than local. New technologies allow purchasing to link to production within an integrated supply chain, changing forever supplier–customer relationships. Concerns over global warming, sustainability, and environmental practices give rise to new laws, standards, and shifts in consumer preferences for products and firms that exhibit superior environmental performance. A competitor succeeds in attracting an organization's largest customer and upsets management's assumptions about the marketplace. Each of these external happenings will drive and push the need for change. These factors are summed up in the acronym PESTE. **PESTE factors** include political, economic, social, technological, and ecological/environmental factors that describe the environment or context of an organization.

These are not simply private sector realities. Not-for-profits, hospitals, schools, and governments all experience these environmental challenges as the world shrinks and the seeming pace of change accelerates and increases in complexity. Not-for-profits or NGOs (nongovernmental organizations) and various governmental bodies respond to hunger in war-torn Somalia and Syria, public universities and hospitals respond to for-profit competitors. Governments around the world deal with issues related to enhancing their economic competitiveness and attract employment, hopefully in sustainable and socially responsible ways. No one is immune.

Sometimes organizations are caught by surprise by environmental shifts, while other organizations have anticipated and planned for new situations. For example, management may have systems to track the perceived quality and value of its products versus its competition's. Benchmarking data might show that its quality is beginning to lag behind that of a key competitor or it might be instrumental in identifying product changes that can lead to market advantages. These environmental scanning and early warning systems allow for action before customers are lost or provide paths to new customers and/or new services. Toyota had such systems in place, but management appears to have responded inadequately.

DID TOYOTA OR GM KNOW ABOUT THE SAFETY DEFECTS?

Misreading the Environment and Associated Risks

On April 5, 2010, the U.S. government's transportation department stated it would seek $16.4 million from Toyota for not notifying the government about potential accelerator pedal problems. "In taking the step, federal authorities are sending the strongest signal yet that they believe the carmaker deliberately concealed safety information from them."[10]

(Continued)

Did Toyota know about these deficiencies and respond by denying they existed and covering up? If so, this is an example of an inappropriate organizational response to environmental stimuli.

The same question could be asked of General Motors concerning ignition switch problems in the Cobalt and other brands. By GM's admission, they first became aware of this problem in 2001. It was the subject of a technical service bulletin in 2005, but there was no recall until 2014, in the aftermath of multiple deaths and injuries, mounting public scrutiny, and lawsuits. The global recall totaled 2.6 million vehicles by May 2014, there have been humiliating U.S. congressional hearings, Mary Barra (GM's new CEO) has publically apologized, and GM is seeking immunity from the courts for lawsuits related to periods before its 2009 bankruptcy. To say this has the potential to undermine confidence in GM and its brand would be a gross understatement and points to the danger of failing to act and implement needed changes in a timely manner.[11]

It's beyond the scope of this book to provide an in-depth treatment of all of the various trends and alterations in the environment. However, we will highlight below some of the important trends to sensitize readers to their environments. As is always the case, organizations find themselves influenced by fundamental forces: changing social, cultural, and demographic patterns; spectacular technological achievements that transform how we do business; concerns about the physical environment and social responsibility that are producing demands for changes in our products and business practices; a global marketplace that sends us competing worldwide and brings competition to our doorsteps; political and legal forces that have the potential to transform the competitive landscape; continued political uncertainty in many countries that has the potential to introduce chaos into world markets; and the aftermath of the economic turmoil that rocked the world economy in 2008, 2009, and 2010.

THE RISKS OF EXCESSIVE PUSH FROM THE EXTERNAL ENVIRONMENT

The financial crisis of 2008 occurred because banks failed to comprehend the risks they took with asset-backed securities and other derivatives. Incentive systems drove bankers to take on excessive risks for excessive profits. They denied the evidence presented to them, and when the bubble burst, the results were catastrophic. For example, when warned by his chief risk officer, who proposed shutting down the mortgage business in 2004, the head of Lehman Brothers threatened to fire him! This rush for profits drove many banks. Chuck Prince, the head of Citigroup at the time, just before the credit markets seized up in August 2007, said: "As long as the music is playing, you've got to get up and dance. We're still dancing."[12]

Clearly both bankers misread the ethical and business implications of what was going on inside their firms. Either there was collective myopia at work with respect to mounting evidence of excessive risk from very credible sources[13] or the rewards and short-term performance pressures were such that they chose not to attend to the warning clouds.

The Changing Demographic, Social, and Cultural Environment

Age Matters. The social, cultural, and economic environment will be dramatically altered by demography. Demographic changes in the Western world and parts of Asia mean that aging populations will gray the face of Europe, Canada, China, and Japan.[14] The financial warning bells are already being sounded. Even before the huge government deficits of 2009 and beyond that Western nations have been digging themselves out from under, Standard & Poor's predicted that the average net government debt-to-GDP ratio for industrialized nations will increase from 33% in 2005 to 180% by 2050, due to rising pension and health care costs,[15] if changes are not undertaken.

Although the United States will age less quickly, Europe and Japan will face a dependency crisis of senior citizens requiring medical care and pension support. By 2050, the median age in the United States is projected to be 36.2 versus 52.7 in Europe. The United States will keep itself younger through immigration and a birth rate that is close to replacement level,[16] though even here growth assumptions have come under question as the rate of immigration has declined in the aftermath of the economic slowdown and questions around emigration policies remain highly politicized. Even with this influx, if nothing changes, Standard & Poor's estimates the U.S. governmental debt-to-GDP ratio will grow to 472% of GDP by 2050, due mainly to pension and health care costs.[17] Aging European countries will be around 300–400% of GDP, despite older populations, due to more cost-efficient approaches to these areas. On the high side, Japan is predicted to reach 729%. Europe's population is projected to peak in 2015 at around 400 million, while the United States passes that number in 2020 and continues to grow thereafter.

Throughout the world, fertility rates are falling and falling fast.[18] In 1974, only 24 countries had fertility rates below replacement levels. By 2009, more than 70

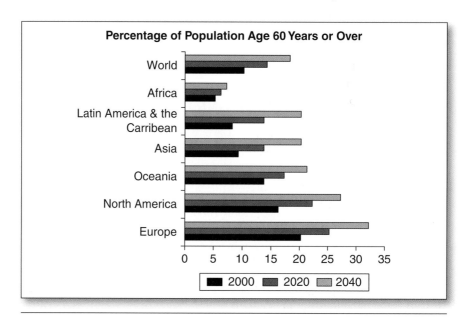

Source: U.N. Population Division.

countries had rates below 2.1. In some countries, the swings are dramatic. The fertility rate in Iran dropped from 7 in 1984 to 1.9 in 2009, a huge shift.

Some see a close tie between female education, fertility rates, and economic growth. When economies are poor, the fertility rate is high and there are many young dependents relying on working adults and older siblings for sustenance. When fertility rates drop, there is a bulge of people, meaning the ratio of working adults to dependents increases, leading to an increase in per capita wealth. Mexico and China are examples of this currently. When this bulge ages, dependent, non-working seniors become a larger percentage of the population, so these advantages tend to disappear over time, as incomes rise and fertility rates fall.[19] As discussed above, this has happened and is happening in Europe and Japan. India, Africa, and Mexico are examples of areas with a smaller proportion of dependents (the young and the old) relative to their working populations, and this is something referred to as an economic dividend. However, it is only a dividend if the population has the skills and abilities needed, and there is infrastructure and policies in place to support such employment—something many developing nations are finding very challenging.[20]

These demographic shifts can take decades to work their way through, and the economic implications for organizations are significant. Imagine 400 to 500 million relatively wealthy Americans and the impact that will have on global economic power, assuming that pension and health care challenges are effectively managed. Consumer spending in emerging economies is expected to more than double from $4 trillion to more than $9 trillion in the next 10 years.[21] Also imagine the impact of a graying Europe and Japan's declining workforce. Some estimates put the fiscal problems in providing pensions and health care for senior citizens at 250% of national income in Germany and France.[22]

Pension costs can become a huge competitive disadvantage at the company level as well. At General Motors, there were 2.5 retirees for every active worker in 2002. These so-called "legacy" costs were $900 per vehicle at that time due to pension and health care obligations. These costs rose to $1,800 by 2006[23] and retired employee–related costs were one of the key reasons that GM sought bankruptcy relief in 2009.

Companies appear to be ill prepared to deal with this aging population.[24] Both private and public sector employers are waking up to these pressures and attempting to bring about changes to their pension programs that will be more sustainable, but the journey will not be easy. Public pushback to reductions in pension income and other entitlement programs has been strong, and even relatively modest proposals for shifts to policies such as increasing the age of retirement by a year or two have faced widespread resistance. This is resistance that scares politicians because these are also people who are most likely to vote and who are also feeling vulnerable as they find their savings are insufficient to sustain their lifestyle.[25]

An aging population also provides new market opportunities—would you have predicted that the average age of a motorcycle purchaser would be over 49? That's Harley-Davidson's experience.[26]

With aging populations, organizations can expect pressures to manage age prejudice more effectively. Subtle discrimination based on age will not be accepted.

Innovative solutions will be welcomed by aging members of the workforce and an increasing necessity for employers. See the story below.

OLDER WORKERS CAN'T BE IGNORED

"The day is coming when employers are going to embrace the value of older workers. They don't have a choice," writes Kerry Hannon. Demographic and fiscal realities are making the retention of older members of the workforce escalate in importance and give rise to the innovations in working relationships, from full time to flexible work relationships and contract positions. Some employers are realizing the benefits that these employees can bring with them and are recognizing the importance of investing in them before their knowledge walks out the door. Employers that fail to adjust their approach to older employees could find themselves seriously at risk as U.S. labor markets reflect the demographic realities.[27]

KPMG has publically recognized the benefits, noting that "older workers tend to be more dedicated to staying with the company, a plus for clients who like to build a relationship with a consultant they can count on to be around for years."[28]

Diversity Matters

Other demographic issues will provide opportunities and challenges. In the United States, Latinos will play a role in transforming organizations. The numbers of Latinos jumped from 35.3 million during the 1990s, to 50.5 million or 16% of the population in 2010 (up from 13% in 2000), making them the largest ethnic/racial group in the United States. They are also much younger (27 versus the national average age of 37.2), and 63% of its members have been born in the United States. Significantly, the largest growth often is in "hyper-growth" Latino destinations such as Nevada and Georgia,[29] some of which have seen an increase of more than 300% in Latino populations since 1980. The immigration component of this growth rate was adversely affected by the U.S. economic downturn and improvements in the Mexican economy, but it is predicted to continue upward due to domestic population growth, plus the impact that a return to economic health will have on immigration. One of the outcomes of hyper-growth in certain urban areas has been an imbalance of Latino males and females. In the non-Latino population, the ratio of males to females is 96:100. In the Latino population, ratios as high as 118:100 are seen in the hyper-growth destinations.[30] While the specific implications for businesses are unclear, the general need for response and change is not. Notions of cultural norms (including those around English literacy and dominant language used) and markets could be shattered by such demographic shifts.

There have also been significant demographic shifts in Europe and parts of Asia, as people move from disadvantaged areas (economic, social, and political) in search of greater opportunities, security, and social justice. These trends are likely to continue, and as in the United States, they provide both challenges and opportunities. For countries like France and Austria, they help to moderate the effects of an aging population by providing new entrants to the workforce and new customers for products and services. However, they also represent integration challenges in terms of needed services and there has been a backlash from some groups, who see them as both an economic and social threat. Resistance to immigration reform in the United States, the tightening of emigration rules in Canada, and the rise of anti-immigration political parties in Western Europe are evidence of this.

Our assumptions about families and gender will continue to be challenged in the workplace and marketplace of the future. Diversity, inclusiveness, and equity issues will challenge organizations with unpredictable results. The heated debates that occurred in the United States in 2006 concerning legislation related to illegal or undocumented immigrants, temporary workers, and family unification continue to provoke passionate positions and no resolution as of 2014. In Europe, debate around these topics has given rise to some electoral success by what used to be fringe parties, and isolated examples of violence. Some nations have implemented laws around certain religious practices (typically associated with dress and visible symbols in schools and workplaces) that are viewed by many as discriminatory.[31] Matters related to same-sex marriage, gender identity, and gender equity continue to be challenging for many organizations, as laws and behavioral norms related to what is acceptable slowly evolve. The front-page coverage devoted to the drafting by the St. Louis Rams of Michael Sam, the first openly gay professional football player, testifies to the attention and emotions these matters can generate.[32] In too many parts of the world they represent life and death issues.

In some nations, employment- and human rights–related legislation have gone a long way toward advancing the interests and acceptance of diversity, by providing guidance, rules of conduct, and sanctions for those who fail to comply. However, issues related to race and diversity still need to be attended to by organizations. Participation and career advancement rates and salary level differences continue to attract the attention of politicians, the public, and the courts. Further, they constrain the development of talent in organizations and have adverse consequences on multiple levels—from the ability to attract and retain to performance and attitudinal outcomes that can, in turn, influence the culture and work climate of the firm.[33]

What happens when this boils over? In 2014 the intense news coverage and disciplining of Donald Sterling, the owner of the Los Angeles Clippers NBA franchise, for racist comments made during a private conversation, point to the extreme distress it caused members of the team and the reputational and brand consequences his behavior had on the franchise and the league itself. Only the swift actions of NBA Commissioner Adam Silver contained the damage, facilitated the sale of the franchise, and clearly signaled what was expected of owners.[34]

Risks in this area are not just related to the actions of senior management. Social media exposure extends the risks to all levels of the firm, where postings from organizational members can and do go viral with adverse consequences (more will be said about this later). Employees in the United States have certain protections when it comes to discussing working conditions with others online. In the case of fast-food restaurants, this has manifested itself into a very public national campaign to increase the minimum wage from $7.50 to $15.00 per hour. This campaign began on social media and firms are finding they must respond very carefully, in part because of the public's connection to a workforce where matters of age, gender, race, ethnicity, and economic fairness are very visible.[35]

When employee postings go over the line on matters of race, gender, diversity, and equity, firms need to act and be seen to be acting quickly and appropriately in order to control damage.[36] Being viewed as proactive and progressive in these areas can create advantages for firms in terms of attraction, retention, and the commitment levels of employees and customers. Firms such as TD Bank communicate this commitment very publically and have been recognized as one of the best employers by Diversity Inc., Corporate Knights, and the Human Rights Campaign.[37] Multinational corporations, such as IBM, view workforce diversity management as a strategic tool for sustaining and growing the enterprise.[38] That doesn't mean it is easy. Google has sought to increase the diversity of its workforce for several years. In May 2014 it publically recognized its current lack of diversity (30% women, 2% black, and 3% Hispanic), and committed itself to aggressively address this through significant external and internal initiatives geared to attracting more individuals from these groups to technical careers and Google.[39] Smaller and medium-size firms (particularly tech start-ups) are increasingly recognizing the importance of this, as they attempt to scale their operations.

Race, gender, age, and diversity-related challenges multiply once organizations extend their footprints internationally. Differing rules, regulations, cultural norms, and values add to the change leadership challenges that need to be managed, as people learn to work with one another in efficient, effective, and socially appropriate ways. Think of the workforce challenges that a North American, Brazilian, or Indian firm needs to address when establishing their presence in a different part of the world. How will they deal with norms and values in these areas that run contrary to their core values? This is not just an issue for larger organizations. Increasingly, smaller firms find themselves facing international challenges as they seek to grow. These come in many forms—from managing virtual, globally dispersed teams and supply chains, to dealing with the complexities of joint ventures. While the challenges can seem daunting, an increasing number of small and mid-size companies are succeeding on the global stage. A study of 75 such firms highlights the strategies and tactics that have produced positive results. Change leadership skills in these firms play a critical role in their survival and success.[40]

The Physical Environment and Social Responsibility Matters

Concerns over global warming, the degradation of the environment, sustainability, and social responsibility have escalated societal pressure for change at the intergovernmental, governmental, multinational and national corporate, and community levels. Accountability for what is referred to as the "triple bottom line" is leading firms to issue audited statements that report on economic, social, and ecological performance with the goal of sustainability in mind.[41] The 2013 fire and building collapse involving garment suppliers in Bangladesh (1,100 workers killed) and the 2014 spread of the Ebola virus in West Africa intersect with questions about the role of multinational corporations in the health and safety of people in developing countries. The 2010 pictures of BP's oil well gushing millions of gallons into the Gulf of Mexico combined with pictures of oil-coated pelicans, drought, extreme heat, storm-related flooding, and disappearing ice masses reinforce the message that action is urgently needed. These pressures will intensify in the years ahead. There is also mounting evidence of the advantages that can accrue to organizations that think about these issues proactively and align their strategies and actions with their commitment to sustainability and corporate social responsibility.[42]

New Technologies

In addition to responding to environmental and demographic changes in the workplace and marketplace, organizations and their leaders must embrace the trite but true statements about the impact of technological change. Underpinning technological change is the sweeping impact that the digitization of information is having. The quantity of data available to managers is mind-boggling. It is estimated that digital data will grow from 400 billion gigabytes of Web-enabled data in 2013 to 40 trillion gigabytes by 2020.[43] The explosion in the amount of data available will be aided by the impact of inexpensive nano-scale microelectronics that will allow us to add sensors and collection capacity to just about anything. *Data mining* is becoming an increasingly common function in organizations that seek to transform data into information.[44]

The following list of technological innovations points to the breadth of changes we can anticipate. This is not the stuff of science fiction. In most of these areas applications are already present and costs are declining rapidly:

- Software that writes its own code, reducing human error
- Health care by cell phone and laptop
- Vertical farming to save space and increase yield[45]
- Mobile Internet, the Internet of Things, cloud technology, and crowd sourcing
- The automation of knowledge work
- Advanced robotics, from industrial applications to surgery
- Wearable computing, from basic data gathering to human augmentation and computer–brain interfaces
- Autonomous and near autonomous vehicles
- Next-generation genomics, from agricultural applications to substance production (e.g., fuel) and disease treatment applications
- Renewable energy and energy storage breakthroughs that will change energy access and cost equations
- 3-D printing for applications as varied as the production of auto parts and human body parts
- Advanced materials (e.g., nano technology) for a host of applications that will result in dramatic reductions in weight and improvements in strength, flexibility, and connectivity
- Advanced oil and gas exploration and recovery technologies[46]

Technology has woven our world together. The number of international air passengers rose from 75 million in 1970 to an estimated 2.9 billion in 2012.[47] The cost of a 3-minute phone call from the United States to England dropped from more than $8 in 1976 to less than $0.06 in 2014 when VoIP (voice over Internet protocol) is used for a call to a landline or cell phone. The number of transborder calls in the United States was 200 million in 1980.[48] Estimates of the numbers today are in the tens of billions. VoIP has disrupted traditional long-distance telephone markets dramatically, and the proliferation of alternative communication channels, including SMS texting, BBM (Blackberry Messenger), Facebook, and their equivalents on other platforms have transformed the communication landscape. There were a total of 6.8 billion cell phones in use in 2013, meaning one for almost every person alive.[49] In 2013, an estimated 968 million smartphones were shipped, meaning access to digital information and apps for everything from weather forecasts to online purchasing and the transfer of funds. Even those without access to a bank or smartphone can transfer cash safely and securely on a regular cell phone in some developing parts of the world—google "M-Pesa" for an example of this.[50]

Our embrace of digital technology and connectedness has opened the world to us and made it incredibly accessible, but it has come with costs. Security concerns related to viruses and hacking have also escalated, and serious breaches are a common occurrence. The Ponemon Institute estimates that in the United States alone, 110 million adults had their personal information exposed by hackers during a 12-month period in 2013. The cost to firms responding to these threats and breaches are in the billions, and that doesn't include the damage done to customer trust/loyalty. Costs related to online fraud and identity theft are in the billions and growing rapidly. These issues will not go away any time soon.[51] Issues related to the loss of privacy, industrial espionage, and sabotage involving both firms and government agencies have also become common.[52] On a business-to-business level, supply chains woven together through software allows them to operate effectively and efficiently, while at the same time opening them to risks.[53]

With the Internet, students around the globe can access the same quality of information that the best researchers have, if it is in the public domain (which is increasingly the case) and if their government hasn't censored access to it. At the same time, the technology that has made the world smaller has also produced a technological divide between haves and have-nots that has the potential to produce social and political instability. Aspects of the gap are closing, as is seen in the growth of cell phones, smartphones, and Internet access in the developing world. Laptops and tablets are now available at well under $100, and the cost in India has dropped to below $50.[54] Lack of access to clean water, sufficient food, and needed medication is less likely to be tolerated in silence when media images tell people that others have an abundance of such resources and lack the will to share. Events such as the Arab Spring, Occupy Wall Street, and the 2014 election of Narendra Modi as India's prime minister point to the power this technology has in mobilizing public interest and action. Technology transforms relationships. Facebook, LinkedIn, Twitter, and their equivalents keep us connected, a third of U.S. newlyweds in 2012 were reported to have met online, and people have even been found attempting to text in their sleep.[55]

THE NEW CHANGE TOOL ON THE BLOCK

Social media has fundamentally altered thinking about change management. It has changed how information is framed, who frames it, and how quickly it migrates from the few to the many. It can stimulate interest, understanding, involvement, and commitment to your initiative. Or it can create anxiety and confusion and be used to mobilize opposition and resistance by those opposed. The one thing it can't be is be ignored!

Our purpose is not to catalogue all new and emerging technologies. Rather, our intent is to signal to change leaders the importance of paying attention to technological trends and the impact they may have on organizations, now and in the future. As a result of these forces, product development and life cycles are shortened, marketing channels are changing, and managers must respond in a time-paced fashion. Competitors can leapfrog organizations and drop once-market-leaders into obsolescence through a technological breakthrough. The advantages of vertical integration can vanish as technical insights in one segment of the business drive down the costs, migrate the technology through outsourcing to other segments, or otherwise alter the value chain in other ways that had not been anticipated.

Is this overstating the importance of paying attention to how rapidly technological and social change can alter the competitive landscape? BlackBerry went from creating and dominating the smartphone business to less than 3% market share in five years. Dramatic downsizing and reinvention are now the order of the day, as the BlackBerry executives search for new paths forward and renewed market relevance.[56] Now shift your thoughts to the automotive sector. What will the emergence of self-driving electric vehicles mean for manufacturers and their suppliers and distributors? What will they mean for city planners, urban transit, and the taxi driver? Prototypes are currently driving on the streets of Mountain View, California, and expectations are that these sorts of vehicles will be for sale in a few years.[57]

The watchwords for change leaders are to be aware of technological trends and to be proactive in their consideration of how to respond to organizationally relevant ones.

Political Changes

The external political landscape of an organization is a reality that change leaders need pay attention to and figure out how to engage. Even the largest of multinationals has minimal impact on shaping the worldwide geo-political landscape and the focus of governing bodies.[58] However, if they are attentive and nimble, their interests will be better served.

The collapse of the Soviet Empire gave rise to optimism in the West that democracy and the market economy were the natural order of things, the only viable option for modern society.[59] With the end of communism in Russia, there was the sense that there was no serious competitor to free-market democracy and the belief existed that the world would gradually move to competitive capitalism with market discipline.

Of course, this optimism was not realized. Nationalistic border quarrels (India–Pakistan, for example) continue. Some African countries have become less committed to democracy (Zimbabwe and Ethiopia). Nation-states have dissolved into microstates (Yugoslavia and Sudan) or had portions annexed as in the case of Crimea. While American power may be dominant worldwide, September 11, 2001 (9/11), demonstrated that even the dominant power cannot guarantee safety. Non–nation–states and religious groups have become actors on the global stage. The Middle East, North Africa, and Central Asia continue to be in turmoil, creating political and economic uncertainty.

Changes in the economic performance of nations have also altered the geopolitical landscape. Growth in China and India, though it has slowed, continues to advance much more than twice the rate of the developed world.[60] They led the world out of the 2007–2008 crash, and have now been joined by other African and Asian nations that are experiencing more rapid economic growth than the developed world. However, grinding poverty rates, though improving, are still the reality for hundreds of millions of people who live in these areas.[61]

As organizations become global, they need to clarify their own ethical standards. Not only will they need to understand the rules and regulations, they will also have to determine what norms of conduct they will work to establish for their organizational members, and what constitutes acceptable and unacceptable behavior. Peter Eigen, chairman of Transparency International, states: "Political elites and their cronies continue to take kickbacks at every opportunity. Hand-in-glove with corrupt business people, they are trapping whole nations in poverty and hampering sustainable development. Corruption is perceived to be dangerously high in poor parts of the world, but also in many countries whose firms invest in developing nations."[62] Left unaddressed, this political corruption becomes imbedded in organizations. Transparency International finds bribery most common in public works/construction and arms and defense as compared with agriculture.[63] The accounting and governance scandals of 2001 to 2002 (Enron and WorldCom), followed by an almost uninterrupted series of major ethical lapses in global financial services/banking, pharmaceutical, and government sectors (to name just three), have created public demands for more transparency, accountability, regulations with teeth, and heightened expectations that firms should be expected to behave in socially responsible manners. Some companies, Hewlett-Packard, H&M, Tesco, Loblaw, and Apple, for example, have responded by requiring that they and the participants in their supply chain adhere to a set of specified ethical standards. Further, they are committed to working with their suppliers to ensure they reach these standards.[64]

The politics of globalization and the environment have created opportunities and issues for organizations. The United States' Obama administration appears committed to the introduction of new green energy initiatives. The desire to reduce the environmental impact and the United States' dependence on foreign oil and coal has meant subsidy programs for new technologies and opportunities for businesses in those fields. It has also led to an explosion of energy recovery methods such as fracking, which bring with them their own ethical issues. Some organizations are restructuring themselves to seize such opportunities. For example,

Siemens has reorganized itself into three sectors—industry, energy, and health care—to focus on megatrends.[65] Senge and his colleagues argued that the new environmentalism would be driven by innovation and would result in radical new technologies, products, processes, and business models.[66] The rapid rates of market penetration for such technologies and the decline in their costs are evidence that Senge was right.

The politics of the world are not the everyday focus of all managers, but change leaders need to understand their influence on market development and attractiveness, competitiveness, and the resulting pressures on boards and executives. Firms doing business in jurisdictions such as Russia, China, and Argentina know this all too well. Issues related to climate change, water and food security, power, urbanization/smart cities, public transport, immigration, health care, education, trade, employment, and our overall health and safety will continue to influence political discussion and decision making at all levels—from the local to the international context. A sudden transformation of the political landscape can trash the best-laid strategic plan.

Successful change leaders will have a keen sense of the opportunities and dangers involved in global, national, and local political shifts. If they are behaving in a manner consistent with corporate social responsibility, they will also have a keen sense of the opportunities and dangers related to the issues themselves.

The Economy

In 2007, the world economy crashed into financial crisis and appeared headed for a 1930s depression. Trillions of dollars of asset-backed paper became valueless, seemingly overnight. Investors and pension funds lost 20% of their value. Global stock markets shrank by $30 trillion, or half their value.[67] The American housing market, which provided an illusory asset base, collapsed and led to the credit crisis. Firms that were chastised for having too much cash on hand and were seen as missing opportunities suddenly became the survivors when credit vanished. At the individual firm level, the economic crisis led to layoffs and bankruptcies. Firms saw their order books shrink and business disappear. Entire industries, such as the automotive industry, were overwhelmed and certain large automotive manufacturers perhaps would have vanished if not for government bailouts. An example of the impact on one small firm is shown in the story below.

THE IMPACT OF THE 2007–2009 RECESSION ON A SMALL BUSINESS

Serge Gaudet operates a wholesale/retail drapery and window blind business in the small Canadian town of Sturgeon Falls, Ontario. The world economic crisis suddenly became real when banks would no longer extend him credit. In his

(Continued)

(Continued)

words, "I had signed orders, contracts in hand, and my bank refused my line of credit so that I could buy the inventory. How was I to finance this deal? I had the contract and it was with a government hospital. Surely, this was credit worthy? What else could I do?"

Mr. Gaudet managed through the crisis by negotiating newer, tougher terms with his bank. But the lack of credit was not his only problem. "Normally, I bid on requests for proposals and win a reasonable percentage of them," he reported. "Suddenly, there was nothing to bid on. Nothing. Every institution that was going to buy blinds was waiting—waiting for government aid that was very slow in coming. It was touch and go whether I could last until new contracts came in."

Mr. Gaudet's story is typical of the situation faced by many small businesses as they struggled through the economic crisis of 2007–2009. Many did not survive. Those that did were able to do so because they had low overhead and debt.[68]

Governments responded to the economic crisis with Keynesian abandon. G20 countries ran huge deficits as governments tried to stimulate their economies out of recession. America's federal deficit hit 10% of GDP in 2009, and the overall debt to GDP went from 65% in 2007 to over 100% in 2012.[69] In December 2010, economists were talking about a slow recovery in America and an almost nonexistent one in Europe, and they were right.[70] Economists also predicted that China would have an 8.6% GDP growth and 11.1% investment growth, with significant growth also predicted for India and the other BRIC nations. While growth in these economies has not been as robust as expected, most have performed relatively well. Clearly, there has been a shift in the economic order of the world.[71]

The lessons from the economic crisis are centered on risk management and capacity building. In a world where everything is interconnected, organizations need to be able to respond quickly. In order to do so, organizations need the capacity to weather such challenges. Ideally, organizations will incorporate the mechanisms to anticipate these challenges and adapt into management, leadership, and the underlying social fabric of the firm. In many situations, these anticipatory mechanisms will not be available and organizations will need to rely on their ability to adapt and change as the environment shifts.

See **Toolkit Exercise 1.2** to practice thinking about environmental forces facing your organization and their implications.

The Implications of Worldwide Trends for Change Management

The economic globalization of the world, the demographic and social shifts in the Western and developing world, technological changes, environmental and ecological pressures, and the upheaval and political and economic uncertainties that flair up around the globe form the reality of organizational environments. Predicting specific short-run changes is a fool's errand. Nevertheless, change leaders need to have a keen sense of just how these seemingly external events impact internal organizational dynamics. "How will external changes drive strategy and internal adjustments and investments?" has become a critical question that change leaders need to address. For example, the rise of the sharing economy has disrupted traditional business structures of the hotel and taxi business. Airbnb and Uber have both capitalized on globalization trends and technological innovations to improve access to information relevant to travelers, increase social trust, and through these mechanisms change the way that people travel.[72]

Barkema, Baum, and Mannix suggest that macro environmental changes will change organizational forms and competitive dynamics and, in turn, lead to new management challenges.[73] (Table 1.1 summarizes Barkema and colleagues' article.)

Table 1.1 New Organizational Forms and Management Challenges Based on Environmental Change

Macro Changes and Impacts	New Organizational Forms and Competitive Dynamics	New Management Challenges
Digitization leading to: faster information transmission lower-cost information storage and transmission integration of states and opening of markets geographic dispersion of the value chain All leading to globalization of markets	Global small and medium-sized enterprises Global constellations of organizations (i.e., networks) Large, focused global firms All leading to spread of autonomous, dislocated teams; digitally enabled structures; intense global rivalry; and running faster while seeming to stand still	Greater diversity Greater synchronization requirements Greater time-pacing requirements Faster decision making, learning, and innovation More frequent environmental discontinuities Faster industry life cycles Faster newness and obsolescence of knowledge Risk of competency traps where old competencies no longer produce desired effects Greater newness and obsolescence of organizations

Source: Adapted from Barkema, H. G., Baum, J. A. C., & Mannix, E. A. (2002). Management challenges in a new time. *Academy of Management Journal, 45*(5), 916–930.

They describe three **macro changes** facing us today: digitization of information, integration of nation states and the opening of international markets, and the geographic dispersion of the value chain. These are leading to the globalization of markets. This globalization, in turn, will drive significant shifts in organizational forms and worldwide competitive dynamics.

The early decades of the 21st century suggest accelerated change in comparison to the latter part of the 20th century. Diversity, synchronization and time-pacing requirements, decision making, the frequency of environmental discontinuities, quick industry life cycles and in consequence product and service obsolescence, and competency traps all suggest greater complexity and a more rapid organizational pace for today and tomorrow. Barkema et al. argue that much change today deals with mid-level change—change that is more than incremental but not truly revolutionary. As such, middle managers will play increasingly significant roles in making change effective in their organizations in both evolutionary and revolutionary scenarios.

Four Types of Organizational Change

Organizational changes come in many shapes and sizes: mergers, acquisitions, buyouts, downsizing, restructuring, outsourcing the human resource function or computer services, departmental reorganizations, installations of new incentive systems, shutting particular manufacturing lines or opening new branches in other parts of the country, and the list goes on. All of these describe specific organizational changes. The literature on organizational change classifies such changes into two types, episodic or discontinuous change and continuous change. That is, change can be dramatic and sudden—the introduction of a new technology that makes a business obsolete or new government regulations that immediately shift the competitive landscape. Or change can be much more gradual, such as the alteration of core competencies of an organization through training and adding key individuals.

Under dramatic or episodic change, organizations are seen as having significant inertia. Change is infrequent and discontinuous. Re-engineering programs are examples of this type of change and can be viewed as planned examples of injecting significant change into an organization. On the other hand, under continuous change, organizations are seen as more emergent and self-organizing, where change is constant, evolving, and cumulative.[74] Japanese automobile manufacturers have led the way in this area with *kaizen* programs focused on encouraging continuous change. In the technology sectors, collaborative approaches, facilitated by social networks that extend beyond corporate boundaries and even crowd sourcing, are giving rise to continuous change models for organizational adaptation, growth, and renewal.[75]

A second dimension of change is whether it occurs in a proactive, planned, and programmatic fashion or reactively in response to external events. Programmatic or planned change occurs when managers anticipate events and shift their organizations as a result. For example, Intel, a multinational semiconductor chip maker headquartered in California, anticipates and appears to encourage a cycle of computer chip obsolescence.[76] As a result, the organization has been designed to handle this obsolescence. Alternately, shifts in an organization's external world lead to a reaction on the part of the organization. For example, the emergence of low-cost airlines has led to traditional carriers employing reactive strategies, such as cutting routes, costs, and service levels in an attempt to adapt.[77]

Nadler and Tushman combine these two dimensions in a useful model illustrating different types of change (see Table 1.2). They define four categories of change: tuning, adapting, redirecting or reorienting, and overhauling or re-creating.

Table 1.2 Types of Organizational Change		
	Incremental/Continuous	**Discontinuous/Radical**
Anticipatory	**Tuning** Incremental change made in anticipation of future events Need is for internal alignment Focuses on individual components or subsystems Middle-management role Implementation is the major task For example, a quality improvement initiative from an employee improvement committee	**Redirecting or Reorienting** Strategic proactive changes based on predicted major changes in the environment Need is for positioning the whole organization to a new reality Focuses on all organizational components Senior management creates sense of urgency and motivates the change For example, a major change in product or service offering in response to opportunities identified
Reactive	**Adapting** Incremental changes made in response to environmental changes Need is for internal alignment Focuses on individual components or subsystems Middle-management role Implementation is the major task For example, modest changes to customer services in response to customer complaints	**Overhauling or Re-creating** Response to a significant performance crisis Need to reevaluate the whole organization, including its core values Focuses on all organizational components to achieve rapid, system-wide change Senior management creates vision and motivates optimism For example, a major realignment of strategy, involving plant closures and changes to product and service offerings, to stem financial losses and return the firm to profitability

Source: Adapted from Nadler, D. A., & Tushman, M. (1989, August). Organizational frame bending: Principles for managing reorientation. *Academy of Management Executive, 3*(3), 196.

Tuning is defined as small, relatively minor changes made on an ongoing basis in a deliberate attempt to improve the efficiency or effectiveness of the organization. Responsibility for acting on these sorts of changes typically rests with middle management. Most improvement change initiatives that grow out of existing quality-improvement programs would fall into this category. **Adapting** is viewed as relatively minor changes made in response to external stimuli—a reaction to things observed in the environment such as competitors' moves or customer shifts. Relatively minor changes to customer servicing caused by reports of customer dissatisfaction or defection to a competitor provide an example of this sort of change, and once again, responsibility for such changes tends to reside within the role of middle managers.

Redirecting or reorienting involves major, strategic change resulting from planned programs. These frame-bending shifts are designed to provide new perspectives and directions in a significant way. For example, a shift in a firm to truly develop a customer service organization and culture would fall in this category. Finally, **overhauling or re-creation** is the dramatic shift that occurs in reaction to major external events. Often there is a crisis situation that forces the change—thus, the emergence of low-cost carriers forced traditional airlines to re-create what they do. Likewise, the credit crisis bankrupted General Motors and forced a complete overhaul and downsizing of the company.

The impact of the change increases as we move from minor alterations and fine-tuning to changes that require us to reorient and re-create the organization. Not surprisingly, reorienting and re-creating an organization is much more time-consuming and challenging to lead effectively. They also have a greater impact on individuals who must reorient themselves. Regardless of difficulty, the financial crisis and recession of 2008–2009 forced companies to react. While there are no data that we know of to confirm this, anticipatory organizational change does not seem to be sufficient to prepare organizations for the dramatic shift in the global business environment presented by 2008–2009. While planning can help organizations think about risk and opportunities, it was their sense of awareness and adaptive capacity that allowed firms to respond and survive the crisis.

An examination of the history of British Airways provides a classic example of a single organization facing both incremental and discontinuous change while both anticipating issues and being forced to react.[78]

BRITISH AIRWAYS: STRATEGIC AND INCREMENTAL CHANGE

Todd Jick's case study describes the crisis of 1981. British Airways' (BA's) successful response in the 1980s was revolutionary in nature. During that period, BA revolutionized its culture and its view of the customer with outstanding results. In the 1990s, BA entered a period of slow decline as the systems and structures at BA became increasingly incongruent with the new deregulated environment and the successful competitors that were spawned

(Continued)

by that environment. Major upheavals in international travel pushed BA into a reactive mode following 9/11, and the results of management's attempts to develop new strategies were unclear for a considerable period. A strike in the summer of 2003 created more uncertainty for the firm.[79] The dramatic rise in oil costs during 2007 and 2008 forced BA to cut costs and implement a merger with Iberia. These strategic moves to cut costs were matched by more incremental internal actions to limit the wages of cabin staff, to match those of its competitors. These changes led to limited strike action in 2010 and a negotiated resolution in 2011, which was facilitated by the arrival of new chief negotiators on both sides—Keith Williams, BA's new president, and Len McCluskey, the union's new general secretary. Fleet renewal (their first Airbus A380 was put into service in 2013), along with ongoing changes to systems, processes, and procedures, mark the continuance of their change journey, marked by both strategic and incremental change initiatives.[80]

Nadler and Tushman raise the question: "Will incremental change be sufficient or will radical change be necessary in the long run?" Suffice it to say that this question has not been answered. However, the Japanese provided a profound lesson in the value of incremental, daily changes. Interestingly enough, it was a lesson the Japanese industrialists learned from North American management scholars such as Duran and Deming. If one observes employee involvement and continuous improvement processes effectively employed,[81] one also sees organizational team members that are energized, goal directed, cohesive, and increasingly competent because of the new things they are learning. Such teams expect that tomorrow will be a little different from today. Further, when more significant changes have to be embraced, these teams are likely to be far less resistant and fearful of them because of their earlier experiences with facilitating change within group structures. Organizational change is part of daily life for them.

Many think of **incremental/continuous change** and **discontinuous/radical change** as states rather than a perspective or a spectrum of change size. From the organizational a point of view, a departmental reorganization might seem incremental. However, from the department's perspective, it may seem discontinuous and radical. As Morgan puts it:

A mythology is developing in which incremental and quantum change are presented as opposites. Nothing could be further from the truth … True, there is a big difference between incremental and quantum change when we talk of results (but) incremental and quantum change are intertwined. As we set our sights on those 500% improvements, remember they're usually delivered through 5, 10, and 15% initiatives.[82]

The perception of the magnitude of the change lies in the eye of the beholder. Incremental changes at the organizational level may appear disruptive and revolutionary at a department level. However, as noted earlier, those who are accustomed to facing and managing incremental change on a regular basis will likely view more revolutionary changes in less threatening terms. Those who have not faced and managed change will be more likely to view even incremental changes as threatening in nature.

Organizational members need to learn to accept and value the perspectives of both the adaptor (those skilled in incremental change) and the innovator (those skilled in more radical change).[83] As a change agent, personal insight regarding your abilities and preferences for more modest or more radical change is critical. The secret to successful organizational growth and development over time lies in the capacity of organizational members to embrace both approaches to change at the appropriate times and to understand that they are, in fact, intertwined.

Planned Changes Don't Always Produce the Intended Results

To this point, it is clear that change—from simple fine-tuning to radical reconstruction—is a necessary prerequisite to organizational survival. However, successful change is extremely difficult to execute as the scope and complexity increases. Many types of change initiatives have failed: reengineering, total quality management, activity-based costing, joint optimization, strategic planning, and network structures.[84] If change leaders were to fully consider the failure rates when designing interventions or acquisitions, fear would trump action. As one manager put it, "The opportunity has turned out to be 10 times what I thought it would be. The challenges have turned out to be 20 times what I thought they were"![85]

Fortunately or unfortunately, inaction and avoidance are no solution. Maintaining the status quo typically does not sustain or enhance competitive advantage, particularly in troubled organizations. Delays and half-hearted efforts that begin only after the problems have become critical increase costs and decrease the likelihood of a successful transformation. As Hamel and Prahalad put it: "No company can escape the need to re-skill its people, reshape its product portfolio, redesign its process, and redirect resources."[86] Organizations that consistently demonstrate their capacity to innovate, manage change, and adapt over the years are the ones with staying power.[87]

Hamel and Prahalad believe that restructuring and re-engineering, on their own, do little to increase the capabilities of the firm. These two Rs increase profitability and can enhance competitiveness but "in many companies . . . re-engineering (and restructuring) . . . are more about catching up than getting out in front."[88] Hamel and Prahalad argue that companies need to regenerate their strategy and reinvent their industry by building their capacity to compete. These transformations and realignments that result are sustained marathons, not quick fixes. Skilled change leaders provide a coherent vision of the change and do all that they can to help people adapt and embrace the changes with realistic expectations. When change recipients understand that things will often get worse before they get better, but also believe that the benefits are well worth the effort, change initiatives are more likely to be sustained.[89] For example, as costs rise in China, the environment is shifting manufacturing elsewhere, including a rebirth of manufacturing in the United States. This trend demands a continuing evolution of strategy as well as reshaping of supply chains to alter ingrained overseas production practices that have evolved over the past 15 years—changes that manufacturing and supply chain managers may have difficulty adjusting to.[90]

Radical solutions both terrify and fascinate managers. Often managers are comfortable with relatively small technological fixes as the source of products, services, efficiency, and effectiveness. However, they tend to fear interventions that seem to reduce their control over situations, people, and outcomes. When organizations embrace technology but not people, they pay a steep price. They reduce the likelihood that the change will produce the desired results and they fail to take advantage of the collective capacity of organizational members to improve operations, products, and services. To say the least, this practice is extremely wasteful of human capacity and energy, causing them to atrophy over time. And recent evidence suggests that true productivity increases come only when the forms are reorganized, business practices reformulated, and employees retrained. Investment in infrastructure alone is insufficient.[91]

Organizational Change Roles

Without a sense of vision, purpose, and engagement, it is easy to become the passive recipient of change. As a passive recipient, you see yourself as subject to the whims of others, as relatively helpless, perhaps even as a victim. As a passive recipient, your self-esteem and self-efficacy may feel as if they are under attack.[92] Your perception of power and influence will diminish and you will feel acted on. Years ago, Jack Gordon talked about aligning employees. That is, once top management has decided on the strategic direction, employees need to be aligned with that direction. We cannot help but think that if you are the recipient of change, "being aligned" just won't feel very good.[93]

Who are the participants in organizational change? Many employees will step up and make the change work. They will be the **change implementers**, the ones making happen what others, the **change initiators**, have pushed or encouraged. Change initiators, or champions, also frame the vision for the change and/or provide resources and support for the initiative. Or they could be on the receiving end of change, **change recipients**. Some will play a role in facilitating change—**change facilitators** won't be the ones responsible for implementing the change, but they will assist initiators and implementers in the change through their contacts and consultative assistance.

Of course, one person might play multiple roles. That is, a person might have a good idea and talk it up in the organization (change initiator); take action to make the change occur (change implementer); talk to others to help them manage the change (change facilitator); and, ultimately, be affected by the change too (change recipient). In this book, we use the terms **change leader** and **change agent** interchangeably.

Change initiators, change implementers, and change facilitators represent different roles played by the change leader or change agent. At any given moment, the person leading the change may be initiating, implementing, or facilitating. Table 1.3 outlines the roles that people need to play in organizational change.

Change Initiators

Change initiators get things moving, take action, and stimulate the system. They are the ones seeking to initiate change to make things better. They identify the need for change, develop the vision of a better future, take on the change task, and champion the initiative. Change initiators may face considerable risk in the organization. To use a physical metaphor, action creates movement, movement creates friction, and friction creates heat! And creating heat may help or hurt one's career. Change agents need to take calculated actions and be prepared to undertake the work needed to create and support the powerful arguments and coalitions to effect change in organizations from the top or the middle of the organization.

Change initiators will find useful aids for change in this book. We, as authors, cannot supply the passion and powerful vision needed by initiators, but we can point out the requirements of successful change: planning, persuasion, passion, and perseverance. And we can provide frameworks for analysis that will enhance the likelihood of successful change.

Table 1.3 Managerial Roles and Organizational Change	
Roles	**Role Description**
Change leader or change agent	The person who leads the change. He/she may play any or all of the initiator, implementer, or facilitator roles. Often, but not always, this person is the formal change leader. However, informal change leaders will emerge and lead change as well. (Note: In this book, change leader and change agent are used interchangeably.)
Change initiator	The person who identifies the need and vision for change and champions the change.
Change implementer	The person who has responsibility for making certain the change happens, charting the path forward, nurturing support, and alleviating resistance.
Change facilitator	The person who assists initiators, implementers, and recipients with the change-management process. Identifies process and content change issues and helps resolve these, fosters support, alleviates resistance, and provides other participants with guidance and council.
Change recipient	The person who is affected by the change. Often the person who has to change his or her behavior to ensure the change is effective.

Change initiators need to be dogged in their desire and determination. Those who succeed will earn reputations for realistic, grounded optimism, for a good sense of timing, and for not giving up. If nothing else, the opposition may tire in the face of their persistence. Better yet are those who have the uncanny ability to creatively combine with others into a coalition that turns resisters into allies and foot draggers into foot soldiers and advocates for change.

Change Implementers

Many would-be and existing managers find themselves as change implementers. Others, including their bosses, may initiate the change, but it is left to the implementers to make it work. This role is critical. Pfeffer argues that effectiveness doesn't come from making the critical decision but rather from managing the consequences of decisions and creating the desired results.[94] As he says, "If change were going to be easy, it would already have happened." The change implementer's role is important and needed in organizations. Without it, there is no bridge to the desired end state—no sustained integrated approach.[95]

Change implementers will find much in this book to assist them. They will find guidance in creating and increasing the need for the changes that change initiators are demanding. They will find tools for organizational diagnosis and for identifying and working with key stakeholders. And they will find concepts and techniques to facilitate the internal alignment of systems, processes, and people; improve their action plans and implementation skills; and help them sustain themselves during the transition.

At the same time, we encourage and challenge change implementers to stay engaged, to stay active, and to initiate change themselves. Oshry identifies the dilemma of "middle powerlessness," where the middle manager feels trapped between tops and bottoms and becomes ineffective as a result.[96] Many middle managers transform their organizations by recognizing strategic initiatives and mobilizing the power of the "middles" to move the organization in the direction needed.

Change Facilitators

Today's complex organizational changes can fail because parties lock into positions or because perspectives get lost in personalities and egos. In such cases, an outside view can facilitate change. Change facilitators understand change processes and assist the organization to work through change issues. As such, they sometimes formally serve as consultants to change leaders and teams. However, many of those who act as change facilitators do so informally, often on the strength of their existing relationships with others involved with the change. They have high levels of self-awareness and emotional maturity, and are skilled in the behavioral arts—using their interpersonal skills to work with teams or groups.

In this book, change facilitators will discover frameworks that will help them to understand change processes. With these frameworks, they will be able to translate concrete organizational events into understandable situations and so ease change. And their knowledge and interpersonal skills will provide change perspectives that will allow managers to unfreeze their positions.

Common Challenges for Managerial Roles

Table 1.4 highlights common sources of difficulty that change initiators, implementers, and facilitators face when attempting to implement planned changes. While there are external factors that can frustrate progress in unanticipated and undesirable directions, this table focuses on ways in which change leaders act as their own worst enemies, self-sabotaging their own initiatives. They stem from predispositions, perceptions, and a lack of self-awareness. The good news is that they also represent areas that a person can do something about if he or she becomes self-aware and chooses to take the blinders off.

Table 1.4 Common Managerial Difficulties in Dealing With Organizational Change

1. Managers are action oriented and assume other rational people will see the inherent wisdom in the proposed change and will learn the needed new behaviors. Or managers assume that they will be able to replace recalcitrant employees.

2. Managers assume they have the power and influence to enact the desired changes, and they underestimate the power and influence of other stakeholders.

3. Managers look at the transition period activities as a cost, not an investment that increases the prospects for success and mitigates failure risks.

4. Managers are unable to accurately estimate the resources and commitment needed to facilitate the integration of the human dimension with other aspects of the change (e.g., systems, structures, technologies).

5. Managers are unaware that their own behavior, and that of other key managers, may be sending out conflicting messages to employees and eventually customers.

6. Managers find managing human processes unsettling (even threatening) because of the potential emotionality and the difficulties they present with respect to prediction and quantification.

7. Managers simply lack the capacity (attitudes, skills, and abilities) to manage complex changes that involve people. When those managing the change get defensive, the minds of others tend to close rather than open.

8. Managers' critical judgment is impaired due to factors related to overconfidence[97] and/or groupthink.

Change Recipients

Change recipients are those who find themselves on the receiving end of change. Their responses will vary from active resistance, passivity, to active support, depending upon their perceptions of the change, its rationale, and its impact. When people feel acted upon and with little or no voice or control in the process, dissatisfaction, frustration, alienation, absenteeism, and turnover are common responses to demands for change.[98]

This book provides guidance that will help recipients to better understand what is happening to them and their organizations. Further, it will identify strategies and approaches that will help change recipients to take an active role and increase the amount of control they have over organizational events.

Regardless of your role in the organization—change recipient, change implementer, change initiator, or change facilitator—this book contains useful tools. Change recipients will understand what is happening to them and will learn how to respond positively. Change implementers will develop their capacity to use tools that increase their effectiveness, and change initiators will learn to take more effective actions to lever their change programs. Change facilitators will find themselves with new insights into easing organizational change.

See **Toolkit Exercise 1.3** to think about change roles you've played in the past.

Gary Hamel of Harvard talks about "leading the revolution"—anyone can play the change game. Anyone can seek opportunities, ask questions, challenge orthodoxies, and generate new ideas and directions! And in doing so, individuals from virtually anywhere in an organization (or even outside of it) can become change leaders.[99] The leadership that started Facebook and Google came from dorm rooms. The local heroes nominated by CNN viewers come from all walks of life.[100] Change leaders foment action. They take independent action based on their analysis of what is best for the long-term interests of their organizations, and they recognize the many faces of change and the crucial next steps necessary to meet their long-term change goals. Finally, they recognize who needs to play what roles in order to advance needed change. As such, at different points in time they fulfill the roles of change initiator, implementer, and facilitator, depending upon the needs of the situation, their skills and abilities, and their beliefs about what is required at a point in time to advance the change.

The Requirements for Becoming a Successful Change Leader

Successful change leaders balance keen insight with a driving passion for action. They have that sensitivity to the external world described above and will be skilled anticipators of that world. They have a rich understanding of organizational systems—their system in particular and the degree to which continuous or strategic changes are appropriate. They understand themselves and their influence and image in their organizational context. They have special personal characteristics—a tolerance for ambiguity, emotional maturity, self-confidence, comfort with power, a keen sense of risk assessment, a need for action and results, and persistence grounded in reasoned optimism and tenacity. Finally, while they are curious and have a strong desire to learn, they also have a deep and abiding distrust of organizational fads and recognize the negative impact of fad surfing in organizations.[101] Change leaders who see the world in simple, linear terms will have more difficulty creating effective change.[102]

Change leaders understand the rich tapestry that forms the organizational culture. They understand the stakeholder networks that pattern organizational life. They recognize the impact and pervasiveness of organizational control systems (organizational structures, reward systems, measurement systems). They know and can reach key organizational members—both those with legitimate power and position and those with less recognizable influence. And they understand which tasks are key at *this* point in time given *this* environment and *this* organizational strategy.[103]

Successful change leaders know their personal skills, style, and abilities and how those play throughout the organization. Their credibility is the bedrock on which change actions are taken. Because change recipients will often be cynical and will examine how worthy the leaders are of their trust, change leaders must be aware of their personal blind spots and ensure these are compensated for whenever needed.

Change leaders also embrace the paradoxes of change:[104]

They are involved in both driving change and enabling change. Change leaders understand the need to persist and drive change through their organization. Without such determination, organizational inertia will slow change and other organizations will race ahead. At the same time, change leaders recognize that getting out of the way might be the most helpful management action to be taken. When those around a manager are following a passion, the best thing might be to help in whatever way possible or to provide resources to make things happen.

They recognize that resistance to change is both a problem and an opportunity. Change resistance happens in planned change. Overcoming such resistance is frequently necessary to make progress. However, change leaders recognize that there are often good reasons for resistance—the person resisting is not just being difficult or oppositional, he or she often knows things or has perspectives that cast doubt on the wisdom of change. Change leaders need to recognize this and work actively to overcome this paradox.

Good change leadership focuses on outcomes but is careful about process. Far too often, change programs get bogged down because a focus on results leads change implementers to ignore good process. At the same time, too much attention to process can diffuse direction and lead to endless rituals of involvement and consultation. Good change leaders learn how to manage this balance well.

Change leaders recognize the tension between getting on with it and changing directions. The environment is always changing. Leaders can always modify their objectives and respond to the environment. But if this is done repeatedly, they never settle on a design and direction and as a result will fail to get things done. Keeping the focus on the overall long-term direction while making adjustments can make sense. The trick is to understand and balance this tension.

Change leaders understand the need to balance patience and impatience. Impatience may prove very helpful in overcoming inertia and fear, generating focus, energizing a change, and mobilizing for action. However, patience can also prove a valuable tool in reducing tension and establishing focus and direction, by providing time for people to learn, understand, and adjust to what is being proposed.

Finally, today's change leader knows that in today's global competition, what matters is not the absolute rate of learning but rather the rate of learning compared to the competition. And if your organization doesn't keep pace, it loses the competitive race.

Summary

This chapter defines organizational change as a planned alteration of organizational components to improve the effectiveness of the organization. The forces that drive change today are classified under social, demographic, technological, economic, and political forces. Environmental shifts create the need for change in organizations and drive much organizational change today. Four types of organizational change—tuning, reorienting, adapting, and re-creating—are outlined. Finally, the nature of change leaders is discussed and some of the paradoxes facing them are examined.

This chapter outlines the change roles that exist in organizations: change initiator, change implementer, change facilitator, and change recipient. Change leaders or change agents could be any of the four roles, initiator, implementer, facilitator, or recipient.

Finally, the chapter outlines a summary checklist and critical questions that change leaders need to consider when thinking through matter related to how to change and what to change. See **Toolkit Exercise 1.1** for critical thinking questions for this chapter.

Key Terms

Organizational change—for the purposes of this book, organizational change is defined as a planned alteration of organizational components to improve the effectiveness of the organization. By organizational components, we mean the organizational mission and vision, strategy, goals, structure, process or system, technology, and people in an organization. When organizations enhance their effectiveness, they increase their ability to generate value for those they are designed to serve.

Change management—is based in a broad set of underlying disciplines (from the social sciences to information technology), tends to be strategy driven, with attention directed to whatever factors are assessed as necessary to the successful design and implementation of change.

PESTE factors—the political, economic, social, technological, and ecological/environmental factors that describe the environment or context in which the organization functions.

Macro changes—large-scale environmental changes that are affecting organizations and what they do.

Tuning—defined as small, relatively minor changes made on an ongoing basis in a deliberate attempt to improve the efficiency or effectiveness of the organization.

Adapting—viewed as relatively minor changes made in response to external stimuli—a reaction to things observed in the environment such as competitors' moves or customer shifts.

Redirecting or reorienting—major, strategic change resulting from planned programs. These frame-bending shifts are designed to provide new perspectives and directions in a significant way.

Overhauling or re-creation—the dramatic shift that occurs in reaction to major external events. Often there is a crisis situation that forces the change.

Incremental/continuous changes—organizational changes that are relatively small in scope and incremental in nature. They may stem from the fine-tuning of existing practices or represent an incremental adaptation to environmental changes. Depending on the perspective of the change recipient, incremental change can be perceived as discontinuous/radical change.

Discontinuous/radical changes—changes that are broad in scope and impact and that may involve strategic repositioning. They usually occur in anticipation of or reaction to major environmental changes and are discontinuous in that they involved changes that are *not* incremental in nature and are disruptive to the status quo.

Change implementer—the person responsible for making certain the change happens, charting the path forward, nurturing support, and alleviating resistance.

Change initiator—the person who identifies the need and vision for change and champions the change.

Change recipient—the person who is affected by the change. Often the person who has to change his or her behavior to ensure the change is effective.

Change facilitator—the person who assists initiators, implementers, and recipients with the change-management process. Identifies process and content change issues and helps resolve these, fosters support, alleviates resistance, and provides other participants with guidance and council.

Change leader or **change agent**—these two terms are used interchangeably in the text to describe those engaged in change initiator, implementer, or facilitator roles. All those involved in providing leadership and direction for the change fall within their broad coverage.

END-OF-CHAPTER EXERCISES

TOOLKIT EXERCISE 1.1

Critical Thinking Questions

Please find the URLs for the videos listed below on the website at study.sagepub.com/cawsey3e. Consider the questions that follow.

1. <u>Did You Know 2013</u>—4:56 minutes

Excellent video to visualize the rate of change in the environment.

- Choose one fact and discuss how it may impact change initiatives for an organization you're familiar with.

- Which fact listed do you think will have the most long-term implications for organizations in the future?

- Brainstorm what similar facts you think may be true in 5 years, 15 years, and 25 years.

2. <u>IBM Study: Making Change Work</u>—2:57 minutes

Interesting discussion of IBM study that only 60% of change projects succeed. Discusses factors that seem to increase the chances for success.

- List reasons (both in the video as well as those not mentioned) that change projects often fail.

- Can you think of similar instances of change project failure from your own experience?

- What are the main takeaways about how to increase the success of a change initiative?

For more information, study.sagepub.com/cawsey3e for a link to the IBM report that is the focus of the video.

3. Individually or in groups, pick a product or service and then go to the Web and explore what technological and/or geopolitical changes are occurring that could seriously disrupt existing organizations in that sector. Then pick an organization that would be affected and identify the changes you'd undertake to help it adapt and thrive.

   For example, if you owned a taxi firm in New York City, how would you prepare for the potential arrival of self-driving cars?

TOOLKIT EXERCISE 1.2

Analyzing Your Environment

Select an organization you are familiar with. What are the key environmental issues affecting this organization? List the factors under each subheading and their implications for the organization.

Factors	Proactive Implications	Reactive Implications
Political		
Economic		
Ecological		
Social		
Technological		

Please see study.sagepub.com/cawsey3e for a downloadable template of this exercise.

TOOLKIT EXERCISE 1.3

Change Roles in Your Organization

Think about organizations that you are familiar with—organizations for which you have worked, schools you've attended, and organizations you've volunteered for such as a baseball league or a church.

Think about changes, large or small, that have taken place in those organizations. Take a moment to describe a situation when you filled each of the change roles (Return to Table 1.4 on page 29 for definitions of each role). How did the role feel? What did you accomplish in the role?

- When did you play the role of a change initiator?

- When did you play the role of a change implementer?

- When did you play the role of a change facilitator?

- When did you play the role of a change recipient?

Please see study.sagepub.com/cawsey3e for a downloadable template of this exercise.

CHAPTER 2

Frameworks for Leading the Process of Organizational Change

"How" to Lead Organizational Change

An organization's ability to learn, and translate that learning into action rapidly, is the ultimate competitive advantage.

—Jack Welch, CEO, General Electric (1981–2001)

CHAPTER OVERVIEW

- In this chapter we discuss frameworks that illustrate the process of how to create organizational change; in Chapter 3 we examine what aspects of an organization might need to be changed. Change leaders must understand and do both.
- We present six models that provide dissimilar and complementary insights into the process of planned, purposeful change:

  1. The first model is a basic step model, that is, the leader takes an organization through step 1 before step 2; this is Lewin's three-stage model.

  2. Kotter's eight stages of organizational change provide a highly structured, finish-one-stage-before-the-next-stage approach to change.

3. The third model is Gentile's *Giving Voice to Values* methodology, which supports individuals taking effective ethical action when a situation so demands.

4. The fourth model is Duck's five-stage model that focuses on people and the range of their emotional responses to change.

5. Fifth, there is a modified version of Beckhard and Harris's change-management model that concentrates on process issues.

6. We end this chapter with The Change Path, our four-stage model that concentrates on process issues and is used as a guiding framework throughout the book. The four stages of this model are: Awakening, Mobilization, Acceleration, and Institutionalization.

Just as an athlete needs different types of training and equipment to play and succeed at different sports (think of the difference between a professional baseball player and a downhill skiing professional), so too does the change leader need different frameworks to apply to specific situations.

These models will help change leaders articulate their approach to leading organizational change and provide guideposts for instituting that change.

S weeping demographic changes, technological advances, geopolitical shifts, and demands to be sensitive to our physical environment are combining with concerns for security and organizational governance to generate significant pressure for organizational change. Awareness of the political, economic, sociological, technological, and ecological/environmental (PESTE) aspects of any organization's external environment forewarns managers for the need to pay attention to multiple factors. Furthermore, it alerts managers to attend to their organizations' environmental contexts and to decide whether they need to take some action as a result.

McDonald's has been one of many organizations that scanned its environment and made changes to its products as a result of shifts in its environment. The recession of 2008 to 2009 put pricing pressure on the restaurant business. McDonald's responded with a continuous stream of new products. Since 2004, it has introduced the snack wrap, several salads, specialty coffees, and, most recently, the Angus burger, a 1/3-lb. burger.[1] These product innovations have led to store sales increases and improved profits. Recently, McDonald's has embraced the "green movement" with major initiatives in the areas of sustainability and corporate social responsibility, and public reporting of their progress. They also piloted the placement of charge points for electronic vehicles in one store in 2009, and this initiative has now been extended to a few other locations.[2] One trend that has challenged McDonald's creativity is the "eat local" movement, where consumers are encouraged to eat locally grown foods. In the international market, McDonald's has created a variety of partnerships to create a more localized experience for its consumers. McDonald's now offers Red Bean Pie in Hong Kong, a Parmigiano Reggiano burger in Italy, and Caldo Verde soup in Portugal.[3] In the United States, McDonald's has tried to use a message about locally grown foods in its advertising, but it has so far failed to commit to using verifiable metrics to support these claims.[4]

To make these product decisions, McDonald's managers had to evaluate environmental shifts and assess their relevance to the organization's strategy and the probability of its continued effectiveness. The healthy food trend meant that McDonald's needed different products and different approaches to developing and sustaining its markets. McDonald's executives examined these trends and decided that product changes were necessary. If one takes the McDonald's example and generalizes it to all managers, then changes in the external environment provide important clues and cues for change leaders. Diagnosing and understanding those clues and cues provides the basis for a new vision and direction for change.

Each person has ideas about how organizations work. For some, this model is explicit—that is, it can be written down and discussed with others. However, many managers' views of organizational functioning are complex, implicit, and based on their personal experiences. Deep knowledge and intuition, so-called tacit knowledge, about the functioning of an organization is invaluable. However, tacit knowledge or intuition is intensely personal, often difficult to communicate, and almost impossible to discuss and challenge rationally. As a result, this book takes an explicit approach and provides ways to articulate unspoken models of how organizations work and to use several models to think systematically about how to change an organization.

Differentiating *How* to Change From *What* to Change

The complexity of change can be simplified somewhat by recognizing that there are two distinct aspects of organizational change that must be addressed. Managers must decide both *How* (process) to lead organizational change and *What* (content) to change in an organization. The example below highlights the difference between the how and what of change. Imagine that you are the general manager of a major hotel chain and you received the following customer letter of complaint:

A LETTER OF COMPLAINT

Dear Sir:

As a customer of yours, I wanted to provide you with our experiences at ATMI, your London, England, hotel.* I have reflected on my experience and decided to provide you with feedback—particularly given your promise on your website—the Hospitality Promise Program.

———————————

*The hotel name is disguised.

(Continued)

(Continued)

My wife and I arrived around 10 P.M. after a flight from North America and the usual tiring immigration procedures, baggage check, and finding our way to your hotel. The initial greeting was courteous and appropriate. We were checked in; the desk person asked if we wished a room upgrade. After I clarified that this would cost money, I declined that proposal.

We then went to our room on the 3rd floor, I believe, and discovered it was a disaster, totally not made up. I phoned the switchboard and was put through to reception immediately. There were profuse apologies and we were told that someone would be up immediately with another key.

Within 5 minutes, someone met us with a key to a room on the 5th floor, a quick, fast response. However, when we got to the new room, it was not made up!

Again I phoned the switchboard. The operator said, "This shouldn't have happened. I will put you through to the night manager." I said that was not necessary, I just wanted a room. However, the operator insisted and I was put through to the night manager. Again, there were profuse apologies and the manager said, "This shouldn't have happened, I will fix this and get right back to you." I indicated that I just wanted a room—I didn't want the organization fixed, just a room. The manager repeated, "I will get right back to you."

We waited 5, 10, 15 minutes. Inexplicably, the manager did not return the call even though he said he would.

Finally, around 20 minutes later, I phoned switchboard again. I said we were waiting for a room and that the night manager had promised to call me back. The operator said, "This is probably my fault as I was doing work for the assistant manager." I did not and do not understand this part of the conversation but again, I was told that they would call right back. Again, I repeated, "I just need a room."

I waited another 5 minutes—it was now 11 P.M. and we were quite tired—there was no return phone call.

My wife and I went down to reception, waited, and after a brief time were motioned forward by the person who registered us initially. I explained that we needed a room. He said, "You were taken care of. You got a room." I stated that "No, I did not have a room, I just had two rooms that were not made up and we needed a clean one for the night."

Again there were profuse apologies. The reception person then said, "Excuse me, just for a moment, so I can fix this." I said, "Really, I just would like a room." The person at the reception desk went around the corner and began to berate someone working there. This went on for several minutes. He then returned to his station, called me forward again, apologized again, and located a third room for us. As well, he gave us coupons for a complimentary breakfast.

This third room was made up. It was "more tired" than the previous rooms but it was clean and we were delighted to find a spot to sleep.

In the middle of the night, as is the norm in many places, the invoice was delivered to our room. To our surprise, a £72 charge was added to the price of the room for a "room change."

(Continued)

Of course, early the next morning, I queued up to discuss this charge. The same reception person was still on duty. He motioned me forward and then immediately left to open up all the computer stations in the reception area. He had a tendency to not make eye contact. This may have been a cultural phenomenon or it may have been his dismay at having to deal with me again. I cannot say.

I showed him the invoice. He said, "Oh, there will be no charge for that room." I said that I was concerned as the invoice did show the charge. He said, "It is taken care of." I said, "Regardless, I would like something to prove that there would not be another charge to my credit card." After one further exchange and insistence on my part, he removed the charge from my invoice.

My wife and I had a pleasant breakfast and appreciated it being complimentary.

We thought that you would want to know of our experience. Customer service is a critical part of the hospitality industry and I am certain that ATMI would wish feedback on experiences such as these.

I am interested in such things and look forward to your reply.

Yours truly,

The list of things done poorly and the organizational issues that exist at this hotel are extensive. Identifying this list of *what* needs attention is relatively easy. The desk clerk has twice assigned rooms that were unmade. This indicates that the system used to record and track information on the condition of the rooms is either non-existent or not working properly. One wonders if someone is responsible for monitoring the housekeepers' performance. There are managerial issues—a manager promises to get back to a customer and doesn't. There are organizational culture issues—the excuses by the switchboard operator and yelling by the reception person. There are further system issues or customer service problems as indicated by the £72 charge for a room change. There are some service training issues—the responses by the receptionist were variable. He was quick to send up a second room key but left the customer standing while he turned on computers. He was reluctant to reverse the extra room charge. There is some hint that there might be other cultural issues that are pertinent.

However, it is not clear *how* the general manager should proceed with needed changes. First off, how accurate is the letter? Can the general manager accept it, or does he have to investigate? Assuming the letter reflects the experiences of more than one unhappy customer, then the general manager still faces the "how" question. If the computer system for tracking room availability does not exist, then it is relatively simple to create and install one. However, if the system exists but is not being used, how does the general manager get the staff to use the system effectively? Closer supervision might work, but who can do that and who will pay for it? Even more difficult are the organizational and cultural issues. The norm among employees appears to be to make excuses and to "berate" others when things go wrong. A manager can tell employees that these behaviors are inappropriate, but how does one persuade employees not to respond abusively? And how will the general manager know if and when the changes are implemented? Is there a system in place to track customer and employee satisfaction? Are these several systems worth the cost they impose on the organization?

Clearly, managers must know what needs to change. However, how to go about making change happen requires careful thought and planning. The models provided below help you think about the process of change and how to make it happen.

The Processes of Organizational Change

As suggested above, many leaders know what they need to achieve, but they just don't know how to get there. An examination of competitors' initiatives and accomplishments, customer behavior, and other data from environmental scans will often provide cues as to what is needed, but moving one's own organization to successfully addressing these factors and related opportunities is difficult.

Why is it so difficult to accomplish change?

There is always a web of tightly woven factors that make organizational change difficult. However, one common cause might lie in practices that were effective in the past and that are no longer appropriate; this can be called the "failure of success." Organizations learn what works and what doesn't. They develop systems that exploit that knowledge and establish rules, policies, procedures, and decision frameworks that capitalize on previous successes. Further, they develop patterned responses (habits), assumptions, attributions, and expectations that influence the ways employees think about how the world works.[5] These beliefs and ingrained responses form a strong resistant force, which encourages organizations and people to maintain old patterns regardless of feedback or input suggesting that they are no longer appropriate. In many respects, this is where the questions of what to change and how to change intersect.

Charles Handy describes some of these dilemmas by examining the pattern of success over time.[6] As he so aptly said: too often "by the time you know where you ought to go, it's too late" (p. 50). He describes a **sigmoid curve** that outlines where one should begin changing and where it becomes obvious that one needs to change (see Figure 2.1). This curve depicts the outcomes of a system as a curve that increases during early-stage development and growth phases, flattens at maturity, and shifts into decline over time. Consider the path tracked by successful technological innovations. Once an innovation demonstrates its value to key early adopters, then sales take off. As others see the benefits of the innovation, they adopt it as well. Patents and proprietary knowledge provide some protection, but over time competitors launch similar products, profit margins become squeezed, and sales growth slows due to increased competition and the level of market saturation. This leads to a flattening of the curve, referred to as the maturity phase. Decline follows as the market becomes increasingly saturated and competitive, and this decline accelerates with the arrival of a new, disruptive innovation that attracts customers away from the existing product or service. Think of what happened to the VCR players when DVD players arrived on the scene. Consider how prices fell for DVD players in the face of competition. Now, video streaming has eclipsed the market for DVDs. DVDs are becoming obsolete as more companies offer streaming services.

The time to introduce change is at point B when the system is growing. The dilemma is that in the short run, the costs are likely to be greater than the benefits. It is only when the new changes are adopted and the system is working well that the outcomes' curve turns upward again. One dilemma is that the costs of change are real and include adding people and shifting production lines, while the benefits of change are uncertain. Managers believe the changes will improve productivity and profits, but that may not occur. By holding off investing in change, an organization may improve its profits in the short run. However, if environmental conditions continue to change and the organization fails to adjust in a timely fashion, executives can quickly find themselves lagging behind their competitors, scrambling to adapt, and running to catch up. If management waited too long to adapt, then an organization may find it impossible to do so.

By the time the system reaches point A, the need for change is obvious, but it may also be too late for the organization to survive without experiencing significant trauma. Positive planned change needs to be commenced sooner in the process—before things deteriorate to a crisis or disaster stage. Unfortunately, change typically comes with costs that appear to lessen the positive outcomes in the short run. As many know, convincing anyone that they should incur costs, make investments, and initiate changes now for long-run benefits is a difficult selling task, particularly if things are going well. This is depicted as the shaded space between the solid and dotted lines beginning at point B in Figure 2.1. The costs of change appear certain and are tangible. But the benefits are uncertain and often vaguely defined. The time after point B is a time of two competing views of the future, and people will have difficulty abandoning the first curve (the one they are

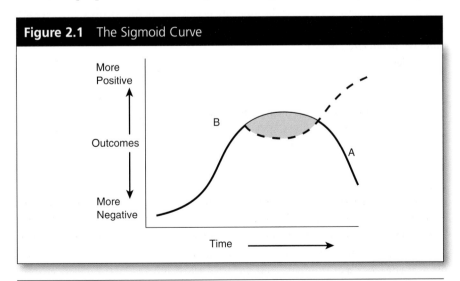

Figure 2.1 The Sigmoid Curve

Source: Adapted from Charles Handy, *The Age of Paradox* (Boston, MA: Harvard Business School Press, 1994), 50.

on) until they are convinced of the benefits of the new curve. In concrete terms, creating change at point B means convincing others about the wisdom of spending time and money now for an uncertain future return.

In the following pages we present six models of organizational change. These models are both discrete and complementary. Below is an overview of what you will find in these models.

- Lewin's model is simple, making it useful for communicating the overall change process to participants.
- Kotter's provides a detailed map of the change process in terms of what each step needs to achieve (i.e., the key success factors of a change initiative), which is useful for planning and implementation.
- Gentile provides individual-level guidance for pushing back and responding skillfully and effectively to people and situations that contradict a person's values; this approach may or may not make systemic change.
- Duck offers guidance for people and emotional issues within a step framework of change.
- Beckhard and Harris provide an action-oriented overview that indicates the sets of activities that should be completed within the steps Kotter identified (roughly).
- The Change Path Model maps sets of activities within a systems-level view (following Lewin) that also reflects organizational-level factors (e.g., operations, control, and measures).

The models have more similarities than differences.

- Each is a process model (i.e., they all depict *how* change should happen).
- Two are descriptive (Lewin and Duck), three are prescriptive (Kotter, Gentile, and Beckhard and Harris), and our Change Path Model combines both.
- One is system-level (Lewin); three are organizational-level (Kotter, Beckhard and Harris, and our Change Path Model); and two are individual-level (Gentile and Duck).
- The models describe many of the same processes, but describe them at varying levels of granularity and with different lenses (e.g., emotions with Duck, managerial tasks with Kotter).

Organizational change most often requires changing at three levels: individual, team or unit, and the organization. Learning and applying more than one model will give the change manager a large set of tools to work with.

(1) Stage Theory of Change: Lewin

Our first model is a basic step model. Sixty years ago, Kurt Lewin[7] wrote about the problem of how to bring about change. He described a three-stage model of change:

Unfreeze → Change → Refreeze

Lewin stated that we need to understand the situation and system as a whole as well as the component parts that make up the system. Before change can occur, an unfreezing process must happen within that system. **Unfreezing** focuses on the need to dislodge the beliefs and assumptions of those who need to engage in systemic alterations to the status quo. The unfreezing process might occur because of some crisis. For example, new competitive products that are attacking the major profit centers of a private enterprise might be a sufficient shock to the organization to "unfreeze" patterns. In this example, the balance in the system must be disrupted or broken in order to permit conditions for change to develop. Some top managers even talk about "creating a crisis" in order to develop the sense of urgency around the need for change.[8]

When this unfreezing occurs, the people who are embedded in the systems become susceptible to **change**. Systems and structures, beliefs, and habits become fluid and thus can shift more easily. Once the change has been completed, these systems, structures, beliefs, and habits can **refreeze** in their new form.

To illustrate Lewin's model, refer back to the Letter of Complaint and examine the comments below.

Unfreeze

Will this letter of complaint be sufficient to "unfreeze" the general manager and move him to action? If this is a single letter, it is highly unlikely that change will occur. If complaints are common for this hotel, this might be seen as just one more letter in a pile—background noise in running the hotel. The letter suggests that this might be an airport hotel in London, England. The location of the hotel might be such that customer service shortfalls might not make a difference to occupancy rates, whereas minimizing costs would be crucial to the hotel's profitability. In all the above scenarios, no unfreezing would take place.

However, this letter may represent an initiative that captures managerial attention and promotes action. The general manager might be facing declining occupancy and view this letter as a signal of where problems may lie. A comparison with other hotels on measures of profitability and customer satisfaction might demonstrate a dramatic need for change that the letter foreshadowed. In this situation, the general manager's views on the existing system are more likely to be unfrozen, and he would be ready for change.

Note that the unfreezing must take place at many levels. The general manager might be ready for change, but the persons at the reception desk might think things are just fine. Their perceptions need unfreezing as well! The integration and interdependence of systems and people require us to think about the unfreezing of the organizational system as a whole.

Change

Assume that the general manager accepts the need to improve the system that indicates that rooms are ready. He or she must now decide what else needs to be changed to bring about the needed improvements. This could begin by hiring a quality-control person who is charged with inspecting and certifying all rooms before they are entered into the system as "ready to use." Some computer programming may need to be done so that rooms are flagged when they are ready, and the quality-control person might be given responsibility for managing that flag subsystem. The quality-control person will have to be recruited, hired, and trained if management cannot promote an appropriate person from within. Once the room-quality system has been designed and procedures are in place, all receptionists will have to be trained. This change could be a participatory process with the involvement of staff, or the general manager could have it designed and order its implementation. The change process would be reasonably complex, involving a number of people and systems.

During this phase, there would be considerable uncertainty. The new system could well be ready before the quality-control person is hired and trained. Or the reverse—the person may be hired and trained but the room-quality system is not ready. Employees might see opportunities to improve what is being proposed and make suggestions regarding those improvements. Regardless of the specifics, the system would be in flux.

In addition to a quality-control person alternative, many other possible solutions exist—some may be much more participative and job enriching than the above. The questions the general manager must answer are which alternatives he will select, why, and how they will be implemented (who will do what, when, where, why, and how).

Refreeze

Once the changes are designed and implemented, employees will need to adapt to those changes and develop new patterns and habits. The new flag system will alter how those at reception and in housekeeping do their work. They may informally ask the quality-control person to check certain rooms first as these are in higher demand. The general manager will follow up to see how the system is working and what people are doing. New reporting patterns would be established, and the quality-control person might begin passing on valuable information to hotel maintenance and housekeeping regarding the condition of particular rooms. At this point, the system settles into a new set of balances and relative stability. With this stability comes refreezing, as the new processes, procedures, and behaviors become the new "normal" practices of the organization.

What do we mean by this notion of relative stability and predictability that comes with refreezing? It stems from the observation that organizational systems, composed of tasks, formal systems, informal systems, and individuals, develop an interdependent state of balance over time called homeostasis. Perturbations or shifts in one part of the system are resisted, or swings away from balance are countered and balance is regained. As suggested earlier, managers may introduce change initiatives only to have those initiatives fail because of existing systems, processes, or relationships that work against the change. Planned changes in structures and roles may be seen as decreasing the power and influence of informal groups, and these groups may react in complex ways to resist change. For permanent change, new structures and roles are needed and new points of balance or homeostasis developed.

The image of a spider's web can help to depict the phenomenon. That is, view the organization as a complex web of systems, relationships, structures, assumptions, habits, and processes that are interconnected and interdependent over time. Altering one strand of the web is not likely to alter the pattern or overall configuration significantly. To do that requires a breaking of many interconnected items—the "unfreezing" in Lewin's terms.

This simple model has stood the test of time. Change agents find it useful both because of its simplicity and because it reminds us forcefully that you can't expect change unless the system is unfrozen first! We may need other, more complex models of the organization to be able to think through what must be unfrozen and changed, but Lewin forces us to recognize the rigidity that comes with stability and interconnectedness within existing systems, relationships, and beliefs.

However, several concerns prevent us from wholeheartedly embracing this model. First, the model oversimplifies the process of change and suggests that change is linear. The reality is that change tends to be complex, interactive, and emergent. Second, the creation of the need for change deserves more attention. It is not merely a matter of moving individuals away from their assumptions about the current state. Rather, they need to have a vision of a future desirable state. Finally, the model implies that refreezing is acceptable as a frame of mind. This seems problematic because it implies that change is a discrete event, rather than a continuous process. In today's rapidly changing world, organizations find that pressures to adapt mean they are never "refrozen"—and if they are, they are in trouble.

Organizations that freeze too firmly may fail to thaw when new markets and customers appear. They may refuse to incorporate feedback in making useful changes. Continuous improvement programs may appear faddish, but they reflect a realistic view of what is needed in a dynamic environment because they enhance an organization's adaptive capacity. Thus, there is concern with the image created by the word *refreeze*, as this is likely too static a condition for long-term organizational health. In discussions with managers, we find the phrase "re-gelling" to have appeal as a state between total fluidity of a liquid and the excess rigidity of a solid. Since Lewin articulated his framework of organizational change in the early 1950s, it is likely that he, too, would have modified his framework for change.

(2) Stage Model of Organizational Change: Kotter

This second model describes a highly structured step-by-step process that overcomes the problem of simplification of Lewin's model. In 1996, Harvard Business School Professor John Kotter published *Leading Change.*[9] His eight-stage process argues that an organization must successfully go through each phase in sequence. For example, failing to establish a sense of urgency throughout an organization (step 1), may explain a leader's inability to communicate effectively a vision for change (step 4). Kotter's framework helps managers know what they should do, when they should take specific actions, and when and how they are ready to move to the next stage.

Kotter's Eight-Stage Process

1. **Establish a sense of urgency:** In older, well-established organizations a sense of complacency may have set in. Leaders need to illustrate the threats to the system and move enough organizational members from a sense of invulnerability to vulnerability.

2. **Create a guiding coalition:** Select a significant number of people (10 to 50) who have titles and lead divisions and departments, have the respect of their colleagues, and relevant knowledge. This group should be aligned and know that change is needed.

3. **Develop a vision and strategy:** People need an overarching dream of an inspiring future. From this vision comes the implementation plans and steps.

4. **Communicate** the change vision: Capture the hearts and minds of most employees by communicating through multiple channels and multiple times the vision for change.

5. **Empower employees** for broad-based action: Large numbers of employees need to embrace the vision and then organizational structures, human resources systems, and a myriad of other internal organizational mechanisms need to support, rather than block, the change.

6. **Generate short-term wins**: Large-scale organizational change may take three to five years and yet employees need to see evidence of successful change within to 18 months (p. 11). Highlight short-term gains to keep employees motivated.

7. **Consolidate gains and produce more change:** Since it takes years for organizational change to become a part of an organization's DNA, many leaders stop too soon. Keep pressing forward until the change seeps into the deepest recesses of an organization.

8. **Anchor new approaches** in the culture: Make sure that the change is embedded in the organization's cultural norms and values.

(3) Giving Voice to Values: Gentile

The third model focuses on the ethical implications of organizational change. Pick up any newspaper or magazine and one finds stories about personal, corporate, or governmental malfeasance; accounts of injustice; and reports of individual violence against peers and society's vulnerable members. In the past these stories included accounts of people such as Bernie Madoff and his elaborate Ponzi scheme, which robbed many investors of their money; and HealthSouth's CEO Richard Scrushy, who was convicted of bribery. In 2014, a scandal has been brewing over scheduling practices at Veterans Administration hospitals across the United States. An underlying issue in most of these situations is an organizational climate that does not effectively manage individual behavior. To minimize the chances of malfeasance, organizations sometimes have to change operating practices, incentives, monitoring systems, and most importantly, underlying values. The first step is recognizing that something is wrong (identify the need to change), and often that requires someone to speak up—the purpose and power of *Giving Voice to Values.*

With numerous examples of corruption and fraud, educator and research scholar Mary Gentile decided to develop a program, at first for business students, to support people's development of confidence and skills that would allow them to speak and act their values—effectively—when faced with a situation that runs counter to their principles. Gentile's *Giving Voice to Values* (GVV) curriculum[10] takes people through a learning process that prepares them to expect values conflicts and provides the tools to intervene when they perceive wrongdoing. (See http://www.babson.edu/Academics/teaching-research/gvv/Pages/home.aspx for a detailed description of the curriculum and its many dimensions.)

The GVV curriculum focuses on the practical application of skills needed to push back and respond skillfully and effectively to people and situations that contradict a person's values. The GVV curriculum consists of three parts that represent the process individuals need to work through to advocate for the need to change: the clarification and articulation of one's values; post-decision-making analysis and implementation plan; and the practice of speaking one's values and receiving feedback.

1. **Clarification and articulation of one's values:** The GVV curriculum invites participants to consider the notion that there is a universality of values and some researchers, such as Martin Seligman and Rushworth Kidder, have found a commonality of core values across cultures and religions. Kidder, who conducted a cross-cultural survey, identified a "list of five widely shared values: honesty, respect, responsibility, fairness, and compassion" (p. 30). The first step requires participants to articulate their values and the impact of acting on those values. This exercise encourages participants to take their often implicit principles and make them explicit and public, an important first step in bringing about change.

2. **Post-decision-making analysis and implementation plan:** The GVV curriculum requires participants to examine case studies of protagonists who have been clear about their values and have effectively voiced their principles in difficult situations (all GVV cases are available through the website). The protagonists of GVV cases have concluded what is right, and the cases walk readers through their thinking and actions—to a point: then readers are invited to figure out what the protagonist might

do to voice her values effectively. For example, in the "Not Even an Option" case, readers meet Ajith, a pharmaceutical representative in a developing country. Ajith is clear that paying bribes is not an option for him (read his story at the end of this book). And, yet, it seems that he and his company will not succeed unless he succumbs to societal norms and pays bribes to government officials to review and accept his company's registrations for the drugs. Participants analyze Ajith's situation and ask: given Ajith's unwillingness to pay bribes, what should he do and say, and to whom? These situations start from the point where the protagonist knows his values and what is right for him to do. GVV is, then, a curriculum about taking actions post-decision-making.

The analytical work can be further subdivided into three parts. First, participants engage in a stakeholder analysis. This is not the traditional "stakeholder analysis" that encourages a utilitarian weighing and making of trade-offs, but rather is an effort to understand how to effectively influence key people. Second, people need to anticipate how stakeholders might respond to the protagonist's questioning of the stakeholders' actions. Gentile calls this the "reasons and rationalization" that a protagonist might expect from others. And, third, Gentile asks: what levers can a protagonist use to persuade stakeholders to join the protagonist's vision?

3. The practice of speaking one's values and receiving feedback: One of the central tenets of GVV is the importance of "pre-scripting." As noted above, the GVV cases often invite readers to decide to whom the protagonist should talk and what she should say. Gentile believes that participants' practice in speaking their values after they have analyzed a situation "is both a cognitive exercise as well as a behavioral and emotional one" (p. 173). Participants write out a script, speak the script in front of another participant, and receive feedback from a third participant–observer who acts as a peer coach to the participant who is articulating the script. Delivering a script challenges participants to articulate often vaguely formed ideas, which deepens their sense that they will take action in difficult, future situations.

GVV and Organizational Change

An assumption of this GVV training is that prepared individuals will speak up and in their speaking up people will change the course of events in units, organizations, or even societies. The GVV cases provide numerous examples of people shifting the direction of their organizations. In the Helen Drinan case, for example, Drinan pushes back and speaks up when it seems that a CEO of a hospital system will be let off the hook even though several women have accused the CEO of sexual harassment.[11] The publicity surrounding this case led the attorney general of Massachusetts to note the problems with governance of the hospital system; eventually the Catholic Diocese of Boston was pushed to sell the hospitals. In the "Naivete or Boldness" case, the protagonist changes the course of her organization when she challenges her CEO and his consultant on their assumptions, numbers, and analysis.[12] The point is this: When people think tactically and strategically about how to most effectively create change around a values conflict, the person or group can be successful. Sometimes this process involves speaking up and at other times the process involves gathering data, asking questions, building a coalition, and/or making alliances with key people. The point of the GVV curriculum is to prepare people to expect conflicts in values and then to take effective action for individual and organizational change.

(4) Emotional Transitions Through Change: Duck

The fourth model captures the people and their emotional responses to the change process. In *The Change Monster: The Human Forces That Fuel or Foil Corporate Transformation & Change,*[13] consultant Jeanie Daniel Duck argues that organizational change evolves in a fairly predictable and manageable series of phases that she calls the "**Change Curve**." This Change Curve is a "simplification and an approximation" of complex, ambiguous, and volatile human emotions that accompany all types of organizational change, from externally driven mergers and acquisitions to internally planned and managed new programs.

Duck's Five-Stage Change Curve

1. **Stagnation** occurs when people have their heads in the sand and have an insufficient sense of threat or challenge from the external world. This can only end with a forceful demand for change from the external environment, such as a merger or acquisition, or from internal pressures for change from a strong internal leader or group. It is the leader's role to push people to see the truth of their situation and to wake them up.

2. **Preparation** begins with a dramatic announcement of change from an internal person, such as the CEO, or from an external force, such as an announcement of a takeover. Immediately, some people feel anxious or jittery; others may be hopeful that needed change is coming; while still others will retreat to cynicism and will not take the announcement seriously. When this rush of emotion occurs, productivity often goes down.

   This phase requires a tremendous amount of planning and operational work by the leaders. In addition, organizational leaders must be aligned for the planned change to succeed.

3. **Implementation** is when the journey begins. It includes designing new organizational structures, job descriptions, and lots of other detailed plans. However, operational changes are not enough: Implementation also requires changing people's mindsets and work practices—in other words, people's emotional maps and habits.

4. **Determination** kicks in when people realize that the change is real and they will need "to live their work lives differently" (p. 30). Duck argues that "people long for an excuse to quit the hard path of transformation," requiring leaders to recognize this emotional trap and to pursue the new vision with high energy and enthusiasm.

5. **Fruition** is the time when the hard work pays off and the organization seems new. "The employees feel confident in themselves; they're optimistic and energized, and they're able to get their work done with less hassle, in less time, and with better results" (p. 34). Leaders need to make sure that this basking in the satisfaction of the change does not lead to napping and future stagnation.

In 1969, Elizabeth Kübler-Ross observed and wrote in *On Death and Dying* about the five predictable emotional stages in terminally ill patients: denial, anger, bargaining, depression, and finally acceptance. She later said that these observable stages apply to children whose parents are going through divorce and to people who experience traumatic losses, such as parents whose child dies. Although Duck does not reference Kübler-Ross, Duck focuses on predictable human emotional responses to organizational change. In reality, people embrace change differently and at dissimilar speeds; Duck argues, however, that individuals go through similar emotional responses to change. It is the savvy leader who monitors his own emotional response to change, anticipates and articulates underlying negative and positive emotional responses to change, and then pulls the group through the negative to excitement and satisfaction with the new order.

(5) Managing the Change Process: Beckhard and Harris

The fifth model of change, outlined by Beckhard and Harris,[14] has a strong **focus on process**. Building on the work of Kurt Lewin, Beckhard and Harris propose a process model that begins with an assessment of why change is needed. Here the forces for and against change are analyzed and understood. A thorough understanding of the organization and its stakeholders will assist in this analysis. Following the recognition of the need for change, leaders are faced with the task of defining and describing a desired future state in contrast to an organization's present reality. This process is called a **gap analysis**. This second step in the change process involves both determining the need for change and creating a powerful change vision A desired future state allows leaders to identify the gap between the present and the future and how they propose to close the gap. This is one of the most important steps in the Beckhard and Harris Model and one that change leaders need to attend to. The discussion of how to get from the present to a desired future state represents the action or implementation state. The final step in the change process is to **manage the transition**. Beckhard and Harris provide a useful elaboration of how the process of change occurs. What is not so clear is how to bring the various stages of the model to life, in order to see change through to a successful outcome. The Change Path Model addresses this matter.

(6) The Change Path Model: Cawsey–Deszca–Ingols

Extracting from the preceding models, years of consulting work, and decades of teaching and talking with managers and executives about change, the Change Path Model combines process and prescription: There is more detail and direction than Lewin and less instruction than Kotter. We recommend that managers also use Gentile's model to act effectively, especially if there is a conflict in values. Duck reminds us about the all too often neglected side of change: the emotional impact of change. Beckhard and Harris remind us of the power of a well-executed gap analysis. (Figure 2.2 sets the out the change Path Model.)

Step 1: The first process is **Awakening**, which begins with a Critical Organizational Analysis (like Beckhard and Harris). Leaders need to scan continuously both their external and internal environments and understand the forces for and against any particular organizational shift. The most powerful drivers for change tend to originate outside organizations. These forces range from new legislation, new products launched by competitors, and new population trends to new technologies; in fact, it is usually an interlocking web of external factors that make environmental shifts so challenging for organizations to respond to effectively. Leaders *also* need to understand deeply what is going on inside their own organizations. For example, are people with critical competencies leaving the organization? If yes, why is the turnover rate disturbingly high? Managers need data from all significant parts of their organization and stakeholders to understand the dynamics internal to their institutions. Once external and internal data is compiled, leaders need to examine their organizations' situation and talk about how the new challenges from the external and internal environments impact their institutions. (Chapter 3 addresses how to diagnose an organization's problems and Chapter 4 focuses on identifying and clarifying the need for change, assessing the organization's readiness for change, and developing the vision for the change.)

Step 2: The second step in the process is **Mobilization**, which includes several significant actions. The determination of what specifically needs to change and the vision for change are further developed and solidified by additional analyses and by engaging others in discussions concerning what needs to change and nurturing their participation in the change process. Many assume that the need for change is easily recognizable, obvious, and evident from the environment. Sometimes this occurs, but often it is not the case. For example, if bankruptcy risks are rising or if profits have declined some people in the organization may believe things must change, but others may not, thinking that what is needed is to simply stay the course until conditions improve. However, once change leaders are convinced of the need for change, it is their job to convince others from the top of the organization to the frontline staff.

Change leaders also need to recognize that there is often a lag between what they know, as the results of their assessments, and what is known by others in different parts of the organization. This lag in information requires change leaders to engage others through multiple communication channels, so that they become convinced of the importance of changing now and not continuing to operate as they have in the past.

The development of the analysis of the present state and the definition of a desired future state leads to the solidification of the gap analysis—an image of the differences between where an organization presently is and where it needs and wants to go. A manager, for example, might have data that employee morale is low. To take appropriate action to improve employee morale, managers need to understand the root causes of the problem. Is it the pay system? Is it the performance appraisal system? Is the problem found across the organization, or is it confined to certain divisions? The answers to these and other questions may suggest different courses of action. In Chapter 3, several frameworks are described for readers to develop a sophisticated checklist for organizational diagnosis. The gap analysis allows change leaders to clearly address the questions of why change is needed and what needs to change. Being able to clearly and succinctly communicate this, along with the vision for the change, is critical to building shared understanding and support for the change in the organization. Think of this as the value of a clear, succinct, and compelling "elevator pitch" of what you have in mind and why it is worth undertaking.

The analyses of (a) formal structures, systems, and processes; (b) the power and cultural dynamics of the organization; (c) the various stakeholders; (d) the recipients of the change; and (e) the change agents themselves, all help to complete an understanding of the situation and the gaps that need attention. In addition to identifying the gaps that must be addressed, these analyses also help change leaders to understand how the existing situation can be leveraged in order to increase the prospects for success. For example, change leaders need to consider how existing systems and processes can be used to advance the change and how influence can be exercised and support built for the undertaking. Further, they need to assess how their own skills and abilities are best deployed to advance the changes.

Step 3: Acceleration involves action planning and implementation. It takes the insights gained in earlier chapters and translates them into the development and activation of a detailed plan for action, in order to bring the change to life. Appropriate tools are deployed to manage the plan, build momentum, and manage the transition. People are systematically reached out to, engaged and empowered to advance the change. Needed new knowledge, skills, abilities, and ways of thinking are developed in others to support the change. Finally, small wins and the achievement of milestones along the way need to be celebrated.

While the stages of the change process, including acceleration, are depicted as linear and straightforward, the reality is usually quite different. Managing change while operating the organization is like changing the tire on a moving car. Conditions can change in unanticipated ways and change leaders need to be able to learn, and adapt their understanding of the situation and what is needed, as they go. The vision for the change may also need to be adapted in ways that contribute to the accomplishment of desired outcomes. Transition management is the important practice of doing just that.

Step 4: Institutionalization involves the successful conclusion of the transition to the desired new state. This is aided by the sophisticated monitoring of progress along the way, including the assessment of when the changes have been incorporated into the fabric of the organization. Measurement can play a very useful role in this area. Understanding the impact of the particular organizational changes we are trying to achieve depends on our ability to measure such change and this sets the stage for future change initiatives. Measurement also plays important roles in earlier phases of the change process.

Figure 2.2 The Change Path Model

Awakening
Chapter 4

1. Identify a need for change and confirm the problems or opportunities that incite the need for change through collection of data.
2. Articulate the gap in performance between the present and the envisioned future state and spread awareness of the data and the gap throughout the organization.
3. Develop a powerful vision for change.
4. Disseminate the vision for the change and why it's needed through multiple communication channels.

Mobilization
Chapters 5 through 8

1. Make sense of the desired change through formal systems and structures and leverage those systems to reach the change vision (Chapter 5).
2. Assess power and cultural dynamics at play and put them to work to better understand the dynamics and build coalitions and support to realize the change (Chapter 6).
3. Communicate the need for change organization-wide and manage change recipients and various stakeholders as they react to and move the change forward (Chapter 7).
4. Leverage change agent personality, knowledge, skills and abilities, and related assets (e.g., reputation and relationships) for the benefit of the change vision and its implementation (Chapter 8).

Acceleration
Chapter 9

1. Continue to systematically reach out to engage and empower others in support, planning, and implementation of the change. Help them develop needed new knowledge, skills, abilities, and ways of thinking that will support the change.
2. Use appropriate tools and techniques to build momentum, accelerate and consolidate progress.
3. Manage the transition, celebrate small wins and the achievement of milestones along the larger, more difficult path of change.

Institutionalization
Chapter 10

1. Track the change periodically and through multiple balanced measures to help assess what is needed, gauge progress toward the goal and to make modifications as needed and mitigate risk.
2. Develop and deploy new structures, systems, processes and knowledge, skills and abilities, as needed, to bring life to the change and new stability to the transformed organization.

Application of the Change Path Model

Let's return to the hotel guest's letter presented earlier in this chapter and use it as an opportunity to apply the Change Path process model to an organization that appears to need to change.

Awakening: Why Change?

The general manager might have very good reasons for interpreting the letter as a signal not to change. The hotel already might be in the midst of a computer systems modification and be overwhelmed with this change. Or, the general manager may have a tracking system that indicates that most hotel guests are very satisfied and that this is an unusual occurrence. Or, the general manager may be under pressure to reduce costs and views change as leading to increased costs. Or, the general manager might see himself as exiting the organization and does not want to put the time and energy into changing systems.

On the other hand, the general manager may have the opposite reaction. The letter could trigger the manager to note inefficient processes that cause higher costs (i.e., it is more costly to clean a room twice or have to return to a room to deliver missing towels). If this letter were sent to Trip Advisor, Yelp, or another travel-related website, then the hotel could experience the loss of customers and a damaged reputation, particularly if it were one of a number expressing dissatisfaction.

Even if the general manager accepts the need for change, the employees might not. At this point in time, they know nothing about the letter. They may feel that their performance is good and no change is needed. They might have a department manager who doesn't follow up on directives and, thus, they could believe that no action is necessary. Or they might be new to their jobs and be poorly trained in customer service.

The challenge for the change leader is to articulate "why change" and their initial vision for the change to key stakeholders in ways that they will understand and move them to positive actions.

Mobilization: Gap Analysis of Hotel Operations

The present state of the hotel operations has several dimensions that could be addressed. The following gaps might exist:

- A gap in information between room readiness and the information that the desk clerk has
- A gap between what the hotel's managers say they will do and what they actually do
- A gap between the appropriate bill and the bill given to the customer
- A gap between the desired interpersonal relationships between employees and customers and that which exists
- A gap between the desired handling of hotel guests and that which occurs

Each of these gaps could require different action plans for change. Careful analysis will demonstrate that there are underlying issues that need to be dealt with. For example, if the organization's culture has evolved to one that is not focused on customer care and relationships, the individual gaps might be difficult to correct without a systematic approach. This gap analysis, then, needs to be used by change leaders to further develop and frame the vision for change. This vision plays a critical role in helping others understand the gap in concrete terms by contrasting the present state with the desired future state.

Taking an organization through the process of change requires going through predictable stages of change. Some organizational change experts, such as Kotter (1996)[15] and Duck (2001),[16] argue that a leader must successfully take the organization through each stage before moving to the next stage. While our experiences suggest that context matters and we challenge a rigid prescription of stages of change, we do believe that there is a predictable beginning, middle, and end process of change, and these set the stage for future pressures for change. Things don't stand still.

Acceleration: Getting From Here to There

In this phase, specific actions are undertaken to advance the implementation of the desired changes. Several planning tools can be used (see Chapter 9). If the general manager in the hotel case decided that the issue to be tackled is computer systems, then the implementation plan and actions might include the following steps:

- Discuss the need for change, the gap analysis, and the vision for change with involved staff to develop a consensus concerning the need for action.
- Form a users' task force to develop the desired outcomes and usability framework for a new computer system.
- Contact internal information systems specialists for advice and assistance on improving the hotel's information system.
- Identify the costs of systems changes and decide which budget to draw on and/or how to fund the needed systems' changes.
- Work with the purchasing department to submit a "request for proposal," promoting systems' suppliers to bid on the proposed system.
- Contact human resources to begin staffing and training plans.
- Implement the plans.

This list of sample tasks lays out the actions needed to accomplish the change. In Chapter 9, we identify tools that help in planning. For example, there are tools to assign responsibilities for different aspects of projects and others for contingency plans. Other tools illustrate how to manage during the transition. Organizations usually don't stop what they are doing because they are changing! In the hotel, for example, rooms will need to be made up, allocated, and assigned while the information system is being modified. In particular, receptionists will need to ensure a seamless transition from the old to the new system. In many system changes, parallel systems are run until the bugs in the new system are found and corrected. Hotel receptionists need to be trained on the new system. How and when that will be done in this implementation phase is part of the managerial challenge during the transition state.

Institutionalization: Measuring Progress Along the Way and Using Measures to Help Make the Change Stick

The final aspect of the model deals with the measurement of change and the metrics used in that measurement. How will the general manager know that the changes implemented are working? Managers can measure inputs easily, such as the number of hotel receptionists who are trained on the new system. But management will also need to track the number of times rooms are misallocated. This is a more difficult problem because the staff could be motivated to prevent accurate reporting from such a system, if the results could put the staff in a negative light. Chapter 10 talks about measurement and control methods that can assist change managers in navigating the path forward.

Models improve change managers' abilities to plan and implement organizational change and to predict outcomes. The Change Path Model provides a practical framework that lays out a linear process for change. This model, like others, risks having change managers oversimplify their challenges. Cause–effect analysis is complex because organizations are nonlinear, complex entities and the constantly shifting external environment impacts an organization's customers and resources. An overreliance on superficial thinking can lead to errors in judgment and unpleasant surprises. Organizations are more surprising and messier than people often assume.

Coordination and control of change may appear fairly straightforward. However, the reality is that organizations often undertake multiple change projects simultaneously. For example, a factory may be shifted toward a continuous improvement process while other parts of the organization are being restructured. Different managers are working on separate change projects to make things better. Under such complexity, control is difficult and likely involves multiple layers of authority and systems. Difficult yes, but coordination and integration of efforts towards shared goals can be accomplished when approached carefully, thoughtfully, and empathetically. See **Toolkit Exercise 2.2** to examine a change initiative through the Change Path process and differentiate between the how and what of change.

Summary

This chapter differentiates what to change from how to change and uses several models to explicitly consider how to change. Successful change management requires attention to both process and content. The Change Path Model serves as the organizing framework for the chapter sequence is laid out using the model. See **Toolkit Exercise 2.1** for critical thinking questions for this chapter.

Key Terms

How to change—relates to the process one uses to bring about change

What to change—relates to the assessment of what it is that needs to change—in other words, the content of the change

Sigmoid curve—describes the normal life cycle of something including an initial phase, a growth phase, deceleration, and decline

Lewin's Model of Change: Unfreeze → Change → Refreeze

Unfreezing—the process that awakens a system to the need for change—in other words, the realization that the existing equilibrium or the status quo is no longer tenable

Change—the period in the process in which participants in the system recognize and enact new approaches and responses that they believe will be more effective in the future

Refreeze (or re-gel)—the change is assimilated and the system reenters a period of relative equilibrium

Kotter's Eight-Stage Change Process

Establish a sense of urgency—upend complacency in order to communicate the need for change

Create a guiding coalition—a team of a significant number of people (10 to 50) who have titles and lead divisions and departments, have the respect of their colleagues, and relevant knowledge to lead the change

Develop a vision and strategy—an over-arching dream of an inspiring future and how to get there

Communicate, communicate, communicate—capture the hearts and minds of most employees by communicating through multiple channels and multiple times the vision for change

Empower employees—helping employees embrace the vision and support necessary structural mechanisms

Generate short-term wins—highlight short-term gains to keep employees motivated

Consolidate gains and produce more change—continue pressing forward until the change seeps into the deepest recesses of an organization

Anchor new approaches—embed the changes in the organization's cultural norms and values

Gentile's Giving Voice to Values

Clarification and articulation of one's values—articulation of one's own values and the impact of acting on those values, making implicit principles explicit

Post-decision-making analysis and implementation plan—understanding how to voice opinions in difficult situations

The practice of speaking one's values and receiving feedback—pre-scripting situations in order to practice voicing values

Duck's Five Phases of People's Reaction Model

Change Curve—a simplification of the complex, often volatile, human emotion that accompanies change

Stagnation—occurs when people have an insufficient sense of threat or challenge from the external world

Preparation—requires a tremendous amount of planning and operational work and alignment of leaders

Implementation—includes designing new organizational structures, job descriptions, and lots of other detailed plans as well as changing people's mindsets and work practices

Determination—motivation to continue the long path to transformation

Fruition—is the time when the hard work pays off and the organization seems new

Beckhard and Harris's Change-Management Process

Focus on process—is key to this model with a step-by-step prescription for change

Gap analysis—describing a desired future state in contrast to an organization's present reality

Manage transition—the final step in the process key to a successful change initiative

The Change Path—Cawsey-Deszca-Ingols

Awakening—the stage of the process in which the need for change is determined and the nature of the change or vision is characterized in terms others can understand

Mobilization—the identification of the distance between the desired future state and the present state at which the system operates

Acceleration—the stage of the process in which plans are developed for bridging the gap between the current mode of operation and the desired future state and the means by which the transition will be managed. A key part of this stage includes action planning and implementation.

Institutionalization—the process of making the change inherent in organizational processes. Also, a consideration of how to measure change and what measures will be used to help identify where the organization is and the level of success achieved.

END-OF-CHAPTER EXERCISES

TOOLKIT EXERCISE 2.1

Critical Thinking Questions

Please find the URL for the video listed below on the website at study.sagepub.com/cawsey3e. Consider the questions that follow.

1. **Giving Voice to Values:**

Please read Case 3 on page 438, "Not an Option to Even Consider: Contending With the Pressures to Compromise," and consider the following questions:

- Who are the important stakeholders that Ajith needs to work with?

- What are the main arguments that Ajith will need to counter? In other words, what are the reasons and rationalizations that Ajith should expect to encounter with the different stakeholders?

- What levers can Ajith pull to increase the chances that Laurent's drugs will be registered? In other words, what power and/or influence does Ajith have to get what he wants?

2. Gentile talks about the importance of Giving Voice to Values in order to frame and address ethical issues and change. Meet in small groups and discuss an issue organizations have to deal with that has conflict of values imbedded in it. Would positive change be advanced if we were to adopt the methodology recommended by Gentile?

This chapter explored a number of change models. Pick one of them and discuss their implications for change leaders.

3. Kotter's Eight-Step Organizational Change Model: Sydney Boone, Ayushmaan Baweja, and Steven Thomsen—12:57 minutes

This video delves more deeply into Kotter's process model of change.

- What are the key lessons or takeaways you got from the video?

- How do they help you think about the process of leading change?

- Compare this approach with the Change Path Model. What are their similarities and differences, and how would you work with both models if you were leading change?

Please study.sagepub.com/cawsey3e for a downloadable template of this exercise.

TOOLKIT EXERCISE 2.2

Analyzing a Change Process Through the Change Path Model

Part I

Interview a manager at any level who has been involved in change with his or her organization. Ask the person to describe the change, what he or she was trying to accomplish, and what happened. Use the following questions as guides for the interview.

- How was the desired change identified? What was the reason for the change?
- Describe the gap between the organization's current performance and the desired future state.
- What was the vision for the change? How was that vision communicated throughout the organization?
- How were the formal structures, systems, and processes involved in the change?
- How were the recipients of change and other key stakeholders engaged in order to get them on board with the change?
- What tools and trainings were used as the change was implemented, and how did the leadership make the change stick?
- What challenges surfaced that weren't accounted for in the original change plan?
- What were the results of the change process? Did the results reflect the original vision? How was measurement used to facilitate change at different stages of the process?

Part II

After the interview, describe the process of the change by answering the following questions that are related to *how* they managed the process:

- How did the manager work to make things happen?
- Who was involved?
- How did they persuade others?
- What resources did they use?

Also describe *what* was being changed? Why were these things important? How did these changes help the organization?

- As you reflect back on the interview, which do you feel was more important to the impact of the change: how things were changed or what was changed?

Please see study.sagepub.com/cawsey3e for a downloadable template of this exercise.

CHAPTER 3

Frameworks for Diagnosing Organizations

"What" to Change in an Organization

There is nothing as practical as a good theory.

—Kurt Lewin

CHAPTER OVERVIEW

- Change leaders need to understand both the process of making organizational modifications (the *how* to change as outlined in Chapter 2) and the ability to diagnose organizational problems and take actions to change an organization.
- Determining what needs changing requires clear organizational frameworks. Change leaders need to comprehend the complexity and interrelatedness of organizational components: how analysis needs to occur at different organizational levels, and how organizations and their environments will shift over time, requiring further analysis and action.
- This chapter outlines several frameworks that one can use to analyze organizational dynamics:

  (1) Nadler and Tushman's Congruence Model balances the complexity needed for organizational analysis, and the simplicity needed for action planning and communication, and provides the over-arching structure for this book;

(Continued)

(2) Sterman's Systems Dynamics Model views the nonlinear and interactive nature of organizations;

(3) Quinn's Competing Values Model provides a framework that bridges individual and organizational levels of analysis;

(4) Greiner's Phases of Organizational Growth Model highlights organizational changes that will—inevitably—occur over time in organizations, from their infancy to maturity; this model is particularly useful for entrepreneurs who sometimes need to be reminded that change needs to occur, even in their small start-up organizations; and

(5) Stacey's Complexity Theory is introduced to highlight the interactive, time-dependent nature of organizations and their evolutionary processes.

- Each framework aids a change agent in diagnosing a particular kind of organizational issue and suggests remedies for what ails an institution.

I n Chapter 2, we considered the process of change (the Change Path). In this chapter, we deal with what aspects of an organization to change. Differentiating the process from the content is sometimes confusing, but the rather unusual example below will highlight the difference.

> Bloodletting is a procedure that was performed to help alleviate the ills of mankind. . . . In the early 19th century, adults with good health from the country districts of England were bled as regularly as they went to market; this was considered to be preventive medicine.[1]

The practice of bloodletting was based on a set of assumptions about how the body worked—bloodletting would diminish the quantity of blood in the system and thus lessen the redness, heat, and swelling that was occurring. As a result, people seemed to get better after this treatment—but only in the short term. The reality was that they were weakened by the loss of blood. As we know today, the so-called science of bloodletting was based on an inaccurate understanding of the body. It is likely that bloodletting professionals worked to improve their competencies and developed reputations based on their skills in bloodletting. They worked hard at the *how* aspects of their craft. Advances in medicine prove that they did not really understand the consequences of *what* they were doing.

Bruch and Gerber differentiate *the what* and *the how* in a leadership question—"What would be the right action to take?"—and a management question—"How do we do it right?"[2] They analyzed a strategic change program at Lufthansa that took place from 2001 to 2004. This program generated more than €1 billion in continuing cash flow. The *how* questions focused on gaining acceptance of the change: focusing the organization, finding people to make it happen, and generating momentum; and the *what* questions were analytical, asking what change was right, what should be the focus, and what can be executed given the culture and situation. Bruch and Gerber concluded that a focus on implementation was not sufficient. A clear grasp of the critical needs, the change purpose or vision, was also essential.[3]

The two foundational models of this book are the Change Path Model (Chapter 2) and the Nadler and Tushman's Congruence Model (Chapter 3). The latter helps in the analysis of what is going on in an organization and what components of an organization need to be changed. That is, it is the "what to change" model. In any organizational change, both process (how to) and content (what) are important. Thus, we embed the Nadler and Tushman model in the four-stage Change Path Model. Nadler and Tushman help us to understand what gaps exist between where the organization is and where we want the organization to be. Like all models, the Nadler and Tushman's Congruence Model captures organizational reality from one perspective; consequently, Chapter 3 describes four additional organizational models designed to assist change leaders in their thinking about organizations and the reality that they represent.

For strengths, the Nadler and Tushman's Congruence Model gives us a comprehensive picture of an organization, its component parts, and how they fit together. That is, it asks us to examine organizational tasks (the work of the organization), people, informal organization (often thought of as the culture), and the formal organization (structures and systems) in the context of an organization's environment, resources, history, and inputs. Organizations are dynamic and highly interactive with their constantly changing environments. Change one aspect of an organization and other things are affected. Change the compensation system, for example, and we expect motivation and efforts of employees to change as well—which they might or might not do.

Our second model in this chapter, Sterman's Systems Dynamics Model, helps us to understand underlying dynamics and to see potential unanticipated consequences before they happen. Sterman asks managers to discard their linear, rational, causative view of organizations and to expand their perspectives to complex, interactive, multi-goal viewpoints.

Much of the change literature and thinking focuses on the change leader or manager or on those who may be resisting change. Note that this perspective is at the individual level. If we focus only at that individual level, we will miss major environmental factors and system or organizational-level matters. Our third model of this chapter, Quinn's Competing Values Model, reminds us to think of both levels. This model captures much of the dual reality. It categorizes organizations into four cultural types with matching roles and skills needed to effectively operate in each of the organizational cultures.

So, we know that we need to have a process to change (the Change Path helps). We need to know what to change (Nadler and Tushman help). We need to understand how systems are interactive and dynamic (Sterman helps). And we need to think about levels of analysis: individual and organizational (Quinn helps). But we also know that both the internal and external environment changes over time.

In order to help us think about time, our fourth model, Greiner's Phases of Organizational Growth Model, helps. Greiner posits a series of predictable stages that occur in the life of an organization. While the empirical evidence to support this model is weak, many managers find this prescriptive stage model helpful in thinking about organizations and how they change over time and growth.

Finally, our fifth model recognizes just how complex organizational systems are. Stacey's Complexity Theory provides a set of propositions about organizations that helps us to capture the implications of intricacies and convolutions.

In summary, to be a successful change leader we need to understand both how to change and what to change. We need to know that organizations are dynamic, they can be viewed at different levels of analysis (individual or organizational), they change over time, and they are complex. Each model described in this chapter builds our conceptual toolkit to better lead change.

Open Systems Approach to Organizational Analysis

Organizations interact with their environments in complex and dynamic ways. This **open systems perspective** is based on the following assumptions:[4]

- Open systems exchange information, materials, and energy with their environments. As such, a system interacts with and is not isolated from its environment.
- A system is the product of its interrelated and interdependent parts and represents a complex set of interrelationships rather than a chain of linear cause–effect relationships.
- A system seeks equilibrium: when it is in equilibrium, it will only change if some energy is applied.
- Individuals within a system may have views of the system's function and purpose that differ greatly from the views held by others.
- Things that occur within and/or to open systems (e.g., issues, events, forces) should not be viewed in isolation, but rather should be seen as interconnected, interdependent components of a complex system.

The adoption of an open systems perspective allows managers to identify areas of misalignment and risk between the external environment and the organization's strategy and structure. Open systems analysis helps practitioners to develop a rich appreciation for the current condition of an organization, and plausible alternatives and actions that could improve it. For example, when people, products, or services within systems have operated without considering their environment for extended periods of time, they risk becoming seriously incongruent with the external environment.[5] Or, if an environment changes rapidly, the results can prove disruptive and, in some cases, disastrous for an organization. Consider how the innovations and actions at Apple and Google disrupted the smartphone market in ways that left Blackberry and Nokia scrambling to revive and reinvent themselves as relevant technology providers. Innovation by one company led to significant disruption and change for other organizations. Disruptions can shake organizations to their foundations, and they also have the potential to sow the seeds for renewal (hence the term *creative destruction*, coined by Joseph Schumpeter[6]).

In summary, organizations should not be analyzed as if they exist in a bubble, isolated from their environments. But rather, organizations should be analyzed as to how effectively and efficiently they garner resources from the external environment and transform these resources into outputs that the external environment welcomes. Nadler and Tushman's Congruence Model does just that.

(1) Nadler and Tushman's Congruence Model

In this book, the Nadler and Tushman model is used as a framework to assist in structuring change leaders' organizational analysis. The model has a reasonably complete set of organizational variables and presents them in a way that encourages straightforward thinking. It specifically links environmental input factors to the organization's components and outputs. As well, it provides a useful classification of internal organizational components and shows the interaction among them. Nadler and Tushman's model is one example of an open systems model.

Nadler and Tushman[7] provide a conceptual scheme that describes an organization and its relationship to its external environment. The Congruence Model is based on the principle that an organization's performance is derived from four fundamental elements: tasks (or the work of the organization), people, formal organization (structure and systems), and informal organization (part of which is the "culture"). The more congruence there is among these four components, and the more aligned they are with the external environmental realities and the strategy of the organization, then the better the organization's performance will be in the external marketplace—whether it is the quality of services for at-risk youths offered by a local school board, or a new electric vehicle an automobile firm hopes will achieve market acceptance.[8] An adaptation of their model is depicted in Figure 3.1. This model is used as a framework for this book. Inputs are transformed to outputs, and the feedback links make the model dynamic and the components highly interdependent.

History and Environment

From its start-up phase, leaders of an organization make choices concerning where they want to locate themselves, what they want to do, and which resources they want to buy, access, or otherwise develop and deploy. These historical decisions set the stage for future actions and outcomes, and which human, technological, and capital resources they subsequently seek from the environment. The history of an organization provides insights into how it evolved its mission, culture, strategy, and approach to how it organizes and manages itself. 3M's early experience, for example, as a near bankrupt mining company set the stage for a sustained culture that highly values flexibility and innovation as keys to its resilience and success.

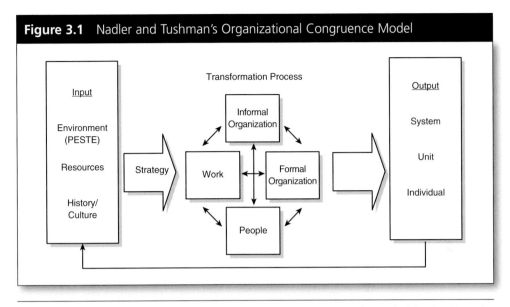

Figure 3.1 Nadler and Tushman's Organizational Congruence Model

Source: From Nadler, D.A. & M.L. Tushman, "Organizational Frame Bending: Principles for Managing Reorientation." *Academy of Management Executive,* 1989, Volume III, Number 3, pp. 194–204.

In addition to history and resources, external environmental factors play a huge role in influencing what organizations choose to do. These include political, economic, social, technological, and ecological factors. For example, if a competitor launches a more attractive product/service, if new environmental regulations are enacted that create risk or opportunity for your products/services, or if an attractive new foreign market is emerging due to changing economic and demographic conditions, organizations will need to consider such environmental factors and trends as they decide upon their strategic approach. All organizational leaders must deal with an organization's history, and recognize the impact and constraints, as they deal with the current external environment and seek to align their resources with the strategy to produce the desired results. In thinking about what to change, all inputs may be sources of opportunity and constraint.

For change leaders, an ability to analyze the organization's external environment and see implications for action in the organization is a central change skill.

Strategy

An analysis of the organization's competencies, strengths, and weaknesses, in light of the environmental threats and opportunities, leads to the strategy that organizational leaders decide to pursue. Strategic choices lead to the allocation of resources. Sometimes the strategy is consciously decided. At other times, it is a reflection of past actions and market approaches that the organization has drifted into. When there is a gap between what leaders say their strategy is and what they do (i.e., the actual strategy-in-use), one needs to pay close attention to the strategy in use. In Chapter 4, we discuss strategy in depth.

For change leaders, the change strategy is a critical focus of their analysis. What are the purposes and objectives of the planned change in the context of the organizational strategy? Is it of the fine-tuning variety, to better align resources with the strategy, remove an obstacle, and more effectively deliver the desired results, or does the change involve something much more substantial, including changes to the strategy itself?

The Transformation Process

The next elements of the model are what Nadler and Tushman define as the transformation process. This is where the organization's components are combined to produce the outputs. They include the work to be done, the formal structures, systems and process, the informal organization, and the people.

Work

The work is the basic tasks to be accomplished by an organization and its subunits in order to carry out the organization's strategy. Some of these tasks are key success factors that the organization must execute in order to successfully implement its strategy. An organization's work may be described in a very discrete way, listing, for example, the duties of a particular position, or, at the polar extreme, the basic functions such as marketing, production that the organization performs in its transformation processes. Tasks may be nested in teams, requiring coordination and integration, or be separated and independent from one another. The work may be designed to require a wide range of sophisticated skills and abilities or require a narrow set of basic skills. The work may require sophisticated judgment and decision making or require people to follow standardized procedures. Existing task designs reflect past decisions concerning what needs to be done and how best to do things. These designs often reflect cultural beliefs in the organization and are, to a degree, a matter of choice. Chapter 5 deals with how the work is formally structured and organized.

In change situations, change leaders should think through the necessary shifts in key tasks in order to carry out the change initiative. This will assist in developing a specific gap analysis and change plan.

The Formal Organization

The formal organization includes the "organizational architecture, a term that describes the variety of ways in which the enterprise structures, coordinates, and manages the work of its people in pursuit of strategic objectives."[9] Once tasks are identified and defined, they are grouped to form reporting relationships, the formal organizational chart of roles, responsibilities, departments, divisions, and so on. The purpose of a structure is to enable efficient and effective task performance. The systems of an organization are the formal mechanisms that help the organization accomplish its work and direct the efforts of its employees. These include an organization's human resource management systems (recruitment and selection, reward and compensation, performance management, training and development); information systems; measurement and control systems (e.g., budget, balanced scorecard); production systems; and so forth. Chapter 5 deals with designed systems and structures.

Change leaders need to understand how the formal systems and structures influence people's behaviors and how structures can be used to facilitate change. Often formal systems, such as budgeting systems, need to be used to gather data for change.

The Informal Organization

The informal relationships among people and groups in the organization, the informal way things get done, and the norms accepted by organizational members reflect the way the culture manifests itself in the organization. While managers define the work necessary to accomplish the strategy and then structure those tasks in formal ways, many things occur that are unplanned, unanticipated, and/or evolve over time. For example, friendly relationships between individuals often ease communications; groups form and provide support or opposition for the accomplishment of tasks; and individuals and teams adapt procedures to make things easier or more productive.* The informal system will include an organization's culture, the norms or understandings about "how we do things around here," values (e.g., about the importance of customer service), beliefs (for example, about why the organization is successful), and managerial style (a "tough boss" style, for example). It will also reflect the informal leadership and influence patterns that emerge in different parts of the organization.

Culture is a product of both the organization's history and its current organizational leadership. It acts as a control system in the sense that it defines acceptable and unacceptable behaviors, attitudes, and values and will vary in strength and impact, depending upon how deeply held and clearly understood the culture is. Other elements of the informal organization that are important to analyze when considering how to create change include power relationships, political influence, and decision-making processes. Chapter 6 deals with informal systems, power, and culture.

Change leaders need to make explicit the oftentimes implicit norms and behaviors of individuals and groups. Identifying the currently useful and dysfunctional norms and dynamics is a critical change agent activity.

People

The people in an organization perform tasks using both the organization's designed systems and structures, and the informal cultural processes that have evolved. It is important that the attitude, knowledge, skills, and abilities of each person match the individual's role, and that their responsibilities and duties match

---

*For an interesting perspective on the relational aspect of an informal system, see either M. Hutt, et al., "Defining the Social Network of a Strategic Alliance," *Sloan Management Review 41*, no. 2 (2000): 51–62, or D. Krackhardt and J. R. Hanson, "Informal Networks: The Company Behind the Chart," *Harvard Business Review 74*, no. 4 (1993): 104–111.

the organization's needs. Understanding the individuals in the organization and how they will respond to the proposed change will be significant in managing the change process. The role of stakeholders and change recipients is discussed in Chapters 4, 6, and 7.

Within every organization, certain key individuals are critical to its success. Often we think of the formal leaders as those who are most important in terms of accomplishing the mission, but others may be crucial. These people might have special technical skills or might be informal leaders of a key group of employees. People such as these, acting as change leaders, are described in Chapter 8.

Change leaders need to understand the impact of proposed changes on the organization's employees. Further, they need to identify key leaders in the organization who can facilitate the needed changes.

Outputs

The outputs of an organization are the services and products it provides to generate profitability or, especially in the case of public sector and nonprofit organizations, to meet mission-related goals. Additional outputs are also important: the satisfaction of organizational members, the growth and development of the competencies of the organization and its members, and customer satisfaction (to name just three). These outputs need to be defined and measured as attentively as profitability, return on investment (ROI), or numbers of clients served.

The above model reflects how one would look at the organization as a whole. However, this same approach can be adapted to look at internal parts of an organization that supply inputs or services for another part of the enterprise. The success of the organization in producing desired outputs should become part of the feedback loop and a new input to the organization. In a well-functioning organization, feedback could provide pressure to modify the strategy or internal alignments. Chapter 10 focuses on the measurement of change.

Change leaders need to recognize that "what gets measured is what gets done." They need to select key measures that will track the change process.

In their work, Nadler and Tushman make three critical statements. First, the system is dynamic. This means that a diagnosis of how the organization should operate will change over time with different concerns and objectives. Second, the "fit" or congruence between components is significant in diagnosing why the organization performs well or poorly. And third, the better the fit is among organizational components and their alignment with the environment, the more effective the organization is. The organizational change challenge is to align the system's components to respond to changing external and internal conditions.

The System is Dynamic

When an organization's environment shifts, so must its diagnosis, in order to identify the changes needed to effectively realign its people, formal systems and processes, tasks, and culture to that environment and produce the desired outcomes.

For example, when inflation was running at 1,100% per year in Brazil,[10] the influence of financial executives soared because financial management played a pivotal role in sustaining firms. When inflation slowed and stabilized in the range of 10 to 20%, power shifted away from finance and toward sales, marketing, and production. If the external environment alters significantly, the internal organization needs to change also. While this may seem like a statement of the obvious, it often goes unobserved in practice. Managers develop patterns of thinking about organizational performance that served them well in the past, but over time these patterned approaches may impair their ability to see when conditions change. Since the external environment is dynamic, the internal systems also need constant tuning, or even transformation.

The "Fit" Between and Among Organizational Components Is Critical

Nadler and Tushman argue that there are many different ways to think about the components of an organization. However, they choose to focus their model on four major components: "1) the task, 2) the individuals, 3) the formal organizational arrangements, and 4) the informal organization."[11]

A change agent needs to understand these four components of an organization and how they fit together and influence one another. Congruence is a measure of how well pairs of components fit together. For example, executives in an organization who restructure and ignore the knowledge and skills of people who will fill the newly created jobs do so at some risk. Restructured organizations with newly defined jobs either require the retraining of employees, or the hiring of new employees with the requisite skills. Or, if managers create structures to fit several key people and then those people leave, there may be a significant loss of fit between the structural components and the new key people.

Organizations With Good Fit Are More Effective Than Those With Poor Fit

Nadler and Tushman argue that effective organizations have excellent "fit" or "congruence" between components. Further, they argue that the strategy needs to flow from an accurate assessment of the environment and respond to or take advantage of changes occurring in that environment. Similarly, the strategy needs to fit the organization's capabilities and competencies. If all of these are not aligned reasonably well, the strategy will fail and the organization will be less effective than it could have been. Inside the organization, the four components (tasks, designed structure and systems, culture, and people) must fit each other. For example, if an organization hires motivated, highly skilled individuals and assigns them routine tasks without challenge or decision-making opportunities, those individuals will likely be bored. There will be a lack of fit and productivity will suffer. Or, if the strategy demands the adoption of new technology and employees are not provided with the necessary training, fit is lacking. Within categories, elements might not fit. For example, an organization might decide to "empower" its employees to improve performance. If it fails to adjust the supervisory approach and reward system to reinforce the desired behaviors, this lack of fit could easily lead to a failure of the empowerment strategy.

Overall, lack of fit leads to a less effective organization. Good fit means that components are aligned and the strategy is likely to be attained.

For many managers, the notion of fit is easiest to understand as they follow the flow from strategy to key tasks to organizing those tasks into formal structures and processes to accomplish the desired objectives. This is a rational approach to management and appeals to one's logic. At the same time, the reality of organizations often means that what appears to management as logical and necessary is not logical to employees. Managerial logic may be viewed by employees as against their interests or unnecessary. Peters recognizes the importance of the so-called nonrational aspects of organizations.[12] He argues that managers should tap into the power of teams to accomplish results and that individuals can be challenged to organize themselves to accomplish tasks. Thus, while fit is easiest to picture in logical terms, change agents need to consider it in terms of the informal system and the key individuals in the change process who will influence its success.

In a typical scenario, changes in the environment require leaders to rethink the organization's strategy. This, in turn, results in changes in key tasks and how managers structure the organization to do those tasks. In developing a new strategy and in redesigning an organization's systems and structures, managers need to become aware of and understand the influence of key individuals and groups.

Nadler and Tushman's Congruence Model framework helps practitioners in three ways. First, it provides a template to assist in an organizational analysis. Second, it gives one a way of thinking about the nature of the change process— environmental factors tend to drive interest in the organization's strategy, which, in turn, propels the transformational processes. These, then, determine the results. Third, the congruence framework emphasizes that, for organizations to be effective, a good fit among all elements in the process is required from environment to strategy through to the transformation process. Fit is also necessary within the transformation process; this is a constant challenge for incremental change initiatives such as continuous improvement programs. An emphasis on the internal fit between organizational components often focuses on efficiency. An emphasis on the external fit between the organization and its environment is an effectiveness focus. See **Toolkit Exercise 3.2** to practice examining a situation through Nadler and Tushman's model.

An Example Using Nadler and Tushman's Congruence Model

Over the past several years, Dell Computers has transformed itself. Dell made its name by selling low-cost computers directly to customers. The company was renowned for an efficient supply chain that allowed it to receive payment for its computers before it incurred the cost of building them. The Dell story outlines the company's attempt to reorient itself.

DELL COMPUTERS REORIENTS ITSELF[13]

For years, Dell focused on being the low-cost, efficient producer of computers. As one report put it, "Dell long stuck with its old playbook of cranking out PCs as efficiently as possible." Dell had focused on making the computer a commodity and sold online using generic parts. Dell focused on optimizing the business it already had while the market shifted. Its competitors, Hewlett-Packard, IBM, Apple, and others, marketed newer, sleeker laptops with better Internet capabilities using retail stores for distribution.

In 2007, company founder Michael Dell returned as CEO after three years of relative distance from operations. He replaced his senior management team, added new products and services, and focused on what customers wanted. However, the marketplace was changing radically as smartphones and similar products became the hot, new focus.

The troubles for Dell had begun when the market shifted. Growth in the corporate market lessened while the consumer sector flourished. As well, developing markets overseas became critical—markets that were less willing to buy over the Internet and use direct delivery. Additional processing power became less critical, and consumers demanded special features and more attractive machines. Dell saw the clear need to alter what it was doing. A diagnosis of what would work led to an overhaul of its products and the company.

After taking over, Michael Dell responded to the marketplace. He set up mechanisms to get customers' input. He shifted Dell's distribution strategy to sell in retail outlets, too. This required a shift in mindset for Dell managers, as they had to establish new distribution systems and manage their relationships with retailers. New machine designs were created and new hardware, including smartphones, were offered. Dell began selling mini-notebooks to appeal to overseas markets. And the company responded to changes in the corporate sector by providing systems solutions, not just computers.

To implement his strategy, Michael Dell installed a new senior management team. One of his first moves was to hire Ron Garriques, the executive who introduced Motorola's Razr phone, as head of Dell's consumer business. Garriques shut down work on the Mantra, a standard line of Dell products. As well, he stopped the introduction of Dell specialty stores and developed relationships with retailers. Product design became a new, central focus.

Michael Dell also brought in Brian Gladden from GE. Gladden believed that Dell needed to be restructured, that its systems and processes were not sophisticated enough for a company of its size. One major move was to shift how Dell focused on external markets by organizing around market segments, such as consumers, corporations, small- and mid-sized businesses, and governments and educational buyers.

Culture change was necessary to shift Dell to a more responsive, flexible company. Group leaders had clear financial targets but were given significant discretion in determining how to achieve these targets.

New products were developed and Dell began selling what in 2010 was the world's thinnest notebook. Design and style were emphasized, along with "tech appeal." Smartphones were also introduced, but Dell announced it was exiting this product category in December 2012 as they continued to search for a strategy that would work in this very competitive sector.

(Continued)

(Continued)

While Dell Inc. remained one of the leading companies in the technology indus-try, key financial ratios from 2006 and 2010 illustrate its problems: profit margins fell from 6.5% in 2006 to 2.7% in 2010. In 2006 Dell reported revenue growth at 13.6%; in 2010 the company reported a 13.4% decline in revenue.[14] Ever-the-optimist CEO Michael Dell said the business climate was improving and "repeated his expectations for a 'powerful' hardware refresh cycle beginning next year (2010)."[15] Somewhere in the 2011–2013 period, Michael Dell decided to take his eponymous company private. He had concluded that further changes were needed and that being a publically listed firm was getting in the way of accomplishing the longer-term objectives. By November 2013, he was celebrating his public to private deal with 350 employees in Silicon Valley. As one of the world's richest men, Dell mixed in "his 16% ownership, valued at more than $3 billion, and another $750 million in cash, with $19.4 billion from Silver Lake Partners (a private equity firm) for a 75% stake in Dell Inc."[16] Time will tell if Michael Dell can transform Dell Inc.

During its rapid growth years in the 1990s, Dell provided unrivalled service to its markets. Corporations wanted reliable equipment with good prices and excellent service. Dell provided this with online ordering and fast delivery. Its manufactur-ing, inventory management, and distribution systems were designed to deliver built-to-order PCs at a low cost. Speed of production became critical in order to minimize the delay between customer order and shipment to that customer. Relationships in the market were with customers, not retailers. While major clients (governments, etc.) had clout, as long as Dell delivered quality products and pro-vided good technical service, the clients were satisfied. The key tasks, to use Nadler and Tushman's terminology, were production and distribution.

During this growth phase, Dell's organization was aligned well with its market. Internally, the production orientation fit those market needs. Systems were designed for efficiency and simplicity. There was no need for retail management. Inventories were minimized as Dell built to order. Finances were simple because customers paid as they ordered and before Dell incurred the costs of production. Dell's management team excelled at getting efficiencies from this system, and the results showed for many years.

As the market shifted, the Dell organization became increasingly out of sync with the marketplace. Dell's strategy was no longer a good fit as the marketplace shifted away from corporate demand to consumers, from machine power to design, from hardware to software and the Internet, from America to developing nations. The clean, straightforward organization that Dell had built could not meet the more complex market expectations.

Note how Michael Dell responded. All components of the company changed. First, the strategy shifted. Design was emphasized. Retailers became key parts of the distribution network. Product variety increased. With that strategic shift, the key success factors or critical tasks changed. Design became more important. Management of retail distribution became crucial and introduced an entirely new set of skills at Dell. As the product range increased, skills in the introduction and timing of new products became more important. To manage this, the company was reorganized into four divisions, each focused on one major customer segment. Financial systems would need to be overhauled to manage this complexity. New formal and informal networks were established as the company's focus changed. Key executives were replaced by others with the skill sets demanded by this new strategy. In short, a new state of congruency was sought so that the internal operations fit the new strategy better.

Dell's reorganization provides an excellent example of how the Nadler and Tushman model's notions of congruency can be used to help to understand and analyze organizations. These efforts to introduce new key people, redesign organizational systems, modify the company's strategy, and alter the product mix have shown mixed results—at the time of the writing of this book, it is too early to tell if they will yield desired results.

Nadler and Tushman's model enables a change agent to think systematically about the organization. It serves as a checklist to ensure practitioners consider the critical components that must be matched with the strategy and environmental demands. Since the system is dynamic, the environment, the people, the competition, and other factors change over time, and part of that change is due to how the components interact with each other. Second, the fit between organizational components is critical. Dell's products, organization, systems, and culture had become misaligned with the emerging environment. Finally, organizations with good fit are more effective than those with poor fit because they will be able to more efficiently and effectively transform inputs into outputs. The moves that Michael Dell made improved the fit and led to a modest turnaround in sales and margins in the short term, but subsequent competitive challenges suggest much more is needed—hence the move to take the company private so that needed changes could be made away from the glare of stock market pressures for short-term results.

Like any living entity, an organization survives by acting and reacting effectively to its external environment. Unless it adjusts with appropriate changes to its approach and, when needed, its strategy, it reduces its capacity to thrive. When one part of the organization is changed, then other parts also need to adapt to maintain the congruence or fit that leads to effectiveness. Michael Dell and his new management team have begun the realignment at Dell Computers. Whether Dell and his team made enough savvy changes for the long term will be demonstrated by the company's future performance. Critical to this will be Dell's ability to innovate and change in the face of shifts in its environment.

Evaluating Nadler and Tushman's Congruence Model

Are the assumptions made by Nadler and Tushman's Congruence Model reasonable ones? For example, should strategy always dictate the organization's structure and systems? While that is one of the traditional views of how to achieve organizational effectiveness, it is not unusual to see the reverse where changes in the structures and systems drive alterations to strategy. For example, FedEx used its systems and expertise that it built to deliver packages to its own customers to provide logistical services to other companies. Amazon got into the cloud storage business by taking advantage of its capability to run large server farms. Thus, the implied direction of the Nadler and Tushman model is appropriate, but any analysis must recognize how dynamic and interactive organizational factors are. For many change agents, particularly those in middle management, the strategy of their organizations will be a given and their role will be to adapt internal structures and systems. Alternatively, change agents may attempt to influence the strategy directly (e.g., participation in a strategic task force) and/or indirectly (initiate activities that lead to the development of new internal capacities, learning, awareness, and interest that make new strategies viable).

Has the importance of fit been overstated? Probably not. For example, in an investigation into the mixed results achieved by total quality management (TQM) initiatives, Grant, Shani, and Krishnan found that "TQM practices cannot be combined with strategic initiatives, such as corporate restructuring, that are based on conventional management theories. The failure of one or both programs is inevitable."[17] Thus, they found that the strategy, the structure, and new TQM processes need to fit with each other. Another example of issues of fit emerged following September 11, 2001, when the U.S. government created the Department of Homeland Security, which combined 22 government entities. However, reports subsequently emerged that suggested the secretary of the department had few levers needed to do his job: the formal structure had been created, but not the systems and processes that were necessary to give him leverage to be successful.[18] In both of these examples, a lack of alignment undermined the efforts to effectively change these organizations.

The need for change may not always be identified by looking at an organization's environment. Problems surface in a variety of ways. There might be problems in the organization's outcomes or outputs, indicating that some aspect of performance needs to be addressed. Further, there is the question of the magnitude of the change. The organization may decide to change its strategy, its culture, or some other core element. Generally, the more fundamental the change, the more other elements of the organization will need to be modified to support the desired change. For example, a change to one aspect of an organization may create a domino effect, requiring other changes to structure, systems, culture, and people. Mary Barra, GM's new CEO appointed in 2014, is living with this challenge. While alignment has improved significantly since emerging from bankruptcy in 2009, as evidenced by positive product reviews and dramatic improvements in sales and profitability, GM's leaders still deal with legacy cultural issues: Ignition switch design defects that resulted in deaths were not addressed for a decade. Internal investigations and congressional hearings report an organizational culture that promoted silence on such issues. Barra appears to be serious about acting on the dysfunctional aspects of GM's culture. She has fired 15 executives found to have been involved with the situation, spoken about it with greater candor than ever before, and instituted a corporate-wide change initiative called "Speak up for Safety."[19] She has affirmed that more recalls are likely as they search through their files: She stated that an "aggressive stance on product recalls is the new norm at GM" and that it is unacceptable for employees to stay silent on safety issues.

Finally, does better fit always increase the likelihood of effectiveness? This depends upon the measure of effectiveness. In the short run, fit focused on efficiency might mean increased profits as the organization reduces costs and becomes efficient. However, an innovation measure might show that fit focused primarily on efficiency has led to declining creativity. Efficiency is important but so is the development of appropriate adaptive capacities in an organization. It can be argued that in the long run, tight congruence in a stable environment leads to ingrained patterns inside the organization. Individuals and organizations develop formal systems and structures, as they should, but these can lead to ritualized routines and habits. Such patterns can be change resistant and can be hugely ineffective when the environment changes. Dell Computers suffered from this prior to Michael Dell's reintroduction in 2007. If the pace of change an organization must deal with is rapid, then an overemphasis on getting congruence "just right" can lead to delays that put the health of the firm at risk. In a rapidly changing environment, approximations are appropriate: don't make it perfect; get it acceptable and move on. Nevertheless, for most analytical purposes, the assumption that an increasing fit is a good objective is appropriate.

As with other congruence or alignment-oriented models, the Nadler and Tushman model must deal with the criticism that "too much emphasis on congruence potentially (could have) an adverse or dampening effort on organizational change."[20] The key lies in balancing the need for flexibility and adaptability with the need for alignment. This balance point shifts as environmental conditions and organizational needs change. To emphasize the dynamic nature of organizations, we next examine Sterman's Systems Dynamics Model.

(2) Sterman's Systems Dynamics Model[21]

As discussed, Nadler and Tushman's Congruence Model acknowledges the dynamic nature of systems but the authors focus more on the importance of alignment. In contrast, Sterman's model, below, focuses on the interplay of dynamic forces of the environment, managerial decisions, and actions of others. Sterman believes that managers should handle increased complexity by increasing the number of variables that they consider. The dynamic nature of the variables and the interactions among the variables over time may lead to counterintuitive results.

Sterman argues that managers often take a linear view of the world—a rational, causative model where managers identify a gap between what is and what is desired, make a decision, and take action, expecting rational results. If sales are low, for example, management might increase advertising, thinking that sales will flow. However, because of complex, interactive, nonlinear dependent variables, this linear view can be inaccurate and limiting. What management may get are counterintuitive results that are often policy or change resistant. If Company A, for example, increases its advertising, then Companies B, C, and D may increase their advertising as well. The result may be increased costs and static revenues. Managers may fail to anticipate the side effects of their decisions and how their actions lead to competitive responses that neutralize their first round of actions.

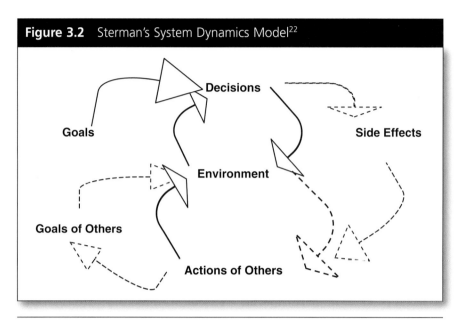

Figure 3.2   Sterman's System Dynamics Model[22]

Source: Reprinted from the *California Management Review,* "Systems Dynamic Modeling", Sterman, J., Vol. 43, No. 4, Summer, 2001. Copyright ©2001, by The Regents of the University of California.

Consider the following example. Managers change the incentive structure for employees, anticipating that this will lead to higher productivity. However, employees might see increased productivity as leading to layoffs (if we produce more, they will need fewer of us), and thus resist increasing outputs. Or employees will begin to focus on quantity and neglect crucial quality concerns. This, in turn, creates negative customer reactions that cause management to create new control systems around quality. Such control systems take additional paperwork and effort that increase costs and potentially defeat the original objective of increasing productivity.

Another point Sterman makes is that many problems result from time lags and delays, inventories and buffer stocks in the system, and attribution errors. Thus, another possible outcome in our above example is that employees may increase their efforts to generate new sales as the result of the changed rewards. However, there could be a significant lag before sales increase. Some sales cycles take months and even years before producing results. Thus, management's initial observation might be that the change in the reward system did not work. Small changes in demand may get exaggerated because of inventory buffers that automatically adjust. And finally, humanity's need to attribute cause might mean that managers assume causal links that don't exist.

Sterman's model heightens the awareness of the complexity involved with change and the challenges involved in developing alignments that will produce desirable results in the short and long term and not result in unpleasant surprises. As such, Sterman's model builds on the work of Argyris and Schön,[23] identifying the importance of organizational analysis through double-loop and triple-loop learning. Single loop is essentially adaptive learning within the organization's operation. Internal data are assessed and modifications are made, but the original objectives are not questioned. Double loop goes beyond making incremental modifications and challenges the assumptions, standards, policies, values, and mode of operation that gave rise to the standards and objectives. Triple-loop learning extends this analysis and exploration of possibilities further and questions the underlying rationale for the organization and why it exists. Triple-loop learning is also consistent with the work of Senge[24] on how organizations should be designed and managed in order to enhance organizational learning, innovation, and change.

In Figure 3.2, decisions lead to side effects as well as intended effects. These interact with the environment and the goals of others to create a more complex set of outcomes than were anticipated.

At McDonald's at the beginning of the 21st century, management decided to increase the number of corporate-owned stores and decrease costs. In the short term, this led to improved results: higher sales and improved profits. However, it also led to a decreased focus on store cleanliness as stores reduced staff. With more stores, overall revenues increased. With less time and effort focused on cleanliness, operating costs decreased and, in turn, increased profits. However, over time, customers became aware of the lack of cleanliness and stopped going to McDonald's. These unintentional side effects created more pressure for short-term profits due to a decline in sales. The cycle would repeat until management became aware of this self-defeating cycle.[25]

When a firm lowers its prices to increase market share and profitability, management may do so without thinking through the implications of its decisions. Its actions may lead to competitor responses that lower prices further and sweeten sales terms and conditions (e.g., no interest or payments for 12 months or improved warranties) in an effort to respond to its competitors and win back market share. Thus, the planned advantages coming from the price cuts may end up adding a few new sales, shrink margins, condition customers to see the product in primarily price terms, and lock the organization into a price-based competitive cycle that is difficult to escape.[26]

Sterman cautions managers to avoid the trap of thinking in a static, simplistic way. Increasingly, successful managers are resorting to systems thinking and more complex, nonlinear modeling to improve their diagnostic skills. *The Economist* argues, "Better understanding is the key" to improved productivity.[27] The promise of "big data" is that it will allow us to engage in much more sophisticated modeling of what is going on and why, so that more accurate assessments and effective courses of action can be undertaken. However being awash in increasing mounds of data won't help unless we learn how to model it in ways that more accurately reflect the complexity of what is going on, including the lag effects our actions in one area can have on other areas.

In doing a diagnosis, managers need to recognize their assumptions and values that underlie their implicit understanding of organizational dynamics and the nature of the environment and the market place. Picture marketing people in a meeting with operations or R&D people and you can imagine the value clashes. Marketing people are often externally oriented while operations people are concerned with internal dynamics. A model by Quinn helps to frame these issues and points to the value of a diversity of perspectives when approaching organizational and environmental analysis.

(3) Quinn's Competing Values Model

How managers think about organizations will largely determine what they think needs changing. The level of analysis that a manger examines can range from the individual to team/department to organizational level. A psychologist, for example, analyzes individuals and small groups and suggests changes at that level. In contrast, an economist uses econometric models to analyze on the organizational or societal level. Quinn provides a model that bridges the individual, team, department, and organizational levels and encourages change agents to think about the interaction between the systems at these levels.[28]

Quinn's Competing Values Model outlines four frames relevant to organizations. Each frame is based on a set of values and assumptions about the organization and how it works. Quinn argues that two dimensions underlie and help define these four frames: an internal-external dimension and a control-flexibility dimension. That is, underlying the perceptions of organizations are assumptions about the importance of the inside versus the outside of the organization and the need for control versus the need for adaptability. Plotting these two dimensions forms four quadrants, each of which provides a different "frame" or view of the organization. The Competing Values Model is portrayed in Figure 3.3.

As a manager, do you think about the organization in internal terms and how it operates? Or do you think of the organization's environment and the fit between that environment and the organization? Do you focus your attention on how the organization adapts and changes? Or is your emphasis more on ensuring that the direction is under control and that people do what is needed? Quinn argues that these dimensions form the four value orientations: Open Systems View, Rational Economic View, Internal Process View, and Human Resources View. Further, he states that while all orientations are needed in an organization, each person will tend to operate from one quadrant more than the others. As well, because the values underlying each quadrant are in conflict, individuals will have difficulty having a "natural" perspective from more than one quadrant. Individuals will tend to adopt one set of internally consistent values and find their views in conflict with or competing with those individuals with perspectives from other quadrants.

One of the strengths of Quinn's model is that it links individual and organizational levels of analysis. That is, managers can examine an organization's processes and determine whether they are focused on external adaptation, internal adaptation, and so forth. At the same time, Quinn suggests managerial roles and skills that are needed for each quadrant. To increase the focus on a quadrant, one needs to have managers develop the competencies needed and design systems to reinforce those skill behaviors. Of specific interest to change leaders are those skills that help with change processes. (See Chapter 8 on change leaders for more on this.)

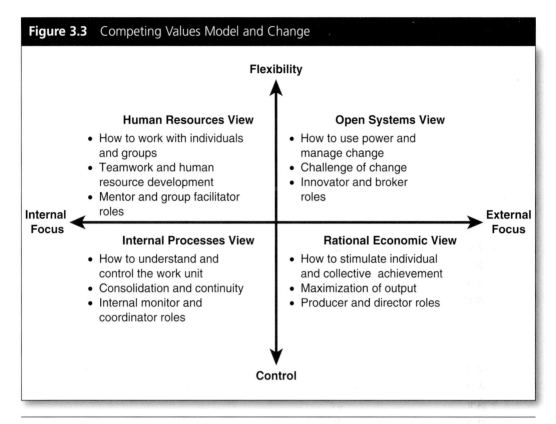

Figure 3.3 Competing Values Model and Change

Flexibility

Human Resources View
- How to work with individuals and groups
- Teamwork and human resource development
- Mentor and group facilitator roles

Open Systems View
- How to use power and manage change
- Challenge of change
- Innovator and broker roles

Internal Focus ← → External Focus

Internal Processes View
- How to understand and control the work unit
- Consolidation and continuity
- Internal monitor and coordinator roles

Rational Economic View
- How to stimulate individual and collective achievement
- Maximization of output
- Producer and director roles

Control

Source: Quinn R. E. et all. (2003). *Becoming a master manager.* New York: John Wiley & Sons.

Quinn labels the internal/flexibility quadrant the Human Resources View of organizations. Similarly, the external/flexibility quadrant is the Open Systems View, the external/control quadrant is the Rational Economic View, and the internal/control quadrant is the Internal Processes View. Each of these quadrants can be associated with a particular way of thinking about organizations with roles that managers need to play and skill sets managers can learn that enable them to play the roles.[29]

Every organization needs to attend to all four quadrants to know what is going on internally while also understanding its external environment. It needs to control its operations and yet be flexible and adaptable. At the same time, too much emphasis on one dimension may be dysfunctional. That is, organizations and leaders need to be flexible, but too much flexibility can bring chaos. Conversely, too much control can bring rigidity and paralysis. In the end, organizations need to balance these in ways that are congruent with their external environmental realities.

Each quadrant provides a value orientation needed in organizations and suggests managerial roles and skills that will support those value orientations. For example, Quinn argues that innovator and broker roles are needed in the Open Systems quadrant. The innovator roles demand an understanding of change, an ability to think creatively to produce change, and the development of risk taking. The broker role involves the development and maintenance of a power and influence base, the ability to negotiate solutions to issues, and the skills of persuasion and coalition building. Care must be taken not to be trapped into adopting one view and ignoring alternate perspectives. Too much focus on internal stability led IBM to miss the PC revolution for many years. Too much focus on the external world led many dot-coms to spin out of control in the technology boom of the early 2000s.

Quinn's model can be used in several ways: to characterize an organization's dominant culture, to describe its dominant tasks, to portray the focus of its reward systems, or to describe a needed shift in task emphasis or in the types of people that it must recruit. To refer again to the Dell example, the company was striving to become more consumer oriented while maintaining its production efficiencies. Because these two value orientations are not joined easily, change leaders will know that the concurrent development of these two initiatives will require careful management.

Quinn's model provides both a framework that bridges individual and organizational levels of analysis and a framework to understand competing value paradigms in organizations. While these perspectives are useful, they suggest a relatively static situation, not a dynamic one that Sterman argues for. In particular, Quinn's framework does not encourage managers to consider possible changes that occur in organizations over time. Greiner's model, described below, provides a framework for predicting the stages of change that occur within organizations over time as they grow from entrepreneurial ventures to multidivisional, multinational entities.

(4) Greiner's Model of Organizational Growth

As discussed in Chapter 1, the magnitude of organizational changes can vary markedly—from small, evolutionary changes to large, revolutionary ones[†]. Evolutionary shifts are, by definition, less traumatic for organizational members and less disruptive to the organization. Since they typically involve small, incremental shifts in existing systems and behaviors, they are easier to plan and execute. However, they may not be what the organization needs in order to maintain health and vitality. For incremental, evolutionary change, the challenge might be convincing people of the need and tweaking systems and processes to reinforce the desired outcomes. For disruptive, revolutionary change, the issue may well be keeping the organization operating while making significant alterations to how the organization views the world, its strategy, and how it goes about transforming inputs into outputs that its customers desire.

Greiner believes that organizations pass through periods of relative stability, punctuated periodically by the need for radical transformations of practices.[30] During the periods of relative stability, organizations tend to be in equilibrium, and evolutionary approaches to change are adopted in order to incrementally improve practices. Then a crisis occurs, such as the rapid growth of the enterprise or the

---

[†]The determination of the size of the change is, of course, somewhat dependent upon organizational level and perspective. An incremental change, according to a CEO, may well be viewed as transformational by the department head that is directly affected by the change.

introduction of a disruptive technology by a competitor, and the crisis demands revolutionary change. In the "crisis of leadership" stage, the founding leader of an entrepreneurial adventure may be pushed aside for the hiring of professional managers. Greiner describes these alternating periods of evolutionary and revolutionary change as natural as an organization grows over time.[‡] Figure 3.4 outlines Greiner's model.

In Greiner's view, over time, managers will change their views on how to operate a business incrementally. These become less effective as conditions change and the business becomes increasingly less well aligned or congruent with its internal and external realities. (In Nadler and Tushman's terms, the organizational strategy and/ or the transformational components—task, formal organization, informal organization, and people—become increasingly out of sync with the environment.) Once the pressure builds sufficiently, it produces the need for more radical transformations of the organization. Pressures build until a breaking point is reached and change is forced.[31] This relatively rapid and discontinuous change over most or all domains of organizational activity is referred to by Greiner as the revolutionary change period.[32]

As shown in Figure 3.4, Greiner outlines a model of typical stages of growth in an organization. He suggests that these patterns are progressive and logical as the organization grows. Greiner is prescriptive in that he claims the organization must pass through these crises in order to grow and develop. The transitions may be caused by a variety of issues: the death of the founder; the need for a functional organization to develop specialties; the emergence of disruptive market forces and/ or technologies; the need to decentralize into divisions to keep closer to the customer; and, finally, the need to become more flexible to enable the organization to use the potential of all employees.

This framework is appealing because of its straightforwardness, logic, and simplicity. However, the model is suggestively prescriptive. Not all organizations follow Greiner's patterns. In today's world, a small entrepreneurial venture may become a global competitor of reasonable size by using the Internet and collaborating with partners around the world. In other words, organizations need not develop as Greiner claims. The model does not seem open to the possibility of the broker organization, one that makes money by connecting organizations to each other. Nevertheless, the framework is valuable in highlighting many of the crises faced by organizations and in relating those crises to the growth stages of the organization. The model reinforces the notion of the competing values that managers must keep in an appropriate state of dynamic tension. For example, as managers move from the crisis of autonomy to growth through delegation, there should be a shift in values and perspectives, from control to flexibility in Quinn's terms.

In the Dell example, the company shifted from a control and functional specialty stage to one where the company was organized into relatively autonomous divisions

---

[‡]Eisenhardt believes that organizations can force incremental change by "time pacing"—setting up targets and deadlines that require regular periodic change. See S. Brown and K. Eisenhardt, "The Art of Continuous Change: Linking Stacey's Complexity Theory and Time-Paced Evolution in Relentlessly Shifting Organizations," *Administrative Science Quarterly 42,* no. 1 (1997): 1–34, or K. Eisenhardt and B. N. Tabrizi, "Accelerating Adaptive Processes: Product Innovation in the Global Computer Industry," *Administrative Science Quarterly 40,* no. 1 (1995): 84–110.

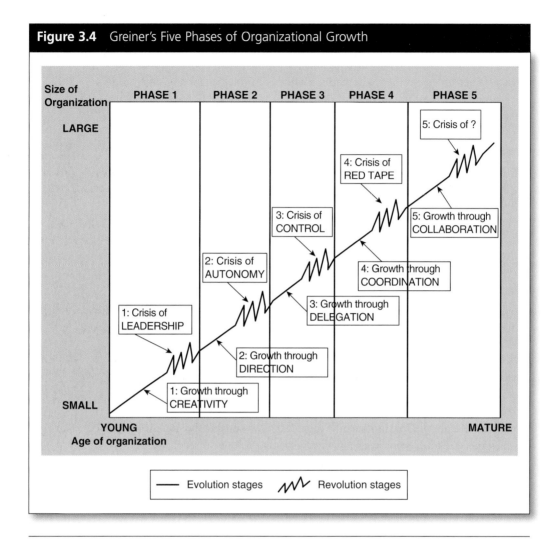

Figure 3.4   Greiner's Five Phases of Organizational Growth

Source: Reprinted with permission from "Evolution and Revolution as Organizations Grow" by Larry Greiner in *Harvard Business Review*, July-August 1972.

focused on customer segments. While Greiner's model suggests that certain tensions predominate during different growth phases, such tensions might not vanish. As such, Dell will continue to struggle with the previously successful efficiency focus that its managers held.

While Greiner's model is prescriptive, it captures many of the issues faced by organizations both in responding to growth and in dealing with the human side of organizational change. Too often, managers are trapped by their own perspectives. They fail to recognize that regardless of who has what title or authority, others will see things differently and have different criteria to judge potential outcomes. An important key in identifying what to change is to embrace multiple perspectives, recognizing that each comes with its own biases and orientation on what needs to be done. By developing an integrated, comprehensive assessment process and being conscious of one's own biases and preferences, the change leader is likely to achieve a holistic understanding of what change will produce the necessary re-alignment for organizational success.

(5) Stacey's Complexity Theory

Many models of organizational change rely on a gap analysis as the description of what needs to change,[33] just as this book does. While this has the advantage of simplicity, change agents need to move beyond this to recognize the importance of interdependence and interrelationships.[34] This chapter began by describing organizations as open systems, and frameworks have been presented for analysis that can account for the dynamic, multilevel, time-dependent nature of organizations. As well, change leaders have been encouraged to recognize that different situations require different levels of analysis, and the appropriate analytic tools are dependent on that level. The importance of moving away from seeing change in primarily simple, rational, cause-and-effect terms should not be underestimated. Change leaders must learn how to cope with complexity and chaos as realities.

Another branch of organizational theorists argues that organizations are complex, paradoxical entities that may not be amenable to managerial control. In this theory, called Stacey's Complexity Theory, Stacey[35] identifies the following as the underlying propositions (adapted below):

- Organizations are webs of nonlinear feedback loops that are connected with other individuals and organizations by webs of nonlinear feedback loops.
- These feedback systems can operate in stable and unstable states of equilibrium to the point at which chaos ensues.
- Organizations are inherently paradoxical. On one hand, they are pulled toward stability by forces for integration and control, security, certainty, and environmental adaptation. On the other hand, they are pulled toward instability by forces for division, innovation, and even isolation from the environment.
- If organizations give in to the forces for stability, they become ossified and change impaired. If they succumb to the forces for instability, they will disintegrate. Success is when organizations exist between frozen stability and chaos.
- Short-run dynamics (or noise) are characterized by irregular cycles and discontinuous trends, but the long-term trends are identifiable.
- A successful organization faces an unknowable specific future because things can and do happen that were not predicted and that affect what is achieved and how it is achieved.
- Agents within the organization can't control, through their actions, analytic processes and controls, the long-term future. They can only act in relation to the short term.
- Long-term development is a spontaneous, self-organizing process that may give rise to new strategic directions. Spontaneous self-organization is the

product of political interaction combined with learning in groups, and managers have to pursue reasoning through the use of analogy.

- It is through this process that managers create and come to know the environments and long-term futures of their organizations.

Some complexity theorists would argue that the managed change perspective that underpins this book is fundamentally flawed. They would do so because it focuses on management of complexity and renewal through environmental analysis and programmatic initiatives that advance internal and external alignment, and through them the accomplishment of the goals of the change. Those who adopt a complexity perspective would view the change leader's job as one of creating conditions and ground rules that will allow for innovation and efficiency to emerge through the encouragement of the interactions and relationships of others.

Advocates believe this approach can unleash energy and enthusiasm and allow naturally occurring patterns to emerge that would otherwise remain unseen (i.e., they self-organize into alignment). Vision and strategy are still valued by complexity theorists because they can supply participants with a sense of the hoped-for direction. However, they are not viewed as useful when they attempt to specify the ultimate goal.

A close review of the complexity ideas, though, shows that this perspective is not far from the one advocated by this book. This book adopts an open systems perspective and argues that the environment is characterized by uncertainty and complexity and that organizations are more likely to be successful over time if they develop adaptive capacities. This means that openness to new ideas and flexibility need to be valued and that organizations need to learn how to embrace the ideas, energy, and enthusiasm that can be generated from change initiatives that come from within the organization. The book recognizes the value that teams (including self-managed teams) can contribute to successful change, from needs assessment to the development of initial ideas and shared vision through to strategy development and implementation. Further, it acknowledges that too much standardization and reduction of variance could drive out innovation. Finally, it notes that greater uncertainty and ambiguity gives rise to greater uncertainty over how things will ultimately unfold, thereby highlighting the importance of vision and strategy as directional beacons for change initiatives as opposed to set directives or rules.

An important idea that comes from Stacey's Complexity Theory is that small changes at key points early on can have huge downstream effects. But can one predict with any certainty where those changes and leverage points will be or what downstream results will emerge as the result of actions we take today? Often the answer is no. Motorola likely had no clear idea where wireless technology would take the world when it began work on cellular phone technology in the 1960s. Likewise, Monsanto probably had little sense of the magnitude of the marketplace resistance that would build for genetically modified seeds when its research and development program was initiated in the 1980s.

We may not be able to predict precisely what will transpire over the long term, but we can make complex and uncertain futures more understandable and predictable if we do our homework in an open systems manner, look at data in nonlinear as well as linear terms, engage different voices and perspectives in the discussion, and rigorously consider different scenarios and different approaches to envisioning what the future might look like.

When organizations do this, they are likely to get a sense of what is possible from a visionary, directional, and technological perspective. Further, through the engagement and involvement of many, change leaders are in a strong position to initiate change with a shared sense of purpose. They are also more likely to have identified critical actions and events that must occur and where some of the potentially important leverage and resistance points exist. As a result, they are more aware of how things may unfold and are in a stronger position to take corrective or alternative action as a result of their ongoing monitoring and management of the process.[36] As well, change agents will recognize the importance of contingency planning as unpredictable, unplanned events occur.

It may not be possible to predict absolute outcomes. However, it is possible to generally predict where an organization is likely to end up if it adopts a particular strategy and course of action. The identification of the direction and the initial steps allow an organization to begin the journey. Effective monitoring and management processes allow leaders to make adjustments as they move forward. The ability to do this with complex change comes about as the result of hard work, commitment, a suitable mindset (e.g., openness and flexibility), relevant skills and competencies, appropriate participation and involvement approaches, access to sufficient resources, and control and signaling processes. In the end, the authors of this book subscribe to the belief that "Luck is the intersection of opportunity and preparation."[37]

Summary

In this chapter, change agents learned about five different organizational models that will help them to develop a well-grounded sense of what needs to change in an organization. This book uses Nadler and Tushman's model as its main framework. The model focuses on achieving congruence among the organization's environment, strategy, and internal organizational components to achieve desired outcomes. In addition, it helps managers categorize the complex organizational data that they must deal with. It examines the tasks, people, structures, and culture of organizations. Finally, it fits neatly into a process approach to organizational change, helping to merge what needs to be changed with the process of how change might occur.

While the book relies on both Nadler and Tushman's framework and the Change Path Model, change leaders must be particularly sensitive to the dynamic nature of organizations, to the need for multiple levels of analysis, and to the shifts that organizations make over time. Sterman's, Quinn's, and Greiner's models take a systems' perspective and are presented to reinforce subtle differences in focus. As well, we discuss Stacey's Complexity Theory. This theory challenges a simple goal-oriented approach that many change managers might take and encourages an emergent view of organizations.

Change leaders must recognize the assumptions and biases underlying their analysis and whether the assumptions they make limit their perspectives on needed change. Their diagnosis should recognize the stage of development of the organization and whether it is facing evolutionary, incremental change, or, at the other end of the change continuum, revolutionary, strategic change. By developing an in-depth and sophisticated understanding of organizations, change leaders will appreciate what has to be done to enhance an organization's effectiveness. See **Toolkit Exercise 3.1** for critical thinking questions for this chapter.

Key Terms

Open systems perspective considers the organization as a set of complex, interdependent parts that interacts with the external environment to obtain resources and to transform the resources into outputs.

Models of Organizations

Nadler and Tushman's Congruence Model—views organizations as composed of internal components (tasks, designed structures and systems, culture, and people). The model states higher effectiveness occurs when the organization is congruent with its strategy and environment. This model forms the framework for this text.

Sterman's Systems Dynamics Model—describes organizations as interactive, dynamic, and nonlinear as opposed to the linear, static view that many individuals hold of organizations.

Quinn's Competing Values Model—describes organizations as based on opposing values: flexibility versus control and external versus internal. These two dimensions lead to four competing views of organizations: the Human Resources View, the Open Systems View, the Rational Economic View, and the Internal Process View.

Greiner's Model of Organizational Growth—hypothesizes that organizations move through five states of growth followed by five stages of crisis.

Stacey's Complexity Theory—argues that organizations are webs of nonlinear feedback loops that connect individuals and organizations that can lead to self-organization and alignment among parts.

END-OF-CHAPTER EXERCISES

TOOLKIT EXERCISE 3.1

Critical Thinking Questions

Please find the URLs for the videos listed below on the website at study.sagepub.com/cawsey3e. Consider the questions that follow.

1. How Organizations Change: Henrik Marten—7.07 minutes

   Presentation by H. Marten on how learning is necessary for organizational change.

   - Explain Marten's key takeaways about how an organization can best learn.

   - Discuss any change experience you've had and how it may compare to Marten's description of organizational learning.

2. Eddie Obeng: Smart Failure for a Fast-Changing World—12:33 minutes

   Obeng talks about our ever-changing world, how our learning has changed and the importance of smart failures.

   - Describe how you perceive failure.

   - Describe how others you've worked with in the past have dealt with failure in themselves as well as people around them.

   - Discuss how you might begin changing an organization to treat failure as learning, as Obeng describes in the video.

Please see study.sagepub.com/cawsey3e for access to the videos and downloadable template of this exercise.

TOOLKIT EXERCISE 3.2

Analyzing Your Organization Using
Nadler and Tushman's Congruence Model

Use the congruence model to describe your organization or any organization you are familiar with.

1. Describe the key input factors that influence the organization:

   a. The external environment (including political, economic, social, technological, and ecological factors).

   b. The organization's history (including its culture) and the resources it has access to.

2. What is the strategy of the organization? Is it in line with the organization's environmental inputs and its history (including its culture) and resources?

3. Are the components of the transformation processes well aligned with the input factors and the strategy? These elements include:

   a. The work

   b. The formal organization

   c. The people

   d. The informal organization (part of which is the culture that manifests itself in different parts of the organization)

   e. How do they interact with one another in ways that influence the outputs produced by the organization?

4. What outputs are being achieved? Are these the desired outputs?

5. When you evaluate your organization's outputs at the individual, group, and organizational levels, what issues should the organization address?

6. Are there any aspects of how your organization works that you have difficulty understanding? If so, identify the resources you would need to access to help with this analysis.

7. Use your answers to fill in the visual model.

Exercise 3.2

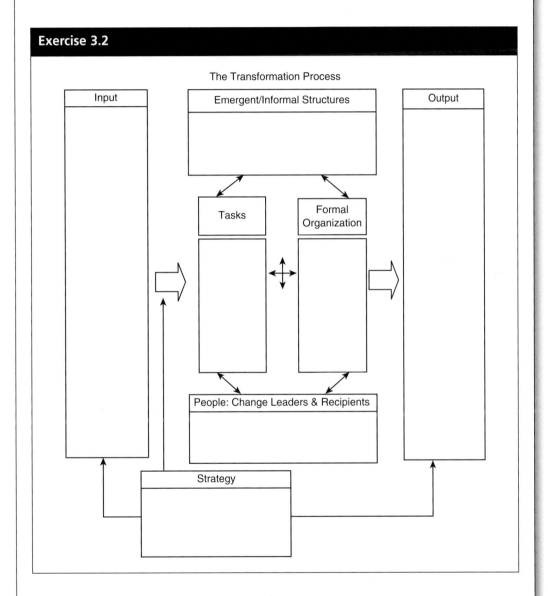

Please see study.sagepub.com/cawsey3e for a downloadable template of this exercise.

CHAPTER 4

Building and Energizing the Need for Change

You never want a serious crisis to go to waste.

—Rahm Emanuel, President Obama's
Former Chief of Staff and the Mayor of Chicago[1]

CHAPTER OVERVIEW

This chapter asks the question, "Why change?"

- It develops a framework for understanding the need for change based on making sense of external and internal organizational data, and the change leaders' personal concerns and perspectives.
- The chapter describes what makes organizations ready for change and provides a questionnaire to rate an organization's readiness.
- It outlines how change leaders can create awareness for change.
- Finally, the chapter outlines the importance of the change vision and how change leaders can create a meaningful vision that energizes and focuses action.

In Chapter 2, we discussed the concept of unfreezing as a precondition to change. How can an organization and its people move to something new if their current mindset and response repertoire are not open to alternative paths and actions?

> You are in a large auditorium filled with people when suddenly you smell smoke and someone yells, "Fire!" You leap to your feet, exit the building, and call 911.

This situation above is straightforward. A crisis makes the **need for change** clear and dramatic. It demands an immediate response and the required action is understood—even more so if the institution has taken fire-safety planning seriously. Most people know the key actions: Where to exit? How to avoid panic? Who should be notified? Who should do the notifying?

However, in many situations, the need for change is vague and appropriate action is unclear. For example, even in an emergency, if there have been no "fires" for a considerable period but there have been false alarms, people may have become complacent, warning systems might be ignored or even have been deactivated due to improper maintenance, and emergency action plans forgotten. A parallel to this might explain the lack of action prior to the mortgage meltdown in the United States in 2007 and the contagion it caused in global financial markets. Some economists and financial experts had raised alarms as early as 2003[2] (including the FBI in 2004[3]) over flawed financial practices and regulations. However, their warnings about the need to regulate mortgage lenders were ignored. The prevailing perspective within the Bush administration was that regulations needed to be minimized because they got in the way of free markets and the generation of personal wealth. Before the meltdown, the need for change was evident to only a few people. In addition, powerful financial institutions and their executives had huge incentives to ignore such warnings and silence those in their own firms who were raising alarms. Self-interest, blind spots, and/or misguided views of the greater good can sometimes blind people to strengths, weaknesses, opportunities, and risks. It is a primary reason for the rise in the importance of risk management and the requirements around risk reporting that publically traded firms must comply with.[4]

Past experiences may cause people to become not only complacent but also cynical about warnings. If false alarms have been regular occurrences, people will come to ignore them. If employees are told that there is a crisis when similar alerts in the past have proven to be false alarms, they will tend to discount the warning. If people are busy and they don't want to be sidetracked, they won't prepare for events that they think aren't going to happen. Remember the press reports concerning the H1N1 flu pandemic in the summer and fall of 2009 and how they changed by the winter of 2010? In the fall, there was a sense of panic, with people lining up overnight to get inoculated. By February, journalists were writing that the World Health Organization (WHO) had overstated the threat, as they had with Bird Flu. As such reports multiply and become the fodder for watercooler and Internet conversations, will the public take WHO warnings as seriously next time?[5] Concerns related to creating complacency may help to explain the careful way that WHO framed the warnings related to the outbreaks of Ebola in West Africa and the SARS-like virus in Saudi Arabia in 2013–2014.[6]

When leaders are perceived to cry "wolf" too often, who will take them seriously when the threat comes to fruition? However, when risks manifest themselves into reality, the blaming always begins with whether or not warning signs were ignored. Such were the responses following both the Sandy Hook School Shooting, in Newtown, Connecticut, in December 2012, and the bombing at the Boston Marathon in April 2013. This, in turn, may lead us to treat symptoms rather than underlying causes, as we look for quick solutions and misinterpret correlations for causality. Even trained professionals can miss obvious cues, as in the story below.

> A few years ago, my father was in intensive care, hooked to a heart monitor. Shortly after I arrived to visit him, the emergency alarm went off, but no one responded. I ran for help but was told not to worry—the alarm goes off all the time—just hit the reset button. The health care professionals had clearly adjusted their behavior to discount false alarms, but needless to say, I was left feeling anything but secure concerning the quality of the system designed to monitor the need for change in my dad's treatment. What if it hadn't been a false alarm? (G. Deszca)

Change agents need to demonstrate that the need for change is real and important. Only then will people unfreeze from past patterns. This is easier said than done. From 2008 through to the winter and spring of 2009, General Motors (GM) struggled to convince the United Auto Workers Union (UAW) that they needed significant financial concessions to survive. The UAW initially took the position that GM had signed a deal and should live up to it. However, the collapse of consumers' demand for automobiles in the summer of 2008 led to fears of bankruptcy. Political pressure from the U.S. and Canadian governments on both GM and their employee unions in the United States (the UAW or United Auto Workers) and Canada (the CAW or Canadian Auto Workers) escalated in the wake of bailout requests. As a result of this pressure, the UAW abandoned its position that "We have done our share." Concessions followed during the next nine months, covering everything from staffing levels, pay rates, and health care benefits to pensions.[7] The CAW followed suit, shortly thereafter. When it comes to raising alarms concerning the need for change, it is sometimes tough to know when and how to get through to people. With GM, it took going to the edge of the precipice and beyond. They had to go bankrupt!

Many change-management programs fail because there is sustained confusion and disagreement over (a) why there is the need for change and (b) what needs changing. Ask organization members—from production workers to VPs—why their organization is not performing as well as it could and opinions abound and differ. Even well-informed opinions are often fragmentary and contradictory. Individuals' perspectives on the need for change depend on their roles and levels in the organization, their environments, perceptions, performance measures and incentives, and the training and experience they have received. The reactions of peers, supervisors, and subordinates as well as an individual's own personality all influence how each person looks at the world. When there has been no well-thought-out effort to develop a shared awareness concerning the need for change, then piecemeal, disparate, and conflicting assessments of the situation are likely to pervade the organization.[8]

Look at the responses of different constituencies to the big issues of our day, and examples of the above proliferate. Take air quality. The adverse effects of poor air quality on public health are well documented. However, if you review the ongoing debate concerning the urgency of the problem and how we should go about addressing it, you will see various stakeholders with different vested interests and perspectives, marshal evidence to advance their point of view and protect their position. As a result, meaningful problem solving is delayed or sidetracked. Appropriate analyses, actions, and interventions are delayed, with predictable consequences, unless a disaster, very visible near disaster, or a seismic shift in public opinion occurs that galvanizes attention and precipitates action.

People often see change as something that others need to embrace and take the lead with. One hears: "Why don't they understand?" "Why can't they see what is happening?" or "They must be doing this intentionally." But stupidity, blindness, and maliciousness are typically not the primary reasons for inappropriate or insufficient organizational change. Differences in perspective affect what is seen and experienced. As the attributions of causation shift, so too do the beliefs about who or what is the cause of the problems and what should be done.[9] A common phenomenon called responsibility diffusion often occurs around changes. Responsibility diffusion happens when multiple people are involved and everyone stands by, assuming someone else will act.[10]

In terms of the change-management process, the focus of this chapter is on the "Awakening" box contained in Figure 4.1. To address this, change leaders need to determine the need for change and the degree of choice available to them and/or the organization about whether to change. Further, they need to develop the change vision and they need to engage others in these conversations so that a shared understanding develops. Without these in hand, they are in no position to engage others in conversations about the path forward.

This chapter asks change leaders, be they vice presidents, line operators, or volunteers at their local food bank, to seek out multiple perspectives as they examine the need for change. There is typically no shortage of things that could be done with available resources. What, then, gets the attention and commitment of time and money? What is the compelling reason for disrupting the status quo? Are there choices about changing and, if so, what are they? In many cases, it is not clear that change is needed. In these cases, the first step is for leaders to make a compelling case for why energy and resources need to be committed to a particular vision. Addressing these concerns advances the unfreezing process, focuses attention, and galvanizes support for further action.

But recognizing the need and mobilizing interest are not sufficient—a change leader also needs to communicate a clear sense of the desired result of the change.

Figure 4.1 The Change-Management Process

The Change Path Model

Awakening
Chapter 4
1. Identify a need for change and confirm the problems or opportunities that incite the need for change through collection of data.
2. Articulate the gap in performance between the present and the envisioned future state, and spread awareness of the data and the gap throughout the organization.
3. Develop a powerful vision for change.
4. Disseminate the vision for the change and why it's needed through multiple communication channels.

Mobilization
Chapters 5 through 8
1. Make sense of the desired change through formal systems and structures, and leverage those systems to reach the change vision (Chapter 5).
2. Assess power and cultural dynamics at play, and put them to work to better understand the dynamics and build coalitions and support to realize the change (Chapter 6).
3. Communicate the need for change organization-wide and manage change recipients and various stakeholders as they react to and move the change forward (Chapter 7).
4. Leverage change agent personality, knowledge, skills and abilities, and related assets (e.g., reputation and relationships) for the benefit of the change vision and its implementation (Chapter 8).

Acceleration
Chapter 9
1. Continue to systematically reach out to engage and empower others in support, planning, and implementation of the change. Help them develop needed new knowledge, skills, abilities, and ways of thinking that will support the change.
2. Use appropriate tools and techniques to build momentum, accelerate and consolidate progress.
3. Manage the transition, celebrating small wins and the achievement of milestones along the larger, more difficult path of change.

Institutionalization
Chapter 10
1. Track the change periodically and through multiple balanced measures to help assess what is needed, gauge progress toward the goal, and to make modifications as needed and mitigate risk.
2. Develop and deploy new structures, systems, processes and knowledge, skills, and abilities, as needed, to bring life to the change and new stability to the transformed organization.

Change leaders do this by creating a compelling vision of the change and what life will look like after it is implemented. This approach to creating momentum is the focus of the latter half of this chapter.

Understanding the Need for Change

The change process won't energize people until they begin to understand the need for change. People may have a general sense that things are amiss or that opportunities are being missed, but they will not mobilize their energies until the need is framed, understood, and believed. An organization may have amassed data on customers, production processes, suppliers, competitors, organization financials, and other factors, but nothing will happen until someone takes the information and communicates a compelling argument concerning the need for change. Advancing the change agenda is aided by being able to address the following questions:

DEVELOPING AN ASSESSMENT OF THE NEED FOR CHANGE

1. **What do you see as the need for change and the important dimensions and issues that underpin it?** How much confidence do you have in your assessment and why should others have confidence in that assessment? Is the appraisal of the need for change a solid organizational and environmental assessment, or is it a response to your personal needs and beliefs?

2. **Have you investigated the perspectives of internal and external stakeholders?** Do you know who has a stake in the matter and do you understand their perspectives on the need for change? Have you talked only to like-minded individuals?

3. **Can the different perspectives be integrated in ways that offer the possibility for a collaborative solution?** How can you avoid a divisive "we/they" dispute?

4. **Have you developed and communicated the message concerning the need for change in ways that have the potential to move the organization to a higher state of readiness for and willingness to change?** Or have your deliberations left change recipients feeling pressured and coerced into doing something they don't agree with, don't understand, or fear will come back to haunt them?

The challenges at this stage for change leaders are to develop the information they need to assess the situation, develop their views on the need for change, understand how others see that need, and create awareness and legitimacy around the need for change when a shared awareness is lacking. To make headway on these questions and challenges, change leaders need to seek out and make sense of external data, the perspectives of stakeholders, the internal data, and their own personal concerns and perspectives. (Figure 4.2 outlines these factors.)

Seek Out and Make Sense of External Data

Change leaders should scan the organization's external environment to gain knowledge about and assess the need for change. Getting outside one's personal

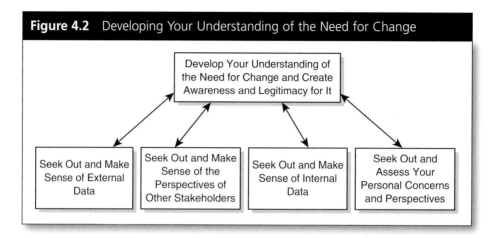

Figure 4.2 Developing Your Understanding of the Need for Change

perceptual box helps to avoid blind spots that are created by "closed-loop learning."[*][11] Change agents may make incremental improvements and succeed in improving short-term results. However, change leaders may not be doing what is needed to assess the risks and opportunities and to adapt to the environment over the long term.[12] Executives tend to spend too little time reflecting on the external environment and its implications for their organizations.[13]

An organization that is experiencing an externally driven crisis will feel the sense of urgency around the need for change. In this case, the change initiator's task will be easier.[14] This crisis can be used to mobilize the system and galvanize people's attention and actions. Without this, many within the organization may not perceive a need for change even though the warning clouds or the unaddressed opportunities may be keeping the change leader awake at night.

The value of seeing organizations as open systems cannot be underestimated. This analytic approach and the learning it promotes play an important role in the development of awareness, improved vision, and flexibility and adaptability in the organization.[15] Often the question becomes for the change leader: "Which external data do I attend to?" A change agent can drown in information without a disciplined approach for the collection, accumulation, and integration of data. Consider how complex the innocuous-sounding task of benchmarking can become.[16] The absence of a disciplined approach to data gathering may mean that time is wasted, that potentially important data go uncollected or are forgotten, or the data are never translated into useful information for the organization.

Some sources for data will be concrete (trade papers, published research, and news reports), while others will be less tangible (comments collected informally from suppliers, customers, or vendors at trade shows). Data collection can take a variety of forms: setting aside time for reading, participating in trade shows and professional conferences, visiting vendors' facilities, and/or attending executive education programs. Just as important, the change leader should consider engaging

---

*Closed-loop learning is learning that focuses on current practices and perspectives rather than developing a deeper understanding of the complex interactions underpinning the situation, including the impact of the external environment.

others in processes related to framing the questions, identifying and collecting data, and systematically interpreting the results in a timely fashion. This makes the task more manageable, increases the legitimacy of the data and the findings, builds awareness and understanding of the need for change, and creates a greater sense of ownership of the process.

Working without awareness of the external environment is the equivalent of driving blind. And yet it happens all the time. For a variety of reasons, ranging from a heavy workload or a sense of emergency, to complacency or arrogance, organizational leaders can be lulled into relying on past successes and strategies rather than investigating and questioning. In so doing, they risk failing to develop an organization's capacity to adapt to a changing environment.[17]

Seek Out and Make Sense of the Perspectives of Stakeholders

Change leaders need to be aware of the **perspectives of key internal and external stakeholders** and work to understand their perspectives, predispositions, and reasons for supporting or resisting change. This will inform and enrich a change agent's assessment of the need for change and the dynamics of the situation, and allow them to frame their approaches in ways that have a greater chance of generating needed support. Without such work, it is impossible to accurately assess perceptions of the situation and frame responses to questions that will resonate with those stakeholders—questions such as why change and what's in it for me?[18]

Externally, these stakeholders may include suppliers, bankers, governmental officials, customers, and alliance and network partners. Internally, the stakeholders will include those individuals who are directly and indirectly affected by the change. If the change involved a reorganization of production processes, the internal stakeholders would include production supervisors, employees, union officials, human resources (recruitment and training implications), finance (budget and control processes), sales and marketing (customer service implications), IT (information implications), and engineering managers.

The point of view of the person championing the need for change will likely differ from the perspectives of other stakeholders. What is interesting and important to those stakeholders will vary, and this will affect what data and people they pay attention to and what they do with the information. If the change leader hopes to enlist their support or at least minimize their resistance, the leader needs to capture and consider their perspectives and the underlying rationale.[19] Particular stakeholders may still remain ambivalent or opposed to the change, but not seeking them out and listening is likely to make things worse. Why create resistance if you don't have to?

All of this highlights the importance of doing preparatory analysis and having a purposeful discussion, if possible, with affected stakeholders and those who understand their perspectives and can potentially influence them. It will increase the change leader's awareness and sensitivity to the context, inform and strengthen the analysis, and indicate blind spots and alternative explanations and paths.

CHANGE VISION AT AN INSURANCE FIRM

When a North American insurance firm acquired one of its competitors, the senior manager in charge of integrating the acquisition was determined to have every employee understand the need for change, the new vision, and its implications. On the day the deal was announced, she made a live presentation (along with the CEO and other key officials) to employees at the head office of the acquisition and streamed the meeting live to all of the acquisition's branch offices and facilities, as well as into the parent organization. She honored the acquisition's senior management team, who were present, communicated the reasons for the acquisition and its implications for change, took questions, and encouraged employees to contact her with questions or concerns. She set up a special website and phone line to answer questions in a timely and direct manner and followed this with visits to all the offices, key customers, and suppliers over the next two months. She held two additional town-hall meetings with employees over the next year to communicate the status of integration activities and reduce anxiety.

An integration team from the acquiring firm was deployed to the acquired firm the day the deal was announced. After introducing themselves and their mandate, specific initiatives were commenced with staff to align key systems and processes and develop strategic and tactical plans. Leaders from the integration team visited key groups at all levels in the acquired organization to discuss the need for change, to discuss their current position in the marketplace, and to review how the roles and responsibilities were currently organized. Integration team members communicated what they knew, listened hard, and made firm commitments to get back with answers by specific dates. The integration team honored those commitments, including the communication of the new organization's strategic and tactical plans and clarification of each person's employment status, within 90 days of the acquisition. Like the senior manager responsible for the integration of the acquisition, the integration team communicated candidly, listened, and adjusted to assessments of the need for change and the strategic path forward, based upon what they learned. The team's approach tapped into the emotional needs of "acquired" employees, reducing their anxieties, instilling hope for the future, and illustrating that their views and concerns were heard. Employee surveys, low absentee and turnover rates, and performance data confirmed this.[20]

The change agents for the insurance firm did their homework when developing and communicating the need for change. They openly engaged stakeholders in dialogue, listened and responded with care and consideration, and then proceeded to the next stage in the change process. Too many executives underestimate the need for communication and the importance of it being two-way. There can never be too much top-level communication and support, but unfortunately, there is often far too little listening. A rule of thumb for managers is to talk up a change initiative at least three times more than you think is needed and listen at least four times as much as you think you should![21] One change leader states that messages need to be communicated 17 times before they get heard![22]

Seek Out and Make Sense of Internal Data

It is no surprise that change leaders need to pay careful attention to internal organizational data when developing their assessment of the need for a particular initiative. Change agents who command internal respect and credibility understand the fundamentals of what is going on within a firm. Change leaders need to know what can be inferred from internal information and measures, how these are currently being interpreted by organizational members, and how they may be leading the firm down the wrong path. Some of this will be in the form of so-called hard data—the sort that can be found in the formal information system and it is often numeric in nature (e.g., customer retention and satisfaction, service profitability, cycle time, and employee absenteeism). Other valuable information will be soft data, the intuitive information gathered from walking around the building and other work areas and having discussions with critical stakeholders. For example, do employees generally pick up litter such as candy wrappers, or is that task left exclusively to the janitorial staff? The former often indicates widespread pride and feelings of ownership in an organization.

Seek Out and Assess Your Personal Concerns and Perspectives

"Know thyself" is a critical dictum for change leaders. Change agents need a good understanding of their strengths and weaknesses, attitudes, values, beliefs, and motivations. They need to know how they take in information and how they interpret and make decisions. They need to recognize their preferences, prejudices, and blind spots. As change agents expand their self-awareness, they are freer to ask questions and seek help when they need it.[23]

> "I think it's a combination of how self-aware people are and how honest they are. I think if someone is self-aware, then they can always continue to grow. If they're not self-aware, I think it's harder for them to evolve or adapt beyond who they already are."
>
> Tony Hsieh, CEO, Zappos.com, Inc.[24]

During the Cuban Missile Crisis, October 1962, Collins and Porras report that President Kennedy was incredibly comfortable with expressing what he did not know and asking many questions before passing judgments.[25] This led to informed decision making that may have saved the world from World War III. Many change leaders have difficulty publically owning the fact that they do not have all the answers and demonstrating a real interest in listening and learning. They likely have noticed that someone who communicates more confidence in their judgment tends to be responded to more positively than a person who is more cautious—particularly if the audience is predisposed to that point of view.

However, behavioral economists have found that this can lead to serious errors of judgment. For example, those individuals in the media who are most self-assured in their judgment are significantly less accurate than those who are more nuanced in their assessments. We may love their bravado and certainty, which helps explain their frequent appearances on TV, but beware of putting too much trust in their conclusions![26] In 2002–2003 Vice President Dick Cheney's confidence in Saddam Hussein and Iraq's possession of weapons of mass destruction was absolute, and yet, U.S. forces found very few.

Reputations for skill, judgment, and success develop over time, and this development is aided by a greater willingness to look, listen, and learn before committing to a course of action. As Daniel Kahneman and his colleagues have noted, dangerous biases creep into important decision making and these need to be guarded against. Taking steps that keep you open to learning and rigorously testing your assumptions and biases can help you avoid decision traps and greatly benefit the quality of the final choice.[27] These actions reinforce the value of looking before you leap in others. They build trust in your judgment, knowing that you've done your homework and considered the situation and options seriously, and show others that a little humility in one's judgment never hurts.[28]

NEW LEADERSHIP AT MICROSOFT

With the selection of Satya Nadella as its CEO in February 2014, Microsoft is signalling a departure from the loudness of Steve Ballmer and a return to someone much more like Bill Gates in his skill sets and approach to management. Nadella is reported to be very competent technically and managerially, and to have demonstrated this over the years at Microsoft, as he has successfully led significant change initiatives, most recently at the Cloud and Enterprise group. People report that he has done so by asking questions, listening, and engaging and energizing participants in ways that allow them to get out of their comfort zone and succeed. Those who have worked with him say he is honest, inclusive, authentic, and caring—generating success by thoughtfully nurturing the involvement and commitment of those around him.[29]

Whenever we, the authors, work with groups of university students, or managers and executives who are attempting organizational change, we caution them not to assume that their perspectives are held by all. They often fail to understand the impact of their own biases, perspectives, and needs and how they differ from those of others involved in a change initiative. They believe that they understand the situation and know what must change; this attitude can create significant barriers to accomplishing the change objectives. The strength of their concerns combined with their lack of self-awareness creates blind spots and causes them to block out dissenting perspectives. When they talk to stakeholders, they may receive polite responses and assume that this implies a commitment to action. Statements such as "That's an interesting assessment" are taken as support rather than as neutral comments. Their inability to read subtle cues or misinterpret legitimate concerns as resistance, rather than thoughtful feedback, leads them astray.

In an extreme attempt to protect himself and his followers from his personal shortcomings and cult-like reputation, Nehru, one of the founding fathers of modern, independent India, used an alias when he wrote the following about himself in a prominent publication in 1937. The backdrop was the struggle for independence from Britain, which was achieved 11 years later.

> What lies behind that mask of his, what desires, what will to power, what insatiate longings? Men like (Nehru) with all their capacity for great work, are unsafe in democracy . . . every psychologist knows that the mind is ultimately a slave to the heart and logic can always be made to fit in with the desires and irrepressible urges of a person . . . (Nehru's) conceit is already formidable. It must be checked. We want no Caesars.[30]
>
> —Nehru writing in the press about himself, using an alias

Nehru's deep commitment to India's independence did not blind him to how his own ego and the burgeoning hero worship that he was experiencing might impair the goal of a democratic India that would need an electorate that exercised thoughtful discourse and informed decision making. As such, he publicly noted the trend toward hero worship and its intoxicating impact on himself and his followers.

This section asks change leaders to consider their readiness for leading a change initiative and the roles that they will play in the process. It asks change agents to assess their skills, abilities, and predispositions to assess and guide the change. In Chapter 8, change agents will again be asked to look in a mirror and assess their predispositions toward various change agent roles. See **Toolkit Exercise 4.2** to understand and diagnose a need for change.

Assessing the Readiness for Change

Understanding the need for change and creating a vision for change are closely linked. Diagnosing where an organization is in the present moment is a prerequisite for figuring out its future direction. Beckhard and Harris[31] argue that addressing the question "Why change?" is a necessary precondition to being able to define the desired future state or the vision. If the question of "Why change?" is never meaningfully addressed, no one should expect the emergence of any sense of a shared vision. The answer to "Why?" is a prerequisite to the "What?" and the "How?" of change.

While dissatisfaction with the status quo by senior managers is certainly very helpful in advancing change, it is unlikely to be a *sufficient* condition. Spector[32] argues that the creation of dissatisfaction among others is needed. This dissatisfaction can be developed by sharing competitive information, benchmarking the organization's performance against others, challenging inappropriate behaviors through highlighting their impact, developing a vision for the future that creates frustration with the present state, and simply mandating dissatisfaction if one has the clout. Being dissatisfied with the status quo helps to ready the organization for change. That readiness depends on previous organizational experiences, managerial support, the organization's openness to change, its exposure to disquieting information about the status quo, and the systems promoting or blocking change in the organization.

Change initiators may understand the need for change, but other key stakeholders may not be prepared to recognize that need or believe it is strong enough to warrant action. Newspaper accounts of the failure to react in time are all too common (e.g., Chrysler in the auto industry,[33] Target (Canada) and Kmart in retailing,[34] Yahoo and BlackBerry in the digital world[35]). Though a litany of reasons are offered in the press, two common themes emerge: (1) Management failed to attend to the warning clouds or the opportunities that were clearly visible, often well in advance; and (2) when management took actions, they did too little too late. Past patterns of success can lead to active inertia (doing more of the same), flawed environmental scanning and assessments, and other factors that will be discussed later in the chapter that sabotage organizational members' capacity to successfully adapt.[36]

Organizational readiness for change is determined by the previous change experiences of its members; the flexibility and adaptability of the organizational culture; the openness, commitment, and involvement of leadership in preparing the organization for change; and member confidence in the leadership. It is also influenced by the organizational structure, the information members have access to, reward and measurement systems, resource availability, and the organization's flexibility and alignment with the proposed change.[37] This theme goes back to Chapter 3's discussion of Nadler and Tushman's Congruence Model and the importance of alignment. Readiness is advanced when organizational members can see how the existing alignment is getting in the way of producing better outcomes and believe that the needed realignment can be achieved. An organization's readiness for change will influence its ability to both attend to environmental signals for change and listen to internal voices saying that change is needed.[38]

Previous experiences affect **individual readiness for change**. If organizational members have experienced more gain than pain from past change initiatives, they will be more predisposed to try something new. However, there is also the risk that they may resist changes that divert them from initiatives that have worked in the past.

If previous change experiences have been predominantly negative and unproductive, employees tend to become disillusioned and cynical ("we tried and it didn't work" attitude).[39] However, under the right conditions, this situation may produce increased resolve concerning the need for change. (Reactions to past change experiences will be discussed further in Chapter 7.)

Writers regularly report that the development and maintenance of top management's support is crucial to change success.[40] If senior managers are visibly supporting the initiative, are respected, and define and tie their success to the change initiative, then the organization is likely to be receptive to change. However, it is not unusual to find differences of opinion concerning change at the senior management level, so a lack of initial support is a reality that many change leaders must navigate. The beginning of any change journey can feel quite lonely, because though you and a few others have become convinced of the need for change, others may have quite different opinions about the need or not yet have given the matter much thought. This includes senior management. Perhaps more troubling situations than the lack of visible support occur when senior management assures change agents of support but fails to provide it at crucial moments because it isn't one of their priorities or they choose to engage in passive forms of resistance.

Organizations that have well-developed external scanning mechanisms are likely to be aware of environmental changes. Cultures and systems that encourage the collection and objective interpretation of relevant environmental, competitive, and benchmark data tend to be more open to change and provide members of the organization with the information they need to provoke their thinking concerning the need for change.[41] If the culture supports environmental scanning and encourages a focus on identifying and resolving problems rather than "turf protection," organizations will be more open to change.

READYING AN ORGANIZATION FOR CHANGE

Armenkis and his colleagues[42] identified factors for **readying an organization for change**.
   Their list includes:

1. The need for change is identified in terms of the gap between the current state and the desired state.

2. People believe that the proposed change is the right change to make.

3. The confidence of organizational members has been bolstered so that they believe they can accomplish the change.

4. The change has the support of key individuals the organizational members look to.

5. The "what's in it for me/us" question has been addressed.

Holt was concerned about an organization's readiness for change and developed a scale based on four beliefs among employees: They could implement a change, the change is appropriate for the organization, leaders are committed, and the proposed change is needed.[43] Judge and Douglas were also interested in calibrating an organization's readiness for change and utilized a rigorous approach to identify **eight dimensions related to readiness**:

1. Trustworthy leadership—the ability of senior leaders to earn the trust of others and credibly show others how to meet their collective goals

2. Trusting followers—the ability of nonexecutives to constructively dissent or willingly follow the new path

3. Capable champions—the ability of the organization to attract and retain capable champions

4. Involved middle management—the ability of middle managers to effectively link senior managers with the rest of the organization

5. Innovative culture—the ability of the organization to establish norms of innovation and encourage innovative activity

6. Accountable culture—the ability of the organization to carefully steward resources and successfully meet predetermined deadlines

7. Effective communications—the ability of the organization to effectively communicate vertically, horizontally, and with customers

8. Systems thinking—the ability of the organization to focus on root causes and recognize interdependencies within and outside the organization's boundaries.[44]

Table 4.1 contains a readiness-for-change questionnaire. It reflects the questions and issues raised in this section and provides another method for helping change leaders assess an organization's readiness for change.[45] By considering what is promoting and inhibiting change readiness, change agents can take action to enhance

Table 4.1 Rate the Organization's Readiness for Change

Readiness Dimensions	Readiness Score
Previous Change Experiences	
1. Has the organization had generally positive experiences with change?	If yes, Score +1
2. Has the organization had recent failure experiences with change?	Score −1
3. What is the mood of the organization: upbeat and positive?	Score +1
4. What is the mood of the organization: negative and cynical?	Score −2
5. Does the organization appear to be resting on its laurels?	Score −1
Executive Support	
6. Are senior managers directly involved in sponsoring the change?	Score +2
7. Is there a clear picture of the future?	Score +1
8. Is executive success dependent on the change occurring?	Score +1
9. Has management ever demonstrated a lack of support?	Score −1

Readiness Dimensions	Readiness Score
Credible Leadership and Change Champions	
10. Are senior leaders in the organization trusted?	Score +1
11. Are senior leaders able to credibly show others how to achieve their collective goals?	Score +1
12. Is the organization able to attract and retain capable and respected change champions?	Score +2
13. Are middle managers able to effectively link senior managers with the rest of the organization?	Score +1
14. Are senior leaders likely to view the proposed change as generally appropriate for the organization?	Score +2
15. Will the proposed change be viewed as needed by the senior leaders?	Score +2
Openness to Change	
16. Does the organization have scanning mechanisms to monitor the environment?	Score +1
17. Is there a culture of scanning and paying attention to those scans?	Score +1
18. Does the organization have the ability to focus on root causes and recognize interdependencies both inside and outside the organization's boundaries?	Score +1
19. Does "turf" protection exist in the organization?	Score −1
20. Are the senior managers hidebound or locked into the use of past strategies, approaches, and solutions?	Score −1
21. Are employees able to constructively voice their concerns or support?	Score +1
22. Is conflict dealt with openly, with a focus on resolution?	Score +1
23. Is conflict suppressed and smoothed over?	Score −1
24. Does the organization have a culture that is innovative and encourages innovative activities?	Score +1
25. Does the organization have communications channels that work effectively in all directions?	Score +1
26. Will the proposed change be viewed as generally appropriate for the organization by those not in senior leadership roles?	Score +2
27. Will the proposed change be viewed as needed by those not in senior leadership roles?	Score +2

(Continued)

Table 4.1 (Continued)

Readiness Dimensions	Readiness Score
28. Do those who will be affected believe they have the energy needed to undertake the change?	Score +2
29. Do those who will be affected believe there will be access to sufficient resources to support the change?	Score +2
Rewards for Change	
30. Does the reward system value innovation and change?	Score +1
31. Does the reward system focus exclusively on short-term results?	Score −1
32. Are people censured for attempting change and failing?	Score −1
Measures for Change and Accountability	
33. Are there good measures available for assessing the need for change and tracking progress?	Score +1
34. Does the organization attend to the data that it collects?	Score +1
35. Does the organization measure and evaluate customer satisfaction?	Score +1
36. Is the organization able to carefully steward resources and successfully meet predetermined deadlines?	Score +1
The scores can range from −10 to +35.	
The purpose of this tool is to raise awareness concerning readiness for change and is not meant to be used as a research tool.	
If the organization scores below 10, it is not likely ready for change and change will be very difficult.	
The higher the score, the more ready the organization is for change. Use the scores to focus your attention on areas that need strengthening in order to improve readiness.	
Change is never "simple," but when organizational factors supportive of change are in place, the task of the change agent is manageable.	

Source: Adapted from Stewart "Rate Your Readiness to Change" scale, *Fortune*, Feb 7, 1994, p 106–110, Holt, D. "Readiness for Change: The Development of a Scale", *Organization Development Abstracts*, Academy of Management Proceedings, 2002, and Judge, W., & T. Douglas, "Organizational Change Capacity: the Systematic Development of a Scale," *Journal of Organizational Change Management*, Vol.22, #6, 2009, 635–649.

readiness—a change task in and of itself. For example, if rewards for innovation and change are seen to be lacking, or if employees believe they lack the needed skills, steps can be taken to address such matters. When considering rewards, remember these include intrinsic as well as extrinsic rewards. The impact of rewards on judgment and behavior needs to be considered carefully, because it can be complicated. For example, excessive rewards for success or excess punishment for failure are more likely to produce unethical behavior.[46] Alternatively, intrinsic rewards and moderate levels of equitable extrinsic rewards that are nested in teams can heighten information sharing, motivation, and commitment.[47] More will be said about this in later chapters. Change readiness must be consciously developed, aligned with supportive systems and structures, and then put to use as a source of competitive advantage. Developing change readiness is an important matter in both public and private organizations.[48]

Heightening Awareness of the Need for Change

When an organization is open to change, thinking individuals will still want to critically assess the evidence concerning the need for change. The change leader may experience blanket resistance and defensiveness, or may experience more localized opposition. Individuals may recognize the need for change in some departments and functions but be resistant to recognizing the need for change as it gets closer to home. If they see only the unraveling of what they've worked to accomplish and/or unpleasant alternatives ahead for them, they will be very reluctant to embrace change proposals. Even when the need for change is broadly recognized, action does not necessarily follow.

FROM BAD TO WORSE: GARBAGE SERVICES IN NAPLES, ITALY

Naples, Italy, has lived with a garbage problem for years. Poor management, organized crime, and ineffective political leadership allowed the matter to fester and escalate. In 2008, worldwide coverage of the problem drew attention and political promises for action, as 55,000 tons of uncollected garbage filled city streets, and 110,000 to 120,000 tons awaited treatment in municipal storage sites. Though the streets are now cleaner, resolution has been slow and suspect. Untold tons of irresponsibly (some would argue criminally) handled waste continue to reside in illegal landfills that dot the countryside, or they have been shipped elsewhere for questionable "disposal." The results have fouled the environment, endangered health, seriously harmed Naples' economy, and required deployment of the army in 2008 and 2011 to deal with uncollected garbage.[49] In November 2013, the legacy created by decades of mismanagement and corruption erupted very publicly yet again—this time in the form of burning trash heaps on the outskirts of Naples that were producing toxic fumes and threatening water quality and food safety in the region.[50]

In the story above, the need for change seems obvious. However, the politicians of the city and other levels of government were reluctant to take the difficult steps needed to deal with the problems. Clearly, Naples and her citizens were not yet prepared to undertake the type of change needed.

Once change leaders understand the need for change, they can take different approaches to heighten the awareness of the need throughout the organization. Change leaders can:

1. Make the organization aware that it is in or near a crisis or creating a crisis that needs to be solved.

2. Identify a transformational vision based on higher-order values.

3. Find a transformational leader to champion the change.

4. Take the time to identify common or shared goals and work out ways to achieve them.

5. Use information and education to raise awareness of the need for change.

The first method is a form of shock treatment and involves either *making the organization aware that it is in or near a crisis or creating a crisis that needs to be solved*. Many of the dramatic turnaround stories that are reported are successful because the actions of people were galvanized and focused by the necessity for action. In the face of crisis, people find it difficult to deny the need to change and to change *now*. When the crisis is real, the issue will be one of showing others a way out that they will follow if they have any confidence in its viability, given that the alternatives are far from attractive.[51]

At times, managers will be tempted to generate a crisis, to create a sense of urgency to change and mobilize staff around a change initiative that may or may not be fully justified. Creating a sense of crisis when one does not really exist must be approached with care.[52] If mishandled, it may be viewed as manipulative and result in heightened cynicism and reduced commitment. The change leader's personal credibility and trustworthiness are then at stake. The reputation developed in and around change initiatives casts a long shadow, for better or worse. The currencies that change agents use are credibility and trustworthiness. These take a long time to develop and can be quickly squandered.[53]

An extension of the crisis is the "burn or sink your boats approach." In this case, the change leader takes the process one step further and cuts off any avenue of retreat. That is, there is no going back. This approach is based on the belief that this will lead to increased commitment to the selected course of action. While it may aid in focusing attention, this approach can increase many of the risks outlined above. In particular, individuals may resent being forced into a situation against their will. It may produce compliant and even energized behavior in the short term due to the absence of alternatives, but it can give rise to undesirable long-term consequences if the actions come to be viewed as being inappropriate or unfair. Consequences can include elevated levels of mistrust, reduced commitment, and poor performance.[54]

CREATING URGENCY AT NEW YORK CITY'S METROPOLITAN TRANSIT AUTHORITY (MTA)

In October 2012, Hurricane Sandy left huge challenges for NYC's MTA. MTA used the sense of urgency to motivate staff to think in creative ways to get the most essential job done. The priority was to get the city connected and moving after the storm. Despite there being no emergency handbook for this kind of situation, the MTA was able to get partial service up within days and full lines running within a week.[55]

In the wake of Hurricane Sandy, the transit system was underwater in many areas, infrastructure had been destroyed, and virtually nothing was running. The crisis faced by Joseph Leader, the subway's chief maintenance officer, and all the other executives and staff, was both real and devastating. They knew tough decisions were needed around the alignment and coordination of resources, and that a huge amount of work would be required to get the city's transit system operational. A competent and highly motivated staff, combined with the powerful shared goal of getting the trains moving, allowed them to mobilize, sort out what needed to be done, and act—even in the absence of protocols.

Urgency is straightforward when there is an event such as Sandy. However, it can prove more difficult when it evolves more slowly, such as deteriorating market conditions, or in the case of not-for-profits such as government agencies, deteriorating service standards or relevance to the public. With the right use of data and influence approaches, people can be woken up. Creating a sense of social/political urgency through advocacy approaches has proven powerful in the public square, as seen in the Arab Spring in Tunisia and Egypt during 2010–2012 and pressure for change in the Department of Veterans Affairs in the United States.[56] Likewise, approaches that disrupt existing perspectives, challenge past learning, and hasten the adoption of new perspectives through creating a sense of urgency have been shown to help new product development teams get out of ruts and become more effective, though they do have to guard against information and knowledge loss in the process.[57]

A second approach to enhancing people's awareness of the need for change is by *identifying a transformational vision based on higher-order values*, such as the delivery of superb service and responsiveness. Transformational visions tap into the need for individuals to go beyond themselves, to make a contribution, to do something worthwhile and meaningful, and to serve a cause greater than themselves. These appeals can provide powerful mechanisms to unfreeze an organization and create conditions for change. In addition, transformational visions pull people toward an idealized future and a positive approach to needed change.

Cynics in an organization may reject these vision appeals for several reasons. They may see them as superficial, naive, ill-advised, off-target, or designed simply to serve the interests of those making the pronouncements. If organizational members have previously heard visionary pronouncements, only to see them ignored or discarded, they may believe the most recent iteration is simply the current "flavor of the week" approach to change.

Change agents need to ask themselves if they are really serious about following through on the values and action orientation that underlie their visionary appeals. If they are not, then they should stop rather than contribute to the build-up of organizational cynicism and alienation that accompanies unmet expectations. Nevertheless, the power of truly transformational visions should not be underestimated. How else do we understand the response to the visionary perspectives provided by change leaders such as Mahatma Ghandi and Nelson Mandela?

A third approach to enhancing the need for change is through *transformational leadership*. Leadership in general and transformational leadership in particular continue to command attention in the change literature—not surprising, given its stature in Western culture and mythology.[58] From George Washington to Adolf Hitler, from Nelson Mandela and Mother Teresa to Saddam Hussein, we've elevated the heroes and condemned the villains.

The same is true for the corporate world. Steve Jobs's resuscitation of Apple, Mukesh Ambani's leadership at Reliance (one of India's most valuable companies), Anne Mulcahy's transformation of Xerox, Thomas Tighe's work at Direct Relief International (a not-for-profit organization), Oprah Winfrey's growth of a media empire, Richard Branson's entrepreneurial initiatives at Virgin, and Elton Musk's development of PayPal, SpaceX (private sector rocket firm that delivers supplies to the space station), and the Tesla automobile . . . they all provide examples of the work of successful transformational leaders. The appeal of charismatic and transformational individuals is powerful. In addition to effectively framing the change vision as noted above, they have the capacity to create strong, positive personal connectedness and a willingness to change in followers that often overrides the followers' personal concerns. However, corporate scandals (e.g., Bernie Ebbers of WorldCom, Bernie Madoff of Madoff Investment Securities, Angelo Mozilo of Countrywide Financial, and Lance Armstrong and the Livestrong Foundation) remind people of the risks of idolizing transformational exemplars. Even GE's Jack Welch's image took a beating with published reports of his divorce battles and the size and nature of his retirement package.[59]

Caution is needed if you are relying on charisma to induce followers to change an organization. In an example cited earlier in this chapter, Nehru's concern over the impact of his charisma caused him to take public steps to rein it in. If the use of charisma is thought to be helpful, certain questions come to mind. First of all, do you have the necessary skills? Many people lack the capacities needed to create a charismatic response in others, and they may also lack access to someone who supports the change and possesses those skills. More important, is this the best approach to mobilizing people around a vision of change? Charismatic appeals can prove powerful and helpful (Barack Obama's successful 2008 and 2012 presidential campaigns attest to this), but there are good reasons for people to be suspicious of charismatic appeals because history demonstrates that personal magnetism is not always directed toward desirable outcomes.

It is important to note that many leaders are very effective change agents without being particularly charismatic. Some of those who have proven to be most influential in nurturing long-term organizational success have been much quieter in their approach.[60] Such a list would include Meg Whitman, CEO of HP; Satya Nadella, CEO of Microsoft; Warren Buffett of Berkshire Hathaway; Michael Latimer, president and CEO of OMERS, a large Canadian pension fund; Ursula Burns, CEO of Xerox; and Ellen Kullman, CEO of DuPont.

A fourth way of stimulating awareness of a need for change is by *taking the time to identify common or shared goals and working out ways to achieve them.* Finding common areas of agreement is a very useful way to avoid and/or surmount resistance to change. Instead of focusing on what might be lost, an examination of the risks of not taking action and what will be gained by taking action can create momentum for change. This is often achieved by having people seriously consider their longer-term interests (rather than their immediate positions) and the higher-order and longer-term goals that they would like to see pursued. If the change leader can focus on the needs of resisting individuals or groups, new and interesting perspectives on change can emerge. Shared interest in and commitment to higher-order or superordinate goals can provide a powerful stimulus for commitment and mobilization.

Fifth, *information and education can be used* to raise awareness of the need for change. In many respects, this is the inverse of the "sink your boats" command-and-control approach to change, because it seeks to build awareness and support through information rather than edict. Reluctance to change may be a result of lack of information or confusion about multiple and sometimes conflicting sources of information. This can be overcome with a well-organized communications campaign that provides employees with the needed information (e.g., best practices, benchmark data about the practices and approaches of others, visits with others to see and hear about their practices, competitive data, and other research).[61] Research on effective organizations can provide a compare-and-contrast picture to an organization's current mode of operation and that process can stimulate discussion and facilitate change.

EDUCATING PROGRAMMERS AT GTECH

GTECH was an extremely successful gaming technology and services company, but in 2002 Richard Koppel, VP of Advanced Technologies, knew change was needed. "Our systems were old, inflexible, and highly proprietary . . . Unless the company overhauled its technology platform, we wouldn't be able to innovate quickly or affordably enough to meet customers' needs." The executives at GTECH supported him, but there was stiff resistance from below. To create a sense of urgency, he and other executives repeatedly communicated and visited with the product developers to educate them about what was at risk. Discussions during regular staff meetings, dissemination of articles, and having GTECH's software developers talk about the issue with peers in other high-tech organizations

(Continued)

(Continued)

further reinforced the message concerning the need for change.[62] Resistance was reduced as a result of these actions, and the subsequent changes contributed to significant improvements to their financial performance over the next several years.

Once again, the change agent's credibility is crucial. If employees are suspicious of the motives of the change agent, the accuracy of the information, or there has been a history of difficult relationships, then the information will be examined with serious reservations. When employees come to accept the information and related analyses, the ground is fertile for the development of a shared sense of the need and the vision for change.

Factors That Block People From Recognizing the Need for Change

Giving voice to the need for change can create awareness in employees. However, future directions are not always obvious and an organization's history and culture can be strong impediments to creating awareness of the need for change. It took Hewlett-Packard a number of years of poor performance, problematic acquisitions, and related stumbles under different CEOs (most notably Carly Fiorina) until they recognized that cobbling in poorly fitting acquisitions to boost market share, and focusing primarily upon efficiency and cost reduction by playing with structures and product/service portfolios, would not reverse the fortunes of their business. Meg Whitman, the retired CEO of eBay, stepped into this very difficult situation and has led the revitalization of storied HP by valuing its roots, leading the conversation around the need for change, working to create a sense of urgency and hope, and taking actions to remove some of the obstacles in the way.

REVERSING THE DEATH SPIRAL AT HEWLETT-PACKARD

Hewlett-Packard had demonstrated commitment over the years to the belief that long-term success was grounded in the "'HP Way"—a cultural perspective that celebrated technical expertise, flexibility, and innovation; placed high value on their collegial, teamwork-based environment; saw employees as their most important resource; and had a strong customer orientation and commitment to act with integrity at all times. However in 1999, following a period of lackluster performance, HP hired Carly Fiorina as their CEO. Fiorina's top-down leadership style put results as the number one priority and arguably devalued employees. Her autocratic and aggressive style left her workforce demoralized. The ill-conceived merger with Compaq and a number of other major actions such as the restructuring of the enterprise into a much more hierarchical one, generated sustained, deepening disappointment on the performance front.

(Continued)

It could be argued that Fiorina suffered from tunnel vision concerning how to act on the need for change and manage the path forward. This blocked her from realizing how to value what was there, respond constructively to the challenges they faced, and modify her management style to facilitate needed changes. The results of her actions demoralized members of the firm, generated significant turnover, and adversely affected the entire organization.

Following Fiorina's dismissal in 2005 and subsequent flawed efforts to get things back on track, the board appointed Meg Whitman as CEO in 2011. At that point, many believed HP was operating on borrowed time. A number of the members of the existing senior management team were reported to have been very unhappy with her appointment. Whitman was an outsider, and some of them had been jockeying for the top job.

Whitman knew that hard choices were needed. These included making major changes to her senior management team, to get rid of infighting and promote much-needed cooperation and constructive engagement. Major job cuts (34,000) had to be made to address cash flow and market realities. However, she also clearly signaled a return to the organization's roots, by restoring funding and executive support for what was then a gutted and demoralized R&D function, symbolizing their commitment to innovation. She made the need for change salient to organizational members and created a sense of urgency. The enterprise was restructured to better align it with the emergent strategy, and she reinforced the importance of having a clear customer focus rather than one driven solely by cost-cutting pressures. Further, she created a vision for the future that offered employees reasons for hope and regenerated shared commitment through the focus on teamwork, collaboration, excellence in execution, and shared celebrations of success. Changes of this magnitude do not happen overnight. HP's impressive return to cultural and financial health by 2014 (stock price up 300% since 2011; being recognized as one of the 100 top employers in Canada in 2014) show that they appear to be well on their way.[63]

All too often, strategists will introduce a new direction and seek to change the organizational culture without attending to the question of the impact of cultural artifacts on the desired change.[64] Cultural artifacts are the stories, rituals, and symbols that influence employees' attitudes and beliefs; they are important because they help to define and give life to the culture. If change agents continue to tie themselves to those artifacts, they may reinforce the old culture they wish to change. However, being dismissive of the past can also be problematic because it may send signals that things done in the past are no longer valued. The challenge is: how do you value the past and its positive attributes without trapping yourself in the past? In 1994, Bethune and Brenneman faced this challenge when they tackled the turnaround of Continental Airlines, taking the firm from near bankruptcy and the worst customer service ratings in the industry to success on all fronts over the next decade.[65] One of the major reasons that they were successful in implementing a turnaround was their introduction of new cultural artifacts that reinforced service as a key value rather than staying anchored to those artifacts that signaled poor service.

CULTURAL CHANGE AT CONTINENTAL AIRLINES

A new reward system was put into place at Continental that focused on improved service. Performance-reward systems, in and of themselves, are not necessarily cultural artifacts, but this new reward system contrasted with past practices. It was tied directly to corporate performance, and the financial rewards were paid in a separate check to employees to draw attention to the relationship between performance and rewards. This reward system not only reinforced a new value at Continental, but it also became a symbol to employees of the importance of high levels of performance in the new Continental, as opposed to the acceptance of poor performance, as had been the case in the old Continental. In addition, stories were told throughout Continental about how the new CEO told jokes to employees, answered questions honestly, and was an all-around good guy to work for. These and numerous additional artifacts replaced old ones that had reinforced bureaucracy and the acceptability of poor performance and that had led to unbelievably low employee morale.[66] They succeeded in sustaining positive changes in customer service and fleet performance over the years, and their financial performance reflected their success in this very competitive industry. In 2009, *Fortune* magazine named Continental the world's most admired airline, and the World Airline Awards recognized it as the best North American airline.[67] In 2010 United Airlines acquired Continental.

Both the Continental and HP examples show that the existing culture can impair organizational members' capacity to either recognize the urgency of the need for change, or believe that there is the organizational will to constructively respond. Even if organizational members recognize the need, culture can impede their ability to take appropriate actions until things occur that weaken the existing beliefs and open the way to new thinking about the organization, the current situation, and its leadership. When this occurred at Continental and HP, the door was opened to meaningful change. Actions that created reasons for hope and reinforced the development and strengthening of new cultural beliefs ensured that the organization would continue its journey in a positive direction and wouldn't regress to old patterns.

Culture can get in the way of recognizing the need for change in poorly performing firms. However, it can represent an even more difficult barrier in successful firms. Consider Unilever, which had great brands and a long history in emerging markets and yet was falling behind competitors in those same markets. They knew they needed to change something but were mentally locked into the business practices that had become sources of disadvantage.[68] In 2004, they finally recognized the sources of the problem and by 2006 were reaping the benefits in terms of renewed growth and profitability. Unilever's performance was adversely affected by the 2008 recession, along with all their major competitors, but their renewed competitive capacities facilitated their recovery by 2010 and led to all-time share price highs in 2014.[69]

Sull argues that organizations trapped in their past successes often exhibit lots of activity (this was true for Unilever), but the outcome is "active inertia," because they remain essentially unchanged.[70] Even when organizations recognize that they need to change, they fail to take appropriate actions. He believes this occurs because:

- **Strategic frames**, those mental models or sets of assumptions of how the world works, become blinders to the changes that have occurred in the environment;
- Processes harden into routines and habits, becoming ends in themselves rather than means to an end;
- Relationships with employees, customers, suppliers, distributors, and shareholders become shackles that limit the degrees of freedom available to respond to the changed environment; and
- Values, those deeply held beliefs that determine corporate culture, harden into dogma, and questioning them is seen as heresy.

During periods of financial difficulty or decline, senior management teams may become polarized in their positions, isolate themselves from data they need, and incorrectly assess the need for change. Senior management teams may prevent critical information from surfacing as they self-censor, avoid conflict, and/or are unwilling to solicit independent assessments as they attempt to preserve cohesion and commitment to a course of action.[71] These are conditions that lead to groupthink[†] and can result in disastrous decisions that flow from the flawed analysis.[72] Change agents need to be vigilant and take action to ensure that groupthink does not cloud a team's capacity to assess the need for change or impair the judgment of the teams with which they are working. If change agents are dealing with a cohesive team exhibiting the characteristics of groupthink, the agents need to take action with care, considering how to make the group aware of factors that may be clouding the group's judgment. Change agents who attempt to alert such teams to these realities are often dealt with harshly, since "shooting the messenger" is a speedy way for teams to protect themselves from difficult data. Strategies for avoiding groupthink include:

- Have the leader play an impartial role, soliciting information and input before expressing an opinion.
- Actively seek dissenting views. Have group members play the role of devil's advocate, challenging the majority's opinion.

[†]Groupthink is "a mode of thinking that people engage in when they are deeply involved in a cohesive in-group, when the members' striving for unanimity overrides their motivation to realistically appraise alternative courses of action." Retrieved December 2010 from wps.prenhall.com/wps/media/objects/213/218150/glossary.html

- Actively pursue the discussion and analysis of the costs, benefits, and risks of diverse alternatives.
- Establish a methodical decision-making process at the beginning.
- Ensure an open climate for discussion and decision making, and solicit input from informed outsiders and experts.
- Allow time for reflection and do not mistake silence for consent.[73]

Additional factors that obstruct managerial judgment over the need for change and the inability to develop constructive visions for future action have been highlighted in both the business and academic press. Ram Charan and Jerry Useem summarize such factors in their 2002 *Fortune* magazine article on the role executives play in organizational failure:

- They have been softened by past success.
- They see no problems or at least none that warrant serious change (internal and external blindness).
- They fear the CEO and his or her biases more than competitors.
- They overdose on risk and play too close to the edge. This is often tied to systems that reward excessive risk taking.
- Their acquisition lust clouds their judgment.
- They listen to Wall Street more than to employees and others who have valuable insights they should attend to.
- They employ the "strategy du jour"—the quick-fix flavor of the day.
- They possess a dangerous corporate culture—one that invites high-risk actions.
- They find themselves locked in a new economy death spiral—one that is sustained and accelerating.
- They have a dysfunctional board that fails in its duties around governance.[74]

Developing a well-grounded awareness of the need for change is a critical first step for change leaders when helping organizations overcome inertia, rein in high-risk propensities, address internal and external blind spots, disrupt patterns of groupthink, and view their environment in ways that open organizational members to change.

So far, this chapter has outlined the variety of perspectives that will exist regarding the need for change. It emphasizes that the perspective of the change leader may not be held by others and that often change leaders need to develop or strengthen the need for change before trying to make specific changes. One of the ways to enhance the perceived need for change and begin to create focused momentum for action is to develop a clear and compelling change vision.

Developing a Powerful Vision for Change

A **vision for change** clarifies the road ahead. It specifies the purpose of the change and provides guidance and direction for action. It can provide a powerful pull on employees to participate positively in the change process.[75] As Simons says, "Vision without task is a dream world and task without vision is drudgery."[76]

Visions can be used to strengthen or transform existing cultures. At a micro level, visions are used to focus awareness, energy, and initiative around local issues, processes, and opportunities. At their best, change visions provide well-grounded, challenging reasons for hope and optimism. At their worst, they are trite bromides that accelerate organizational cynicism, hallucinations that are confusing or misguided, or specific directions that are simply inappropriate or counterproductive.

Change leaders use visions to create and advance the mental pictures people have of the future and to provide directional guidance for stakeholders whom change agents need to enlist in the enterprise. Creating the vision is a key part of defining a future state and, in turn, it is central to any gap analysis done by a change leader.

Understanding the foundational components of **organizational vision** is important. In an ideal world, it is closely connected to the mission of the organization (its fundamental purpose or reason for existence) and informs the core philosophy and values of the institution. It addresses such questions as, "What does this organization stand for?" Vision identifies the desired ideal future. From this should flow the strategies, goals, and objectives.[77] When change leaders have fully developed a change process, the strategies, goals, and objectives flow from the vision and will address three essential questions for an enterprise: What business are we in? Who are our target customers, and what is our value proposition to them? How will we deliver on our value proposition?

Change agents often create change visions or "sub-visions" in order to generate emotional energy, commitment, and directional clarity for the organizational change as the process proceeds from planning through to implementation in different departmental units. These allow the overall change vision to be adapted to reflect how it manifests itself within specific areas of the organization. If FedEx's overriding commitment to its customers for its express service is "absolutely, positively overnight," then a change leader's vision concerning a logistics support initiative might deal with enhancing accuracy in package tracking to reduce error rates to below .00001%.

Beach states:

> Vision is an agenda of goals . . . vision is a dream about how the ideal future might be . . . it gives rise to and dictates the shape of plans . . . vision infuses the plan with energy because it gives it direction and defines objectives. Even the most unassuming vision constitutes a challenge to become something stronger, better, different.[78]

Approached properly, it can mobilize and motivate people[79] and have a positive impact on performance and attitudes.[80]

Change leaders need to know *how* to develop a vision. Jick outlines three methods for creating vision: leader-developed, leader–senior team-developed, and bottom-up visioning.[81] As the name suggests, **leader-developed vision** is done largely in isolation from others. Once it has been created, it is announced and shared with others in the organization. **Leader–senior team-developed vision** casts a broader net. Members of the senior team are involved in the process of vision formation. Once completed, it is then shared with others. **Bottom-up visioning**, or an employee-centric approach, is time-consuming, difficult, *and* valuable in facilitating the alignment of organizational members' vision with the overall vision for change. If a change leader can articulate a compelling vision that captures a broad spectrum of organizational members, then a leader-developed vision is likely appropriate. If, on the other hand, employees are diverse and have mixed feelings about the vision, then the change agent's job will be difficult and a bottom-up approach will be necessary. If employees both "get it" (i.e., the vision) and "want to get it," subsequent support for change will prove much easier to develop, leverage, and implement.[82] This is particularly important when cultural changes are involved.[83]

What does it take to develop an effective change vision? According to Todd Jick, good change visions are:[84]

- Clear, concise, easily understood
- Memorable
- Exciting and inspiring
- Challenging
- Excellence centered
- Stable but flexible
- Implementable and tangible

The process of creating a vision statement encourages change agents to dream big. Paradoxically, when visions become too grand and abstract, they can cease to have much impact. Alternatively, they may provide guidance that energizes and mobilizes individuals to undertake initiatives that unintentionally work at cross purposes to other initiatives that have been embarked upon or that may even have the potential to put the organization at risk.[85]

FOOD BANKS CANADA

"A Canada Where No One Goes Hungry"

Food Banks Canada is the national body that plays a leadership role with its 450 affiliated nonprofit food banks across the country and 10 provincial associations. Its corporate vision is to relieve hunger in Canada every day by raising food and funds to share with food banks nationally, delivering program and services to Canadian food banks, and influencing public policy to create longer term solutions. This vision provides guidance that underpins specific change initiatives to promote coordination and cooperation among local food banks and

(Continued)

the provincial bodies, enhance press and community awareness of food bank initiatives and hunger issues, build support in the corporate community, and influence relevant governmental organizations and departments on matters related to hunger and food security. The vision grew out of restructuring and revitalization initiatives by the food bank community around 2006. At that time the new CEO and other staff members were recruited, the board and its governance processes were restructured, branding activities for the national organization were undertaken, and the approaches to advocacy and outreach were revitalized. As the result of these initiatives, Food Banks Canada has improved its reputation with government, national private sector organizations (e.g., grocery chains and food manufacturers), and affiliated local food banks as a credible and respected national voice on hunger issues, and an effective deliverer of related services. Donations (food, money, and related services such as trucking) are significantly stronger now. Awareness levels related to domestic hunger have also increased. The release of their data-rich annual publication, *HungerCounts*, now generates significant media attention and commentary by the sorts of individuals who can make a difference.[86]

Lipton provides a pragmatic view of what makes for an effective vision statement. He argues that it needs to convey three key messages: (a) the mission or purpose, (b) the strategy for achieving the mission, and (c) the elements of the organizational culture that seemed necessary to achieving the mission and supporting the strategy.[87] He believes a vision will be more likely to fail when:

- Actions of senior managers are incongruent with the vision. They fail to walk the talk.
- It ignores the needs of those who will be putting it into practice.
- Unrealistic expectations develop around it that can't possibly be met.
- It is little more than limited strategies, lacking in a broader sense of what is possible.
- It lacks grounding in the reality of the present that can be reconciled.
- It is either too abstract or too concrete. It needs to stimulate and inspire, but there also needs to be the sense that it is achievable.
- It is not forged through an appropriately messy, iterative, creative process requiring a combination of "synthesis and imagination."
- It lacks sufficient participation and involvement of others to build a consensus concerning its appropriateness.
- Its implementation lacks "a sense of urgency . . . and measurable milestones."[88]

Lipton's list provides change leaders with a set of factors to consider when developing and operationalizing their vision for change. Are their actions aligned with the vision? Have they considered the needs of those who will be putting it into practice? If not, Lipton would argue that you are lowering the motivational and directional value the change vision can provide. Conversely, if they are present, the power of the change vision is enhanced.

Change visions need to paint pictures that challenge the imagination and enrich the soul. Too many vision statements are insipid and dull. Too often they represent generic pap—right-sounding words but ones devoid of real meaning, designed for plaques and outside consumption and not rooted in the heart of the organization. Such visions focus on the lowest common denominator, something politically neutral that no one could object to. By trying to say everything or appeal to everyone, they say nothing and appeal to no one![89]

Table 4.2 contains the Handy-Dandy Vision Crafter, a cynical view of organizational vision statements and how they are developed. While many statements may

---

Table 4.2   The Handy-Dandy Vision Crafter

Just fill in the blanks with the words that best suit your needs!

We strive to be the: _____

(Premier, Leading, Preeminent, World-class, Dominant, Best of class . . .)

Organization in our industry. We provide the best in: _____

(Committed, Caring, Innovative, Expert, Environmentally friendly, Reliable, Cost-effective, Focused, Diversified, High-quality, On-time, Ethical, High-value-added . . .)

(Products, Services, Business Solutions, Customer-oriented Solutions . . .)

To: _____

(Serve Our Global Marketplace; Create Customer, Employee, and Shareholder Value; Fulfill Our Covenants to Our Stakeholders; Exceed Our Customers' Needs; Delight Our Customers . . .)

Through _____ employees

(Committed, Caring, Continuously Developed, Knowledgeable, Customer-focused . . .)

In the Rapidly Changing and Dynamic: _____

(Industry, Society, World)

---

end up containing words similar to those in the model, the Handy-Dandy Vision Crafter ignores the hard work and the difficult creative process and activities that organizations go through to develop a vision statement that works for them. In many ways, the process of developing the change vision is as important as the vision itself. However, too many vision statements read as if the Vision Crafter had been used to create them.

Sometimes a quick statement, a slogan, can serve as a vision proxy. Consider the following statements:

- Every life deserves world-class care (Cleveland Clinic)
- Think differently (Apple Computers)
- Saving people money so they can live better (Walmart)

- Inspire the world, create the future (Samsung)
- To organize the world's information and make it universally accessible and useful (Google)
- The greatest tragedy is indifference (Red Cross)
- Grace, space, pace (Jaguar)
- Play on (Lego)

These slogans are tied to statements of mission and vision, and they provide messages that are clear to employees and customers alike. They are meant to reflect underlying values that the organization holds dear and can help provide continuity with the change vision. Consider, for example, the one adopted by the Cleveland Clinic. If you were to take the words at their face value and were an associate there, change initiatives that facilitate access for the poor at the Cleveland Clinic are more likely to be viewed as positive change initiatives than ones focused solely on improving profitability, because they have the potential to be consistent with what the organization is all about.

The slogan "Quality is job #1" was used by Ford to symbolize its determination to improve quality in the 1980s. In the aftermath of quality and safety concerns that buffeted Ford, the automaker successfully used these words, with an accompanying concerted program of action, to refocus employee and public perceptions of the importance of quality to Ford and, ultimately, the excellence of its products. This major initiative spanned several years and was ultimately successful in taking root in the minds of employees and the public. However, the Ford Explorer/Firestone controversy in 2000[90] concerning vehicle stability in emergency situations reopened public questions of Ford's commitment to quality and safety and put extreme internal and external pressure on Ford and Bridgestone (Firestone's parent organization) to restore the public trust. The lesson to draw from Ford's experience is that an image built on a vision that took years to develop can be shattered quickly. Ford appears to have learned from the experience and their recent slogan, "Drive Further," is intended to address customer concerns around quality by committing to deliver products that are up to the challenge.

GM is relearning this lesson now, due to its decade-long failure to address an ignition switch problem that has resulted in a number of deaths, lawsuits, and the recall of approximately 18 million cars in North America in 2014. Mary Barra (the new CEO) is working hard to get out in front of this horrible situation, be transparent with the internal and external investigations, take concerted action to address the issue, and restore public confidence that inaction such as this will not recur under her watch at the "new" GM.[91]

Johnson & Johnson's response to the 1982 Tylenol deaths and tampering of bottles scare[92] and Procter & Gamble's[93] response to inappropriate competitive intelligence activities related to hair care products provide two examples of how clear vision can help organizations develop change initiatives that respond effectively to potentially damaging events. In the case of Tylenol, this best-selling brand was pulled from store shelves until the company was confident it had effectively addressed the risk of product tampering, at the cost of tens of millions of dollars. In the Procter & Gamble situation, when the CEO found out, he fired those involved, informed P&G's competitor that it had been spied upon, took appropriate action with respect to knowledge that P&G had inappropriately gained, and negotiated a multimillion-dollar civil damage payment to the aggrieved competitor. The actions of these two firms demonstrated their commitment to their respective visions of how they should operate and reinforced public and employee confidence in the firms and what they stood for.[‡]

Compare Procter & Gamble's and Johnson & Johnson's responses with Toyota's initial reactions to safety concerns in 2009 and 2010. The Toyota vision in 2010 was to become the most successful and respected car company in each market around the world by offering customers the best purchasing and ownership experience. However, one wonders if the desire to become the largest and most successful auto firm got in the way of the vision for respect that would be linked to quality and the willingness to put the needs of customers ahead of the company's own. The response to safety concerns was initially slow and defensive, and Toyota paid a very heavy price in lost sales and damaged reputation and brand.[94] It was ranked the seventh most admired company in the world by *Fortune* in 2010, dropped to 33 for 2011 and 2012, and is slowly regaining ground, landing 29th on the list in 2013.[95]

As noted earlier, companies can be trapped by the existing vision of their organization.[96] Goss, Pascale, and Athos argue that (a) narrow definitions of what the company is about, (b) failure to challenge the accepted boundaries and assumptions of the company, and (c) an inability to understand the context leads to inadequate or mediocre visions. They show the problems that can occur when a vision is achieved—now what? Once the vision is achieved, motivation is lost. It is a bit like a team whose vision was to "make it to the Super Bowl"—it is at a distinct disadvantage when playing against a team whose vision is to "win the Super Bowl."

Once the vision is clear, the issue becomes one of enactment by employees. Storytelling is a technique employed by change leaders to communicate a vision and mobilize awareness and interest. Because people identify with and remember stories, change agents can use stories in several ways: to create contextual awareness of how an organization got to its problematic condition; to demystify data; to clarify a change initiative and why a particular course of action makes sense; to relieve or increase tension and awareness; and finally, to instill confidence.[97] The multiple uses of stories make storytelling a critical skill for change leaders. Some have referred to this as ways to increase the stickiness or memorableness of the message and enhance its meaningfulness. To increase the stickiness, Cranston and Keller recommend framing the stories five different ways. By this they mean not stopping the message for change after the traditional data-based approach that either demonstrates shortfalls (here is how we're falling behind and need to improve) or opportunities. In addition to this, they recommend also framing the stories in terms of the impact of the change vision on society, the customer, the work team, and the individuals. Which messages are you more likely to remember—stories about positive impacts on you, your work team, your customers, and society,

---

[‡]Johnson & Johnson's credo can be found at www.jnj.com/connect/about-jnj/jnj-credo/. Procter & Gamble's mission, vision, and values can be found at: www.pg.com/en_US/downloads/media/PVP_bro chure.pdf.

or ones that speak solely to 5% improvements to margins and 10% increase in sales levels?[98]

Wheatley argues that one must "get the vision off the walls and into the halls"![99] She claims that people are often trapped by a mechanical view of vision, one that is limited to only a directional component of vision (vision as a vector). She argues that vision should be viewed as a field that touches every employee differently and is filled with eddies and flux and shifting patterns. This view emphasizes the need to understand how each individual "sees" or "feels" the vision. As Beach says, "Each member (of the organization) has his or her own vision."[100] Somehow, these individual visions need to be combined into an overall sense of purpose for the organization. The active engagement and involvement of employees (or their representatives) in the development, communication, and enactment of the vision for change is a strategy that has been effectively used to advance the creation of a shared sense of purpose.[101] Twenty-six centuries ago, Lao Tzu observed that "the best change is what the people think they did themselves."

The Difference Between an Organizational Vision and a Change Vision

While the rules for crafting a vision remain the same, the focus of the vision shifts depending upon the level and position of the change leader. Different parts of the organization will focus the vision for their areas in ways that reflect the aspirations for their part of the enterprise. They should be aligned with the overarching vision but differentiated in ways that generate meaning and energy for those involved with that part of the enterprise. Whereas the corporate vision is about the longer-term future, the change vision is shorter term in its perspective, and more specific as to the targets for change, the tangible outcomes to be achieved, and the anticipated impact. In other words, it is focused on the specific changes to be implemented. By definition, they are designed to contribute to the vision of the organization but are more focused in their scope, and often require the cooperation of others to bring them to fruition.[102]

This is easy to understand when the divisions are involved with different products/services and/or different markets, but it also holds for other functions within the organization, such as manufacturing, marketing, or accounting services. For example, a staff support function such as HR will have a change focus that is largely internal to the organization, because that is where most of its customers and products/services lie. However, a vision for change focused on improving HR's ability to successfully recruit and retain external talent would involve an external focus plus the needed alignment of internal systems and processes to produce the desired results for the organization. If you are an organization needing to scale your operations rapidly, change initiatives that facilitate the recruitment, development, and retention of talented employees takes on added urgency—something firms such as Infosys and Tata Consulting, know all too well.[103] In 2014, Infosys reported they were planning to add 3,500 employees to just two of their Indian development centers and were striving to keep their attrition rate at 12% or lower. To promote their image as a desirable employer, they had, among many internal and external initiatives, undertaken specific outreach initiatives to educational institutions and had distributed 10,000 electronic notebooks to students studying in government schools in regions near the two development centers.[104]

Change leaders' goals are advanced when they develop compelling messages that appeal to the particular groups of people critical to the change initiative. However, in practice, there will be tensions between the changes proposed and what other parts of the organization are attempting to accomplish. For example, the sales force may be focused on how quickly it is able to respond to customers with the products they require, while manufacturing may be rewarded for how efficiently it is able to operate rather than how quickly it is able to respond to a customer order. These tensions need to be recognized and managed so that the needed changes do not flounder, and various approaches for handling this will be addressed in subsequent chapters.

When change leaders develop their vision for change, they are challenged with the question of where to set the boundaries. A narrower, tighter focus will make it easier to meet the test of Jick's characteristics of effective vision for a specific target audience, but it may also reduce the prospects for building alliances and a broad base of support for change. As the need for change extends to strategic challenges and the cultural dimensions of a firm, this issue of building a larger constituency for the change becomes increasingly important. Two questions must be answered: First, where, if anywhere, do common interests among stakeholders lie? Second, can the vision for change be framed in terms of the common interest without diverting its purpose to the point where it no longer delivers a vision that will excite, inspire, and challenge?

This was a challenge that Dr. Martin Luther King met superbly. In 1963, King stood on the steps of the Lincoln Memorial and delivered his famous "I Have a Dream" speech on the 100th anniversary of the publishing of the Emancipation Proclamation by President Lincoln. This was a critical point in the Civil Rights Movement, and Dr. King succeeded in seizing that moment by enunciating a compelling vision that embraced a large coalition. Attention to the coalition is apparent in his words:

> The marvelous new militancy which has engulfed the Negro community must not lead us to distrust all white people, for many of our white brothers, as evidenced by their presence here today, have come to realize that their destiny is tied up with our destiny and their freedom is inextricably bound to our freedom. We cannot walk alone.

Dr. King then went on to set out a vision in language all would understand: "I have a dream that one day this nation will rise up and live out the true meaning of its creed: We hold these truths to be self-evident: that all men are created equal."[105]

A broadly stated vision will potentially appeal to a broader range of people and engage a more diverse group in a change process. For example, the National Campaign to Prevent Teen Pregnancy appealed to a very broad range of groups, from Catholics who opposed abortion to Planned Parenthood who accepted abortion.[106] Regardless of their specific positions, all groups wanted to prevent teen pregnancy. However, each of these groups had different ideas about the strategies for prevention. The risk of a broad change vision is that their appeal to particular groups may either be watered down, or the coalitions attracted to them may subsequently break down when the vision gets translated into actions.

Coalitions that can develop around a common vision can be surprising. Who would have thought that Ted Olson, a very prominent conservative Republican lawyer, and David Boies, a prominent liberal lawyer, who had faced off in courts over the matter of hanging chads in the 2000 U.S. presidential election, would become co-councils in the successful litigation efforts to defeat the Defense of Marriage Act and California's Proposition 8, that culminated in a decision in their favor in the Supreme Court of the United States?[107] Likewise, the ability for environmentalists and conservative Republicans to forge a common cause around the reduction of fossil fuel consumption is not something many expected, but it now exists. Though their perceptions of the underlying rationale for the need for change are different, they were able to identify a common vision for change:

REDUCING FUEL CONSUMPTION AS A COMMON VISION

Environmentalists and groups of conservative Republicans are stepping up a campaign to promote alternative-fuel vehicles and wean the USA from dependence on foreign oil. While still skeptical about links between autos and global warming, the conservatives have concluded that cutting gasoline consumption is a matter of national security.

Right-leaning military hawks—including former CIA Director R. James Woolsey—have joined with other conservative Republicans and environmental advocates such as the Natural Resources Defense Council to lobby Congress to spend $12 billion to cut oil use in half by 2025. Their vision is to end America's dependence on foreign oil, build a sustainable energy system, and, in the process, create millions of jobs. The alliance highlights how popular sentiment is turning against the no-worries gas-guzzling culture and how alternative technologies such as gas–electric hybrids are finding increasingly widespread support.

"I think there are a number of things converging," said Gary L. Bauer, a former Republican presidential candidate and former head of the Family Research Council who has signed on to a strange-bedfellows coalition of conservatives and environmentalists called Set America Free. "I just think reasonable people are more inclined right now to start thinking about ways our country's future isn't dependent on . . . oil from a region where there are a lot of very bad actors."[108]

Examples of Organizational Change Visions

In the past, visions have generally been viewed as organization-level statements. However, change programs can benefit from a clear sense of direction and purpose that vision statements provide. The most powerful visions tap into people's need to be part of something transformative and meaningful. Mundane but important change programs involving restructuring or profit-focused issues need clear, concise targets.

Here are some examples of organizational change visions:

Google's Implied Vision for Change in Telecommunications

Give carriers less control over what they can and cannot do with their networks through promoting net neutrality, developing Google's own mobile phone and operating system, and through forcing the carriers to build more high-speed networks through the threat that Google will do it if they don't.[109]

Xerox's Vision for Creating Agile Business Processes

Our research in ethnography, computer vision, natural language, and machine learning aims to automate business processes via flexible platforms that run on robust and scalable infrastructures. By implementing our solutions on state-of-the-art, cloud-based frameworks, we enable scalability and availability, while ensuring security and integrity of vital corporate assets.[110]

IBM—Diversity 3.0

IBM has a long history of commitment to diversity and has consistently taken the lead on diversity policies long before it was required by law. It began in the mid-20th century, grounded in Equal Opportunity Legislation and compliance (Diversity 1.0). We moved forward to Diversity 2.0 in the 1990s with a focus on eliminating barriers, and understanding regional constituencies and differences between the constituencies. As our demographics changed, we adapted our workplace to be more flexible and began our focus on work-life integration. In addition, over the past 5 years, we've introduced IBM's Values, which links to our diversity work.

This strong foundation brings us to where we are today—Diversity 3.0. This is the point where we can take best advantage of our differences—for innovation. Our diversity is a competitive advantage and consciously building diverse teams helps us drive the best results for our clients.[111]

Ronald McDonald House Charities (RMHC) Vision

We believe that when you change a child's life, you change a family's, which can change a community, and ultimately the world.

As pioneers of providing family-centered care, RMHC strives to be part of the solution in improving the lives of children and their families, providing programs that strengthen families during difficult times.

In 2014, we launched the three-year "RMHC Impact Strategy," with a goal to serve one million more children and their families per year. This strategy not only builds on our success over the last 40 years, but also gives us the foundation to be stronger and more efficient than ever.

In order to do this, we are focusing on three strategic priorities:

- Expanding our reach by both creating and growing existing programs—including Ronald McDonald Houses and Ronald McDonald Family Rooms
- Strengthening our global network through staff development and education, and ensuring the financial sustainability of RMHC and its Chapters around the world
- Mobilizing support to increase the understanding of RMHC programs; thereby allowing us to support more children and families around the world

Through the strong network of RMHC Chapters around the world collectively we are able to identify needs and carry out the RMHC mission on the ground. But we can't do it alone. We rely on our strong relationships with the medical community to provide access to health care. We rely on the RMHC Mission Partner, McDonald's, including the corporation, owner/operators, suppliers and customers, as well as other important corporate partnerships. And, we rely on strategic alliances with organizations that have the knowledge and infrastructure to extend our reach. Most of all, we rely on you—our donors, volunteers, staff, and friends.[112]

Tata's Vision for the Nano

Ratan Tata's 2003 Vision to his engineering team, led by 32-year-old star engineer Girish Wagh:

Create a $2,000 "people's car." It has to be safe, affordable, all weather transportation for a family. It should adhere to regulatory requirements, and achieve performance targets such as fuel efficiency and acceleration.

The result of this vision is the Tata Nano. It gets 50 miles to the gallon, and seats up to five. And at $2,500 before taxes it is the most inexpensive car in the world. In March 2012, Mr. Tata stated that the original vision for the Nano had been achieved, and that the vision had now shifted to further upgrading and refinement of the product.[113]

World Wildlife Fund: Vision for Its Community Action Initiative—Finding Sustainable Ways of Living

At the World Wildlife Fund (WWF) we protect wildlife, preserve habitats and empower people to conserve resources while improving their livelihoods. We understand the close relationship between humans and the environment, and incorporate elements of governance, gender relations, health, and education into our conservation work. Our community conservation program links improving human lives with conserving biodiversity. Through WWF initiatives, communities are given the opportunity to reduce poverty, improve socio-economic conditions and become environmental stewards for the natural places WWF works to conserve.

> Our vision: Build a sustainable balance between people and nature by empowering local communities to reduce poverty, enhance their opportunities and well-being, and strengthen their role as environmental decision makers.[114]

Vision for the "Survive to 5" Program

Save the Children, World Vision, UNICEF and other not-for-profits, have taken up the challenge posed by the World Health Organization, to reduce child mortality by two-thirds, by 2015. Mortality rates had been reduced by 41% between 1990 and 2011, but the refugee crises that have been created by wars and environmental disasters were complicating efforts, giving rise to a call for the United Nations for a redoubling of efforts.[115]

Vision: We believe all children should live to celebrate their fifth birthday.

The Survive to 5 campaign supports Millennium Development Goal 4—to reduce child mortality by two thirds by 2015 and save the lives of over 5 million children under 5 who are dying of preventable and treatable diseases.[116]

> In order to help reduce preventable deaths, Survive to 5 will work in countries where basic health care is inaccessible to large numbers of children. Working with government and private sector health care systems, we will develop policy environments that are conducive to community-based care and train a cadre of local health care workers to increase health care coverage and ensure linkages and referrals to facilities for more complicated cases. Research shows that simple interventions—including vaccines, oral rehydration therapy, antibiotics for pneumonia and sepsis and medicine to treat malaria—could save some two-thirds of the children who currently do not survive. Clean practices at birth and improved immediate newborn care, such as breastfeeding and special care for low birth weight babies would also contribute to saving young lives.[117]

Change Vision for "Reading Rainbow"

In 2014, LeVar Burton used the crowdsourcing website "Kickstarter" for a campaign to raise $5 million. The short-term change vision is to work together to bring back the "Reading Rainbow" show to PBS, and provide free access to 7,500 classrooms.

> The broader vision is to leverage the existing free Reading Rainbow app and make its existing and future content available for free, to each and every web connected child, by developing a web-enabled reading rainbow for the home, create a classroom version with the tools teachers need, and subsidize the cost so it is available to schools for free.[118]

Visions for change from the starting point for the chain of vision → objectives → goals → activities.[§] To make the change vision tangible, change agents also need to specify measurable goals for their change efforts. The research on goal setting has been quite clear on the benefits of SMART (specific, measurable, attainable, relevant, and time-bound) goals.[119] The provision of direction with measurable results for feedback galvanizes many people to pursue desired aims. This is easy to say, but defining the right measurable goals is not straightforward. Perhaps a critical task is to persuade a key stakeholder to view the change positively. How does one assess when such attitudes are beginning to change and capture the progress? Identifying interim goals, indicators of progress, and key milestones that demonstrate progress toward the end goals of the change vision are challenges that will be dealt with in subsequent chapters. See **Toolkit Exercise 4.3** to practice writing a vision statement, then move on to **Toolkit Exercise 4.4** to combine your understanding for the need for change and your newly crafted vision statement.

Summary

In summary, change occurs when there is an understanding of the need for change, the vision of where the organization should go, and a commitment to action. Change leaders need to address the question "Why change?" and develop both a sound rationale for the change and a compelling vision of a possible future. Unfreezing organizational members is advanced when these have been effectively executed.

The rationale for change emerges from a sound understanding of the situation: the external and internal data that point to a need for change, an understanding of the perspectives of critical stakeholders in the organization, internal data in the organization that affects any change, and the personal needs and abilities of the change leaders themselves. Critical in this is an understanding of the organization's readiness for change and the awareness of the need for change throughout the organization. Finally, the chapter discusses the creation of powerful visions and how to develop a specific change vision.

In addition to creating appealing visions of the future and demonstrating a compelling need for change, change agents need to understand the particular contexts of the major individuals in the change events. These stakeholders, or key players, will have an impact on the change situation, so their motives and interests need to be analyzed. Likewise, the impacts of formal structures, systems, and processes on the change need to be assessed and understood. The next two chapters explore these topics. See **Toolkit Exercise 4.1** for critical thinking questions for this chapter.

[§]We use the following definitions. *Mission* means the overall purpose of the organization. *Vision* means the ultimate or ideal goal pursued. Thus, for a social service agency, the mission might be to look after the homeless and improve their health outcomes. The vision could be to eradicate homelessness and related health issues in the community by 2020. The change vision related specifically to accommodations might then be to provide access to safe, affordable housing for 60% of the homeless in the community within the next three years.

Key Terms

Need for change—the pressure for change in the situation. This need can be viewed as a "real" need, that demonstrated by data and facts, and a "perceived" need, that seen by participants in the change.

Developing a perspective on the need for change is aided by (a) seeking out external data, (b) seeking out the perspective, (c) seeking out data internal to the organization, and (d) reflecting upon personal concerns and perspectives of the change leader.

Perspectives of key internal and external stakeholders—the unique point of view of important participants in the change process. Understanding this perspective is critical to recognizing why this stakeholder supports or resists change.

Readiness for Change

Organizational readiness for change—the degree to which the organization as a whole perceives the need for change and accepts it.

Individual readiness for change—the degree to which the individual perceives the need for change and accepts it.

Readying an organization for change—can be done through the use of a variety of strategies, including (a) creating a crisis, (b) developing a vision that creates dissatisfaction with the status quo in the organization, (c) finding a champion-of-change leader who will build awareness of the need for change and articulate the vision for change, (d) focusing on common or superordinate goals, and (e) creating dissatisfaction with the status quo through education, information, and exposure to superior practices and processes of both competitors and non-competitors. Different strategies have different strengths and weaknesses associated with them.

Eight dimensions related to readiness—trustworthy leadership, trusting followers, capable champions, involved middle management, innovative culture, accountable culture, effective communications, and systems thinking.

Strategic frames—the mental models or sets of assumptions held by change participants about how the world works. These can block the recognition for the need for change.

Vision

Vision for change—the idealized view of the short-term future after a specific change has been enacted. Change visions are more specific than organizational visions and have some element of a time constraint.

Organizational vision—the idealized view of the future. The vision needs to be: (a) clear, concise, easily understood; (b) memorable; (c) exciting and inspiring; (d) challenging; (e) excellence centered; (f) stable but flexible; and (g) implementable and tangible.

Leader-developed vision—developed directly by the change leader.

Leader–Senior-team-developed vision—developed by the senior management group in conjunction with the change leader.

Bottom-up visioning—engages a broader spectrum of organizational members in the vision framing process. The change vision is developed through the active participation of those responsible for implementing the change, including those on the front line.

A Checklist for Change: Creating the Readiness for Change

1. What is the "objective" need for change? That is, what are the consequences to the organization of changing or not changing? Are people aware of these risks?

2. Are organizational members aware of the need for change? Do they feel the need for change, or do they deny its need? How can they be informed?

3. Remember that individuals are motivated toward change only when they perceive the benefits as outweighing the costs. How can you, as a change leader, help employees see the benefits as outweighing the costs?

4. If individuals believe the benefits outweigh the costs, do they also believe the probability of success is great enough to warrant the risk taking, including the investment of time and energy that the change will require?

5. What change alternatives are people predisposed to? What are the costs, benefits, and risks that make them attractive? How should these alternatives be addressed by the change leader?

END-OF-CHAPTER EXERCISES

TOOLKIT EXERCISE 4.1

Critical Thinking Questions

Please find the URL for the video listed below on the website at study.sagepub.com/cawsey3e. Consider the questions that follow.

1. David Logan: Tribal Leadership—16:36 minutes

This video focuses on five kinds of tribes that people naturally form and how they influence behavior.

- Describe Logan's theory on tribes.

- Compare Logan's ideas with tribes you've been a part of in the past.

- Reflect on how Logan's idea of Tribal Leadership may affect how to approach change.

2. There are lots of great examples of leaders communicating their vision for change, such as Martin Luther King, Nelson Mandela, Malala Yousafzai, Steve Jobs, Howard Schultz, Indra Nooyi, Hilary Clinton, and Melinda Gates.

- Go to the Web and find a powerful vision for change speech that resonates with you. What is it about the one you selected that resonates with you?

- Does it share the characteristics of an effective vision statement outlined in the text?

Please see study.sagepub.com/cawsey3e for a downloadable template of this exercise.

TOOLKIT EXERCISE 4.2

Developing the Background to Understand the Need for Change

As suggested earlier in this book, a careful diagnosis is essential for successful organizational change. Much of this diagnosis is needed to understand the need for change that the organization faces and then to engage and persuade organizational members concerning the need for change.

1. Consider an example of an organizational change that you are familiar with or are considering undertaking. What data could help you understand the need for change?

2. Have you:

   a. Understood and made sense of external data? What else would you like to know?

   b. Understood and made sense of the perspectives of other stakeholders? What else would you like to know?

   c. Understood and assessed your personal concerns and perspectives and how they may be affecting your perspective on the situation?

   d. Understood and made sense of internal data? What else would you like to know?

3. What does your analysis suggest to you about the need for change?

Please see study.sagepub.com/cawsey3e for a downloadable template of this exercise.

TOOLKIT EXERCISE 4.3

Writing a Vision Statement[120]

Think of an organization you are familiar with that is in need of change. If you were the change leader, what would be your vision statement for change?

1. Write your vision statement for the change you are striving for.

2. Evaluate your vision. Is it:
   - Clear, concise, and easily understood?
   - Memorable?
   - Exciting and inspiring?
   - Challenging?
   - Excellence centered?
   - Stable and yet flexible?
   - Implementable and tangible?

3. Does the vision promote change and a sense of direction?

4. Does the vision provide the basis from which you can develop the implementation strategy and plan?

5. Does the vision provide focus and direction to those who must make ongoing decisions?

6. Does the vision embrace the critical performance factors that organizational members should be concerned about?

7. Does the vision engage and energize as well as clarify? What is the emotional impact of the vision?

8. Does the vision promote commitment? Are individuals likely to be opposed to the vision, passive (let it happen), moderately supportive (help it happen), or actively supportive (make it happen)?

9. Now assess your vision on a scale of 1 to 5 (5 being the highest) relative to the factors set out below.

   a. Actions of senior managers are congruent with the vision. They walk the talk.

      1   2   3   4   5

   b. It pays attention to the needs of those who will be putting it into practice.

      1   2   3   4   5

   c. Realistic expectations develop around it that are challenging but can be met.

      1   2   3   4   5

   d. It communicates a broader sense of what is possible.

      1   2   3   4   5

   e. It is grounded in the reality of the present and can be reconciled with it.

      1   2   3   4   5

   f. It is neither too abstract nor too concrete. It has the potential to stimulate and inspire, but it also communicates the sense that it is achievable.

      1   2   3   4   5

   g. It has been forged through an appropriately messy, iterative, creative process requiring a combination of "synthesis and imagination."

      1   2   3   4   5

   h. It has sufficient participation and involvement of others to build a consensus concerning its appropriateness.

      1   2   3   4   5

   i. Its implementation contains "a sense of urgency . . . and measurable milestones."[121]

      1   2   3   4   5

10. Given your assessment of the above items, what would you recommend be done in order to strengthen the value of the change vision?

Please see study.sagepub.com/cawsey3e for a downloadable template of this exercise.

TOOLKIT EXERCISE 4.4

Putting the Need for Change and the Vision for Change Together

For any change to be successful, the need for change must be real and must be perceived as real. If the organization does not accept the need for change, the chances of anything substantive happening are negligible. Thus, developing the need for change is vital. Understanding the gap between what is and what is desired is important in order to accurately describe the need for change.

Think of the situation you were considering in Exercise 4.2.

1. What is the gap between the present state and the desired future state?

2. How strong is the need for change?

3. What is the source of this need? Is it external to the organization?

4. Is there tangible evidence of the need for change in that there is concrete evidence of the need or a crisis situation that demonstrates the need for change?

5. If the change does not occur, what will be the impact on the organization in the next two to six years?

6. What is the objective, long-range need to change?

People can be motivated by higher-order purposes, things that relate to fundamental values. Change visions can be crucial in capturing support for change and in explaining the nature of change to others. Creating such a change vision is tricky. If one aims too high, it taps into higher values but often fails to link with the specific change project or program. If one aims too low, the vision fails to tap into values that motivate us above and beyond the ordinary. Such a change vision looks like and feels like an objective.

7. Return to the change vision you developed in Exercise 4.2. Does it capture a sense of higher-order purpose or values that underpin the change and communicate what the project is about?

8. Explain how the vision links the need for change.

Please see study.sagepub.com/cawsey3e for a downloadable template of this exercise.

CHAPTER 5

Navigating Change Through Formal Structures and Systems

If you're going to sin, sin against God, not the bureaucracy; God will forgive you but the bureaucracy won't.

—H. G. Rickover, U.S. Admiral[1]

We shape our buildings; thereafter they shape us.

—Winston Churchill[2]

CHAPTER OVERVIEW

- This chapter discusses the basics of how organizations structure themselves.
- It outlines how change leaders can diagnose the strengths and weaknesses of existing systems and structures.
- It examines how the formal structure and systems can foster, impair, and facilitate the acceptance of change initiatives.
- It lays out ways to manage systems and structures to gain approval for change initiatives. Formal, coalition-building, and renegade approaches are discussed.
- Finally, it reviews the ways to develop more adaptive systems and structures to increase the likelihood of continuous improvement.

Any discussion of organizational change needs to pay careful attention to the role of formal systems and structures. They influence what gets done, how it gets done, the outcomes that are achieved, and the experiences of the people who come into contact with the organization. While organizations define their systems and structures, the systems and structures shape the behavior of organizational members. Formal systems and structures play important coordination, communication, and control roles, and they influence how decisions are made about change. Sometimes systems and structures represent what needs to change.

An organization's formal structure is defined by how tasks are formally divided, grouped, and coordinated.[3] Formal **structures** are designed to support the strategic direction of the firm by enhancing order, efficiency, effectiveness, and accountability. They serve as guides and controls on decision-making authority, coordinate and integrate operations, provide direction to internal governance, and attempt to promote desired behavior and organizational outcomes.[4] The organizational chart is the common document of organizational design.

Formal **systems** include planned routines and processes such as strategic planning, accounting and control systems, performance management, pay and reward systems, and the information system. Collectively, these set out how things are supposed to be done, the rules and procedures to be followed, how information is collected and disseminated, how individuals are to be compensated, and all the other formalized systems and processes that are used for coordination, integration, and control purposes. They provide the formal infrastructure that operationalizes the organizational structure.

Organizations vary in their need for complexity in their structures and systems, but all require some degree of formalization to be sustainable. These are modified over time as conditions change and they need to bring them into alignment with external conditions, strategy, and other internal factors. The corner grocer needs simple systems for accounting, staffing, and managing its suppliers, pricing, and inventory management. Walmart, on the other hand, requires sophisticated systems and structures to efficiently and profitably handle $473 billion in net sales, processed by 2 million associates in 11,000 retail units that operate in 26 countries.[5] This includes $10 billion in online sales in 2014, an increase of 30% over 2013.[6]

One reason that Walmart dominates the consumer retail market is its logistics systems that coordinate all aspects of inventory management, from ordering through to shipping, warehousing, shelving, and final disposition. Its knowledge-management system, Retail Link, provides Walmart and its suppliers with data that allow them to identify emerging opportunities for their products. Their systems are continuously improved in order to better drive business results, and they are demonstrating their ability to effectively extend their technical reach to the world of online retailing. It is systems like this that allow Walmart to satisfy multiple stakeholders and maintain its competitive position in the industry.[7]

The purpose of this chapter is to describe the roles that formal systems and structures play in advancing change. It also provides guidance in identifying the gap between the existing structures and systems, and what is needed to bring about alignment after the change. Figure 5.1 outlines where this chapter fits in the change-management process. This chapter is the first of four that detail how change leaders can advance a sophisticated gap analysis and deploy it in pursuit of change. This chapter deals with formal systems and structures, and the

---

Figure 5.1   The Change-Management Process

The Change Path Model

Awakening
Chapter 4
1. Identify a need for change and confirm the problems or opportunities that incite the need for change through collection of data.
2. Articulate the gap in performance between the present and the envisioned future state, and spread awareness of the data and the gap throughout the organization.
3. Develop a powerful vision for change.
4. Disseminate the vision for the change and why it's needed through multiple communication channels.

Mobilization
Chapters 5 through 8
1. **Make sense of the desired change through formal systems and structures, and leverage those systems to reach the change vision (Chapter 5).**
2. Assess power and cultural dynamics at play, and put them to work to better understand the dynamics and build coalitions and support to realize the change (Chapter 6).
3. Communicate the need for change organization-wide and manage change recipients and various stakeholders as they react to and move the change forward (Chapter 7).
4. Leverage change agent personality, knowledge, skills and abilities, and related assets (e.g., reputation and relationships) for the benefit of the change vision and its implementation (Chapter 8).

Acceleration
Chapter 9
1. Continue to systematically reach out to engage and empower others in support, planning, and implementation of the change. Help them develop needed new knowledge, skills, abilities, and ways of thinking that will support the change.
2. Use appropriate tools and techniques to build momentum, accelerate and consolidate progress.
3. Manage the transition, celebrating small wins and the achievement of milestones along the larger, more difficult path of change.

Institutionalization
Chapter 10
1. Track the change periodically and through multiple balanced measures to help assess what is needed, gauge progress toward the goal, and to make modifications as needed and mitigate risk.
2. Develop and deploy new structures, systems, processes and knowledge, skills, and abilities, as needed, to bring life to the change and new stability to the transformed organization.

chapters that follow will cover the informal aspects of organizations, change stakeholders and recipients, and change leaders themselves.

Change leaders need to develop a deep understanding of how existing structures and systems are currently influencing outcomes and how they are likely to facilitate or impede the proposed changes. Once that understanding is developed, change leaders need to put that system and structural awareness to use to promote and enact change. To advance this agenda, the chapter is divided into four sections:

1. Making sense of organizational structures and systems

2. Diagnosing the strengths and weaknesses of existing systems and structures

3. Understanding how structures and systems influence the approval process of a change initiative and how they then facilitate or hinder the acceptance of change

4. Designing adaptive structures and systems to enhance future change initiatives

Making Sense of Formal Structures and Systems

The structural frame,[8] to use the language of Bolman and Deal, outlines an internal blueprint for how managers assign tasks, roles, and authority to produce products or services for the external marketplace. Wrapped around this structure are all the formal systems and processes that are designed to bring the structure to life and make it possible for the organization to deliver on its strategy and value proposition.

To make sense of structures, it is useful for change leaders to understand and be able to work with core concepts in this area. Some of the more common elements used include:[9]

1. *Differentiation:* The degree to which tasks are subdivided into separate jobs or tasks. This concept deals with who does what and asks about the degree to which jobs are specialized and distinctive from one another on both the horizontal and vertical organizational axes. The differentiation of tasks is an early step in the life of an entrepreneurial adventure as it grows from one to two and then three people, with further differentiation of tasks as the number of employees increases. As organizations grow and add more people, tasks are divided and subdivided. Large organizations, as a consequence, are often characterized by highly specialized jobs, leading to silos of similar and separate tasks and job categories.

2. *Integration:* The coordination of the various tasks or jobs into a department or group. This is the extent to which activities are combined into processes and systems, pulling together all the disparate pieces of tasks and jobs into a coherent whole. Small organizations are typically structured in a simple and straightforward manner, organized by functions such as production, accounting/finance, sales and

marketing, and human resources. As they grow and become more complex, they look for more efficient and effective ways to group tasks and activities. Departments or divisions may be organized geographically or by product category, customer segment, or some other hybrid approach such as networks that seem to offer the best way to organize activities at that point in time. Sometimes they may even be spun off as separate, stand-alone entities. In large organizations, such as Boeing, there are integrative roles with people and teams who specialize in coordinating and communicating in order to bring together the disparate parts of the enterprise.

3. *Chain of command:* The reporting architecture in a hierarchical organization. This concept defines how individuals and/or units within an organization report to one another up and down the organizational ladder. It reflects the formal power structure and where decision responsibilities lie within the hierarchy.

4. *Span of control:* The number of individuals who report to a manager. This notion questions the optimal ratio of workers to managers in an organization. Since there is no one correct way to answer this question, part of the art of organizational design is to figure this out, given the culture, strategy, and what needs to be done. An organization that gives managers too little span of control runs the risk of creating a costly and top-heavy administrative structure and encouraging its managers to micromanage too few employees. On the other hand, managers who have too many employees reporting to them run the risk of inadequate supervision, feedback, and employee development.

5. *Centralization vs. decentralization:* How and where decision making is distributed in an organizational structure. The more centralized the approach, the more the decision making gravitates to the top of the organization. Conversely, the more decentralized it is, the more the decision making is delegated to lower levels of employees. In general, organizations flatten their hierarchies when they adopt a more decentralized approach and vice versa.

6. *Formal vs. informal:* The degree to which organizational charts exist, are codified, and are followed. This is the extent to which structures and processes of the organization are set down in writing and expected to be followed.[10]

To practice understanding change on existing structures and systems see **Toolkit Exercise 5.2.**

Impact of Uncertainty and Complexity on Formal Structures and Systems

Another way of thinking about structural alignment is to begin by reflecting on the environment they operate in. Beginning with the work of Thompson in the 1960s,[11] researchers have explored the impact of uncertainty and complexity on why organizations structure their systems and processes as they do and the impact these configurations have on their capacity to successfully adapt to the environment over time.[12] When examining the structural dimensions, organizations have often been classified into two types: (1) those that are more formal, more differentiated, more centralized, and more standardized, and (2) those that are less formal, less differentiated, more decentralized, and less standardized. The terms that are applied to this organizational typology are *mechanistic* and *organic*. Table 5.1 outlines the characteristics of mechanistic and organic organizational forms as opposite ends of a continuum.[13]

Mechanistic organizations rely on formal hierarchies with centralized decision making and a clear division of labor. Rules and procedures are clearly defined and employees are expected to follow them. Work is specialized and routine. Mechanistic organizations tend to be concentrated in industries where the risk of getting it wrong is high. For example, nuclear power suppliers or pharmacy industries will be extremely mechanistic in order to manage the high risk and detailed logistics of their business.

Organic organizations are more flexible. They have fewer rules and procedures, and there is less reliance on the hierarchy of authority for centralized decision making. The structure is flexible and not as well defined. Jobs are less specialized.

Table 5.1 Mechanistic and Organic Organizational Forms

More Mechanistic ———————————————————————————— More Organic

Tasks are broken down into separate parts and rigidly defined and assigned	Flexible tasks that are adjusted and redefined through teamwork and participation
High degree of formalization, strict hierarchy of authority and control, many rules	Relatively little formalization, less reliance on a hierarchy of authority and control, few rules, greater participation and decentralization
Narrow span of control with reliance on hierarchies of people in specialized roles	Wide span of control
Knowledge and control of tasks are centralized at the top of the organization, limited decision making at lower levels	Knowledge and control of tasks are decentralized and located throughout the organization; highly decentralized decision making
Communication is vertical	Communication is horizontal and free flowing, with many integrating roles
Simple, straight-forward planning processes	Sophisticated environmental scanning, planning, and forecasting, including the use of scenarios and contingency thinking

Source: Adapted from Daft, R.L., *Organization Theory and Design*, 9th ed. Ohio: South-Western, 2007, pg.152.

Communication is more informal, and lateral communications are more accepted. Many start-up companies and companies in creative fields will be more organic, allowing increased communication and flexibility in day-to-day tasks. While it may appear that one structural form is more appealing than the other, both can be effective depending upon their fit with the environment. When efficiency is critical to success and ambiguity and uncertainty are low to moderate, a more mechanistic structure will fit best. However, when an organization's ability to respond to its environment with flexibility and adaptiveness is critical to its success, a more organic structure will make more sense.[14]

Formal Structures and Systems From an Information Perspective

A third way of thinking about the impact of systems and structures on how and why firms operate as they do is to look at how they formally manage information. One of the primary purposes of formal structures and systems is to place the right information in the hands of appropriate individuals in a timely fashion so that they can do what is needed. Information technology has been instrumental in allowing organizations to develop structures and systems that are more robust, dynamic, and flexible.

Supply chains, distributed manufacturing, flattened hierarchies with empowered workgroups, and networked organizations all owe their growth to improvements in this area. It has let organizations such as Dell to move from mass-production models to mass customization, with little productivity loss.[15] By extension, technology has also allowed us to think differently about structures and systems when planning and managing organizational change. For example, telecommunication advances mean virtual teams distributed around the globe can be created, meet "face to face," access and share information in real time, and move projects forward in ways that were not possible 10 years ago.

Jay Galbraith defines this as the **information-processing view of organizations**.[16] If the organization is to perform effectively, there needs to be a fit between the organization's information-processing requirements and its capacity to process information through its structural design choices. The better the fit between these, the more effective the organization will be. As **uncertainty** increases, the amount of information that must be processed between decision makers during the transformation process increases. The organization must either increase its capacity to handle that information or restructure itself to reduce the need for information handling. Figure 5.2 outlines Galbraith's work.

As uncertainty increases, the traditional vertical information strategies for uncertainty reduction will prove increasingly less effective, and the organization will require methods that either reduce the need for information processing or increase the capacity of the organization to process information.[17] Organizations can reduce their information-processing challenges by adding slack resources to act as buffers (e.g., extra people and inventory) and/or by creating self-contained tasks

Figure 5.2 An Information-Processing View of Organizational Structure

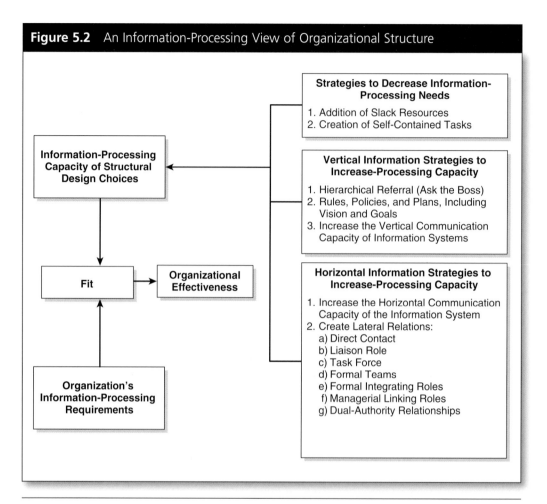

Source: Adapted from Galbraith, J.R., Organization Design. Reading, Mass.: Addison-Wesley, 1977; and Daft, R.L., Organization Theory and Design, 8th Edition. Cincinnati, Ohio: South-Western, 2003.

(e.g., divisions organized around product categories, geography, or customers). For example, extra inventory means that increased variation in demand for a product will be handled by drawing down or increasing inventory levels. Similarly, separating an organization into divisions operating as profit centers means that the divisions may not need to coordinate their activities as much. This reduces the information-processing requirements.

Initially, organizations attempt to increase their information-processing capacity by using the hierarchy. That is, if you are uncertain what to do, ask your boss. If the situation becomes repetitive, create a decision rule to guide the decision. If the subordinate knows more about the situation than the boss, they can agree on a set of objectives or goals or focus on the organizational vision, which allows the subordinate to act independently and handle the uncertainty. These represent what Galbraith calls vertical information strategies. A further vertical information strategy is when organizations increase their capacity to process information by investing in vertical information systems (e.g., computer-generated performance reports, decision support systems).

Organizations also can improve their information-processing ability by increasing their horizontal communication capacity (e.g., e-mail systems, intranets, electronic bulletin boards, texting, and various forms of social media). Finally, they can increase the capacity to process information horizontally by creating lateral relationships that vary in complexity from something as simple as direct, informal contact, to more formal networks and complex, formal structures such as a matrix that are intended to facilitate the horizontal flow of information.

The role of the information systems is to develop needed information and get it to the individuals who most need it in a timely manner for decision making. Interdepartmental and interdivisional boundaries and jurisdictional disputes can impede the flow of information. The investigation of the 9/11 tragedy pointed to examples of this.[18] Information was present in various departments and agencies that would have assisted in alerting officials to the danger, but communication impediments kept it from being shared and integrated in a timely fashion. Removing impediments is easier said than done in larger, more complex organizations. Issues such as privacy, data and system security, decision rights (who is supposed to do what with the information), and protection of intellectual property must be sorted out. Questions related to where information resides, in what forms, and who should have access to it need to be tackled before it can be pulled together.

Galbraith identified seven types of lateral relations that will help overcome boundaries that impair information flow. These are:

- direct contact between affected individuals (e.g., a product designer and a manufacturing engineer);
- use of individuals in liaison roles to bridge groups;
- multidepartment task forces;
- formal teams;
- integrating roles such as a product managers with cross-department authority;
- managerial linking roles (similar to the integrating roles but with more formal decision authority); and
- structures with dual-authority relationships such as are found in a matrix organization.

If the organization is to perform effectively, this model points to the importance of congruence or fit between the firm's strategy, its information-processing requirements (e.g., market and competitive information, operational information), and the information-processing capacity that the firm's design choices have given rise to.

Change leaders need to be aware of the impact of vertical and horizontal information strategies on information flows and organizational performance when assessing what needs to change. Further, sensitivity to these issues needs to extend to the actual management of the change process. This is because even well-managed change will increase uncertainty in at least the short term, and major changes will significantly increase it for longer periods of time. This will give rise to information-processing needs that change leaders will need to manage.

Research reported by McKinsey and Company point to the value of making greater use of social media technologies and paying more attention to networks to advance change initiatives.[19] When change leaders don't pay sufficient attention to their information-processing needs the lack of fit may impair the effectiveness of the change initiative. Often multiple strategies are needed—extra resources to increase the capacity to process information, a focus on understanding the goals and purposes, and a significant increase in lateral relations.

Aligning Systems and Structures With the Environment

The structural variables and models outlined above provide change leaders with an introduction to the multiple perspectives they can use when assessing structures and the formal systems that are developed to bring them to life. This can prove helpful when evaluating the internal consistency of structures and systems and their alignment with an organization's strategy, vision, culture, and environment. When cost strategies in a traditional manufacturing context are critical, a more mechanistic approach is often appropriate. When innovation is key, organic approaches provide a better fit with an organization's strategy.[20]

For change leaders, the importance of this material lies in the fact that organizations need to align their formal structures and systems with their environments. In 2008, ITT, an engineering firm serving the energy, transportation, and industrial markets, took a hard look at the alignment of its formal structures. This led ITT to drop its organization-wide performance rating system when management realized it was having an adverse impact on employees in different parts of the company's global operations and was not accomplishing its purpose. For example, a "3" or average on its 5-point rating scale of performance was viewed negatively by its Chinese employees, who saw it as a loss of face. This resulted in increased dissatisfaction and turnover. ITT realigned its formal performance rating system globally to reflect cultural differences and removed this global rating scale. In China, turnover was halved following the change.[21] In Nadler and Tushman's terminology, there needs to be congruence between the outside world, the strategy, and how the inside world is formally organized. By understanding the nature of the external environment and the organization's strategy, history, and resources, a change leader gains insight into the types of structures and systems that have the most to offer. By understanding the formal organizational arrangements, the leader gains insights on where and how decisions are made and how these can be leveraged to advance change.

Change leaders also need to be aware that even in a fairly mechanistic organization, different departments and divisions may face very different information-processing needs and will therefore need to be structured and managed differently. For example, a firm's R&D department's environment may be more dynamic and uncertain than that faced by the production department. As a result, R&D may need a more organic structure, whereas the production department will benefit from a more mechanistic one that leverages well-developed, standardized processes. Likewise, those involved with the launch of a new product or expansion into a new market will have to deal with higher levels of uncertainty and complexity than those responsible for mature markets, where concerns for structures and systems that enhance efficiency are likely the norm.

Structural Changes to Handle Increased Uncertainty

From a structural perspective, the quest for enhanced organizational effectiveness starts by looking at what needs to change in the organization and deciding how best to break things down and allocate the work. These differentiation approaches include aspects such as division of labor and departmentalization. If this has already been done, the challenge usually shifts to a discussion of how to integrate the components so that they can accomplish the intended results. The vertical and horizontal information linkage strategies identified by Galbraith in Figure 5.2 are examples of such integrating approaches.

Boeing's redesigned approach to the development and manufacturing of its aircraft provides an excellent example of the application of structural changes in a very complex business. The aircraft manufacturer realized that it had to change its approach to compete with Airbus, and it did so in its approach to the development of the 787.

BOEING RESTRUCTURES ITSELF

Before the 787, Boeing did all the engineering design work itself. The main reason to change, says Mike Bair, head of the 787 development team, was that the company realized it had to trawl the world and find the best suppliers in order to compete with its main rival in the market for commercial aircraft, the increasingly successful Airbus.

Airbus, a joint European venture involving French, German, British, and Spanish partners, started from scratch. Almost by accident it stumbled on an organizational architecture that, along with generous subsidies, helped it overtake the giant of the business in less than two decades.

Boeing's reorganized commercial plane development operations now look more like the approach used by Airbus. It scoured the globe for new partners and found some in Europe, some in Japan, and some not far from its home base in the United States. Whereas with the 777 aircraft the company worked with 500–700 suppliers, for the 787 it chose just under 100 "partners."

The difference is not just in the numbers, but in the relationship. Their supplier partners now share greater responsibility for the success of the project. For over six months in 2005, teams of people from the various 787 partners met at Boeing's base in Everett, north of Seattle, to work together on the configuration of the plane—something that until then Boeing had always done by itself. Partners then went back to their own bases, responsible for all aspects of their piece

(Continued)

(Continued)

of the puzzle. The partners built their own production facilities for their bits of the aircraft. As Bair said at the time, "it puts a high premium on the choice of partners in the first place."

It also put a high premium on the management of that network of partners. Boeing held a partners' "council meeting" every six weeks, and set up a network to facilitate global collaboration that made it possible for designers all over the world to work on the same up-to-the-minute database.

The company also put great faith in videoconferencing and set up high-band-width facilities that were in constant use. People came into their offices in the middle of the night to have virtual meetings with colleagues in different time zones. Technically, the 787 is an American plane; but in reality it is a global one.[22]

The 787 was designed to be a breakthrough product, with features that would dramatically improve its performance on all fronts—from fuel consumption to customer comfort. However, breakthroughs with sophisticated technologies and systems do not come easy, and the project was 3½ years late in making it into the hands of its initial customers. When it did arrive, there were problems with the batteries that required grounding until they were sorted out.

There have been severe hiccups and reputational damage to manage along the way, but Boeing now seems to be well on its way to success with the plane. By the end of 2013, the 787 had carried over 10 million passengers, flown 100 million miles in service, and there were back orders for more than 800 planes. Delivery delays have frustrated both customers and suppliers, and there have been problems with batteries and certain other components that continue to present challenges for Boeing. However, most analysts report such issues are to be expected with a new design such as this and that they expect the 787 will perform well over the long term. Insiders point to the delays experienced by the Airbus A380 during its development and subsequent problems with wing cracks. From a customer perspective, the plane's overall performance has met with mostly positive reviews.[23]

Boeing provides a graphic illustration of how structural approaches are changing in response to increasing complexity and ambiguity. In the aircraft maker's case, this included a radical reappraisal of where and how aircraft design and manufacturing should be undertaken, the role of suppliers and Boeing in the process, the treatment of intellectual property, and how the process should be managed. It recognized that its past approach was making it uncompetitive, and it has worked to break down silos and bring its suppliers into the design process as part of a dynamic network. This has necessitated a cultural shift toward treating its carefully selected suppliers as trusted contributing partners in the design and manufacturing challenges, and it has required the use of information-processing strategies to link it all together.

Boeing's structural and systemic transformation around the 787 has not been without its challenges and setbacks. It has logged record advanced orders, but its revolutionary use of composite materials to replace aluminum and its innovations on the global design and manufacturing front resulted in more than a 3½-year delay in the delivery of the first planes. There have been difficulties getting its global supply chain to work as expected, and a 2-month strike at Boeing exacerbated matters.[24] It entered commercial service in August 2011, but fires related to battery electrical issues have grounded the plane at times and battery-related matters continue to surface from time to time. At the same time, the order backlog is impressive, pointing to carrier confidence in the product and those that will emerge from this new platform.

Boeing has demonstrated a willingness to tackle fundamental questions of how best to deal with the structural challenges of differentiation and integration in order to enhance its performance. Wetzel and Buch[25] argue that organizations are more comfortable with increasing both differentiation and integrating mechanisms than with other approaches, and tend to overuse these strategies. For example, a need for specialized response leads to a more structurally differentiated organization. This in turn leads to a need to coordinate or integrate more. An alternate strategy would be to decrease the need to differentiate, easing information-processing needs in Galbraith's terms.

Wetzel and Buch believe that it is useful to consider the benefits of such a reduction in the amount of structural differentiation in the organization, through such mechanisms as flattened structures, multiskilled workers, automated processes, and self-managed teams. By reducing their reliance on differentiating structural solutions, organizations can reduce their need for integrating mechanisms and increase the likelihood of developing congruent interventions. From an information-processing perspective, this falls into the category of strategies to ease information-processing linkage needs (see Figure 5.2).

Boeing provides an example of this approach at the enterprise level. At a more micro level, this approach was used by a medical regulatory body. By automating the certification-checking process and having physicians directly enter their professional certification data, the need for both differentiation and integrating mechanisms was reduced by the regulatory body, and efficiency and effectiveness were significantly enhanced, without a loss of control.[26] The new system produced personnel cost efficiencies through automation and allowed up-to-date information to be shared quickly and thoroughly.

Making Formal Structure and System Choices

An organization's design impacts the behavior of its members. In universities, faculty in the schools of management, government, and education may all teach courses on leadership, but these faculties may never speak with one another or teach one another's students. And yet these differentiated faculties may teach the same concepts and use the same textbooks. Similarly, in many large universities, each school or faculty often has its own specialized library and librarians, a costly arrangement. In fact, these diverse libraries might house the same journals and books in different physical locations across a campus or subscribe to the same electronic data sets that provide access to online journals. Faced with significant budget cuts, the Harvard College Library took steps in 2009 to streamline services and foster collaboration with the sharing of research librarians across library facilities. Rather than only looking at cuts to fixed costs and personnel, the library administration chose to "encourage structural efficiency as a means of wringing savings from their ledgers."[27]

Every formal structure and system design has strengths and weaknesses associated with it. Bolman and Deal[28] argue that all organizational designs present structural dilemmas, or insolvable predicaments, that managers must deal with and reconcile. These fundamental design issues confront managers with enduring structural dilemmas: "tough trade-offs with no easy answers."[29] Bolman and Deal define, for example, the differentiation versus integration conundrum as:

> The tension between allocating work and coordinating sundry efforts creates a classic dilemma. . . . The more complex a role structure (lots of people doing many different things), the harder it is to sustain a focused, tightly coupled enterprise. . . . As complexity grows, organizations need more sophisticated—and more costly—coordination strategies. Rules, policies, and commands have to be augmented.[30]

Bolman and Deal identify other structural dilemmas. Another, for example, is the *gaps versus overlaps* dilemma. If tasks are not clearly assigned, then they can easily fall through the organizational cracks. If, on the other hand, managers overlap assignments, then they may create "conflict, wasted effort, and unintended redundancies."[31] The point is for change agents to understand these structural dilemmas, know the costs of mismanagement of these structural issues, and analyze if and how a gap has become an organizational liability that needs to change. Once a preferred structural option has been selected, weaknesses related to it can be alleviated and internal alignment improved through the design or modification of the formal policies, processes, structures, and systems.

Change leaders need to understand their organizations' strategy, how the formal structures and systems/processes are aligned with it, and the impact of those arrangements on the outcomes achieved. This is true at the macro or organizational level, and it is equally true down to the work-unit level. How can the formal structures and systems be modified to enhance the capacity of the organization to deliver on its strategy? If a change in strategy is needed, how do the formal structures and systems need to be realigned to contribute to the strategic change agenda? Wischnevsky and Damanpour found that sustained poor performance was likely to produce strategic change, and this in turn was likely to drive structural change.[32]

At the team or departmental level, change leaders have the option of creating several types of reporting structures depending upon the need under different conditions. For example, when new perspectives and ideas are sought, brainstorming sessions can be used to promote a free flow of ideas among all members of the group, with no hierarchical impediments. All ideas are equally welcomed. While brainstorming structures are good at generating ideas and engaging broad-scale participation, moving to the implementation stage typically requires the concentration of authority and decision making into fewer hands. This could take the form of a team or task force charged with making such decisions, or it could be delegated to a specific individual—more often than not, the manager responsible for the activity.

Mechanistic organizations can create structures and processes that allow them to either temporarily or permanently suspend hierarchical practices under certain conditions and constraints to advance creativity and innovation. The goal is to create spaces in which frank and open dialogue is encouraged, and learning and organizational improvement advanced. Continuous-improvement teams within call centers, event-debriefing processes used by Special Forces units in the military, and innovation task forces within government are all examples of attempts to encourage reflection and innovation in more mechanistic structures. Decisions that lie beyond the authority and responsibilities of those who generate the analyses and insights can then be reviewed by the appropriate senior individuals. Approved initiatives can then be further developed and/or implemented on a broader scale where warranted. This is essentially what occurs at LifeSpring Hospitals.

AN EFFICIENT HIERARCHY WITH WELL-DEVELOPED, STANDARDIZED SYSTEMS AND PROCESSES

Maternity-related deaths total 2 million babies a year in India, but LifeSpring is bringing hope through pre- and postnatal counselling and delivery at $80 per birth (price in 2010). This is a 50–50 joint venture between the Acumen Fund, a U.S.-based nonprofit venture philanthropy fund, and HLL Lifecare, a government of India–owned corporation that is the largest manufacturer of condoms in the world. Twelve small maternity hospitals (20–25 beds) were in place by the fall of 2013, and they have plans to raise funds for another 150. The Acumen Fund reports that the hospitals are ISO certified, have treated 300,000 people, and have delivered 18,500 healthy babies. Acumen's investment in this joint venture is $2 million.

The experience of the poor with public hospitals in India has not inspired confidence. Care can be of questionable quality, difficult to access, and sometimes requires bribes. In contrast, LifeSpring hospitals are bright and inviting, and mothers-to-be (plus those who accompany them) have their own private space. Doctors and nurses are in ready attendance, and services include staffed operating rooms, in the event that a cesarean section is required. Over 90 standardized processes have been developed to ensure consistent high-quality care for all, and replicability as new hospitals are added. Careful staff selection and training reinforces these quality practices and high standards of care. There is an extensive ongoing commitment to the professional development of medical staff internally and with external bodies. Staff is involved in continuous improvement initiatives, to ensure that standards of care and related standardized processes continue to improve. There are also strong commitments to transparency and the building of strong customer relationships through community outreach.[33]

How does LifeSpring deliver such consistent, high-quality service to the poor, at 30–50% of the normal cost in Indian public hospitals? The keys lie in clearly focused values, vision, value proposition and strategy; structures, systems, and processes that are well aligned with the service delivery model; and committed, well-trained staff that pursue continuous improvement on an ongoing and systematic basis.

Change leaders must understand these important points about formal structures and systems:

- There is no one best way to organize.
- Structural decisions should follow strategic decisions because the structure will then be there to support the strategy.
- All structures present leaders with dilemmas that they must manage. Today's trade-off may seem too costly in the future and will suggest a reorganization to fit tomorrow's external environment.
- Once structural choices are made, formal systems and processes need to be aligned so that weaknesses are addressed and the internal alignment with the strategy is supported.
- Organizational structures shape and impact people's behavior. A task force or committee, for example, that formally brings people together to analyze and report on a particular issue forces its members to cross organizational boundaries and to learn about and collaborate with people beyond their silo.

Using Structures and Systems to Influence the Approval and Implementation of Change

Using Formal Structures and Systems to Advance Change

Formal structures and systems must be leveraged to advance change. For example, industry-wide standard practices have long inhibited change in the airline industry. At United, American, Air Canada, British Airways, and other traditionally organized air carriers, air routes were organized in what is called a "hub-and-spoke" design. That is, passengers were collected at many points and delivered to a central hub, where they changed planes and were sent out on a different spoke to their final destination. Different types of planes were purchased to service different routes, cabins were divided between business and economy class, and services were very similar across airlines. For many years, this strategy delivered cost savings to the airlines and served them well. Union agreements escalated labor costs over this period as employees sought to share in the success.

However, discount airlines, such as Southwest Air, WestJet, and Ryanair, came along and opted for a different strategic approach. They adopted a single type of plane to ease maintenance challenges, offered a single no-frills service level in the cabin, and structured other aspects of their operations to lower labor and capital costs per passenger mile. Most important, they restructured their air routes to provide point-to-point service, used less expensive airports (where appropriate), and had more efficient schedules that advanced load factors and processes that reduced the time required before the plane was back in the air. The changes to the traditional airline practices evolved from cultural and strategic differences and were anchored in new structures, systems, and processes designed to support the new value proposition. Because of these changes, they were able to fly passengers directly to their destinations at a lower price and, in the case of Southwest, WestJet, and Ryanair, become very profitable in the process. The traditional airlines' structures and systems that were designed to facilitate the efficient and effective delivery became a problem and contributed to their recent financial challenges that they now seem to be overcoming.

Poor financial performance has led to growing demands for major improvements from banks, shareholders, pension funds, and other stakeholders. Structural and system realignment to lower labor costs and other cost drivers have been key targets of change. Those who have sought to resist the changes, such as the airline labor unions, have attempted to leverage existing structures and systems to advance their interests. The following example provides a fascinating but different look at the role that existing structures can play in organizational change.

COMPETITIVE EFFICIENCY AT UNITED AIRLINES

One of the ways that the board at United Airlines (UAL) responded to the competitive realities and the disastrous financial results was to use formal processes to replace a number of key executives[34] and charge senior management with responsibility for turning things around. Staffing arrangements, work rules, and labor costs were among the many areas that attracted the attention of senior management tasked with effecting change. In 2002, management analyzed and then used existing systems and structures (including formal judicial components) to advance and legitimize changes to their collective agreements and, by extension, changes to staffing levels, the organization of work, and related terms and conditions of work.

In response, employee groups enlisted formal (as well as informal) systems and structures to protect their interests—actions that airline executives saw as resisting needed changes. UAL's use of existing structures and systems to effect change was viewed by employee groups as adversarial, generating serious resentment in what was obviously a very difficult context. Despite the dissatisfaction of employees and their representatives with the imposed changes, they were enacted because the formal structures and rules that governed the situation allowed management to do so.

Similar hard-nosed change tactics were employed at Air Canada in 2003 when it entered bankruptcy protection[35] and British Airways in 2010 as it responded to huge financial losses.[36] They show the use of existing structures and systems to advance change through the exercise of formal power and authority from the top of the organization and/or through the imposition of action by outside agents such as banks, courts, or regulators.

Approaches that leverage formal structures and systems to advance change do not have to result in a war with one's employees. Rather, their application can be undertaken in a manner that facilitates understanding, builds support (or lessens resistance), and legitimizes change among those who have serious reservations. Agilent, an electronic test and measurement business, had to downsize in 2002, laying off 8,000 employees.[37] Management was seen by its employees as having acted responsibly and humanely. Openness and honesty characterized how the financial and strategic issues were approached and how the appropriate systems and structures were applied by the executives. Employees believed all reasonable options were explored and that layoffs were undertaken as a last resort. Those exiting Agilent reported that they were treated with respect and dignity, while those remaining were left with hope for the future of the firm and confidence in the leadership. To go through this level of downsizing and still be ranked #31 on *Fortune*'s 100 Best Companies to Work For in the following period is no small accomplishment! Agilent has faced other challenges in subsequent years, but it continues to be regarded as an innovative leader in scientific measurement and a desirable employer. Various awards from around the globe point to its innovativeness, positive employment practices, and corporate citizenship. It employed approximately 20,000 people and generated net sales of $6.8 billion in 2013. Its share price has met or exceeded its peer group of firms, the S&P 500, and all other major North American indexes for the past 10 years.[38]

Using Systems and Structures to Obtain Formal Approval of a Change Project

Change is made easier when the change leader understands when and how to access and use existing systems to advance an initiative. In larger organizations, **formal approval processes** for major initiatives are often well defined. For example, in universities, significant academic decisions usually require the approvals of department councils, faculty councils, and university senates in the form of formal motions and votes. The change agent's task is to engage in tactics and initiatives that will increase the likelihood of a positive vote for the proposed change through these various formal bodies.

Any significant change initiative will cost money. To maximize the chances of receiving resources for a change initiative, change leaders will need to understand the budget process and how to garner support for the proposed change through departments and individuals who approve the financial support. Timing is important. The likelihood of approval in the short term is less if the organization is in the middle of the budget cycle and available funds have already been allocated. Efforts to build interest and support should begin well in advance of when significant funds are needed, building to coincide with key decision dates.

Earlier in this book, two dimensions of change were considered: the magnitude or size of the change and the proactive–reactive initiation dimension. Change projects that are incremental will normally require fewer resources and lower levels of organizational approval. As the change increases in magnitude and strategic importance, change leaders will find that they need to pay more attention to formal approval processes, eliciting the support of more senior individuals prior to enacting the change. However, exceptions to this general pattern are often found in areas with safety and regulatory compliance implications. In these situations, significant change decisions (e.g., mandated changes to work practices) may be delegated to appropriate frontline staff due to the risk of not responding quickly enough. Once the urgency abates, decisions may be reviewed by more senior managers and other paths forward adopted. Reactive strategic changes tend to attract the greatest attention because of the risk, visibility, and criticality of such changes to the future of the organization.[39]

When senior decision makers believe the change initiative has significant strategic and/or financial implications and risks, the change will typically require the formal approval of the organization's senior executive team or its board of directors. A savvy change leader knows the approval levels and hurdles associated with different types of changes—that is, at what level does an issue become a board matter, a senior executive decision, or an issue that can be dealt with at a local level? What will they be looking for in the way of analysis and support?

No two organizations will be the same. Organizations in which there are significant negative consequences of failure (e.g., a nuclear power plant or a pharmaceutical manufacturer) will usually require more senior levels of approval for what may appear to be a relatively modest undertaking in a mission-critical area. Likewise, the hurdle levels are likely to be rigorous in organizations with senior managers and/or cultures that have a low tolerance for ambiguity.

Using Systems to Enhance the Prospects for Approval

Change leaders have a variety of factors they need to consider concerning the use of systems to increase the likelihood of approval.

First, they need to ask themselves if formal approval is required or if the change decision already rests within their span of control. If no approval is required, they may choose to make people aware of their intent and engage them in discussions to increase downstream acceptance. However, why initiate activities that trigger unnecessary formal approval systems and processes when they are not required? Figure 5.3 outlines the various considerations regarding positioning the approval of a change proposal.

In all cases:

a. When there is a decision maker, identify his or her attitude to the change and attempt to work with that person.

b. Demonstrate how the change project relates to the strategy or vision of the organization.

c. Use good process to legitimize the change proposal.

If formal approval is required, change leaders need to demonstrate that the initiative is aligned with the vision and strategy of the organization, advances the organization's agenda, and has benefits that exceed the costs. If the needed changes modify the vision, strategy, or key elements that make up the organization, the change leader will need to demonstrate how such changes will enhance organizational health and have downstream benefits that exceed the costs and risks associated with these significant organizational changes. Included in such a calculation should be the costs and risks of doing nothing.

Another good strategy to obtain approval through formal systems is to introduce change initiatives early. Even though proposals may not be fully developed at an early stage, it can be beneficial to introduce key points at this stage, especially when there may be competing ideas. Once others agree with a proposal it becomes harder to change their minds and convince them to change direction. If ideas are presented early, the challenge is to engage people from their neutral standpoint, rather than the much more difficult task of convincing them to abandon a commitment to another proposal.

If changes are more extreme and if there is sufficient time, leaders can frame and introduce the change in ways that increase management's familiarity and comfort with the proposal. They can do this incrementally, using vehicles such as staged agreements on the purpose and scope of the change (e.g., defining the scope of Stage 1, followed by defining the scope of Stage 2 once Stage 1 has been completed, etc.), preliminary studies, task force reviews, consultants' reports, and pilot projects prior to the request for formal approval of the larger initiative. This, in turn, reduces perceived risks, enhances a sense of the benefits, and essentially conditions the organization to embrace (or at least not resist) more fundamental changes to the aligned systems.

If time is of the essence due to a crisis or emerging threats, the change leader can act with urgency and use the danger to focus attention, facilitate approval of the initiative, and generate motivation to proceed. Formal approval processes often have expedited processes available for dealing with imminent threats and emergencies.

When formal approval is required, a change leader will need to know whose agreement is needed. However, if broader acceptance is important before gaining formal approval, then those involved in approval discussions will need to be expanded accordingly. Approval and **acceptance** are generally enhanced when people are involved in the discussion and feel that they have been heard. They are also enhanced when there is the perception that the analysis and discussion around the alignment systems (e.g., vision, strategy, goals, balance scorecards, and strategy maps) have been discussed thoroughly.[40]

Acceptance is sometimes increased among the uncommitted and more resistant when they believe that there has been a rigorous review process in place for the assessment of a change. That is, the procedures are thorough and complete. Further, when there is active involvement of those individuals or their representatives in the planning and approval processes, their understanding and acceptance of the change tend to rise. Some may see this as a co-option strategy.

Figure 5.3 Positioning the Change for Formal Approval

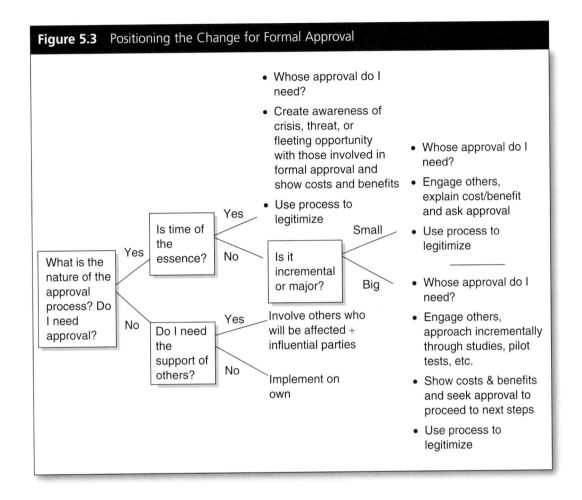

Formal approval systems, therefore, can increase the perception that a change has been assessed appropriately and is worthy of support. However, those who are opposed to a proposal may usurp the process and intentionally erect procedural and approval barriers to an initiative. The oppositions' motives in doing this may be unsullied (the desire for due diligence, due process, and careful review), they may be firmly convinced that the change is not in the organization's best interests, or their motives may be to obstruct out of self-interest. Change leaders will need to carefully assess the motives of the opposition before deciding on how best to respond.

Ways to Approach the Approval Process

Mastering the Formal Approval Process

Howell and Higgins[41] identified three different ways of approaching the formal approval process. The first involves the straightforward rational approach. Proposals are typically developed and brought forward for consideration, and they are reviewed for inclusion on the agenda. Once the proposal is presented and discussed, it is approved, rejected, or sent back for further study or rework. The likelihood of gaining approval is increased when change leaders:

- Have a well-placed sponsor
- Know their audience members and their preferences
- Understand the power and influence dynamics and the implications of the project for the organization and for those involved in the approval process
- Do their homework with respect to their detailed knowledge of the change project, its scope and objectives, its costs and benefits, and risk areas
- Informally obtain needed approval and support in advance
- Have the change project presented persuasively by an appropriate individual
- Have a good sense of timing concerning when best to bring it forward[42]

The systems associated with obtaining formal approval for planned changes vary greatly. In organic or entrepreneurial organizations, the process may be loose and idiosyncratic. As organizations mature, even very entrepreneurial firms tend to systematize and formalize the approval processes in order to increase control.

The decision making associated with formal approval processes takes many forms (e.g., formal voting by an executive committee, consensus mechanisms, and go/no-go decisions controlled by individual executives). While the exact approval process will be unique to the firm, the level of rigorousness and formality used to assess proposed changes usually varies with the magnitude of the change, the levels of perceived risk and uncertainty, the preferences of those involved with the decision, and the culture and power dynamics at work in the organization.

When the proposed change lies in an area in which much is known, decision makers tend to focus on concrete information (e.g., benchmark data, industry patterns, and performance data). They then use this data to help make a decision.[43] When the changes reside in areas that are inherently ambiguous, attention turns to an assessment of the quality of the analysis and the logic and reputation of the advocate for the proposal. In essence, the decision makers need to decide whether or not they trust the judgment of the change leader and the skills and abilities of the change team.[44]

As organizations mature, they often adopt a staged approval process for changes that are viewed as strategically significant, expensive, wide-reaching in their impact, and potentially disruptive. A staged approach establishes decision-approval steps that do not prematurely dismiss ideas worthy of further exploration while controlling the ever-increasing commitment of time and resources if the change were to progress to the next stage.[45] The goal is to provide focus through vision and strategic alignment, allow proposed initiatives to be explored and assessed in a rational manner, avoid unpleasant surprises, manage risk, and keep an eye on the portfolio of change initiatives to ensure the organization does not become overwhelmed with change initiatives.

As one proceeds through the approval stages, the assessment process becomes increasingly rigorous and the hurdles that must be met before proceeding to the next stage rise. When the process is working well, it should stimulate innovative thinking and initiatives, enhance the quality of assessment, reduce the cycle time from ideation to implementation, and reduce the likelihood of dysfunctional political behavior.

The formal approval process does more than ensure that the decision making concerning change is thorough and reasoned. If the process is viewed as legitimate by others in the organization, its decisions will lend legitimacy to what changes are pursued and enhance acceptance. When an incremental or staged approval process has been adopted to gain approval (e.g., commencing with concept and initial plan approval, followed by a field experiment or a pilot test, a departmental trial, and a final review prior to large-scale adoption), then the outcomes achieved and reactions to the results (e.g., the credibility of the data and the reaction of opinion leaders) will play an important part in building support for approval and downstream acceptance by others.

In addition to addressing the traditional hierarchical approach, Howell and Higgins identified two other ways to use system awareness to advance change: strategies based on **creeping commitment** and **coalition building**; and strategies involving simply forging ahead without formal approval.

Encouraging "Creeping Commitment" and Coalition Building

As an alternative to directly pursuing formal approval for a change initiative, change leaders can employ a strategy of creeping commitment (the foot-in-the-door approach[46]) and coalition building. Initiatives such as customer and employee surveys, benchmark data, pilot programs, and other incremental system-based approaches can be used to acclimate organizational members to the change ideas. Such initiatives can be used systematically to clarify the need for change, refine the initiative, address concerns, reduce resistance, and increase comfort levels. As well, they can create opportunities for direct involvement that will build interest and support for the change within key groups. This, in turn, will reduce resistance and increase the prospects for support if and when formal approval is sought. This strategy also captures commitment by reducing energy that may be spent on other options or directions.

Coalitions can be extremely important during a formal approval process. Change leaders need to understand key players to develop influential coalitions that will support the changes. Often in systems or technological changes, if key user groups want to adopt new software or systems, management will be more willing to accept the innovation. In other situations, developing the coalition provides the political clout to move the decision in a favorable direction.

The intent of this approach is to create the momentum needed to reach a tipping point[47] that significantly enhances the likelihood of approval. When formal approval is required, the support from key coalition members and stakeholders should make the process more manageable. If the change has been accepted by a sufficient number of key stakeholders, it may make the approval process all but automatic.

Developing coalitions for change often makes a great deal of sense when seeking formal approval. However, coalition building is not without its risks. This approach takes time and adds complexity (more fingers are in the pie) that may impede the approval process. It can also become quite political and divisive, with coalitions developing in opposition to the change that will need to be managed. Change leaders should avoid getting trapped in tactics that seriously harm relationships, diminish their integrity, and/or compromise long-term objectives.

Bypassing the Formal Approval Process: Just Do It!

The need to seek formal approval can sometimes be bypassed entirely. Peter Grant, a banker who changed the demographic of employees at his bank over a 30-year period, never sought formal permission. He understood the systems in his organization and used this awareness to quietly advance a change agenda over 30 years. Through this approach, he dramatically altered the nature of his organization. He would appear to have followed the classic change dictum, "Don't ask, just do it."

PETER GRANT'S "JUST DO IT" APPROACH

Peter Grant was a black manager, one of the few in the firm when he joined. Over his career, he pursued his personal goal of bringing more women and minorities into the firm. Each time he had the opportunity, he hired a qualified minority. And he encouraged others to do the same. Over his career, he was instrumental in having 3,500 talented minority and female members join the organization.[48]

When the scope of the change is manageable, defensible, and arguably within their scope of authority, change leaders should seriously consider proceeding on their own without seeking formal approval. Key people such as supervisors should be kept sufficiently in the loop so that they are not unpleasantly surprised or left with the belief that someone acted in an underhanded fashion.

When the "just do it" strategy is effectively applied, the dynamics can be powerful. Those who might otherwise be predisposed to oppose the change may not notice it or be lulled into acquiescence as the change proceeds in a lower-key fashion during the initial phases (e.g., data gathering, preliminary experimentation). This approach allows for change refinement, the generation of supportive data, and the building of momentum for change that is difficult to stop.

Howell and Higgins refer to this as the renegade process.[49] It grows out of the premise that it is often easier to gain forgiveness than permission to do something in organizations. This tactic can prove helpful in the early stages of product innovation, but Frost and Egri[50] argue that securing permission is an important contributor to success when social innovations are involved. When using a **renegade approach**, one must be careful not to create enemies unnecessarily or engage in tactics that create long-term damage to your reputation and credibility or the reputation of the firm.

The renegade method does not mean the chaotic introduction of disturbances merely to shake things up. Most organizations are already experiencing enough turbulence. Nor does it mean acting in organizationally naïve ways. Rather, this approach begins with a careful assessment of organizational and environmental factors, including the needs and preferences of key individuals who have the potential to harm or assist the change and the change leader. Finally, it asks change leaders to recognize the power and influence that they have to get things done through launching the initiative on their own and, when the situation is appropriate, to "just do it!" This attitude and propensity toward making these decisions also sets the precedence for similar decisions in the future.

Aligning Strategically, Starting Small, and "Morphing" Tactics

Gaining approval for change becomes less daunting when you are able to show how the change aligns with the organization's mission, vision, and strategy. When a change plan is being developed, questions of its relationship to these dimensions and its alignment with other existing systems need to be addressed.

If the case can be made that the change initiative adds value over other alternatives *and* fits within the context of the mission, vision, strategy, and significant downstream systems (e.g., information and reward systems, organizational structure), the likelihood of acceptance and adoption of the change is enhanced. If the resources required for the change seem relatively minor relative to the benefits, approval is also more likely. For example, consider a proposed change in the level of customer service offered by call center personnel that has high potential to increase customer satisfaction and significantly reduce the need for call-backs. The likelihood of approval and acceptance is higher if the only required actions are an additional half day of training, the development of needed support materials, the modification of a couple of decision support screens, the presence of supervisory support, and the modification of performance metrics to reinforce the desired change. In effect, the change leader will have demonstrated that there is little to fear because the change is incremental, is not particularly disruptive in nature, is consistent with the vision and the strategy, and contains benefits that outweigh the costs.

Change leaders often find it is useful to frame changes in ways that reduce the sense of incongruence with existing structures and systems. In general, this approach makes it easier to gain approval because it reduces the sense of disruption and risk that the change will entail. For example, if the end state of a change were to move from mass marketing to relationship-focused, one-to-one marketing, this would be a huge change. The perceived risk can be reduced by breaking the change down into a number of smaller, manageable stages that begin with exploratory research and evaluation, followed by a pilot project, assessment of learning and system alignment challenges, extension to a customer group that was particularly well suited to the approach, and so forth. By starting small and minimizing the incongruence with existing systems, the change leader can move in a systematic fashion in the desired direction, learning and modifying systems and structures in ways that look incremental in the short term but have significant long-term effects.

As momentum and the critical mass of support build for a revolutionary change that is positioned as incremental, the change may take on a life of its own. When those smaller change elements are added together over time, the cumulative changes will look far more significant in retrospect than they did at any point along the way. The term "morphing" captures the sense of this approach to change because it depicts a slow and steady transformation of the organization over time.[51] Abrahamson refers to this as the "change without pain" approach, though not all recipients would share this sentiment.[52] The earlier example of Peter Grant, who was instrumental in the hiring of 3,500 women and visible minorities at his bank, falls into this category. The lesson is that approval can often be advanced by avoiding the depiction of the change as a marked departure of heroic proportions. An evolving series of ten 5% changes in organizational performance over the course of five years produces a total change of 50% in organizational performance, and that does not include the compounding effects!

See **Toolkit Exercise 5.3** to reflect on an approval process you're familiar with.

The Interaction of Structures and Systems With Change During Implementation

Structures and systems not only have an impact on a change leader's ability to gain acceptance for a change project; they can also have a significant impact on the success of the implementation process. Sometimes there are existing systems and structures that change agents have to work with, while at other times they may represent aspects of the actual change. The transformation at MASkargo, a state-of-the-art Malaysian air cargo facility, provides an example of system-enabled changes. Tens of millions of dollars had been invested in the late 1990s in systems and technology designed to support the creation of a premier air cargo–handling center. However, performance fell far short of expectations. Rather than panic, MASkargo opted for a change path that began by working with and assessing existing systems and structures. It then used the learning from that assessment to modify and extend those systems and structures to improve existing services and develop new initiatives.

MASKARGO'S ADVANCED CARGO CENTER DELIVERS ON ITS PROMISE

Malaysia's state-of-the-art one-stop air cargo–handling facility had, in its first two years of operation, been plagued by system failures, bottlenecks, and misplaced shipments that proved extremely costly. However, MASkargo was able to correct these issues by fine-tuning the formal systems and processes and ensuring that employees developed their ability to work with the new structures and systems. Systemic cargo-handling glitches were identified and rectified. Workers developed greater familiarity with the fully automated operational process, and results improved. MASkargo recorded a RM52 million profit in the 2002–2003 third quarter to sharply turn around from an RM242.86 million loss for the whole of 2001–2002.

MASkargo's vision was to "keep business moving." The specific changes they made included the establishment of performance benchmarks for their key operations (e.g., cargo is processed in just 90 minutes for uploading to connecting aircraft to 100 destinations across six continents). More important, they took action when benchmarks were not achieved. "If a process takes longer than specified, agents may immediately lodge a complaint and we will take action," said Mohd Yunus Idris (a former general manager of Operations and CEO until June 2014). Rising tonnage, their ability to handle very diverse cargo effectively and efficiently (from day-old chicks to elephants and Formula 1 cars), profitability, and high levels of customer satisfaction over the years, suggested their improvement changes have, for the most part, worked well. MASkargo has been publically recognized in the last decade for its cargo-handling accomplishments through multiple awards, including Best Air Cargo Carrier (Asia), Airline of the Year (Cargo—most recently in 2012), Best Air Cargo Terminal Operator (Asia), and Best Cargo Airport. "Our selling points are reliability and efficiency. All the sophisticated equipment will come to naught if we cannot deliver," said Idris.

As of 2014, they had the capacity to handle up to a million tons annually and had deployed advanced cargo-handling technology to ensure things got to where they were supposed to go in a timely and cost effective manner. This included challenges related to handling intermodal cargo (e.g., air ↔ ships). They offer a 6-star animal hotel, significant perishable storage capacity, a priority business center that forwarding agents can access, and have their own fleet of cargo aircraft. They provide connections to 100 destinations globally, are ISO certified, and have sophisticated services related to supply chain integrity and cargo security.

However, a winning alignment does not last forever. Since the 2008 economic downturn, MASkargo has faced rising competitive pressures and resultant revenue and profit challenges. Recently their parent, Malaysia Airlines, reported that MASkargo had experienced financial losses. Some customers report that these problems can be traced to poorer service levels being delivered by new vendors (appointed in 2012), and are caused by manpower shortages.[53] Reading between the lines, the vendor changes may have been precipitated by competitive cost pressures at MASkargo, and continuing performance issues mean further change initiatives are underway to address these challenges.

The change task at MASkargo in the 2000–2002 period was made easier by the fact that the facility was new, systems were well documented, and participants understood that refinement and improvement initiatives were to be expected and embraced. MASkargo recognized the value of aligning systems and structures with the vision and strategy, and used this to promote the needed changes. Further, they avoided getting bogged down in finger pointing and other defensive tactics when things didn't pan out initially. Such actions can derail progress in even what appears to be a relatively straightforward problem.

Diagnosis of the nature and impact of structures and systems during implementation puts change leaders in a strong position to identify when and where these may present challenges that will need to be managed and where they can be used to facilitate change. The MASkargo and Peter Grant change examples involved approaches that refined and exploited existing systems in support of the desired changes.

In summary, change agents need to understand the approval processes for their particular projects. They need to know the key players and how formal the process is. Does it require a vote? Will the go-ahead be authorized at a management or executive meeting? Alternatively, can the change agent act to develop a coalition first, or just act using available resources and power? In the next section, we will explore the role of systems in change approval, change acceptance, and change implementation.

Using Structures and Systems to Facilitate the Acceptance of Change

Change agents may be tempted to breathe a sigh of relief and relax once a change project is approved. However, gaining formal approval is not the same as gaining generalized acceptance of the change. Too often, the anticipated chorus of excitement fails to materialize and, in its stead, change agents experience begrudging cooperation, or covert or overt resistance. The assumption that approval will automatically lead to acceptance is a dangerous one.

> **CUSTOMER RELATIONSHIP MANAGEMENT**
>
> Complex implementations, failure to yield desired results, and escalating maintenance costs have all marred the reputation of customer relationship management (CRM) programs; 50% of CRM implementations generally fail and almost 42% of CRM software licenses bought end up unused. In 2013, a survey of 352 U.S.-based executives found that failure rates of CRM had risen to 63%. While some fault lies with the vendors, sometimes it is, unfortunately, the business that gets itself in a rut. An analysis of failure implementations found a lack of clear ownership for the initiative 53% of the time, followed by a lack of management bandwidth (43%), a lack of executive support (38%), and the lack of a sense that it was an IT priority (38%).[54]

Despite their best intentions, change leaders often have less-than-stellar success in bringing approved change to fruition. Lack of awareness for and acceptance of the change within the organization, lingering doubts and half-hearted commitments at senior levels, confusion as to who is supposed to do what, issues of skill/ability, and lack of time or resources often play roles in this. Systemic factors in an organization can be used to ease the legitimization and acceptance of a change initiative and provide access to needed resources. They facilitate the assignment of authority and responsibility, provide needed training and bandwidth, publicly affirm commitment and needed resourcing at the senior and middle levels, and ensure that the output of the changes are put to use and not ignored, because they have not been part of past practices. However, they can also derail progress when not properly deployed. The inappropriate delegation of sponsorship, structures that fail to provide sufficient access to needed resources, and the misapplication of systems are three of the most commonly cited mistakes made by top management in change initiatives.[55]

Paul Tsaparis, formerly of Hewlett-Packard, did not make the mistake of underestimating the role that systems and structures can play.

SYSTEMS AND STRUCTURES AT HP (CANADA)

In May 2002, Paul Tsaparis, 42, president and CEO of Hewlett-Packard (Canada) Ltd., began managing the massive integration of Hewlett-Packard and Compaq in Canada. The new 6,800-person organization had annual revenues in excess of $3 billion (Canadian). As is often the case with organizational integration, staff reductions were involved.

Tsaparis approached the integration challenge by getting out and putting a human face on the challenges and changes. He needed to communicate the vision and corporate strategy and let people know what was happening to their employment situation as soon as possible. He needed to reassure other key stakeholders (customers, suppliers) that they would not be lost in the shuffle. Tsaparis knew he needed to develop organizational structures, systems, and processes that would support HP's strategy, reinforce the integration change initiative, and increase the likelihood of longer-term organizational success. He created a team of individuals to facilitate the organizational changes. This, in turn, required structures, systems, and processes that would support the change team in the pursuit of its objectives. Tsaparis remained the president of HP Canada until 2010, when he was promoted to VP of Technology Support for the Americas, a position he left in June 2012.[56]

Tsaparis faced significant structural and systemic challenges to change. Each organization, HP and Compaq, had its own way of doing things. And many of those systems and structures would have explicit as well as implicit implications—ways of doing things that might not even be written down but were firmly embedded in the habits of organizational members. As a result, the conscious development of structures and systems that would support HP's strategy represented an important step in the building of an infrastructure that would support change and promote acceptance. Conflicting and misaligned structures and systems needed to be identified and addressed so that the resulting web of structures and systems were aligned. Staying true to HP's core values and principles provided critical guidance for the massive change initiative. Tsaparis reports that the more these are aligned with your own core values, the more likely you, as leader, are to succeed.

Change agents need to understand the effects of structures and systems from the perspective of the person who is on the receiving end of the change—the actual person who will be asked to behave differently. If people do not accept the change (whether they like it or not), they are unlikely to modify their behavior in the desired direction, no matter how excellent the change project is.

Interestingly, acceptance or compliance does not necessarily mean attitude change. That is, attitude change need not come first. It may well evolve after the needed behavior is obtained. That is, if systems can be used to promote the desired behavior in individuals (e.g., through having them live with new structural or systemic arrangements), their attitudes toward what they are doing may adjust over time in the desired direction as they live within the new context.[57]

The effective use of the formal communication, performance management, and reward systems can play useful roles in gaining acceptance and commitment. Clarity of purpose and direction, combined with employee involvement and rewards for desired behavior, can all be used to advance the engagement and involvement of employees in change-related initiatives. A top-down directive that orders change may lead to less information sharing, reduced risk taking, less acceptance of change, and greater employee turnover.[58] Unless the employees buy into the legitimate authority of executives and the legitimacy of the change, they may not accept it and instead may engage in actions that slow, disrupt, or sabotage progress.

Much of the change leaders' difficulty in thinking through the impact of structure on acceptance flows from their assumptions. One sees clearly the need for change and the rationale underlying the change and believes the change is immensely logical. From that position, it is much too easy to assume that others will see and accept the logic of the change agent! But the logic falls flat for organizational members facing a formal reward system that works against the change or an organizational structure that emphasizes characteristics contrary to the desired change (e.g., cost controls rather than customer focus).

The passage of time, in conjunction with the use of formal systems, can also influence the acceptance of change. When a change initiative has been the subject of formal discussion and review for an appropriate interval, this gestation period may allow the idea to become more familiar and acceptable. Initiatives that are shocking at first may appear less threatening after a period of reflection. Alternatively, if approval has been granted and there seems to be little activity or visible progress, acceptability and support may diminish.

In summary, systems and structures, properly deployed, can play an important role in the speed and rate of acceptance of change. People don't resist all change. Lots of things have the potential to be seen as worth doing, and people tend to respond positively to change initiatives that they understand and believe are worth the effort and risk. The way that systems and processes are deployed will influence the perception of the change.[59]

Developing Adaptive Systems and Structures

The ability of organizations to adapt to change is aided by their ability to learn. Nevis suggests that organizations can be viewed as learning systems that acquire knowledge, disseminate it through the organization, and use that knowledge to accomplish their missions.[60] Learning is facilitated when organizational members do the following:

1. Systematically and deliberately scan their external environment and learn from it

2. Demonstrate the desire to question existing approaches and always improve

3. Have a concern for measurement of performance and shared perceptions of the gap between the current and desired levels of performance

4. Develop an experimental mindset where they try new things

5. Create an organizational climate of openness, accessibility, honesty, and active discussion and debate

6. Engage in continuous education at all organizational levels

7. Use a variety of methods, appreciate diversity, and take a pluralistic view of competencies

8. Have multiple individuals who act as advocates for new ideas and methods and who are also willing to exercise their critical judgment in the review of ideas

9. Have an involved, engaged leadership

10. Recognize the interdependence of units and have a systems perspective

Many of these learning actions are influenced by organizational structures and systems. The presence of formal early-warning systems and opportunity-finding systems advance the scanning capacity of the organization. The presence of a formal strategy and environmental review process, complete with performance metrics, will increase the likelihood that firms will systematically review where they are and where they want to go. Systems that reward innovation and information sharing will increase the prospects for openness and exploration. Systems that fund and reinforce development will open people to continuous education. Likewise, appropriately designed systems and processes can be used to advance diversity and the exploration of new ideas. Finally, systems can be used to increase the prospect that interdependencies are recognized and that a systems perspective is brought to problem solving.

Organizations that are flexible and adaptive have an easier time adjusting to incremental and upending changes than do bureaucratic ones.[61] As the complexity and turbulence of organizational environments increase, more flexible, **adaptive systems and structures** will be required.[62] Essentially, they need to become more "change ready."[63]

In a study of strategic planning in an international nongovernmental development organization, the need for adaptive capacity manifested itself in an interesting way. Rather than opt for an unambiguous course of action, this organization tended to develop multiple strategies that were both ambiguous and ambitious. What looked like strategic drift to outsiders provided managers with flexibility in how they responded to changing conditions. Appropriate ambiguous strategies were used as metaphors to promote consensus and legitimacy with key stakeholder groups and allow for learning and the adjustment of change plans as they proceeded forward.[64]

To cope with turbulence and complexity, organizations are being designed in unconventional ways. These include the increasing use of formal and informal networks to link individuals in the organizations with external individuals and organizations to promote shared initiatives. For example, supply chain networks are increasingly being used to leverage supplier talents in dealing with design and engineering challenges, finding ways to enhance quality, and identifying opportunities for cost reduction. Designer, supplier, producer, and distributor capabilities of different organizations are being brought together in networks to increase flexibility, adaptability, and innovative results. Thus, a product might be designed in Italy, built in Korea from Brazilian materials, and distributed in the United States by a Scandinavian firm. Think IKEA for this type of network.[65] The network partners are held together by market mechanisms such as contracts, just-in-time logistics, shared market intelligence and production systems, shared purposes, and customers' demands rather than by organizational charts and traditional controls.[66]

The need for greater flexibility and adaptiveness is moving organizations away from command and control structures, and giving rise to the increased use of collaborative structures and processes to promote trust, communications, information sharing, and shared ownership of the undertaking. At a micro level, this may come in the form of self-managed work teams, cross-functional teams and task forces, and other approaches that facilitate intra-organizational communication and cooperation. At the organizational level, it may take the form of flattened structures, systems processes and technologies that promote collaboration, and leadership styles and the promotion of cultural norms that foster greater collaboration, transparency, and shared sense of purpose.[67] When people are geographically dispersed and collaboration is needed, virtual teams are increasingly being deployed, along with enabling technologies to allow them to build needed trust and effectively work together. In some organizations, the physical design of office space is being reimagined, in order to bring people from different functions together and promote collaboration, rather than isolate them from one another.[68] One example of a company employing a flatter more democratic structure is Zappos.com. While a democratic system or "holacracy" made up of self-organizing teams has certainly garnered attention, there are doubts as to whether it will become a tried-and-true management structure.[69]

Collaborative relationships and their associated networks are taking new and interesting forms that extend far beyond traditional organizational boundaries. Open-sourced design and development, shared content creation initiatives such as that associated with Wikipedia, customer co-creation, online advisory groups, and other forms of cooperative input and information sharing are creating fascinating opportunities for individuals and organizations of all sizes that did not exist in the past.[70]

In matters of organizational change, the formal use of social technologies and the degree to which they are used to advance the change have been found to contribute to successful implementation.[71] This is not surprising when one thinks of the power of social technologies for communicating information and aligning the interests and efforts of dispersed individuals. Research has found that greater organizational learning and knowledge creation are associated with more organic organizational structures rather than more mechanistic ones.[72] Collaborative networks have been found to be powerful contributors to how people respond to change, but more will be said of this later.[73]

One of the roles of the change agent is to help organizations learn from the past and evolve systems and structures that are likely to help them succeed in the future. Focusing on how organizations acquire knowledge and spread it throughout the organization can be a valuable diagnostic tool in this regard. By facilitating the development of adaptive systems and processes (keeping in mind the competitive realities and the need for congruence with the environment), change agents will succeed in enhancing the capacity of the organization to adjust to change in the future.

Summary

Formal systems and structures influence how change initiatives evolve and succeed. Change leaders need to understand them, how they operate, and how they influence the change process. In addition, change leaders need to know how to manage the approval process for initiatives so that they can work with, through, and/or around them in order to increase the prospects of the change being adopted. Formal systems and structures can be used to advance acceptance and implementation of the change in the organization. And finally, formal systems and structures increasingly need to be flexible and adaptive, to promote learning and set the stage for needed changes. See **Toolkit Exercise 5.1** for critical thinking questions for this chapter.

Key Terms

Organizational **structure** and **systems**—how the organization formally organizes itself to accomplish its mission. Structure is how the organization's tasks are formally divided, grouped, and coordinated. The structure would include the organizational hierarchy, the structure of any manufacturing operation, and any formal procedures such as the performance appraisal system, as well as other structures. Systems are the formal processes of coordination within the organization.

Formal approval process—the formal procedure that change agents must follow for organizational approval of a change project.

Mechanistic organizations—exhibit machinelike qualities. They rely on formal hierarchies with centralized decision making and a clear division of labor. Rules and procedures are clearly defined, and employees are expected to follow them. Work is specialized and routine.

Organic organizations—exhibit organism-like qualities as they are more flexible. They have fewer rules and procedures, and there is less reliance on the hierarchy of authority for centralized decision making. The structure is flexible and not as well defined. Jobs are less specialized. Communication is more informal and lateral communications more accepted.

The **information-processing view of organizations**—considers organizations as information-processing mechanisms. This view argues that the better the fit between the information-processing capabilities of the organization and its environment, the more effective the organization.

Environmental **uncertainty**—measures the degree of variability of the environment. Duncan suggests two dimensions of uncertainty: degree of complexity of the environment and degree of dynamism.

The formal approval process—the traditional approach in which a person or persons develop a proposal and bring it forward for assessment and formal approval by the appropriate organizational members.

Acceptance of change—the degree to which change participants accept or "buy into" the change that has been implemented.

Creeping commitment—the gradual increase in commitment by change participants toward the change project. Such an increase is often obtained by involving participants in decision making.

Coalition building—the forming of partnerships to increase pressures for or against change.

The renegade approach—when change is initiated without having first obtained formal approval. This is often done in conjunction with creeping commitment and coalition-building tactics. The intent of the approach is that the change is advanced to the point that it cannot easily be reversed by those with formal authority.

Adaptive systems and structures—those that are relatively ready for change compared to others.

Checklist: Change Initiative Approval

1. What does a review of documents related to relevant formal structures and systems reveal about the formal approval process and who has formal authority for approving the change initiative?

2. What are the key points in the process that a change leader needs to pay attention to: timing of meetings, getting on the agenda, cycle time, types of decisions made, and where decisions are made?

   a. How are the relevant systems and structures interconnected? How do they influence one another?

3. Develop a process map that tracks the change idea from start to finish.

   a. What role (and person) has formal authority and decision-making responsibility for this initiative?

   b. What are the decision parameters that are normally applied, and are there zones of discretion available to decision makers?

   c. What are the power and influence patterns around particular systems and structures? Who has direct and indirect influence on how the systems and structures are applied?

   d. How should the change leader manage these formal systems and structures to reduce resistance? And how can they be managed to advance the change initiative?

END-OF-CHAPTER EXERCISES

TOOLKIT EXERCISE 5.1

Critical Thinking Questions

Please find the URLs for the videos listed below on the website at study.sagepub.com/cawsey3e. Consider the questions that follow.

Please read Case 2 on page 417 "Food Banks Canada: Revisiting Strategy 2012" and consider the following:

1. Food Banks Canada is a growth and change story about a not-for-profit national organization that was created by its affiliated members to better address hunger issues and get needed food to the poor. In response to decline and poor performance, it altered its governance process, opted for a federated structure, renewed its leadership and staff, and put a renewed vision and strategy to work. Five years have passed and the CEO is considering what they should do next. Please read the Food Banks Canada case at the end of the book and consider the following:

   • Katharine Schmidt is reflecting on Food Banks Canada's accomplishments and challenges of the last five years and considering what they should strategically target now. Should they stay with their current strategy or alter course?

   • As you analyze the Food Banks Canada case to better understand their current situation, consider carefully the nature of their formal structure and decision-making process, its strengths and weaknesses, and why they selected it as their governance structure.

   • What do you think Schmidt should recommend they do? To accomplish this, will there need to be changes to their structure or governance approach?

   • How should Schmidt go about generating needed support and approvals from the National Board, her staff, the Member Council, and affiliated food banks?

- How should she turn those approvals into successful actions and outcomes?

2. <u>Food Banks Canada Hunger Count 2010</u>—2:19 minutes

Consider this video in conjunction with the Food Banks Canada case at the end of the book.

- Comment on how the video inspires a vision for change in Canada.

- How did the video use data to engage listeners?

3. <u>Dr. John Kotter: Accelerate! The Evolution of the 21st Century Organization</u>—6:07 minutes

In this video, Kotter provides a prescription for how organizations need to structure themselves to be able to evolve successfully today.

- What do you think of his prescription?

- Think of an organization you are familiar with (it could be public, private, a not-for-profit, or a branch of government). What are the change implications for it, if it were to adopt this approach?

- What do you think this organization should do to enhance its flexibility and readiness for change?

Please see study.sagepub.com/cawsey3e for a downloadable template of this exercise.

TOOLKIT EXERCISE 5.2

Impact of Existing Structures and Systems on Change

Think of a change you are familiar with.

1. How did the organization use structures and systems to deal with the uncertainty and complexity in the environment?

   Was this an appropriate response?

   How could the existing structures and systems have been approached and used differently to advance the desired change?

   How did existing structures and systems affect the ability of the change leader to bring about the desired change?

   a. What systems/structures were involved?

   b. How did these systems/structures influence what happened?

   Was this related to how they were formally designed or was this related to how they actually came to be used in practice?

   c. Who influenced how the systems/structures were used, and how did this affect the outcomes that ensued?

   1. What role could incremental strategies that were nested with existing systems and structures have played? Would they have really moved the process forward or simply avoided the real changes that needed to be addressed?

   2. What role could more revolutionary strategies have played? Would they produce issues related to their alignment with existing systems and structures?

   How would you manage the challenges created by this?

Please see study.sagepub.com/cawsey3e for a downloadable template of this exercise.

TOOLKIT EXERCISE 5.3

Gaining Approval for the Change Project

Consider a change project in an organization with which you are familiar.

1. What is the approval process for minor change initiatives?

   For major change initiatives?

   Can you describe the processes involved?

   a. If a project requires capital approval, are there existing capital budgeting processes?

   b. If the project needs dedicated staff allocated to it or if it will lead to additions to staff, what are the processes for adding people permanently, and selecting and developing staff?

   c. Does the project alter the way work is organized and performed?

   d. What are the systems and processes used for defining jobs and assessing performance?

   e. Can the project be approved by an individual? Who is that person? What approval power do they have?

2. Are there ways that the perceived risks of the change could have been reduced by the way the change leader staged the project and managed the approval process?

Please see study.sagepub.com/cawsey3e for a downloadable template of this exercise.

CHAPTER 6

Navigating Organizational Politics and Culture

In organizations, real power and energy is generated through relationships. The patterns of relationships and the capacities to form them are more important than tasks, functions, roles, and positions.

—Margaret Wheatley[1]

CHAPTER OVERVIEW

- Change leaders recognize the importance of understanding the informal components of an organization—power and culture—which are key forces at play within an organization, impacting important stakeholders in the change situation.
- Understanding the power dynamics in an organization is critical to a successful change process. Different sources of power are described so change leaders can gain leverage in their organizations.
- Force field analysis and stakeholder analysis are two key tools to use to advance the understanding of the informal organizational system and how to change it.
- Know yourself as a change leader and stakeholder in the process.

C hange leaders' understanding of both the present and desired future state of organizations depends on an analysis of multiple dynamics within organizations. Chapter 5 looked at the formal structures and systems, noting how they impact change initiatives. Chapters 7 and 8 will examine the impact of key individuals in the organization on the change process. This chapter provides the background on the less tangible but no less real aspects of organizations: political dynamics and culture (see Figure 6.1).

It is important to note that in evaluating stakeholders in your organization, you are also a stakeholder in this process. To get a full picture of the **informal organization**, it is important to use these tools to evaluate yourself as a part of that system.

Figure 6.1 The Change Path Model

Awakening
Chapter 4

1. Identify a need for change and confirm the problems or opportunities that incite the need for change through collection of data.
2. Articulate the gap in performance between the present and the envisioned future state, and spread awareness of the data and the gap throughout the organization.
3. Develop a powerful vision for change.
4. Disseminate the vision for the change and why it's needed through multiple communication channels.

Mobilization
Chapters 5 through 8

1. Make sense of the desired change through formal systems and structures, and leverage those systems to reach the change vision (Chapter 5).
2. **Assess power and cultural dynamics at play, and put them to work to better understand the dynamics and build coalitions and support to realize the change (Chapter 6).**
3. Communicate the need for change organization-wide and manage change recipients and various stakeholders as they react to and move the change forward (Chapter 7).
4. Leverage change agent personality, knowledge, skills and abilities, and related assets (e.g., reputation and relationships) for the benefit of the change vision and its implementation (Chapter 8).

Acceleration
Chapter 9

1. Continue to systematically reach out to engage and empower others in support, planning, and implementation of the change. Help them develop needed new knowledge, skills, abilities, and ways of thinking that will support the change.
2. Use appropriate tools and techniques to build momentum, accelerate and consolidate progress.
3. Manage the transition, celebrating small wins and the achievement of milestones along the larger, more difficult path of change.

Institutionalization
Chapter 10

1. Track the change periodically and through multiple balanced measures to help assess what is needed, gauge progress toward the goal, and to make modifications as needed and mitigate risk.
2. Develop and deploy new structures, systems, processes and knowledge, skills, and abilities, as needed, to bring life to the change and new stability to the transformed organization.

Be sure to ask yourself how your own personality impacts you as a stakeholder. Evaluate your motivations and understand how you will benefit from the change.

DAIMLER-BENZ AND CHRYSLER

Merger Failure

When Daimler-Benz and Chrysler Corp. announced their $36 billion "merger of equals" in 1998, it was hailed as a marriage made in heaven. At the time, Chrysler was the world's most profitable and cost-efficient carmaker, while Daimler was renowned as the planet's premier luxury carmaker. DaimlerChrysler became the new model for a global automotive powerhouse, and its stock soared into triple digits, forcing rival automakers into mergers of their own. But in remarkably short order, the mass/class union hit the skids, undermined by a transatlantic culture clash and a damaging exodus of talent. Virtually the entire "dream team" of Chrysler executives that built the hot models and big profits of the 1990s departed, leaving behind a chaotic American operation where costs were spinning out of control.[2]

To begin, two cases of significant organizational change—the merger of Daimler-Benz and Chrysler and the changes to 3M brought about by CEO McNerney—set the stage for this chapter.

The DaimlerChrysler merger provides a classic example of the impact of organizational cultural clashes leading to "divorce." On May 7, 1998, the CEOs of Daimler-Benz AG and Chrysler publicly announced that they had decided to "get together in a merger of equals,"[3] creating a colossus company of $132 billion in annual revenues and consummating the largest industrial merger the world had seen. Since the companies had complementary product lines (Daimler produced luxury cars and Chrysler mass-market vehicles) and geographical market coverage (Daimler primarily in Europe and Chrysler largely in the USA), the merger was hailed as having great potential for synergies. When the automotive industry had consolidated and globalized in the mid-1990s, Daimler-Benz AG, a valued brand by any standard, had found itself a "tiny player by global standards" (p. 2). As the number three auto manufacturer in the United States, Chrysler faced a similar problem in entering and succeeding in global markets. The merger seemed to make good business sense.

Quickly, however, the merger floundered on the different cultures of the two companies and different executive compensation systems, as well as poorly articulated and communicated goals. Reflecting their commitment to luxury products, Daimler-Benz executives flew first class and stayed in first-class hotels. In contrast, Chrysler executives generally flew coach class and stayed in inexpensive hotels to save money. The reverse marked their compensation systems: In 1996, Chrysler's CEO earned $9.8 million, and Daimler-Benz's entire management board earned $11 million that same year.[4] A shared vision failed to materialize, with Chrysler engineers predicting that German beer would be sold in their Detroit vending machines and Daimler engineers saying that over their dead bodies Mercedes would be built in Chrysler factories.[5]

DaimlerChrysler executives officially announced the divorce on May 15, 2007. Cerberus Capital Management paid Daimler $7.4 billion for 80.1% of the Chrysler unit, ending "nine years of management agony and billions of dollars in losses."[6] Why did this marriage fail? Pundits observed different problems. One Merrill Lynch auto analyst said: "The problem is not the concept of the partnership but the execution. . . . This is a partnership where the two companies haven't partnered."[7] Another argued: "It (the merger) missed a basic building block from the start: honesty . . . the leaders of the two companies billed the so-called marriage as a merger of equals. That was a scam."[8]

If corporate mergers are the ultimate in change-management challenges, then the arrival of a new CEO may also challenge embedded power dynamics and cultural patterns. In December 2000, CEO Jim McNerney arrived at 3M's 28-building, 430-acre, suburban Maplewood (MN) campus. Interestingly, McNerney was the first outsider to lead 3M in all of its 98-year history. 3M's CEOs usually rise from within, after being steeped in the corporation's culture and philosophy. However, 3M employees found that the new CEO was able to work with those around him.

MCNERNEY ENTERS 3M

Jim McNerney's style has let employees to feel that they, not McNerney, are driving the changes. He was able to introduce data-driven change without forcing his ideas from General Electric onto the organization.

McNerney was able to rely on existing 3M management rather than importing other GE executives. "I think the story here is rejuvenation of a talented group of people rather than replacement of a mediocre group of people," he says. As part of his change plan, he avoids giving orders and reinforces the 3M culture whenever he can. "This is a fundamentally strong company. The inventiveness of the people here is in contrast with any other place I've seen. Everybody wakes up in the morning trying to figure out how to grow. They really do." This diplomacy generally played well with the 3M faithful. "He's delivered a very consistent message," says Althea Rupert, outgoing chair of Technical Forum, an internal society for all 3M technical people. "There's a sense of speed and a sense of urgency."[9]

In the 3M case, McNerney shows a clear understanding of the players, their perspectives, and their needs, and this made the implementation much easier to accomplish. Perhaps McNerney had no choice. But he did act in ways that involved people, focused their attention and interest, and brought them along rather than attempting to impose an outside set of views.

While the stories of the DaimlerChrysler merger–divorce and the installation of a new leader within a fully functional 3M are quite different, they demonstrate the impact of power dynamics and the influence of an organization's culture. How change leaders deal with power and behavioral organizational norms and the difficult-to-define, amorphous organizational culture will affect the speed and nature of the change.

When assessing possible responses to change initiatives, be it a merger, the installation of a new CEO, or a more modest undertaking, leaders need to recognize the impact that individual and organizational history can have. Employees may have had significant experience with change that leads them to be wary. They may have also worked with the existing approaches and have their own perspectives on what change is needed, so ambivalence and concern are natural—particularly in individuals who have demonstrated commitment to the organization and the quality of the outcomes achieved.[10] Some change projects are downsizings in disguise and yet change leaders somehow expect employees to welcome such initiatives with open arms. Surely, such optimism is naïve!

Power Dynamics in Organizations

Mention the words "organizational politics," and many people roll their eyes, throw up their hands, and say: "I don't want to have anything to do with politics!" The assumption is that organizational politics is inherently dirty, mean-spirited, destructive, and that organizations and their members would be better off without "politics." In order to understand this, we need to clarify what "politics" really means. In this context, politics is the act of brokering power to meet one's own goals.

And, of course, many times this assumption is accurate. It is clear that if some people have enough power, they bully others and get their way, regardless of the impact on the organization. However, **power** can be used strategically to influence organizations toward healthier ends. Power, regardless of its tainted image, is essential to making things happen. Robbins, Langton, and Judge define power as the capacity to influence others to accept one's ideas or plans.[11] Bolman and Deal make a persuasive argument that organizational "politics is the realistic process of making decisions and allocating resources in a context of scarcity and divergent issues. This view puts politics at the heart of decision making."[12] Academic experts agree: There is nothing inherently good or bad about power. Rather, it is the application and purposeful use of power and its consequences that will determine whether it is "good" or "bad."

In fact, the power to do things in organizations is critical to achieving change. Power is a crucial resource used by change agents to influence the actions and reactions of others. The knowledgeable change agent asks multiple power-related questions, such as: What power do I have and what are the sources of my power? What am I authorized to do by virtue of my title and position? What signatory authority and what dollar limits of expenditure does my position have? For example, can I hire someone based on my signature alone, or do I need to obtain approval for the hiring? These questions help change agents to diagnose their formal authority and power.

While organizations confer specific authority and power on particular positions, change agents also need to be perceived as influential. Change agents need to articulate positive beliefs about power—and to be aware of others' perception of their power. There are both internal psychological and external, reality-based roadblocks to exercising power. Clearly, power can be real—one can influence people with knowledge, persuade them by strength of personality and integrity, or use rewards and punishments to direct people's behaviors. But the perception of power is just as important, if not more important, than the actual resources that a manager holds. If others do not believe that a person is influential, then the facts will have little impact until those perceptions are changed. The rookie manager has the same formal power as the experienced one. However, the perception of their power and influence are generally very different. Often the perception that an individual has power to act is all employees need. When individuals have the trust of their CEOs, for instance, they want to maintain that trust and are therefore not likely to use inappropriate influence tactics on their boss.[13]

What gives people power in organizations? Individuals have power because of the position they hold, who they are (character and reputation), and who and what they know. When position, reputation, and expertise combine in one individual, that individual is likely to be powerful. These individual sources of power are classified in Table 6.1.[14]

Table 6.1 Types of Individual Power	
Positional Power	• Resides in the legitimate authority of the title and position; includes control and access to resources and the ability to formally reward and punish organizational members. The formal right to make decisions is a major source of power.* • In today's egalitarian world of flattened hierarchies and virtual organizations, this type of power is lessening in effectiveness as people demand to know the "why" of things. This is most true in cultures where deference to positional power is lower.[15]
Network Power	• Connection power results from the informal network of connections of people that permits them to access and pass on information. • People with large networks of colleagues across organizational levels and boundaries have access to more information and to be perceived as more influential
Knowledge Power	• Can be expert and/or information power. • Expert power is the possession of a body of knowledge essential to the organization; credentials provide independent certification of expertise and increase one's ability to influence. • Information power is clout gained through the flow of facts and data: by creating, framing, redirecting, or distorting information and by controlling who receives the information.
Personality Power	• The ability to inspire trust and enthusiasm from others (charisma) provides many leaders with significant individual power. • Reputation, which comes from people's experiences with the person, including reports of success (or failure), influences personal power.

*Another way of looking at power is in terms of "yea-saying" or "nay-saying" power. Yea-saying means that a person can make it happen. For example, he or she could decide who would be hired. Nay-saying power means that a person could prevent something from happening. Thus, nay-saying power would mean that someone could prevent a particular person from being hired but could not decide who would be hired.

Departmental Power

In addition to personal influence, departments within an organization have different levels of power. This power is dependent on the centrality of the work the department does, the availability of people to accomplish the task, and the ability of the department to handle the organization's environment. These can be categorized as:

- *Ability to cope with environmental uncertainty*: Departments and individuals gain power if they are seen to make the environment appear certain. Thus, marketing and sales departments gain power by bringing in future orders, diminishing the impact of competitors' actions, and providing greater certainty about the organization's future vitality in the marketplace. During times of economic turbulence, finance departments gain power through their ability to help the firm navigate its way. Likewise, other departments and functions either enhance or diminish their power based upon their ability to absorb uncertainty and make the world more predictable and manageable for the organization.
- *Low substitutability*: Whenever a function is essential and no one else can do it, the department has power. Think, for example, of the power of human resources departments when no one else can authorize replacement of positions or the power of data processing departments prior to the advent of the personal computer.
- *Centrality*: Power flows to those departments whose activities are central to the survival and strategy of the organization or when other departments depend on the department for the completion of work. In most large white-collar organizations, systems people have power because of our dependence on the computer and the information derived from it. Close the management information systems and you shut down the organization. Highly regarded and well-developed information systems anchor the success of firms such as Federal Express, Dell, Walmart, Statistics Canada, The Bank of Montreal, Scotland Yard, and BMW.

Hardy added to our understanding of the sources of power with her classification.[16] She described three dimensions of power:

1. *Resource power*—the access to valued resources in an organization. These include rewards, sanctions, coercion, authority, credibility, expertise, information, political affiliations, and group power. Resource power is very similar to the individual power listed above.

2. *Process power*—the control over formal decision-making arenas and agendas. Examples of process power would be the power to include or exclude an item on a discussion agenda. Nominating committees have significant process power as they determine who gets to sit on committees that make decisions.

3. *Meaning power*—the ability to define the meaning of things. Thus, the meaning of symbols and rituals and the use of language provide meaning power. For example, a shift from reserved parking and large corner offices for executives to first-come parking and common office space can symbolize a significant move away from the reliance on hierarchical power.

Hardy's introduction of process and meaning power adds significantly to the understanding of how one might influence a change situation. Anyone who has tried to get an item added to a busy agenda will understand the frustration of not having process power. And when your supervisor states that having e-mail on your phone is "optional" but you're held accountable for responding to e-mails outside of normal business hours, this is a clear use of meaning power.

While many sources of power exist, the type of power used by managers can have different effects. Some types of power or influence are used more frequently than others. One research study found that managers used different influence tactics depending on whether they were attempting to influence superiors or subordinates. Table 6.2 outlines the usage of these **power tactics**. It shows that managers claim they use rational methods in persuading others. The use of overt power, either by referring something to a higher authority or by applying sanctions, is not a popular tactic.

Change agents, like all managers, need to think of themselves as "politicians."[17] Defining oneself as an organizational "politician" will suggest the need to negotiate, develop coalitions, build and use alliances, deal with the personality of the decision maker, and using contacts and relationships to obtain vital information. Savvy change leaders do not underestimate the need for power and influence in their determination to make something happen. Examples in the last chapter on the leveraging of formal structures and systems to advance change speak to this reality. See **Toolkit Exercise 6.2** to assess different kinds of power.

Table 6.2 Usage Frequency of Different Power Tactics		
	When Managers Influenced Superiors	**When Managers Influenced Subordinates**
Most Popular Tactic ↑ ↓ Least Popular Tactic	Using and giving reasons	Using and giving reasons
	Developing coalitions	Being assertive
	Friendliness	Friendliness
	Bargaining	Developing coalitions
	Being assertive	Bargaining
	Referring to higher authority	Referring to higher authority
		Applying sanctions

Source: Kipnis, D. et al. "Patterns of Managerial Influence: Shotgun Managers, Tacticians and Bystanders," *Organizational Dynamics.* Winter, 1984.

Organizational Culture and Change

Organizational culture: What does it mean?

The concept of organizational culture is fairly new. While psychologists talked about group "norms" and social climates in organizations as early as 1939,[18] the concept of "culture" only began to attract organizational behavior researchers in the 1980s and 1990s.[19] Now, the idea is widely used among academics and practitioners alike: A 2014 search on Amazon books by the words "organization culture" yielded a listing of over 47,000 plus books.[20]

The widespread use of the term has not, unfortunately, created a standard definition. However, Ed Schein's definition, which has been published in four editions of his book *Organization Culture and Leadership* (1992, 1996, 2004, & 2010), dominates the field and is quite useful in thinking about the phenomenon. Schein defined culture as:

The culture of a group can now be defined as (1) a pattern of shared basic assumptions (2) that was learned by a group (3) as it solved its problems of external adaptation and internal integration, (4) that has worked well enough to be considered valid and, (5) therefore, to be taught to new members (6) as the correct way to perceive, think, and feel in relation to those problems (the numbers were added by the authors).

Note the complexity of this definition with its six sub-parts. Schein is concerned with a group and its learning; with how an organization adjusts to the external environment's ever-evolving demands and how internal players respond coherently and in alignment to those challenges; the fact that these ways of behaving are taught to new members "in a socialization process that is itself a reflection of (the) culture"; and that the culture promotes a particular way of thinking and feeling about problems.

How to Analyze a Culture

To analyze a culture, Schein identified three levels. The first level is the visible aspect—or artifacts—of the organization. These include everything from how employees dress, the design of an organization's buildings, to its structures and processes. While artifacts are easy to see, their meaning can be difficult to decipher and an observer needs to be careful to ascribe meaning to a single artifact or observation. The second level is an organization's "espoused beliefs and values"; this second level includes an organization's articulated mission, values, and strategy. Most change agents begin to change an organization by starting at this level of culture. The third level is the "basic underlying assumptions" that have become so ingrained and so much a part of a group's thinking and perspective on the world that they are not questioned. Since these assumptions remain largely unarticulated, they are also non-debatable, making them extremely difficult to change. For example, a university faculty may see itself as caring passionately about the quality of the classroom experience, and protect its beliefs by actions which serve to silence anyone who raises questions or concerns in this area.

Many founders of organizations explicitly set out to establish a culture that is compatible with their beliefs about how organizations operate best and the values that should be embedded in the organization. For example, Gretchen Fox, founder and former CEO of FOX Relocation Management Corp., Boston (see the website for this case), had worked in excessively hierarchical law firms before she started her relocation firm. At law firms she had observed large, physically fit men who were senior partners in the firm and whereby held high-level positions in the organization's hierarchy ignore low-level women staff as they lifted and carried heavy boxes and bottles of water. For Gretchen, the human thing for the men to do would have been to help with the heavy lifting. Gretchen decided then and there that when she built her business, she would establish a flat, non-hierarchical firm. This belief was embedded in the layout of offices (Gretchen's office was a regular-sized office in a row of offices, leaving the light-filled sunny corner spaces for employees); in the minimal use of titles; in a collective, decision-making process for hiring new employees; and in a rational approach to work that did not involve status in the hierarchy.

As FOX Relocation grew, some of the observable artifacts—such as titles—needed to change to accommodate folks in the external world's understanding of who did what inside the firm. The question became: What else, if anything, needed to change inside the firm to adapt to the external environment and to maintain the integrity of the culture?

Tips for Change Agents to Assess a Culture

A change agent, then, needs to assess a culture at three levels. Such an analysis may lead to innovative ways to change a culture.

1. *Observe the artifacts.* How do people dress? How are offices arranged? What is the space differential for offices between top-level executives and other people who work in the organization? How are parking lots and spaces assigned, and who pays and does not pay for a space? How do members of the organization interact and relate to one another? Where and how are meals eaten? Is there an executive dining room and separate food for executives? What is the pay and reward differential for people at the top of the firm and those at the bottom? (This information can be difficult to impossible to obtain for some organizations.)

2. *Read documents and talk to people to learn espoused beliefs and values:* What does the organization say about itself on its website and social media platforms? What are the articulated mission, values, and strategy statements? What does it brag about in its press releases? Ask five to ten people: What does this organization value and believe in?

What, if any, of these documents have changed in the past five years? How have they changed, and are these changes in alignment with changes in the artifacts of the organization?

3. *Observe and ask people about underlying assumptions:* Since these are often unarticulated and their origins developed years before, it may be difficult for people to express the organization's fundamental suppositions. Observers need to look for clues on fundamental issues: What is the basic orientation to time in terms of past, present, and future? What time units are most relevant for the conduct of the organization's business? For example, colleges and universities orient around the quarter or semesters, units of time that are not relevant to most businesses but would be to bookstores that serve universities and landlords who rent to students. A second example would be the nature of human being: "are humans basically good, neutral, or evil, and is human nature perfectible or fixed?"(p. 429).[21] It is important to consider these fundamental issues, and then search for and develop hypotheses about what needs to change to improve the outcomes experienced and how to go about it.

CLASHING WORKPLACE CULTURES

Training & Careers, Inc. (TCI), a small nonprofit agency, focused on job training and placement for low-income residents included programs in culinary arts, janitorial work, and hotel and hospitality training. Due to financial issues, TCI merged with Careers, Inc. (CI), a national nonprofit that had a similar mission and programs. TCI, headquartered in Boston, had a relaxed and autonomous work culture. Careers, Inc. (CI), headquartered in New York City, had a regimented and tightly supervised workforce. As the organizations began to merge their operations, they neglected to address the differences in their workforce cultures. TCI was made up of white-collar staff, 25% of whom held a master's degree in social work. TCI was able to attract this talent by offering flexible work schedules, three weeks of paid vacation, and letting the staff out early most Fridays. CI's workforce, on the other hand, attracted largely blue-collar workers who led the janitorial training programs. This workforce had strict time reporting guidelines and few vacation incentives, as their compensation was commensurate with their high school or associate's level education.

As the organizations attempted to merge, TCI experienced significant pushback from its employees as CI eliminated early-release Fridays and proposed cutting vacations. TCI moved away from staff autonomy by adopting CI's time clock system, which required employees to punch in and out each day. Because the leaders of the two organizations did not sufficiently understand the cultural differences and take these into account during the merger, TCI experienced a 43% turnover of frontline staff following the merger. Remaining staff were disgruntled and openly sought other job opportunities outside the organization.

This vignette suggests three levels of organizational culture. The time clock system, requiring employees to punch in and out each day, is an artifact that was present in one of the organizations, but not the other. The espoused beliefs and values were discernable in the comparable missions and programs of the two organizations and pointed to potential friction points. Further, the underlying assumptions of who to hire and how to manage them suggests differences at the third level of culture. At Careers Inc., executives believed that staff needed to be tightly controlled and supervised to make sure that they do a day's work. By contrast, the underlying assumption of TCI was that staff accepted lower pay in return for more autonomy and time off perks. When this assumption was challenged, the results were disastrous.

To create one organization and one culture, the executives at CI required all of its employees to use the time clock, punching in and out daily. In making this requirement, CI executives sent a signal about their core beliefs about the nature of human beings and how they should be managed.

Understanding the Perceptions of Change

Individuals choose to consider and adopt a proposed organizational change—or choose not to. Sometimes they do this willingly and other times they choose reluctantly, either feeling forced or mixed about their decisions. This perspective is valuable when thinking about increasing the success of organizational change, for it is at the individual level that people decide to change. Their choices depend on their views of the situation and how it impacts their lives.

In the recent past, many change programs have been focused on cost cutting, including the downsizing of the number of employees in an organization. People are bright. They understand what is happening. And if a program will cost them their jobs, why would you expect them to be enthusiastic and positive? Such resistance demonstrates the point that individuals will choose to cooperate or not depending on their personal circumstances and their assessment of how the change will impact them personally. Individuals will adopt or accept change only when they think that their perceived personal benefits are greater than the perceived costs of change. This can be summarized as follows:

CHANGE OCCURS WHEN

Perceived Benefits of Change > Perceived Cost of Change

This simple formula highlights several things. First, change agents have to deal with both the reality of change and its perceptions. Again, perception counts as much as reality. Second, in many situations, the costs of changing are more evident than the benefits of change. In most change situations, first the costs are incurred and then the benefits follow. The perceived benefits of change depend on whether people think the benefits are likely—that is, the probability of the change being successful in ways that count for them. As well, the benefits of change depend on the state of "happiness" or dissatisfaction with the status quo. Interestingly, people also tend to focus on the consequences of the change rather than the consequences of not changing and remaining the same. The more dissatisfied people are, the more they as individuals will be willing to change. The **change equation** can be modified to capture this as follows:

CHANGE OCCURS WHEN

Dissatisfaction × **Benefits** × **Success** > **Cost**

Where

> Dissatisfaction = Perception of Dissatisfaction With the Status Quo
> Benefits = Perception of the Benefits of Change
> Success = Perception of the Probability of Success
> Cost = Perceived Cost of Change

Thus, change agents need to build the case for change by increasing the dissatisfaction with the status quo by providing data that demonstrate that other options are better, demonstrating that the overall benefits are worth the effort of the change, and showing that the change effort is likely to succeed. Doing your homework and early successes become part of the change agent's toolkit.

It is important to differentiate between the costs and benefits to the organization and the costs and benefits to individuals. Too often, change leaders focus on the organizational benefits and miss the impact at the individual level. The earlier example highlighted this. If an individual sees that the change will increase profits and result in job loss, why would a manager expect support? It takes very secure people who feel they have alternatives and are being equitably treated to be positive under these circumstances even if they believe the change is needed for the organization.

Table 6.3 captures this. It contrasts the impact on individuals with the impact on the organization to predict the resulting support for a change initiative. The purpose of Table 6.3 is to encourage change leaders to avoid the trap of assuming that positive organizational outcomes will automatically be supported by individuals.

In addition to considering the direct impact of a change on a person, individuals will also think about and be influenced by the effects of the change on their coworkers and teammates. The strength of interpersonal bonds, including the shared values, goals, and norms within an organization, can have a significant impact on attitudes and actions. The traditions of how work is divided, how people and departments interact or do not, and simply the way of doing business create a culture within an organization. The desire to maintain the organization's traditions, even if there is a mutual understanding for a need to move on, can hinder the acceptance of changes. This challenge is greater if there are shifts in roles and responsibilities and therefore a shift in power. A change leader needs to understand and respect individuals' and organizational history and the individual members' perceptions of that history to effectively negotiate the change process and appropriately engage all stakeholders.

Table 6.3 Organizational and Individual Consequences and the Support for Change

Perceived Impact of the Change on the Organization	Perceived Impact of the Change on the Individual	Direction of Support of the Change
Positive consequences for the organization	Positive outcome for the individual (e.g., less work, better work)	Strong support for change
Positive consequences for the organization	Negative outcome for the individual (e.g., more work, worse work)	Indeterminate support for change but very possibly resistance
Neutral consequences for the organization	Positive outcome for the individual (e.g., less work, better work)	Positive support for change
Neutral consequences for the organization	Negative outcome for the individual (e.g., more work, worse work)	Resistance to change
Negative consequences for the organization	Positive outcome for the individual (e.g., less work, better work)	Indeterminate support for change
Negative consequences for the organization	Negative outcome for the individual (e.g., more work, worse work)	Resistance to change

Change agents need to think of the impact on individuals—particularly people critical to the change. When doing so, consider also the people who will actually have to change and how they will view the change equation and assess the benefits, costs, and risks. A general manager may decide that new systems are needed, but it is the individual who will be operating the systems who will have to learn how to work with them and change his or her behavior. To consider the perceived impact of change see **Toolkit Exercise 6.3**.

Identifying the Organizational Dynamics at Play

Each of the organizational models introduced in Chapters 2 and 3 assumed that organizations consist of people, systems, and structures that interact according to the forces at play. In organizational change, the key is to understand the forces and how they respond to shifts in pressure. In system terms, the technical term is *homeostasis,* meaning a system has a tendency toward a relatively stable equilibrium among its interdependent factors. Organizations are as they are because the forces involved are in balance. If one force is changed, it could affect many things and may well be resisted. Alternatively, it may give rise to unanticipated support for the change.

Two tools are particularly useful in helping change leaders to understand such forces and why the organization changes (or doesn't).

1. **Force field analysis**—a process of identifying and analyzing the driving and restraining forces impacting an organization's objectives

2. **Stakeholder analysis**—a process of identifying the key individuals or groups in the organization who can influence or who are impacted by the proposed change and then of working with those individuals or groups to make them more positive to notions of change

Once these tools have been deployed, it is important to integrate them. Stakeholders will show up in the force field analysis as forces that need to be considered, and an in-depth assessment of them in the stakeholder analysis will put the change agent in a stronger position to manage those forces in ways that will advance the change.

Force Field Analysis[22]

The force field analysis identifies the forces for and against change. In situations that are stable or in equilibrium, the forces for change (driving forces) and the forces opposing change (restraining forces) are balanced. To create change, the balance must be upset by adding new pressures for change; increasing the strength of some or all of the pressures for change; reducing or eliminating the pressures against change; or converting a restraining force into a driving force. Figure 6.2 depicts a force field analysis chart.

Pressures for change come in many shapes and include both internal and external sources. External factors often are the initial triggers that give rise to internal

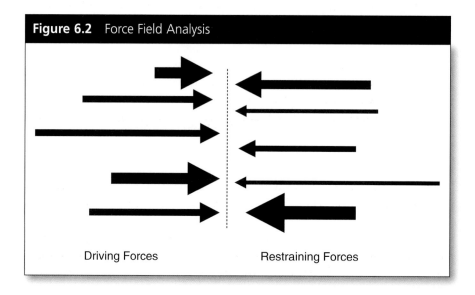

Figure 6.2 Force Field Analysis

Driving Forces   Restraining Forces

pressures. External driving forces could include benchmark data and various market forces that are putting pressure on senior management to improve their performance in the private sector. Politicians concerned about increased costs or declining service levels could generate driving forces in the public sector. Alternatively, external factors may involve opportunities for future growth or access to special incentives (e.g., tax relief) designed to promote certain activities. Internal pressures, such as the vision of a champion, work group attitudes and norms, and internal systems (e.g., the reward system) that are aligned with the change have the potential to act as driving forces.

Restraining forces for change might come from power dynamics, cultural norms, and formal organizational systems that are incongruent with the change. For example, if innovation is part of the desired change, control systems that focus on efficiency and minimize experimentation or variance from standards to reduce costs will act as a restraining force. Changes that are seen as threats to individuals will lead to resistance. Habits or patterns of behavior that could impede the change might be difficult to alter, even when individuals are supportive. The longer those habits have been in place, the more difficulty individuals will have in extricating themselves from those patterns. Work group norms, informal leadership patterns, and workplace culture may act as either driving or restraining forces, depending on the situation.

To do a force field analysis:

1. Identify the forces acting in the situation and estimate their strength. Both the immediate and the longer-term forces need to be considered. The immediate forces are the ones that are acting now and have a more immediate impact (e.g., quarterly sales targets). The longer-term forces are those that may have less immediate effect but whose impact may linger longer, such as customer satisfaction or employee morale.

2. Understand how the forces might be altered to produce a more hospitable climate for the change and develop strategies that will maximize your leverage on the driving and restraining forces with the minimum effort. Conserving your energy and resources is important because change management is a marathon, not a 100-yard dash.

3. Look beyond the immediate impact and identify ways to increase support and reduce resistance. Consider unanticipated consequences that may result from what is implemented. For example, you may be able to reduce resistance by throwing financial rewards at individuals, but in doing so you may inadvertently promote unethical behavior, reduce organizational commitment, and destroy your compensation system.

In the 3M example mentioned earlier, the appointment of McNerney created a new force in the organization. The Six Sigma system he introduced from GE was data based and thus appealed to the values of 3M employees. At the same time, he reduced defensiveness as a force by praising the 3M culture and showed how the employees could achieve more by focusing on the data and explicit goals. All of these things added to forces for change and reduced or eliminated forces against change. As positive outcomes began to ensue from these initiatives, the process provided sustaining reinforcement.

Strebel suggests looking at force field analysis graphically. That is, consider the forces for and against change separately—not necessarily opposing each other directly but operating orthogonally (at right angles).[23] Figure 6.3 shows this.

Strebel's view of the change arena allows us to plot where forces for and against change are in balance. The change arena helps us to identify four areas with which many change agents are familiar: areas of constant or **continuous change**, areas of high resistance, areas of "breakpoint" change, and areas of "sporadic" or "flip-flop" change. With **breakpoint change**, pressures are significant and the resistance will be strong. Under these circumstances, resistance will prevent change until the driving forces strengthen to the point that the system snaps to a new configuration. For example, World War II was seen by many Americans to be someone else's battle until the attack on Pearl Harbor dramatically altered the status quo. When breakpoint change occurs, it will be radical and create significant upheaval because of the strength of the changes involved. The situations faced by General Motors and the UAW in 2006 and 2009 are classic breakpoint situations. The market pressures on General Motors were very strong. The UAW faced equally strong resistance forces from both active and retired members, who wished to protect their health benefits and their pension plans.[24] In 2006, this led to significant concessions from the UAW, but these were a pale imitation of those obtained in 2009 after GM exercised breakpoint change through declaring bankruptcy and seeking court protection while it restructured.

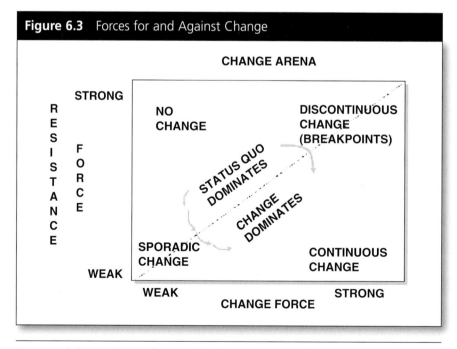

Figure 6.3 Forces for and Against Change

Source: Strebel, P., "Choosing the Right Change Path," *California Management Review.* Winter, 1994, 29–51.

In **flip-flop changes**, forces are weak and change events are not very important, and the situation could change only to reverse itself easily. Flip-flop changes tend to occur when participants have shifting preferences or are ambivalent concerning matters that are of only modest importance to them.

Force field analysis requires careful thinking about the dynamics of the situation and organization, including how people, structures, and systems affect and are affected by what is happening. How will these factors assist or prevent change?

Toolkit Exercise 6.4 asks you to do a force field analysis in order to develop your skills in this area.

Such analysis does lead individuals to think in relatively linear ways—forces are either for or against change. Their influence is linear and direct. However, a different, more nonlinear perspective is often needed. A tool called stakeholder analysis is valuable in gaining insights into a more nonlinear interactive view of organizations.

Stakeholder Analysis

Stakeholder analysis is the identification of those who can affect the change or who are affected by the change. Included in this is the analysis of the positions, the motives, and the power of all key stakeholders. Stakeholder management is the explicit influencing of critical participants in the change process. It is the identification of the "entanglements" in the organization, the formal and informal connections between people, structures, and systems.

The purpose of stakeholder analysis is to develop a clear understanding of the key individuals who can influence the outcome of a change and thus be in a better position to appreciate their positions and recognize how best to manage them and the context. A useful starting point is to think carefully about who will be affected and who has to change their behavior in order for the change to be successful. An obvious but often overlooked point is exactly that—someone or some people will be affected and some will have to change their behavior!* Once the key person or persons are identified, change leaders must focus on who influences those people and who has the resources and/or power to make the change happen or to prevent it from happening.

In doing a stakeholder analysis, the first step is to identify those people who need to be concentrated on. A change leader can identify those people by asking the following questions:

- Who has the authority to say "yes" or "no" to the change?
- Which areas or departments or people will be impacted by the change? How will they likely react, and who leads and has influence in those areas and departments? Note that the stakeholders relevant to a change do not always reside in the organization and can include customers, suppliers, communities, government bodies, and so on.

---

*We are reminded of the old definition of insanity: Doing the same thing over and over, but expecting a different result!

- Who has to change their behavior or act differently for the change to be successful? This is a key question—the change ultimately rests on having these people doing things differently.
- Who has the potential to particularly ease the path to change, and who has the potential to be particularly disruptive?

Savage developed a model that plots stakeholders on two dimensions: their potential for threat and their potential for cooperation.[25] If a stakeholder has high potential for both threat and cooperation, Savage suggests that a collaborative approach should be developed. In this way, the stakeholder is brought onside and his or her support obtained. If the stakeholder is supportive, that is, has high potential for cooperation and low potential for threat, Savage argues for a strategy of involvement where the change agent maximizes support from the stakeholder. A stakeholder who is nonsupportive, that is, has limited potential for cooperation but high potential for threat, should be defended against. Finally, a marginal stakeholder, one with limited potential for either cooperation or threat, should be monitored to ensure the assessment is correct.

Once these vested interests are mapped, the change leader can examine the effects of organizational systems and structures. Only with this deep understanding can change be managed well.

Change agents need to know who the key participants are, their motivations, and the relationships between them. Creating a visual picture of the key participants and their interrelationships can be helpful to understanding the dynamics of the situation. A **stakeholder map** lays out the positions of people pictorially and allows the change agent to quickly see the interdependencies. In drawing stakeholder maps, some add complexity: Members of the same groups can be encircled; different thickness of lines can be used to signify the strength of the relationship; different colors can be used to signify different things (e.g., level of support or resistance); or arrows can be used to point to influence patterns, with their thickness often used to characterize the strength of the relationship. The only constraint on the construction of a stakeholder map is one's ability to translate data into a meaningful visual depiction of the key stakeholders and their interrelationships. As noted earlier, it is critical to not leave out stakeholders that are external to the organization. External stakeholders create and are a part of important dynamics, and understanding their connection to the organization as well as their power and influence will help the change agent in plotting the complete landscape.

Some of the factors that are useful to depict are:

- their wants and needs,
- their likely responses to the change,
- how they are linked,
- their sources and level of power and influence,
- the actual influence patterns,
- how they currently benefit from the status quo,
- how they may benefit from the change, and
- how they may be worse off from the change.

Figure 6.4 shows a hypothetical stakeholder map.
Cross and Prusak classify organizational members as:

- **Central connectors**—people who link with one another. For example, Stakeholder #4 links Stakeholders #2, #3, and #6.
- **Boundary spanners**—people who connect the formal and/or informal networks to other parts of the organization. In the map, the change agent and Stakeholder #4 are both serving as boundary spanners.
- **Information brokers**—people who link various subgroups. In Figure 6.4, the change agent has the potential to play that role.
- **Peripheral specialists**—people who have specialized expertise in the network.[26]

Once the stakeholder map is developed, change agents can visually see groupings and influence patterns, levels of support and resistance, and the strength of existing groupings and relationships. They can use this map to assess their assumptions concerning the stakeholders by soliciting input and feedback from others. Action plans can be reviewed relative to the map and to see if the strategies and tactics are likely to produce stakeholder responses that will contribute to the desired results. These are just a few of the ways these maps can be applied.

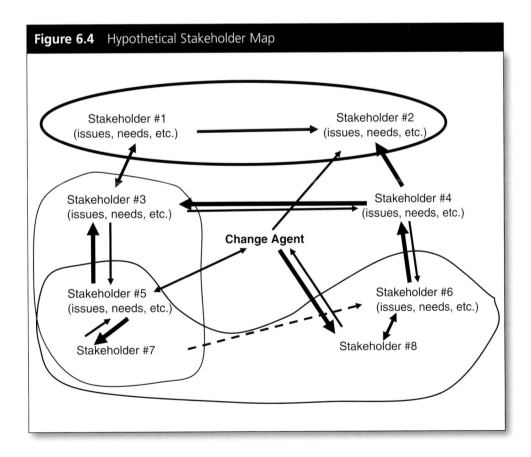

Figure 6.4   Hypothetical Stakeholder Map

Understanding the positions of key players or stakeholders is essential if a change agent is to alter the forces that resist change and strengthen those that promote change. One can think about moving each stakeholder on **a change continuum** from an **awareness** of the issues to **interest** to a **desire for action** to **taking action** or supporting action on the change. One also wants to guard against unnecessarily driving them to actively resist the change.

Awareness → Interest → Desire for action → Take action

Classifying stakeholders according to this continuum is useful because it can guide what change tools you should use. For example, in the initial stages of a change process, the issue may be one of creating awareness of the need for change. Here, one-on-one communication to organization-wide publicity counts. Articles in an internal organizational newspaper can educate people. Forums or open sessions discussing the issues can play a role. Addresses by senior executives can both inform and generate interest in a topic. Benchmark data can convince skeptics that change is necessary, and a special budgetary allocation or a pilot project can pave the way for people to try out a change program. Which tactics are most appropriate to use at different points in time will depend on the situation; the people affected; the change agent's skills, abilities, reputation, and relationships; as well as on the organization's culture and previous experiences with change.

As a general rule, change leaders should shift from low-intensity forms of communication to higher-intensity forms as individuals shift from awareness to interest and action. Impersonal but educational messages might inform, but persuasion often takes direct one-on-one action.

For example, in one organization, the CEO wanted independent sales agents to adopt a new and relatively expensive software program. Persuasion efforts about the costs and benefits had limited success. Finally, the change agent identified two things: First, the key influencers were the managers of the sales agents and second, these managers could be classed as supportive, neutral, or negative. The change agent had the CEO phone each manager directly, emphasize the strategic importance of the adoption of the software, query them about concerns they might have, and then directly ask them for their support. Clearly, this was a very powerful and persuasive technique, using all of the power and prestige of the president along with his considerable interpersonal skills.[27]

Stakeholders will vary not only in their **readiness to change** but also in their attitudes toward or predisposition to change. Some individuals tend to be inherently keener about change and fall into the categories of **innovators** or **early adopters**. Others will wait until the first results of the change are in—they follow the initial two groups of adopters and form the **early majority**. The **late majority** wait longer before adopting. They want more definitive data concerning the change and the reactions of others before they are prepared to commit. Finally, some will, by their nature, resist change until late in the process and can be classified as **laggards** or **late adopters** and **non-adopters**. Table 6.4 lists people's predisposition to change.

Table 6.4 Individual Predispositions to Change	
Innovators or early adopters	Individuals who seek change and want variety
Early majority	Individuals who are receptive to change but are not first adopters
Late majority	Individuals who follow others once the change has been introduced and tried
Laggards or late adopters	Individuals who are reluctant to change and do so only after many others have adopted
Non-adopters	Individuals who will not change or adapt under most circumstances

In most organizations, we tend to know the innovators. They are constantly trying something new, including new products and services. Risk and novelty seem to provide the adrenalin they need to get through the day! Change comes easily and is sought. In contrast, we also know those who tend to be uncomfortable with new things. These individuals have a strong preference for order and routine. Change is to be avoided and when it must happen, it happens only after most others have shown the way and the status quo is no longer viable.

Change agents need to identify and work first with innovators and early adopters. There is no sense trying to shift someone whose personality resists change until others have adopted. It may be useful to keep certain stakeholders informed of your activities even though they are typically later adopters so as to avoid unnecessary backlash. However, the simple act of keeping people informed is not the same as working closely with innovators and early adopters to advance the initiative. Early in any change program, change agents must anticipate that they will lack support. Few people will know about the change, let alone support it. The process of adoption will often be gradual until a critical mass of support exists. This will be explored in greater detail in Chapter 9 when the topic of the tipping point is introduced.

While the willingness to change can be viewed, in part, as a personality variable, it is also dependent upon the degree to which someone understands the change and his or her commitment toward the change. Floyd and Wooldridge differentiated between understanding and commitment.[28] In their view, someone could have high or low understanding of the change and have high, low, or negative commitment to the change.[†] This provides a matrix of possibilities that helps us to think about stakeholders and their positions. Change agents need to consider those who actively oppose the change as well as those who are positive in their commitments. Being neutral or skeptical due to ambivalent feelings about the change is not the same as being an informed opponent of the change. See Table 6.5.

[†]Another way of looking at commitment is to categorize people as "make it happen," "help it happen," "let it happen," or "keep it from happening."

Table 6.5 Stakeholder's Understanding and Commitment

	High Understanding of the Change	Low Understanding of the Change
High, positive commitment to the change	Strong consensus	Blind devotion
Low, positive commitment to the change	Informed skeptics	Weak consensus
Negative commitment to the change	Informed opponents	Fanatical opponents

Floyd and Wooldridge stress that change agents need to understand people's perspectives of the initiative and that there is no one "right" position. Often we assume that it is best to have people who both understand the change and are committed to it. This is the "strong consensus" cell in Table 6.5. Floyd and Wooldridge argue that at different times, blind devotion, informed skepticism, or a weak consensus is desirable. That is, at times we may need people to be blind devotees—if the change is a strategic secret, people need to accept the change and be committed to act and not ask questions because the change leaders are not in a position to answer them. On the other hand, when beginning a project and testing out ideas for action, change leaders may well want informed skeptics—people who understand the situation well and who are not too committed. These people may well give valuable advice regarding change tactics and strategies as well as contribute to the actual design of the change.

Table 6.6 provides a grid that allows each stakeholder's position and degree of resistance and awareness to be plotted. This form provides a systematic analysis of stakeholders. In the second column, each stakeholder's predisposition toward change can be noted. Is the person typically an innovator or an early adopter, or does that individual wait and see how others are reacting? If the person waits, is he or she normally a part of the early majority of adopters or the late majority group, or does he or she tend to lag further (i.e., the laggards and non-adopters)?

The second column can also be used to assess the stakeholder's current **commitment profile**. Is this person currently resistant, ambivalent, neutral, somewhat predisposed, or supportive of the change, or is he or she already committed to the initiative? The change agent can then consider power and influence patterns and develop strategies and tactics that will move the individual stakeholders along the adoption continuum (aware, interested, desiring the change, and taking action). The movement of the stakeholders can be plotted in the appropriate columns, with attention given to learning (e.g., what was the impact of the action undertaken?) and the refining of strategies and tactics in the future. In the end, the objective is to move key stakeholders along the adoption continuum, or at minimum, prevent them from becoming significant obstacles to the success of the change initiative.

Table 6.6	Analysis of Stakeholder's Readiness to Take Action				
	Predisposition to Change (innovator, early adopter, early majority, late majority, laggard)				
	Current Commitment Profile (resistant, ambivalent, neutral, supportive or committed)	**Aware**	**Interested**	**Desiring Change**	**Taking Action**
Stakeholder's Name					
Jones					
Smith					
Douglas					

Summary

Change agents need to understand the power structures and informal dynamics in their organizations, including culture. They must recognize that **resistance to change** is likely and is not necessarily a bad thing—there is potential to use resistance in a positive way. It is important to know the forces impacting the organization and the individuals within them, as well as the internal and external stakeholders that will impact and will be impacted by the change process.

Two powerful tools to help us think through the organizational situation are force field analysis and stakeholder analysis. Force field analysis helps change agents to plot the major structural, systemic, and human forces at work in the situation and to anticipate ways to alter these forces. Stakeholder analysis helps us to understand the interactions between key individuals and the relationships and power dynamics that form the web of interactions between individuals. See **Toolkit Exercise 6.1** for critical thinking questions for this chapter.

Key Terms

Informal organization—represented by those structures, systems, and processes that emerge spontaneously from the interaction of people within the formal systems and structures that define the organizational context. They include: informal leadership, communication, and influence patterns; norms and informal roles; and, at a macro level, the culture of the organization that emerges and influences behavior.

Power—the capacity to influence others to accept one's ideas or plans. The chapter set out a number of sources from which power can be derived.

Power tactics—strategies and tactics deployed to influence others to accept one's ideas or plans.

The change equation—says that change occurs when the perception of dissatisfaction with the status quo times the perceived benefits of the change times the perceived probability of success is greater than the perceived cost of the change.

Force field analysis—a process of identifying and analyzing the force field in an organization and then altering those forces to accomplish your change. The force field is made up of driving and restraining forces.

Stakeholder analysis—the identification and assessment of those who can affect the change or who are affected by the change. Included in this is the analysis of the positions, motives, and power of all key stakeholders. It is the identification of the relationships in the organization, the formal and informal connections between people, structures, and systems. Stakeholder management is the explicit influencing of critical participants in the change process. As such, it is common to see stakeholders also reflected in the force field analysis.

Continuous change—occurs continuously because the forces for change are strong and the resistance forces are weak.

Breakpoint change—change that occurs in a context defined by strong forces for change and strong sources of resistance. When things occur that heighten the change forces and/or weaken the resistance forces, the system is snapped into a new configuration.

Flip-flop change (or sporadic change)—change that occurs within a context of weak change forces and resistance forces. Within this context, the change is not viewed as particularly important and as a result, change may occur, only to be easily reversed.

Stakeholder map—a visual representation of the key stakeholders, their interrelationships, influence patterns, wants, needs, issues, and predispositions toward the change.

Central connectors—people who link with one another.

Boundary spanners are people who connect the formal and/or informal networks to other parts of the organization.

Information brokers—people who link various subgroups.

Peripheral specialists—people who have specialized expertise in the network.

Change continuum—describes the four stages stakeholders may progress through during a change project. The stages are awareness, interest, desire for action, and taking action.

Awareness—the first stage in the change continuum and describes stakeholders who are only just aware of the change initiative.

Interest—the second stage in the change continuum and describes stakeholders move from general awareness to active interest in the initiative.

Desire for action—the third stage in the change continuum and describes stakeholders move from an interest to a desire to take action. It is important in this stage to make action steps clear for stakeholders.

Taking action—the final stage in the change continuum and describes stakeholders who are fully committed to the change and taking action for the change.

Readiness to change—a person's predisposition toward change in general. Is the individual generally an innovator, an early adopter, a member of the early majority, a member of the late majority, or a laggard?

Innovators or **early adopters**—individuals who seek change and want variety. They have a natural predisposition to change.

Early majority—individuals who are receptive to change, but are not the first adopters.

Late majority—individuals who follow others once the change has been introduced and tried

Laggards or **late adopters**—individuals who are reluctant to change and do so only after many others have adopted. They have a very low predisposition to change.

Non-adopters—individuals who will not change or adapt under most circumstances. These individuals will actively resist change efforts.

Commitment profile—a person's orientation toward the specific change in question. Is the individual resistant, ambivalent, neutral, supportive, or committed to the change?

Resistance to change—the desire to *not* pursue the change. Resistance can stem from a variety of sources, including differences in information, perceptions, needs, and beliefs. In addition, existing informal and formal systems and processes have the potential to act as impediments to change.

Checklist: Stakeholder Analysis

1. Who are the key stakeholders in this decision or change effort?

2. Is there a formal decision maker with the formal authority to authorize or deny the change project? Who is that person (or persons)? What are his/her attitudes to the project?

3. What is the commitment profile of stakeholders? Are they against the change, neutral (let it happen), supportive (help it happen), or committed champions of the change (make it happen)? Do a commitment analysis for each stakeholder.

4. Are they typically initiators, early adopters, early majority, late majority, or laggards when it comes to change?

5. Why do stakeholders respond as they do? Does the reward system drive them to support or oppose your proposal? What consequences does your change have on each stakeholder? Do the stakeholders perceive these as positive, neutral, or negative?

6. What would change the stakeholders' views? Can the reward system be altered? Would information or education help?

7. Who influences the stakeholders? Can you influence the influencers? How might this help?

8. What coalitions might be formed among stakeholders? What alliances might you form? What alliances might form to prevent the change you wish?

9. By altering your position, can you keep the essentials of your change and yet satisfy some of the needs of those opposing change?

10. Can you appeal to higher-order values and/or goals that will make others view their opposition to the change as petty or selfish?

END-OF-CHAPTER EXERCISES

TOOLKIT EXERCISE 6.1

Critical Thinking Questions

Please find the URLs for the videos listed below on the website at study.sagepub.com/cawsey3e. Consider the questions that follow.

1. Please read Case 1 on page 397, "Building Community at Terra Nova Consulting," and consider the following questions:

   - What is the need for change at Terra Nova?

   - What are the cultural barriers to change?

   - What are the political barriers to change?

   - What alternatives does O'Reilly face?

   - How should O'Reilly go about making desired changes?

2. <u>GM Edgar Schein on Corporate Culture</u>—3:18 minutes

   - According to Schein, how should leaders deal with organizational culture?

- How has Schein's thinking on culture evolved over time?

- What do you think of Schein's advice on how to better prepare yourself for dealing with culture?

3. <u>Simon Sinek: If You Don't Understand People, You Don't Understand Business</u>—30:40 minutes

   - According to Sinek, how is trust built?

   - How does understanding people help us better understand business?

   - What is Sinek's case for authenticity?

Please see study.sagepub.com/cawsey3e for a downloadable template of this exercise.

TOOLKIT EXERCISE 6.2

Assessing Power

Personal:

1. What sources of power do you have access to?

   Your personal style and comfort zone will affect your choice of tactics. What tactics have you used in the past?

2. Consider a particular context in which you regularly find yourself (e.g., work, school, church, community group). What could you do to increase the power you have available to you in that context?

   What types of power are involved?

3. As it is important to know exactly the sources and limits to your power, it is also very important to understand the key players, structures, and systems in your situation. How do these influence the types and amount of power available to you?

   What could you do to change this?

Organizational:

1. Pick an organization you are quite familiar with. What were the perceptions around power in the organization?

In particular, what factors led to the assumption of power?

Which departments carried more weight and influence? What behaviors were associated with having power?

2. Think of a change situation in the organization. What types of power were at play?

Who had position, knowledge, and personality power? What individuals and departments handled uncertainty, were central, and were not very substitutable?

3. In Hardy's terms, who controlled resources?

Who had process power—that is, set the agendas, managed the nomination or appointment process to key committees, etc.? (Define what things meant and how important they were.)

4. Who had yea-saying power? On what issues?

Who had nay-saying power?

Please see study.sagepub.com/cawsey3e for a downloadable template of this exercise.

TOOLKIT EXERCISE 6.3

Perceived Impact of Change

1. Consider the impact of a change on an organization you are familiar with and then consider the impact on the individuals concerned. What were the impacts on the organization? What were the impacts on the individuals?

   Were these impacts both positive? Are you certain they were perceived that way?

2. What were the perceived costs of change? Who perceived these?

   Were the perceptions accurate? How could they be influenced?

3. What were the perceived benefits of change?

   Were the perceptions accurate?

   What was the probability of achieving these benefits?

   Were the employees and managers dissatisfied with the present state? Why? What were the costs of not changing?

4. Did the organization incur the costs of change prior to the benefits? If so, why did the organization agree to this risk? (i.e., incurring rather definite costs but indefinite benefits)

Please see study.sagepub.com/cawsey3e for a downloadable template of this exercise.

TOOLKIT EXERCISE 6.4

Understanding the Forces for and Against Change: The Force Field Analysis

Consider an organizational change situation you are familiar with. Use the following questions to guide you through the process of drawing a force field analysis.

1. What are the forces for change? Include external forces as well as a consideration of key individuals or groups. How strong and committed are these forces? (Who will let it happen; who will help it happen; who will make it happen?)

2. How could these forces be augmented or increased? What forces could be added to those that exist?

3. What are the forces that oppose change? Include structural forces such as reward systems or formal processes in the organization. Consider as well the effect of informal processes and groups or the culture of the organization.

4. How could these forces be weakened or removed? What things might create major resentment in these forces?

5. Can you identify any points of leverage that you could employ to advance the change? For example, deploying key well-respected individuals who support the change or providing low-cost guarantees related to serious concerns.

Please see study.sagepub.com/cawsey3e for a downloadable template of this exercise.

CHAPTER 7

Managing Recipients of Change and Influencing Internal Stakeholders

If there is any one secret of success, it lies in the ability to get the other person's point of view and see things from his angle, as well as from your own.

—Henry Ford

Reasons lead to conclusions. Emotions lead to action.

—William Magee, Operation Smile

CHAPTER OVERVIEW

- People respond to change in many ways. Some embrace it. Others are ambivalent. Some view change negatively. Reactions depend on the nature of the change, the situation, the individuals involved, and how it is approached. Change leaders need to understand why people react to change as they do, gathering data to understand individuals' situations and their responses.
- Change leaders need to rethink their assumptions about resistance to change. Employees often have good reasons for resisting the change leaders' proposals, and these reasons need to be understood and learned from.
- Change leaders can rethink the language that they use, seeing employees as "stakeholders and participants in the process." This new language implies a different stance toward power and the legitimacy of employees to voice their opinions during the change process.

(Continued)

(Continued)

- Change leaders need to be aware of the established psychological contract between the organization and its employees and to recognize that changes to the psychological contract need to be handled carefully.
- People usually respond emotionally to change directives, and leaders need to prepare themselves for the emotional upheaval, even though the need for change is often driven by rational factors.
- A present-day challenge is to make change the norm and encourage people to become change leaders or change implementers themselves. This capacity can be thought of as organizational agility and resilience.

It was 2003 and the women of Liberia changed their status and role from recipients of change to stakeholders in the national political process of their country. Charles Taylor, president of Liberia since 1997, controlled about one third of the country, and the Liberians United for Reconciliation and Democracy (LURD) and other rebel factions controlled the rest of the country. All groups were accused of a range of atrocities, from creating child soldiers and the raping of women and young girls to painful maiming of enemies. No one was safe, and many were starving and homeless. In these desperate circumstances, the women of Liberia united. Christian and Muslim women, rather than seeing their differences and continuing their exclusive affiliation with their own religious and ethnic rebels, recognized that a change in political party from Taylor's National Patriotic Front of Liberia (NPFL) to LURD would not change their lives since violence was the permanent and lasting legacy of all the fighting factions.

The women's political slogan became PEACE. They dressed in white and sat in the fields in the sun, the rain. At first they were ignored. Then their persistent presence was finally noted and President Taylor recognized the women as individuals who could no longer be dismissed. However, he did too little, too late. By the fall of 2003, Taylor was forced to resign and go into exile in Nigeria. (It should be noted that there were multiple forces, including but not limited to the Economic Community of West African States [ECOWAS], the United Nations, and the United States of America's government, that demanded Taylor's exile.) In 2005, Ellen Johnson-Sirleaf was elected president of Liberia with the support of the women's peace movement, Women of Liberia Mass Action for Peace. She took office in January 2006, and was reelected in 2011. She was awarded the Nobel Peace Prize in 2011, jointly with Leymah Gbowee of Liberia and Tawakkol Karman of Yeman, for their nonviolent initiatives to advance women's rights to safety and full participation in the peace process. India honored her in 2013 by awarding her the Indira Gandhi Peace Prize, and in 2014 *Forbes* listed her as the 70th most powerful woman in the world.[1]

This remarkable story is told eloquently in *Pray the Devil Back to Hell.*[2] From the perspective of change leaders, it is important to note that these Liberian women upended their status as recipients of change and violence, and established themselves as powerful stakeholders in the national political process. While most organizational change situations are not about physical violence, change leaders need to acknowledge that change can require people to modify their personal or professional identities, skill sets, and other deeply held beliefs and expectations. It is to legitimize these struggles of internal stakeholders that we use this language.

The reality of people's lives is that they are often on the receiving end of change, often called "the **recipients of change**." This chapter suggests how recipients of change may react and how change agents can incorporate this understanding to improve their change plans. The chapter deals with the reality of those who find themselves on the receiving end of change. It will consider different reactions to change: support or enthusiasm, mixed feelings or ambivalence, and opposition or **resistance to change**. While positive responses toward change are fairly common, depending upon the nature of the change and how it is introduced, the chapter focuses on people who are mixed or negative toward change. The chapter helps managers understand the phases people as recipients of change go through. As well, the chapter considers the factors that influence how people respond to change: their personalities, their coworkers or teams, and their leaders or managers. It recognizes that both the content (the what) of change and the process (the how) of change matter. Change leaders need to ensure that what they do is based on sound analysis and that the process of change (the how), allows for and encourages the involvement and input of others in both the assessment and implementation phases. Finally, this chapter looks at how change leaders can reduce the negative effects of change initiatives on recipients. Figure 7.1 summarizes the change model and highlights the key issues in dealing with recipients of change and influencing internal stakeholders.

Stakeholders Respond Variably to Change Initiatives

Not Everyone Sees Change as Negative

Many managers assume that resistance is inevitable in change situations. It is time to dispel this myth. Employees do not always react negatively and in many situations will react quite positively. Will they raise questions and experience a sense of uncertainty or ambivalence when change is introduced? Of course they will. They are thinking individuals, trying to make sense out of the change and its impact. This questioning often is perceived as resistance but is not necessarily change resistance. Often if resistance arises, it does so after people resolve their mixed feelings. If they conclude that the benefits to them clearly outweigh the costs, have high personal relevance, and are consistent with their attitudes and values, support for the change is highly likely.[3] As was noted in Chapter 6, negative reactions to change increase in frequency and intensity when people believe that the potential costs and consequences to them and the things they value outweigh the benefits.

A second myth that needs dispelling is the belief that age and resistance to change go hand in hand. Research shows that is not the case, and in a recent study

Figure 7.1 The Change Path Model

Awakening
Chapter 4
1. Identify a need for change and confirm the problems or opportunities that incite the need for change through collection of data.
2. Articulate the gap in performance between the present and the envisioned future state, and spread awareness of the data and the gap throughout the organization.
3. Develop a powerful vision for change.
4. Disseminate the vision for the change and why it's needed through multiple communication channels.

Mobilization
Chapters 5 through 8
1. Make sense of the desired change through formal systems and structures, and leverage those systems to reach the change vision (Chapter 5).
2. Assess power and cultural dynamics at play, and put them to work to better understand the dynamics and build coalitions and support to realize the change (Chapter 6).
3. **Communicate the need for change organization-wide and manage change recipients and various stakeholders as they react to and move the change forward (Chapter 7).**
4. Leverage change agent personality, knowledge, skills and abilities, and related assets (e.g., reputation and relationships) for the benefit of the change vision and its implementation (Chapter 8).

Acceleration
Chapter 9
1. Continue to systematically reach out to engage and empower others in support, planning, and implementation of the change. Help them develop needed new knowledge, skills, abilities, and ways of thinking that will support the change.
2. Use appropriate tools and techniques to build momentum, accelerate and consolidate progress.
3. Manage the transition, celebrating small wins and the achievement of milestones along the larger, more difficult path of change.

Institutionalization
Chapter 10
1. Track the change periodically and through multiple balanced measures to help assess what is needed, gauge progress toward the goal, and to make modifications as needed and mitigate risk.
2. Develop and deploy new structures, systems, processes and knowledge, skills, and abilities, as needed, to bring life to the change and new stability to the transformed organization.

age was found to be negatively related to resistance. In other words, resistance decreased as age increased.[4] To understand people's reaction to change, look well beyond their chronological age. The causes likely lie elsewhere.

Some researchers have suggested that "resistance to change" is a term that has lost its usefulness because it oversimplifies the matter and becomes a self-fulfilling prophecy. We agree. That is, if change leaders assume resistance will occur, it becomes more likely. Change leaders should focus on trying to understand why people react to the change as they do and how those reactions are likely to evolve over time.[5]

When changes are introduced, people often find themselves pulled in different directions. Family, friends, relatives, coworkers, and subordinates may hold divergent views concerning the proposed change, and organizational leaders and managers may deliver ambiguous or conflicting messages concerning its rationale and implications. If things become polarized around the change, people who have come to a decision may view those who are of a different opinion with suspicion and disapproval. All of these pressures can lead stakeholders to feel ambivalent about the change.

These mixed feelings can be magnified by concerns about the impact of the change on (a) their relationships with others, (b) their ability to do what is being asked of them, (c) the fit with their needs and values, and (d) their job security and future career prospects. These concerns are further intensified when people lack confidence that the change will produce the intended results. When employees see themselves as relatively powerless, a variety of less constructive coping responses, including avoidance, alienation, passivity, absenteeism, turnover, and sabotage may result.[6]

The perceptions of costs and benefits of change depend on what people are concerned about, what they have experienced in the past, and what they think they know. Sometimes relatively small changes will produce strong responses in one group due to the perceived consequences. In another group, more significant changes might produce mild reactions because of perceptions that the impact on them will not be significant or they are simply more comfortable with change.[7] Consider the reactions of employees of Desjardins Group to the selection and subsequent actions of their new CEO in 2008.

MONIQUE LEROUX AND CHANGE AT DESJARDINS

If cultural change in for-profit, publically traded organizations is difficult, consider the challenges inherent in doing so in a 100-plus-year-old financial services cooperative, made up of over 500 independent, affiliated member branches with strong rural roots, governed by over 6,000 elected officers in Quebec, Canada. Monique Leroux is a chartered accountant who was one of the first female partners at Ernst & Young and the senior Quebec VP for the Royal Bank of Canada before joining Desjardins in 2001. She became its CFO in 2004 and successfully ran for election as its CEO in 2008, being selected over several other candidates by the 256 voting members who represented the affiliated branches.

Her election surprised many. Desjardins was viewed as an "old boys club," and her earlier career experiences meant that she was still an outsider to many. However, her ability to articulate the challenges, constructively engage employees and members in conversations about what was needed, and her managerial

(Continued)

(Continued)

and leadership skills resonated. A majority of those voting believed she represented the best leadership option, given her skills and her commitment to Desjardins, its members, and its heritage. Leroux took office just prior to the financial crisis of 2008. She successfully helped the organization navigate the crisis and then undertake the significant changes needed to effectively compete in the financial services industry—one dominated by large, sophisticated, and successful firms in Canada.

Desjardins had a strong, customer-oriented culture and had been successful at attracting and retaining membership in its core rural communities, but the world of financial services was changing rapidly. Its Quebec membership was graying and the population was becoming more urban. Furthermore, the Quebec economy was not performing well and suffered from relatively high levels of unemployment. Leroux recognized that significant adaptations of their business model were needed if they were to continue to successfully serve their members, grow, and not become an anachronism. The organization operated in a fairly fragmented manner due to the independence of its member affiliates, and the lack of integration needed to be addressed if customers were to be served effectively and efficiently. This in turn required systems and processes to better integrate services, manage costs, and evolve their online presence and portfolio of services. Leroux based her campaign to be CEO on the need to develop the organization and its services in order to compete effectively, while staying true to their core values as a cooperative. She believed it was important to extend Desjardins' reach outside of Quebec, but they would first have to deal with needed changes to their internal structure, system, processes, and service offerings.

Soon after her appointment as CEO, the autonomous and close-knit culture of the Desjardins' network of independent branches and associated divisions came face to face with Leroux's approach to change. It was one grounded in the active engagement of members and employees in consultative processes, often through the use of teams. Consultation was followed by decision making, and between 2008 and 2012 this led to a flattening of the hierarchy, the successful restructuring and realignment of services and processes, and a reduction in the number of VPs from 250 to 112 and the number of senior VPs from 40 to 12. It also led to 1,000 job cuts. These waves of consultation and engagement also gave rise to initiatives related to new lines of business, staff and managerial development, diversification of the managerial and executive group, the establishment of separate groups outside the cooperative structure (e.g., business units targeting commercial markets) but owned by the cooperative, and a more performance-driven and customer-oriented approach to service delivery. To support these initiatives, Leroux actively built her management team so that it contained the diversity of perspectives, skills, and values needed to respond effectively to the challenges. The combination of restructuring and issues of individual fit or alignment with the new organization led to turnover in the executive and managerial ranks.

Leroux was well aware of the fact that employees and members had valid concerns for what these changes might do to their cooperative culture. She believed in the value of the cooperative movement, was committed to it, and

(Continued)

was very respectful of Desjardins' roots—as indicated by her approach to change which was characterized by the active engagement and involvement of others, rich communication of ideas and perspectives, and listening. However, once decisions were made and it was time to move to action, she actively promoted and reinforced the expected changes. Leroux is reported to have said, "I will not go for bitterness or backstabbing, and fights, and territorial management. You guys are responsible to make it happen and work as a team" (pg. 7, Harvard Business School case).

Leroux adopted an approach that allowed organizational members to see the need for change themselves and to actively participate in its development and implementation. Some had difficulty adjusting to the changes and the pace. Dissatisfaction, lower morale, and turnover were reported by managers in some divisions, particularly with those who had experienced title reductions or a disruption of work relationships they valued.

The changes pursued under Leroux's leadership were challenging for the recipients of change, but they have proven very successful. By 2012, Desjardins had moved into new markets and lines of business (e.g., payroll services, commercial and investment services, insurance), increased the number of employees from 17,000 to 45,000, increased their total assets from $152 billion to $190 billion, and increased their cash distributions or dividends to their 5.8 million members from $215 million in 2008 to $401 million to 5.6 million members by 2012. In terms of bank safety, they were rated number 3 in North America by Global Finance and were assessed as the 13th strongest bank in the world in 2013. They were rated highest in investor satisfaction for three years in a row when evaluated against other discount brokerage firms by J. D. Power, and were named one of Canada's 10 best companies to work for by the *Financial Post*. By 2014, they were underway with the expansion of their services outside of Quebec, as seen in their acquisition of the largest network of insurance brokers in Western Canada in 2010, the acquisition of Vancouver-based Qtrade Financial Group in 2013, and their 2013 opening of an office in Canada's financial heartland in downtown Toronto, Ontario.[8] They were also actively engaged in conversations with other financial services cooperatives in Canada and internationally, to explore ways they might be able to leverage one another's strengths and capacities.[9]

Leroux was elected to a second term in 2012, and under her leadership Desjardins has continued to experience steady progress on all fronts. In addition to being Desjardins' CEO and chair of its board, she sits on a number of other cooperative boards and advisory groups nationally and internationally, as well as several educational and not-for-profit advisory bodies. She is a member of the Order of Canada and the recipient of many other national and international honors that recognize her expertise, contributions, and commitment to the betterment of society.[10]

How employees perceive change will depend upon their assessment of the situation. If they see themselves *and* the organization benefiting from the change, they are more likely to embrace the change. If they see themselves as involved and participating in the initiative, they are more likely to be supportive.[11] If the outcomes are viewed as likely to be negative for the organization and the individuals, they will be unsupportive of the change. If their views are mixed, they will experience **ambivalence to the change**.[12]

The successes achieved at Desjardins under Leroux's leadership were due, in part, to her engagement of people in the renewal of the organization's services, systems, processes, and structures. Leroux was transparent when she brought the challenges to the employees, and worked hard to create a shared understanding of the need for change and to think through what change could look like. She used change tools such as stakeholder engagement, environmental and organizational analyses, participative teams, active communication through diverse channels, goal setting, and change teams, to bring needed changes to life and to help reinforce commitment to a renewed culture that was congruent with Desjardins' cooperative roots. Along the way, she succeeded in converting many skeptics and resistors into becoming partners in the change process.

The range of possible perceptions and responses is complex, as people assess the change against their interests, attitudes, and values. What Monique Leroux and her team were able to accomplish can be attributed to their engagement of both recipients of change and new recruits in helping to define the problem, design solutions, and implement them. This was aided by their use of hard data that all could understand; institutionalizing the change through projects, systems, and processes; and sustaining the change by creating a structure to promote collaboration and accountability. It was critical that the company's internal systems and processes catch up, and the proof of their success lies in the organization's improved financial performance and the growth of its capabilities and capacity to deliver.

However, even in the face of improved performance on multiple fronts, not all ambivalence concerning the changes disappeared, and pockets of resistance remained at Desjardins. A number of employees reported in 2011 that they were still concerned that the pace of change had been too fast and that too high a price had been paid in the form of the deterioration in employee morale and elevated levels of turnover in some areas.

Recipients' understanding and responses to the change will evolve over time as the change unfolds. As a result, the approaches used by change leaders will need to vary over the course of the change process. Whereas factual information delivered in a speech or a consultant's report may be useful when dealing with beliefs concerning the need for change and developing initial awareness, informal discussions and social support may be much more useful when ambivalence is stemming from conflicting emotions.[13] If downsizing or relocation is required, it will take more than the rational presentation of data or delivery of equitable relocation packages or early retirement provisions to alleviate distress. Often, executives have had months to consider the changes, and employees need time to adjust.

If resistance occurs, it may stem from those in middle and/or more senior roles, since they often have the most to lose, which happened at Desjardins. They may be seeking to maintain power and influence, sustain their capacity to perform, or avoid what they perceive to be a worsening of their position.[14] Change leaders need to be aware of this as they manage the situation. Finally, attribution errors may cause change leaders to fixate on individual resistance rather than probe more deeply for causal factors. For example, behavior that is being categorized as individual resistance may be due to misaligned structures and systems rather than individual opposition.[15] As well, many managers are predisposed to expect resistance in subordinates. Care needs to be taken that a self-fulfilling prophecy is not created.

Responding to Various Feelings in Stakeholders

Positive Feelings in Stakeholders: Channeling Their Energy

As noted earlier, many individuals welcome change. A change initiative can represent a chance for personal growth or promotion. Some people enjoy variety and seek opportunities to create. Others want the challenge of new situations. Still others imagine a change is needed to improve the situation. When people are feeling positive, engaged, informed, and hopeful, these emotions can be harnessed in support of the change.[16]

It is important, however, to anticipate the risks that may accompany the positive feelings in some stakeholders while others remain uncertain. Blind acceptance by some employees may lead to a lack of reflection in both them and others. Strong positive support of organizational initiatives from respected individuals may cause others to censor their doubts and give rise to the risk of groupthink. This potential tyranny of the minority or majority may lead to a stereotyping of those ambivalent to or opposing the change as "the enemy." This can lead to infighting rather than thoughtful analysis and the productive pursuit of organizational benefits.

Change leaders need to:

- channel the energy in positive ways, not letting the enthusiasm for change overwhelm legitimate concerns;
- "name" the problem of mixed feelings and the need to understand the different reactions to change;
- appoint highly respected, positively oriented stakeholders to chair significant committees or other change initiative structures, and ensure they have the skills and resources required to fill these roles in ways that don't stifle needed discussions and debate. Transparency, openness to learning, and the willingness to translate learning into practice will advance recipient openness to change; and
- manage the pace and remember that going too slow can dampen support for change with enthusiasts, while going too fast will create anxiety in those who are doubtful and fatigue.

Ambivalent Feelings in Stakeholders: They Can Be Useful[17]

It comes as no surprise that employees are likely to have mixed feelings about change, as it often gives rise to perceptions of increased complexity, uncertainty, higher risk, and the disruption of agreed-to work responsibilities and relationships. People's beliefs about a change and its potential impact can be both positive and negative and can vary in intensity. To illustrate this, consider the example of an industrial paint manufacturer that changed how it handled its major customers by moving key technical service representatives from the head office to the customers' plants. The change provided staff with desired opportunities for increased responsibility, autonomy, and pay, but it required their relocation to a new workplace and the disruption of their cohesive work group. Naturally, their feelings were mixed. Some were excited and others anxious about their new responsibilities. Some were sad about leaving close friends behind.[18] This also created change in role definition, as the new duties required service representatives to play a much more active client-management role. These were activities that customer service representatives had viewed as belonging to sales personnel.

When ambivalence is prevalent, change leaders should create conditions that will increase the likelihood that people will voice concerns. They need to create an environment that welcomes feedback. Piderit states that people are more likely to speak up when the ambivalence stems from conflicting beliefs. When conflicting emotions are involved, though, she notes that individuals often have more difficulty giving voice to negative emotional responses. She hypothesizes that "they would be more likely to wrestle with their ambivalence alone or to avoid the subject entirely."[19]

Ambivalence generates discomfort for people, causing them to seek resolution of the feeling. Once this resolution occurs, subsequent changes to attitudes become more difficult. People protect their attitudes by employing a variety of strategies:

- turn to habits and approaches that have served them well in the past.[20]
- engage in selective perception (actively seeking out confirming information and avoiding disconfirming data).[21]
- selectively recall (being more likely to remember attitude-consistent rather than inconsistent data).[22]
- Deny in the form of counterarguments geared to support and strengthen one's position.[23]

More extreme defensive responses can include sarcasm, anger, aggression, and withdrawal. Since attitudes become much more difficult to change once they solidify, there is all the more reason to invest the time needed at the front end of the change in order to effectively process people's reactions to change.

Rather than interpreting mixed feelings as resistance, change leaders are better served by:

- focusing on helping people make sense of the proposed changes;
- listening for information that may be helpful in achieving the change;

- constructively reconciling their ambivalence; and
- sorting out what actions are now needed.

It is almost always in the best interest of change agents to actively engage people in meaningful discussions early in the change process and help to align their interpretations with the process.[24] Employees' input can prove invaluable in identifying potential problems and risk points.[25] Their engagement and involvement can allow concerns to be addressed.[26] Meaningful engagement can increase the likelihood of the formation of supportive attitudes toward the change and perceptions of fairness as they attempt to make sense of what they are being asked to do.[27] Desjardins' organizational change was effective due to the adoption of approaches such as these, by highly skilled and respected change champions.

Balogun and Johnson note that once the blueprint for more complex change is set out, it is brought to life through the interpretations and responses of employees. As a result, these authors argue that "managing change is less about directing and controlling and more about facilitating recipients' sense-making processes to achieve an alignment of interpretation."[28] As this evolves, so too does the change that subsequently unfolds. All this points to the importance of employee perceptions of organizational support for what lies ahead. When they feel this is present, perceptions of uncertainty are reduced because they have a greater sense that they know what is going on and that support will be available, if and when they need it. As a result, adaptability increases, and job satisfaction and performance rise relative to what is seen when such support is lacking. In essence, recipients have a clearer sense that they know what is going on; someone has their "back"; there is open, supportive communication to sort through matters as they arise; and that there are reasons for hope concerning what lies ahead.[29]

Negative Reactions to Change by Stakeholders: These Too Can Be Useful

Change leaders undertake an initiative because they believe the benefits outweigh the costs. However, anticipate that stakeholders may have a range of different perspectives, from feeling imposed upon and unprepared, to perceiving the change is ill advised and/or poorly designed and likely to fail, to feeling anger and rage. Table 7.1 outlines the causes of negative reactions to change.

Concerns and negative reactions toward change develop for a variety of reasons:

- *Perception of negative consequences of the change may be a reality.* The change may be fundamentally incongruent with things the people deeply value about their jobs (e.g., autonomy, significance, feedback, identity, and variety[30]) or the workplace (e.g., pay, job security). The loss of work is likely the most extreme form of this. When significant job losses are involved, such as when the major employer in a town decides its plant needs to be closed for the good of the corporation, the costs are all too real for the recipients. In such situations, it is difficult,

---

Table 7.1 Causes of Negative Reactions to Change

1. Negative consequences appear to outweigh the benefits.

2. The communication process is flawed, leading to confusion and doubt.

3. There is concern that the change has been ill conceived, insufficiently tested, or may have adverse consequences that are not anticipated.

4. The recipients lack experience with change and its implications or have habituated approaches that they rely upon and remain committed to.

5. The recipients have had prior negative experience with a similar change.

6. The recipients have had prior negative experience with those advocating the change.

7. The negative reactions of peers, subordinates, and/or supervisors whom you trust and respect and with whom you will have to work in the future influence your views.

8. The change process is seen to be lacking procedural justice and/or distributive justice and breaching the recipient's sense of their employment contract.

9. The recipients fear that they don't have the necessary skills and competencies to perform well after the change has been implemented.

---

if not impossible, for people to see positive consequences ensuing from the change.[31] The closing of the Fishery Products International plant provides an example of employment loss.

JOB LOSS AT FISHERY PRODUCTS INTERNATIONAL

The 2008 closing of the Fishery Products International (FPI) processing plant in Harbour Breton, Newfoundland, is "devastating," says Earle McCurdy, president of the Fish, Food and Allied Workers Union. "This closing has put 350 people out of work in a community of 2,100. You don't have to be a Ph.D. to determine the size of the impact," he says. "And it's not only Harbour Breton; it's the entire peninsula."

FPI officials blame the closing on an independent report that claims "the plant has major structural problems and is no longer safe for occupancy." However, FPI spokesman Russ Carrigan released a statement saying, "The entry of China into the market for headed and gutted cod has driven the commodity price up dramatically—well beyond the point of our commercial viability."[32]

In this example, recipients would have difficulty accepting the corporate perspective on the need for change.

- *Communication processes may be flawed*, and people may be left feeling ill informed or misled.[33] Support for management is less likely when people feel they lack the information they need to make an informed judgment or lack the supervisory support needed to successfully follow through on the proposed course of action. The prospects for support diminish further and faster when employees feel that information has been intentionally and arbitrarily withheld or manipulated. In our FPI example, there appears to be confusion over the reasons for the closure. Is it the structural problems or the entry of Chinese competition to the marketplace?

- *People may have serious doubts about the impact and effectiveness of the change.* They may be concerned that the change initiative has not been sufficiently studied and tested, or they may believe that the change will have adverse consequences that have not been thought through.[34] For example, a move by a head office to consolidate warehouse operations and trim inventory levels may be seen as a surefire way to increase efficiency, but it could cause serious concerns in sales and marketing about the firm's ability to effectively service its customers.

- *People may lack experience with change and be unsure about its implications or their capacity to adjust.* When conditions in an organization have been stable for long periods, even modest changes can seem threatening. During extended periods of stability, people tend to develop well-engrained habits, and the patterned behavior can result in negative reactions to change. Habituated approaches represent strategies that we believe have served us well in the past and that we are often not even conscious of. The Desjardins example earlier in the chapter demonstrated this, as the culture of the independent branches prior to 2008 had resulted in issues of service fragmentation and inefficiency and insufficient awareness that this was a pressing issue that needed to be dealt with.

- *People may have had negative experiences with change initiatives or approaches that seem similar to the one being advocated.* To use an old adage, once burned, twice shy. If stakeholders have learned that change initiatives lead to layoffs or that the initiatives begin with great fanfare but are never completed, people will be more negative. They have learned that they should be skeptical about change and its consequences.[35]

- *They may have had a negative experience with those advocating the change.* They may mistrust the judgment of those promoting the change, their ability to deliver on promises, their access to resources, their implementation skills, or their integrity.

- *People may be influenced by the negative reactions of peers, subordinates, or supervisors* whom they trust and respect and/or whom they have to work with in the future. These opinion leaders can have a significant impact.

- *Last but not least, there may be justice-related concerns.* People may see the process as lacking in procedural justice (i.e., was the process fair; did people have an opportunity to question change leaders, voice opinions, and suggest options). For example, an absence of participation and involvement may leave employees feeling ignored and relatively powerless.[36] In addition to concerns about procedural fairness and the trustworthiness of leaders,[37] they may also believe that distributive justice was lacking (i.e., the final decision was fundamentally unfair).[38] Matters related to this will be discussed in the section in this chapter dealing with the psychological contract the recipients feel they have, involving their working relationship.

When things do not unfold as planned, resistance is often flagged as the cause. Rather than assess the situation carefully and objectively, managers responsible for change are quick to lay the blame at the feet of those thought to be acting as obstacles.[39] The dynamics of this likely increases resistance as each blames the other and tensions rise. When managers and employees point fingers at each other as the cause of change difficulties, the focus is not on advancing the agenda for change. The key question is not who is to blame, but rather what is happening, why is it happening, and what does this tell us about what we should do now?

Kotter notes that impediments to change are much more likely to come from problems related to the misalignment of structures and systems than from individuals engaged in resistance.[40] For example, if existing systems continue to reward competitive behavior, why would you expect employees to behave in a cooperative manner?[41] Likewise, if critical information or resources are not available, how can individuals implement the change program? Change leaders need to be aware of the tendency to focus on individuals and not the roles that the existing structures, systems, and processes may be playing in impeding progress and influencing people's reaction to the initiative.

For successful change management and implementation, there needs to be engagement and open conversation, especially in the face of resistance. Such communications can create a shared understanding of different perspectives, and have the potential to be a valuable resource when approached constructively, by identifying new ways of thinking about the situation and possible paths forward.[42] Alignment also needs to exist between what is communicated and the systems and structures of the organization. When the change leader asks you to do "A," but other systems and structures tell you that "B" is what you should do, one should expect ambivalence and/or resistance until issues of alignment are addressed. If resistance is based on different definitions of the issues, then leaders need to return to the framing and analysis of the underlying problems and attempt to resolve the differences. If the resistance is based on differing views of the consequences, the reasons need to be understood and change plans modified if appropriate.

Make the Change of the Psychological Contract Explicit and Transparent

The organizational context plays a role in determining reactions of people to change. The **psychological contract** that people have with the organization can be a critical contextual variable.[43] The psychological contract represents the sum of the implicit and explicit agreements we believe we have with our organization. It defines our perceptions of the terms of our employment relationship and includes our expectations for ourselves and for the organization, including organizational norms, rights, rewards, and obligations. As such, they both influence and are influenced by the culture of the organization.[44]

Much of the psychological contract is implicit. Because of this, change initiators may be unaware of it when they alter existing arrangements. In effect, leaders often don't recognize the impact such changes may have on the psychological contract. They fail to realize that employees may have a very different view than they do of what constitutes "their deal," their employment contract, including what they have a right to expect and what is fair and equitable. The perceptions of sudden and arbitrary changes to the psychological contract of employees can lead to trouble.

While most people recognize that psychological contracts will have to adapt to changing conditions, they don't react well to surprises and unilateral actions that fail to consider their input or that of their representatives. Changes that threaten our sense of security and control will produce a loss of trust, fear, resentment, and/or anger.[45] People need to devote time and effort to absorbing the change and its implications. Even unilateral changes that will have a positive impact on employees may be resisted because of factors such as suspicion over the "real agenda" and concerns about a reduced sense of control or the capacity to perform.

When dealing with psychological contracts, remember that they do not exist in a vacuum. Changes to one person's contract can have an impact on the psychological contracts of others, including the managers involved and the change leaders themselves. Effectively managing the interpersonal as well as personal dynamics when dealing with changes to psychological contracts represent important work that change leaders need to address.[46]

Ideas related to supervisory support, communications, and issues of fairness that have been discussed earlier will assist change leaders in dealing with the impact of the change on the psychological contract. Dmitriy Nesterkin argues that negative emotions and resistance to changes in the contract are reduced "by implementing and sustaining socially supportive and interpersonally just organizational environment, led by an emotionally intelligent management staff (p. 573).[47] This includes following through and delivering on both the transactional commitments related to the change, as well as the relational elements of the contract.[48]

THE WASHINGTON SUBURBAN SANITARY COMMISSION

In 2002, Washington Suburban Sanitary Commissions (WSSC) new general manager, John Griffin, was brought in to implement change given the threat of privatization that the organization faced. As an outsider hired into this role, he engaged in open and honest communication immediately, asking questions and being transparent with all stakeholders. Griffin led the organizational change with structural reorganization. As a manager working closely with Griffin, Steve Gerwin told his employees: "Don't worry, when the change comes, there will be a job for you and even a better one than you have now. But if you think the job you used to have is going to be there, you're wrong."[49]

Gerwin explicitly communicated that there was going to be a significant change in the psychological contract. "If you want to come to work and read the newspaper, talk to your friends and fill up space and get your paycheck, that job is gone. But if you want a challenge and something to do, there may be an opportunity there." He used language the people could understand and remember: They could not have their old jobs after the reorganization, but they could have a challenging job.[50]

Predictable Stages in the Reaction to Change

Change is inevitable—growth is optional

—from a bumper sticker

Change can be thought of as occurring in three phases: before the change, during the change, and at the end of the change. The **stages in the reaction to change** typically begin in advance of the actual change initiative as individuals worry about what will happen and what their personal consequences will be. The reaction can continue until long after the change initiative has been completed as people work through the feelings created by the change. When experiencing traumatic changes and transitions, people tend to go through a predictable sequence of stages similar to those outlined by Elizabeth Kübler-Ross in her work on grieving.[51] The model suggests that emotionally healthy people will work through issues until they accept the change. From a change agent's perspective, this is sometimes referred to as helping others work through the "valley of despair." Table 7.2 integrates her insights with those of Fink,[52] Jick,[53] and Perlman and Takacs.[54]

Before the change: People who are anticipating significant change may experience pre-change anxiety. At this stage, people think something is in the wind, but they don't know exactly what it is or how it will show itself. Uncertainty escalates and people often find themselves agonizing over the impact it could have on them as well as its impact on others. For many, the anticipation phase can be debilitating. In their desire to reduce uncertainty and anxiety, many will search for signs of what might be on the horizon. Rumors may abound. Others will deny the signs and signals of change, finding it too threatening to think about. During this phase, the organizational rumor mill often moves into high gear and increases anxiety levels. The confusion and uncertainty created often continue long after the change has been announced and may be coupled with fear, anger, alienation, defensiveness, and a variety of other responses that have strong attitudinal and performance implications. Ambivalent feelings described earlier are often generated at this point and are evident in comments and actions. As noted earlier in this chapter, people are more likely to speak up when the mixed emotions stem from conflicting beliefs. When conflicting emotions are involved, though, individuals often have more difficulty giving voice to negative emotional responses.[55]

Once change is announced: Even though people know that change is coming, many still experience shock when it actually arrives. Individuals at this stage may feel overwhelmed by events to the point of immobilization. Some people will engage in defensive retreat, holding onto the past and experiencing anger over the

Table 7.2 Stages of Reactions to Change

Before the Change	During the Change	After the Change
Anticipation and anxiety phase	Shock, denial, and retreat phase	Acceptance phase
Issues: Coping with uncertainty and rumors about what may or may not happen	Issues: Coping with the change announcement and associated fallout; coping with uncertainty and rumors; reacting to the new "reality"	Issues: Putting residual traumatic effects of change behind you, acknowledging the change, achieving closure, and moving on to new beginnings—adaptation and change
1. Pre-change anxiety—Worrying about what might happen, confusion, and perhaps significant denial of what change is needed or likely	2. Shock—Perceived threat, immobilization, no risk taking 3. Defensive retreat—Anger, rejection and denial, compliance; sense of loss, risk taking unsafe 4. Bargaining 5. Depression and guilt, alienation	6. Acknowledgment—Resignation, mourning, letting go, energy for risk taking begins to build 7. Adaptation and change—Comfort with change, greater openness and readiness, growing potential for risk taking

changes. Insecurity and a sense of loss and unfairness are common reactions. People will often try to avoid dealing with the real issues and try to reduce their risk by lowering their exposure and relying on habituated responses that have worked in the past. The sense of betrayal will be strongest for those who placed their greatest trust in the firm and who feel their psychological contract with the organization has been violated. Their trust in the leadership will typically decline. Some individuals may agree outwardly, announcing their willingness to cooperate ("We're behind you all the way!"), only to act in a noncompliant manner when they are out of sight of those advocating the change. This behavior can sometimes extend to sabotage. Some people will engage in bargaining behavior, negotiating to make the change go away or to minimize its negative impact on them. Depression and guilt, stress and fatigue, and reduced risk taking and motivation have been regularly reported to follow such unsuccessful attempts to reverse the tide. Alienation can result.

At the end: Finally, people begin to accept the change and acknowledge what they have lost. They begin to let go of the past and start to behave in more constructive ways. At this point, they can again take risks—not those associated with getting even, but rather those associated with liberation from the past and moving on. As risks are rewarded with success, confidence builds in the change. During the adaptation and change stage, people become more comfortable with or accepting of the change, internalize it, and move on.

People need to work their way through their reactions to the change phases in a systematic fashion to avoid becoming stalled. The same is true for the change process itself, which needs to happen in the appropriate order, according to Kotter. As the subtitle of his article *Leading Change: Why Transformation Efforts Fail* says, "Leaders who successfully transform businesses do eight things right (and they do them in the right order)." This order is as follows: establishing a sense of urgency, forming a change team, creating a vision for change, communicating the vision of change, empowering others to act, planning for and creating short-term wins, consolidating wins to reinvigorate the process, and institutionalizing the change. Skipping steps, Kotter says, only creates an illusion of speed and never produces a satisfying result.[56] Both what you do and how you do it are important. See **Toolkit Exercise 7.2** to think about the phases of change.

Even when people recognize the need for difficult decisions, they may have difficulty emotionally accepting and adapting to the consequences of change decisions.[57] This emotional distress can be true regardless of the consequences. For example, even those who are retained after organizational downsizing will experience emotional upset. The **survivor syndrome** is a term that refers to the reaction of those who survive a poorly handled, traumatic change such as a downsizing.[58] Survivor syndrome effects include lower levels of job satisfaction, motivation, and organizational loyalty; greater stress; greater ambiguity; vulnerability about one's future position; a sense of entrapment in a negative situation; and guilt about being retained while others have been let go.[59] To avoid some of the traps related to the survivor syndrome, individuals remaining with the organization need to understand the reasons for the decisions, feel people have been fairly dealt with, and that there are solid reasons for hope in the future of the organization and its positive implications for them.

As Jick and Peiperl point out, the sequence described in Table 7.2 provides a prescriptive, optimistic, and simplistic view of how individuals adjust to disruptive change.[60] Some will move through the stages quickly, others will move more slowly, some will get stuck, and some will move more quickly than they should, taking unresolved issues with them. As an example, consider the actions of a senior executive who lost his job as the result of a merger. During the eight months it took him to find a new position, he focused on maintaining a very positive attitude. Friends marveled at his resilience, though some questioned whether he was living in denial. Upon joining a new firm as a vice president, he became increasingly critical and bitter about his new employer. His hostility had little to do with the organization he had joined or his new position. It was unresolved anger and other baggage related to his earlier dismissal. His inability to recognize and deal with this ultimately cost him the new position.[61] When individuals get "stuck" in the early and middle stages, extricating themselves can prove very difficult.

Individual reactions to organizational change will be related to perceptions of the potential outcomes, and most changes will not be as severe and disruptive as those envisioned above. In the next section, the chapter explores three specific factors that have an influence on how people adapt to change:

- personality and experience with the rate of change
- the reactions of coworkers and teammates
- experience with and trust in leaders

See **Toolkit Exercise 7.3** to consider your personal reactions to a change situation.

Stakeholders' Personalities Influence Their Reactions to Change

Some individuals (innovators, early adopters, or members of the early majority) are generally more predisposed to change (see our discussion in Chapter 6). Others tend to review carefully the experience of others and commit later in the process (the late majority and late adopters). Finally, there are those who resist adopting change until the bitter end.[62] These **predispositions to change** are influenced by individual factors such as susceptibility to the social influence of others, tolerance for risk and ambiguity, and self-image (e.g., innovator versus cautious adopter). See **Toolkit Exercise 7.4** to think about your natural predisposition to change.

As the above suggests, individuals' perceptions of the change experience and the risk of change will be influenced by their personalities.[63] People who have a low **tolerance for turbulence and ambiguity** tend to be most comfortable in stable environments.[64] As the rate of change accelerates, they will experience increased stress as they attempt to cope and adjust. At low to moderate levels, though, this increased stress may also lead to increased job satisfaction if people experience success with change. However, when change comes to be seen as increasingly disruptive or radical, the resulting stress and strain will tend to produce increasingly elevated levels of anxiety and fear, defensiveness, fatigue, and ultimately hopelessness, alienation, and resignation. Levels of absenteeism and turnover, errors and accidents, and depressed levels of work satisfaction are commonly observed to escalate as such stressors rise.[65]

People who have a high tolerance for turbulence and uncertainty will find stable and unchanging environments unsatisfying after a period of time. When they find novelty and challenge lacking, concerns grow that their careers have stalled,[66] and they experience increasing levels of boredom, frustration, absenteeism, and turnover.[67] As the rate of change increases to moderate levels, so will their levels of satisfaction and interest, particularly if they become directly engaged with the change initiative. As the rate of change and the accompanying levels of turbulence and uncertainty intensifies to levels that are outside their comfort zones, effects similar to those seen in low-tolerance individuals are observed, although the effects occur later at higher rates of change (see Figure 7.2).

Take a few moments to revisit the question of how you react to change and reflect on your experience. What is your predisposition to accept change? You can also use this to help understand your stakeholders (see **Toolkit Exercise 7.5**).

Prior Experience Impacts a Person's and Organization's Perspective on Change

Previous experience with change will affect a person's view and behavior. Long periods of stability and minimal change will lead to people seeing change as more unsettling and risky than those with somewhat more frequent encounters with change.[68] Even those who are thinking "thank goodness, we're finally doing something!" may at first experience elevated levels of perceived risk and stress from exposure to even moderate levels of change.

A sustained period of continued success with a particular strategy can cause individuals and organizations to become trapped by those strategies and tactics that have served them well. The tendency to rely on competencies and strategies that have worked in the past is referred to as a **competency or a complacency trap**.[69] Faced with the need for change, they rely on those approaches that have worked well in the past, even though the old strategies are no longer effective because they are no longer well aligned with their environment. Breaking out of these traps is not easy.

If organizations and their employees have adapted successfully to ongoing experiences with moderate levels of change, then those employees are likely to be more open and flexible. The organization's change "muscles" are toned. Those who have regular, ongoing exposure to moderate amounts of positive change (e.g., through continuous improvement) tend to find change to be less unsettling and hence less risky because they become accustomed to believing that tomorrow will likely be different from today and that this is not something to be avoided.[70]

However, when organizations and employees live in an environment with extended periods of major upheavals and uncertainty, the sense of personal risk escalates and remains high. Under these conditions, employees may become exhausted and feel increasingly vulnerable to the next wave of change. They become jaded and alienated if earlier promises and hopes for improvement have gone unmet. Those who have not exited the firm may resign themselves to adopting a strategy of keeping their heads down to avoid personal risk. Under these extreme conditions, the perceived risk attached to a particular change initiative may actually diminish. Like those in danger of being swept overboard in a storm, individuals may be prepared to grasp onto any plausible change initiative that looks like it could serve as a lifeline, unless their alienation is such that they have effectively given up.

Figure 7.2 depicts a hypothetical connection between past rates of change experienced by people in an organization and the degree of perceived risk with an anticipated change. It illustrates the adaptability and resilience that individuals exhibit as a result of their experience with the previous rates and types of change within an organization. For example, if people have experienced long periods of minimal change, they will likely perceive higher risks with the proposed change. The perceived risk of the proposed change declines if there has been a moderate rate of change within the organization and a general normalization and level of comfort associated with past changes. As the normal rate of change increases in intensity and/or becomes drawn out, the perception of risk associated with the new change begins to rise again. When the rate and level of intensity of change reach a certain point, those involved will be ready to grasp at anything with the potential of offering a way out (see drop-off line in Figure 7.2). This pattern can be seen when participants recognize that the organization is in a crisis state, and they become unfrozen and ready to change. In a crisis situation, one can expect initial defensiveness followed by openness to change if a viable path forward can be offered.[71]

As has been discussed, both personality and past experiences with change affect how people view proposed changes. Table 7.3 outlines the hypothesized interactions between an individual's need for change, tolerance for ambiguity, and the frequency and magnitude of the change experience.

Coworkers Influence Stakeholders' Views

Our views of change are also influenced by the comments and actions of those around us—particularly those whose opinions and relationships we value (see Table 7.4). Trusted mentors, managers, and friends can be particularly influential. If those we trust are positively predisposed toward a change initiative, we may be influenced in that direction. Similarly, if they are experiencing serious concerns about the change or are opposed to it, they will influence us to consider factors that may move us in the opposite direction.[72]

Consider, for example, the reactions of the immediate supervisor who is on the firing line when it comes to implementing change. Have they been involved in

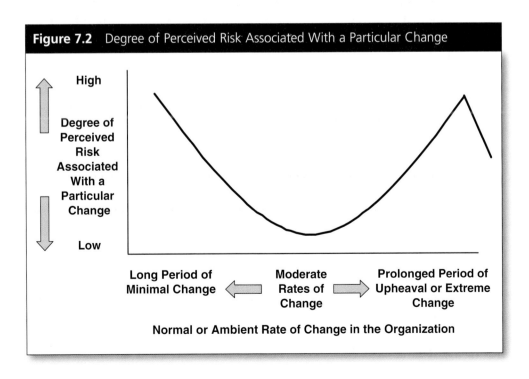

Figure 7.2 Degree of Perceived Risk Associated With a Particular Change

Table 7.3 The Interaction of Personality With the Experience of Change

Individual Difference	Change Experience			
	Low	**Some**	**Frequent**	**Chaotic**
	No change experience for an extended period, a belief that this job will last indefinitely	Some change experience that demonstrates both the difficulties and survivability of change	Frequent change experience, nothing static, major upheavals and uncertainty	Chaotic environment characterized by temporary systems, fluid environments, and constant change
Individuals who have higher tolerance for ambiguity, novelty, and change	Restlessness; boredom, attempts to create change or to disrupt routines	Grappling with change issues; feelings of invigoration and new meaning in the job, expectation of improvement	Stress showing, coping strategies being developed, energy still present but fatigue starting, voicing of concerns; the desire to exit increases	Stress effects, fear, and fatigue as they attempt to cope; voicing of concerns exists, but the likelihood of resignation, alienation rises; and/or a willingness to grasp onto a plausible course of action as a way to reduce the chaos
Individuals who have a lower tolerance for ambiguity, novelty, and change	Acceptance of the situation, buy-in to the steady state, no preparation or anticipation of change	Stress effects present, concerns voiced, but a willingness to adjust to moderate amount of change present	Significant coping difficulties; stress effects, including fear, fatigue, and alienation often present; increased willingness to grasp on to a plausible course of action to reduce the chaos	Severe coping difficulties and resultant stress and strain, alienation, resignation and/or exit at high levels and/or elevated willingness to grasp at plausible courses of action to reduce the chaos

developing the change and/or do they feel fully informed about the need for and nature of the change, and its implications? Do they feel that they have been listened to? Research shows that supervisors/managers have a significant influence on how the change is perceived and reacted to by their direct reports. It comes as no surprise to find that managers who are more committed to the change are more likely to generate more positive responses to the change in those who report to them.[73] Yet all too often, frontline managers report that they found out about the change at the same time as their direct reports. They see themselves as being expected to explain and voice support for the change but feel ill-informed about it and excluded from the process until the very end. Ignoring them is a mistake to be avoided. Engaging them as valued contributors to the change process increases the likelihood that they will communicate support for the change with those they influence, and constructively participate in its implementation.[74]

Coworkers and work groups play a critical role in how people sort out their own reactions to change, because these individuals live in a similar organizational world and their relationships are bound together by norms, roles, and shared obligations and experiences. When coworkers are ambivalent on the desirability of a particular change, one can expect to see **skepticism** in others as they sort out their own feelings about the matter. The importance of coworkers' reactions increases as the strength of relational ties rises. The more coworkers see themselves as part of a cohesive team, the greater will be their influence.[75] Even groups that seem to be in conflict will often become cohesive and turn on the "outsider" who is seen to be threatening group members. Change leaders who ignore cohesion, norms, and varying levels of ambivalence do so at their own peril.

Table 7.4 Impact of Trusted Peers on Recipients		
Opinions of Those Trusted by Recipients	**Recipients' Initial Attitude to the Change**	**Possible Implications on the Attitude of the Recipients**
Positive toward the change	Positive toward the change	Very motivated to support and predisposed to get involved
	Negative toward the change	Opposed to the change but potentially open to other perspectives because of new information and peer pressure
Negative toward the change	Positive toward the change	Support of the change may become more tempered due to information and the perspectives offered by trusted peers. Will often experience pressure to reconsider their support or perhaps be silenced by peer pressure
	Negative toward the change	Opposed to the change and reinforced in those views by trusted peers and the peer group

Feelings About Change Leaders Make a Difference

How employees view and react to change is influenced by their perceptions of the change leaders. If people believe their perspectives and interests are recognized and they trust these leaders, then they are likely to respond positively to the suggestions for change.

When change leaders talk about significant change, they often focus on the rationale, including the costs and benefits of changing. They may pay some attention to the costs of *not* changing, but usually little focus is given to the benefits of the status quo. Followers, on the other hand, assessing change at a personal level, will often reflect on the benefits of not changing and discount the costs of staying with the status quo. The followers may prefer the devil they know to the unknown one. They can estimate, and sometimes inflate, the costs of changing but may feel far less certain about the benefits. As a result, change leaders and followers' estimates of the benefits and costs can differ dramatically.

If change leaders recognize and deal with the issues factually, constructively, and sensitively, they will help people interpret the context in a more predictable manner and concerns can be brought to the surface and addressed.[76] From a procedural justice and a personal efficacy point of view, people want their voices to be heard, even if it doesn't result in a change in the decision. In 1998, when the president of Continental Airways told employees that he was closing their airport's operations, his candor, combined with his positive reputation as a leader, resulted in an acceptance of the change.

CANDOR AT CONTINENTAL AIRWAYS

I met with the employees and their families—about 600 people in all. Along with explaining the details of the closing and relocation plans (the company had doubled the financial aspects of the relocation package over what was required by the contract), I also shared with them my vision for Continental and how far we had come. I then opened the floor to questions and answers.

For about five minutes, employees expressed appreciation that I had personally come to give them the news and had developed a financial package to meet their needs. But then the pilots walked in—in full uniform—with their families. They surrounded the room and refused to sit down. A pilot came to the microphone to express how incompetent he felt management was and how Continental was once again making the wrong decision. The rest of the pilots applauded.

Do you know what happened? The rest of the employees, led by a baggage handler who was also being relocated, stood up and defended me, one after another, for 20 minutes. They told the pilots that they should feel lucky that Continental finally had a senior management team that treated them with enough respect to deliver the bad news—as well as the good relocation package—in person. I left to a standing ovation.[77]

How change leaders handle the perceptions and the alterations to the psychological contract will matter to employees. The president of Continental was more successful in managing the shift in psychological contract with the ground employees than with the pilots. Perceptions of his promises may have been influenced by the employees' views that they were being treated reasonably under the circumstances—procedural and distributive justice was upheld.[78] The fact that he was personally present to deliver the news also mattered. People react positively to courage, empathy, honesty, and sound logic and these are better conveyed in person than when they are relegated to talking points or a report. When people feel steamrollered by the pressure exerted on them rather than reasonably engaged, resistance may go underground and resurface at a later date in the form of resentment for the change leader.[79]

Integrity Is One Antidote to Skepticism and Cynicism

Some people believe change leaders when they promise a bright future or state that there is no alternative except what is offered. However, others are more skeptical—often for good reasons. Followers may believe that the promises are suspect, particularly if the leader is relatively unknown or untested. If followers have received promises before and found them wanting, then people will be skeptical. Followers sometimes report that change leaders have said the right things but acted in ways that advanced their own self-interest, ignoring what was good for most employees and the organization. That was the concern about Thorsten Heins (CEO, BlackBerry) that was voiced quietly at first, when people read about his compensation arrangements in required public disclosures. It was voiced much more loudly when he departed BlackBerry with a $22 million severance after less than two years of rapidly deteriorating performance and the unsuccessful sale of the firm.[80]

Skepticism can shift to **cynicism** (a real loss of faith) and heightened pessimism when people whose opinions we value share a similar negative belief.[81] The consequences of such cynicism include reduced satisfaction, reduced organizational commitment, and less motivation to work hard. It results in an increase in accidents and errors, a lessened desire and will to engage in future change initiatives, and decreased leader credibility. As Reichers, Wanous, and Austin say, "People do not deliberately become cynical, pessimistic and blaming. Rather these attitudes result from experience, and are sustained because they serve useful purposes. Cynicism persists because it is selectively validated by the organization's mixed record of successful change, and by other people in the organization who hold and express similar views."[82]

The perceived trustworthiness and integrity of the change leader play important roles in the judgments made by the recipients. When change leaders are viewed as credible and trustworthy, their vision of the future reduces the sense of uncertainty and risk and increases the sense of hope in recipients as they put their faith in the leader's judgment. People often turn to credible leaders and colleagues to help them absorb uncertainty and make sense of confusion.[83] Leader efforts to actively involve recipients in the change initiative further reduce the chances of cynicism developing.[84]

Periods of transition represent a time when the ethical and reputational risks for leaders are particularly high. The "best course of action" is far from clear. Offering hope and direction without misleading or overstating the case is the narrow path that change leaders must navigate. As one CEO noted, the difference between a visionary leader and a huckster is the thin edge that is integrity.[85]

Avoiding Coercion But Pushing Hard: The Sweet Spot?

Change leaders may find that they have to resort to the use of coercion. Kramer argues that under certain circumstances, intimidating leaders apply their political intelligence to creatively push followers to higher levels of performance than would otherwise have been achieved.[86] Importantly, Kramer specifically notes that while such individuals are tough and demanding, they are not simply bullies. Their initial coercion is to unfreeze the situation and achieve initial shifts in position. However, leaders who rely primarily on the application of fear and force to gain commitment to change are taking significant risks.[87] While it may be true that "if you have them by their throats, their hearts and minds will follow,"[88] any release of the throat risks resistance and revolt. Effective change must be about more than the leader's power.

Monique Leroux at Desjardins challenged the employees, but she did so with a mix of encouragement, active engagement, occasional ultimatums around unacceptable behavior, staff changes and dismissals when necessary, and modeling the desired change through her own behavior. She used metrics and other information to make the business challenges visible to everyone in ways they could understand and relate back to their work and the company they were committed to. The use of such information was not only to help senior management understand the business, the underlying problems, the paths forward, and progress along the way; the metrics and related information and stories had a psychological effect with the broader organization as well, increasing employee awareness of what they were working toward and why it was important.

At times, employees respond to leaders out of fear of what will happen if they don't comply. While fear can motivate, leaders who rely primarily on fear or coercion are following a risky path—both ethically and pragmatically (i.e., will the support be there when the stick or threat is no longer present).[89] In his book *From Good to Great*, Collins refers to this "doom loop" as the enemy of effective leadership.[90]

Leaders, frustrated by a lack of progress, are attracted to the use of punishment and fear, because these tools are available, are immediate in their short-term effects, and carry the illusion of control through obedience and compliant behavior.[91] However, we do *not recommend* the use of such strategies in most situations. Years ago, Deming noted that the move to total quality could not be achieved through fear, and evidence in the intervening years continues to demonstrate the lack of effectiveness of fear.[92] While activity controls like fear may produce compliance in the short run, they have proven to be ineffective over the intermediate to longer term.[93] Further, such techniques can create undesirable side effects (e.g., frustration, withdrawal in the form of absenteeism and turnover, aggression, and sabotage). A much more desirable and less risky course of action is through the positive engagement of people through initiatives that enhance the recipients' capabilities to deal effectively with the change.[94] At the same time, managers can use their power to make expectations and standards explicit in order to challenge employees.

Creating Consistent Signals From Systems and Processes

While the leader's words and deeds are important, so too are other parts of the organizational context. A leader's credibility will be either enhanced or diminished by the extent to which organizational systems and processes send a consistent message or are themselves the focus of changes that will bring them into alignment with the change vision.

Credibility and trust are diminished when the leader's words say one thing (e.g., quality is critical) but the systems and processes signal something else (e.g., ship now, fix later). In *Built to Last*, Collins and Porras found that firms with staying power possess resilient cultures that have the capacity to adjust and realign their systems and processes in response to changing conditions. This resilience was made functional by the underlying value set and supportive systems and processes that were installed by leaders.[95] As such, they provided continuity for organizational members while at the same time contributing to the adaptability and change of existing systems and processes. This reflects an interesting and important paradox for the change leader. The successful management of change is enhanced by giving voice to factors that develop the sense of continuity, the connection between the past and the future, as well as by giving voice to the need for and nature of the change.[96]

Steps to Minimize the Negative Effects of Change

Those who have been involved in significant changes know that how people view the change will have a profound impact on the ultimate success or failure of a change initiative.[97] Success is aided when change recipients become willing implementers. Therefore, the effects of change on recipients need to be approached with care during the initial planning phases and throughout the change process, including the post-change period.

Engagement

Trust is increased and rumors are reduced when leaders share story after story about the problems that are driving the need for change, what is known and not known, process, action plans, and timelines.[98] When coupled with the personal involvement of engaged leaders and executives and a meaningful degree of employee involvement in decisions that affect them (at minimum, the ability to ask questions, voice concerns, and receive answers that reduce uncertainty), individual adaptation and acceptance are advanced.[99] People want to know where things are going, why, and what the implications are on the organization, their parts of the operation, and on them personally. When change leaders don't know the answers to questions that are raised, people should be given a timetable detailing when they can expect to hear and the commitments to follow up should be honored.

Timeliness

Employees often want to vent their concerns and frustrations, and, at times, grieve what has been lost. If this is to be handled constructively, they need to hear in a timely fashion and be given time to constructively process what they have heard. No one benefits when recipients first hear about a particular change on the evening news or in the local coffee shop. When this happens, the information needs to be quickly and credibly dealt with through internal communication channels. The more that critical messages can be communicated in a timely, face-to-face manner (backed up by appropriate documents and systems/processes, as needed, to handle complexity and retention), the better. Otherwise the rumor mill will shift into overdrive as people attempt to make sense of new and potentially conflicting information.[100] Once the message is in their hands, they may need time and assistance to make sense of what they have heard and constructively react, both on their own and with their peers. Otherwise, they may well come to believe that they have not been fairly dealt with by the change leaders or organization.

Two-Way Communication

Change communication needs to be two-way, as change leaders need to be open to learning as much from exchanges as followers. A variety of communication channels are available to change leaders, and multiple channels are best. Redundancy is clearly preferable to gaps. Communicating through executive-staff briefings, teams, task forces, recipient representatives, advisory groups, video, newsletters, hotlines, and the creative use of the intranet (including bulletin boards, blogs, and e-mail to monitor concerns and expedite the delivery of answers) all have a role in helping people learn about and adapt to change. When coupled with transparency, authenticity, and minimal levels of executive defensiveness, these communication approaches advance recipient engagement and adaptation to change.

Exposure to employees' feedback and reactions allows change leaders to adapt strategies and approaches in an informed and sensitive manner. For example, tracking themes from e-mails, postings on bulletin boards, social media, and surveys results can provide insights into how followers are interpreting and responding to the change. The importance of such feedback proves the adage that leaders who think they know it all have a fool as their advisor. To quote the movie director Blake Edwards, "Every time I think I know 'where it's at,' it's usually somewhere else."

Table 7.5 Strategies for Coping With Change	
Recipients	**Change Leaders**
Accepting Feelings as Natural • Self-permission to feel and mourn • Taking time to work through feelings • Tolerating ambiguity	**Rethinking Resistance** • As natural as self-protection • As a positive step toward change • As energy to work with • As information critical to the change process
Managing Stress • Maintaining physical well-being • Seeking information about the change • Limiting extraneous stressors • Taking regular breaks • Seeking support	**Giving First Aid** • Accepting emotions • Listening • Providing safety • Marking endings • Providing resources and support
Exercising Responsibility • Identifying options and gains • Learning from losses • Participating in the change • Inventorying strengths • Learning new skills • Diversifying emotional investing	**Creating Capability for Change** • Making organizational support of risks clear • Providing a continuing safety net • Emphasizing continuities, gains of change • Helping employees explore risks, options • Suspending judgment • Involving people in decision making • Teamwork • Providing opportunities for individual growth

Source: Adapted from Jick, T., & Peiperl, M. A. (2003). *Managing change, cases and concepts* (2nd ed.). New York: McGraw-Hill.

Jick and Peiperl have identified a number of strategies that can assist both the recipients and their managers in coping with different stages of the change (see Table 7.5).

Change recipients can develop support networks to facilitate letting go and moving on if they know and understand the stages of change. Change leaders need to develop an understanding of the dynamics around change and recognize the need to work through the change-management process in a systemic and supportive fashion. Often, followers' understanding for the need for change lags behind that of change leaders. By definition, those leading change have diagnosed the need for change, mourned the loss of the old, understood and embraced the new vision, and moved to action. Those impacted by the change need to work through the same process—but are lagging behind their leaders and lack their direct involvement. As change leaders, we need to give them time to adapt and catch up! See **Toolkit**

Exercise 7.6 to analyze a time when you were a change recipient and the quality and actions of change leadership.

Make Continuous Improvement the Norm

One way that organizations can reduce the perceived threat of change is to adopt managerial approaches that challenge everyone to regularly question the status quo and seek to improve existing practices as part of their ongoing activities. If organizational members routinely question and initiate continuous improvement projects, then shifts in the environment will not be seen as threatening events. Leaders generate an atmosphere in which change is experienced as a naturally occurring condition by creating an organizational climate in which incremental changes are sought out and embraced. The fact that tomorrow is unlikely to be exactly the same as today becomes the expected norm as opposed to an unexpected shock.[101]

One benefit of continuous improvement approaches such as Six Sigma is the legitimization of ongoing changes in ways that provide continuity with the past. Rather than searching for the silver bullet that will produce the cure for current organizational ills, these approaches seek to advance less heroic, ongoing initiatives that will enhance organizational health in incremental ways.[102] In so doing, these approaches make revolutionary changes less likely and threatening because the real and perceived magnitude of the change is reduced.

If the organizational culture promotes an ongoing and constructive embrace of change, perceptions of the threat related to change are bound to be reduced. Abrahamson refers to this as dynamic stability and points to firms like GE as exemplars of the approach.[103] The experience tells organizational members that changes are normal and tend to work out for the best.

Even when the news is bad, an approach of ongoing employee engagement with change can lead to lower levels of uncertainty, quicker response times (people know what they are facing), improved outcomes (e.g., less undesirable employee turnover), and higher levels of satisfaction than likely would otherwise have occurred. If people (or their representatives) have participated in the analysis, planning, and/or implementation efforts, this tends to further reduce the fear and uncertainty.[104]

Creating organizational agility and resiliency enables organizations to be more prepared for change. Agility allows an organization to be more open to change while resiliency strengthens the core—common purpose, shared beliefs, and identity—to thoughtfully and strategically guide a change process. This requires the establishment of a knowledge-sharing system, commitment from top leadership, and cross-training of employees. In addition, there needs to be a commitment to organization-wide reevaluation and the use of all successes and failures as learning opportunities.[105] Today's and future organizations need to be designed to institutionalize change. This can be done through the promotion of organizational modularity, quick anticipation and response to external forces, construction of conflict-management processes, and building of organizational coherence around values and culture rather than structure.[106]

A final approach to reducing the perceived threat of change is to use approaches that do not cause people to believe they have to bet the farm. One can do this through encouraging the use of experimentation and pilot programs and through ensuring that the perceived rewards and punishments associated with success and failure are not excessive. Again, experience has demonstrated that a series of smaller, interrelated changes by dedicated change agents over time can produce substantial, even revolutionary changes in the organization—sometimes without the organization even knowing they were underway.[107]

Encourage People to Be Change Agents and Avoid the Recipient Trap

It is clear from this chapter that being a change recipient is not as energizing or exciting as being a change agent! Change agents are active and involved. Change recipients find themselves on the receiving end and may experience a lack of power and control. One way to reduce the negative effects of change is to take risks, get more involved, and become a change agent.

When people attempt to influence the events swirling about them, they are, in effect, acting as their own change agents. Since they are often in subordinate roles and dependent, to varying degrees, on the actions of others, skilled people manage the influence process by recognizing whom they are dependent on,[108] engaging in appropriate stakeholder analysis, followed by actions that reflect what they've learned. By demonstrating initiative, presenting ideas, taking action, and attempting to make a difference, potential change recipients can gain power in both real and perceived terms. And they will be viewed differently in the organization. As you will have recognized by now, these notions of agency and active involvement in change by organizational members, from awareness creation to ideation and implementation, are themes upon which this book is built.

Summary

This chapter has dealt with how people react and why they respond positively, negatively, or with ambivalence to change initiatives. It suggests that change leaders use feelings of ambivalence as opportunities to influence stakeholders. Change agents need to understand ambivalence and resistance to change and use the awareness of these to develop a better appreciation for the change environment.

The chapter outlines the prescriptive model of change phases that people go through when disruptive changes are involved. Knowing the model may provide useful insights as to how to act. The chapter deals with the factors that affect how people view change: their personalities, their experiences with change, their coworkers, the organization, and the change leaders themselves. Finally, the chapter ends by considering what change agents and leaders can do to manage the process and minimize the negative impact of change. See **Toolkit Exercise 7.1** for critical thinking questions for this chapter.

Key Terms

Recipients of change—find themselves on the receiving end of a change initiative and have little power to alter the direction or content of a change initiative.

Resistance to change—includes actions that are intended to slow or prevent change from happening. Resistance arises when an individual comes to believe that the costs outweigh the benefits and that opposition is warranted. Actions can vary from the expression of concern and "go slow" responses through to more active forms of resistance, including coalition building, formal protests, and even sabotage. Too often managers expect resistance and it becomes a self-fulfilling prophecy.

Ambivalence to change—the mixed emotions that a change initiative can trigger. Ambivalence arises from uncertainty and occurs when we are asked to act in ways that are inconsistent with our existing attitudes. These mixed emotions generate discomfort that we seek to resolve. There is evidence that suggests we have an easier time giving voice to mixed feelings involving conflicting beliefs than we do when negative emotional responses are involved. Once the individual has resolved his or her ambivalence, subsequent changes to those attitudes become much more difficult until a new sense of ambivalence arises.

The **psychological contract**—represents the sum of the implicit and explicit agreements we believe we have with key individuals and the organization concerning our employment relationship. These ground our expectations concerning ourselves and the organization, concerning terms and conditions, norms, rights, rewards, and obligations.

The **stages in the reaction to change**—typically must progress through when coping with a more traumatic change are the anticipation and anxiety phase, the shock, denial, and retreat phase, and the acceptance phase.

Survivor syndrome—refers to the reaction of those who survive a poorly handled, traumatic change such as a downsizing.

Predisposition to change—relates to our general inclination toward change. Are we typically innovators, early adopters, members of the early majority of adopters, members of the late majority, or in the group of individuals who are very late adopters or non-adopters?

Tolerance for turbulence and ambiguity—involves our comfort level with these conditions. Individuals who have higher tolerance levels generally will be more comfortable and open to change, while those who have lower tolerance levels will prefer more stable and predictable environments.

Competency or a complacency trap—the tendency to rely on competencies and strategies that have worked in the past.

Skepticism relates to doubts and concerns we may have concerning the capacity of the change to deliver the promised results. These may be rooted in the change itself, the adoption process, concerns about the change leadership, or unease about the organization's and other key stakeholders' responses to the change.

Cynicism occurs when we fundamentally lose faith in the change, the adoption process, the key individuals involved, or the organization.

Checklist: How to Manage and Minimize Cynicism About Change[109]

1. Keep people involved in making decisions that affect them.

2. Emphasize and reward supervisors who foster two-way communication and good working relationships and show consideration and respect for employees.

3. Keep people informed about ongoing change—when, why, and how—and include honest appraisals of risks, costs, benefits, and consequences.

4. Keep surprises to a minimum through regular communication about changes, anticipating questions and concerns.

5. Enhance credibility by:

   a. Using credible spokespersons who are liked and trusted

   b. Using positive messages that appeal to logic and consistency

   c. Using multiple channels and repetition.

6. Acknowledge mistakes, accept responsibility, apologize, and make amends.

7. Publicize successful changes and progress.

8. Use two-way communication in order to see change from the employees' perspectives and use this awareness to help with planning and future communications related to change.

9. Provide opportunities for employees to express feelings and receive validation and reassurance. Ensure you address the concerns raised.

10. Ensure existing structures, systems, and processes are not sending conflicting messages, obstructing the change, and creating cynicism in the process. If they are, recognize their impact, discuss them openly, and take steps to address the issue and either bring them into alignment with the change or minimize their negative impact.[110]

END-OF-CHAPTER EXERCISES

TOOLKIT EXERCISE 7.1

Critical Thinking Questions

Please find the URLs for the videos listed below on the website at *study.sagepub.com/cawsey3e*. Consider the questions that follow.

1. Please read Case 4 on page 444 "Diego Curtiz at Highland State University" and consider the following questions:

   - What has Diego Curtiz done well in managing the SSA project?

   - Where could Curtiz have done better in managing the SSA project?

   - What challenges does Curtiz face now that the SSA implementation is at its midpoint?

   - What does Tainer mean when she tells Curtiz "You have *got* to get Ken on board"? Do you agree with her?

   - What should Curtiz do next regarding Ken Cullen?

   See the case "Travelink Solutions," which can be found on the website: study.sagepub.com/cawsey3e

2. Travelink Solutions describes an organization that is experiencing change initiatives that are producing negative outcomes for both the organization and the recipients of change. William, a young staff member, sees multiple problems within this 24/7 travel business. As a low-level, sixteen month employee, William has documented and discussed the situation with his friend, Robert, a marketing manager who has been with the organization for three years. William and Robert both must decide if they will shift from being recipients of change to

becoming change agents. They must decide if and how they might bring the organizational problems and possible solutions, to the attention of management.

- If you found yourself in William or Robert's situation, what would you do?

- Have you ever been in a situation where you were a recipient of change and things were going poorly? How did it affect you and others in the organization?

- What is your assessment of the situation at Travelink and the underlying causes?

- If you found yourself in William or Robert's situation, what would you do?

3. The Power of Vision: Dreaming of Peace

View *Pray the Devil Back to Hell* (Information about documentary available at http://www .praythedevilbacktohell.com/).

This is the story of how Liberian women who were recipients of a harsh political regime and leader became leaders of change within their country.

- Why did the women dress in white and sit in the marketplace for days on end? What did they hope to accomplish? Why were they successful in reaching their goal of petitioning the dictator, Charles Taylor?

- How did the Liberian women, who were not a formal part of the negotiating teams in Ghana, impact the negotiation processes? Who were the important allies of the Liberian women during the negotiations?

- Would you agree that the Liberian women went from being recipients of change to being leaders of change? Which of their strategies and tactics do you think other powerless groups can use to become powerful and lead change?

4. The "X" Model of Employee Engagement: Maximum Satisfaction Meets Maximum Contribution—7:43 minutes
   Consider the following:

   - How can you engage employees in each area to increase their engagement to the organization and an organizational change effort?

   - Which group are your greatest allies within the change, and how can you use them?

   - Think about jobs in the past and describe your engagement using this model.

Please see study.sagepub.com/cawsey3e for the above case and a downloadable template of this exercise.

TOOLKIT EXERCISE 7.2

Working Through Emotional Responses to Change

1. Consider a significant and disruptive change situation that you know about (or talk to a friend or relative about such a change situation). Identify the different phases of change.

2. Can you identify strategies that people used or could have used to help them work their way through the different phases?

3. Can you identify strategies that change leaders used or could have used to help people work their way through the different phases?

	Are recipients aware of how they are reacting? Yes/No	Strategies recipients can use to work through an emotional response to a change initiative	Strategies change leaders can use to help recipients work through an emotional response to a change initiative
• Prechange anxiety			
• Shock			
• Defensive retreat			
• Bargaining			
• Depression, guilt, and alienation			
• Acknowledgment			
• Adaptation and change			

Does the model hold? Why or why not?

What other consequences of change can you identify?

Please see study.sagepub.com/cawsey3e for a downloadable template of this exercise.

TOOLKIT EXERCISE 7.3

Personal Reactions to Change

1. Think through your organizational experiences at school and at work when you have been a recipient of change. How have you typically responded to these changes? What were the factors that led to those responses?

   To help you think about these questions, ask yourself the following concerning three to four such changes:

   a. What was the change, and how was it introduced?

   b. What was the impact on you?

   c. What was your initial reaction? Enthusiasm? "Wait and see" attitude? Ambivalence, due to conflicting reactions? Cynicism?

   d. Did your attitudes change over time? Why or why not?

2. Was there a pattern to your response?

   a. Under what circumstances did you support the change? When did you resist? What can you generalize from these experiences?

   b. If you experienced ambivalence, how did you resolve it and what happened to your attitudes toward the change once the ambivalent feelings were resolved?

3. Overall, have your earlier experiences with change been largely positive, largely negative, or mixed?

Have these experiences colored your expectations and feelings toward change in the future?

Please see study.sagepub.com/cawsey3e for a downloadable template of this exercise.

TOOLKIT EXERCISE 7.4

Your Normal Reaction to Innovation and Change

When you find yourself dealing with matters of innovation and change, how do you typically react?

1. Do you find that you fall into the category of innovator or early adopter, readily considering and often adopting new approaches, well in advance of most people?

2. Or do you generally fall into the category of the early majority? If the initial responses and experiences of the early adopters are generally positive, you are willing to take the risk and adopt the new approach.

3. Or are you generally in the category of the late majority? You wait until the innovation or new approach has been tried and tested by many people before you commit to adopt.

4. Or are you a person who typically does not adopt the innovation or new approach until the vast majority of people have done so? In other words, are you a late adopter or even a non-adopter until forced to do so?

5. What is your tolerance for change? What level of turbulence and ambiguity in a work situation do you find most stimulating and satisfying?

6. How do you react when the rate of change is quite low and is likely to remain there?

7. How do you react when the rate of change is at a moderate level? What constitutes a moderate level for you? Are your tolerance levels lower or higher than those of others you know?

8. What price do you find you pay personally when the rate of turbulence and ambiguity exceeds what you are comfortable with? When it is either too low or too high?

9. Have you had to cope with prolonged periods of serious upheaval or periods of extreme turbulence? Have these experiences affected your acceptance of change?

Please see study.sagepub.com/cawsey3e for a downloadable template of this exercise.

TOOLKIT EXERCISE 7.5

Disruption of the Psychological Contract

Think about a change initiative that you are aware of. What happened or will likely happen to the psychological contracts of recipients?

1. What is the existing psychological contract? (If in the past, what was the contract?)

2. What were the explicit and implicit pieces?

3. In what ways did the change disrupt the existing psychological contract? To what extent was this perception real? (If in the past, in what ways did the change actually disrupt the psychological contract?)

4. Given the individuals and the context, what reactions to these disruptions to the psychological contract do you anticipate? (If in the past, what were the reactions?)

5. Are there steps that could be taken to reduce the negative effects stemming from the disruption? (If in the past, could anything have been done?)

6. How should a new psychological contract be developed with affected individuals? (If this is in the past, how could this have been done?)

7. If you are the recipient of change, what steps could you take to better manage your way through the development of a new contract? (If this is in the past, what could you have done?)

Please see study.sagepub.com/cawsey3e for a downloadable template of this exercise.

TOOLKIT EXERCISE 7.6

Leadership and Change Recipients

Think more specifically about an example of change leadership that you know.

1. What was the nature of that leadership?

2. Was the leader trusted?

3. Did he or she deserve the trust given?

4. What kind of power did the leader use?

5. How were the messages about the change conveyed? Were they believable messages?

6. Did organizational systems and processes support, or at minimum, not impair the change leader's messages?

7. Was there a sense of continuity between the past and the anticipated future? How was that sense of continuity developed and communicated? What was the impact?

8. What can you learn about the impact of the leader on people and stakeholders as a result of your responses to the above questions?

9. What can you learn about the impact of organizational systems and processes on the people and stakeholders?

10. Talk to others about their experiences. Can you generalize? In what way? What cannot be generalized?

Please see study.sagepub.com/cawsey3e for a downloadable template of this exercise.

CHAPTER 8

Becoming a Master Change Agent

Never doubt that a small group of thoughtful, committed individuals can change the world. Indeed, it's the only thing that ever has.[1]

—Margaret Mead

Leadership is the art of getting someone to do something you want done because they want to do it.

—Dwight D. Eisenhower

CHAPTER OVERVIEW

- The success of a change agent involves knowing your strengths and weaknesses and how these interplay among the person, the situation, and a vision.
- Successful change agents have a set of skills and personal characteristics: interpersonal, communication, and political skills; emotional resilience and tolerance for ambiguity and ethical conflicts; persistence, pragmatism, and dissatisfaction with the status quo; and openness to information, flexibility, and adaptability. They act in a manner likely to build trust. Change agents develop their skills with experiences in change situations.
- This chapter describes four change agent types: the Emotional Champion, the Developmental Strategist, Intuitive Adapter, and the Continuous Improver. Each has a different preference for his or her method of persuasion (vision versus analytical) and orientation to change (strategic versus incremental).
- This chapter considers different change roles: an internal change agent, an external consultant, and a member of a change team.

This chapter examines what makes a change agent. It looks at change agents' individual characteristics and how these interact with a situation and vision to determine change agent effectiveness. We contrast change managers from leaders and examine how change leaders develop. Four types of change leaders are identified: the Emotional Champion, the Developmental Strategist (particularly important for a transformational change), the Intuitive Adapter, and the Continuous Improver. We examine the skills of internal change agents, the roles of the external change agents, and the usefulness of change teams. The chapter ends with rules of thumb for change agents from the wisdom of organizational development and change agent experts. Figure 8.1 highlights this chapter's place in the Change Path.

The role of change agent is a double-edged sword. While it can prove exciting, educational, enriching, and career enhancing, it can also be hazardous to your career, frustrating, and demoralizing when risks escalate and failure looms. In general, people who become change agents will improve their understanding of organizations, develop special skills, and increase their networks of contacts and visibility in the organization.[2] Those who choose not to respond to the challenge of leading change, on the other hand, run the risk of becoming less central and relevant to the operation of their organizations.

When changes fail, there is the sense that the change agent's career has ended. However, this is seldom the case. While failure experiences are painful, change agents are resilient. For example, when Jacques Nasser left Ford in 2001, many thought he was a spent force. However, about a year after leaving Ford, he took over as chairman of Polaroid after it was acquired by One Equity Partners in a bankruptcy auction. In 2½ years, Nasser turned it around and its resale resulted in a $250 million gain for One Equity.[3] In August 2009, Nasser again hit the business press news when he was nominated chairman of BHP Billiton, the world's largest mining company, and took office in early 2010.[4] The skills and personal attributes that Nasser developed at Ford have served him well since he left in 2001.

Many individuals find it difficult to identify where and how they fit into the change process. They believe that they cannot ignite change with their low- or mid-level roles and titles, and minimal experiences in organizations. Years of autocratic or risk-averse bosses and top-down organizational cultures make it hard to believe that this time the organization wants change and innovation. Critics of present-day educational systems have suggested that schools encourage dependent rather than change-agent thinking. If teachers and professors see the students' role as absorbing and applying within prescribed boundaries rather than raising troubling questions, independent and innovative thinking will not be advanced.

In the turbulent years that have defined the first couple of decades of the 21st century, however, individuals find themselves living in organizations that challenge them to take up one of the roles of change agency: initiator, implementer, facilitator, and/or task force team member. Leaders in organizations are asking people to step forward and make a difference. While the specific roles will vary over time and context, moving to a more active role is critical. Simply providing information or offering armchair solutions seldom produces meaningful change. To disrupt inertia and drift, some individuals must move from an observer status to active. Those

Figure 8.1 The Change Path Model

Awakening
Chapter 4
1. Identify a need for change and confirm the problems or opportunities that incite the need for change through collection of data.
2. Articulate the gap in performance between the present and the envisioned future state, and spread awareness of the data and the gap throughout the organization.
3. Develop a powerful vision for change.
4. Disseminate the vision for the change and why it's needed through multiple communication channels.

Mobilization
Chapters 5 through 8
1. Make sense of the desired change through formal systems and structures, and leverage those systems to reach the change vision (Chapter 5).
2. Assess power and cultural dynamics at play, and put them to work to better understand the dynamics and build coalitions and support to realize the change (Chapter 6).
3. Communicate the need for change organization-wide and manage change recipients and various stakeholders as they react to and move the change forward (Chapter 7).
4. **Leverage change agent personality, knowledge, skills and abilities, and related assets (e.g., reputation and relationships) for the benefit of the change vision and its implementation (Chapter 8).**

Acceleration
Chapter 9
1. Continue to systematically reach out to engage and empower others in support, planning, and implementation of the change. Help them develop needed new knowledge, skills, abilities, and ways of thinking that will support the change.
2. Use appropriate tools and techniques to build momentum, accelerate and consolidate progress.
3. Manage the transition, celebrating small wins and the achievement of milestones along the larger, more difficult path of change.

Institutionalization
Chapter 10
1. Track the change periodically and through multiple balanced measures to help assess what is needed, gauge progress toward the goal, and to make modifications as needed and mitigate risk.
2. Develop and deploy new structures, systems, processes and knowledge, skills, and abilities, as needed, to bring life to the change and new stability to the transformed organization.

who wish to add value to their organizations and make a difference will challenge themselves to take on change leadership roles.

For many, their implicit model of change assumes that they must have the involvement and support of the CEO or some other senior sponsor before they can create meaningful change. There is no question that if a change initiative has the commitment and budget of a senior change champion, the job is immeasurably easier. However, for many individuals acting from subordinate organizational roles (e.g., technical professionals, first-line and middle managers, frontline staff), the changes they want to promote require them to question existing systems and processes, with little top-level, visible support when they begin.

In *Leading the Revolution*, Hamel argues that every "company needs a band of insurrectionists" who challenge and break the rules and take risks.[5] One teacher provides an example.

REFLECTIONS ON A TEACHER

The teacher that influenced me the most was concerned with our learning and not with the power and influence of the administration. For example, when *Catcher in the Rye* was deemed unfit for our youthful eyes, he informed the class that this book was classed as unsuitable. This teacher reported that the book by J. D. Salinger should be avoided and while it was recognizable because of its red cover with yellow print and found in most bookstores, libraries, and magazine stores, we should not seek it out. Later, the same teacher was instructed to black out certain risqué phrases from one of the assigned books for class. Of course, he marched into the class, described that the phrases on p. 138, lines 7 and 8, that were to be blacked out and that he was enlisting the class's help to do the work for him.

Anonymous caller, CBC Radio, January 2004.

Testing orthodoxies will become critical in the drive to keep pace with environmental demands.[6] The individuals wanting to remove student exposure to the perceived immorality in the books likely thought they were change agents as well. However, by doing so, they were limiting student access to information and the opportunity to think about common realities. For the teacher in the example, this was viewed as violating the prime purposes of a school system—educating the students and instilling a desire for learning. It drove him to action.

With the ever-increasing need for innovation and change in organizations, there is the recognition that change management is an essential part of every good manager's skill set.[7] Change agency has shifted from notions of "lone ranger," top-down heroic leadership to ones involving leaders who enable change teams and empower workers to envision change and make it happen.[8] As Jick points out, "implementing their own changes as well as others."[9] While we might think that change is led from the top, Jick and others dispute this. "Most well-known change initiatives (*that are*) perceived as being 'top-down' or led by a senior executive or the CEO, probably started at the bottom or the middle, years earlier."[10]

As Rosabeth Moss Kanter states, real change is for the long haul. It "requires people to adjust their behavior and that behavior is often beyond the direct control of top management."[11] Bold strokes taken by top management likely do not build the long-term capabilities of the organization unless they are buttressed by a concerted commitment to an underlying vision. Bold strokes can reduce, reorganize, and merge organizations, but each of these takes a toll on the organization. Unfortunately, the long-term benefits can prove to be illusory if the initiative fails to sustainably embrace the hearts as well as the heads of organizational members in ways that generate internal and external environmental congruence.

Factors That Influence Change Agent Success

The Interplay of Personal Attributes, Situation, and Vision

Images of organizational change agents often revolve around personalities that appear to be bigger than life: Jack Welch, former CEO of GE; Bill Gates, former CEO of Microsoft; and Meg Whitman, former CEO of eBay and CEO of HP. If such grand standards are the benchmarks employed to assess personal qualities and potential as a change agent, most people will inevitably fall far short of the mark.

However, history suggests that leading change is about more than just the person. In the 1930s, Winston Churchill was a politician in decline. When World War II began, suddenly his skills and personality matched what was needed, and the British public believed he was uniquely qualified to be prime minister. Churchill did not change who he was, but the situation changed dramatically and, as prime minister, Churchill projected a vision of victory and took actions that changed history and his reputation. This match of person and situation is further highlighted by the fact that Churchill experienced electoral defeat in the postwar environment despite his enormous popularity during the war.

In other words, it was the person *and* it was more than the person. **Change agent effectiveness** was a function of the situation, the vision the person had, and the actions he or she took. A robust model for change considers the interaction between personality, vision, and situation. Michael J. Fox exemplifies a person who became a change agent extraordinaire in the fight against Parkinson's disease.

Fox's basic personality didn't change with the onset of Parkinson's. But suddenly he

---

MICHAEL J. FOX BECOMES A CHANGE AGENT

Most people get Parkinson's disease late in life. Michael J. Fox, a television/movie star, contracted it when he was 30. Before his disease, Fox was focused on his career. Within a year, Fox had created the Fox Foundation that has become an exceptionally effective organization in fundraising and in shaping the research agenda for Parkinson's disease.[12]

---

was faced with a situation that generated a sense of purpose and vision that both transcended his self-interest and captured the attention and emotions of others. This powerful vision was crucial to Fox's transformation from movie star to change agent.

He deployed his energy, interpersonal skills, creativity, and decision-making skills to pursue this vision. His contacts, profile, and reputation gave him access to an influential board of directors. In record time, he recruited a key executive director and created a foundation that became a funding force. Most important, he chose to act. He articulated values that resonated with key stakeholders and raised awareness and interest through his strategies and tactics. The ability to create alignment among stakeholders on the values front has been shown to be very valuable in reducing resistance and advancing change.[13] His is far from an isolated incident. From Paul Newman's social entrepreneurship and philanthropy with salad dressing[14] to Andrea Ivory's initiative to bring early breast cancer detection to uninsured women in Florida,* individuals from all walks of life are choosing not to accept the status quo and are making a difference.

In the above cases, the interaction of the person, situation, and powerful vision transformed a person into a change agent. This can be summarized in the following equation:

Situations play a crucial part in this three-way interchange. Some situations

> Being a Change Agent = Person × Vision × Situation

invigorate and energize the change agent. Enthusiasm builds as coalitions form and the proposed change gains momentum and seems likely to succeed. Other situations suck energy out of the change agent and seem to lead to a never-ending series of meetings, obstacles, and issues that prevent a sense of progress. Borrowing from the language of chemical reactions, Dickout calls the former situations **exothermic** change situations. Here energy is liberated by actions.[15] Conversely, the latter situations he calls **endothermic**. Here the change program consumes energy and arouses opposition—which in turn requires more energy from the change agent.

Change agents need exothermic situations that "liberate the energy to drive the change."[16] However, they will experience both exothermic and endothermic periods in a change process. Initial excitement and discovery are followed by snail-paced progress, setbacks, dead ends, and perhaps a small victory. The question is: Do the agents have the staying power and the ability to manage their energy flows and reserves during this ultra-marathon? Do they have a team to help replenish their energy and keep them going? Or do they run out of energy and give up? Colleagues who serve as close confidantes can play an important role in sustaining energy. They help to keep things in perspective, enabling the change leader to face future challenges and pitfalls. While action taking is the defining visible characteristic of change, discussion and reflection play important and often undervalued roles in the development and maintenance of change leaders.[17] Reflection as a critical practice of change leaders is discussed later in this chapter.

---

*CNN's Heroes Project seeks to inspire people to take action by annually recognizing the change initiatives of everyday people in their communities and celebrating the impact they are having. Their initiatives are highlighted on http://www.cnn.com/SPECIALS/us/cnn-heroes.

Change Leaders and Their Essential Characteristics

An examination of the literature on the personal characteristics of change leaders yields a daunting list of personal attributes ranging from emotional intelligence to general intelligence, determination, openness to experience, and so forth.[18] Textbook treatments of leadership provide lists of the traits and behaviors that prove difficult to reconcile. While most of the literature is inconclusive about attributes that matter and can be generalized, six stand out as particularly relevant for change leaders.

1. Commitment to Improvement

The essential characteristic of **change leaders** is that they are people who seek opportunities to take action in order to bring about improvement. They possess restlessness with the way things are currently done, inquisitive minds as to what alternatives are possible, and the desire to take informed risks to make things better. Katzenbach argues that change leaders are significantly different in their orientation from traditional managers.[19] For Katzenbach, the basic mindset of a "real change leader" is someone who does it, fixes it, tries it, changes it, and does it again—*a trial-and-error approach* rather than an attempt to optimize and get it perfect the first time.

2. Communication and Interpersonal Skills

Doyle talks about potential change agents and argues that they need sophisticated levels of interpersonal and communication skills to be effective.[20] He describes change agents as requiring emotional resilience, tolerance for ethical conflicts and ambiguities, and they need to be politically savvy. Conflict goes with the territory when stakeholders believe the changes will negatively impact them, and researchers have noted the importance of conflict-facilitation skills in change agents, including skills related to constructive confrontation and the development of new agreements through dialogue and negotiation.[21] Barack Obama's soaring oratorical skills allowed him to speak directly to the American people and bypass much of the Washington establishment when he was pushing for changes to the American health system in 2009. This set the stage for the difficult discussions, negotiations, and tactical maneuvers that followed and resulted in new health care legislation. Kramer maintains that this political awareness about what needs to be done may lead, in certain situations, to abrasive, confronting, intimidating behavior.[22] Such challenging behavior may be what is needed to "unfreeze" a complacent organization. Stories of Churchill's arrogant behavior, appropriate in wartime, cost him the prime ministry in the postwar election.

The communication and interpersonal skills needed to navigate the political environment and awaken the organization to needed action receive a lot of attention. However, this more muscular image of the transformational communications skill of change leaders is but a subset of the range of approaches they may deploy in this area. Not all change leaders have a gift for rhetoric, and many are not charismatic in the traditional sense of the term.[†] In his book *From Good to Great*, Jim Collins[23] explores the skill sets of change leaders who successfully transformed their average organizations into great ones. He highlights the quiet, humble, grounded, and committed way in which many of these change leaders interacted with others on a day-to-day basis and the influence this had on the outcomes their organizations were able to achieve. Their positive energy was clearly visible, and frustration didn't give rise to the communication of cynicism that can taint the perspectives of others and derail a change.[24]

McCall and Lombardo identified a number of other characteristics that derail change leaders when they are communicated to others: being cold and aloof, lacking in critical skills, displaying insensitivity to others, being arrogant, being burned out, lacking trustworthiness, and being overly ambitious from a personal perspective.[25] When Malcolm Higgs looked at the question of bad leadership, he identified four recurring themes: abuse of power, inflicting damage on others, overexercise of control to satisfy personal needs, and rule breaking to serve the individual's own purposes. He saw these actions as caused by narcissism in the leader—a view of oneself as superior, entitled, and central to all that happens.[26]

3. Determination

Change agents need a dogged determination to succeed in the face of significant odds and the resilience to respond to setbacks in a reasoned and appropriate manner. After all, in the middle of change, everything can look like a failure. Change agents need to be able to persist when it looks like things have gone wrong and success appears unlikely.

4. Eyes on the Prize and Flexibility

Change agents also need to focus on the practical—getting it done. They must have a constant focus on the change vision, inspiring others and keeping others aligned with the change goal. Change agents must keep their eyes on the prize to avoid getting bogged down in other day-to-day stresses and abandoning the change vision. At the same time, they must be ready to take informed risks, modify their plans to pursue new options, or divert their energies to different avenues as the change landscape shifts—sometimes because of their actions and sometimes because of the actions of others or shifts in other factors in the environment. Doggedness is balanced by flexibility and adaptability, and impatience is balanced by patience. Time for dialogue and reflection on the change process is needed to give perspective and make informed judgments.[27] Change agents must reflect this delicate balance of being driven of the change vision, but not so much that they are unwilling to make modifications to the process as the environment inevitably shifts along the way.

[†]Charisma is defined as a trait found in persons whose personalities are characterized by a personal charm and magnetism/attractiveness along with innate and powerfully sophisticated abilities of interpersonal communication and persuasion (http://en.wikipedia.org/wiki/Charisma).

5. Experience and Networks

Given their desire to make things happen, it is not surprising to find that experience with change is an attribute common to many successful change agents. These individuals embrace change rather than avoiding it and seeing it as "the enemy." They are constantly scanning the environment, picking up clues and cues that allow them to develop a rich understanding of their organization's situation and the need for change. As the situation shifts, they are aware of those shifts and respond appropriately to them. They make this easier for themselves by ensuring that they are part of networks that will tell them what they need to hear—not what they want to hear. They build these networks over time through their trustworthiness, credibility, and interpersonal skills and through the value other members of these networks derive from them. Networks don't work for long if others don't feel they are getting value from them. To ensure that members of the networks and others continue to communicate with them, change leaders are well advised to remember to never be seen as shooting the messenger. If messengers believe the act of communicating will put them at risk, they will alter their behavior accordingly.[28]

6. Intelligence

Intelligence is needed to engage in needed analysis, to assess possible courses of action, and to create confidence in a proposed plan.[29] In general, one has more confidence in a proposal developed by a bright individual than one brought forward by a dullard. However, traditionally defined intelligence is not enough. Interpersonal skills, empathy, self-regulation, a positive and yet realistic outlook, attention to detail, and the motivational drive to see things through are needed to frame proposals effectively and implement them. These factors make up what is called emotional intelligence and it is often highlighted in discussions of change agent characteristics.[30]

In his investigation of the characteristics of change leaders, Caldwell differentiates the attributes of change leaders from those he calls **change managers**.[31] Table 8.1 outlines his view of the differences. Caldwell argues that change leaders operate from a visionary, adaptable perspective while change managers are much more hands on and work with people. Of course, there is nothing that says a change agent cannot possess the attributes of both change leaders and change managers (as defined by Caldwell). In fact, they will need access to both, depending upon their role(s) and the change challenges they are addressing.

Another way to think about the various attributes of change agents is to consider the sorts of behaviors they give rise to. The following three categories of change behaviors are a helpful way of grouping their actions:[32]

- *Framing behaviors:* behaviors oriented toward changing the sense of the situation, establishing starting points for change, designing the change journey, and communicating principles
- *Capacity-creating behaviors:* behaviors focused on creating the capacity for change by increasing individual and organizational capabilities and creating and communicating connections in the organization

Table 8.1 Attributes of Change Leaders and Change Managers

Attributes of Change Leaders	Attributes of Change Managers
• Inspiring vision	• Empowering others
• Entrepreneurship	• Team building
• Integrity and honesty	• Learning from others
• Learning from others	• Adaptability and flexibility
• Openness to new ideas	• Openness to new ideas
• Risk taking	• Managing resistance
• Adaptability and flexibility	• Conflict resolution
• Creativity	• Networking
• Experimentation	• Knowledge of the business
• Using power	• Problem solving

Source: Adapted from Caldwell, R. "Change Leaders and Change Managers: Different or complementary?" *Leadership & Organization Development Journal.* 24/5, 2003, 285–293.

The attributes were ranked by experts. The most highly ranked are at the top of the list, with the others following in order. Note that Table 8.1 identifies attributes not specifically mentioned in the preceding pages.

- *Shaping behaviors:* actions that attempt to shape what people do by acting as a role model, holding others accountable, thinking about change, and focusing on individuals in the change process

Higgs and Rowland examined such behaviors and discovered that "framing change and building capacity are more successful than shaping behavior."[33] They suggested that change leaders should shift from a leader-centric, directive approach to a more facilitating, enabling style in today's organizations.

Finally, Kouzes and Posner provide interesting thinking about the characteristics of effective change leaders in behavioral terms. In their book, they argue that leaders who are adept at getting extraordinary things done know how to: (1) challenge the process or the status quo, (2) inspire a shared sense of vision, (3) enable others to act, (4) model the way, and (5) encourage the heart of those involved with the change.[34] The authors do an excellent job setting out how to accomplish these things, and their book is recommended reading for those interested in pursuing these ideas further. See **Toolkit Exercise 8.2** to rate yourself as a change leader.

Developing Into a Change Leader

Intention, Education, Self-Discipline, and Experience

Many change leadership skills can be learned, which means that they can be taught.[‡] The acquisition of concepts and language establishes mental frameworks for

---

[‡]Like many fields, formal study and education play their role in developing change leaders—thus this book!

want-to-be change leaders. Reading about best practices and landmines can alert novices to predictable success paths and mistakes. The Center for Creative Leadership[35] is one of a number of organizations that produce publications about relevant leadership challenges and practices. In a 2007 article, Corey Criswell and Andre Martin identified a number of trends that future leaders need to be aware of that are creating change to the way business is done. They include (a) more complex challenges, (b) a focus on innovation, (c) an increase in virtual communication and leadership, (d) the importance of authenticity, and (e) leading for long-term survival.[36] The awareness of these macro-level trends will help change agents better understand the environment and use and develop necessary skills to lead change internally.

Change leaders also need to understand and embrace the notion of experiential learning. It is rare that someone is a change agent only once. Change leadership capacities are a sought-out skill set. These skills are developed similarly to the way individuals strengthen their physical skills. Once you start toning a muscle set, it feels good and you strive to continue to maintain and develop that muscle. But performance typically is tied to our capacity to have our muscles act interdependently. When one set of muscles develops, you may find others that need strengthening to improve your overall capacity to perform. Similarly within an organization, change agents seek opportunities to continuously improve both themselves and their organizations. They may have great interpersonal skills, but they need expertise in crafting financial arguments, or vice versa. Over time, this process of development becomes part of one's professional identity. The journey never ends.

As part of this process, self-discovery, discipline, and reflection are critical to ongoing success and growth. Jeanie Daniel Duck argues that an organization will not change if the individuals within that organization do not develop themselves. As a change leader, if you intentionally model reflective behavior, you will encourage others to do the same. The key questions to ask, according to Duck, are:

- Which of your behaviors will you stop/start or change? Identify this behavior and replace it with something else.
- What, specifically, are you willing to do? Brainstorm different actions and how you might measure them.
- How will others know? Help yourself by engaging others to hold you accountable.
- How might you sabotage yourself? Identify ways in which you might hold yourself back.
- What's the payoff in this for you? Construct a reward and motivate yourself.[37]

Bennis describes four rules that he believes change leaders should accept to enhance their self-development:

1. You are your own best teacher.

2. You accept responsibility and blame no one.

3. You can learn anything you want to learn.

4. True understanding comes from reflection on your experience.[38]

Bennis's fundamental message is to take responsibility for your own learning and development as a change leader. This requires reflection. Of course, reflection implies something to reflect on—thus, the role of experience. It is through reflection that a change leader hones existing skills and abilities, becomes open to new ideas, and begins to think broadly, widening the lens through which he or she looks at the situation at hand. In a disciplined manner, a would-be change leader needs to establish personal change goals and write them down. This calls for intentional reflection and continuous learning, which are important for both the individual level, as described by Duck, as well as the organizational level, in developing the ability to change.

What Does *Reflection* Mean?

Organizations are able to change more effectively when individuals and change leaders within the organization shift their mental maps and frameworks, and this requires openness and reflection. The skill of communication is essential here, as it is through conversation and open dialogue that change occurs. There is a need to think *with* others in a reflective way to see change happen. In order to do this, an individual needs to understand what the group thinks and why. The group then needs to identify its shared assumptions, seek information, and develop a mutual understanding of the current reality. This involves open and honest communication in a space where no one is wrong and there is a commitment to finding that common ground—for the present situation and the vision for the future. Change leaders are in the position to create safe spaces for reflection where members of the organization have a voice that is listened to and valued.

Appreciative inquiry (AI), a concept introduced by Dr. David L. Cooperrider at Case Western Reserve University, is critical in these conversations of reflection. AI is the engagement of individuals in an organizational system in its renewal. If you can find the best in the organization and individuals—that is, appreciate it—Cooperrider argues that growth will occur and renewal will result. Through AI, people seek to find and understand the best in people, organizations, and the world by reflecting on past positive experiences and performance. In doing so, the positive energy and commitment to improve is embraced.[39] By framing positively, a different type of energy is found within the organization to move forward in the direction of change.

AI provides an interesting approach for change agents to consider when thinking about how best to approach change, because it recognizes the value of ongoing individual and collective reflection to the enactment of effective change. In order for reflection to add value, there can't be a "wrong" understanding. Everyone must strive to fully understand people's perceptions, assumptions, and visions through discussing and challenging one another's views. In a global society with relationships developing and evolving at all levels, organizations operate in an ever-changing context, making the development of shared understanding and mutual respect all the more important.

Developmental Stages of Change Leaders

Miller argues that there are **developmental stages of a change agent.** He believes that individuals progress through stages of beliefs about change, increasing in their complexity and sophistication.[40] (See Table 8.2 for an outline of his belief stages.) He believes that movement from Stage 1, Novice, to Stage 2, Junior, to Stage 3, Experienced, might be learned vicariously—by observing others or by studying change. However, movement to Stage 4, Expert, requires living with a change project and suffering the frustrations, surprises, and resistance that come with the territory.

There is evidence that these change agent skills and competencies can be acquired through the systematic use of developmental assignments.[41] See **Toolkit Exercise 8.3** to evaluate your development as a change agent.

Table 8.2 Miller's Stages of Change Beliefs	
Stage	**Description**
Stage 1 Novice	Beliefs: People will change once they understand the logic of the change. People can be told to change. As a result, clear communication is key. Underlying is the assumption that people are rational and will follow their self-interest once it is revealed to them. Alternately, power and sanctions will ensure compliance.
Stage 2 Junior	Beliefs: People change through powerful communication and symbolism. Change planning will include the use of symbols and group meetings. Underlying is the assumption that people will change if they are "sold" on the beliefs. Again, failing this, the organization can use power and/or sanctions.
Stage 3 Experienced	Beliefs: People may not be willing or able or ready to change. As a result, change leaders will enlist specialists to design a change plan and the leaders will work at change but resist modifying their own vision. Underlying is the assumption that the ideal state is where people will become committed to change. Otherwise, power and sanctions must be used.
Stage 4 Expert	Beliefs: People have a limited capacity to absorb change and may not be as willing, able, or ready to change as you wish. Thinking through how to change the people is central to the implementation of change. Underlying is the assumption that commitment for change must be built and that power or sanctions have major limitations in achieving change and building organizational capacity.

Source: Adapted from Miller, David. "Successful change leaders: What makes them? What do they do that is different?," *Journal of Change Management.* Vol. 2, 4, 383.

Four Types of Change Leaders

Regardless of their skill sets, change agents' ability to sense and interpret significant environmental shifts is of particular importance to their capacity to respond. Part of such an ability comes from the deep study of a field or industry. As well, some might have the intuition to understand significant changes in the environment by their ability to detect and interpret underlying patterns.[42] Take, for example, Glegg Industries of Glegg Water Treatment Services.

GLEGG WATER SYSTEMS[43]

In 2000, GE bought Glegg Industries. Glegg Water Treatment Services had been an entrepreneurial organization that grew at a compound growth rate of 20 to 25% in the 1980s and 90s. The executives had a clear and strong vision: "pure water for the world." They used this vision to pull the organization in the direction they wanted. They were tough, realistic analyzers of data that provided a sophisticated understanding of the company's market. Three times in their history, the leadership forecasted a decline in growth rates in the technology that the organization was using—so they shifted into completely new but related areas. For example, the organization delivered water treatment systems for power industries. As that market matured, the company shifted to produce high-quality water systems for computer makers. Later, it shifted to a new membrane technology, which permitted integrated systems to be sold.*

---

*The company has since been sold to GE and its operations closed.

What is significant in the Glegg example is the change leaders' abilities to anticipate strategic shifts, manage that magnitude of change, *and* continuously improve and grow between these significant changes. The levels of skill required to manage in these different situations is high. Maintaining this is difficult.

At Glegg Water Treatment Services, change leaders understood the strategic shifts in the industry and what that implied for their organization. Between these major disruptions, they worked incrementally to improve operations and to change the organization for the better. To do this, they motivated people by reinforcing their belief in the importance of what they were doing—providing the purest water possible. However, they did not just use these visionary or emotional appeals, they also used data to persuade. Hard, calculated numbers pushed their perspectives forward and provided convincing evidence of the need for change and the value of the vision.

Much of the change literature differentiates between the types of change that Glegg experienced: strategic or episodic change followed by incremental or continuous change.[44] Episodic change is change that is "infrequent, discontinuous, and intentional." Continuous change is change that is "ongoing, evolving and cumulative." Weick and Quinn suggest that the appropriate model here is "freeze, rebalance and unfreeze." That is, change agents need to capture the underlying patterns and dynamics (freeze the conceptual understanding); reinterpret, relabel (reframe and rebalance those understandings); and resume improvisation and learning (unfreeze).[45] Further, Weick and Quinn suggest that the role of change agents shifts depending on the type of change. Episodic change needs a prime mover change agent—one who creates change. Continuous change needs a change agent who is a sense maker who is then able to refine and redirect the organization's actions.

The Glegg Water example also shows that change agents and their agendas can act in "pull" or "push" ways. *Pull actions* by change agents create goals that draw willing organizational members to change and are characterized by organizational visions of higher-order purposes and strategies. *Push actions,* on the other hand, are data based and factual and are communicated in ways that advance analytical thinking and reasoning and that push recipients' thinking in new directions. Change agents who rely on push actions can also use legitimate, positional, and reward-and-punishment power in ways that change the dynamics of situations.[46] At Glegg Water, markets were assessed and plans were created and implemented based on the best data available.

As a further example of both push and pull tactics, the School of Management (SOM) faculty at Simmons College, Boston, MA, evolved its work patterns and foci over a seven-year period with the intention of achieving the Association to Advance Collegiate Schools of Business (AACSB) International accreditation. In spring 2009, the SOM reached its goal because a diverse faculty was united in its purpose and met the multiple standards set by AACSB. While facts and analytical thinking allowed the faculty to figure out its tactics and strategies to reach its goal, it was the strategic importance of the vision that pulled people together.

Table 8.3 outlines a model that relates the motivational approaches of the change agent (analytical push versus emotional pull) to the degree of change needed by the organization (strategic versus incremental). The model identifies four change agent types: the Emotional Champion, the Developmental Strategist, the Intuitive Adapter, and the Continuous Improver. Some change agents will tend to act true to their type due to the nature of their personalities, predispositions, and situations. Others will move beyond their preferences and develop greater flexibility in the range of approaches at their disposal. The latter will therefore adopt a more flexible approach to change, modifying their approach to reflect the specific situation and the people involved.

The Emotional Champion has a clear and powerful vision of what the organization needs and uses that vision to capture the hearts and motivations of the organization's members. An organization often needs an emotional champion when there is a dramatic shift in the environment and the organization's structures, systems, and sense of direction are inadequate. To be an emotional champion means that the change agent foresees a new future, understands the deep gap between the organization and its future, can articulate a powerful vision that gives hope that the gap can be overcome, and has a high order of persuasion skills. When Glegg Water Treatment Services was faced with declining growth and needed to find new

Table 8.3 Change Agent Types

**Strategic Change and Incremental Change *versus*
Vision Pull and Analytical Push**

Strategic Change

Emotional Champion   *Developmental
                                          Strategist*

Vision Pull   Analytical Push

Intuitive Adapter   *Continuous Improver*

Incremental Change

growth markets, it needed the visionary who could picture the strategic shift and create an appealing vision of that future.

An Emotional Champion:

- is comfortable with ambiguity and risk;
- thinks tangentially and challenges accepted ways of doing things;
- has strong intuitive abilities; and
- relies on feelings and emotions to influence others.

The Developmental Strategist applies rational analysis to understanding the competitive logic of the organization and how it no longer fits with the organization's existing strategy. He or she sees how to alter structures and processes to shift the organization to the new alignment and eliminate the major gap between the organization and the environment's demands. Again, in Glegg Water, the strategic shifts resulted not only from the capturing of a new vision but also from market intelligence and analysis. Hard-nosed thinking enabled Glegg Water to see how to take its company to a new level by finding a new market focus.

A Developmental Strategist:

- engages in big-picture thinking about strategic change and the fit between the environment and the organization;
- sees organizations in terms of systems and structures fitting into logical, integrated components that fit (or don't) with environmental demands; and

- is comfortable with assessing risk and taking significant chances based on a thorough assessment of the situation.

The Intuitive Adapter has the clear vision for the organization and uses that vision to reinforce a culture of learning and adaptation. Often the vision will seem less dramatic or powerful because the organization is aligned with its environment and the change agent's role is to ensure the organization stays on track. The change agent develops a culture of learning and continuous improvement where employees constantly test their actions against the vision. At Glegg Water, continuous improvement was a byword. Central to this were the people who understood the pure water vision and what it meant to customers. Efficiency was not allowed to overrule a focus on quality.

An Intuitive Adapter:

- embraces moderate risks;
- engages in a limited search for solutions;
- is comfortable with the current direction that the vision offers; and
- relies on intuition and emotion to persuade others to propel the organization forward through incremental changes.

The Continuous Improver analyzes micro environments and seeks changes such as re-engineering systems and processes. The organization in this category is reasonably well aligned with its environment and is in an industry where complex systems and processes provide for improvement opportunities. At Glegg Water, information systems captured data on productivity and processes. These data were used to improve efficiency and profits.

A Continuous Improver:

- thinks logically and carefully about detailed processes and how they can be improved;
- aims for possible gains and small wins rather than great leaps; and
- is systematic in his or her thinking while making careful gains.

The purpose of this model is to marry types of change with methods of persuasion. Each change agent will have personal preferences. Some will craft visions that could sweep employees onto the change team. Others will carefully and deliberately build a databased case that would convince the most rational finance expert. Change agents will have their preferred styles but, as noted earlier, some will be able to adapt their approach and credibly use other styles as the situation demands. By knowing your own level of flexibility, you can undertake initiatives that will develop your capacity to adapt your approach as a change agent in a given situation. Alternatively, if you're concerned about your own capacity to respond, you can ally with others who possess the style that a particular situation demands.

In Chapter 1, we briefly discussed the preferences of adaptors (those with an orientation toward incremental change) and innovators (those who prefer more radical or transformational change).[47] Kirton's work with these two orientations points out that individuals tend to have clear preferences in their orientation and sometimes fail to recognize the value present in the alternative approach to change as they focus on what they are most comfortable with. When this occurs, there may be an inappropriate fit of approach with the situation or the people involved. Alternatively, when individuals with both preferences are present, this can lead to disagreement and conflict concerning how best to proceed. While constructive disagreement and debate about alternatives is valuable, managers need to avoid dysfunctional personal attacks and defensive behavior. This points again to the importance of developing greater awareness of the different change styles and the benefits of personal flexibility. When managers lack the needed orientation and style, they need access to allies with the requisite skills.

Many organizations expect their managers to develop skills as change agents. As a result, managers need to improve their understanding of internal change agent roles and strategies. Internal organizational members need to learn the team-building, negotiating, influencing, and other change-management skills to become effective facilitators. They need to move beyond technical skills from being the person with the answer to being the person with process-management change skills: the person who helps the organization find the answers and handles the complex and multivariate nature of the reality it faces.[48]

Hunsaker identified four different internal roles a change agent can play: catalyst, solution giver, process helper, and resource linker.[49] The **catalyst** is needed to overcome inertia and focus the organization on the problems faced. The **solution giver** knows how to respond and can solve the problem. The key here, of course, is having your ideas accepted. The **process helper** facilitates the "how to" of change, playing the role of third-party intervener often. Finally, the **resource linker** brings people and resources together in ways that aid in the solution of issues. All four roles are important, and knowing them provides a checklist of optional strategies for the internal change agent. See **Toolkit Exercise 8.4** to find your change agent preference.

Internal Consultants: Specialists in Change

Internal change agents involved with leading projects often have line responsibilities for the initiative. However, larger organizations also advance change through the use of individuals who are internal consultants. Organizational-development specialists, project-management specialists, lean or Six Sigma experts, and specialists from other staff functions such as accounting and IT are examples of this. When internal change agents are operating from a consulting role, Christopher Wright found that they manage the ambiguity and communicate the value associated with such roles by developing a professional persona that highlights their distinctive competencies as well as reinforces their internal knowledge and linkages.[50]

Internal change agents are critical to the process because they know the systems, norms, and subtleties of how things get done, and they have existing relationships that can prove helpful. However, they may not possess needed specialized knowledge or skills, lack (or be seen to be lacking) objectivity or independence, have difficulty reframing existing relationships with organizational members, or lack an adequate power base. When there are concerns that these gaps cannot be sufficiently addressed by pulling in other organizational members to assist with the process, organizational leaders may believe that it is necessary to bring in external consultants to assist with the project. Sometimes the external consultants are sought out by the internal change agents, while at other times they are thrust upon them. Wise organizational leaders know that external consultants need strong credentials if they are to win over the skeptics about a change project. In fact, poorly performing consultants can create resistance to a change initiative.

In general, external consultants may be used to provide subject-matter expertise, facilitate the analysis, and/or provide guidance to the path forward.

External Consultants: Specialized, Paid Change Agents

Provide Subject-Matter Expertise

External change agents are often hired to promote change through the technical expertise and credibility they bring to an internal change program. This was the case at Simmons College.

> ### USING AN EXTERNAL CONSULTANT AT SIMMONS COLLEGE[51]
>
> In 2006, the School of Management (SOM), Simmons College, Boston, turned to an external consultant when working to gain AACSB International accreditation. The faculty had floundered for several years about how to assess students' learning of the overall management curriculum. Required by the AACSB's Standards to illustrate that its graduating students have learned a program's curriculum, some schools institute standardized tests to assess students' learning. However, the SOM wanted a customized approach to evaluate the unique aspects of its management curriculum. The faculty struggled to envision methodologies and content to reach its goals. Finally, Katherine Martell, an assessment guru, was hired, bringing with her knowledge of how 50 other business schools conducted their assessment processes. When she left the school after two days of working with the faculty, the assessment processes and plans were in place and readily implemented in the following months.

Katherine Martell, the external consultant, was able to help faculty solve the "assessment of learning" problem that had stalled their progress in attaining AACSB accreditation. She did so by helping them work their way through the issues and find a solution. In addition to her technical skills and professional credibility, she was also retained because she possessed well-developed team-process skills that were instrumental in helping them work their way through the problem. When internal change agents or their teams feel they lack the technical skills needed in these areas, they often turn to external expertise.

Bring Fresh Perspectives From Ideas That Have Worked Elsewhere

Too often, insiders find themselves tied to their experiences, and outside consultants can help extricate them from these mental traps.[52] Much can be learned from the systems and procedures that others have used elsewhere. In the following example, the leadership team at Knox Presbyterian Church (Waterloo) recognized it had a problem with how to approach fundraising and turned to RSI Consulting, who had helped many other churches address similar challenges through the use of established procedures. Once it had examined RSI's approach, the church's leadership team retained Craig Miller's services and was able to successfully adopt the approach.

> ### EXTERNAL CONSULTANTS AS PROCESS EXPERTS[53]
>
> When Knox Presbyterian Church, Waterloo, Canada, was planning a new building, church leaders decided they needed a capital campaign to bring life to their change initiative. However, the coordinating team knew that their view of fundraising was tied to past approaches and they recognized that these would not be able to raise the funds required. They searched out and hired RSI Consulting, specialists in church campaigns, with more than 9,000 conducted in 38 years. Craig Miller of RSI brought standard templates, which he used to guide church volunteers in framing the campaign and organizing their fundraising work. Knox had the vision and the manpower but lacked the expertise and structure in how to handle the fundraising. By hiring RSI, they did not have to design the structure for a capital campaign; they borrowed it. As a result, Knox church members raised more than $2.3 million in pledges, in the 90th percentile of results for that size of church, and they did so very economically.

Provide Independent, Trustworthy Support

To help them manage the change process, internal change agents may find they need access to outside consultants who are viewed as independent, credible, competent, and (most importantly) trustworthy by others in the organization. In addition to guidance, they may be able to lend external credibility and support for analyses or actions that advance the change initiative. Such consultants can prove extremely helpful with internal and external data gathering and the communication of the findings and their implications. Organizational members may feel more comfortable sharing their thoughts and concerns with the consultants than they would with internal staff. Finally, the external validation their analyses and conclusions provide may be the nudge needed to generate higher levels of support for the change and action.

Limitations of External Consultants

External consultants can be instrumental in helping foster an atmosphere conducive to change by leveraging their reputations and skill sets through the way they manage the process. However, they have their limitations. They lack the deep knowledge of the political environment and culture of the organization that the inside change agents should have, and in the end it is the organization that needs to take responsibility for the change, not the external consultant. As a result, external change consultants may be able to assist internal agents, but they cannot replace them. Final decision making needs to reside with the internal change leader and the organization.

How an internal change leader selects, introduces, and uses external consultants will have a lot to do with the ultimate success or failure of a change initiative. Consultants come in many forms, with different backgrounds, expertise, price tags, and ambitions. They often come with prescribed methodologies and offer prepackaged solutions. As a result, some consultants are insensitive to the organization's culture or needs. The provision of ready-made answers not based in specific organizational research can be frustrating, and prescription without diagnosis is arguably malpractice.[54] Responsibility for this failure will fall back on the manager who retained the consultant, since he or she is accountable for managing this relationship.

Another risk factor is that consultants may receive signals that they are expected to unquestioningly support the position of the leader of the organization that brought them in, even when the external consultants have serious concerns with the course of action being undertaken. When external consultants lose their ability to provide independent judgment, their value and credibility are seriously reduced and their reputations may suffer irreparable harm if they succumb to pressure and the change subsequently fails in a very public manner.[55]

In spite of these and other risks, many organizations continue to use external consultants to advance their change agendas and mitigate the risks of failure. One study reports that 83% of organizations that used consultants said they would use them again.[56] To increase the chances of success, consider the following advice on how to select an external consultant.

HOW SHOULD YOU SELECT AN EXTERNAL CONSULTANT?[57]

Since the appropriate consultant or consulting team will either advance or detract from the success of your change initiative, selecting a suitable one is a critical step. The following process is recommended for complex organizational change situations:

(Continued)

1. Ensure that you have a clear understanding of what you want from the consultants. Too often organizations hire consultants without thinking through exactly what value they can and will bring. Know who they will report to, what roles they will play, and how much you are willing to pay for their services.

2. Talk with multiple (up to five) consultants and/or consulting organizations. Internal change leaders will learn a great deal about the organization's problems and how they might be solved by talking with multiple vendors. They will also be able to compare and contrast the consultants' working styles, allowing them to gauge the chemistry between the change leader and team and the consultant. The internal change leader needs to ask: Do we have complementary or similar skills and outlook? Does this consultant bring skills and knowledge that I lack internally? Does the organization have the budget that is needed to engage this consultant?

3. Issue a request for proposals (RFP). Only ask those consultants with whom you would like to work, since writing and responding to RFPs is a time-consuming and labor-intensive process. Ask the internal leaders of the change process to objectively review the RFPs and provide you with feedback.

4. Make your decision and communicate expectations. Indicate clearly to the internal change leaders, the consultant(s), and all stakeholders the time line, roles, expectations, deliverables, and reporting relationships.

Change Teams

To balance access to needed perspectives, organizational leaders are moving toward the use of **change teams** that embody both internal and external perspectives. Change initiatives that are large require the efforts of more than one change agent. Outside consultants may be able to help, but as was noted earlier, they may lack credibility and often lack the deep knowledge of the political environment and culture of an organization. As a result, change agents look to extend their reach by using change teams. Worren suggests that teams are important because "employees learn new behaviors and attitudes by participating in ad-hoc teams solving real business problems."[58] Further, as change agents become immersed in the change, the volume of work increases and the roles and skills required of them vary. A cross-functional change team can be used to bring different perspectives, expertise, and credibility to bear on the change challenge inherent in those different roles.[59]

Organizational downsizing and increasing interest in the use of self-managed teams as an organizing approach for flattened hierarchies and cross-functional change initiatives have spurred awareness of the value of such teams.[60] Involvement in self-managed teams gives people space and time to adjust their views and/or influence the change process. It moves them out of the role of recipient and makes them active and engaged stakeholders.

In a benchmarking study focused on the best practices in change management, Prosci describes a good change-management team member as:

- Being knowledgeable about the business and enthusiastic about the change
- Possessing excellent oral and written communications skills, and a willingness to listen and share
- Having total commitment to the project, the process, and the results
- Being able to remain open minded and visionary
- Being respected within the organization as an apolitical catalyst for strategic change[61]

Some of these characteristics of a good change team member appear contradictory. For example, it is tricky to be simultaneously totally committed and open minded. Nevertheless, skilled change leaders often exhibit paradoxical or apparently contradictory characteristics. For example, the need to both be joined with and yet separate from other members of the change team in order to maintain independence of perspective and judgment is a difficult balance to maintain.[62] See **Toolkit Exercise 8.5** to analyze your skills as a change team member.

Working with and in teams and task forces is a baseline skill for change leaders. They must not only work to achieve the change, but they must also bring the change team along so that it accepts, is enthusiastic about, and effectively contributes to the implementation of the change initiative. Many might believe that this requires individuals who are adept at reducing stress and strain in the team, but once again, this is not always the case. The most effective response will depend upon the needs of the situation. Bill Gates, for example, developed high-performance change teams in spite of a dominating personality and awkward social skills because of his abilities in the areas of vision and his capacity to attract and motivate highly talented individuals.

BILL GATES: TEAM LEADER

Gates rarely indulges in water-cooler bantering and social niceties that put people at ease. But while Microsoft's former CEO and chairman was not considered a warm, affable person, he was an effective hands-on manager, says one former employee. "Bill is an exceptional motivator. For as much as he does not like small talk, he loves working with people on matters of substance," says Scott Langmack, a former Microsoft marketing manager.[63]

In the summer of 2008, Gates announced that he would cease full-time work at Microsoft to focus on his charitable foundations.[64] With this announcement, change agents and teams within Microsoft faced a new set of challenges related to managing this transition. Teams are essential components in making change happen.

A SUCCESSFUL CHANGE TEAM AT CASE WESTERN RESERVE UNIVERSITY

Many years ago, a group of students at Case Western Reserve University decided that there had to be better ways of teaching organizational change and development. This small group dedicated itself to changing the system. In two years, they transformed parts of Case Western and created the first doctoral program in organizational development with themselves as potential graduates. They planned and plotted. They identified key stakeholders and assigned team members to each stakeholder with the responsibility of bringing that stakeholder onside—or at least neutralizing their opposition. It was the team that made the change happen. They put into practice what they were learning as students.[65]

Creating the conditions for successful change is more than having an excellent change project plan. Equally important is recognizing the different change roles that need to be played and then developing a strong change team. This section covers the different change roles that team members play and how you design an excellent change team.

Possible Roles Within Change Teams[§]

Many change examples point out the need for a **champion** within the team who will fight for the change under trying circumstances and will continue to persevere when others would have checked out and given up. These change champions represent the visionary, the immovable force for change who will continue to push for the change regardless of the opposition and the resistance to change. Senior managers need to ensure that those to whom the change is delegated possess (and are seen to possess) the energy, drive, skills, resilience, credibility, and commitment needed to make it happen. If these are lacking, steps need to be taken to ensure that they are either developed or appropriate team members need to be found to champion the implementation of the change.

Change champions should consider two further organizing roles that are often better operationalized through the use of two separate teams: a **steering team** and a **design and implementation team**. The steering team provides advice to the champion and the implementation team regarding the direction of the change in light of other events and priorities in the organization. As suggested by the name, it plays an advisory and navigational function for the change project. It is also involved in determining and providing direction to the team's mandate, resourcing requirements, higher-order policies, and major go/no-go decisions.

The design and implementation team plans the change, deals with the stakeholders, and has primary responsibility for the implementation. The responsibilities of the different team members will vary over time, depending upon what is needed and their skill sets. The team will often have a **change project manager** who

---

[§]In Chapter 1, we discussed the roles that an individual can play: change recipient, initiator, facilitator, and implementer. These same roles are looked at here in relation to change teams.

will coordinate planning, manage logistics, track the team's progress toward change targets, and manage the adjustments needed along the way.

Senior executives who act as **sponsors** of change foster commitment to the change and assist those charged with making the change happen.[66] Sponsors can act visibly, can share information and knowledge, and can give protection. **Visible sponsorship** means the senior manager advocates for the change and shows support through actions (i.e., use of influence and time) as well as words. **Information sharing and knowledge development** has the sponsor providing useful information about change and working with the team to ensure that the plans are sound. Finally, sponsors can **provide protection** or cover for those to whom the change has been delegated. Without such protection, the individuals in the organization will tend to become more risk averse and less willing to champion the change.[67]

Developing a Change Team

Developing the team is an important task for the change leaders because the ability to build teams, motivate, and communicate are all predictors of successful change implementation.[68] If change teams can be developed that are self-regulating or self-managed, change can often be facilitated because teams leverage the change leader's reach. The engagement and involvement of team members tends to heighten their commitment and support for the initiative,[69] and because they operate independently, self-managed teams can reduce the amount of time senior managers must commit to implementation-related activities. Self-managed teams share an understanding of the change goals and objectives, sort out the differentiation and execution of tasks, and have control over the decision quality.

Wageman has identified the following seven factors as critical to team success with self-managed teams:

- clear, engaging direction;
- a real team task;
- rewards for team excellence;
- the availability of basic material resources to do the job, including the abilities of individual team members;
- authority vested in the team to manage the work;
- team goals; and
- the development of team norms that promote strategic thinking.[70]

A similar list was developed by the Change Institute and is set out in Table 8.4.[71]

The dedication and willingness to give it their "all" is the most obvious characteristic of highly committed change teams. The dogged determination to make changes regardless of personal consequences because of a deep-rooted belief in a vision creates both the conditions for victory and the possibilities of organizational suicide. In the earlier example at Case Western Reserve University, if the changes were not successful, the individuals involved would have sacrificed several years of their lives to no organizational effect. In the case of Lou Gerstner's turnaround at IBM,[72] there was a distinct possibility that the firm would not survive and members

Table 8.4 Design Rules for Top Teams

1. Keep it small: 10 or fewer members.

2. Meet a minimum of biweekly and demand full attendance—less often breaks the rhythm of cooperation. How the team meets is less important—it may be face to face or through virtual means.

3. Everything is your business. That is, no information is off-limits.

4. Each of you is accountable for your business.

5. No secrets and no surprises within the team.

6. Straight talk, modeled by the leader.

7. Fast decisions, modeled by the leader.

8. Everyone's paid partly on the total results.

of his inner circle would be forever known as the individuals who oversaw the collapse of this American corporate icon. Instead, they will be known as the inner circle who helped Gerstner turn around IBM from losing $8.1 billion in 1993 to renewal, profitability, and growth. At the time of his retirement in 2002, the value of a share of IBM's stock had risen from $13 to $80, adjusted for splits. Wanting to create one "Big Blue," Gerstner re-organized the corporation from individual fiefdoms to one integrated organization and tied the pay of his top 10 executives (his inner circle) to the overall company's performance. In reflecting upon his success in transforming IBM, Gerstner stressed "how imperative it was for a leader to love their business and to 'kill yourself to make it successful.' There is no substitute for hard work and the desire to win. CEOs face a multitude of choices, often peddled by a multitude of self-interested advisors, but they need to focus on exploiting competitive advantages in core businesses" (p. 2).[73]

In forming a change team, the personalities and skills of the members will play a significant role in the team's success. The change process demands a paradoxical set of skills: the ability to create a vision and the intuition to see the connections between that vision and all of the things that will need to be done. This includes identifying who will need to be influenced, thinking positively about stakeholders while recognizing what will influence them and why they may resist you, caring passionately for an initiative yet not interpreting criticism and opposition as a personal attack, and translating broad strategy or vision into concrete change plans. Having the capacity to deal with these paradoxes requires comfort and skill in dealing with ambiguity and complexity.

While those tasks around change demand the paradoxical expertise explained above, functional and technical competencies also play a very important role. It is difficult to imagine a team establishing credibility if it lacks such basics. However, the personalities present in the team will influence how the team interacts and performs, including its ability to manage the inherent paradoxes. While it is usually not necessary for the team to be highly cohesive, cohesion, rooted in a shared sense of purpose, will lend strength to the change effort and focus the team's activities. Implementing change requires considerable energy and can be frustrating and exhausting. At such times, having access to a cohesive and committed team can be invaluable in sustaining you during difficult times.

The boxed insert below describes how Federal Express systematically develops a team approach to change.

DEVELOPING CHANGE TEAMS AT FEDERAL EXPRESS[74]

Federal Express has developed a checklist for using change teams.

1. Ensure that everybody who has a contribution to make is fully involved, and those who will have to make any change are identified and included.

2. Convince people that their involvement is serious and not a management ploy—present all ideas from management as "rough" ideas.

3. Ensure commitment to making any change work—the team members identify and develop "what is in it for them" when they move to make the idea work.

4. Increase the success rate for new ideas—potential and actual problems that have to be solved are identified in a problem-solving, not blame-fixing, culture.

5. Deliver the best solutions—problem-solving teams self-select to find answers to the barriers to successful implementation.

6. Maintain momentum and enthusiasm—the remainder of the team continues to work on refining the basic idea.

7. Present problem solutions, improve where necessary, approve, and implement immediately.

8. Refine idea, agree upon, and plan the implementation process.

Adapted from Lambert, T. (2006). Insight. MENAFN.com. Retrieved May 2010 from http://www.menafn.com/qn_print.asp?StroyID=129531&subl=true.

The checklist that follows the Key Terms section in this chapter sets out factors to consider when structuring work on a change team.

Change From the Middle: Everyone Needs to Be a Change Agent

Increasingly, successful organizational members will find that they need to act as change agents in their organizations. As Katzenbach suggests, the real change leader will take action—do things, try them out, and then do it again while getting better.[75] While this book applauds this type of initiative, remember the first rule for change agents: *Stay alive.*

When managers find themselves involved with change, most will be operating from the middle of the organization. At times, they will have those above them attempting to direct or influence change while they are trying to influence those superiors about what needs to be initiated and how best to proceed. At other times, those middle managers will need to deal with subordinates and peers, those who will be on the receiving end of the change or who are themselves trying to initiate activities.

Oshry recognized the feelings of **middle powerlessness** that many feel when operating in the "middle" and outlined strategies for increasing one's power in these situations.[76] Problem ownership is one of the key issues. Far too often, managers insert themselves in the middle of a dispute and take on others' issues as their own when, in fact, intervention is not helpful. As well, when the issue is the managers, they may refuse to use their power. They need to take responsibility, make a decision, and move on. Or they need to refuse to accept unreasonable demands from above and attempt to work matters out rather than simply acquiesce and create greater problems below.

Oshry's advice to those in the middle is to:

1. "Be top when you can and take responsibility for being top."

2. "Be bottom when you should." Don't let problems just flow through you to subordinates.

3. "Be coach" to help others solve their own problems so they don't become yours.

4. "Facilitate" rather than simply carry messages when you find yourself running back and forth between two parties who are in conflict.

5. "Integrate with one another" so that you develop a strong peer group that you can turn to for advice, guidance, and support.

Whether a manager uses logic or participation to engage others in a change initiative, or acts on his or her own,[77] the message is clear: Managers are increasingly being held accountable for either taking action or helping to make change happen. Scanning the environment, figuring out what will make things better, and creating initiatives are the new responsibilities today's managers carry. This text argues that any change agent role—initiator, implementer, facilitator, or team member—is preferable to constantly finding yourself only on the receiving end of change. A strategy of passively keeping one's head down and avoiding change increases a person's career risk because he or she will be less likely to be perceived as adding value.

FROM A CHANGE EXPERT

Greg Brenneman has made a career out of turning large companies around and encourages people to work with sick organizations. "If you have a chance of working for a healthy or a sick one, choose the sick one. The sickest ones need the best doctors and it's a lot easier to stand out in a company that needs help,"

(Continued)

(Continued)

he said to MBA students in 2008.[78] These companies are the ones where you really get into the work and help a company truly succeed. The successful ingredients in turnarounds, according to Brenneman, are: healthy financials; developing and sticking to a clear strategy, especially in a time of crisis; identifying new leaders from the industry to lead the company; and plain hard work.

Rules of Thumb for Change Agents

How should managers act as change agents? Several authors have proposed useful insights and wisdom from their experiences and analysis of change leaders. These **rules of thumb for change agents** which have been integrated, combined, and added to, are listed below:[79]

- **Stay alive**—"Dead" change agents are of no use to the organization. The notion that you should sacrifice yourself at the altar of change is absurd unless you truly wish it. At the same time, the invocation to "stay alive" says you need to be in touch with those things that energize you and give you purpose.
- **Start where the system is**—Immature change agents start where they are. Experienced change agents diagnose the system, understand it, and begin with the system.
- **Work downhill**—Work with people in the system in a collaborative fashion. Confront and challenge resisters in useful ways. Don't alienate people if at all possible. Work in promising areas and make progress.
- **Organize, but don't overorganize**—Plans will change. If you are too organized, you risk becoming committed to your plan in ways that don't permit the inclusion and involvement of others.
- **Pick your battles carefully**—Don't argue if you can't win. A win/lose strategy deepens conflict and should be avoided wherever possible. The maxim "If you strike a king, strike to kill" fits here. If you can't complete the job, you may not survive.
- **Load experiments for success**—If you can, set up the situation and position it as positively as possible. Change is difficult at the best of times—if you can improve the odds, you should!
- **Light many fires**—High-visibility projects often attract both attention and opposition. Work within the organizational subsystems to create opportunities for change in many places, not just a major initiative.
- **Just enough is good enough**—Don't wait for perfection. Beta test your ideas. Get them out there to see how they work and how people react.
- **You can't make a difference without doing things differently**—Remember that definition of insanity—"doing things the same way but expecting different results"! You have to act and behave differently to have things change. Hope is not an action.

- **Reflect**—As individuals, as change teams, and as organizations, a commitment to learning from each experience and creating space for reflection on both positive and challenging moments is essential to effective and productive change.
- **Want to change; focus on important results and get them**—Not only does success breed success, but getting important results brings resources, influence, and credibility.
- **Think and act fast**—Speed and flexibility are critical. Sensing the situation and reacting quickly will make a difference. Acting first means others will have to act second and will always be responding to your initiatives.
- **Create a coalition**—Lone ranger operatives are easy to dismiss. As Gary Hamel says, an "army of like-minded activists cannot be ignored."

Summary

This chapter describes how anyone, from any position in the organization, can potentially instigate and lead change. Assuming a change agent role is a matter of personal attributes, a function of the situation, and the vision of the change agent. Four types of change leaders are described: the emotional champion, the intuitive adapter, the continuous improver, and the developmental strategist. Finally, the use of change teams was discussed and advice was provided to managers on how to handle the middle role they find themselves in when dealing with change.

The management of change is an essential part of the role of those who want to manage and lead. It will tax your skills, energize and challenge, exhaust, depress, occasionally exhilarate, and leave you, at times, with a profound sense of accomplishment. What it will not do is leave you the same.

The demands of organizations are clear—managers are expected to play an increasingly significant role in the management of change. Earlier, this book advised managers to know themselves, assess the situation carefully, and then take action. The next chapter outlines action planning to assist leaders of change. See **Toolkit Exercise 8.1** for critical thinking questions for this chapter.

Key Terms

Change agent effectiveness—a function of the person, his or her vision, and the characteristics of the situation.

Exothermic—describes a change situation when energy is liberated by actions.

Endothermic—describes a change program that consumes energy and arouses opposition, which then requires more energy from the change agent.

Change leaders—pull people to change through the use of a powerful change vision.

Change managers—create change by working with others, overcoming resistance, and problem solving situations.

Developmental stages of a change agent—vary from a novice stage to an expert stage through successful experiences with increasingly complex, sophisticated change situations.

Types of Change Leaders

The Emotional Champion—has a clear and powerful vision of what the organization needs and uses that vision to capture the hearts and motivations of the organization's members.

The Developmental Strategist—applies rational analysis to understanding the competitive logic of the organization and how it no longer fits with the organization's existing strategy.

The Intuitive Adapter—has the clear vision for the organization and uses that vision to reinforce a culture of learning and adaptation.

The Continuous Improver—analyzes micro environments and seeks changes such as re-engineering systems and processes.

Hunsaker's Change Roles

The **catalyst**—needed to overcome inertia and focus the organization on the problems faced.

The **solution giver**—knows how to respond and can solve the problem as well as convince others to pursue their solutions.

The **process helper**—facilitates the "how to" of change, playing the role of third-party intervener often.

The **resource linker**—brings people and resources together in ways that aid in the solution of issues.

An **internal change agent**—an employee of the organization who knows the organization intimately and is attempting to create change.

An **external change agent**—a person from outside the organization trying to make changes. Often this person is an outside expert and consultant.

The **change team**—the group of employees, usually from a cross-section of the organization, that is charged with a change task.

The **champion**—the person within the change team who will fight for the change under trying circumstances and preserve throughout adversity.

The **steering team**—plays an advisory and guidance role to change leaders and design and implementation teams.

The **design and implementation team**—responsible for the actual design and implementation of the change initiatives.

The **change project manager**—coordinates planning, manages logistics, tracks the team's progress toward change targets, and manages the adjustments needed along the way.

A sponsor of change—senior executive who fosters commitment to the change and assists the change agents who are actively making the change happen.

Visible sponsorship—entails actions including leveraging of influence and time to advocate for the change.

Information sharing and knowledge development—when the sponsor provides useful information to the change team and ensures that the team's change plans are sound

Sponsors may also **provide protection** for those who are delegated with change tasks, allowing change agents to be less risk averse and more willing to champion the change.

Middle powerlessness—the feeling of a lack of power and influence that those in middle-level organizational roles often experience when organizational changes are being implemented. Pressure comes from above and below and they see themselves as ill-equipped to respond.

Rules of thumb for change agents—things for change agents to keep in mind to ensure their survival and success over the long term.

Checklist: Structuring Work in a Change Team

Once the nature of the change initiative has been set out, team members will need to sort out what needs to be done when and who will do it.

A shorthand designation, BART, is a useful way to structure tasks among a working group. Talking about BART in the context of a newly forming team can make the roles and responsibilities among people clear and decrease conflict among group members.

To be a useful tool, start with *Tasks* and end with *Boundaries*. It is wise to have a conversation about these issues, put what has been agreed-upon in writing, and then revisit the structure at a designated time.

1) Tasks: This is the work that needs to be completed in a particular situation. Make a comprehensive list of tasks; next, assign the tasks to specific roles; then decide how much authority an individual has in the role; and, finally, describe how one role interfaces with another.

2) Authority: This is the scope of decision making that a particular team member has in her or his role.

3) Roles: These are the parts that individual team members have been explicitly assigned to be responsible for in the execution of specific tasks.

4) Boundaries: The edge where one person's responsibilities ends and another's begins.

In addition to the above items, team members need to come to agreement on how they will operate as a team. This includes:

(a) values the team shares and norms of behavior,
(b) performance expectations they have for themselves and for one another,
(c) how they will communicate with and support one another,
(d) how they will manage and resolve conflicts,
(e) how they will manage documents and reports,
(f) how they will track and measure progress, and
(g) how they will otherwise manage their team processes.

Once again, it is useful to put what has been agreed-upon in writing and then revisit it, as needed.

END-OF-CHAPTER EXERCISES

TOOLKIT EXERCISE 8.1

Critical Thinking Questions

Please find the URLs for the videos listed below on the website at study.sagepub.com/cawsey3e. Consider the questions that follow.

1. Please read Case 5 on page 449, "Ellen Zane—Leading Change at Tufts/NEMC" and consider the following questions:

   - Describe the health care environment in Massachusetts in the 1990s. What were the driving forces for change that were pushing the industry? What impact did these forces have on Tufts/New England Medical Center?

   - What happens within Tufts/NEMC as the external environment gyrates with change? What data in the case supports your claim?

   - What's wrong with Tufts/NEMC as Zane takes over as CEO in January 2004?

   - How did Zane gain skills as a leader of change?

   - Which type of change would you prefer to lead? Why?

2. <u>Ellen Zane on Negotiating</u>—11:13 minutes

- What kind of power did Zane have when she was negotiating with insurers?

- What did Zane do to prepare for this emergency?

- How did Zane facilitate a solution?

3. <u>Gene Deszca's Talk: Leading Change</u>—14:59 minutes

- Evaluate yourself on the core competencies mentioned in the video.

- What do you think that you need to do to improve on your skills or create a situation where you can be a successful change agent?

Please see study.sagepub.com/cawsey3e for a downloadable template of this exercise.

TOOLKIT EXERCISE 8.2

Myself as Change Agent

1. The following list of change agent attributes and skills represents an amalgam drawn from the previous section. Rate yourself on the following dimensions:

Attributes of Change Leaders From Caldwell

Low 1 2 3 4 5 6 7 High

- Inspiring vision *1 2 3 4 5 6 7*
- Entrepreneurship *1 2 3 4 5 6 7*
- Integrity and honesty *1 2 3 4 5 6 7*
- Learning from others *1 2 3 4 5 6 7*
- Openness to new ideas *1 2 3 4 5 6 7*
- Risk taking *1 2 3 4 5 6 7*
- Adaptability and flexibility *1 2 3 4 5 6 7*
- Creativity *1 2 3 4 5 6 7*
- Experimentation *1 2 3 4 5 6 7*
- Using power *1 2 3 4 5 6 7*

Attributes of Change Managers From Caldwell

- Empowering others *1 2 3 4 5 6 7*
- Team building *1 2 3 4 5 6 7*
- Learning from others *1 2 3 4 5 6 7*
- Adaptability and flexibility *1 2 3 4 5 6 7*
- Openness to new ideas *1 2 3 4 5 6 7*
- Managing resistance *1 2 3 4 5 6 7*
- Conflict resolution *1 2 3 4 5 6 7*
- Networking skills *1 2 3 4 5 6 7*
- Knowledge of the business *1 2 3 4 5 6 7*
- Problem solving *1 2 3 4 5 6 7*

Change Agent Attributes Suggested by Others

- Interpersonal skills *1 2 3 4 5 6 7*
- Communication skills *1 2 3 4 5 6 7*

- Emotional resilience   *1 2 3 4 5 6 7*
- Tolerance for ambiguity   *1 2 3 4 5 6 7*
- Tolerance for ethical conflict   *1 2 3 4 5 6 7*
- Political skill   *1 2 3 4 5 6 7*
- Persistence   *1 2 3 4 5 6 7*
- Determination   *1 2 3 4 5 6 7*
- Pragmatism   *1 2 3 4 5 6 7*
- Dissatisfaction with the status quo *1 2 3 4 5 6 7*
- Openness to information   *1 2 3 4 5 6 7*
- Flexibility   *1 2 3 4 5 6 7*
- Capacity to build trust   *1 2 3 4 5 6 7*
- Intelligence   *1 2 3 4 5 6 7*
- Emotional intelligence   *1 2 3 4 5 6 7*

2. Do you see yourself as scoring high on some items compared to others? If so, you are more likely to be comfortable in a change agent role. Lack of these attributes and skills does not mean you could not be a change agent—it just means that it will be more difficult and it may suggest areas for development.

3. Are you more likely to be comfortable in a change leadership role at this time, or does the role of change manager or implementer seem more suited to who you are?

4. Ask a mentor or friend to provide you feedback on the same dimensions. Does the feedback confirm your self-assessment? If not, why not?

Please see study.sagepub.com/cawsey3e for a downloadable template of this exercise.

TOOLKIT EXERCISE 8.3

Your Development as a Change Agent

Novice change leaders often picture themselves as being in the right and those that oppose them as somehow wrong. This certainty gives them energy and the will to persist in the face of such opposition. It sets up a dynamic of opposition—the more they resist, the more I must try to change them, and so I persuade them more, put more pressure on them, and perhaps resort to whatever power I have to force change.

1. Think of a situation where someone held a different viewpoint than yours. What were your assumptions about that person? Did you believe they just didn't get it, were wrong headed, perhaps a bit stupid?

   Or did you ask yourself, why would they hold the position they have? If you assume they are as rational and as competent as you are, why would they think as they do? Think back to Table 8.2. Are you at Stage 1, 2, 3, or 4?

2. Are you able to put yourself into the shoes of the resister? Ask yourself: What forces play on that person? What beliefs does he or she have? What criteria is he or she using to evaluate the situation?

3. What are the implications of your self-assessment with respect to what you need to do to develop yourself as a change agent?

Please see study.sagepub.com/cawsey3e for a downloadable template of this exercise.

TOOLKIT EXERCISE 8.4

What Is Your Change Agent Preference?

1. How comfortable are you with risk and ambiguity?

   Do you seek order and stability or change and uncertainty?

   Describe your level of comfort in higher-risk situations.

   Describe your degree of restlessness with routine, predictable situations.

2. How intuitive are you?

   Do you use feelings and emotion to influence others? Or are you logical and systematic?

   Do you persuade through facts and arguments?

3. Ask someone who knows you well to reflect on your change preferences and style. Does that person's judgment agree or disagree with yours?

Why? What data do each have?

4. Given your responses to the above, how would you classify yourself? Are you:

- An Emotional Champion
- An Intuitive Adapter
- A Developmental Strategist
- A Continuous Improver

5. How flexible or adaptive are you with respect to the approach you use?

Do you always adopt the same approach, or do you use other approaches, depending on the needs of the situation?

Which ones do you feel comfortable and competent in using?

Again, check out your self-assessment by asking a significant other for comments. Comment on their response.

Please see study.sagepub.com/cawsey3e for a downloadable template of this exercise.

TOOLKIT EXERCISE 8.5

Your Skills as a Change Team Member

1. Think of a time when you participated in a team. What was the team's goal?

   How well did the team perform? Were the results positive?

   Why or why not?

2. Did the team members exhibit the characteristics listed by Prosci, below? Rate your team members' performance on these characteristics.

   - Being knowledgeable about the business and enthusiastic about the change
   - Possessing excellent oral and written communications skills and a willingness to listen and share
   - Having total commitment to the project, the process, and the results
   - Being able to remain open-minded and visionary
   - Being respected within the organization as an apolitical catalyst for strategic change[80]

3. What personal focus do you have? Do you tend to concentrate on getting the job done—a task focus? Or do you worry about bringing people along—a process focus?

4. How would you improve your skills in this area? Who might help you develop such skills?

Please see study.sagepub.com/cawsey3e for a downloadable template of this exercise.

CHAPTER 9

Action Planning and Implementation

When it is obvious that the goals cannot be reached, don't adjust the goals, adjust the action steps.

—Confucius[1]

CHAPTER OVERVIEW

- Change leaders recognize the usefulness of plans and the imperative of action. Prepare, take action, and learn from the results. Change initiators have a "do it" attitude.
- Action planning and implementation involves planning the work and working the plan. "Right" decisions mean approximately "right" as change agents obtain feedback from action and make adjustments as they act.
- Change agents learn to specify who does what, when, and how to monitor and track their change initiatives. Agents use a variety of management tools, such as responsibility and project planning charts, surveys and survey feedback, and critical path methods, to successfully plan and implement their change programs.
- Successful change agents develop detailed communications plans and understand how to manage transitions from the present to a future desired state.

This book has a philosophical bias for taking action. Rather than passively waiting or complaining from the sidelines, change agents get engaged. However, the goal is not action simply for novelty and excitement. Action must increase the likelihood of positive change. Great ideas don't generate value until they are effectively executed. One of the ways to improve the quality of action is to use proven tools to execute a change agenda.

Tools in Chapter 9 translate plans to action. If this were a political campaign, these tools would be steps that are deployed after the candidate has been selected, the platform finalized, and the election called. The chapter provides advice on implementation tactics and project management tools. It addresses communication and influence tactics during the change process. And finally, the management of transition, or the process of keeping the organization operating while implementing the change, is detailed. In terms of the model in Figure 9.1, these are the implementation issues of "getting from here to there"—assessing the present in terms of the future, determining the work that needs to be done, and implementing the change.

Without a "Do It" Orientation, Things Won't Happen

Many major change initiatives start in the C-suite. Boards of directors and executives at the top of organizations have access to all of the data that an organization generates, and from this perspective and input they can observe a myriad of organizational problems and envision viable solutions. Two examples of boards who hired strong, change agent CEOs are IBM's board when they brought in Lou Gerstner in 1993 and the board of New England Medical Center, Boston (now called Tufts Medical Center) when they hired Ellen Zane in 2002 to lead the transformation of the then-foundering nonprofit hospital (see cases at the end of this book or on the website for the story about Zane's turnaround of the medical center). Gerstner and Zane were seasoned executives when they took on the extremely difficult task of pushing change from the top down into the basements of their organizations. Both had a **"do it" orientation** and both were authorized by their boards and by their titles, jobs, and positions to lead change within their institutions. Having the authority to act makes certain aspects of the job of change agent easier than working from the middle. Gerstner, for instance, when he claimed the title of CEO, quickly changed the reward system for his top executives, focusing their attention on the performance of IBM as a whole, rather than just their divisions or areas. Such quick structural change is unlikely in a mid-level role.

In an ideal world, change leaders located in the middle of the organization will also find support for their projects. They need ready access to supportive executives who provide directional clarity, ensure their organizations are ready for change, approve needed resources, provide other modes of support, and cultivate broad employee commitment for the change. In some instances, this is not the case. Many executives will have little or no knowledge of the initiative or its value and implications. If they have heard of the idea, they may lack interest because of other priorities and political realities; some may have heard of it and have concerns, while others will simply want to distance themselves from the change in the event it doesn't work out. Some will fail to understand the important role they have to play in nurturing innovation from within the organization; others will not see it as their role.

Figure 9.1   The Change Path Model

Awakening
Chapter 4
1. Identify a need for change and confirm the problems or opportunities that incite the need for change through collection of data.
2. Articulate the gap in performance between the present and the envisioned future state, and spread awareness of the data and the gap throughout the organization.
3. Develop a powerful vision for change.
4. Disseminate the vision for the change and why it's needed through multiple communication channels.

Mobilization
Chapters 5 through 8
1. Make sense of the desired change through formal systems and structures, and leverage those systems to reach the change vision (Chapter 5).
2. Assess power and cultural dynamics at play, and put them to work to better understand the dynamics and build coalitions and support to realize the change (Chapter 6).
3. Communicate the need for change organization-wide and manage change recipients and various stakeholders as they react to and move the change forward (Chapter 7).
4. Leverage change agent personality, knowledge, skills and abilities, and related assets (e.g., reputation and relationships) for the benefit of the change vision and its implementation (Chapter 8).

Acceleration
Chapter 9
1. Continue to systematically reach out to engage and empower others in support, planning, and implementation of the change. Help them develop needed new knowledge, skills, abilities, and ways of thinking that will support the change.
2. Use appropriate tools and techniques to build momentum, accelerate and consolidate progress.
3. Manage the transition, celebrating small wins and the achievement of milestones along the larger, more difficult path of change.

Institutionalization
Chapter 10
1. Track the change periodically and through multiple balanced measures to help assess what is needed, gauge progress toward the goal, and to make modifications as needed and mitigate risk.
2. Develop and deploy new structures, systems, processes and knowledge, skills, and abilities, as needed, to bring life to the change and new stability to the transformed organization.

Organizations are complex systems, and their prospects for successful adaptation are advanced when they can also learn and grow from the bottom up. This is one of the reasons that firms such as 3M, Procter & Gamble, and Deloitte have demonstrated such staying power: They grow from within and from the bottom up. Wise senior managers know how to nurture and leverage employees' adaptive energy.

Wise change agents know how to save short-sighted senior managers from themselves. If you work in an organization such as 3M, then "lucky you!" If you do not, an early task is to seek—and hopefully acquire—senior-level support for your initiative, if it is needed. An e-mail from the CEO or SVP announcing her support for your project will help garner support from other organizational members.

INNOVATION AND CHANGE AT 3M

Front-line freedom to innovate and senior-level support have been critical ingredients to 3M's success. Technical and marketing employees commit 15% of their time to work on projects of their own choosing, without supervision. The environment is open and informal, input from customers and lead users is sought, and collaboration and inquisitiveness are valued. Social media facilitates front-line collaboration and helps to overcome the communication barriers that organizational size and complexity bring. At the same time, 3M's culture is demanding, and the process for funding new ideas is highly structured.

The degree of management scrutiny and oversight increases as new ideas evolve to require significant resources. Products that are eventually successful in the marketplace are typically rejected several times in management's funding process before receiving funds, requiring persistence from innovators. Management and employees embrace and learn from failures because innovation won't happen otherwise. George Buckley, 3M's CEO and a Ph.D. in engineering, is deeply interested in innovation. He regularly visits the labs to find out what people are exploring, believing that "creativity comes from freedom, not control."[2] This commitment to innovation allows new products and services to percolate and develop from the ground up.[3]

If senior-level support for change is unlikely to develop in the near future, change initiators may feel that abiding by formal organizational protocols and waiting for official support will slow progress unduly. Faced with this situation, change agents may choose to follow the advice of Rear Admiral Grace Hopper, a pioneering female software engineer in the U.S. Navy, who said "it is easier to seek forgiveness than permission."[4]

Pfeffer and Sutton state "actions count more than elegant plans or concepts" and that "there is no doing without mistakes." They ask, however, a crucial question: "What is the company's response?"[5] If the organization's response to reasoned initiatives and honest mistakes is to scapegoat and blame, people quickly learn not to take risks that might lead to mistakes. Or they learn to cover up mistakes. Either way, the organization suffers.* However, beliefs about likely organizational responses can also become a convenient excuse for inaction and the avoidance of risk taking (e.g., What if my idea really won't work or what will I do if it does work?). If such beliefs are never challenged, their stability will produce self-fulfilling prophecies.

---

*This does lead to an accountability paradox. Accountability is a needed and useful attribute. However, there needs to be a fine balance between holding change leaders accountable for what they do and encouraging the risk-taking behavior that leads to needed learning and change.

Effective executives and managers of change are aware of the consequences of their actions and intuitively test their organizational assumptions by engaging in an action–learning–reaction cycle.[6] Sayles recognized this when he wrote, "working leaders instead of simply waiting for and evaluating results seek to intervene. And the interventions they undertake require a more intimate knowledge of operations, and more involvement in the work than those of traditional middle managers."[7]

For employees lower in the hierarchy, action is also key. Instead of being discouraged by lack of authority or reach, one must fully understand the resources and tools they have at their disposal. Dr. Ross Wirth, chair of Business, Franklin University, reflected on his 32-year career at Citgo Petroleum with the following wisdom:[8] "Traditional thought says that nothing happens without top management's approval (but) change need not be something that is 'done to you.' Here is another way to think of it: empowerment is something you grasp until you find its limits. I tell people that they can constantly test the limits of their empowerment, carefully reading internal politics to see when they are pushing up against a boundary. Too many people think they are not empowered, but actually they have failed to test their limits."

The reality of much organizational life is somewhere between an environment that punishes those who dare to challenge the status quo and one in which all such initiatives are unconditionally embraced and rewarded. Organizational members who choose not to wait on formal permission and undertake reasonable self-initiated change initiatives may experience some chastisement for not first seeking approval, particularly if the initiative runs into difficulty. However, in many organizations, they are also commended for showing initiative and having a positive impact. The organization's culture and the personality of a boss (e.g., managerial style and tolerance for ambiguity) will obviously influence what response the initiator receives, but most managers value initiative.

What can be done to increase the likelihood that taking action will produce desired results? The following sections address this question by exploring a variety of planning and implementing tools. The purpose of these tools is to assist change leaders in designing and then managing their initiatives in ways that increase their prospects for success.

Prelude to Action: Selecting the Correct Path

Any action plan for change needs to be rooted in a sophisticated understanding of how the organization works and what needs to be achieved. Since there are a variety of action paths available, how do you decide which to take? Mintzberg and Westley provide guidance in this matter by setting out three generic approaches: thinking first, seeing first, and doing first:[9]

- **Thinking first strategy** works best when the issue is clear, data are reliable, context is structured, thoughts can be pinned down, and discipline can be established as in many routine production processes. The introduction of an initiative such as Six Sigma is an example where management needs to think first.

- **Seeing first strategy** works best when many elements have to be combined into creative solutions, commitment to those solutions is key, and communication across boundaries is essential. New product development is an example of the need to see first.
- **Doing first strategy** works best when the situation is novel and confusing, complicated specifications would get in the way, and a few simple relationship rules can help people move forward. For example, if a manager is testing an approach to customer service and wants feedback about what works, then doing first is appropriate.

As complexity and ambiguity rise, Mintzberg and Westley argue that the preferred approach to action shifts. Thinking first fits when the situation is well structured, a manager has the needed data, and there is not much confusion about how to proceed. As ambiguity and complexity rise, though, certainty over how best to proceed becomes less clear. Seeing first approaches the challenge by experimentation, prototyping, and pilot programs so that commitment can be gained by having others see and experience an initiative. Doing first is a response to even more ambiguous situations and takes the process of exploration further in the search for new paths forward. As these paths begin to emerge, the approach can then be altered to seeing first or doing first, depending on what is suitable for the next stage.

Nitin Nohria offers a slightly different assessment of the generic change strategies available.[10] He identified three strategies, defined their characteristics, explained the typical implementation, and highlighted their risk points. **Programmatic change** (similar to Mintzberg and Westley's thinking first change) involves the implementation of straightforward, well-structured solutions. It is best suited to contexts that are clear and well defined and where the magnitude of the change is incremental in nature. Risks with this approach lie in potential problems with inflexibility, overreliance on a "one-size-fits-all" solution, and a lack of focus on behavior.

Discontinuous change involves a major break from the past. If the environment is shifting dramatically and a continuation of activities based on existing assumptions will not work, then discontinuous, top-down change may be fitting. Organizational restructuring due to downsizing, rapid growth, or the realignment of markets is an example of this category. Risks with this approach come from political coalitions that may form and derail the change, a lack of sufficient control to enforce the change, and the loss of talented people who become frustrated and quit.

Emergent change (similar to Mintzberg and Westley's doing first change) grows out of incremental initiatives and can create ambiguity and challenge for staff members. An employee-centered change initiative to modify the culture of the organization that emerges from customers' and staff's feedback would be an example. If the organization has a talented, knowledgeable workforce that understands the risks and possibilities, utilizing an emergent change approach may be appropriate. Risks with this approach come in the form of confusion over direction, uncertainty as to the impact of the change, and slow progress (See Table 9.1).

Table 9.1 Three Generic Change Strategies			
Change Type	**Characteristic**	**Implementation**	**Issues or Concerns**
Programmatic change	Missions, plans, objectives	Training, timelines, steering committees	Lack of focus on behavior, one solution for all, inflexible solutions
Discontinuous change	Initiated from top, clear break, reorientation	Decrees, structural change, concurrent implementation	Political coalitions derail change, weak controls, stress from the loss of people
Emergent change	Ambiguous, incremental, challenging	Use of metaphors, experimentation, and risk taking	Confusion over direction, uncertainty and possible slow results

Source: Adapted from N. Nohria and R. Khurana, "Executing Change: Three Generic Strategies," *Harvard Business School* Note. #494–039. August 24, 1993.

To counteract the pitfalls of programmatic or "thinking first" change, consider using employee engagement and feedback to connect with those on the receiving end, learn from their experiences, and decentralize decision making to allow for adaptation to local conditions. The pitfalls (including unintended consequences) from change will be lessened by processes that reduce ambiguity, promote feedback and learning, and build support by enhancing member understanding of the change and why it was undertaken.

The issues related to emergent or "doing first" change may be managed through the use of field experiments and task forces to provide engagement and feedback on an ongoing basis. These can be used to create clarity concerning what is emerging and build understanding and support for the next steps in the change process. In metaphorical terms, this points to a move from "ready—aim—fire" to "ready—fire—aim—re-fire—re-aim"[†] for an emergent approach to planning. In fast-moving contexts, it is likely that a traditional planning process will be too lengthy and that by the time the planning is finished, the opportunity may have been missed. This metaphor recognizes that significant information can be obtained from action feedback. When a change leader initiates action, reactions will occur that can provide insight into how to respond and take corrective actions.

A third approach to thinking about change strategies is found in the unilateral versus participative approaches to change. Advocates of a **unilateral approach** to

---

[†]The managerial use of this metaphor is usually credited to T. Peters and R. H. Waterman Jr., *In Search of Excellence* (New York: Harper & Row, 1982). Our understanding is that its presence in its modified form has its roots in missile defense. If you are defending against incoming missiles, you don't have time to wait and plan a response. You do need to fire before you aim your missile. Then once you have things in motion, you can re-aim your missile based on new, current information.

change believe that if one first changes systems and structures, forcing behavioral changes, that action will in turn produce changes in attitudes and beliefs over time. Those who promote a **participative approach** believe the opposite. They argue that you first need to engage and change attitudes and gain acceptance of an initiative before restructuring systems and organizational structures.

Waldersee and Griffiths note that change initiatives have been traditionally grouped into two broad categories. **Techno–structural change** refers to change that is based in structures, systems, and technology. **Behavioral–social change** is focused on altering established social relationships. After investigating 408 change episodes, they concluded that the unilateral approach was perceived to be more appropriate for techno–structural change, while participative approaches were seen as more appropriate when behavioral–social changes such as cultural change were involved.[11] When Australian managers were asked about the perceived effectiveness of these two change approaches, they saw unilateral methods as more effective in bringing about successful change, regardless of the type of change. What does all of this mean for action planning? Waldersee and Griffiths concluded that:

> Concrete actions taken by change managers are often superior to the traditional prescriptions of participation.[12] Forcing change through top-down actions such as redeploying staff or redesigning jobs may effectively shift employee behavior. With the context and behavior changed, interventions targeting attitudes may then follow. (p. 432)

While a unilateral approach may have appeal for those who want to ensure that things are done, such an approach can be risky and needs to be managed with care. When implementation lacks sensitivity, stakeholders may feel that their perspectives and concerns have been ignored. This can result in fallout and resistance that could have been avoided, and missed opportunities for valuable input.

What conclusions can be drawn from this material on a "do it" orientation and change strategies? Start a change process rather than waiting to get things perfect. Be willing to take informed risks and learn as you go. Finally, pick your change strategy with care and remember to take steps to manage the risks associated with the adopted approach. Regardless of how difficult change appears to be, Confucius was right—"a journey of a thousand miles begins with a single step."[13] You need to plan your work and work the plan.

Plan the Work

If the change leader's approach to planned change has followed what this book suggests, then much planning will have already been done. In addition, Beer, Eisenstat, and Spector[14] offer a prescriptive list of "steps to effective change." Beer et al.'s steps are:

1. Mobilize commitment to change through joint diagnosis of business problems.

2. Develop a shared vision of how to organize and manage for competitiveness.

3. Foster consensus for the new vision, competence to enact it, and cohesion to move it along.

4. Spread revitalization to all departments without pushing it from the top.

5. Institutionalize revitalization through formal policies, systems, and structures.

6. Monitor and adjust strategies in response to problems in the revitalization process.

For many change situations, this checklist provides valuable guidance in the development of an action plan. However, assuming a "one-size-fits-all" approach to change is risky. For example, the above list assumes a fundamental cooperative orientation. That is, there is sufficient commonality of goals that a shared vision is possible. The list also suggests that change should evolve and not be pushed down by top management. However, change agents will need approaches that allow them to face situations in which cooperation and commonality of goals is weak or absent and where changes are being pushed from the top. The table below compares Beer et al.'s steps with the prescriptions of others, which may be helpful in thinking about planning through multiple perspectives.[15]

As well, the need for contingent thinking needs to be addressed. That is, an action plan depends significantly upon the action-planning context. In complex and ambiguous situations, plans and tactics must be able to adapt as events unfold. As such, it is useful to remember the old saying: "No plan survives first contact."[16]

In summary, while careful planning is critical, change leaders must also recognize that planning is a means—not an end in itself. Don't ignore vital emerging information just because it does not fit with carefully conceived plans. The abilities

Table 9.2 A Comparison of Four Models of Change

Beer et al.'s Six Steps for Change (1990)	Jick's The Ten Commandments (1997)	Kotter's Eight-Stage Process for Successful Organizational Transformation (1996)	Lueck's Seven Steps for Change (2003)
Mobilize commitment to change through joint diagnosis of problems.	Analyze the organization and its need for change.	Establish a sense of urgency.	Mobilize energy, commitment through joint identification of business problems and their solutions.
Develop a shared vision of how to organize and manage for competitiveness.	Create a vision and a common direction.	Create a guiding coalition.	Develop a shared vision of how to organize and manage for competitiveness.

(Continued)

Table 9.2 (Continued)

Beer et al.'s Six Steps for Change (1990)	Jick's The Ten Commandments (1997)	Kotter's Eight-Stage Process for Successful Organizational Transformation (1996)	Lueck's Seven Steps for Change (2003)
Foster consensus for the new vision, competence to enact it, and cohesion to move it along.	Separate from the past.	Develop a vision and strategy.	Identify the leadership.
Spread revitalization to all departments without pushing it from the top.	Create a sense of urgency.	Empower broad-based action.	Focus on results, not activities.
Institutionalize revitalization through formal policies, systems, and structures.	Support a strong leader role.	Communicate the change vision.	Start change at the periphery, then let it spread to other units, pushing it from the top.
Monitor and adjust strategies in response to problems in the revitalization process.	Line up political sponsorship.	Generate short-term wins.	Institutionalize success through formal policies, systems, and structures.
	Craft an implementation plan.	Consolidate gains and produce more change.	Monitor and adjust strategies in response to problems in the change process.
	Develop enabling structures.	Anchor new approaches in the culture.	
	Communicate, involve people, and be honest.		
	Reinforce and institutionalize change.		

Source: Based on Todnem, R. (2005). Organisational change management: A critical review. *Journal of Change Management, 5*(4), 369–381; and Beer, M., Eisenstat, R., & Spector, B. (1990, November -December). Why change programs don't produce change. *Harvard Business Review, 1000*, 158–166.

to think contingently, consider alternative paths forward, and adapt are important contributors to enhanced adaptive capacity.[17]

Engage Others in Action Planning

Occasionally, change planning must be undertaken under a cloak of secrecy, such as when a merger is in the works and the premature release of information would significantly affect the price and the level of competitive risk. In general, though, the active involvement of others and information sharing enhances the quality of action planning for most change strategies. Consider one of the experiences of Barbara Waugh, who spent 25 years as a change agent at Hewlett-Packard:

CHANGE AT HP LABS

Barbara Waugh's campaign for change at HP Labs began when its director asked her, "Why does no one out there consider HP Labs to be the best industrial research lab in the world?" Rather than propose answers, she and the director began by asking questions through a survey. The inquiry generated 800 single-spaced pages of feedback related to programs (e.g., too many projects and too few priorities), people (e.g., poor performers are not removed quickly enough and researchers lack sufficient freedom to do their jobs well), and processes (e.g., the information infrastructure is inadequate).

The feedback, says Waugh, was "800 pages of frustrations, dreams, and insights." But how could she capture and communicate what she learned? She drew on her experience with street theater and created a play about HP Labs. She worked passages from the surveys into dialogue and then recruited executives to act as staff members and junior people to act as executives. The troupe performed for 30 senior managers. "At the end of the play, the managers were very quiet," Waugh remembers. "Then they started clapping. It was exciting. They really got it."[18]

Waugh's approach is instructive because it illustrates the power of presenting potentially boring data in an engaging and compelling manner. This was not the first time she nurtured change in an emergent, grassroots fashion. Her approach leveraged listening and questioning, built networks with individuals with complementary ideas, and when needed, arranged for access to financial resources for worthy endeavors.[‡]

Underlying planning-through-engagement strategies are assumptions regarding top-down (unilateral) versus bottom-up (participative) methods of change. Although

---

[‡]In planning the work, interviews, surveys, survey feedback, and appreciative inquiry (a rigorous commitment to active listening, feedback, mutual development, and renewal) are powerful action planning tools. They come from the Organizational Development (OD) approach to change. For more information, two good sources are: D. L. Cooperrider, D. Whitney, and J. M. Stavros, *Appreciative Inquiry Handbook: For Leaders of Change* (Brunswick, OH: Crown, 2008); and T. G. Cummings and C. G. Worley, *Organization Development and Change* (Mason, OH: South-Western, 2009).

Waldersee and Griffiths's study[19] showed that unilateral implementation methods have much to offer, the success of a change is enhanced when people understand what it entails, why it is being undertaken, what the consequences of success and failure are, and why their help is needed and valued. All too often, techno–structural changes have floundered because of design problems getting tangled up with acceptance and implementation issues that never get sorted out.

Regardless of the change strategy preferred, the plan needs to be examined carefully for logic and consistency. The next section outlines a series of questions to improve change agents' abilities in this area.

Ensure Alignment in Your Action Planning

Change agents often understand what needs to be done but get the sequence of activities wrong. They might leave a meeting after a productive discussion but fail to sort out who is responsible for what. Sometimes critical steps in the plan are risky and alternative strategies need to be considered in case things do not go as planned. At other times, change agents may over- or underestimate the available resources and constraints, the time and energy required by various steps, or their own power and competence. Table 9.6 (later in this chapter) provides a checklist of questions to use when reviewing an action plan. This checklist tests the viability of the plan and asks for a rethinking of the connections between the analysis of the situation and the plan itself. Tough-minded thinking can improve the coherence and thoughtfulness of action plans.

Action Planning Tools

This section explores a selection of action planning tools that change agents find particularly useful (see Table 9.3). Selecting the appropriate tool is both an art and science: An art as the story of Waugh at HP illustrated (see above), and a science as one analyzes data carefully and makes an appropriate selection.

1. To-Do Lists

When managers engage in action planning, they often begin by outlining in detail the sequence of steps they will take initially to achieve their goals. That is, they make a list. A **to-do list**, a checklist of things to do, is the simplest and most common planning tool. Sometimes this is all the situation requires. As the action planning becomes more sophisticated, simple to-do lists will not suffice and responsibility charting provides more control.

2. Responsibility Charting

Responsibility charting can be a valuable tool to detail who should do what, when, and how. As well, it can be used to help keep projects on track and provide

Table 9.3 Tools for Action Planning

1. To-do list—a checklist of things to do

2. Responsibility charting—who will do what, when, where, why, and how

3. Contingency planning—consideration of what should be done when things do not work as planned on critical issues

4. Surveys, survey feedback, and appreciative inquiry—capturing people's opinions and tracking their responses, observations, and insights over time, to assist in identifying what needs changing, nurturing engagement and support, and in tracking progress

5. Project planning and critical path methods—operations research techniques for scheduling work. These methods provide deadlines and insight as to which activities cannot be delayed to meet those deadlines.

6. Force field and stakeholder analysis—examination of the forces for and against change and the positions of the major players and why they behave as they do

   a. Commitment charts—an evaluation of the level of commitment of major players (against, neutral, let it happen, help it happen, make it happen)

   b. The adoption continuum or awareness, interest, desire, adoption (AIDA) analysis—examination of major players and their position on the AIDA continuum related to the proposed changes

7. Leverage analysis—determination of methods of influencing major groups or players regarding the proposed changes

a basis for record keeping and accountability. Table 9.4 provides an example responsibility chart. The process begins by defining the list of decisions or actions to be taken. Then individuals are assigned responsibility for achieving specific actions at specified deadlines.

3. Contingency Planning

Contingency planning is the importance of thinking through what should be done should events not go as planned. Two tools that aid in contingency planning are decision tree analysis and scenario planning.[§]

Decision tree analysis asks change agents to consider the major choices and the possible consequences of those alternatives. Analysts are then asked to plan for the possible next actions and consider what the consequences of those actions might be. Such alternating action–consequence sequences can be extended as far as reasonable. As well, probabilities can be assigned as to the likelihood of each consequence. For

---

[§]Readers are encouraged to consult standard operations research texts for further information on these tools.

Table 9.4 Example Responsibility Chart

Decisions or Actions to Be Taken	Responsibilities			
	Susan	Ted	Sonja	Relevant Dates
Action 1	R	A	I	For meeting on Jan. 14
Action 2		R	I	May 24
Action 3	S	A	A	Draft Plan by Feb. 17; action by July 22
Etc.				

Coding:

R = Responsibility (not necessarily authority)

A = Approval (right to veto)

S = Support (put resources toward)

I = Inform (to be consulted before action)

Note that if there are a large number of *As* on your chart, implementation will be difficult. Care must be taken to assign *As* only when appropriate. Likewise, if there are not enough *Rs* and *Ss*, you will need to think about changes needed here and how to bring them about.

Source: Refer to Beckhard, R, *Organizational Transitions*, Addison-Wesley, Reading, Massachusetts, 1987 (p104) for a further discussion on responsibility charting.

many applications, a simple scale (*very likely, likely, possible, unlikely,* or *very unlikely*) is sufficient. This approach helps model the possible consequences to change decisions and assess the benefits and risks associated with the different pathways.

A second tool that helps managers with contingency planning is **scenario planning**. Here a change strategy is formed by first developing a limited number of scenarios or stories about how the future may unfold and then assessing what the implications of each of these would be to the organization.[20] Change leaders typically frame these around an issue of strategic and/or tactical importance. For example, if a firm producing paper forms is concerned about the long-term viability of its business model, then management could develop scenarios of what a paperless form producer would look like. Once the scenarios were developed, managers would ask themselves: how likely is this scenario? What would need to happen to make the scenario a reality? And what contingencies might arise that would need to be addressed? If one or more of these future scenarios seemed worth investing in, then management would develop its plans accordingly. To open people's minds to possibilities and avoid blind spots, external parties are often brought into the process to offer data and insights (often from other perspectives), challenge assumptions, and stimulate thinking, discussion, and informed analysis.

Scenario planning is different from forecasting. Forecasting starts in the present and uses trend lines and probability estimates to make projections about the future. Scenario planning starts by painting a picture of the future and works backward, asking what would have to happen to make this future scenario a reality and what could be done.[21]

While most uses of scenario planning are at a strategy level, the principles can be applied to frame possible visions for change and develop the action pathways that will increase the likelihood that the vision will be achieved. Royal Dutch Shell[22] was one of the first users of scenario planning. The firm used it as a way to link future uncertainties to today's decisions.

4. Surveys and Survey Feedback

Change agents may find it is helpful to use surveys to capture people's attitudes, opinions, and experiences at a particular point in time and then possibly track those attitudes over time. Tools in this area can provide anonymity to the respondents and make it possible to capture the opinions of a larger proportion of the participants than might otherwise be possible. Political agendas don't disappear with the use of a survey, but they may make it possible for people to say things that they would not feel comfortable stating publically. Services such as SurveyMonkey.com and EmployeeSurveys.com have made the design, delivery, and analysis easy to manage.

Surveys are used to access the opinions of internal and external stakeholders and assess attitudes and beliefs of relevance to the change. For example, how do customers view the firm's service levels, innovativeness, and product performance? What ideas do they have concerning new product offerings or service improvements? Employees can be sampled to assess the organization's readiness for change, the culture or work climate, their satisfaction and commitment levels, or what is helping or hindering their ability to do their jobs. Sometimes surveys are deployed to develop options and assess opinions on their viability. Later in the change process, surveys may sample understanding and knowledge levels, emerging attitudes and issues, and levels of acceptance and satisfaction with the change. The possible applications are restricted only by imagination, people's willingness to respond, and legal and ethical considerations.

Ready-made surveys are available on virtually any topic. Some are publically available at no cost, while others are proprietary and have charges attached to their use. Costs can vary from a few dollars per survey to thousands of dollars when outside consultants are used to design, administer, assess, and report the findings. When it comes to scoring and interpretation, some are straightforward and easy to interpret, while others require the assistance of a skilled practitioner. Some of these instruments have been carefully assessed for reliability and validity, while others have nothing more than face validity.

The bottom line with respect to surveys is that they can prove very helpful to change agents but need to be approached with care. Their design, administration, and analysis require the assistance of someone well trained in survey research. Even when a change agent is sampling opinions, the ability to frame good questions is a prerequisite to getting useful information. The same holds true for analysis and interpretation.[*]

A powerful use of surveys is an approach called **survey feedback**.[23] It is an action research method developed by organizational development (OD) practitioners as a way to stimulate and advance conversations and insights concerning what is going on in the organization, how members are feeling, and how things could be improved. As the name suggests, it involves the sharing of survey results with the individuals affected by the findings. Those involved in the discussion will have responded to the survey.

Skilled facilitators guide work groups through the discussion of the findings. They use this as an opportunity to enrich their interpretation of what the data means and where things are at, and to more fully explore the implications for action. The process is used to raise awareness and understanding, advance the analysis, and build support and commitment for actions that will benefit both the individuals and the organization. Appreciative inquiry approaches discussed earlier in the book can be married effectively with survey feedback to engage and energize participants, learn from them, and set the stage for future actions.

5. Project Planning and Critical Path Methods

Project planning and critical path methods can provide valuable assistance to change managers as they think about what action steps to take.[**] These methods have been developed into sophisticated operations research techniques to aid the planning of major projects. Critical path methods ask planners to identify when the project should be completed and to work backward from that point, scheduling all tasks that will require time, effort, and resources. These are arranged in time sequence such that tasks that can occur simultaneously can be identified. These tasks are then plotted on a timeline. Sequential tasks are plotted to determine the needed time to complete the project.

With this done, managers can assess bottlenecks, resource requirements, slack at particular points in the process (i.e., more time or resources than the minimum required), and progression paths. The critical path, the path with the least slack time, can be identified and special attention can be paid to it. If there are concerns about the time to completion, the project manager can add resources to speed up the project, revisit the specifications, look for viable alterations to the implementation path, or increase the amount of time required to complete the project. Likewise, if there are concerns over the cost of the project, the project manager can explore alternatives on this front.

---

[*]For further information on survey research, see L. M. Rea and R. A. Parker, *Designing and Conducting Survey Research* (San Francisco: Jossey-Bass, 2005).

[**]Software packages are available in this area. A commonly used one, Microsoft Office Project (http://www.microsoft.com/project/en/us/default.aspx), allows you to track steps, resource requirements, and costs; see the impact of possible changes; trace the source of issues; visually communicate project information to others; and collaborate with them on the plans. Colleges, universities, and organizations such as the Project Management Institute (http://www.pmi.org/Pages/default.aspx) offer professional training in project management.

The critical path method introduces the notion of parallel initiatives. That is, it recognizes that different things may be able to be worked on simultaneously if the work is properly organized. Phase 1 tasks don't have to be totally completed before beginning work on Phase 2 tasks. Care and sophistication are required with this approach because it carries the risk of increasing confusion and redundant effort. When properly applied, though, it can shrink the time required to complete the change. This is readily visible in areas such as new product development. Figure 9.2 gives an example of a sequential and a parallel plan for new product development. In the upper half of the figure, the tasks are plotted sequentially. In the lower half of the figure, the tasks overlap. Concept development begins before opportunity identification ends and the cycle time to completion is reduced.

6. Tools to Assess Forces That Influence Outcomes and Stakeholders

Force field analysis asks change agents to specify the forces for and against change. **Stakeholder analysis** and related maps ask that the key players be identified and the relationships among players and the change initiative be examined.

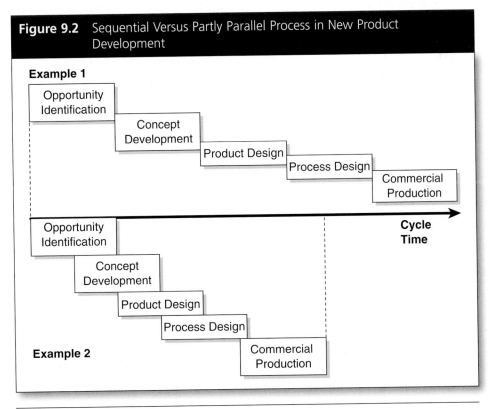

Figure 9.2 Sequential Versus Partly Parallel Process in New Product Development

Source: M. A. Shilling and W. L. Hill, "Managing the New Product Development Process: Strategic Imperatives," *Academy of Management Executive* 12, no. 3 (1998): 67–81.

(See Chapter 6 for discussion of these topics.) Two additional tools that are helpful when planning actions related to stakeholders are commitment analysis charts and AIDA (awareness, interest, desiring, action) charts.

A. Commitment Analysis Charts

Managers can use **commitment charts** to analyze the engagement of each stakeholder. Stakeholders can be thought of as being weakly to strongly opposed (against) to your change project, "neutral" (let it happen), slightly positive (help it happen), or strongly positive (make it happen). Change leaders also need to consider the level of understanding that underpins stakeholders' commitment level. Identifying the existing level of commitment is the first step in planning tactics designed to alter those preexisting patterns. Table 9.5 provides an example commitment chart. (Note that the "X" in the table shows where the person is and the "O" shows where a change agent wants them to be.)

B. The Adoption Continuum or AIDA

Stakeholder analysis will have identified the people who are critical to the change process. With this information in hand, change agents need to consider how they propose to encourage those individuals to move along the **adoption continuum** until the needed stakeholders are aligned with the change, or at least their opposition has been minimized.

As noted in Chapter 6, change agents can think of the process of getting people onside with change as one of first creating awareness and then encouraging them to move from awareness of the issues to interest in the change to desiring action and, finally, to action or adopting the change. This is called the AIDA or adoption continuum. Table 9.6 provides an example of how a change agent might map people on to the adoption continuum as a method of tracking their change attitudes.

Table 9.5 An Example Commitment Chart[24]						
	Level of Commitment					
Key Players	**Opposed Strongly to Weakly**	**Neutral**	**Let It Happen**	**Help It Happen**	**Make It Happen**	**Level of Understanding (high, med, low)**
Person 1		X	→O			Med
Person 2				X	→O	High
Person 3		X	□	→O		Low
Etc.						

Source: Beckhard, R., & Harris, R. (1987). *Organizational transitions* (p. 95). Reading, MA: Addison-Wesley.

Different individuals will be at different points on the AIDA continuum, which makes change strategies complex. For each stage, change agents need to use different tactics. For example, to raise initial awareness, well-designed general communication vehicles such as e-mails, newsletters, reports, and videos can be used. The messages should raise awareness of the need for change, set out the vision for the change, and provide access to thought-provoking information and images that support the initiative.

To move people to the interest phase, managers need to outline how the change will affect stakeholders personally and/or why this change should be of interest to them. Discussion groups on the issue, benchmark data, simulations, and test runs showing results can be effective in stimulating interest. Once interest is aroused, specific tactics to demonstrate and reinforce the benefits and build commitment are needed. Change agents might use one-on-one meetings to influence stakeholders, to persuade them to get directly involved with the change, or to connect them with influential supporters of the change. Change agents might reallocate resources or designate rewards in ways that reinforce adoption. Influencing people one at a time or in small groups can be valuable if influential individuals are identified and the right message is communicated to them.

7. Leverage Analysis

People's position on the adoption continuum is influenced by their general orientation to change—whether they tend to be an innovator, early adopter, early majority, late majority, or laggard in matters related to change. One of the action planning challenges for the change leaders is to sort out people's overall predisposition to change in general and the proposed change in particular.

Moving individuals on the adoption continuum is aided by engaging in **leverage analysis**. Leverage analysis seeks to identify those actions that will create the greatest change with the least effort. For example, if opinion leaders of a key group of individuals can be identified and persuaded to back the proposed organizational change, the job of the change leader is easier. Likewise, if the task is to persuade senior management, one needs to identify influential individuals in this group. Identifying high-leverage methods will depend on the quality of your knowledge of the participants and your analysis of the organization and its environment. (One successful change agent ensured the adoption of a new software system by persuading the CEO

Table 9.6 Mapping People on the Adoption Continuum

Persons or Stakeholder Groups	Awareness	Interest	Desiring Action	Moving to Action or Adopting the Change
Person 1				
Person 2				
Person 3				
. . .				

to personally call every regional manager as they were key stakeholders in the change, and ask for their support!)[25]

Gladwell presents an excellent example of the notion of leverage in his book *The Tipping Point*.[26] Gladwell points out how little things can have large consequences if they occur at the right moment and are contagious. If things catch on and momentum builds, eventually a tipping point is reached. This is the point where a critical level of support is reached, the change becomes more firmly rooted, and the rate of acceptance accelerates. As Burke puts it, change agents need to find the critical few individuals that can connect with others in ways that change the context and tip things into a new reality. The vision needs to be sticky (i.e., cast as a story so that it will stay in people's minds), and change agents need to understand the connectors in the organization to get this message out.[27] Moore notes that one of the biggest challenges to reaching the tipping point is to build sufficient support to allow the acceptance of the change to cross the "chasm" between the early adopters and visionaries and the early majority.[28] Once this gap has been bridged, the rate of progress accelerates. As things accelerate, new challenges emerge, such as how to scale your efforts so that momentum is maintained and enthusiasm is not soured due to implementation failures or stalled progress.

TIPPING POINTS AND THE MOMENTUM FOR CHANGE IN THE OBAMA ELECTION

Barack Obama's path to the presidency was dotted with several tipping points during the state primaries and the federal campaign. Some were related to specific things done by the candidate; some related to the actions of others; and some tied to specific situations (e.g., the mortgage/banking crisis). His creative use of social media (e.g., Facebook) is particularly noteworthy. It allowed him to reach out virally to groups of electors and move them along the commitment continuum at speeds not seen before. This generated grassroots financial support and media buzz that legitimized his candidacy very early on.

During the primaries, Representative James E. Clyburn, a prominent uncommitted South Carolina Democrat, felt the tipping point occurred around midnight on Tuesday, May 6, 2008. "I could tell the next day, when I got up to the Capitol that this thing was going to start a slide toward Obama. I don't believe that there is any way that she (Hillary Clinton) can win the nomination." Contentious remarks by former President Bill Clinton created a rift with African Americans, Obama's 14-point North Carolina victory exceeded expectations, and Hillary Clinton's weaker-than-expected win in the Indiana primary all conspired to take the wind out of her campaign while energizing Obama's.

Super-delegates were still not committing in large numbers to Obama in early May. Clyburn saw this as "the long shadow of the Clintons in the Democratic Party stretching back more than a decade and the reservoir of goodwill." However, he expected to see a steady and significant movement in the days ahead. "That's pretty much where everybody knows it's going to end up." Representative Rahm Emanuel, the Democratic conference chairman, went further and labeled Obama the presumptive nominee.[29]

This discussion of Obama's campaign points to the value that the Internet and social media can play in raising awareness and advancing commitment levels, and politicians of all stripes have recognized this and become increasingly sophisticated. Blogs, Facebook pages, Twitter, Instagram, Pinterest, . . . the terrain continues to evolve, and change agents need to pay attention to how these technologies can be used to leverage their plans. In their global survey of the corporate deployment of social media tools in change initiatives, McKinsey and Company reports their use has become mainstream and that they are playing significant roles in the success of change initiatives. They are being used to communicate with and inform staff; seek feedback; and engage, energize, and otherwise enhance the sense of front-line ownership in change initiatives.[30]

8. Operation Management Tools

The operations management area provides useful planning tools and diagnostic aids: Pareto diagrams (which classify problems according to relative importance), cause–effect diagrams, histograms, approaches to the development of benchmark and normative data, control charts (to show abnormal trends), and scatter diagrams are some of the tools that can be used to manage a change initiative.[31] The selection of which of these tools to use depends upon the nature of the change challenge, the needs of the change agents, and the resources available to them. In general, the value of these tools lies in focusing attention, sorting out patterns and underlying effects, and assessing progress.

The variety of techniques and tools to bring about change continues to grow. Over the years, Darrell Rigby and Barbara Bilodeau have tracked management's use of different change tools on a global basis and assessed managerial satisfaction with them (see Table 9.7 and Figure 9.3).[32] By tracking usage patterns by region and types of firms, differences in the sorts of change issues seen as most needing attention become apparent. This generic listing of change approaches provides a useful touch point for change leaders when they are considering how to proceed given the needs for change that they have identified.

In summary, planning the work asks change leaders to translate the change vision into specific actions that people can take. The plan outlines targets and dates and considers contingencies—what might go wrong (or right), how managers can anticipate those things, and how they can respond. Further, it examines how realistic the chances are for success and how a change agent increases the probabilities for success. Table 9.9 provides you with a checklist of things to think about when developing and assessing your action plan.

Working the Plan Ethically and Adaptively

Working the plan requires change agents to focus, develop support and delivery capacity, test their thinking, see things as opportunities, adapt to changes in the environment, and take appropriate risks. At the same time, change agents need to proceed ethically. Otherwise they risk destroying credibility and the trust others

Table 9.7 Rigby's List of the Best Tools for the Job

Type of Tool	Impact of the Change Tool				
	Financial Results	Customer Equity	Performance Capabilities	Competitive Positioning	Organizational Integration
Customer Retention		++		+	
Customer Satisfaction Measures		++		++	
Customer Segmenting		++			
Cycle Time Reduction	++		+	+	
Growth Strategies	+		+		
Merger Integration Teams					+
Mission and Vision Statements					++
One-to-One Marketing	++	++	++	++	++
Pay for Performance	+				
Strategic Alliances		+		+	
Strategic Planning		+	++	++	
Supply Chain Integration	++			++	++
Total Quality Management		++			
Virtual Teams					++

+ Significantly above the mean in 1 year

++ Significantly above the mean in every year (over 10 years)

Source: D. Rigby, "Management Tools and Techniques: A Survey," *California Management Review,* 43, no. 2 (2001, Winter).

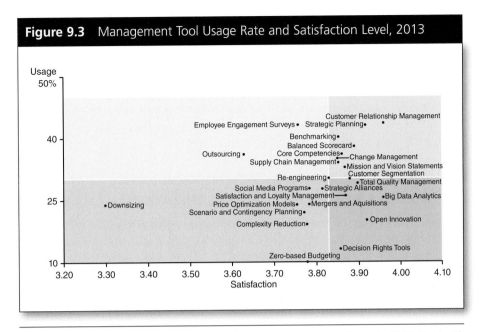

Figure 9.3 Management Tool Usage Rate and Satisfaction Level, 2013

Source: Rigby, D., & Bilodeau, B. (2013, May 8). Management tools and trends, 2013. Used with permission from Bain & Company. www.bain.com

have in them. Relationships can and do recover from strong disagreements, but recovery is less likely if people feel they have been lied to or otherwise ethically abused. A permanent sense of betrayal tends to ensue when you have been dealt with unethically.

Working the plan recognizes the importance of being able to roll with the punches and learn as you go. Chris Argyris warns, "people who rarely experience (and learn from) failure end up not knowing how to deal with it."[33] De Bono echoes this sentiment, saying, "success is an affirmation but not a learning process."[34] Post hoc memories of what led to success (or failure) tend to be selective; valuable learning will be lost if steps aren't taken to actively and objectively reflect on the process as you go. There will be missteps and failures along the way, and a key attribute of a "do it" orientation to working the plan is the capacity to learn and adapt the paths to change along the way.

When working the plan, generating stakeholder and decision-maker confidence in the viability of the initiative is critical. However, it is also important not to be deluded by your own rhetoric. Russo and Shoemaker provide us with guidelines for managing under- and overconfidence; in particular, they differentiate the need for confidence when one is an implementer as opposed to a decision maker. Decision makers need to be realistic; implementers can afford to be somewhat overconfident if it provides others with the courage to change.[35]

Developing a Communication Plan

When implementing a change program, change leaders often find that misinformation and rumors are rampant in their organization. The reasons for change are not clear to employees, and the impact on employees is frequently exaggerated, both positively and negatively. In all organizations, the challenge is to persuade employees to move in a common direction. Good communication programs are essential to minimize the effects of rumors, to mobilize support for the change, and to sustain enthusiasm and commitment.[36] In a study on the effectiveness of communications in organizations, Goodman and Truss found that only 27% of employees felt that management was in touch with employees' concerns, regardless of the fact that the company had a carefully crafted communications strategy.[37]

RUMORS AND REALITY IN ORGANIZATIONAL CHANGE

In an inbound call center of an insurance firm, employees became convinced that the real purpose of an organizational change initiative was to get rid of staff. Management made public announcements and assurances that the reorganization was designed to align processes and improve service levels, not reduce headcount. However, staff turnover escalated to more than 20% before leaders convinced employees that the rumors were false.

Often, much of the confusion over change can be attributed to the different levels of understanding held by different parties. Change agents and senior management may have been considering the change issues for months and have developed a shared understanding of the need for change and what must happen. However, frontline staff and middle managers may not have been focused on the matter. Even if they have been considering these issues, their vantage points will be quite different from those leading the change.

The **purpose of the communication plan for change** centers on four major goals: (1) to infuse the need for change throughout the organization, (2) to enable individuals to understand the impact that the change will have on them, (3) to communicate any structural and job changes that will influence how things are done, and (4) to keep people informed about progress along the way. As the change unfolds, the focus of the communication plan shifts.

Timing and Focus of Communications

A communication plan has four phases: (a) prechange approval, (b) creating the need for change, (c) midstream change and milestone communication, and (d) confirming/celebrating the change success. The messages and methods of communication will vary depending upon which phase your change is in. Table 9.8 outlines the communication needs of each phase.

Prechange phase: Change agents need to convince top management and others that the change is needed. They will target individuals with the influence and/or authority to approve a needed change. Dutton and her colleagues suggest that packaging the change proposal into smaller change steps helps success. She found that timing was crucial in that persistence, opportunism, and involvement

Table 9.8 Communication Needs for Different Phases in the Change Process

Prechange Phase	Developing the Need for Change Phase	Midstream Change Phase	Confirming the Change Phase
Communication plans to sell top management	Communication plans to explain the need for change, provide a rationale, reassure employees, and clarify the steps in the change process	Communication plans to inform people of progress and to obtain feedback on attitudes and issues, to challenge any misconceptions, and to clarify new organizational roles, structures, and systems	Communication plans to inform employees of the success, to celebrate the change, and to prepare the organization for the next change

Source: Based on Klein, "A Management Communications Strategy for Change," *Journal of Organizational Change.* Vol. 9, #2, 1996.

of others at the right time were positively related to the successful selling of projects. Finally, linking the change to the organization's goals, plans, and priorities was critical.[38]

Developing the need for the change phase: When creating awareness of the need for change, communication programs need to explain the issues and provide a clear, compelling rationale for the change. If a strong and credible sense of urgency and enthusiasm for the initiative isn't conveyed, the initiative will not move forward. There are simply too many other priorities available to capture people's attention.[39] Increasing awareness of the need for change can also be aided by the communication of comparative data. For example, concrete benchmark data that demonstrate how competitors are moving ahead can shake up complacent perspectives. Spector demonstrates how sharing of competitive information can overcome potential conflicting views between senior management and other employees.[40] The vision for the change needs to be articulated and the specific steps of the plan that will be undertaken need to be clarified. People need to be reassured that they will be treated fairly and with respect.[41]

Midstream change phase: As the change unfolds, people will want to have specific information communicated to them about future plans and how things will operate. If the organization is being reorganized, employees will want to understand how this reorganization will affect their jobs. If new systems are being put into place, training needs to happen in order to help employees understand and use the systems properly. If reporting relationships are altered, employees need to know who will do what in the organization. Thus, intentional strategies are needed to communicate this information.

In the middle phases of change, people need to understand the progress made in the change program. Management needs to obtain feedback regarding the acceptance of the changes and the attitudes of employees and others (e.g., customers, suppliers) affected by the initiative. Change leaders need to understand any misconceptions that are developing and have the means to combat such misconceptions. During this phase, extensive communications on the content of the change will be important as management and employees begin to understand new roles, structures, and systems.[42] As the newness of the initiative wears off, sustaining interest and enthusiasm and remaining sensitive to the personal impact of the change continue to be important. Change leaders need to remain excited about the change and communicate that enthusiasm often. Recognizing and celebrating progress, achievements, and milestones all help in this regard.[43]

Rumors, gossip, and horror stories will compete with the messages from the change leaders, and their frequency rises when the change leader's credibility declines or ambiguity increases. Employees tend to believe friends more than they do supervisors and tend to turn to supervisors before relying on the comments of senior executives and outsiders. Change agents have a choice: They can communicate clear, timely, and candid messages about the nature and impact of the change or they can let the rumors fill the void. An effective communications campaign can reduce the number of rumors by lowering uncertainty, lessening ambivalence and resistance to change, and increasing the involvement and commitment of employees.[44]

Change websites, electronic bulletin boards, online surveys to sample awareness and opinions, change blogs, and other types of social media can all play useful roles in the communications strategy. However, when uncertainty rises on things of importance, don't forget the power of face-to-face communications. Positive reactions tend to increase and negative reactions are lessened when people have an opportunity to hear from those in authority and ask them questions about the change and its impact.[45]

Confirming the change phase: The final phase of a change program needs to communicate and celebrate the success of the program. Celebration is an undervalued activity. Celebrations are needed along the way to mark progress, reinforce commitment, and reduce stress. They are certainly warranted at the conclusion! The final phase also marks the point at which the change experience as a whole needs to be discussed (more will be said about this in the next section on transition management) and unfinished tasks identified. The organization needs to be positioned for the next change. Change is not over—only this particular phase is.

While change agents attend to the different phases in the change process, they need to match the communications challenge with the communications channel selected.[46] Channel richness ranges from standard reports and general information e-mails at one end through to personalized letters and e-mails, telephone conversations, videoconferencing, and face-to-face communications at the other end. When the information is routine, memos and blanket e-mails can work well. However, when things become more complex, ambiguous, and personally relevant to the recipient, the **richness of the communication channel** needs to increase. A change agent can follow up with a document that provides detailed information, but face-to-face approaches are valuable when matters are emotionally loaded for stakeholders or when you want to get the recipients' attention.

Goodman and Truss suggest using line managers and opinion leaders as lynchpins in the communications strategy, but this requires that they be properly briefed and engaged in the change process. They also stress that change agents need to recognize communication as a two-way strategy.[47] That is, the gathering of information from people down the organizational ladder is as important as delivering the message.

Key Principles in Communicating for Change

Klein[48] suggests six principles that should underlie a communications strategy:

1. Message and media redundancy are key for message retention. That is, multiple messages using multiple media will increase the chance of people obtaining and retaining the message. Too often, management believes that since the message was sent, their work is done. It is the employee's fault for not getting the message! As one author pointed out, it takes time for people to hear, understand, and believe a message, especially when they don't like what they hear.[49] Some change agents believe that it takes 15 to 20 repetitions before a message gets communicated effectively. The value of communicating messages in multiple ways to increase retention and meaningfulness that was discussed in Chapter 7, and the use of social media in change initiatives that was discussed earlier in this chapter, speak to this.[50]

2. Face-to-face communication is most effective. While the impact of face-to-face is highest, the cost is also higher. Face-to-face permits two-way communication, which increases the chance of involvement of both parties and decreases the probability of miscommunication.

3. Line authority is effective in communications. Regardless of the level of participative involvement, most employees look to their managers for direction and guidance. If the CEO says it, the message packs a punch and gets attention.

4. The immediate supervisor is key. The level of trust and understanding between an employee and his or her supervisor can make the supervisor a valuable part of a communications strategy. People expect to hear important organizational messages from their bosses.

5. Opinion leaders need to be identified and used. These individuals can be critical in persuading employees to a particular view.

6. Employees pick up and retain personally relevant information more easily than general information. Thus, communication plans should take care to relate general information in terms that resonate with particular employees.

The importance of communications in helping recipients deal with change was discussed in Chapter 7. Creating a sense of fairness, trust, and confidence in the leadership, and interest and enthusiasm for the initiative is important to the success of change initiatives. Well-executed communications strategies play an important role here.[51] However, change leaders seldom give enough attention to this topic. They intuitively understand the importance of the timely communication of candid, credible change-related information through multiple channels, but they get busy with other matters. As communication shortcomings escalate, so too do downstream implementation difficulties.[52]

Influence Strategies

Influencing others is a key concern for change leaders when working the plan. It involves consideration of how they can bring various stakeholders onside with the change. The sooner this is addressed, the better. When implementing change, there is a tendency to give insufficient attention to the constructive steps needed to foster employee support and alleviate dysfunctional resistance. When considering your communication plan and use of influence strategies, think about who you are communicating with and never underestimate the importance of the reputation (including their competence and trustworthiness) of those who are the face and voice of the change initiative.

Below are seven change strategies for influencing individuals and groups in the organization.[53] These are:

1. **Education and communication:** This strategy involves using education and communication to help others develop an understanding of the change initiative, what is required of them, and why it is important. Often people need to see the need for and the logic of the change. Change leaders may fail to adequately communicate their message through the organization because they are under significant time pressure and the rationale "is so obvious" to them they don't understand why others don't get it.

2. **Participation and involvement:** Getting others involved can bring new energy and ideas, and cause people to believe they can be part of the change. This strategy works best when the change agent has time and needs voluntary compliance and active support to bring about the change. Participation fits with many of the norms of today's flattened organizations, but some managers often feel that it just slows everything down, compromising what needs to be done quickly.

3. **Facilitation and support:** Here change agents provide access to guidance and other forms of support to aid in adaptation to change. This strategy works best when the issues are related to anxiety and fear of change, or where there are concerns over insufficient access to needed resources.

4. **Negotiation and agreement:** At times, change leaders can make explicit deals with individuals and groups affected by the change. This strategy can help deal with contexts where the resistance is organized, "what's in it for me"

is unclear, and power is at play. The problem with this strategy is that it may lead to compliance rather than wholehearted support of the change.

5. **Manipulation and co-optation:** While managers don't like to admit to applying this tactic, covert attempts to influence others are very common. Engaging those who are neutral or opposed to the change in discussions and engaging in ingratiating behavior will sometimes alter perspectives and cause resistors to change their position on the change. However, trust levels will drop and resistance will increase if people believe they are being manipulated in ways not consistent with their best interests.

6. **Explicit and implicit coercion:** With this strategy, as with the previous one, there is a negative image associated with it. Nevertheless, managers often have the legitimate right and responsibility to insist that changes be done. This strategy tends to be used when time is of the essence, compliant actions are not forthcoming, and change agents believe other options have been exhausted. Change leaders need to recognize the potential for residual negative feelings and consider how to manage these.

7. Open systems analysis points to a seventh change strategy—**systemic or system adjustments**. At times, adjustments can be made to formal structures, systems, and processes that reduce resistance while advancing the desired changes. For example, if employee resistance has coalesced in a group of employees who are employed in a particular function, organizational restructuring or the reassignment of group members to other areas may reduce resistance markedly. However, if it is mishandled, it can mobilize and escalate resistance in others.

SYSTEM ADJUSTMENTS (I.E., CLOSING STORES AND ELIMINATING JOBS) AT WALMART

Walmart has used systemic adjustments over the years as a change tool to assist in maintaining managerial discretion in employment practices by retaining their non-union status. In 2005, 200 employees at the store in Jonquière, Quebec, Canada, were attempting to negotiate the first-ever union contract with the firm. However, after 9 days of meetings, over 3 months, Walmart announced it was closing the store because of concerns over its profitability. In 2008, the same approach was adopted when six employees in Gatineau, Quebec, won the right to unionize their small operation within Walmart. Walmart employees in Weyburn, Saskatchewan, voted to unionize, but quickly reversed field and voted to decertify in 2010. The unions in both Quebec and Saskatchewan sued the employer for unfair labor practices and took their respective cases all the way to the Supreme Court of Canada. After years of litigation, the Quebec suit against Walmart's store closure met with limited success (some financial restitution was ordered), but the Saskatchewan case was unsuccessful. Currently no Walmart operation in Canada is unionized. The only other time a unionization drive had been close to succeeding was in 2000. Eleven meat cutters in their Jacksonville, Texas, store voted to join the UFCW. Walmart responded by eliminating the meat cutting job companywide.[54]

See **Toolkit Exercise 9.2** to think about influence strategies you've experienced.

Another way to think about influence strategies is to consider whether they attempt to push people in the desired direction or pull them. **Push tactics** attempt to move people toward acceptance of change through rational persuasion (the use of facts and logic in a nonemotional way) and/or pressure (the use of guilt or threats). The risk with the use of push tactics is that they can lead to resistance and defensiveness. Recipients may oppose the pressure simply because it is pressure and they feel a need to defend their positions.

Alternatively, change leaders can rely on **pull tactics**: inspirational appeals and consultation. Inspirational appeals can arouse enthusiasm based on shared values or ideals. *Consultation* (as it is used here) refers to when you seek the participation of others through appeals to the individuals' self-worth and positive self-concept. Both these approaches are designed to pull individuals in the desired direction.[††]

Falbe and Yukl examined the effectiveness of nine different influence tactics. The most effective strategies were two pull tactics: (1) inspirational appeals and (2) consultation (seeking the participation of others). When considering these, never underestimate the importance of the credibility of the change leader.

The strategies of intermediate effectiveness were a combination of push and pull strategies: (3) rationale persuasion (facts, data, logic); (4) ingratiation (praise, flattery, friendliness); (5) personal appeals (friendship and loyalty); and (6) exchange tactics (negotiation and other forms of reciprocity).

The three strategies that were least effective were push strategies: (7) direct pressure, (8) legitimating tactics (framing of the request as consistent with policy and/or the influencer's authority), and (9) coalition building (creation of subgroups or linkages with other groups to exert pressure).[55]

Nutt categorizes four influence tactics used during implementation: (1) intervention, (2) participation, (3) persuasion, and (4) edict. **Intervention** is where key executives justify the need for change (often through the use of data) and provide new norms to judge performance. **Participation** involves engaging stakeholders in the change process. **Persuasion** is the use of experts to sell a change. And **edict** is the issuing of directives. Table 9.9 summarizes Nutt's data on the frequency of use, initial and ultimate adoption rate, and the time to install for each of these tactics.

This table demonstrates the value of a well-respected sponsor who acts as a lightning rod and energizes and justifies the need for change. The frequency of the use of participation as a strategy is somewhat higher than intervention and may reflect the challenge of managing change from the middle of the organization. Adoption takes longer, but it has the second best success rate. Persuasion is attempted more frequently than the other three tactics, but its success rate is significantly lower than participation and the time to adoption slightly longer. Finally, it is difficult to understand the frequency of use of edict as a tactic, given its poor adoption rate and length of time to install.

[††]These styles are described more fully in Chapter 8.

Table 9.9 Implementation Tactics and Success[56]				
Tactic	**Percentage Use**	**Initial Adoption Rate**	**Ultimate Adoption Rate**	**Time to Adopt (Months)**
Intervention	16%	100%	82%	11.2
Participation	20%	80.6%	71%	19.0
Persuasion	35%	65%	49%	20.0
Edict	29%	51%	35%	21.5

This section has outlined a variety of influence tactics that can be used to build awareness, reduce ambivalence and resistance, and move people to acceptance and adoption of the initiative. In general, it is wise to move as slowly as is practical. This permits people to become accustomed to the idea of the change, adopt the change program, learn new skills, and see the positive sides. It also permits change leaders to adjust their processes, refine the change, improve congruence, and learn as they go. However, if time is of the essence or if going slowly means that resisters will be able to organize in ways that will make change highly unlikely, then change leaders should plan carefully, move quickly, and overwhelm resistance where possible. Just remember, though, that it is far easier to get into a war than it is to build a lasting peace after the fighting ends. Don't let your impatience and commitment to moving the change forward get the better of your judgment concerning how best to proceed.[‡‡] See **Toolkit Exercise 9.3** to think about push and pull tactics.

Transition Management

Change management is about keeping the plane flying while you rebuild it.[57]

When dealing with an ongoing operation, you typically don't have the luxury to put everything on hold while making a major change happen. You can't say "sorry, we aren't able to deliver the product we promised because we are making improvements." Most organizations have many change projects underway simultaneously. One part of the organization may be re-engineering itself. Another might be introducing a quality program while another part focuses on employee empowerment. All of these must be managed concurrently while continuing to produce products and services.

Morris and Raben argue for a transition manager (a change agent or implementer in the language of this book) who has resources, structures, and plans.[58] The

---

[‡‡]These styles are described more fully in Chapter 8.

transition manager has the power and authority to facilitate the change and is linked to the CEO or other senior executive. Resources are the people, money, training, and consulting expertise needed to be successful. Transition structures are outside the regular ones—temporary structures that allow normal activities to take place as well as change activities. The transition plan is the change plan with clear benchmarks, standards, and responsibilities for the change. Figure 9.4 outlines a checklist for transition management.

Transition management is making certain that both the change project and the continuing operations are successful. The change leader and the transition manager are responsible for making sure that both occur. The change leader is visibly involved in articulating both the need for change and the new vision, while others involved in implementing the change manage the organization's structural and system changes and the individuals' emotional and behavioral issues so that neither is compromised to a danger point.[59] Ackerman described the application of a transition management model at Sun Petroleum.[60] She addressed the question, "How can these changes be put into place without seriously straining the organization?" Her solution was to create a transition manager who handled the social system requirements. Ackerman also argued for the use of a transition team to create a transition structure that would enable the organization to carry on operating effectively while the major changes take place.

Beckhard and Harris focus on the transition details in organizational change.[61] They reinforce the importance of specifying midpoint goals and milestones, which help motivate the members of the organization. The longer the span of time required for a change initiative, the more important these midcourse goals become. The goals need to be far enough away to provide direction but close enough to provide a sense of progress and accomplishment and an opportunity for midcourse changes in plans.

A second component of transition management is keeping people informed to reduce anxiety. During major reorganizations, many employees are assigned to new roles, new bosses, new departments, or new tasks. Those individuals have a right to know their new work terms and conditions. Transition managers will put systems in place to ensure that answers to questions (such as "how will I, my co-workers, and my customers be affected?" "Who is my new boss?" "Who will I be working with and where will I be located?" or "What is my new job description?") can be provided in a timely manner. An example of this need occurred in the Ontario (Canada) Ministry of Agriculture, Food and Rural Development. As the designer of a major change in that organization, Bill Allen commented that the Ministry "underestimated the importance of a well thought out transition structure and plan. Employees of the Ministry had hundreds of questions about the organizational change and there was no formal structure to handle these in a consistent and professional manner."[62] The transition manager needs to be authorized and given the capacity to do this.

The final phase in transition management occurs in and around the same time as the celebrations are occurring in recognition of what has been accomplished. Project completion can be a bittersweet time for participants because they may not be working directly with one another in the future. They've worked hard, developed close friendships, and shared emotional highs and lows along the way. The experience can be extremely influential to their future development, and it needs to be processed and brought to closure in ways that do it justice. One way to approach closure (in addition to the celebration) and maximize the learning for all is to conduct an **after-action review**.[63] An after-action review involves reviewing the change experience as a whole and learning from what transpired along the way. There needs to be a candid assessment from multiple perspectives of the change process and the strengths and weaknesses of the various approaches used along the way. It asks: (a) what were the intended results, (b) what were the actual results, (c) why did the actual results happen, and (d) what can be done better, next time? As the participants explore these questions, the approaches, tools, sources of information, and insights that have the potential to improve performance in the future need to be identified, and the knowledge must be codified in ways that will allow others to access and learn from it. This knowledge is potentially the most significant legacy that those involved with the change can leave for themselves and others who will follow.

Figure 9.4 A Checklist for Change: Transition Management

The following questions can be useful when planning transition management systems and structures.

1. How will the organization continue to operate as it shifts from one state to the next?

2. Who will answer questions about the proposed change? What decision power will this person or team have? Will they provide information only or will they be able to make decisions (such as individual pay levels after the change)?

3. Do the people in charge of the transition have the appropriate amount of authority to make decisions necessary to ease the change?

4. Have people developed ways to reduce the anxiety created by the change and increase the positive excitement over it?

5. Have people worked on developing a problem-solving climate around the change process?

6. Have people thought through the need to communicate the change? Who needs to be seen individually? Which groups need to be seen together? What formal announcement should be made?

7. Have the people handling the transition thought about how they will capture learning throughout the change process and share it?

8. Have they thought about how they will measure and celebrate progress along the way and how they will bring about closure to the project at its end and capture the learning so it is not lost (after-action review)?

Summary

"Doing it" demands a good plan and a willingness to work that plan. To advance a "do it" orientation, the chapter assesses several strategies for approaching the change and planning the work. The chapter examines various action planning tools and considers how to handle the communications challenges that arise during a change initiative. Finally, transition management is considered, because the delivery of services and products typically needs to continue while the change initiative is underway. See **Toolkit Exercise 9.1** for critical thinking questions for this chapter.

Key Terms

"Do it" orientation—a willingness to engage in organizational analysis, see what needs to be done, and take the initiative to move the change forward:

1. **Thinking first strategy**—an approach used when the issue is clear, data are reliable, the context is well structured, thoughts can be pinned down, and discipline can be established, as in many production processes.

2. **Seeing first strategy**—an approach that works best when many elements have to be combined into creative solutions, commitment to those solutions is key, and communication across boundaries is essential, as in new product development. People need to see the whole before becoming committed.

3. **Doing first strategy**—an approach that works best when the situation is novel and confusing, complicated specifications would get in the way, and a few simple relationship rules can help people move forward. An example would be when a manager is testing an approach and wants feedback about what works.

4. **Programmatic change**—a traditional approach to planned change; starts with mission, plans, and objectives; sets out specific implementation steps, responsibilities, and timelines.

5. **Discontinuous change**—an approach adopted for a major change that represents a clear break from the previous approach, often involving revolutionary ideas.

6. **Emergent change**—a change that grows out of incremental change initiatives. It often evolves through the active involvement of internal participants. As it emerges, it can come to challenge existing organizational beliefs about what should be done.

7. **Unilateral approach**—top-down change. Change requirements are specified and implemented—required behavioral changes are spelled out, and it is anticipated that attitude changes will follow once people acclimatize themselves to the change.

8. **Participative approach**—bottom-up participation in the change initiative focuses on attitudinal changes that will support the needed behavioral changes required by the organizational change.

   Techno–structural change—includes change initiatives focused on the formal structures, systems, and technologies employed by the organization.

   Behavioral–social change—includes change initiatives focused on altering established social relationships within the organization.

Action Planning Tools

1. **To-do list** is a checklist of things to do.

2. **Responsibility charting** is who will do what, when, where, why, and how.

3. **Contingency planning** is consideration of what should be done when things do not work as planned on critical issues.

4. **Decision tree analysis** asks change agents to consider the major choices and the possible consequences of those alternatives.

5. **Scenario planning** is a change strategy formed by first developing a limited number of scenarios or stories about how the future may unfold and then assessing what the implications of each of these would be to the organization.

6. **Surveys** involve the use of structured questions to collect information from individuals and groups in systematic fashion.

7. **Survey feedback** is an organizational development technique that involves participants in the review and discussion of survey results. The goal is to actively engage them in the interpretation of the findings, the discussion of their implication, and the identification of how best to proceed.

8. **Project planning and critical path methods** are operations research techniques for scheduling work. These methods provide deadlines and insight as to which activities cannot be delayed to meet those deadlines.

9. **Force field analysis** examines the forces for and against change.

10. **Stakeholder analysis** is the position of the major players and why they behave as they do.

11. **Commitment charts** is an evaluation of the level of commitment of major players (against, neutral, let it happen, help it happen, make it happen).

12. The **adoption continuum** is an examination of major players and their position on the awareness, interest, desire, and adoption continuum related to the proposed changes.

13. **Leverage analysis**—determination of methods of influencing major groups or players regarding the proposed changes

Purpose of the communication plan for change—(1) to infuse the need for change throughout the organization, (2) to enable individuals to understand the impact that the change will have on them, (3) to communicate any structural and job changes that will influence how things are done, and (4) to keep people informed about progress along the way.

Four phases in the communications process during change are outlined:

(1) the **prechange phase**—centering on communicating need and gaining approval for the change;

(2) **developing the need for change phase**—focuses on communicating urgency and enthusiasm for the change;

(3) the **midstream phase**—involves disseminating details of the change and should include obtaining feedback from employees;

(4) **confirming the change phase**—communicates and celebrates the success of the program to reinforce commitment.

Richness of the communication channel—different channels vary in the richness of the information they can carry. Standard reports and general-information e-mails represent the lean end of the continuum. Richness increases as one moves to personalized letters and e-mails, telephone conversations, video conferencing, and face-to-face communications (the richest channel).

Alternatives to reducing negative reactions to change and building support developed by Kotter and Schlesinger:

(1) **Education and communication** is a strategy that helps others develop an understanding of the change initiative, what is required of them, and why it is important;

(2) **Participation and involvement** gets others involved and can bring new energy and ideas, and cause people to believe they can be part of the change;

(3) **Facilitation and support** is a strategy that provides access to guidance and other forms of support to aid in adaptation to change;

(4) **Negotiation and agreement** is when change leaders can make explicit deals with individuals and groups affected by the change;

(5) **Manipulation and co-optation** include covert attempts to influence others;

(6) **Explicit and implicit coercion** rests on change leaders' legitimate right and responsibility to insist that changes be done; and

(7) **Systemtic adjustments** are those made to formal systems and processes that reduce resistance while advancing the desired changes.

Push tactics attempt to move people in the desired direction through rational persuasion (e.g., the use of facts and logic) and/or direct or indirect pressure (e.g., guilt, threats).

Pull tactics attempt to draw people in the desired direction through arousing interests and enthusiasm through inspirational appeals, consultation, and their active participation.

- **Intervention** is a strategy of influence identified by Nutt, which involves key executives justifying the need for change and providing new norms to judge performance.
- **Participation** is a strategy of influence identified by Nutt, which involves engaging stakeholders in the change process.
- **Persuasion** is a strategy of influence identified by Nutt, which involves the use of experts to sell a change.
- **Edict** is a strategy of influence identified by Nutt, which is the issuing of directives.

Transition management is the process of ensuring that the organization continues to operate effectively while undergoing change

After-action review is a final phase of the transition-management process. It seeks to bring closure to the experience and engage participants in a process that will allow the learning gained through the change process to be extracted and codified in some manner for future use.

Checklist: Developing an Action Plan

1. Given your vision statement, what is your overall objective? When must it be accomplished?

2. Is your action plan time-sequenced and in a logical order? What would be the first steps in accomplishing your goal?

3. What is your action plan? Who will do what, when, where, why, and how? Can you do a responsibility chart?

4. What would be milestones along the way that will allow you to determine if you are making progress? What is the probability of success at each step?

5. Have you anticipated possible secondary consequences and lagging effects that your plans may give rise to and adjusted your plans accordingly?

6. Do you have contingency plans for major possible but undesirable occurrences? What things are most likely to go wrong? What things can you not afford to have go wrong? How can you prevent such things from happening?

7. Do you have contingency plans in the event that things go better than anticipated and you need to move more quickly or in somewhat different directions than initially planned, to take advantage of the opportunities?

8. Is your action plan realistic given your influence, both formal and informal, and the resources likely to be available to you? What can you do to address shortfalls?

9. Do you and your team have the competences and credibility needed to implement the action steps? If not, how will you address the shortfall?

10. Who does your plan rely on? Are they onside? What would it take to bring them onside?

11. Does your action plan take into account the concerns of stakeholders and the possible coalitions they might form?

12. Who (and what) could seriously obstruct the change? How will you manage them?

END-OF-CHAPTER EXERCISES

TOOLKIT EXERCISE 9.1

Critical Thinking Questions

Please find the URLs for the videos listed below on the website at study.sagepub.com/cawsey3e. Consider the questions that follow.

1. Terms of Engagement—3:32 minutes

Berrett-Koehler Publishers's "Change Authors" Series focuses on four principles: widening the circle of involvement, connecting people to each other and to ideas, creating communities for action, and embracing democracy. *Terms of Engagement: Changing the Ways We Change Organizations* is a B-K Business Book by Richard H. Axelrod.

- Explain the four principles using examples from your own change experience.

- Brainstorm how you might begin to instill one of these principles in an organization you are familiar with.

2. It Starts With One: Changing Individuals Changes Organizations—26:25 minutes

Two professors from INSEAD (Hal Gregersen and Stewart Black) discuss the idea that you can't change organizations if you don't focus on change with individuals first. Investigate three barriers: the failure to see, failure to move (developing the capacity of individuals to do something new), and failure to finish (following through with support until capacities are where they need to be; need champions at the front line as well as elsewhere in the organization, as well as signposts that help people understand where they are in terms of implementing the change initiative). This includes helping leaders to understand the changes required within themselves.

- Which barrier resonated with your experience the most?

- How do you think these principles might facilitate a successful change project?

3. Appreciative Inquiry—4:50 minutes

- What is the basic idea of appreciative inquiry?

- What emotions does this strategy center on?

- How does an appreciative approach change process?

Please see study.sagepub.com/cawsey3e for access to videos and a downloadable template of this exercise.

TOOLKIT EXERCISE 9.2

Action Plans for Influencing Reactions to Change

1. What methods have you seen used in organizations to influence people's reactions to a specific change? Think specifically about a change instance and what was done.

   a. Education and communication

   b. Participation and involvement

   c. Facilitation and support

   d. Negotiation and agreement

   e. Manipulation and co-optation

   f. Explicit and implicit coercion

   g. Systemic adjustments

2. What were the consequences of each of the methods used? What worked and what did not work? Why?

3. What personal preferences do you have regarding these techniques? That is, which ones do you have the skills to manage and the personality to match?

Please see study.sagepub.com/cawsey3e for a downloadable template of this exercise.

TOOLKIT EXERCISE 9.3

Influence Tactics

1. Think specifically of change situations in an organization you are familiar with. What influence tactics did people use? Describe three situations in which three different tactics were used.

   a. Inspirational appeals

   b. Consultation (seeking the participation of others)

   c. Relying on the informal system (existing norms and relationships)

   d. Personal appeals (appeals to friendship and loyalty)

   e. Ingratiation

   f. Rational persuasion (use of facts, data, logic)

   g. Exchange or reciprocity

   h. Coalition building (creation of subgroups or links with other groups to exert pressure)

   i. Using organizational rules or legitimating tactics (framing of the request as consistent with policy and/or your authority)

   j. Direct pressure

   k. Appeals to higher authority and dealing directly with decision makers

2. How successful were each of the tactics? Why did they work or not work?

3. How comfortable are you with each tactic? Which could you use?

Please see study.sagepub.com/cawsey3e for a downloadable template of this exercise.

CHAPTER 10

Measuring Change

Designing Effective Control Systems

What gets measured is what gets done.

—Author Unknown

CHAPTER OVERVIEW

- Measurement and control processes can play a critical role in guiding change and integrating the initiatives and efforts of various parties.
- Four types of management control processes are identified: diagnostic/ steering controls, belief systems, boundary systems, and interactive controls. Different types of controls are needed as the change project shifts from the planning to implementation phases.
- The use of strategy maps as an alignment tool is explored.
- Three measurement tools are presented: the balanced scorecard, the risk exposure calculator, and the duration, integrity, commitment, and effort (DICE) model.

When British Columbia implemented its carbon tax in 2008, a key element in its climate strategy, there was significant anxiety and commentary in the press that it would kill economic development in this resource-rich province of Canada. However, that has not been the experience. This change initiative, designed to be revenue neutral, has resulted in this province having the lowest personal income tax rate in Canada. Fossil fuel use has been reduced by 16%, while consumption in the rest of Canada has risen by 3%, and B.C.'s economy has performed slightly better, on average, than the rest of Canada. These results suggest that carefully designed programs such as this can reduce our appetite for fossil fuels while playing a positive role in economic growth.[1] This example also shows the necessity of measurement and the power it has to dispel commonly held, though inaccurate, beliefs. For British Columbia, despite the fact that the carbon tax worked to improve not only the economy but also sustainability in the province, it took hard measurements to legitimize the change.

Measurements matter. What gets measured affects the direction, content, and outcomes achieved by a change initiative. Measurements influence what people pay attention to and what they do.[2] When organizational members see particular quantifications as legitimate, believe their actions will affect the outcomes achieved, and think those actions will positively affect them personally, the motivational impact increases. But when the legitimacy or impact of the measures is questioned or when people believe they can't affect the outcomes, the measurements are seen as interference and can result in cynicism and alienation. Change agents know that measurement is important, but sometimes they need to understand more fully how measures will be used to help frame and guide the change.[3]

For a variety of reasons, measurement is often given less attention than it deserves during change initiatives. The change is seen as complex, requiring multidimensional measurements tools that seem too complex and difficult to track; measures are not viewed as focusing on what is important; the evolution of change initiatives makes end-point measures difficult to quantify; or end-point measures suggest commitment to a line in the sand that is then difficult to modify to match changing conditions.[4] In addition, change leaders often explain that they lack time to assess outcomes, that they were too busy making the change happen, and/or that they did not get around to thinking fully about measurement of outcomes.

The reality is that **measurement and control systems** incorporated into change initiatives can clarify expected outcomes and enhance accountability. This leaves some change agents feeling vulnerable. They worry that critics will use the measures to second-guess an initiative and even undermine both the change and the change agent.

In spite of these concerns, well-thought-out measurement and control processes provide change leaders with valuable tools. Information from these measurement systems enables change managers to: (1) frame the need for change and the implications of the vision in terms of expected outcomes; (2) monitor the environment; (3) guide the change, gauge progress, and make midcourse corrections; and (4) bring the change to a successful conclusion.[5] Key change leadership skills include identifying assessment measures, building them into the change process, adapting them as needed, and using them as tools to aid in decision making, communication, and action taking.[6] At RE/MAX (described below), the measurement system supported a change to the employment relationship, allowing the firm to attract and retain superior agents.

MEASUREMENT SYSTEMS AT RE/MAX

For RE/MAX, the Denver, Colorado–based real estate franchise network, a redefinition of customers away from industry norms was crucial. Cofounder and chairman David Liniger noted that the firm's success came from the simple idea that RE/MAX customers were the real estate agents themselves, not the buyers and sellers of real estate. More specifically, RE/MAX targeted high-performing agents who represented just 20% of the entire pool of real estate agents but accounted for approximately 80% of all sales.

RE/MAX's focus on high-performing agents originally consisted of changing the industry's traditional 50–50 fee split between broker and agent to a franchise system in which agents kept all commissions after payment of a management fee and expenses. In some cases, that shift changed retention rates of real estate agents as much as 85%. RE/MAX followed the change in the reward system with additional services, including national marketing campaigns, training of agents in sales techniques by satellite, and coordinated administrative support.

The results have been impressive: According to CEO Liniger, in 2003, the average RE/MAX agent earned $120,000 per year on 24 transactions versus an industry average of $25,000 on 7 transactions. "The customer comes second," he says, but hastens to add, "If our emphasis is on having the best employees, we're going to have the best customer service."[7]

The real estate sales meltdown in 2007–2008 and the subsequent slow recovery proved very challenging for the industry, but RE/MAX has rebounded. In North America it was recognized as one of the top 50 franchises for minorities in 2012 and the only real estate firm on the list. It has been named the highest ranked real estate franchise globally for four years in a row in *Franchise Times* Top 200 survey and has also been named the best real estate franchiser by *Entrepreneur* magazine 10 times in the past 14 years. A 2012 assessment of the top 500 brokerages in the industry found that RE/MAX agents averaged twice as many transactions when compared with their major competitors, resulting in an average of $3 million in sales, or 60% more than that achieved by the average of all other agents in the survey. With over 93,000 agents and 6,000 offices in more than 95 countries in 2013, it is arguably the number one brand in its industry.[8]

At RE/MAX, management's strategic realignment was anchored in a change to the reward system from fee-splitting the sales commission to one based on a franchise model. This example demonstrates that what is measured and rewarded will have a major impact on what outcomes are achieved. Sometimes measures are a matter of personal goal setting, as in the case of an athlete who links training metrics to performance goals and then celebrates small steps that lead to the accomplishment of a major milestone. In other situations, assessment grows out of expectations and/or requirements established by others, such as just-in-time measurement and cost reduction systems imposed on suppliers by automobile firms.

Employees' acceptance or rejection of measurements of a change initiative is important. When employees' acceptance of such measures increase, people experience less work stress, more job satisfaction, improved job performance, better work/family balance, less absenteeism, less job burnout, and more organizational commitment.[9] Because RE/MAX's executives structured a win–win strategy for the firm and for higher-performing agents, agents accepted the firm's measures and, in turn, the firm attracted and retained above-average real estate agents.[10] RE/MAX believes that the alignment of its strategy with its measurement system, innovative technology and sales approaches, and an ongoing commitment to agent education has been instrumental to its success.

This chapter looks at the role of measurement in change management and how assessment influences people's behavior. Issues over the development, use, and impact of measures are examined. The role of measurement and control in risk management is discussed, as is the question of what to measure at different stages in the life cycle of the change. Finally, strategy maps and balanced scorecards are introduced to demonstrate how to address the alignment of action with the change vision and strategy. Throughout this chapter, the goal remains the same: to learn how to use measurement and control mechanisms to increase the prospects for successful change.

Figure 10.1 suggests that measurement and control occur at the end of the change process, but in fact measurement and control aspects of a change need to begin at its inception. Change leaders should use these analytic tools throughout the life of the process. They can assist in helping to define the need for change, quantify what is expected from a change initiative, assess progress at specified intervals, and, at the end of the process, evaluate the change initiative's impact. Measures can help change agents in five ways: clarify expectations, assess progress and make mid-course corrections, assess the extent to which initiatives are being internalized and institutionalized, assess what has been ultimately achieved, and set the stage for future change initiatives.[11]

Many managerial discussions of measurement systems and control processes focus on how they impede progress.[12] Though measurement systems can get in the way, well-designed and effectively deployed systems have the potential to overcome organizational barriers and contribute to successful change.

The following case example outlines how change agents at Control Production Systems (CPS) approached their deteriorating market position. The example shows how change agents benefited from consultation with key participants[13] and collaboration with diverse groups[14] and how they used measurement and control processes to frame and reinforce the needed changes.

A CASE STUDY IN THE VALUE OF REALIGNING MEASURES

Control Production Systems (CPS), a mid-sized firm that designs, manufactures, sells, and services customized production control systems, had noticed an erosion of its market share to competitors. Declining customer loyalty, greater difficulty selling product and service updates, and an increased reliance on price to win the business were shrinking margins and making competitive life

(Continued)

difficult, even though product and service offerings were innovative and of a high quality. The firm possessed a strong, positive culture that reflected the values of innovation, quality, and open communications, but recent setbacks had shaken people's confidence.

As a result of a town hall meeting called to discuss the corporation's situation, the CEO acted on a suggestion to form a cross-functional change team to assess the firm's circumstances and recommend a course of action. The team included sales agents and customer support staff and was led by the director of sales and service. The director reported to the senior management team on a monthly basis, and the team was expected to diagnose and analyze the problem and frame recommendations for change within two months, which would be followed by implementation activities. An intranet website facilitated communications about the change, and transparency, candor, and no reprisals were the watchwords for the change team's approach. As well, the team received sufficient resources to allow it to get on with its task.

Prior to the change, sales agents were organized geographically and paid on a salary-plus-commission basis. After a sale, agents handed off responsibility to customer support staff to address order fulfillment and post-sales servicing. The customer support staff was rewarded on the basis of cost control and throughput. If customers never contacted the firm for help, that was considered good because no contact generated no cost and suggested customer satisfaction. Short calls were seen as better than long ones due to cost implications, and standardized responses and online help were preferred over trouble-shooting phone calls for the same cost reasons. The firm kept no systematic record of customer calls and responded to customers on a first-come, first-served basis.

Analysis by the change team showed that customers who had minimal contact with the customer support staff were less likely to develop a relationship with the firm, were likely deriving less value from their purchases, and were less likely to be aware of product and service innovations and applications that could benefit them. In other words, the activities that kept short-term costs low hurt customer loyalty and long-term profitability. Benchmark data concerning service models, customer satisfaction, and purchase decisions confirmed that CPS was falling behind key competitors.

After the diagnosis, the team concluded that there was a need to change the way the firm dealt with and serviced its major customers. The team determined that the way to increase sales and profitability was to ensure that customers saw CPS as a trusted partner who could find ways to enhance customers' productivity and quality through improvements in CPS's control systems.

The company realigned how it managed its relationships with customers. The firm integrated sales and customer support services, created sub-teams with portfolios of customer accounts by industry, and assigned the sub-teams to manage customers as ongoing relationships. The vision was a customer-focused partnership in which one-stop shopping, customer intimacy, service excellence, and solution finding would frame the relationship rather than simply selling and servicing in the traditional manner.

(Continued)

(Continued)

During the change, the change team measured employees' understanding and commitment to the new service model, employees' skill acquisition, and results of pilot projects. Further, the team measured service failures in areas of delivery, response time, quality, and relationship management to identify and deal with problems quickly if they occurred during the transition period. The team searched for systemic problems, developed remedies, encouraged openness and experimentation, and avoided finger pointing. Milestones for the change were established and small victories along the transition path were identified, monitored, and celebrated.

Once the team initiated the changes, it aligned performance measures by focusing on customers' satisfaction with the breadth and depth of services, response time, customers' referrals, repeat sales, and margins. The reward system shifted from a commission base for sales personnel and salary plus small bonus for customer service staff to a salary-plus-team-based performance incentive that included customers' satisfaction and retention, share of the customers' business in their product and service area, and customers' profitability over time. In the three years since implementation, there have been significant improvements in all the targeted measures, and feedback from customer service has become an important influencer of product refinement and development.

The case above demonstrates how measurements can support a change initiative at each stage of the process. At the beginning, change leaders used measurements in problem identification, in root cause analysis, and in the development of awareness for a new vision and structure. The leaders recognized the misalignment between measures that reinforced cost reductions in servicing clients (first-order effects) and the desired but unrealized long-term outcome of customer loyalty and profitability (second-order or lag effects). As the change leaders and team continued to diagnose their organization's structure and systems, at each step data were collected, analyzed, and used to fine-tune plans. Employees came to trust using data to make savvy decisions. In the end, clients' satisfaction with CPS's products and services (first-order effects) gave rise to customer loyalty and follow-up purchases and profitability (second-order effects) that management had not previously measured or achieved.

To make the question of the impact of measures and control processes all the more real, consider a change you are familiar with and complete **Toolkit Exercise 10.2**.

Selecting and Deploying Measures

There is no shortage of possible measurement indicators: cycle time, machine efficiency, waste, sales per call, employee satisfaction, waiting time, market share,

---

Figure 10.1 The Four-Stage Change Process

Awakening
Chapter 4
1. Identify a need for change and confirm the problems or opportunities that incite the need for change through collection of data.
2. Articulate the gap in performance between the present and the envisioned future state, and spread awareness of the data and the gap throughout the organization.
3. Develop a powerful vision for change.
4. Disseminate the vision for the change and why it's needed through multiple communication channels.

Mobilization
Chapters 5 through 8
1. Make sense of the desired change through formal systems and structures, and leverage those systems to reach the change vision (Chapter 5).
2. Assess power and cultural dynamics at play, and put them to work to better understand the dynamics and build coalitions and support to realize the change (Chapter 6).
3. Communicate the need for change organization-wide and manage change recipients and various stakeholders as they react to and move the change forward (Chapter 7).
4. Leverage change agent personality, knowledge, skills and abilities, and related assets (e.g., reputation and relationships) for the benefit of the change vision and its implementation (Chapter 8).

Acceleration
Chapter 9
1. Continue to systematically reach out to engage and empower others in support, planning, and implementation of the change. Help them develop needed new knowledge, skills, abilities, and ways of thinking that will support the change.
2. Use appropriate tools and techniques to build momentum, accelerate and consolidate progress.
3. Manage the transition, celebrating small wins and the achievement of milestones along the larger, more difficult path of change.

Institutionalization
Chapter 10
1. Track the change periodically and through multiple balanced measures to help assess what is needed, gauge progress toward the goal, and to make modifications as needed and mitigate risk.
2. Develop and deploy new structures, systems, processes and knowledge, skills, and abilities, as needed, to bring life to the change and new stability to the transformed organization.

---

profitability per sale, cost of sale, and customer retention, to name a few. If change agents try to measure everything concurrently, they are likely to lose focus. To focus attention, agents need to be clear about the stage of the change process and what dimensions are important to monitor at a particular stage given the desired end results. Here is a list of criteria to help change leaders determine which measures to adopt.

Focus on Key Factors

An accurate analysis of the change challenges will mean that change leaders will know which factors are key and what levers will move people in the direction of the desired change. Measures influence what people pay attention to and how they act, even when they believe those actions are ill advised.[15] Consider the all-too-common practice of trade loading, the inefficient and expensive practice of pushing excess inventory onto distributors and retailers in order to make the manufacturer's numbers look better in the short term.[16] For years, staff at Gillette knew that the practice of trade loading was having a negative effect on pricing, production efficiencies, customer relationships, and profitability. Trade loading meant unsold inventory was hidden from Gillette's eyes in the distribution channels and price discounting was eroding margins (distributors quickly learned how to time purchases to take advantage of such discounts). In spite of the widespread awareness that this practice was ill advised, it continued until new leadership realigned key measures and practices to support the desired changes and finally brought an end to an unhealthy practice.[17]

Knowing the critical measures to develop, deploy, and monitor at the different stages of the change process is a complex issue. In the Gillette case, this involved measures that demonstrated the negative consequences of trade loading, showed the positive consequences of the change vision, and assessed performance in ways that aligned with the change vision and targeted outcomes.

Use Measures That Lead to Challenging but Achievable Goals

Employees need to believe that they can achieve challenging goals. Measurements that note small steps to the larger goal and measures within an individual's control will tap into desired motivations.

Use Measures and Controls That Are Perceived as Fair and Appropriate

Employees' perception of the appropriateness and fairness of the measures and control processes is driven as much by the process used to develop and legitimize them as by the outcomes they deliver.[18] Even reasonable measures may not be acceptable if people feel the measures were forced on them. Good processes will reduce resistance through communication, as communication provides opportunities for input and feedback while building trust and support. Avoid applying measures in ways that punish people who take reasonable actions based on their understanding of the change goals and what is expected of them.

Measurement and control processes are more likely to be accepted if the process used in developing them is seen as reasonable and fair, even if those measures lead to negative outcomes for those being measured (this matter of fair process was discussed earlier and in more detail in Chapter 7). It is very beneficial if individuals who are responsible for delivering on measures see them as relevant and fair.

Avoid Sending Mixed Signals

Measurement systems related to change often send conflicting signals, and it is not unusual for change leaders to say one thing but signal another through what they measure and reward. For example, an organization may initiate changes aimed at enhancing quality and customer satisfaction but then "wink at" the shipment of flawed products to meet just-in-time delivery metrics and avoid exceeding its internal scrap and rework targets. Managers do this even though they know that substandard products will increase warranty work, require customers to do rework, and put the firm's reputation with the customer at risk. The fundamental problem in this example is that measures are not aligned with goals.

Aligning measurements and avoiding mixed signals is tricky because there are always tradeoffs. For example, employees' acceptance of a particular step (as measured by survey results) and the achievement of a particular performance milestone (e.g., going "live" with a new customer service module) may end up conflicting. The firm may have succeeded in going "live" with the new module, but employees and customers may be unaware of or confused about the advantages associated with the new module versus the costs and benefits of remaining with the existing approach. Change leaders need to address such matters by providing advice on how these tradeoffs associated with the change and the potentially conflicting signals generated by different measures should be handled. If this isn't done, change initiatives may flounder in the subsequent confusion.

The Canadian division of a U.S. auto parts firm initiated a change initiative in the form of a new quality program and reinforced it with a gigantic display board preaching, "Quality is important because General Motors demands it!" However, next to this sign sat pallets of completed parts with supervisory tags that approved shipment, overriding quality control inspection reports that had ordered rework prior to shipment. The firm's management had not addressed how to resolve conflicts between the new quality initiative and their just-in-time obligations. Supervisors looked at how they were measured and concluded that delivery trumped quality. Employees looked at how their supervisors reversed decisions on substandard quality and concluded the new quality program was a joke and a waste of money. The inability to reconcile the handling of the quality problems with their delivery obligations led to the loss of the GM contract and the closure of the plant approximately 18 months after the display board was first unveiled.[19]

Employees are very aware of such conflicting messages. Confusion, frustration, sarcasm, and eventually alienation are the natural consequences. When such inconsistencies are built into a change initiative and go undetected or unaddressed by the change leader, cynicism about the change and its supporters increases, and the change process falters. Kerr's well-known paper, "On the Folly of Rewarding A, While Hoping for B," explores many of the issues around measurement and the production of unintended consequences.[20]

Ensure Accurate Data

Employees, customers, and others are likely to supply accurate and timely data when they trust the measurement system and believe that data will not be used to harm them. Excessive rewards for success, undue sanctions for missed targets, or a very stressful work environment can lead to flawed information from carefully designed sets of measures.[21] These pressures create incentives for individuals to report inaccurately or to shade the reality of the situation. To ensure accurate and timely data from the measurement system, those supplying the data need to trust who it is going to and believe that it is their responsibility to comply fully and honestly. Keep pressure at reasonable levels and avoid excessive rewards for success or excessive consequences for not achieving targets.

Match the Precision of the Measure With the Ability to Measure

A measurement motto might read, "Better to be approximately right than precisely wrong!" Change leaders need to match the measures to the environment. If the change is significant, clearly structured, and predictable, leaders can devote time and resources to developing precise, sophisticated measures. However, if the change environment is turbulent and ambiguous, approximate measures are more appropriate.[22] Change agents need to make their choices based upon (a) how quickly they need the information, (b) how accurate the information needs to be, and (c) how much it will cost. Information economics point to the fact that designing the needed information for a change initiative inevitably involves tradeoffs among these three components.[23]

The general rule of thumb is to keep the measures as simple and understandable as possible, and make sure that they attend to the important elements of the change in a balanced way. Table 10.1 looks at the nature of the change context and considers what types of measures will be appropriate.

Regardless of the measures chosen, change leaders need to be seen as "walking the talk." When leaders treat the measures as relevant and appropriate, employees will see that they are serious about what they are espousing. Use sound communication practices when dealing with questions related to what to measure, who to engage in discussions about measurement and control, how to deploy the measures, and how to interpret and use the data effectively to manage the change. Change leaders' behaviors that reinforce perceptions of the fairness and appropriateness of the measures and instill confidence in their proper application are very important in legitimizing measurement as a powerful tool in the change process.[24]

Table 10.1 The Change Context and the Choice of Measures		
Change Context	**Choose More Precise, Explicit, Goal-Focused Measures**	**Choose More Approximate Measures, Focus on Vision and Milestones, and Learn as You Go**
When complexity and ambiguity are:	Low	High
When time to completion is:	Short	Long

Control Systems and Change Management

Robert Simon, an expert in the area of management control systems, believes that managers focus too much on traditional diagnostic control systems developed from management accounting. Managers need to think about four types of control levers as constituting the internal control systems when considering change. That is why strategy lies at the center of his model, because what one attempts to do needs to consider the influence of all four of these control levers.[25]

- **Interactive controls**—the systems that sense environmental changes crucial to the organization's strategic concerns. For example, market intelligence data that helps firms better understand and anticipate competitor actions.
- **Boundary systems**—the systems that set the limits of authority and action and determine acceptable and unacceptable behavior. For example, limits to spending authority placed on managerial levels. These focus on what is unacceptable and identify both what is prohibited and what is sanctioned.
- **Belief systems**—the fundamental values and beliefs of organizational employees that underpin the culture and influence organizational decisions. For example, the stated organization values that often accompany the vision and mission.
- **Diagnostic/steering controls**—the traditional managerial control systems that focus on key performance variables. For example, sales data based on changed selling efforts.

Each of these systems can help in implementing change, but they serve different purposes depending upon where you are in the change process. *Interactive control systems* help sensitize change leaders to environmental shifts and strategic uncertainties and the relevance of these on the framing of the change initiative. This will allow them to modify change plans in the face of environmental factors, and tend to play the biggest role when dealing with issues related to assessing the need for change and vision for the change.

Understanding the organization's *boundary system* means change leaders know what sorts of actions are appropriate and which are inappropriate or off limits. The firm's rules or boundaries need be respected and place limits on what actions are appropriate. If they choose, change leaders can test those boundaries explicitly, but they need to do so in an ethical and transparent manner.

An understanding of the *organization's belief system* informs leaders about the culture and how beliefs and values influence action. This allows change leaders to frame initiatives in ways that are aligned with the core beliefs and the organizations, and the higher-order values of individuals, and use this alignment to help motivate desired actions and overcome resistance to change. Data in this area comes from direct experience with others in the organization, employee surveys and a systematic evaluation of past decisions, practices and behaviors. As in the case of boundary systems, change leaders may wish to address the need to modify those beliefs as part of the change, but should again approach the matter in an ethical and transparent manner. Otherwise they risk being accused of misleading people and acting inappropriately. This will destroy trust in them and the initiative.

Finally, a well-developed *diagnostic control system* helps change agents understand critical performance variables and milestones, and modify their approach to encourage desired behaviors and outcomes while discouraging dysfunctional ones. These are the steering controls and metrics they use to help them navigate their way on the change journey. As you can see, these controls and their related measures address the determination of the nature of the desired change, how it will be framed, and how progress will be monitored and assessed along the way (see Figure 10.2).

Table 10.2 sets out the different elements of the control system and relates them to the measures used at different stages of the change process. As the change progresses from initial planning to wrap-up and review, the control challenges and measurement issues also shift. The key is to align the controls and measures to the challenges posed at each stage of the change and prepare for the next. This helps to ensure that change leaders have the information and guidance they need to assess matters, make decisions, and manage their way forward.[26]

Controls During Design and Early Stages of the Change Project

At the commencement of a major change, mission and vision (i.e., belief systems), interactive control systems (e.g., environmental assessment), and boundary systems

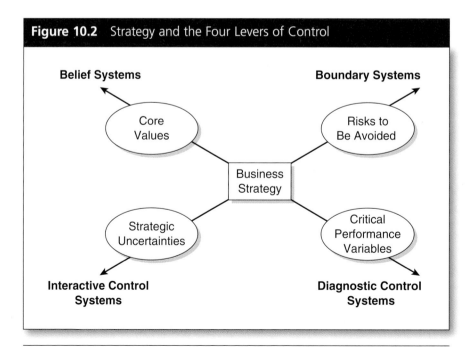

Figure 10.2 Strategy and the Four Levels of Control

Belief Systems

Boundary Systems

Core Values

Risks to Be Avoided

Business Strategy

Strategic Uncertainties

Critical Performance Variables

Interactive Control Systems

Diagnostic Control Systems

Source: R. Simons, "Control in the Age of Empowerment," *Harvard Business Review*, March-April 1995, p.85.

Table 10.2   Control Systems, Measures, and the Stage of the Change

	Controls When Designing and Planning the Change	Controls in Beginning Stages of the Change Project	Controls in Middle Stages of the Change Project	Controls Toward the End of the Change Project
Interactive Controls (Environmental scanning; assessing possible paths and targets)	Assess opportunities and threats; consider possibilities. Test the viability of existing vision, mission, and strategy given the environmental situation, and assess the need for change.	Affirm that the change project is aligned with environmental trends. Assess how to use environmental trends to increase the chances of change success.	Ongoing monitoring. Confirm that environmental assessment continues to support the change.	Obtain feedback regarding the success of change initiative relative to the environmental factors. Ongoing environmental scanning and assessment of organizational strengths, weaknesses, opportunities, and threats (SWOT).
Boundary System (What behaviors are *not* OK?)	Limit the change options to those within the boundary conditions. Test the limits of what is acceptable.	Go/no go guidance as to appropriateness of actions.	Go/no-go guidance as to appropriateness of actions. Reassess risks. Re-establish boundaries if needed. Test new boundaries where appropriate.	Reevaluate the boundary limits.
Belief System (What are our beliefs and values? What is our purpose?)	Assess congruence between core values of the firm, its mission, and the purpose of the change project. Communicate how the change relates to the core values and mission. Consider implications if change involves modifications of the belief system and how to facilitate the change.	Congruence assessment. Appeal to fundamental beliefs to overcome resistance or address need for change in those beliefs.	Congruence assessment. Reaffirm core values throughout the change project and/or assess progress in the needed modifications to the belief system.	Congruence assessment. Reassess and potentially reaffirm the core values and mission based on learning during the change project.
Diagnostic and Steering Controls (Focusing resources on targets; measuring progress; taking corrective action and learning as we go)	Assess the impact of existing controls on the change project. Consider what diagnostic systems will have to be developed and/or altered under the change.	Develop milestones, diagnostic measures, and steering controls. Develop tactics to alter control systems as needed.	Evaluate progress against milestones. Assess whether systems and processes are working as they should. Modify milestones and measures as needed.	Determine when the project has been completed. Confirm that new systems, processes, and behaviors established by the change are working appropriately. Evaluate project and pursue learning on how to improve the change process.

play particularly important roles in clarifying overall direction as options and potential courses of action are explored. Data from secondary research, exploratory discussions, preliminary organizational assessments, and initial experimentation are helpful at this stage because they allow projects and alternatives to be considered in a grounded manner. The organization's readiness for change (discussed in Chapter 4) can be assessed and steps taken to enhance readiness. Information from multiple sources is used to sort out options, assess what should be done next, and make an initial go/no-go decision on whether to proceed in the development of the initiative.

In the early stages, change leaders need to have systems that will identify who to talk to and who will tell them what they need to hear, not what they want to hear. Enthusiasm and commitment on the part of change leaders are beneficial to the change but can create serious blind spots if not tempered by the reality checks that control systems can provide. As go/no-go decisions are made, change agents need to develop and refine the directional and steering control measures and specify important milestones. Project planning tools, such as the critical path method, can play a useful role (see Chapter 9).

Controls in the Middle of the Change Project

Indicators that define the overall purpose, direction, boundary conditions (what actions are acceptable and unacceptable) for the change, and core values and beliefs are still important in clarifying and framing what change is intended. However, diagnostic and steering controls (e.g., budgets and variance reports, project and activity schedules, and tracking of content from e-mails and phone conversations) play an increasingly important role in the middle of the change project. At this point, change leaders want to be able to track and receive timely and accurate feedback on progress. Change leaders need to recognize whether the information produced leads or lags the desired outcomes. As in the example of CPS discussed earlier in this chapter, customer satisfaction was a lead indicator of an improved sales climate, while repeat sales and profitability were lag indicators of the improved situation. If this had not been recognized, initiatives undertaken to improve customer satisfaction may have been discontinued because there was no immediate improvement in sales.

Milestones and road markers need to be developed through project planning and goal- and objective-setting activities. These markers can then be used to track progress and reinforce the initiative of others by recognizing their achievement. For example, if a firm were implementing a new performance management system, the completion and sign off on the design of the system, the completion of a training schedule, the achievement of needed levels of understanding and acceptance of the system (as assessed by measures of comprehension and satisfaction with the system), and the completion of the first cycle of performance reviews (with system evaluation data from those using the system) are possible road markers.

At important milestones, go/no-go controls once again enter the picture, with conscious decisions made about refinements to the change initiative. Change leaders need to make decisions about the appropriateness and desirability of pro-ceeding to the next stage. If milestones are not being achieved, change leaders need to consider what sorts of actions, if any, should be undertaken or they may need to revisit the timeline or refine the measures used to track progress. In that respect, change leaders also need to consider how measures can help them think about contingencies and adapt to unforeseen situations.

Controls Toward the End of the Change Project

As the end of a planned change approaches, diagnostic and steering measures are replaced by concrete outcome measures. What was accomplished and what has been the impact? How do the results compare with what change agents expected at the beginning? What can be learned from the change experience? Change leaders need to capture the observations and insights from those who have been involved in the change, as it will help them prepare for future initiatives.

Toolkit Exercise 10.3 asks you to apply Simon's control systems model to a change initiative.

Other Measurement Tools

Four tools that can assist in planning, deploying, and managing change are dis-cussed in the next section. These are the strategy map, the balanced scorecard, the risk exposure calculator, and the DICE model. They can enhance internal consis-tency and alignment and aid in assessing risk.

Strategy Maps

Once change leaders have framed their vision and strategy for the change, they can develop a visual representation of the end state and the action paths that will get them there. The tool was developed by Robert Kaplan and David Norton and is called a **strategy map**.[27] As can be seen from Figure 10.3, financial outcomes are driven by customer results. These customer results come from the performance of internal systems and processes, which in turn rest on the organization's resources (human, informational, and capital).[28]

Once the change vision and strategy are defined, Kaplan and Norton recom-mend starting with financial goals and objectives and then setting out the objec-tives, initiatives, and paths needed to generate those outcomes. The **financial perspective** drives the goals and objectives.

- If the vision for change is achieved, how will it look from the perspective of the financial results achieved?
- To accomplish these financial outcomes, what initiatives have to be under-taken from a customer perspective to deliver on the value proposition in ways that generate the desired financial results?

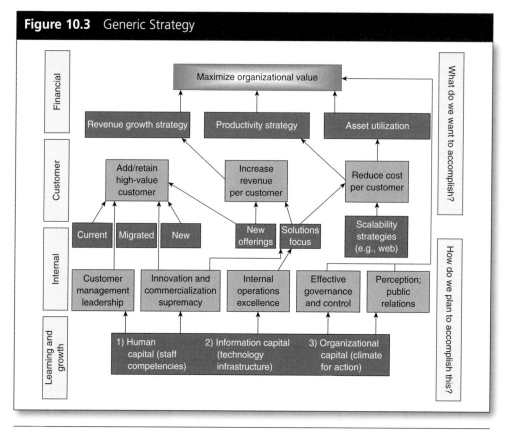

Figure 10.3   Generic Strategy

Source: From H. M. Armitage and C. Scholey, "Using Strategy Maps to Drive Performance," *CMA Management,* Vol. 80, #9, 2007, pg. 24.

- To accomplish these customer outcomes and/or contributions directly to the financial outcomes through efficiencies, what changes must be tackled from an internal business process perspective?
- Finally, to attain the internal process goals and objectives, what must be undertaken from a learning and growth perspective to increase the organization's capacity to do what is needed with the internal processes and customers?

The learning and growth perspective embodies people, information, and organizational capital (e.g., culture, intellectual property, leadership, internal alignment, and teamwork). For not-for-profit organizations, many recommend placing the **customer perspective** at the top of the model (some have relabeled it as the stakeholder perspective), since this is the reason for the organization's existence. Some place the financial perspective parallel with the customer or stakeholder perspective, while others place it below learning and growth or elsewhere. Others have added levels or changed labels on the strategy map. However, the goal remains the same: develop a coherent picture that aligns your change strategy with the organization's purpose so it generates the desired outcomes. It is all about translating the change vision into action, communicating with key constituents, integrating and aligning the specific action plans, implementing, and learning and refining as you go.

The assumption underlying strategy maps in for-profit organizations is that financial outcomes are the end goals that they are striving for and that other objectives within the change program should be aligned to produce and support those desired outcomes. If particular activities and the objectives don't support the changes, they should be seriously questioned and either dropped or reduced in importance. Each of the change initiatives identified by the strategy map will need to be managed as to goals and objectives, success measures, timelines, resource requirements, and an action plan. These, in turn, need to be integrated with the other change initiatives that are embodied in the strategy map.

When properly deployed, strategy maps provide change leaders with a powerful organizing and communication tool.[29] This visualization helps people understand what is being proposed and why. It clarifies why certain actions are important and how they contribute to other outcomes that are critical to achieving the end goals of the change (i.e., cause–effect relationships). It helps people focus and align their efforts and appropriately measure and report progress. It can assist change leaders to identify gaps in their logic, including missing objectives and measures. When Mobil used strategy maps, it helped them to identify gaps in the plans that had been developed for one of their business units. Objectives and metrics were missing for dealers—a critical component for a strategy map focused on selling more gasoline.[30]

To give you a concrete example of how a strategy map can be used to help, one is set out in Figure 10.4. It shows the vision and mission for Control Production Systems, Inc. (discussed earlier in this chapter). Then it shows the specific measures used in each category.

Figure 10.4 Strategy Map for Control Production Systems

Mission for CPS:

Design, manufacture, service, and support industry-leading production control systems that enable CPS to enhance the efficiency and effectiveness of its production processes beyond what is possible through other means. Customer loyalty and long-term profitability are built on a foundation of excellence in these areas.

Vision for the Change in Customer Orientation:

Our valued industrial partners will experience service and performance that delight. We will exceed all our competitors' standards through superbly designed and expertly installed and supported control equipment and software.

We will support our customers through technically competent account representatives who are focused on the challenges and needs of specific industries and customers and committed to ensuring that their success is significantly enhanced through the value derived from the production control systems. Our product leadership combined with superb customer care and excellent technical support will result in highly loyal and committed customers who look to CPS for all their more sophisticated control system needs.

(Continued)

Figure 10.4 (Continued)

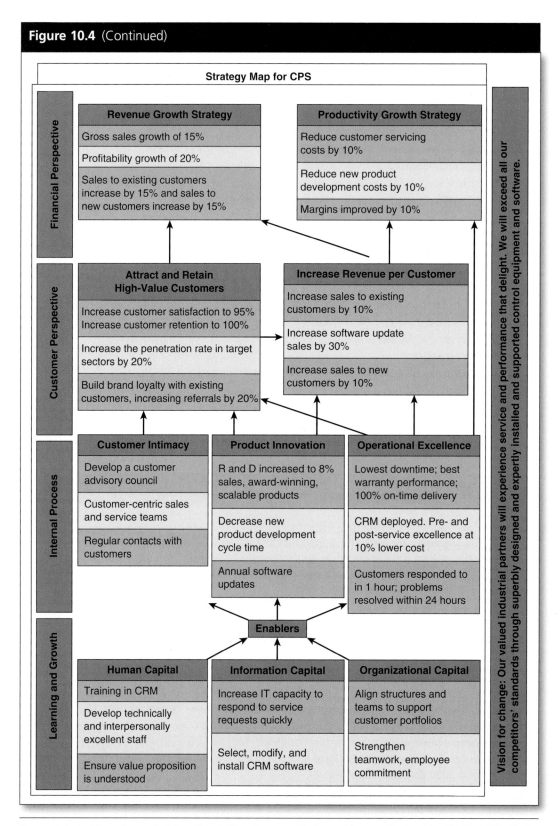

The Balanced Scorecard

If the strategy map links capabilities, change strategies, and outcomes, the **balanced scorecard** integrates measures into a relatively simple way of tracking the critical success factors. Kaplan and Norton argue that four categories of goals and measures need to be highlighted in a balanced scorecard: financial, a company's relationship with its customers, its **internal business process**, and its **learning and growth**. In doing so, management can achieve a balanced, integrated, and aligned perspective concerning what needs to be done to produce the desired strategic outcomes.[31]

Among these indicators, some will lead while others will lag. For example, improvements in service levels such as the response time to a customer's inquiry could be lead indicators of improvements in customer satisfaction. However, this may not immediately translate into new sales and increased profitability. Improvements in such measures will often be lag indicators of improvements in service levels because of the nature of the purchase cycle involved. The balanced scorecard recognizes that not all effects are immediate. By setting out assumptions concerning what leads to what, it makes it easier for the change leader to test assumptions, track progress, and make appropriate alternations as necessary.

When developing a strategy map and balanced scorecard for an internal change initiative, remember that the relevant customers may be employees in other departments of the organization. Kaplan and Norton argue that the use of multiple measures ensure a more balanced perspective on what a successful change will require. The likelihood that multiple measures will inadvertently mislead change leaders about what a successful change will require is much less than if they rely on a single indicator. Figure 10.5 outlines a generic balanced scorecard for a change project. Figure 10.6 outlines the scorecard for Control Production Systems.

Toolkit Exercise 10.4 asks you to construct a strategy map and balanced scorecard for an organization that you know. Remember that customers can be internal or external to the firm.

Risk Exposure Calculator

Robert Simon has developed a **risk exposure calculator** for use in assessing the level of risk associated with a company's actions.[32] Simon argues that risk is related to the rate of growth of the company, its culture, and how information is managed. The tool focuses primarily on internal rather than external environmental risks. Although it was designed for use on the overall organization, it has been modified to assess the risk exposure related to a particular change initiative as well as maintaining the status quo.

The first three risk drivers are grouped under **change pressure**. When the change leader is (a) under significant pressure to produce, (b) there is a great deal of ambiguity, or (c) employees are inexperienced in change, then the risks

Figure 10.5 Generic Balanced Scorecard for Change

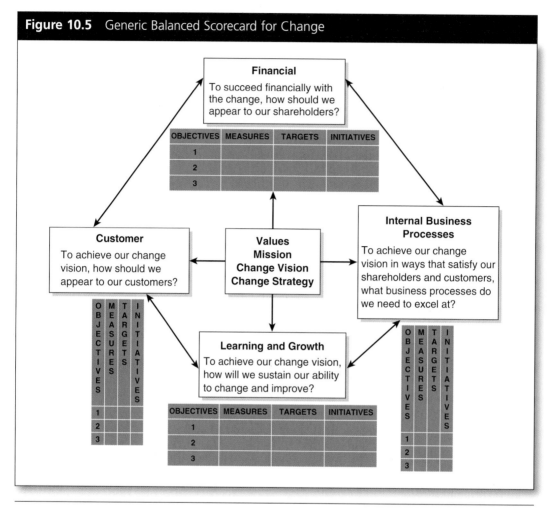

Source: Adapted from R. S. Kaplan and D. P. Norton, "Using the Balanced Scorecard as a Strategic Management System," *Harvard Business Review* 74, no. 1 (1996): 76.

associated with the change initiative will be higher than if those three conditions were less present.

Change culture identifies the second set of risk drivers. If (a) the culture pushes risk taking, (b) executives resist hearing bad news, or (c) there is internal competition, then risks will be further elevated.

The final set of risk drivers is grouped under **information management**. When (a) the change situation is complex and fast changing, (b) there are gaps in diagnostic change measures, and (c) decision making regarding change is decentralized, then risks will rise once again. These risk factors are cumulative in nature. The overall level of change risk rises as the total number of significant risk factors rises.

If Simon's risk calculator had been applied to Enron, AIG's mortgage arm prior to the economic meltdown in 2007–2008, or Lehman Brothers by those knowledgeable about their internal operations, scores indicating extreme risk would have been recorded. The environment at these organizations was complex, fast moving, and

Figure 10.6 Balanced Scorecard for CPS

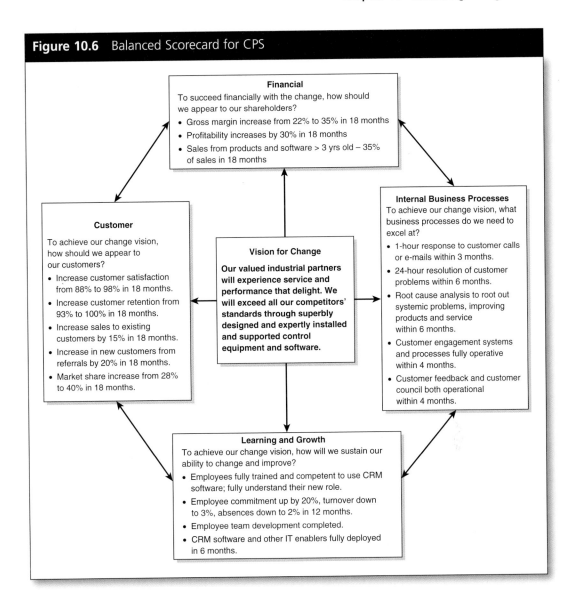

Financial
To succeed financially with the change, how should we appear to our shareholders?
- Gross margin increase from 22% to 35% in 18 months
- Profitability increases by 30% in 18 months
- Sales from products and software > 3 yrs old – 35% of sales in 18 months

Customer
To achieve our change vision, how should we appear to our customers?
- Increase customer satisfaction from 88% to 98% in 18 months.
- Increase customer retention from 93% to 100% in 18 months.
- Increase sales to existing customers by 15% in 18 months.
- Increase in new customers from referrals by 20% in 18 months.
- Market share increase from 28% to 40% in 18 months.

Vision for Change
Our valued industrial partners will experience service and performance that delight. We will exceed all our competitors' standards through superbly designed and expertly installed and supported control equipment and software.

Internal Business Processes
To achieve our change vision, what business processes do we need to excel at?
- 1-hour response to customer calls or e-mails within 3 months.
- 24-hour resolution of customer problems within 6 months.
- Root cause analysis to root out systemic problems, improving products and service within 6 months.
- Customer engagement systems and processes fully operative within 4 months.
- Customer feedback and customer council both operational within 4 months.

Learning and Growth
To achieve our change vision, how will we sustain our ability to change and improve?
- Employees fully trained and competent to use CRM software; fully understand their new role.
- Employee commitment up by 20%, turnover down to 3%, absences down to 2% in 12 months.
- Employee team development completed.
- CRM software and other IT enablers fully deployed in 6 months.

highly ambiguous. Many senior managers lacked knowledge and experience with the high-risk products and services they were responsible for, risk taking and competition were pushed to the extreme, and the bearers of concern and bad news put themselves at risk of being fired.

There are also dangers for the organization when risk levels get too low. Little positive change will occur if there is no pressure for change, little cultural support for risk taking, and very stable and predictable information. With lower risk, the capacity of the organization to be flexible and adapt will atrophy over time. When they are then faced with change that can no longer be ignored, their ability to respond will be compromised.

There is no optimal risk score that fits all organizations. These vary, depending on the nature of the environment, the upside and downside consequences of risk taking (and the probabilities associated with these), and the ability to take steps to alleviate risks. The risk appetites of change leaders should prudently reflect the needs and opportunities for innovation and change balanced by the needs for appropriate levels of caution and oversight. Of course, the organization's resources and capabilities will also determine the degree of risk that is sustainable and desirable.

Change leaders can take advantage of the risk calculator by using the information from it to make the risks manageable during the planning and deployment stages. For example, ambiguity can be reduced by emphasizing the change vision or by creating explicit milestones. Risks related to inexperience can be moderated by adding experienced managers to the change team. Further, it can be used to monitor risk levels as the change proceeds, with steps taken along the way to moderate levels up or down, depending on the situation.

Toolkit Exercise 10.5 sets out a risk calculator based on Simon's work and allows you to calculate a risk score indicating whether the project is in a safety zone or not.

The DICE Model

A process-oriented approach to assessing and managing the risks associated with change projects is offered by Sirkin, Keenan, and Jackson. Based upon empirical data, they have developed a four-factor model for predicting the success of a change initiative. They refer to this as the **DICE framework**.[33]

Duration asks about how frequently the change project is formally reviewed. If the frequency of formal review is less than every 2 months, it receives a score of 1. A score of 2 is awarded when the frequency is from 2 to 4 months; a 3 for a frequency of between 4 and 8 months; and a 4 for time intervals in excess of 8 months. The message is that the risk of failure increases as the time between formal reviews rises. In other words, "out of sight, out of mind" is a bad idea when it comes to assessing and guiding major changes. Providing timely guidance and assistance requires a more rigorous and systematic approach to managing the change—something that won't happen with a "how's it going → just fine" form of cursory assessment.

Integrity asks about the team leader's skills and credibility, and the skills, motivation, and focus of members of the change team. A score of 1 is recorded if: the team leader has the skills needed and the respect of coworkers, if the team members have the skills and motivation to complete the project on time, and if at least 50% of the team members' time has been assigned to the initiative. If the change team and leader are lacking on all dimensions, a score of 4 is recorded. If the factors lie somewhere in between, scores of 2 or 3 are allocated.

Commitment is a two-stage measure. The first part assesses the commitment of senior management. If the words and deeds of senior managers regularly reinforce the need for change and the importance of the initiative, a score of 1 is given. If senior managers are fairly neutral, scores of 2 or 3 are recorded. When senior managers are perceived to be less than supportive, a score of 4 is applied.

Second, the employee or "local level" commitment is evaluated. If employees are very supportive, a score of 1 is given. If they are willing but not overly eager, the score shifts to 2. As reluctance builds, scores shift to 3 and 4.

Effort is the final factor in the DICE model and refers to the level of increased effort that employees must make to implement the change. If the incremental effort is less than 10%, it is given a score of 1. Incremental effort of 10% to 20% raises the score to 2. At 20% to 40%, the score moves to 3, while additional effort in excess of 40% raises the score to 4.

The overall DICE score is calculated in the following fashion: The Integrity and Senior Management Commitment scores are weighted more heavily in the model, with each being multiplied by 2. This is because the scores on these factors have been found to be more significant drivers of risk. Then the scores of all factors are added together.

Overall Dice Score = Duration + (2 × Integrity of Performance) + (2 × Senior Management Commitment) + Local Level Commitment + Effort
The research shows the following about scores:

7–14: high likelihood of success

15–17: worry zone

17+: extremely risky, woe zone, with higher than 19 very unlikely to succeed

This model is useful in assessing risk and also in pointing to concrete things that can be done to make the risks manageable during the planning and deployment phases. For example, risks can be reduced by having more frequent formal project reviews and by the staffing of change initiatives with competent and credible team leaders and members. Likewise, increasing local and senior-level commitment and allocating sufficient time to change leaders will also help in reducing risks.

Toolkit Exercise 10.6 asks you to apply the DICE model to a change you are familiar with.

Summary

Care taken in the selection of measures and control processes helps clarify what the change is about and focuses energy and effort. It also saves change managers a great deal of time later on because it enhances the efficiency and effectiveness of the change process, provides an early warning system of problems, and thus leads to faster attention to needed areas and appropriate midcourse corrections. It also forces change leaders to be honest with themselves and others about what will be accomplished and what it will take to bring these things to reality. There is an old management adage that makes a lot of sense: It is far better to under promise and over deliver than to overpromise and under deliver.

The careful selection and use of metrics can be used to enhance ownership of the change through how the measures are selected (i.e., who participates in their selection) and through ensuring that those involved receive the credit for what is accomplished. See **Toolkit Exercise 10.1** for critical thinking questions for this chapter.

Key Terms

Measurement and control systems—developed to focus, monitor, and manage what is going on in the organization.

Interactive controls—the systems that sense environmental changes crucial to the organization's strategic concerns, for example, market intelligence that will determine competitor actions.

Boundary systems—the systems that set the limits of authority and action and determine acceptable and unacceptable behavior, for example, limits to spending authority placed on managerial levels. These tend to focus on what is unacceptable and identify not only what is prohibited but also the sanction.

Belief systems—the structure of fundamental values that underpin organizational decisions, for example, the stated organizational values that often accompany the vision and mission.

Diagnostic/steering controls—the traditional managerial control systems that focus on key performance variables, for example, sales data responding to changed selling efforts.

Strategy map—the visualization of how the vision and strategy can be systematically brought to fruition. Strategy Maps begin by defining the vision and strategy for change.

Financial perspective—identifies the financial outcomes that the change will give rise to and define the paths that will produce those outcomes.

Customer perspective—focuses on service and customer-oriented goals to acheive financial objectives.

Balanced scorecard—an integrated set of measures built around the mission, vision, and strategy. Measures address the financial perspective, customer perspective, internal business process perspective, and learning and growth perspective. As such, they provide a balanced perspective on what is required to enact the strategy.

Internal business process—perspective focuses on operational and process efficiencies that help accomplish financial goals and objectives.

Learning and growth—details the internal training and development needed to allow staff to reach objectives across the map.

Risk exposure calculator—an assessment tool developed by Robert Simon that considers the impact that specific factors may have on the risk levels faced by the firm.

Change pressure—when change leaders feel significant pressure to produce and accomplish the change, when there are high levels of ambiguity, and the leaders have little experience with change, risk is increased.

Change culture—when the rewards for risk taking are high, when senior executives resist hearing bad news, and when there is internal competition between units, risk is increased.

Information management—necessary when the situation is complex and fast changing, when gaps in diagnosis exist, and if decision-making is decentralized, risk is increased.

DICE framework—a process-oriented approach to assessing and managing the risks associated with change projects.

Duration—measures how frequently the change project is formally reviewed. As duration increases, risk increases.

Integrity of performance is a two-part measure. The first part asks about the team leader's skills and credibility and the second part asks about the skills, motivation, and focus of members of the change team. As skills, credibility, and motivation decrease, risk levels increase.

Commitment is a two-stage measure. The first part assesses senior management commitment. The second part evaluates employee or "local level" commitment. As commitment decreases, risk levels increase.

Effort—measures the level of increased exertion that employees must make to implement the change. As the amount of incremental effort increases beyond 10%, risk levels increase.

Checklist: Creating a Balanced Scorecard

1. State the mission, vision, and strategy for the change.

2. Consider the mission, vision, and strategy of the organization:
   - Is the proposed change consistent with these?
   - If not, what needs to be done with the change or the existing mission, vision, and strategy to bring them into line?

3. Complete the financial component of the scorecard by answering the following questions:
   - If you succeed with the change vision, how will it appear to the shareholders or those responsible for funding the change?
   - How will you know (objectives and metrics)?
   - Are some of these leading indicators while others are lagging indicators?

4. Complete the customer component of the scorecard by answering the following questions:
   - If you succeed with the change, how will it appear to your customers?
   - How will you know (objectives and metrics)?
   - Are there leading and lagging indicators here?

5. Complete the internal business processes component of the scorecard by answering the following questions:
   - If you succeed with the change, how will it appear in your business processes?
   - How will you know (objectives and metrics)?
   - Are there leading and lagging indicators here?

6. Complete the learning and growth component of the scorecard by answering the following questions:
   - If you succeed with the change, how will it appear to your employees and demonstrate itself in their actions?
   - What about the information and organizational capital?
   - How will you and they know (objectives and metrics)?
   - Are there leading and lagging indicators here?

7. Seek feedback from trusted colleagues on the scorecard you've developed. Does it help them to understand the change initiative you have in mind, the key measures that will indicate progress, and what will need to be done to achieve the desired outcomes?

END-OF-CHAPTER EXERCISES

TOOLKIT EXERCISE 10.1

Critical Thinking Questions

Please find the URLs for the videos listed below on the website at study.sagepub.com/cawsey3e. Consider the questions that follow.

1. "Self-Managed Work Teams at South Australian Ambulance Service" is a case available on the book's website that will help you think about the use of measurement to advance change initiatives. Ray Main is partway through a transformational change in this agency and is thinking about what he needs to do to bring the changes to a successful conclusion.

As you assess the case, give careful thought to the role that measurement-related change tools identified in this chapter could play in clarifying what needs to be done, developing plans, setting targets, and in measuring progress so that action plans can be adjusted along the way.

- What do you think Ray should do, and what role should measurement play in his plans?

- Develop an action plan for Ray.

2. The Beauty of Data Visualization—21:27 minutes

This is a TED talk by David McCandless on the value of visualizing data in order to draw new meaning and insights from complex data in order to better design, innovate, make better decisions, and so on. Can be a useful video prior to discussing the development of information and metrics to help frame change, change views, and guide change initiatives.

- Give an example of how the reframing of data might bolster the change process in each of the four stages.

- How might the data presented in the video prompt change? Explain.

3. Susan Colantuono: The Career Advice You Probably Didn't Get—13:57 minutes

- How do the skills Colantuono talks about matter to measuring and implementing change?

- How should organizational leaders imbed the skills that Colantuono talks about into the organization in order to create continuous change?

Please see study.sagepub.com/cawsey3e for access to video and a downloadable template of this exercise.

TOOLKIT EXERCISE 10.2

Reflecting on the Impact of Measures and Control Processes on Change

Think of a change initiative that you are familiar with.

1. What measures and control processes were employed in tracking and guiding the change initiative? Were they consistent with the vision and strategy of the change? Were they viewed as legitimate by those who would be using them?

2. How was the measurement information captured and fed back to those who needed to use it? Was it a user-friendly process, and did the information arrive in a useful and timely form?

3. Did the change managers consider how the measures might need to evolve over the life of the change initiative? How was this evolution managed? By whom?

4. Were steps taken to ensure that the measures used during the change would be put to proper use? Were there risks and potential consequences arising from their use that would need to be managed?

5. Were goals and milestones established to plot progress along the way and used to make midcourse corrections if needed? Were the smaller victories celebrated to reinforce the efforts of others when milestones were achieved?

6. What were the end-state measures that were developed for the change? Were they consistent with the vision and strategy? Were they viewed as legitimate by those who would be using them?

7. How was the end-state measurement information captured and fed back to those who would need to use it? Was it a user-friendly process?

8. Were steps taken to ensure that the measures would be put to proper use? Were there risks and potential consequences arising from their use that would need to be managed?

Please see study.sagepub.com/cawsey3e for a downloadable template of this exercise.

TOOLKIT EXERCISE 10.3

Application of Simon's Control Systems Model

Consider a change you are familiar with.

1. Describe the control processes and measures that were used with the change (i.e., the belief, interactive, boundary, and diagnostic controls). When and how were they used, and what was their impact?

    a. During the earlier stages of the change initiative

    b. During the middle stages of the change initiative

    c. During the latter stages of the change initiative

2. Were there forbidden topics in the organization, such as questions related to strategy or core values? Were those limits appropriate and did anyone test those limits by raising controversial questions or concerns? Were small successes celebrated along the way?

3. What changes could have been made with the control processes and measures that would have assisted in advancing the interests of the change?

Please see study.sagepub.com/cawsey3e for a downloadable template of this exercise.

TOOLKIT EXERCISE 10.4

Aligning the Change With Systems and Building the Balanced Scorecard for the Change

Think about a change you are familiar with.

1. State the mission, vision, and strategy for the change.

2. Consider the mission, vision, and strategy of the organization:

   - Is the proposed change consistent with these?

   - If not, what needs to be done with the change or the existing mission, vision, and strategy to bring them into line?

3. Financial component of scorecard: If you succeed with the change vision, how will it appear to the shareholders or those responsible for funding the change?

   How will you know (objectives and metrics)? Are some of these leading indicators while others are lagging indicators?

4. Customer component of scorecard: If you succeed with the change, how will it appear to your customers?

   How will you know (objectives and metrics)? Are there leading and lagging indicators here?

5. Internal business processes component of scorecard: If you succeed with the change, how will it appear in your business processes?

   How will you know (objectives and metrics)? Are there leading and lagging indicators here?

6. Learning and growth component of scorecard: If you succeed with the change, how will it appear to your employees and demonstrate itself in their actions?

   What about the information and organizational capital? How will you and they know (objectives and metrics)? Are there leading and lagging indicators here?

7. Lay out the scorecard you've designed for your change and seek feedback.

8. Show how the different components are connected to each other by developing a strategy map for the change in the space below.

Please see study.sagepub.com/cawsey3e for a downloadable template of this exercise.

TOOLKIT EXERCISE 10.5

Using the Risk Exposure Calculator

Consider a change initiative that you know is currently being considered for adoption and apply the risk exposure calculator to it.

				Score
Change Pressure	Pressure to produce Low High 1 2 3 4 5 Score:	Level of ambiguity Low High 1 2 3 4 5 Score:	Experience with change High* Low 1 2 3 4 5 Score: *Note: High and Low anchors are reversed for this item.	Out of 15 ___
Change Culture	Degree to which individuals are rewarded for risk taking Low High 1 2 3 4 5 Score:	Degree to which executives resist hearing bad news Low High 1 2 3 4 5 Score:	Level of internal competition Low High 1 2 3 4 5 Score:	Out of 15 ___
Information Situation	Degree to which situation is complex and fast changing Low High 1 2 3 4 5 Score:	Level of gaps that exist in diagnostic measures Low High 1 2 3 4 5 Score:	Degree to which change decision making is decentralized Low High 1 2 3 4 5 Score:	Out of 15 ___
Total Score =				

Using scoring criteria consistent with that developed by Simon:

- If your score is between 9 and 20, you are in the safety zone.
- Between 21 and 34, you are in the cautionary zone.
- Between 35 to 45, you are in a danger zone.

1. Does the organization have an appropriate level of risk taking given the nature of the business it is in? Does it play it too safe, about right, or does it take excessive risks?

2. Does the approach help you in thinking about risk and what factors may be contributing to the overall risk levels?

3. Do the findings help you to think about what can be done to make the levels of risk more manageable?

Source: Adapted from Simon, R. "How Risky is Your Company?," *Harvard Business Review*, Vol. 77, #3, 1999, 85–94.

Please see study.sagepub.com/cawsey3e for a downloadable template of this exercise.

TOOLKIT EXERCISE 10.6

Applying the DICE Model

Consider a change initiative that you know is currently being considered for adoption and apply the DICE model to it.

- Duration: How frequently is the project formally reviewed?

  a) Time between project reviews is less than 2 months—1 point

  b) Time between project reviews is 2–4 months—2 points

  c) Time between project reviews is 4–8 months—3 points

  d) Time between project reviews is more than 8 months—4 points

- Duration Score = _____

- Integrity: How capable is the project team leader? How capable and motivated are team members? Do they have the sufficient time to devote to the change?

  a. Leader is respected, team is capable and motivated, and members have sufficient time to commit to the project—1 point

  b. If leader or team is lacking on all these dimensions—4 points

  c. If leader and team are partially lacking on these dimensions—2 to 3 points

- Integrity of Performance Score: (Your Initial Score × 2) = _____

- Commitment of Senior Management: How committed is senior management to the project? Do they regularly communicate the reasons for the initiative and its importance? Do they convincingly communicate the message and their commitment? Is the commitment to the project shared by senior management? Have they committed sufficient resources to the project?

  a. If senior management clearly and consistently communicated the need for change and their support—1 point

  b. If senior management appears neutral—2 to 3 points

  c. If senior management is reluctant to support the change—4 points

- Senior Management Commitment Score: (Your Initial Score × 2) = _____

- Local Level Commitment: Do those employees most affected by the change understand the need and believe the change is needed? Are they enthusiastic and eager to get involved or concerned and resistant?

  a. If employees are eager to be engaged in the change initiative—1 point

  b. If they are willing but not overly keen—2 points

  c. If they are moderately to strongly reluctant to be engaged in the change—3 to 4 points

- Local Level Commitment Score = _____

- Effort: What incremental effort is required of employees to implement the change? Will it be added on to an already heavy workload? Have employees expressed strong resistance to additional demands on them in the past?

  a. If incremental effort is less than 10%—1 point

  b. If incremental effort is 10% to 20%—2 points

  c. If incremental effort is 20% to 40%—3 points

  d. If incremental effort is greater than 40%—4 points

- Effort Score = _____

  To calculate your overall DICE score: Add the scores from the above:_____

  1. What score did the change project receive? Was it in the low-risk category (7 to 14), the worry zone (between 14 and 17), or the high-risk area (over 17)?

  2. Do the findings help you to think about important sources of risk to the success of the project?

  3. Do the findings help you to think about what can be done to make the levels of risk more manageable?

Source: Adapted from H. L. Sirkin, P. Keenan, and A. Jackson, "The Hard Side of Change Management," Harvard Business Review 91, no. 9 (2005, October): 108–118.

Please see study.sagepub.com/cawsey3e for a downloadable template of this exercise.

CHAPTER 11

Summary Thoughts on Organizational Change

Once you fall in a river, you're no longer a fisherman, you're a swimmer.

—Gene Hill

CHAPTER OVERVIEW

- The chapter begins with a case that illustrates the application of the Change Path Model.
- Individuals wishing to become organizational change agents need to recognize that two main routes exist: sophisticated technical specialists and strategic generalists, with the former often leading to the latter.
- Several paradoxes in the field of organizational change are summarized.
- The chapter ends with a summary checklist of lessons in organizational change.

Change is both normal and pervasive, and the capacity to lead and implement organizational change, denotes a skill set all managers need to possess. In summarizing the practical and theoretical approaches to organizational change, it is important to reiterate that the change process is rarely a straight path. You may begin the process of organizational change aiming at a particular vision and end up at some variation of the original goal. Change processes require adapting, compromising, reevaluating, and having an open mind, while at the same time remaining committed to the vision and persevering to see the change through. The process contains inherent paradoxes that must be managed, and the journey can be confusing and frustrating for both those trying to implement changes and those whose lives are affected by the changes. However, it also has the potential to energize and excite, provide focus and hope. It represents the path through which revitalization and renewal occurs, from smaller incremental modifications to those larger-scale transformational changes that need to be undertaken from time to time.

Change management is not something you simply deal with, then can ignore. Rather, it is a continuing process of seeking to understand what is going on and what is needed, undertaking initiatives with others, and learning from the experiences and outcomes achieved. The completion of one change sets the stage for the changes that lie ahead. In essence, change is the normal state and if an organization is not attempting to challenge the status quo, adapt, and improve, it's likely undergoing less desirable forms of change—stagnation, atrophication, and decline. Developing your capacities to lead and manage this process increases your ability to add value and will enhance your career prospects. The search for talented individuals who can help make positive things happen will only intensify in the years ahead.

Putting the Change Path Model Into Practice

The Change Path Model has provided an organizing framework for this book, and it is presented in its summary form in Figure 11.1. This model argues that change agents move systematically from analyses that stimulate interest in change and awaken the organization, through to mobilization, acceleration, and institutionalization of the change. A summary checklist for change is presented at the end of this chapter.

An important modification has been made to this final presentation of the model. An arrow has been added that links the fourth phase back to the first, to reflect that the enactment of one set of changes sets the stage for the next ones. It's an ongoing process, whose intensity will vary, depending upon the situation, the people, and the magnitude of what is being undertaken. There is no question that we need to rest and reenergize from time to time, celebrate what we've accomplished, and become fully competent in extracting the benefits the changes make possible. But then it's on to the next challenges. We can't change the past, but what we choose to do (or not do) now can change the future. If we choose to do nothing but more of the same—you get the picture!

The case that follows, Harry and the Company Takeover,* provides an opportunity to review the concepts in the model and see each stage of the process played out in a smaller firm. It does not occur in a clean and tidy manner, because this is real life. Some stages overlap with others, due to Harry's approach to change, there are stumbles along the way, and he acts in ways that you may well disagree with at times. However, his commitment to change is clear and the case provides a window on how the process unfolds at this firm.

---

*This case is based on personal experience of the authors.

Figure 11.1 The Change Path Model

Awakening
Chapter 4
1. Identify a need for change and confirm the problems or opportunities that incite the need for change through collection of data.
2. Articulate the gap in performance between the present and the envisioned future state, and spread awareness of the data and the gap throughout the organization.
3. Develop a powerful vision for change.
4. Disseminate the vision for the change and why it's needed through multiple communication channels.

Mobilization
Chapters 5 through 8
1. Make sense of the desired change through formal systems and structures, and leverage those systems to reach the change vision (Chapter 5).
2. Assess power and cultural dynamics at play, and put them to work to better understand the dynamics and build coalitions and support to realize the change (Chapter 6).
3. Communicate the need for change organization-wide and manage change recipients and various stakeholders as they react to and move the change forward (Chapter 7).
4. Leverage change agent personality, knowledge, skills and abilities, and related assets (e.g., reputation and relationships) for the benefit of the change vision and its implementation (Chapter 8).

Acceleration
Chapter 9
1. Continue to systematically reach out to engage and empower others in support, planning, and implementation of the change. Help them develop needed new knowledge, skills, abilities, and ways of thinking that will support the change.
2. Use appropriate tools and techniques to build momentum, accelerate and consolidate progress.
3. Manage the transition, celebrating small wins and the achievement of milestones along the larger, more difficult path of change.

Institutionalization
Chapter 10
1. Track the change periodically and through multiple balanced measures to help assess what is needed, gauge progress toward the goal, and to make modifications as needed and mitigate risk.
2. Develop and deploy new structures, systems, processes and knowledge, skills, and abilities, as needed, to bring life to the change and new stability to the transformed organization.

HARRY AND THE COMPANY TAKEOVER

When Harry decided to help his cousin turn around his business, he had no idea things were in as bad shape as they were. He knew that the banks had called their demand notes, which would put the company into receivership if appropriate

(Continued)

actions were not taken, but he was shocked at the number of problematic issues. In his mind, the company's business model was straightforward: renting out specialized heavy construction equipment (either with or without operators) to a relatively easily identified set of customers (contractors who had need of such equipment). Straightforward, maybe, but there was no question that things were a mess.

Harry's cousin had founded the firm 15 years ago. He had grown it steadily through the first 10 years, followed by accelerated growth over the past 5 years. The bankruptcy of a key competitor and unprecedented growth in the area had resulted in a robust market opportunity. Staff levels had more than doubled during the past 5 years, to 57 employees. Fifteen employees were located in the office area, handling administrative, accounting/finance, and sales functions. The remainder were in the repair shop, in the yard, or on the road, dealing with maintenance, delivery, and equipment operation roles.

In the past year, sales had flattened and moved to a modest decline. Other financial indicators showed worrying trends. For 2 years, operating expenses had risen significantly. While Harry wasn't certain why, he thought that equipment purchases had led to higher interest charges and that labor costs had risen dramatically. It was as if the firm had lost its capacity to manage the growth.

Things had gone from difficult to worse in the past 2 years. The company's bank was demanding repayment of loans. His cousin had varied his management approach from requesting to pleading and finally to avoiding issues at work. Employees referred to him as Waldo (from the children's book *Where's Waldo?*), because he was usually impossible to find when guidance was sought or a decision needed to be made.

Harry agreed that he would try to turn things around in return for his cousin consenting to turn over decision-making power and control while focusing on what he knew best—things related to operations and the equipment. His cousin had grown up with a love for heavy equipment, and family members said that the only reason he was in business was so that he had newer and bigger toys to play with. He had specialized knowledge about which equipment was suitable for which jobs and, prior to the past 2 years, had been adept at developing relationships with customers that generated repeat business.

Their terms were agreed to, but Harry's arrival did not reverse his cousin's disappearing act. He continued to appear depressed and distant, with little appetite for assuming a more active operational role in the business.

Harry believed that the business had solid prospects and should sustain an adequate return on the investment. However, it certainly was not doing so now. He met with the bank and presented a turnaround plan. Based on his reputation as a successful entrepreneur and his willingness to make a significant investment to improve liquidity, the bank agreed to renegotiate the operating loan and line of credit. This would provide the firm with the breathing space needed to execute the turnaround.

Harry moved into his cousin's office and began to take control of the management of the firm. He was shocked to find a culture of permissiveness, waste, and tolerance for corruption. As he walked through the parts and

(Continued)

(Continued)

maintenance areas, he found parts, tools, and equipment scattered about. Grease on the floor made walking a risky proposition. Pizza boxes, pop cans, and bottles were littered around. He thought he smelled liquor on some employees. He observed that lateness and absenteeism were problems. No one seemed to be doing anything about these problems because the labor market for mechanics and operators was tight and supervisors were afraid that people might quit.

The housekeeping within the office/administrative area was somewhat better than other parts of the operation, but it still left much to be desired. Some employees smoked in work areas despite no-smoking rules. While the accounting and finance area appeared to be better organized, they often had difficulty providing the managerial data Harry requested.

After reviewing sales information, Harry also found himself wondering about the source of orders. Most orders came from brokers rather than directly from users of the equipment. He wondered why and after a little probing found that the brokers were taking 15% to 25% off the top for the orders.

In an inspection of the operations shortly after his arrival, Harry found seven brand-new tires and rims stashed behind a building. When he checked purchasing invoices, he learned that nine had been bought the week before. On further investigation, he was told that no new tires had been mounted on any equipment. Harry could not locate those two tires and rims, worth more than $2,000 each.

One of the first things that Harry did was to walk around the operation and talk to people. He would look them in the eye and say, "I want to make money here. What do you want?" At the same time, he started insisting that if people came to him with problems, they should also come with what they wanted out of the situation—a solution to the issue. When they did, he would listen intently, take time to discuss things thoroughly, voice appreciation and support, and approve action, when appropriate, with the words, "Great—let's get on with it. Let me know if you need anything and keep me in the loop with how it goes." The consistent message from Harry was that this operation will be a success and everyone will win—if we exercise more discipline and if everyone shows initiative and contributes to improvements needed to make this operation a winner.

Harry realized that many members of the firm probably wanted to do a good job. That was the sense he got as he visited departments, talked with individuals one on one, and heard about their frustrations. Some employees seemed to come and go as they wished—three even brought their dogs to work. He had listened to one customer complaint about late delivery of equipment and learned that the person delivering the machinery had stopped for 3 hours on route. The driver's excuse was lunch and engine problems that had miraculously resolved themselves. Employees' morale was in the toilet, but turnover had yet to become a problem.

Harry called the employees together during his first week to introduce himself; address the need for improvement; solicit their cooperation, ideas, and effort; and let them know that he planned to be around regularly. Harry also put up flip-chart sheets in the office during the first week and began listing every issue or problem that he or others identified. His list contained 93 items by the end of the third week. However, by the third week, he had also approved four employee-initiated improvement plans.

(Continued)

During his first week, Harry smelled alcohol on the breath of an employee who appeared to be under the influence. He fired him on the spot. He told employees that new rules on attendance would be enforced.

During the third week, Harry called people together for a second plant meeting and summarized some of the problem areas that had been identified that needed attention. He also announced the initial change recommendations that employees had advanced and publicly thanked the initiators. He stated that new rules on work scheduling would be implemented. He stated that housekeeping in both the plant and office had to improve. He said that the business had the potential to be a first-class operation, and it was time for it to quit looking like a pigsty. The shop floors would be degreased, the walls would be repainted, and tools and equipment should be properly stored. If people wanted pizza or anything other than a donut or muffin with their coffee, they would be expected to eat it in the lunchroom or not at all. Major cleanup activities were undertaken over a 3-week period, with floor degreasing and painting occurring during the weekends.

During his third week, Harry went into the workspace of the people with dogs and said, "What are these? Employees or pets?" They vanished from the workplace. After further investigation of the tires he had found stashed, Harry concluded that the person who had signed the purchase order for the nine tires was selling them out the back door, and on the Wednesday of week three, he escorted him off the premises.

During the fourth week, Harry had an opportunity to follow up on his hunch that the company was losing money by relying on brokers. He phoned one of their customers who regularly used their equipment but who went through a broker and asked why they were not placing orders directly. "Because you never called us before" was the answer. Before he ended the conversation, he had a $50,000 work order placed directly. When Harry relayed this conversation and its results to the sales staff, they were at first defensive. Further conversation, combined with his now-standard question ("We want to make money—do you want to be part of it?"), elicited affirmative responses, though they still seemed unsure as to how they should change their sales approach. Harry made a note to himself that they would need further training and guidance (plus improve their performance), or they would need to be replaced.

Harry recalled similar conversations with other employees. For example, in a conversation with a truck driver, Harry said, "We make money when you are delivering equipment to clients. If you stand around when orders are pending, we don't make money. People who work hard and get more equipment to clients are going to make more money. Do you want to be a part of this or not?" "I'm in" was the response.

During the fourth week, Harry noticed that certain pieces of equipment that had been in for repair in week one were still inoperable. He asked why and was told that the maintenance supervisor was in a dispute with the field service foreman and sales staff over the allocation of repair and maintenance charges, and as a result, needed repairs had not been undertaken. This resulted in lost rental sales. The argument had been going on for more than a month, and he was told this was not the first time. Harry reacted with frustration. He called an immediate

(Continued)

(Continued)

meeting of those involved, ordered the equipment repaired as soon as possible, and stated that this was no way to resolve conflicts. He added "unclear responsibilities" to his list of issues on the flip chart.

During Harry's sixth week on the job, he announced that he wanted a system that would give him a profit-and-loss statement for each piece of equipment. "Why do you want that?" was the response. When he explained why to the employees in accounting, they understood, but operational employees saw it as more paperwork that might get in the way of sales and servicing.

When he began to explore equipment repair invoices during week 6, he noted that many expensive repairs had been done on-site at their clients' premises. Much of the work looked routine but was made much more expensive because of the location and because the company had to negotiate with the client over operating losses while the machine was down. Harry wondered why that equipment hadn't been serviced prior to leaving the shop. When he inquired further, he discovered that there was no formal preventive maintenance program established for the equipment.

By week 7, the cleaning and painting of the office area and workplace had been completed and it helped to spruce up the environment. Employees were reacting positively to the improved workplace, as reflected in comments Harry received during his weekly walks through the work areas. Little additional action seemed to be needed from Harry to maintain these improvements. Even the paperwork in the office area seemed to be better organized now, but Harry wondered whether it was simply being put in boxes and hidden from view. When he told employees in the plant that he thought that swearing was unprofessional conduct at work, they just looked at him.

Things seemed to be getting better, but much more needed to be done. He went down his list, noting some of the most pressing items:

1. No formalized preventive maintenance systems

2. Questionable inventory management system, missing parts in some areas, excess inventory in others, and a significant volume of obsolete parts that were held in inventory

3. Missing tools and equipment, including some big-ticket items, such as a $35,000 loader and a $25,000 compressor

4. Sales relationships not actively managed, clients not phoned in a timely manner, customer complaints not acted upon until threats were invoked

5. Logistics/scheduling, customer delivery and pickups, on-site servicing of equipment not handled well. Customers complained about downtime and their inability to predict when things would be done.

6. Lags between order fulfillment and client billing, slow payment of accounts payable

7. Poor relations with suppliers of parts and equipment, due in part to slow payment, disagreements over terms and conditions, and lack of supplier responsiveness to emergency requests

8. Finally, and importantly, there was the lingering question: What role would his cousin play after the company had been revitalized?

Awakening: As one can surmise from the case, Harry's critical organizational analysis provided extensive evidence of *what* needed to change. The list was long: employees drinking on the job, sloppy shop conditions, potential theft of valuable equipment, low performance expectations, a lack of systems and processes in critical areas such as equipment maintenance, and the absence of a disciplined approach to interpersonal conduct and dispute resolution. How to change was not as clear, as the culture of the organization reinforced the negative dynamics. Clearly, Harry needed to change the systems and culture to get things back on track—assuming, of course, that the bank would give him the time to turn the operation around.

The question of "why change?" was evident to Harry and to the bank but was not evident to all the employees. Harry needed to "unfreeze the situation." The initial behavior of some employees indicated complacency, resignation, and in some cases, a desire to milk the company for as long as it lasted. He dealt with the bank by giving them a plan and putting in his own money. This and his reputation as a skilled owner–manager persuaded the bank to work with him. Harry tackled the culture of permissiveness by making his expectations clear to employees (Are the dogs "employees or pets"?). While some of this was unorthodox, the communication was clear. As well, Harry understood that actions counted. By firing people who were abusing the organization, he was making the strongest statements possible about what was not acceptable. Because he was in charge of the operation, he had the power to do this. Note that Harry's cousin also had the formal authority to take such actions, but he had chosen not to act. Over time, Harry's cousin had come to be perceived as powerless. This is clearly *the awakening stage*, as Harry identified the problems and began creating a perception of the need for change throughout the organization.

Harry's vision for change was clear and simple: "I want to make money. This will take individual initiative, discipline, and systems and processes that can support our work. What do you want?" The strategy was to service clients with the rental equipment they needed in a timely and profitable manner. One could argue over the nature of the appeal, but the vision was clear and appropriate to the company situation. At the same time, Harry seemed to have an implicit vision for the longer term. His actions to clean up the workplace; stop employees from swearing and smoking; empower employees to engage in active problem solving; become more customer, cost, and performance focused; and act on their improvement ideas all suggest a new vision for the workplace. The vision he presented to employees of sharing in the success of the business and making money, by being more disciplined in their approach to their work, showing initiative, and taking pride in what they did was motivating to them, even though they may have been more ambivalent about the smaller steps to reaching this goal (i.e., becoming more professional and improving housekeeping).

Mobilization: His visits with the bank, customers, and employees; the review of records and past performance; and insights gained while walking around the facility led to the list of 93 issues. This was his gap analysis and commencement of the mobilization stage. In his view, there would be employees who would want to work and who would welcome being part of a successful company. Those he appealed to directly by outlining how they could make money by helping the company succeed. Those who resisted strongly were fired if their behavior was illegal or unethical, or if they failed to meet standards that he rapidly worked to establish and communicate. Harry recognized and reinforced employees who began to embrace the change. Implicitly, the message was that they could be viewed as change agents working in the employee group.

Harry recognized that an important gap that needed to be addressed was an absence of needed formal structures. The reporting lines and procedures were unclear, as shown by the dispute between the maintenance supervisor and the general foreman and sales staff. Formal systems either were faulty or didn't exist. For example, the accounting system could not track usage and profitability by machine and there was no preventive maintenance system. Harry dealt with key stakeholders in priority: the bank, the employees, and key clients. The aftermath of these contacts created initiatives that raised expectations, began to improve performance, and helped to generate hope for the future.

Acceleration: The case demonstrates nicely the acceleration stage, including action planning and implementation steps. The operation was relatively simple and his plan consisted explicitly of dealing with the list of issues needing attention. He discussed specific problems with employees and demanded that others take action to deal with the issues. This approach changed their way of thinking about their role and gave them a reason to invest in the future of the company—a future that he had defined as a lucrative one. As he learned about the ambitions and competencies of employees, he encouraged them. He also began the process of setting standards, firing those who were engaged in inappropriate behavior or who failed to meet reasonable performance standards. His communications plan was personal, constant, and direct. He celebrated employees who had instigated changes and recognized them publicly, reinforcing this way of thinking and encouraging other late adapters to get on board.

Harry's implementation skills contributed to the success of the organizational change. While the case example provided above only addresses the first few weeks of the change initiative, we can report that he continued to follow through, reversed the decline, and within six months had returned the firm to financial health, as evident in increasing sales, substantially improved margins, and profitability. True to his word, employees were supported in initiating and making needed changes, reasonable standards were enforced, accomplishments were celebrated, and employees shared in the firm's financial success. Morale and commitment rose substantially. Implementation is essential to the process. A study by McKinsey & Company reports that good implementers run more successful change efforts, experience 30% higher financial returns, and sustain twice the value from the change over the long run.[1] The key practices, which are evident in Harry's case, are ownership and commitment to the change, intentional prioritization of time, and company-wide accountability. In addition, a strong flow of information and clear decision rights has proven to be cornerstones of successful execution.[2] No amount of restructuring an organization will make up for confusion over decision rights and lack of appropriate information. See www.simulator-orgeffectiveness.com/ to experiment with your skills in diagnosing organizations and selecting actions that will move them to a state of more effective execution and implementation.

Institutionalization: Because of the size of the operation, Harry was able to measure the changes directly as he institutionalized the changes, integrating them into the fabric of the organization. Some changes he could see. The plant was cleaner. The dogs were gone. Others he could track by looking at sales figures and profit margins. At the same time, he knew that the systems he wanted, such as a system to track profits per piece of rental equipment and a preventative maintenance program, would take longer to install. Through these combined undertakings, he sought to change the culture of the organization to one that was much better aligned with its environment.

Finally, the change initiatives that Harry took were just the beginning. He recognized and rewarded those who joined him in turning the company around. He learned a great deal about the operation and what were critical factors in a successful operation. And finally, he developed a new list of change initiatives that would take the organization to the next level of development. His goals were fluid, were influenced by the opinions of others, and evolved as he learned more about each issue.

Harry exemplifies what this book is about. He was very action oriented but he was not a loose cannon. Importantly, his actions were based on a thorough understanding of the need for change, the gaps that needed to be addressed, key success factors, and the levers that needed pulling to achieve change. He insulated the organization from the environment (through his investment in the firm that created a needed financial buffer) long enough for the change processes to begin to work, and he recognized that both short- and long-term changes were needed. In summary, he was an expert change leader. **Toolkit Exercise 11.2** provides a detailed step-by-step summary for planning a change project.

Future Organizations and Their Impact

Barkema- argues that in the future all organizations will need to be global in orientation.[3] Small- and medium-sized firms will access global markets through the Internet in low-cost/high-information-transmission ways. Others will form organizational networks, partnering with others to complete the value chain. Some will be large, focused global firms with worldwide activities.

Barkema states that organizations will have autonomous, dislocated teams. That is, organizations, large or small, will require motivated teams to coordinate their activities across borders and cultures. At the same time, structures will be "digitally enabled." They will have the electronic systems to facilitate coordination. Scanning systems will transmit sales data from stores and warehouses anywhere to manufacturing facilities in real time and will be used to determine future production levels. Personal communications devices such as the iPhone and other smartphones will mean that people can communicate any time, all the time. Such dispersed systems facilitated by almost instantaneous communications will make it easy for competitors to respond to each other's actions. The world will move faster. We can readily see signs of this increased speed.

Such changes will mean that organizations will need loose/tight controls both within and between firms. Within organizations, critical strategic variables will be closely monitored and controlled. Visions will be articulated and adhered to. At the same time, rapid environmental shifts will demand local responses that will vary by region as well as responses that are broad in their geographic reach. What works in one country won't necessarily work in another. Think of the regional differences in the formulation of branded products such as Coke and McDonald's, and this reality becomes clear. Consequently, managers will need to have the autonomy and loose controls to respond to local needs within the critical boundaries of the firm.

Between organizations, networks of firms will be linked to allow for needed information exchange. What is shared will vary from the purely transactional to the strategic, depending on the levels of trust and intimacy existing between firms. At the same time, these firms will maintain their independence on key strategic dimensions viewed as proprietary and/or sources of competitive advantage critical to their long-term success.

Galbraith suggests that strategy and structure of organizations will continue to be closely tied.[4] Organizations will come in an enormous variety of forms and complexities. Straightforward work that is repetitive and easily understood will disappear and companies will organize around opportunities and resources. The key management tasks will involve innovation and the mastering of complexity. Galbraith classifies potential strategies and suggests matching structures.

According to Galbraith, organizations in the 21st century will become increasingly customer oriented and focused. In the customer-oriented organization, organizations will have three major organizational parts: business units, international regions, and customer accounts. These parts will be linked with lateral processes: teams and networks. Focused organizations will have subunits focused on different key criteria: costs, products, or customers.

Malone argues that tomorrow's organizations will have the benefits of both large and small organizations.[5] Digital technologies will enable economics of scale and knowledge creation while preserving the freedom, creativity, motivation, and flexibility of small organizations. There will be a shift from traditional centralized hierarchies to organizations of loose hierarchies, democracies, and markets—like organizations.

- *Loose hierarchy example:* Wikipedia, the free online encyclopedia that anybody can edit and when errors occur, others will spot and correct them
- *Democracy examples:* W. L. Gore, where you become a manager by finding people who want to work for you, or Mondragon, where employees elect a board of directors to make decisions
- *Market example:* An Intel proposal where plant managers propose to sell futures on what they produce and salespeople buy futures for products they want to sell. Prices fluctuate and will determine what products get produced at what plants and who gets to sell the products.

The above is suggestive of how organizations will evolve in the future. As a result of these and other trends, organizational change and change agents will need to

Table 11.1 The Impact of Organizational Trends on Organizational Change and Change Agents

Organizational Trend	Organizational Change	Change Agent
Globalization—be big, or specialized, otherwise be acquired, squeezed, or eliminated	Strategic global perspective for both large firms and niche SMEs	Pattern finder
Virtual and networked organizations	Knowledge of networks and emergent organizational forms increasingly important	Vision framer Organizational analyst and aligner
Loose/tight controls		Mobilizer, empowerer, enabler, enactor
24/7 response requirement	Knowledge and risk management: ability to use crowd sourcing, online communities, and big data to enhance knowledge creation, innovation, and risk management	Disintegrator and integrator
Cost and quality focus, outsourcing and supply chain rationalization		Corporate gadfly and trend surfer
Crowd sourcing for capital, innovation, and talent		Generalist capacities: facilitation, influencing, negotiating and visioning skills; project management expertise
Rise of big data, algorithms, and artificial intelligence (AI) to inform decision making	Web-enabled communication, change-related blogs, fast response capacity with a human face	Specialist roles, related to expertise needed for specific change initiatives. For example, software system integration, customer relationship management, flexible manufacturing, organizational integration following acquisition
Shortening product life cycles and increasing customer expectations	Negotiation and the development and leveraging of networks to enhance quality, cost leadership, and/or customer focus	
Influential online communities democratizing information access		
Increasing focus on integrated customer services and knowledge management	Creativity, innovation, and rapid deployment capacity	
Rapid technological change fundamentally alters industry structures, in terms of both the "what" and the "how"	Increased importance of empowerment, teams, community engagement, and a strong process focus	Capacity to develop and sustain the trust and confidence of multiple stakeholders
Changing demographic, social, and cultural environment		
Political changes are realigning alliances and the competitive environment		

shift as well. Table 11.1 summarizes these potential changes. The table suggests that change agents will need both a set of generalist capabilities providing basic competencies as well as change skills oriented around critical technical competencies.

In summary, those involved with organizational change need to develop:

- a strong strategic and global perspective;
- knowledge of networks and emergent organizational forms and how they work;

- skills in risk management and knowledge management;
- understanding of the impact of Web-enabled communication, the use of social media in advancing external and internal change, and fast response capacity;
- the ability to communicate worldwide while maintaining a human face;
- perceptiveness of different cultures and norms, and how these factors affect organizational change; and
- the capacity to create, deploy, and work with empowered teams with the right mix of skills and abilities, operating with a focused vision. The teams' boundaries come from the vision and agreed-to expectations concerning performance, modes of operation, and other predefined standards and shared commitments. These capacities will apply to both co-located teams and virtual teams, whose members may be geographically dispersed.

Becoming an Organizational Change Agent: Specialists and Generalists

For many change agents, their initial involvement begins when they are asked to participate in a change initiative (often as a member of a team) due to their particular technical skills, past performance, and interest they have demonstrated in change initiatives. If the change involves the deployment of new sales support software, for example, individuals with appropriate technical competencies concerning both the software's implementation and the nature of the sales process will need to be involved with the project.

Over time, though, the careers of change agents tend to evolve in two different ways: those who are more technically oriented in their change skills and those who possess more generalist change agent skills.

The careers of more technically oriented change agents will be characterized by projects of increasing size and complexity, in their areas of technical expertise. For instance, if their educational background was in computer programming, their initial involvement could be the provision of training for corporate users of a system upgrade. Over time, as their expertise grows, these change agents will find themselves taking on bigger and more sophisticated technical change challenges. At their peak, such individuals who began their careers providing computer training will have become respected change experts in large-scale software system integration projects. Technically oriented change specialists will require some competence in more general change-management skills, such as gap analysis, communication of vision, and interpersonal skills; however, it will be their technical change-management expertise that will be sought after when an initiative lies within their domain—be it software, merger integration, or foreign market development. Individuals pursuing this career path will often be found in consulting firms that specialize in their areas of expertise.

The careers of more general management-oriented change agents are characterized by a shift away from a technically focused path, as they work to develop change-management skills that are appropriate for a wider variety of situations. Those who choose to orient their development around general change-management skills may initially start their careers in technical and functional change management. However, over time, these individuals will develop increasingly sophisticated general change-management competencies associated with the Change Path Model. As a result, over time they will find themselves undertaking diverse challenges of increasing complexity, from turning around a poorly performing division to ramping up an operation to cope with growth, restructuring and integrating merged operations, or tackling cultural changes needed to increase organizational effectiveness in emerging markets.

To be successful, organizations need access to individuals with both technical and more general change-management competencies. At times, certain change skills will be more important than others for obvious reasons, but the management of complex change initiatives benefit from having access to both perspectives and is further aided when the change agents involved respect this need, recognize each other's skills and abilities, and understand what each of them is able to contribute to the initiative. Figure 11.2 outlines these two broad career paths.

An additional complexity to consider in the area of change management was noted in Chapters 1 and 8. Some change agents orient their careers around incremental change initiatives while others orient themselves around the management of more disruptive changes. Once again, it is not a matter of either/or as to which orientation is best. At different points in time, organizations will need access to both of these skill sets. When change agents with different orientations respect and value these differences in approach and recognize what each can contribute, the interests of change are advanced.

Paradoxes in Organizational Change

The field of organizational change has a set of underlying paradoxes that change agents struggle with. Just as quantum physics considers an electron as both a particle and a wave,[†] some aspects of organizational change have two perspectives. Both aspects are important and neither should be rejected.

First, the management of organizations will become more complex as the strategic focus of organizations develops a global perspective. Organizational change will need tools and processes that encourage the systematic management of a wide number of elements (organizational systems, structures, cultures, leadership, technology, etc.) while maintaining the speed of change. Clearly a challenge will be to handle complexity without being overwhelmed and frozen by it. Organizational change as a field needs to handle the paradox of how to maintain the momentum of change (something that may require simplification) while not dismissing the complexity of an organization's environment.

[†]Under certain circumstances, the electron looks like a particle and has the characteristics of a particle (mass, solidity, etc.). Under other circumstances, the electron seems to be a wave. It has a frequency and other wave characteristics. This paradox is only resolved by accepting an electron as both.

Figure 11.2   Organizational Change Agents' Skills

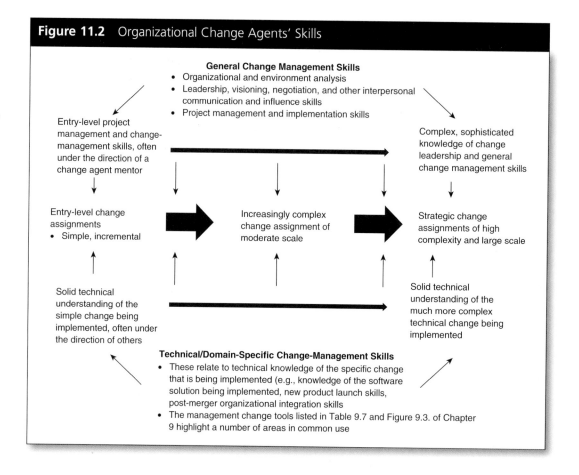

A second paradox involves an organization's need to be simultaneously central-ized and decentralized. Organizations must be centralized to have singularity of strategy, yet also decentralized so that they can remain competitive by responding agilely to changes in the environment. Organizational change agents need to learn how to help organizations understand this paradox and to evolve mechanisms to handle this tension.

As organizational leaders become skilled in promoting decentralized initiatives, they will face the challenge of handling multiple change initiatives simultaneously. Change agents need to consider which change initiatives will block or run counter to others and which ones will support and facilitate others. Interaction effects are not always self-apparent, and sometimes initiatives that look like they are support-ive of other activities in the short run may have adverse consequences over the long term. How can change leaders help an organization institutionalize or finish one project while continuing multiple other ones, and how can they assist in identifying and managing unintended side effects?

Organizational change involves both incremental/continuous and radical/discontinuous change. Depending on how rapidly the environment is changing, organizations may need to engage in both kinds of change. The challenge for change agents will be to develop adaptive, flexible organizations while simultaneously engaging in radical organizational change when it is needed. Organizational change as a field needs to develop insights into this paradox.

Finally, the digital world and the rise of the knowledge worker shift the territory of organizational change from a hierarchical frame to a democratic, participative one. But the essence of many change projects is a new direction that, in the end, is mandated, nondemocratically, from above. Most change projects need input from rank-and-file employees but also need some degree of central direction and management. The tension between participative involvement of many and the pressure to drive change from the top and center of an organization creates potential paradoxes.[‡]

Given these paradoxes, change agents must develop a positive orientation to change that permits them to deal with inherent contradictions.

Orienting Yourself to Organizational Change

Everyone who is a member of an organization will participate in organizational change. Change is a part of living, and opportunities will emerge that involve you in change in various roles. Sometimes your involvement will be mandated, whereas at other times you may choose to seek it out, or your change roles may evolve naturally over time. Sometimes you will be asked to take on the role of change leader or change agent, become a member of a team implementing the change, take on an advisory role, or you may find yourself on the receiving end of a change initiative. Sometimes you will find yourself able to exercise choice as to what roles you play in the change initiative, whereas at other times this will not be the case. As you experience organizational change from whatever role you find yourself in, the following advice will help you deal with it more effectively.

1. Gain perspective and insight by recognizing the dynamism and complexity of your organization. What connections exist between parts and how do they work?

2. Recognize that people's perceptions are critical. The perception of benefits and costs determines a person's reaction to a change proposal.

3. Understand that your perception is only one of many. Your view is neither right nor wrong. It is just your point of view of how things are.

4. Gather people as you go. There are multiple ways to achieve your change (even when you are starting as a recipient), but the ways that bring others with you are easier and more fun. And remember, people can't rock the boat when they are busy rowing.

5. Pull people toward you with a powerful change vision. Push people through argument and rewards when you need to, but gain support through their hearts.

[‡]Organizational change will need to be prepared to use and respond to various social media platforms that discuss openly the issues surrounding change initiatives. Can change leaders accept and deal positively with open criticism that may show up on such media?

6. Get active in pursuit of your vision. If you do something, you will get responses, and you can learn from those. Not doing anything cuts you off from learning.

7. Have a plan oriented around your change vision. Having an explicit plan means your thinking can be discussed and challenged. Know that your plan won't last and will require modification when you start implementing it, but it will certainly be useful in starting a discussion and gaining commitment.

8. Do things that are positive. Actions that suck energy from you and the system are difficult to sustain. Growing your energy as change agent is important.

9. To start meaningful change, you need only a few believers. To continue, you need to develop momentum until a critical mass of key participants is onside. Some will never join in, and that's OK unless they attempt to sabotage or otherwise disrupt agreed-to initiatives.

10. There are many routes to your goal. Find the ones with the least resistance that still allow you to proceed with integrity.

Summary

That's it. It's an evolving list and its further development is up to you. You've been reading and thinking about how to develop your skills as an agent of change. It's time to deploy those ideas; see what works when, where, why, and how; and learn as you go. No excuses. If you want to make things happen, you will have to learn to live with the frustration, excitement, uncertainty, loneliness, and personal development that come with being a change agent. The learning lies in the journey, while joy, a sense of accomplishment, and feelings of fulfillment accompany the completion of milestones and the realization of changes that have a positive impact on the lives of others. See **Toolkit Exercise 11.1** for critical thinking questions on this chapter.

> *And the day came when the risk it took to remain tight in a bud was more painful than the risk it took to blossom.*
>
> —Anaïs Nin

END-OF-CHAPTER EXERCISE

TOOLKIT EXERCISE 11.1

Critical Thinking Questions

Please find the URLs for the videos listed below on the website at study.sagepub.com/cawsey3e. Consider the questions that follow.

1. Please read Case 6 on page 481 "Ellen Zane—Leading Change at Tufts/NEMC" and consider the following questions:

   - Who are the stakeholders that you identified in each sub-story? What do they have at stake?

   - This is a long list of stakeholders who have various needs and interests. What's significant about this list of stakeholders and their interests? What can we learn from this exercise?

   - It is spring 2011 and the nurses at Tufts Medical Center are threatening to strike. As Zane thinks about and plans to negotiate with the MNA, how is this negotiation different from and similar to her negotiation with Blue Cross Blue Shield's CEO?

   - Is Zane's power base different when she is negotiating with Blue Cross Blue Shield than when she is negotiating with nurses at TMC?

   - What do you think happened in the nurses' strike at TMC?

2. <u>Ellen Zane on the Hardest Job</u>—1:12 minutes

   <u>Ellen Zane and the Cherry on the Cake</u>—2:17 minutes

   - What made this change project worth it for Zane?

   - How did she effectively approach the hardest job?

3. Ellen Zane on Rebranding —3:18 minutes

   - What are all the pieces that went into the rebranding plan?

   - How did Zane evaluate the risk involved with the rebranding effort?

4. Choose a recent CNN Hero; think about how they managed to create change.

   - How did the person you chose create successful change?

   - What inspired them to take on the change?

   - Imagine in 10 years you become a CNN Hero. What story will they tell about you?

5. Look also at the We Day website. Consider the vision and success of Craig and Marc Kielburger in their various endeavors.

   - How were the Kielburgers able to create such sweeping change at such a young age?

   - What challenges do you think they may have faced, and how did they overcome them?

   - How are the youth involved in "We Day" working to create change?

   - What is it that you want to change?

Please see study.sagepub.com/cawsey3e for a downloadable template of this exercise.

TOOLKIT EXERCISE 11.2

Developing Your Change Plan

This toolkit exercise applies the tools from all chapters and asks you to develop a complete change plan for a change you want to make happen.

As a first step, develop your statement of the need for change and your vision for the change.

Once the need for change and vision has been articulated, your assignment is to begin the development of an action plan for the change. This will be broken into four parts:

a. The development of a sequence of action steps and the arrangement of them into a critical path with a clearly defined end goal, intermediate targets, and specific first step.

b. The consideration of contingencies—what might go wrong? How will these things be handled?

c. A responsibility chart. That is, who will do what, where, when, and how?

d. A transition plan including a communications plan. How will the transition be managed? Who will make the innumerable decisions required to handle the details? Who will provide information to those affected? As well, how will the change be communicated to organizational members?

The Action Plan

Begin the development of an action plan. What are the critical steps that must be accomplished? Arrange your action steps in sequence. Can some be done simultaneously? What activities cannot begin or should not start until others are completed? What timelines should you observe? Often it is useful to begin at the end of the project and work backward to now.

Who needs to become committed to the project?

Where are key players at on the adoption continuum? Are they even aware of the change? If aware, are they interested or have they moved beyond that stage to either desiring action or having already adopted?

What will it take to move them along the continuum in the direction of adoption?

The AIDA Continuum

Key Player Name	Aware?	Interested?	Desires Action?	Adopter?

What is the commitment to the adoption of those who have reached the adopter stage? That is, are they at the "let it happen" stage, the "help it happen" stage, or the "make it happen" stage?

How can the commitment levels of key stakeholders be increased?

Responsibility Charting[6]

Actions or Decisions	Person #1	Person #2	Person #3	Person #?
Action #1				
Action #2				
Decision #1				
Action #3				
. . . . .				

Who will do what, where, when, and how? Often a responsibility chart can be useful to track these things.

Coding:

R = Responsibility (not necessarily authority)

A = Approval (right to veto)

S = Support (put resources toward)

I = Inform (to be consulted before action)

Note that if there are a great number of *A*s on your chart, implementation will be difficult. Care must be taken to assign *A*s only when appropriate. Likewise, if there are not enough *R*s and *S*s, you will need to think about changes needed here and how to bring them about.

Formulate a transition plan including a communications plan. How will the transition be managed? Who will make the innumerable decisions required to handle the details? Who will provide information to those affected? As well, how will the change be communicated to organizational members?

The Measurement of Change

How will you know that your goal or change project is successfully implemented? (At times, success will be obvious—e.g., a new system in place. At other times, success will be more difficult to measure—e.g., attitudes toward the adoption and acceptance of a new system.)

What intermediate signals will indicate that you are making progress? What is the first step or sequence of steps?

Your end goal is:

You can measure it by:

Intermediate measures and milestones are:

The first step is:

Contingency Planning

Remember O'Brien's Law[§]? Well, it holds, and things will not go as planned. But you can plan for the unexpected.

What are the critical decision points? Who makes those decisions?

What will you do if the decision or event does not go as planned?

What plans can you make to account for these contingencies? If you can, draw a decision tree of the action plan and lay out the decision–event sequence.

Please see study.sagepub.com/cawsey3e for a downloadable template of this exercise.

[§]O'Brien's Law states: Murphy was an optimist.

Case Study 1

Building Community at Terra Nova Consulting

Ken Ogata

Gary Spraakman

York University

Three months after his appointment as president of Terra Nova Consulting, Terry O'Reilly faced his partners at their biennial conference over a weekend in February 2008. After the events of the past year, everyone at the partners' conference had anxiously awaited hearing his plans to turn Terra Nova Consulting around. With that in mind, he had begun to describe his plan to the partners:

> Over the past forty years, Terra Nova has grown into a global firm, an elite firm within our industry, with offices on five continents. It's a firm each of you has had a hand in building, and it's a firm we can all be proud of. We've been successful, and we're respected for our technical excellence and innovative approaches, but now it's time for a change to meet the challenges of the future.
>
> It's time to present a new image to our clients and employees. Something that recognizes our past excellence, while positioning Terra Nova Consulting for the future. It's time for a new name that will be recognizable internationally. While we are proud of our Canadian heritage and the Terra Nova name, I believe it is time to move forward under a new name that can transcend borders.

Source: Reprinted by permission from the Case Research Journal. Copyright © 2014 by Ken Ogata and Gary Spraakman and the North American Case Research Association. All rights reserved The company and all individuals have been disguised. Financial information has also been altered, but reflects the reality of the situation facing Terra Nova. All other details are represented as accurately as possible.

We wish to thank the members of Terra Nova Consulting for their help and cooperation in participating in this study. We would also like to thank Tupper Cawsey, Deborah Ettington, and three CRJ reviewers for their helpful comments and editorial assistance. Finally, we would like to thank Chad Carson, Cynthia Ingols, Mark Julien, Velma Vincent, Stefanie Ruel, Karen Boroff, Ron Camp, Rosemary McGowan, and several anonymous ASAC and NACRA conference reviewers for their helpful comments and suggestions on previous versions of this case.

From now on, Terra Nova Consulting will be known as TNC. And to go with that new name, I propose a new slogan. One that reflects our experience and expertise in both geotechnical engineering and the environmental sciences. One that assures our clients that they have hired the very best. TNC will now be known for having "The greatest minds on earth."

And then Terry experienced the longest two seconds of his life. All he could feel from the podium was stunned silence. Then the room erupted. "Change our name? What the hell do you mean you want to change our name? We've put a lot of work into being recognized as Terra Nova Consulting! We're proud of our heritage!" And the slogan? Even though Terra Nova had won numerous accolades for its prowess in geotechnical (earth) engineering, the company portrayed a quiet confidence. "You can't say that we have the greatest minds on earth! How arrogant! We let our work speak for itself!" The partners as a group had let him know in no uncertain terms that this was too bold, too brash for their Terra Nova.

After that opening, his other ideas for change were summarily dismissed by the partners. Terry had based his ideas for change around rebranding the firm through a new name, logo, and slogan. He wanted Terra Nova to be regarded like McKinsey and Company, as the very best in the consulting industry. He had also hoped that rebranding the firm by shortening its name to an acronym (like IBM—International Business Machines) would present a fresh face to its clients and instill a new attitude among employees. Finally, he hoped that the rebranding initiative would help create a new sense of shared values and identity at Terra Nova, one that would rebuild the former collegial atmosphere.

What Terry didn't get a chance to tell the partners, but which the board of directors and his executive team knew, was that Terra Nova still faced significant financial challenges. Although interim president Matt Ferguson had been able to stabilize the slide in profitability, several projects were still suffering cost overruns and write-offs. An even greater risk involved the lack of investment in company shares. Too many of the junior professionals did not see a long-term future with Terra Nova, and had avoided making the financial commitment of buying shares. Other senior partners had sent a message to the executive team about their dissatisfaction with the company's direction by refusing to increase their stakes. The lack of new equity and working capital had been offset through more expensive bank financing, which had negatively affected profitability. But technical excellence and working harder were no longer enough for success.

While several partners had privately acknowledged to him that change was needed, and the board had chosen Terry as president because of his fresh perspective, his proposals were too much, too fast for the partners. Terry had unknowingly stepped upon a few organizational political land mines. Longtime partner and vice-president Doug Hunter pulled him aside later in the hospitality suite to remind him that this was not how things were done at Terra Nova.

> You've got to start with the top senior people and work your way down through the organization. Any major initiative needs consensus among the shareholders, and particularly the senior shareholders. But consensus isn't simply a majority, it has to be a lot broader than that. You can probably get 50 percent of the people on board in relatively short order, and then 25 percent more sometime after that, and then the next 15 percent to get to around 90 percent, but it takes time, a long time. The process is time consuming. But you can't force change from the top down. The partners won't stand for that.

Doug reminded Terry that consultation was key to decision making at Terra Nova. While administrative matters were usually made in consultation with the senior executive and/or office manager teams, larger strategic decisions needed buy-in and support from the partners. Former interim president Matt Ferguson later echoed Doug's advice:

> Terry, you can't change Terra Nova through an authoritarian top-down style. The senior guys will just ignore your ideas if they don't like them. You need to sell your ideas gradually among the most powerful and influential partners. But you can't force them. It's like herding cats. They will fight you every step of the way if they're so inclined. They need to be convinced to go along like it was their idea all along. Sometimes the best you can hope for is that they won't stand in the way.

While Terry's ideas had not received a positive initial reaction, Matt had reminded him that part of Terra Nova's culture involved challenging new ideas to see if they could pass the test.

> You've got to remember, Terry, that a lot of them come from very critical backgrounds in science and engineering. So the first thing whenever they see anything new, the first they look for is holes, and try to drive tanks through them. Part of that may be human nature, but I think it's stronger in our organization because of the nature of the staff that we've got.

Terra Nova ensured success by challenging new ideas. This was part of their quality assurance process. For Terry, surviving the initial challenge was only the first step. He needed to rework his ideas, and map out a plan, then convince the senior partners of the need for change.

Company History and Past Practices

Terra Nova, a premier engineering consulting firm, was founded in 1970 by a small group of ten engineers. The first office was located in a second floor apartment on King Street in Toronto, Canada. Terra Nova founder Adam Danyluk described the firm as starting as a boutique operation that specialized in geotechnical (earth) engineering consulting related to civil engineering projects. The firm had benefited from a series of major highway projects that required specialized ground engineering technical studies on soil conditions and rock formations. Terra Nova had subsequently expanded by providing engineering design work for other public works projects including subways, bridges, and dams.

In the 1980s, Terra Nova provided geotechnical services to the mining industry, involving ground control issues. Expertise in groundwater and hydrogeology was added to address contaminated soils and site remediation problems. Technical excellence and innovative solutions on these projects led clients and industry partners to regard Terra Nova as an elite firm within the industry. The firm continued to diversify its portfolio of services, and ventured into the biosciences including wildlife habitat, air engineering and modeling, and archaeology, to address the environmental impacts associated with development projects. But Terra Nova's engineering heritage remained its core.

Longtime partners tended to describe the firm as a place where one worked with friends rather than coworkers. Although Terra Nova was regarded as an elite firm, its compensation was only comparable to the industry average. As noted by former Terra Nova junior professional engineer Mark Davis:

> Terra Nova was a great place to work in almost every aspect except pay. I was getting paid well below average for engineers in my graduating year initially. But although Terra Nova paid below average, there are worse companies in this industry . . . While I have no complaints about the management of the company or how I was treated there, I felt that I had to leave Terra Nova.

I could not support my family in the long term with my existing and projected future salary. However, I wish to clarify that for its field (geotechnical and environmental consulting) there is no better place to work. I don't think there's a better company in this industry than Terra Nova.

What attracted staff to Terra Nova was the opportunity to be involved in challenging, innovative projects, which generally were only awarded to technically superior firms. Junior professional staff were given much greater opportunities and responsibilities as members of Terra Nova than their former peers now employed by competitors were given. In addition, they were able to work alongside some of the best engineers in the industry. This allowed them to develop their technical skills and knowledge in ways not possible elsewhere.

Many mid-career staff were attracted by the opportunity to share in the firm's success as shareholders. Several had come from competitors, where only senior partners were allowed to buy shares, and advancement to partner was tightly restricted. Terra Nova afforded them with greater opportunity to not only become owners, but also to reach the partner level. Finally, Terra Nova provided them with the opportunity to become experts within their fields and applauded entrepreneurial initiative to develop new lines of business. Partner and office manager Henry Cooper had briefed Terry about the firm's past as follows:

When this firm started, it was built around strong personalities that were basically sole practitioners in a technical area in a particular geographic location. So what happened was we moved into certain technical areas through the sheer power and motivation of individuals saying, "we're going to do that. I'm going to move into that area of business. I'm going to become the key guy in that area." So we got into rock mechanics through Josh Halladay in Vancouver. We got into the nuclear waste business through

Jeremy Davis in Seattle. We got into the oil sands through Sid Anderson in Calgary. Just by the sheer weight and power of these individuals' personalities. It wasn't a group of people sitting around strategizing. There might have been an element of that, but it took one individual to actually be the champion and drive it.

The firm's growth strategy reflected its philosophy of seeking to meet clients' needs. Clients asked if Terra Nova could do related technical work (e.g., site remediation, environmental impact assessments). Not wanting to turn down additional work, Terra Nova project managers usually agreed, and then sought appropriate partner firms to subcontract the work. As demand in these areas grew, Terra Nova formalized these arrangements through mergers and acquisitions, bringing the relevant expertise in-house. This led the firm into a variety of new industries as different opportunities became available. As Terra Nova expanded and diversified its portfolio, it also employed an increasingly diverse mix of professionals and technical disciplines. Many members held graduate degrees within their respective disciplines (e.g., biology, geology, archeology, engineering), and the firm continued to seek out the top graduates.

Terra Nova's office locations varied considerably in size from under thirty to over 200 personnel, and were typically in suburban, corporate office buildings. Entrance area walls were adorned with firm awards such as best employer, technical excellence, community service, or pictures of the firm's founders. Offices were professional looking, yet modest, with a combination of formal offices and cubicles. Individual offices averaged about 120 square feet in size. There was limited variation in office size between professional staff and partners, such that even retired founder Adam Danyluk did not have a window/corner office, nor was there an executive office suite area at the firm's head office.

Terra Nova generated revenue by charging the working time of its professional staff to competitively acquired projects. Since office chargeability was highly correlated with profitability, chargeability became the key organizational objective and measure of performance. Chargeability targets ranged from 80 percent for partners, 85 percent for project managers, to 90 percent for professional staff. For example, professional staff whose days and weeks were 100 percent charged to revenue-generating projects were deemed to contribute more to Terra Nova than those who were only 90 percent charged out. At the partner level, contribution to the firm was also measured in terms of winning new client projects and developing new lines of business.

Organizational Structure and Management Style

When Terry had joined Terra Nova through a merger five years ago, he had asked some of the other partners for an organizational chart. He discovered that no formal organizational chart existed because according to the other partners, "Terra Nova has a flat organizational structure." Partners, project managers, and professional staff were all assigned to various project teams that sometimes spanned multiple offices.

Terry had found Terra Nova's structure confusing at first. Partner designation was not based upon tenure, but upon technical excellence and contribution to the firm. In addition, owners of acquired firms who decided to stay were often made partners. Partner turnover due to retirement was often uncertain, as many elected to stay on after reaching the age of sixty-five. Accordingly, partners ranged in age from forty to seventy-two years old. Historically, Terra Nova's partnership numbers represented about 15 percent of total staff, while consultants represented about 80 percent of staff.

Partners served as project managers or office managers. Many partners avoided the office manager positions, preferring to be directly involved in project work. Thus, most but not all office managers were partners. Project teams could involve a mix of junior (less than five years experience) and senior professionals, in addition to partners, depending upon the scale, scope, and technical requirements of the project. Finally, shareholders could be found at any level, ranging from receptionist to board member, as ownership was not restricted by position.

Informally, Terry saw five levels at Terra Nova, starting with the board and partners who provided general oversight, then the president, executive team, and office managers, followed by project managers, professional staff (junior and senior by tenure), and administrative support staff. Ultimately, the partners were in charge, as they elected the board of directors. The board in turn appointed the president, and approved the firm's overall strategic direction. The president was responsible for managing the firm's strategic direction with the support of his executive team, and the office managers were responsible for day-to-day operations. Project managers and partners were responsible for identifying, winning, and managing projects, and generating profits by staying within budget and avoiding overruns. Partners tended to be the project managers for larger projects. Professional staff were assigned to one or more projects, and were sometimes responsible for smaller projects. Despite this hierarchy, all members from the newest professional staff person to the most experienced partner participated equally in projects based on their knowledge and skills.

Combined with this flat organizational structure was a small corporate head office. The president's executive team consisted of two vice-presidents, the controller (CFO), and head of HR. Although head office designation was based upon the president's location, several executive team members were located in other offices as their appointments were deemed temporary.[1]

Several partners stated that they had avoided creating organizational charts due to their implicit aversion to bureaucracy and formal management controls. However, many of the junior professionals did not share this view.

Geologist Chris Barker had described his office's (Vancouver) management style as follows:

> In the past, we did it the way Bob [partner] said because Bob's king. And it worked. The firm hired excellent people whom people trusted, and they didn't have a problem following Bob. But now in an office [Vancouver] where there are ten Bobs [partners], and no one is quite sure which one to listen to, you need some protocols in management. Toronto though is a very managed group. They have a lot of training, a lot more corporate structure, so a lot of the junior professionals get a good feeling when they go to Toronto and work there. You know what it's going to take to move up, whereas here in Vancouver it's a bit of sink or swim, struggle to the top.

In contrast to many of the partners, several junior professionals had suggested the need for more structure, including the codification of policies and procedures regarding things like professional development, equipment requests, and international assignments.

Typically, Terra Nova's partners had earned their stripes first as professional staff, then as project managers, and were then promoted through a peer-review process. Some partners had gained advanced standing by virtue of their former positions as senior managers at other firms prior to joining Terra Nova via acquisition. Terry had come to Terra Nova this way. Terry's former partners at RMO Environmental wanted to retire, and had elected to "merge" their firm with Terra Nova. RMO had been a fairly close knit group of about forty biologists, scientists, and hydrologists that specialized in environmental impact assessment studies. The firm had been very much under the control of the founding partners, who typically saw things eye to eye. In contrast, Terra Nova's participatory democracy allowed partners to become involved in corporate level issues such as culture, strategy,

and business planning whenever they disagreed. When and why they chose to exercise this prerogative, Terry had yet to fully understand.

Doug Hunter, partner and vice-president, had told Terry that the cornerstone of the firm's operating philosophy was to provide innovative, high-quality technical solutions on behalf of its clients. Each office operated independently, specializing in certain services in a particular geographic market. Offices were expected to remain profitable by generating their own project revenues and controlling costs. However, offices also operated collectively under the Terra Nova banner, pooling their capabilities and expertise to win and undertake large projects. In this way, Terra Nova leveraged the capabilities and expertise of all employees across the firm, thereby reducing individual office duplication, while facilitating technical specialization, and enabling efficient utilization of available resources across the firm. This collaborative approach also strengthened the ties across offices and promoted a collective mind-set. It was not unusual to have visiting staff dropping in to borrow offices and meeting rooms.

Ownership Structure

Terra Nova was a private, 100 percent employee-owned firm. Unlike traditional partnerships, share ownership was not restricted to partners, but rather was broadly distributed. There was a high level of participation, with over 40 percent of all employees owning shares, resulting in no one owning more than 2 percent of the shares. As such, no single individual or small group of staff could dictate firm direction through a majority position. In accordance with board policies, partners held about 80 percent of the shares available, while other employees held the remaining 20 percent. Although partners had to meet certain minimum share-holding requirements, many partners held more than the minimum as they deemed it to be a good investment, as well as a sign of their commitment to the firm. As noted by two partners, this principle of employee ownership was a central tenet of the firm:

> Employee ownership is number one. I think that if anyone tried to change the employee ownership structure of the firm, then the firm would die, because a lot of people are here for that very reason. It's something we use to attract people, and people come for that reason. If we changed that structure, we would lose a lot of good people. There were rumors floating around about two years ago that the President [Michael Erikson] was going to try and take the firm public, but the partners put a stop to any chance of that happening.
>
> Luis Carbonell (partner)

> There's an emotional attachment to this firm that to a large extent transcends monetary value. I've heard several of the old guys saying, "We didn't build the firm to sell it." I mean every time anything other than employee ownership has been mentioned, nobody was interested in it. We wanted this firm to stay employee-owned.
>
> Henry Cooper
> (partner and office manager)

Terra Nova employees were invited to purchase shares through an annual company-wide memorandum, which indicated the total number of shares available, the price per share (based on book value), and payment terms. The number of shares available in any given year varied, based upon how many treasury shares were available, and how many shares were being sold (due to retirement or termination of employment). Share allocations though, did not always match demand. First call on available shares was reserved for staff who had been promoted to partner but did not hold enough shares to meet their ownership requirement. The remaining shares were then prorated in response to

requests. Financing for share purchases was not available from Terra Nova; nor was there a payroll deduction plan.

Several shareholders had expressed to Terry that employee ownership provided a sense of community, a common bond between employees as the firm expanded, and the basis for a philosophy of acting in the firm's best interest. It also allowed partners and others to "participate" in the firm's success through annual dividends. Finally, the acquisition of shares by staff helped finance the firm's operations, and reduced the need for more expensive external debt financing. However, many junior professionals had declined to commit financially to the firm, and even some of the partners were refusing to increase their stakes.

Without sufficient employee uptake, Terra Nova had to buy back and hold retiree shares, increasing the firm's debt financing requirements and reducing cash flow. The controller had suggested to Terry that the firm consider the idea of going public like other firms in the industry.[2]

Organizational Culture

Like many other professional service firms, management control was not exercised through traditional, top-down hierarchical command. Employees were expected to be self-managed and motivated, but to act in accordance with organizational values, norms, and objectives. Thus, communication, cooperation, socialization, and rigorous hiring practices took on added significance to ensure proper fit and alignment of employee actions with organizational goals.

Terra Nova had traditionally sought like-minded individuals through existing personal contacts, hiring friends, work acquaintances, and referrals from trusted colleagues. In particular, the firm actively sought the best students from top universities. But with growth came the need for recruitment of cold contacts where there was no prior relationship or referral. Even potential merger and acquisition candidates were screened for cultural similarity. Partner and office manager Henry Cooper explained,

> Oh, the fit's everything. Every merger and acquisition that we've undertaken, the cultural fit with us was absolutely paramount. I mean if there's no cultural fit then it's pointless even embarking on the process. Is this firm's value system the same as ours? Are they interested in doing quality work for quality clients? Do their people have an ownership mentality? Are

they going to be comfortable with Terra Nova's fairly flat, non-hierarchical structure? Are they comfortable with a culture of employee ownership? All these things are key. If the cultural fit isn't there then it's pointless proceeding, 'cause it won't work.

Terra Nova's official core values (see **Exhibit 1**), were described as reflective of the founders' personal values, and had been reinforced over time as part of "how we do business."

Exhibit 1	Terra Nova Consulting Cultural Principles and Core Values
Principle	**Core Value**
Employee ownership	Responsible participation in business success and ownership. Sustainability of financial return to shareholders.
Collegiality and self-actualization	Supportive of personal growth, learning, and risk taking. Integrity in relationships, commitments, and service.
Technical excellence	Reliable, innovative, cost-effective solutions. Professional, cultural, and business diversity.

Source: Terra Nova Consulting

Notwithstanding this generally positive characterization of Terra Nova's culture, former president Matt Ferguson described Terra Nova's culture in the past as follows:

> We used to joke that a new arrival was taken by the scruff of the neck and the seat of the pants and dropped into the deepest pool we could find while the senior people stood around and watched to see if he would sink or swim.

Corporate Financial Position

Terry thought back over the events of the past two years. It had begun in mid-2006 with Michael Erikson stepping down after ten years as president. Although the firm was still profitable, it had been suffering declining

financial performance and reduced profitability. Traditionally, Terra Nova had enjoyed income before taxes as a percentage of fee revenue of 15 percent or more (see **Exhibit 2**). Even though fee revenues had continued to increase, project cost overruns, increased overhead, and billing and collection delays had negatively affected earnings. While the financials did not suggest that Terra Nova was in danger of bankruptcy (see Balance Sheet—**Exhibit 3**), Terry was still concerned as he regarded the decline in financial performance as reflective of deeper organizational problems.

The decline in profitability was beginning to restrict Terra Nova's operations. Net profit needed to be about 7–10 percent of fee revenue to fund normal growth. More troubling for Terra Nova though was the lack of interest among employees in purchasing shares. Many of the junior professionals were not prepared to invest and commit to the firm, while older

Exhibit 2   Terra Nova Consulting Income Statements ($000)

	2001	2002	2003	2004	2005	2006	2007 Prelim.
Revenue							
Gross revenue	$91,199	106,916	118,176	127,843	136,711	149,741	159,068
Subcontracts	−6,852	−9,074	−10,354	−12,652	−15,219	−16,010	−14,865
Fee revenue	84,347	97,842	107,822	114,831	121,492	133,640	144,203
Expenses							
Direct labor	−33,907	−39,822	−43,776	−46,736	−47,989	−52,188	−56,727
Gross profit	50,440	58,020	64,046	68,095	73,503	81,452	87,476
Allocated overhead	−22,942	-30,429	−32,670	−36,057	−39,120	−44,101	−46,592
General overhead	−14,339	−18,100	−21,133	−24,000	−27,457	−31,672	−29,510
Chargebacks	1,030	2,456	3,543	2,249	1,280	1,207	1,339
Income before taxes	14,189	11,947	13,786	10,287	8,206	6,886	12,713
Income taxes	−5,676	−4,779	−5,514	−4,115	−3,282	−2,754	−5,085
Net income	**8,513**	**7,168**	**8,272**	**6,172**	**4,924**	**4,132**	**7,628**

Source: Terra Nova Consulting

Note: TNC uses the following definitions:

Fee revenue—actual revenue received from consulting projects.

Direct labor—actual labor costs charged to consulting projects.

Allocated overhead—costs charged to projects.

General overhead—cost of operating groups, corporate office, and other costs.

Chargebacks—to clients (e.g., equipment rentals, printing).

Exhibit 3   Terra Nova Consulting Balance Sheets ($000)

	2001	2002	2003	2004	2005	2006	2007 Prelim.
Assets							
Current assets							
Cash, investments	$5,663	5,865	6,001	6,291	6,647	7,575	6,962
Accounts receivable	13,629	14,038	15,020	15,922	19,628	19,217	21,685

(Continued)

Exhibit 3 (Continued)							
Work in progress	11,582	15,105	20,070	22,883	25,070	24,745	23,294
Prepaid expenses	127	14	2	47	0	0	543
	31,001	35,022	41,093	45,143	51,345	51,537	52,484
Investments	41	44	46	50	904	1,699	3,099
Net fixed assets	6,002	6,336	6,652	6,985	7,218	7,584	7,720
Other assets	797	855	851	872	885	937	1,307
Total assets	$37,841	42,257	48,596	53,050	60,352	61,757	64,608
Liabilities and Shareholders' Equity							
Current liabilities							
Bank overdrafts	$140	92	447	563	980	2,329	1,287
Accounts payable	8,490	8,336	8,772	10,076	14,673	14,343	11,845
LT debt due	0	0	0	0	0	3	737
Deferred revenue	22	80	0	190	0	0	502
	8,652	8,508	9,219	10,829	15,653	16,675	14,371
Long-term debt	6,350	6,350	6,350	6,350	6,350	6,347	5,845
Shareholders' equity							
Capital stock	3,837	3,837	4,337	4,337	5,219	6,001	7,360
Retained earnings	19,002	3,562	28,690	31,534	33,130	32,734	37,034
Total shareholders' equity	22,839	27,399	33,027	35,871	38,349	38,735	44,384
Total Liabilities and Equity	$37,841	42,257	48,596	53,050	60,352	61,757	64,608

Source: Terra Nova Consulting

employees recognized that Terra Nova was unlikely to produce the strong dividend returns of the past. Moreover, older partners needed to divest their shares as they approached retirement, but could not if there were no buyers. Without new investment, it would be difficult for Terra Nova to remain employee owned. Vice-president Doug Hunter explained:

I think what triggered it was that the firm had been going through a period of malaise for about two or three years, a sense that we had lost our direction. There was a sense that something was not right. Shares weren't selling very well at all. The employees were sending a strong message that they weren't interested in making that financial or emotional commitment to the firm. The quantity of shares that we had in trust was becoming a reasonably significant potential financial liability. How long we could let that go on before we had to bring in outside investment was unclear. But that would result in a huge shift in culture.

The lack of employee investment through share purchases had resulted in a buildup of treasury shares. The reduction in shareholder capital had to be covered from other sources, including drawing upon a line of credit with the bank. Exacerbating the situation was the need to buy back shares from retiring partners, some of whom had amassed sizable holdings. These increased financing costs correspondingly resulted in a further drag on profits.

Organizational Assessment

Matt Ferguson had agreed to take over as president on an interim basis in November of 2006, and had managed to improve profitability by reducing project overruns and controlling expenses. Still, a growing number of partners had told Matt that they were concerned that something was still not right at Terra Nova. Several partners had heard from friends at competitors that some of the junior professionals had started exploring their options. Another noted that their academic contacts had become reluctant to recommend Terra Nova to their best graduating students, citing a negative work environment.

In the spring of 2007, Matt Ferguson asked OCI Consulting, an HR specialist firm, to conduct an organizational assessment. OCI Consulting administered an instrument they called an Organizational Cultural Inventory that assessed and mapped out Terra Nova's culture into twelve cultural styles, grouped into three orientations, Constructive, Passive/Defensive, and Aggressive/Defensive. (See **Appendix B** for a description of the Organizational Cultural Inventory.)

Four months ago at a special meeting of selected Terra Nova partners, OCI Consulting had announced the results of its study (see **Exhibits 4 and 5**). Terry had been unable to attend as he was visiting clients in Australia, but had heard about what happened later from his colleagues:

Yeah, it was October 25 of 2007. Dr. Frank Chow, president of OCI Consulting. He was a very credible guy, he had an undergraduate degree in engineering, his PhD was in psychology. He spoke well, he was articulate, and he could really defend himself. You can imagine the subset of Terra Nova folk who are very technical, where they're going to question everything. But we believed what he told us, I think to a person believed it, and came away with a commitment to change.

There were two things that stood out that OCI Consulting told us. One was, the senior people in this firm were completely out of touch, we had developed some bad habits. And the other thing he told us, actually he prefaced it. He said, "Some of what we're going to tell you is our opinion, and we'll tell you if it's our opinion, you can take it or leave it. Some is fact! It's a fact that if you don't change, you'll stop being an elite firm!" And that caught people's attention.

George Garcia (partner)

Oh yeah, those overheads that Chow produced show this dramatic disconnect between what the founders, what the partners and key shareholders of the firm thought and the rest of the firm. Those two overheads were shock therapy of the first order. Jacob [board member] often says, you know, it was OCI Consulting that held our face up to the mirror and made us look at what we were and we didn't like what we saw.

Henry Cooper (partner and office manager)

Jeff Tavere from OCI Consulting had described the meeting to Terry as follows:

At the meeting where the results were presented, there was an initial reaction of denial—the results couldn't possibly be right. Yet as the meeting unfolded, I think there was an awakening—"We had better pay attention to this because this could be quite significant for our future." The meeting was quite animated to say the least in terms of people standing up and verbally throwing things.

OCI Consulting's brutal assessment echoed in Terry's head. Terra Nova would cease to be an elite firm within eighteen months if it did not address its dysfunctional culture, and could even fail! That was the unequivocal message from the HR experts. Nevertheless, he and several of the partners remained skeptical. Surely Terra Nova wasn't in that bad shape, especially since Matt Ferguson had started to turn things around financially. Revenues were up, costs down, and they had managed to retain their key clients. How could this cause the downfall of the entire firm? But he had to admit that the partners did not see eye-to-eye with the next generation of junior professionals regarding the firm's culture. And that was the message already being relayed by some partners to others in the firm.

As it was explained to the general audience in the Toronto office, the OCI Consulting people said, there's some things we're going to tell you that are fact. And if we say they're a fact, you can guarantee they're a fact based upon our however many years of experience and all the studies. Number one fact is, if you don't change, Terra Nova will cease to be an elite firm!

Naveen Jindal (project engineer)

The study had revealed a wide divergence between the actual and desired culture among members. More importantly, the survey revealed a wide gap between the perceptions of partners and others. Jeff Tavere from OCI Consulting explained:

The first thing was a striking disconnect between the senior team and the junior team. By that I mean the partners thought things were fine, everything was going well, while all the others had a very different experience—they felt very disconnected from what was going on.

So the results matched the description that people were using of the environment as a "shark tank." The circumstances disengaged the junior professionals because they didn't know quite how to operate in that environment.

The tables Dr. Chow from OCI Consulting had shown the partners at the meeting were later circulated to the other partners, including Terry. The first table (Exhibit 4) showed the size of the gap between the ideal and actual cultures at Terra Nova for non-partners. The second table (Exhibit 5) indicated where there was agreement (or not) among Terra Nova staff. Weak agreement indicated a lack of consensus or divergent viewpoints, whereas strong agreement indicated what was preferred. Unfortunately, there was more divergence of opinion between the partners and non-partners ratings than there was convergence.

Partners tended to rate the firm's culture high on the Constructive orientation for both the actual and ideal culture. For them, Terra Nova was the ideal place to work. Non-partners including junior professional staff also ideally desired a work culture that was high on the Constructive orientation. However, in contrast to the partners' perception of the firm's espoused culture, non-partners tended to perceive an actual Aggressive/Defensive culture—one high on perfectionism, power, and critique (oppositional). As noted by one project manager:

But for the Calgary Office in 2004, the culture was still the old style for a lot of engineering or special services companies—a very, I don't know what the word is,

Exhibit 4	Summary of Terra Nova's OCI Results		
Style	**Actual**	**Ideal**	**Gap**
Constructive	%	%	
Humanistic/Encouraging	23	95	−72
Affiliative	13	80	−67
Achievement	41	94	−53
Self-Actualizing	29	95	−66
Passive/Defensive			
Approval	37	16	21
Conventional	43	17	26
Dependent	40	7	33
Avoidance	58	21	37
Aggressive/Defensive			
Oppositional	74	75	−1
Power	58	31	27
Competitive	65	40	25
Perfectionistic	61	42	19

Source: OCI Consulting

Note: Percentage represents those responding either "strongly agree" or "somewhat agree." Gap reflects the amount of divergence between the actual and ideal culture for that particular style.

Exhibit 5	Summary of Intensity Variation (standard deviation)			
	ACTUAL		**IDEAL**	
Style	**Std. Dev.**	**Intensity**	**Std. Dev.**	**Intensity**
Constructive				
Humanistic/Encouraging	6.27	Weak	3.87	Strong
Affiliative	6.23	Weak	3.97	Strong
Achievement	5.28	Average	3.54	Very strong
Self-Actualizing	5.21	Average	3.63	Strong

(Continued)

Exhibit 5 (Continued)				
Passive/Defensive				
Approval	5.16	Average	5.22	Average
Conventional	5.73	Average	4.57	Strong
Dependent	6.08	Weak	3.87	Strong
Avoidance	6.06	Weak	3.99	Strong
Aggressive/Defensive				
Oppositional	4.39	Average	5.15	Weak
Power	6.29	Weak	5.60	Average
Competitive	5.80	Average	5.95	Average
Perfectionistic	4.79	Average	4.34	Strong

Source: OCI Consulting study

Note: The standard deviation (intensity) of respondent scores indicated the degree of consistency between respondents' opinions, ranging from weak (low) to very strong (high). High deviations indicate disagreement between members (weak intensity), and reflect the divergence between junior and senior member assessments, while low deviations indicate agreement between members (strong intensity).

aggressive or confrontational, almost, in some respects. It was not unusual to have partners of the firm standing out in the hallway pretty much screaming at each other, and then walk down the hallway and have a coffee with each other.

Luis Carbonell (partner)

Along with the survey, the OCI consultants had also conducted a series of focus group sessions. That exercise had laid bare some of Terra Nova's flaws. Jaegwon Kim, who had recently been appointed as a partner, summed it up as follows, "Over the years, Terra Nova has become a firm that appears to the younger professionals to be very dedicated to the partners, and not so much to the younger staff." Project manager Calvin McClarey observed, "You know, generally, the only management information we ever get as junior professionals is profit and chargeability." Marine biologist Anna

Leung also noted the partners' lip service to espoused company core values,

The firm espouses core values such as sustainability and environmental responsibility, but does not actively demonstrate much commitment to those values if there is any economic or financial impact. The organization and its leadership do seem to mean well . . . [but] the unfortunate result within the Environmental Department is a feeling of slight environmental hypocrisy.

OCI consultants discovered through the focus groups that among the junior professionals there was a strong desire for greater work/life balance. Although hard work, extended out-of-town fieldwork and pressure to meet client deadlines were accepted as parts of the job, younger staff were not prepared to sacrifice their personal lives for the firm. There was also the perception that Terra Nova needed to provide more opportunities for the junior professional staff to develop their knowledge and skills. That combined with the authoritarian style of some older partners had left many junior professionals feeling more like employees rather than colleagues. Moreover, it did not prepare them to take over in the future, a particular concern as the older partners retired or cut back their hours.

Subsequent internal employee satisfaction surveys revealed that whereas staff felt that their pay and benefits were only around the industry average, they were generally satisfied with their benefits (**Exhibit 6**). Many still expressed a desire to have a long-term career with Terra Nova, though admittedly few of the junior staff felt that way. However, there was also agreement that working at Terra Nova offered other important incentives:

- Flexibility to work on a variety of projects, and thereby develop new knowledge and skills
- Ability to work with acknowledged industry experts
- A feeling of accomplishment and satisfaction in the work they did
- The opportunity for career progression to partner
- Terra Nova's reputation for excellence allowed professionals to work on interesting and challenging projects

In response to the surveys, most of the partners suggested that these incentives were still working as they had in the past. Other professional staff, however, perceived it to be very difficult to request projects for development and nearly impossible to get projects with other offices. Therefore, the junior professionals grew frustrated as they did not see any clear career progression.

The shockwave from OCI Consulting's report prompted the board in October of 2007 to seek a new president who could lead Terra Nova into the future. Although Matt Ferguson had done a commendable job addressing the firm's operational issues, even he admitted that he lacked the leadership skills and vision necessary to bridge the gap between the partners and others. Dr. Chow had suggested that a change in leadership might be needed to address Terra Nova's cultural deficiencies. The board initiated a search internally for someone with the necessary vision and innovative perspective to rebuild community within Terra Nova. It had been Terry's ideas about change and how to promote a more collegial environment that had convinced the board to select him as the new president. Bolstering Terry's case was the fact that he was the "youngest" available Terra Nova candidate, having joined through a merger only five years earlier. While he had been exposed to Terra Nova's culture and way of operating, he had not yet been "tainted" by the experience, and was able to bring a fresh perspective and new ideas to the table.

That had set the stage for the partners' conference in February of 2008, and the opportunity for Terry to lay out his plans for changing Terra Nova. But those plans had failed miserably, and now he needed a new approach.

Terry's Challenges

Terry realized that the proposed name change, a new logo, and slogan would not solve Terra Nova's cultural divide. However, he had hoped that it would at least start to change the mind-set of the partners and foster a new attitude at the firm. Terry mulled over some of the challenges that lay ahead.

First, although Matt Ferguson had temporarily managed to rejuvenate Terra Nova's profitability, there was still the need to continue to improve project management procedures to avoid cost overruns and speed up collections in the future. Terry knew that the partners focused more on winning new projects and technical excellence, rather than staying within budget on

Exhibit 6 Employee Satisfaction Survey Results					
	Tenure				
Question	**< 2 yrs.**	**2–5 yrs.**	**6–10 yrs.**	**11–15 yrs.**	**20+ yrs.**
I hardly ever think about leaving this company to work somewhere else	81%	65%	67%	70%	92%
I think the way this company promotes people is fair	81%	62%	64%	49%	42%
Compared to other places I might work, I feel that I am fairly paid	76%	62%	76%	85%	67%
I feel I am fairly paid for the contribution I make to the company's success	79%	59%	67%	76%	75%
My performance has a significant impact on my pay increases	79%	60%	67%	64%	92%
If you have your way, how likely are you to be working at this organization					
one year from now	95%	88%	93%	91%	92%
five years from now	81%	68%	87%	82%	67%
for the rest of your career	53%	54%	67%	73%	83%
Listed below are various factors that may be important to your overall satisfaction					
advancement opportunity	82%	72%	78%	67%	92%
the "work" you do day-to-day	92%	85%	89%	85%	92%
your pay	71%	60%	67%	79%	75%
your benefits	92%	80%	84%	88%	100%
individual recognition (non-financial)	79%	62%	69%	58%	75%
% of Respondents	**29%**	**30%**	**20%**	**15%**	**6%**

Source: Terra Nova Consulting

Note: Original data "missing" 16–20 yr. category.

existing projects, or collecting payment once the projects had been completed.

Second, Terra Nova faced a transition in leadership and experience at the partner/project manager level. Many partners were approaching retirement. They had built strong personal relationships with their clients, who would now be passed on to relatively unknown new partners. Moreover, these retiring partners had considerable technical knowledge and experience, expertise, and intellectual capital upon which Terra Nova had staked its reputation and business strategy. The firm's ability to manage the loss of this knowledge while developing new capabilities would have significant implications for its future success.

Third, many Terra Nova junior professionals had declined to commit financially to the firm. The lack of additional employee investment had increased Terra Nova's debt financing requirements, reducing cash flow and creating a drag on profitability. Although the controller had suggested taking the firm public as a way to lower financing costs, Terry had been cautioned by Doug and Matt against going that route.

Finally, there was the dilemma posed by the OCI Consulting study, and the cultural divide between the partners and junior professionals as a result of a highly negative organizational climate. The partners were reluctant to change, but they did not want to see the firm they had worked so hard to create collapse, or be sold to another firm. The junior professionals though were not committed to the firm, and it was uncertain whether Terra Nova's non-monetary incentives would continue to be sufficient to retain and motivate them.

Dr. Chow had suggested that a number of changes were necessary if Terra Nova was to survive as an elite firm. Among these was developing a more constructive culture, with greater respect for individuals that included work/life balance. Based upon Terry's conversations with founder Adam Danyluk, this had been the climate at Terra Nova when it was a much smaller firm. Dr. Chow had also suggested that Terra Nova move away from being a collection of individual practitioners, to becoming more of a team-oriented firm with shared corporate clients. This would shift the focus away from the older partners as they retired, and build the connection with clients to Terra Nova as a whole.

Terry thought he knew what was needed; what he didn't know was "how" and "when." He had hoped that the ideas he had presented to the partners would kick-start the process, but that now seemed like a non-starter. He knew he needed help with the "how," and hoped that Doug and Matt or some of the younger office managers might be able to help build the support needed for change. With that, he began to sketch out his new plan.

Notes

1. This structure is similar to that of other professional service firms (PSFs), where the majority of work occurs through project teams. (See **Appendix A** for background note on professional service firms.)
2. PSFs may go public for various reasons including to finance expansion, and because of partner resource limitations.

Appendix A: Background Note on Professional Service Firms (Psf)[1]

Professional Service Firms include a variety of firms providing a wide range of services including legal, accounting, engineering, medical, and other services to both businesses and individuals. Traditionally, PSFs have comprised groups of similarly educated and socialized professionals like lawyers, accountants, and doctors, who provide a specific type of service to a particular clientele. As such, single profession firms like law offices and accounting firms are likely to develop homogeneous organizational cultures and operating practices that are reflective of the values and norms of their particular profession.

PSFs have typically been structured as partnerships, where ownership is privately held by a small group of partners. In the case of law firms, this often resulted in naming the firm after the founding partners. Many PSFs typically provide standard or commoditized services like audits or training programs. Thus organizationally, many PSFs fall into the category of professional bureaucracies, where coordination occurs through similar training and certification (e.g., law school and bar exam), and socialization. However, the project-driven nature of consulting work often shifts the focus onto individual projects and temporary project teams, which is more typical of the adhocracy form of organization.

Adhocracies have highly organic structures, with little formalization of behavior. Job specialization is based on formal training. There is a tendency to group the specialists in functional units for housekeeping purposes, but to deploy them in small, market-based project teams for work purposes. There is reliance on liaison devices to encourage mutual adjustment (key coordinating mechanism), within and between these teams. Innovation means breaking away from established patterns, so adhocracies do not rely on standardization for coordination. Of the five configurations (simple structure, machine bureaucracy, professional bureaucracy, divisionalized form, and adhocracy), adhocracies show the least reverence for the classical principles of management, especially unity of command. The adhocracy must hire and give power to experts—professionals whose knowledge and skills have been highly developed in training programs.

In contrast to professional bureaucracies, adhocracies are unable to rely on the standardized skills of experts to accomplish coordination, as that would result in standardization rather than innovation. Instead, adhocracies need to treat extant knowledge and skills as the starting point from which to build new knowledge and skills. In addition, new knowledge and skills presupposes the fusion of existing knowledge and skills. Thus, the specialization of the expert in professional bureaucracies is not appropriate for adhocracies, which must cross over the boundaries of conventional specialization and differentiation. In professional bureaucracies each professional can operate independently, but in adhocracies professionals must fuse their efforts into multi-disciplinary teams working on projects.

Over time though, as these firms engage in business relationships with increasingly larger and more complex multinational firms, the nature of client problems necessitates a corresponding expansion in the scale, scope, and diversity of skills available within a single firm. This in turn leads to an increasing mix of professionals with different technical backgrounds, professional norms, and codes of conduct (heterogeneous culture). It also prompts some firms to go public to acquire the financing needed to expand their operations.

Client engagements (i.e., consulting projects) come in a variety of forms. Consulting firms may be awarded projects as the low cost bidders, particularly where a competitive tendering process (request for proposal) is involved. Firms may also be approached directly by clients where particular expertise is required. Other clients may seek elite firms to provide an element of legitimacy to the final report/recommendations. In addition, client engagements may vary from one-off projects to standing relationships where firms maintain an ongoing relationship. Success on one-off projects may develop into additional contracts or even standing relationships, particularly where favorable working relationships are developed between project managers and their clients. Projects are typically negotiated by partners with prospective clients, and so positive client relations are often critical to firm success. Positive prior working relationships often translate into less complicated negotiations (faster approvals, less rigorous review of proposal, higher mark-ups) as clients are already aware of the firm's ability to meet their needs. This also results in significant cost avoidance as there are no proposals and less legal work involved.

All staff bill clients for their time at their charge-out rates, which tend to be mark-ups of two to three times their actual hourly wages. Higher quality/prestige firms are typically able to command higher charge-out rates. These charge-out rates need to cover direct costs such as staff salaries, firm overhead (administration), and profitability. Key to overall firm success is high chargeability (percentage of staff time available billed to projects) and charge-out rates (mark-up), with minimal write-downs of accounts receivables, staffing costs (optimal use of less costly junior staff), or project cost over-runs (time and expenses). Timely billing and collection of receivables is important to maintain adequate cash flow and reduce firm working capital requirements.

Success requires delivering projects within budget and on time to earn a profit. This includes sound budget projections, proper staffing (number and mix), timely completion of work, and favorable mark-ups. Strong project management is thus critical for success. Typically, project management is handled by partners, while project managers and professionals provide much of the "grunt work," including fieldwork as necessary. Many partners though have achieved their positions through technical excellence within their discipline, and often developed management skills by doing rather than formal training. As such, many partners and project managers often lack knowledge of formal project management approaches, cost or financial accounting, or modern human resource management techniques.

Note

1. This background note is based upon Mintzberg's (1981, 1983) work on organizational structures, where he defines five key configurations: simple structure, machine bureaucracy, professional bureaucracy, divisionalized, and adhocracy.

Appendix B: The Organizational Culture Inventory

Description	OCI Style	Description of OCI Style
Constructive Styles: Healthy balance of task and people orientations. Seek to develop people and aid in attainment of higher order needs. Value and reward quality. Teamwork and quality service to clients.	Achievement	Pursuit of excellence
		Set high goals and seek to achieve
		Enthusiastic about work
	Self-actualizing	Seek self-growth opportunities
		Enjoy their work
		Always try to do their best
	Humanistic-encouraging	Show concern for others
		Encourage work/life balance
		Concern and support for health and safety
	Affiliative	Value teamwork and cooperation
		Friendly and pleasant
		Treat each other fairly and with respect
Passive/Defensive Styles: People emphasis. Seek to avoid conflict and follow the rules. Low employee satisfaction and motivation. Low environmental responsiveness and fit. Status quo organization. Low competition.	Approval	Try to gain the approval of others
		Go along with others
		Seek agreement and avoid conflict
	Conventional	Seek conformity
		Expect people to follow the rules
		Comfortable with the status quo
	Dependent	Expect people to follow orders
		Check decisions with superiors
		Always consult others before deciding
	Avoidance	Management avoids tough decisions
		Avoid risks
		Avoid mistakes/blame
Aggressive/Defensive Styles: Task focus. Individuals dominate. Focus upon power, security, and status. Confrontation and criticism. Perfectionism. Management interests first.	Oppositional	Critical of others
		Oppose new ideas
		Avoid change
	Power	Seek to control subordinates, everything Demand loyalty from employees
		Engage in political behavior
	Competitive	Try to outperform peers
		Competitive
		Always try to be right
	Perfectionistic	Mistakes unacceptable
		Expected to know all the details
		Focus upon work first

Source: OCI Consulting.

Case Study 2

*Food Banks Canada: Revisiting Strategy 2012**

Gene Deszca

Tupper Cawsey

School of Business and Economics, Wilfrid Laurier University

It had been five years since Katharine Schmidt had taken over as Executive Director of Food Banks Canada in late 2007. The organization had made significant progress in that time. Donations of food and funds at the national level were up substantially, strong and committed staff members were now in place, the organization's advocacy activities for the hungry were being received positively and they were becoming better known and respected for their work. However, the reality was that they were still a small organization when compared with the size of other national not-for-profits, and the size of a number of the affiliate organizations that they represented. There was so much that needed to be done to address hunger issues in Canada. Were they going about it in the best way and were they strategically targeting the right sorts of activities?

Schmidt may have stimulated interest in the topic, but she wasn't the only one asking questions about "what next?" Five years seemed about the right time for such a review. Food Banks Canada's Board and Member Council were generally very pleased with the progress achieved under Schmidt's leadership, but they too were pondering what the organization's next steps should be. The Board had formally committed itself to conduct a strategic review and develop a strategic plan for the 2012 to 2017 period. As CEO, Schmidt knew the Board would look to her for leadership on this matter

The current federated structure offered lots of potential, but Schmidt was troubled by how best to reconcile the varying perspectives voiced by certain stakeholders, particularly affiliated food banks. There had been concerns raised privately regarding Food Banks Canada expanding its strategic and operational roles, especially among some of the large food banks. How should they strategically address matters relative to food donations, fundraising, public advocacy and capacity building at the member affiliate level? What should be the roles of Food Banks Canada and what should be the roles of the Provincial and Local affiliates? Were they structured appropriately to deliver on these roles? Finally, if changes needed to be made, how should Schmidt go about managing them?

What counted, of course, was the alleviation of hunger for millions of people, not just the growth and health of Food Banks Canada. As Schmidt reflected on their progress and the options, she wondered "what recommendations should be made to the Board and how should we approach the implementation challenges?"

Hunger in Canada

The first food bank in Canada opened its doors in 1981 in Edmonton, Alberta. While food banks were originally intended to be a temporary measure, the need for them continued— and in fact grew.

Hunger and poverty are inexorably interrelated and the number of people visiting food banks in Canada on a regular basis has continued to climb over the years.

- Almost 900,000 Canadians were being assisted by food banks every month with 93,000 people accessing a food bank for the first time
- Food bank use was 9% higher in 2010 than it was in 2009 and was the highest level of food bank use on record
- 38% of those turning to food banks are children and youth, 52% of households helped receive social assistance and 18% have income from current or recent employment

- 35% of food banks ran out of food during the survey period as a result 55% of food banks cut back on the amount of food provided to each household
- 79% of Canadians believed that hunger was a problem in Canada[†]

Though Canada is a rich, developed country, hunger is a daily reality for a large and growing number of citizens. The people helped include families with children, employed people whose wages are not sufficient to cover basic living essentials, individuals on social assistance, and Canadians living on a fixed income, including people with disabilities and seniors.[‡]

Programs run by food banks that provide essential food and consumer care products include soup kitchens (hot and cold meals), hamper and snack programs, college- and university- based food programs for poor students, and community kitchens and gardens. In addition, the people who turn to food banks often need other types of assistance. Some food banks have responded to such needs by providing services such as skills training and job search assistance, housing and childcare referrals, and community advocacy.

Most food banks and food programs depend heavily on volunteers for much or all of their operational activities. In fact, close to 50% of food banks are run solely by volunteers. Their work is made possible through contributions from individual donors, corporate sponsors, community support, parent organizations, and Food Banks Canada.

The issue of hunger in Canada is being tackled predominantly through a network of over 3000 + food agencies. All food banks in Canada run independently with their own Boards of Directors and charitable status. While the

---

[†]Source: *Food Banks Canada HungerCount 2010: Food Banks Canada's national survey of food banks and emergency food programs* and *Food Banks Canada HungerCount 2011: A comprehensive report on hunger and food bank use in Canada, and recommendations for change.*

[‡]Source: Food Banks Canada website: http://www.foodbankscanada.ca/Learn-About-Hunger/About-Hunger-in-Canada.aspx

majority of food banks chose to be part of the national organization—not all did. Eighty-five percent of the individuals assisted by a food bank are assisted through an affiliated organization to Food Banks Canada. Some of the affiliated food banks, such as Daily Bread in Toronto or the Greater Vancouver Food Banks Society were larger than Food Banks Canada in terms of revenue, the volume of food distributed, and staff levels, but the majority were smaller.

Food Banks Canada: History and Renewal[§]

The organization began as a small group of local Canadian food banks that formed the Canadian Association of Food Banks (CAFB) in 1987. The original goal of the association was to better address household food security by increasing public awareness, lobbying for social policy change on behalf of food banks, and improving access to food for those in need. Local food banks had existed for years, but many had recognized that demand was increasing and they needed to increase their coordination of efforts and to deliver integrated messages across Canada on poverty and hunger. Public awareness of the issues needed to be enhanced, and many food banks wanted to increase their influence on government policy. Further, many national food product manufacturers and distributors asked for national systems for the distribution of surplus food to Canadians struggling with hunger. Some food bank managers believed efforts by the national organization could increase the volume of food available to agencies and provide for more efficient coordination and distribution of the food to member agencies. The formation of the Canadian Association of Food Banks was seen as a step in this direction.

The CAFB was governed by a volunteer Board of Directors who were representatives from food banks across Canada. Often the members of this group had divided loyalties between what was best for the fight against hunger in Canada and what was best for their home food bank.

By 2005, the majority of CAFB Board members believed that the organization was failing to achieve what was possible. Issues related to governance, vision, and mission dogged the national organization. There appeared to be significant challenges with coordination and integration of efforts across the country. Awareness raising and policy lobbying activities were not as effective as hoped. Donations to the national organization appeared undeveloped. CAFB had inadequate resources and uncertain objectives. The Board of the CAFB recognized that change and revitalization were essential. It conducted a strategic review in 2005–2006. After this review, it voluntarily restructured itself (see Exhibit 2) and began the process of rebranding of CAFB. The 2007 national board governance model was designed to encompass broader skills sets, be much more representative of local food banks, and impartially pan-Canadian in its focus while having greater autonomy for forward thinking and strategic implementation.

As a key part of their renewal agenda, the CAFB Board searched for a new Executive Director and in the fall of 2007 hired Schmidt. Her initial mandate was to lead the restructuring and rebranding initiative, reenergize and guide the national organization, and improve the resources at hand. The organization was rebranded through this process from Canadian Association of Food Banks to Food Banks Canada.

By 2012, the rebranding of the Canadian Association of Food Banks into Food Banks Canada had made significant progress. Schmidt and the Board had successfully reorganized its governance structure, refocused

---

[§]An overview of the history of the organization can be found in Exhibit 1.

the organization's strategy, and hired a new staff team to help her achieve a turnaround. The stated mission of Food Banks Canada that was developed in 2007 was to meet the short-term need for food and find long-term solutions to reduce hunger.[5]

As a result of the changes, Food Banks Canada had increased its annual revenues from $1.0 million to over $4.6 million in donations, and delivered two times more donated food per year to affiliated food banks than in 2007. In addition, Food Banks Canada's work in advocacy on hunger-related issues had been advanced through their research, their annual reports on food bank use, and expanded lobbying of the federal government. These actions had heightened national awareness and increased its influence with both the government and major corporations involved with food. Positive media coverage that accompanied the publication of these reports had played a significant role in increased public awareness.

By 2011, Food Banks Canada had more fully developed a number of key programs to advance its agenda. Three of the more significant were:

- National Food Sharing System (NFSS)—this program acquires and shares large industry donations of food and consumer products and coordinates national-level and large-scale food drives for the food bank network of more than 450 affiliate members across Canada.
- Hunger Count Reports—both affiliated and non-affiliated members participate in these research studies on the number of people accessing food banks. These are published annually, distributed to the press and used for government advocacy.
- Hunger Awareness Day—a national initiative with food banks across the country participating, which is designed to heighten public awareness of critical issues

related to food access and security for Canadians living on low incomes.

While Food Banks Canada had grown its profile and was viewed by government and other important stakeholders as a credible professional organization that was having a positive impact, they wanted to do more to enhance their value to the food bank community and the people they served. Direct work on alleviating hunger was done directly by local food banks and Schmidt pondered how best to assist them. In fact, the amount of money and food raised by Food Banks Canada was relatively small, when compared to the total amount of money donated to and the total volume of food collected by local food banks. Major food banks in Canada had more resources than the national body and a few believed they were competing with Food Banks Canada for donations and media attention in ways that were not helpful to their mission.

Katharine Schmidt

Schmidt saw her career path as one marrying her interest in public service, food, and poverty issues. After a BA in Family Studies, she spent ten years with the Ontario Ministry of Agriculture, Food and Rural Affairs, culminating in involvement with the Ministry's strategic plan. Her work in leadership development with rural groups prepared her to head up a strategic initiative by the Ministry, seeking greater cooperation among agricultural producers, food processors, food distributors and retail channels for greater effectiveness within the sector.

A desire for personal change and development led her to take a leave, and enroll in Wilfrid Laurier University's one-year MBA program. Upon graduation, she accepted employment with the Canadian Federation of

---

[5]Please visit www.foodbankscanada.ca for more information.

Independent Grocers, on a one year secondment from the Ministry. This was followed by a move to Food and Consumer Products Canada for seven years. These seven years provided her with a broad exposure to major firms, key influencers, and a heighted awareness of the corporate side of the food sector.

"It was a big decision to leave government after 10 years. I believed it would be a great experience to be able to work for a major national industry advocacy group building on my experience with the agri-food sector. Then, in 2004, I decided it was time for another change—one that would allow me to apply my new experience and contacts while getting back into helping people. When the Food Bank of Waterloo Region was looking for a new Executive Director, I jumped at the opportunity. While in that role I began to really understand some the underlying causes of hunger in Canada, I became aware of the need and importance for a strong national organization that could advocate for Canadians."

Schmidt's work as Executive Director of the Food Bank of Waterloo Region brought her directly into contact with community needs related to household food security and access, the food bank community, and the broader dynamics related to the national food bank organization. She saw that a strong national organization could provide leadership across the country and that it could advocate with the federal government. She was pleased with the decisions made by the membership of CAFB at the 2006 annual general meeting to bring in a new governance structure and new Board as steps to strengthen the organization. The new Board of the national organization hired Schmidt because of her successful performance as Executive Director of the Food Bank of Waterloo Region and her performance while working with Food and Consumer Products Canada and earlier agencies and industry groups.

Food Banks Canada: A Federated Structure

As part of the strategic initiative of 2006, the Board of Food Banks Canada adopted a new federated governance structure. The Canadian Association of Food Banks (CAFB) had been an affiliation of independent food banks run by representatives from each member food bank. As one Board member recalled, "The governance issues facing the CAFB were significant. As designed, each food bank affiliate had a vote on major issues. Quebec had many more food banks than any other province. That meant that Quebec had over a thousand votes, Ontario had around 120 while Alberta had 2 votes, New Brunswick one and Nova Scotia one. Not only was this not representative but it was almost unworkable."

Under the new membership structure, rather than local food banks joining Food Banks Canada directly, local food banks would join a provincial association. Once they joined the provincial association they would become affiliate members to Food Banks Canada. The organization would seek input and involvement from its membership by having each provincial association identify two representatives who would be their nominees on the Member Council.

The Member Council was designed to help ensure that the voices of food banks from across the country were heard by the National Board, and vice versa. It was intended that this body would play an important role in facilitating communications and coordination between the national organization and affiliated member organizations on plans and programs being implemented across the country (see Exhibit 2b). The 20 representatives on the Member Council were drawn from the provincial bodies and affiliated food banks. Many of the 20 representatives placed on Member Council had been on the previous CAFB Board. Schmidt, as CEO of Food Banks Canada (or her nominee) also sat on this council.

The new structure also had a reconstituted National Board that focused on the strategy and governance of the national body. The National Board initially had 16 members, And participation on it shifted to individuals drawn from corporate Canada, the food industry, and highly capable and committed individuals with specific skills needed to advance the interests of the national body (e.g., skills in finance, HR, marketing, communications, strategy, and legal). In order to have affiliate representation on the National Board, two members were drawn from Member Council to serve on the Board. The purpose of the reconstituted National Board was to focus its attention on the advancement of the work of the national organization, which they would be able to do with increased independence, now that they were not there to simply represent the issues of particular geographic areas (see Exhibit 2 and 2a).

Moving Food Banks Canada Forward 2007–2012

Schmidt set out to build an effective management team. From January 2008 to January 2012 she first reduced staff from five-and-a-half full-time equivalent to two and one half. Then, over a period of three years, she added eleven-and-a-half full-time energetic, talented individuals committed to the food bank cause (see Exhibit 3). Concurrent with the hiring of key personnel, Schmidt led the rebranding effort. The name "Canadian Association of Food Banks" implied a collectivity with little central purpose or coordination. The new brand, captured by the new name, Food Banks Canada, became critical to increasing visibility with corporate partners and to symbolize the shift in strategic direction. In early 2007, Food Banks Canada had little visibility with the public or even the food industry. At that time, all food banks strove for visibility and wanted to become the recognizable representative for food and hunger in their respective areas. While Food Banks Canada had complimentary goals as that of the local organizations, some local food banks perceived it as a competitor for recognition and attention, and resources.

Schmidt and the Board believed that their rebranding initiative had met with some success. This was supported by an independent branding study they had commissioned, but the data showed it represented an ongoing challenge. When affiliates marketed their activities under different names it added to the confusion in the public's mind as to who was doing what when it came to providing food for those living in poverty. If you were in Toronto, you would see the Food Banks Canada logo but also that of Daily Bread Food Bank, North York Harvest, and Fort York Food Bank. If you were in Minto, Ontario, Food Banks Canada could be perceived to be competing with the Minto Community Resources Centre, and so on. This natural tension between needing to promote local needs versus creating broader national awareness was often a source of conflict. Some independent food banks' staff questioned whether they wanted Food Banks Canada to be the brand name for hunger relief and what the benefit was to them.

In addition to talent building and rebranding, Schmidt spent time food raising and developing systems to collect and distribute food from national donors. When for example, Kraft Canada phoned and said "We have 70 skids of a product for you if you pick them up today," Food Banks Canada needed the trucking capacity to pick up the goods and then a fair system of distribution of those goods to local food banks. Further, these systems had to be acceptable to member food banks, address risks in the food safety area, and minimize any waste that occurred due to inefficient food handling. As one Food Canada representative said; "a system was in place, but it was poorly and ineffectively run. There were delays, and perhaps, a lack of professionalism and expertise. At the same time, I would say that, before the spike in gas prices in 2008-09, free transportation was much more available to us, particularly via trucking companies."

As a result of problems in this area, the organization developed and implemented training programs on food safety and handling that it operated nationally for people working in food banks, particularly those from small agencies. In 2011, this was the only program that Food Banks Canada operated that was directly supported by federal government money. While training provided part of the reason for the improvement in food quality and quantity, a great deal of the credit went to strengthened relationships with national food companies and new, sophisticated systems for the collection and redistribution of food donated at the national level.

Schmidt spent significant time food and fundraising. In 2009, Food Banks Canada initiated a partner program for corporate donors.** As a result, the amount of food raised at the national level grew from 7 million pounds in 2008 to 14 million pounds in 2011.†† A member of the leadership team stated, "National and even international corporations want to work with an organization that can handle food at the national level. Affiliate members want Food Banks Canada to coordinate things better and help them, but they also wanted to retain their autonomy and manage corporate relationships on their own."

While progress had been achieved with food supply, progress had also been made in fundraising and related systems and procedures. The Director of Development and Partnerships observed: "When I started my role at Food Banks Canada there were no policies or systems. There were a few large, supportive companies with 10 to12 of them giving $10,000 to $12,000 each. Now there are 40 to 50 firms with some giving as much as $50,000 to $100,000. One company's contribution is $250,000 per year" (see Exhibit 4 for a summary of their financial position).

In 2011, Food Banks Canada affiliate members' food banks provided direct services to 85% of the people accessing emergency food programs nationwide. The food and money supplied to them by Food Banks Canada totaled 7% (or 15 million pounds out of 200 million pounds of food) with the remainder coming from food or fundraising initiatives at the local or, to a much lesser extent, provincial level.

Role of Provincial Bodies

By 2012 each of the ten provinces had a provincial association, though these varied widely in their level of development. A few provincial bodies had yet to obtain their charitable status from the government and some had little to no permanent staff. A key challenge Food Banks Canada faced was to identify a strong case for the support of the work of certain provincial bodies by donors. Food Banks Canada had a protocol in place when it engaged with donors to ask them to provide support at all three levels (local, provincial, national). However, they were finding that national donor organizations preferred to give nationally or locally, and were less interested in donating to provincial bodies.

**Partners are companies who have prioritized their commitment to help Canadians who are hungry and have pledged their support to Food Banks Canada. They help in many ways: financially, helping with Hunger Awareness Week, food donations, and transportation system donors.

††One of the ongoing dilemmas faced by Food Banks Canada was the determination of the value of food donations. After extensive research, Food Banks Canada decided to value each pound of food donated to be worth $2.50. This number meant Food Banks Canada could translate food given into dollars equivalents raised. It was a useful marketing tool in that it allowed Food Banks Canada to state the value of food distributed.

Where to Now?

Results of the Member Survey[‡‡]

In the winter of 2011, 410 Canadian food banks were surveyed. One hundred and seventy four surveys were completed and analyzed by an independent survey research firm. Seventy-eight percent of respondents were either a member of a food bank Board, the executive director, or a manager of a food bank.

The survey reported that Food Banks Canada was well known and well regarded by Canadian Food Banks. Ninety-three % of respondents reported that Food Banks Canada provided value in the fight against hunger in Canada and 79% reported that their organizations received direct support from Food Banks Canada.

In general, respondents felt that provincial food bank associations were performing well. Eighty-two percent said they were satisfied with the performance of the provincial associations. Their value lay in direct help and in representing food issues to others. Larger food banks were less likely to say they were "very satisfied" with provincial associations. Of concern was the fact that 19% of respondents reported that Food Banks Canada provided little direct value to them. Those representing communities over 100,000 people saw the least amount of value in Food Banks Canada to their organizations.

Raising awareness of the hunger issue in Canada, at all levels, was viewed as the top priority, with 43% of respondents choosing raising awareness of the hunger issue *in their community* as number one. This was followed by raising awareness of the work the food bank community does and developing fundraising campaigns in their communities. The top priority for Food Banks Canada, while still clear, was more debatable. Raising awareness of the hunger issue *in Canada* was chosen as top priority by 29% of respondents, followed by acquiring large-scale donations and federal government advocacy.

For the most part, program participants were satisfied with the programs/activities Food Banks Canada offered, and in particular, they valued their participation in and use of HungerCount, Hunger Awareness Day, and National Corporate programs. Some programs had high awareness but low participation. More than half said they were aware of but had never participated in programs/activities like the Community Kitchen Fund or the National Membership Conference. Respondents used the Food Banks Canada newsletters and HungerCount and Hunger Awareness Day materials but did not use the Online Resource Centre as much. While respondents reported that they did not use nutrition materials much, those materials were identified as the top priority for new tool development. More materials on fundraising and public service announcements were also wanted. Client story books received the least amount of support. Exhibit 5 reports on the top priorities identified in the survey.

Strategic Choices Being Considered

Members of the Food Banks Canada leadership team differed in where they thought the organization should focus. One member of the leadership team commented: "Over the next five years it will be critical that we increase our efforts advocating at the federal level. Capacity building within the Canadian food bank community is also vital to ensure food is getting to those who need it most, but we also need to maintain and enhance food acquisition and distribution activities." This focus reflected her belief that "food donation programs with bigger organizations lent themselves to being institutionalized and systematized and were effectively underway, potentially freeing some resources for other critical activities." However, she recognized that

---

[‡‡]Source: Presentation materials to Food Banks Canada by harrisdecima, March 2012.

such a shift was not without risks and needed to be managed carefully, so that donors did not feel ignored or undervalued.

Another member of the Leadership Team pointed out the challenges of funding the future priorities based on donor interest and preferences:

> For the foreseeable future, the organization needs to be involved in both advocacy and food and fundraising, including donations in-kind such as transportation services to distribute food. Food is substantive and donors are often interested in supporting food acquisition and sharing. We find that policy development, research and government advocacy is a more difficult "sell" to donors. Over 10 years, we might build up an individual donor base interested in giving to a national organization doing advocacy. But we are a long way from that. With limited resources, and donors being interested in some parts of our mandate more than in others areas, it will be difficult as we move forward.

A third perspective from another member of Food Banks Canada's leadership team believed that: "If Food Banks Canada is going to maintain legitimacy, it has to be seen as an organization that is about getting food to people. It has to protect the charitable aspect of the food bank network from getting lost in a social justice debate,[§§] but at the same time maintain an appropriate level of advocacy." As a result Food Banks Canada needed to be seen as raising food and putting it in the hands of those in need, while retaining its commitment to provide a focus on policy and legislative change. Advocacy needed "to be approached in ways that do not alienate corporate and political figures. As he put it, "Poking one's finger in another's eye is not likely to produce support for one's cause." He

further believed that Food Banks Canada's current model was sustainable.

The Board

The current Food Banks Canada National Board had 16 members, including two representatives from provincial member food banks. The other 14 members were well connected with food producers and government and had demonstrated their commitment, in part, through their past contributions. Board members received no compensation and all were asked to make a financial commitment to Food Banks Canada, according to their means. Board membership required a significant time commitment which all members honored. They were well balanced in their diversity of skills and backgrounds (accounting, finance, marketing, communications, human resources, legal, business, and nonprofit) and geographic representation. The general sentiment of National Board members, national staff members, and most of the affiliated organizations that were on the Member Council, was that the National Board had developed into a hardworking, well prepared, competent, independent, and highly collegial group. Schmidt attended all Board and Board committee meetings but was not a voting member of the Board.

Robin Garrett, elected in 2006 to the Board, became its Chair in 2011. She had a long involvement with the national organization and its predecessor, beginning in the late 1990's when she was with the Food and Consumer Products Manufacturers Association. She had 16 years of management experience working with national and regional organizations and was currently the President and CEO, Tourism Partnership of Niagara.

Garrett believed that Food Banks Canada had come a long way but needed a stronger national presence to exercise influence and attract resources: "The most successful federated

---

[§§]The social justice debate argued for justice for all. Clearly ending food poverty was part of this but many saw a major difference between the specifics of providing people with food and engaging in a broad ranging social justice argument.

not-for-profits, in my belief, are those that have a strong national organization, with clear roles throughout the organization—from the front-line operators, through to the provincial organizations, with the national organization on top. It is about aligning and coordinating work, allocating and maximizing resources so we can give back maximally."

Garrett observed that the roles within the food bank community were developing but that a shared understanding and agreement was not yet fully developed. There was some discomfort at the provincial level as to their roles and ability to deliver on assigned roles. She noted that there were a couple of very strong provinces (Nova Scotia and Quebec), but there were others that were weak and some that had very little infrastructure. In addition, food banks across the country varied tremendously in their sophistication.

Garrett believed the above factors created anxiety over roles and concerns related to the livelihood of paid staff members at the local and provincial levels. These factors also gave rise to some resentment in larger member organizations over the emergence of a strong national body, and the power shift that this entailed. This, in turn, created a real risk of turf wars.

When it came to fundraising and food raising campaigns, Garrett felt that the food banks needed a common message, with Food Banks Canada playing both a lead and coordinating role.

> You get better bang for your buck when there is a clear national campaign focusing on people in need. We can share resources and materials. There are 500 food banks all doing fundraising campaigns. Can you imagine the effectiveness gains and the savings that would be possible, if we combined and integrated our efforts though a national campaign? Food Banks Canada needs to launch national campaigns. We need to go after national corporate donors for such national campaigns. The message and materials need to be developed nationally and then used at the local levels, with Food Banks Canada synchronizing the campaigns. Wow, now all Canadians would hear the same message. Wouldn't it be wonderful if there were a single web site for food banks where money is raised?

However, this was not a sentiment shared by some of the strong food bank members and this expressed itself in resentment over Food Banks Canada ramping up national activities in some of these areas. They saw these as an intrusion on provincial and local food bank responsibilities, where there was a desire to own the direct connection with donors and the delivery system. One of the side effects of this was that donor lists developed by local food banks were not readily shared.

There were significant differences in systems and resources among local food banks, which pointed to the need for capacity building at the local and in some cases, provincial levels. Garrett wondered if there needed to be different approaches to service delivery, so that the smaller food banks could be directly supported by the larger, more sophisticated bodies. Once again, the issue was one of alignment. In the end she believed that Food Banks Canada had to create initiatives in the advocacy, food raising, fundraising, and capacity building areas that demonstrated how it could add value to all, if roles were clarified and aligned.

Brian Fraser, appointed to the Board in 2009 and now Vice Chair, was a corporate lawyer and partner with Gowlings, a major law firm. Fraser was asked for assistance by Food Banks Canada on a branding issue. Pro bono work, combined with a deep interest in what the national organization was attempting to accomplish, along with exposure to Schmidt, led to his recruitment to the National Board.

Fraser believed that the transformation of Food Banks Canada, and even the Board, could be traced to the effectiveness of Schmidt as the Executive Director. He stated that she had played a constructive role in board member recruitment and had been instrumental in building this strong and independent board, providing it with excellent support while at the same time welcoming careful critical assessment, and independent thought. Fraser reported that a key risk area was the potential that Schmidt might leave and the need to prepare for her successor.

He believed good progress had been made in the relationship with the Member Council and with large food banks, such as Toronto's Daily Bread Food Bank. Given the small size and limited resource base of Food Banks Canada, it had to continually work to build its brand as the national "go to" organization in matters related to hunger.

One risk area he mentioned was the competition in fundraising from non-affiliated agencies who sought to raise money and food contributions for the hungry. He believed that while some of these were well intentioned, others were questionable as to motive. As well, they created the risk for fragmentation occurring in the food bank community.

As for the future strategic direction, Fraser's view was that advocacy efforts, which were currently at an early stage of development, should receive increased attention. Capacity building of less capable local food banks was the second priority that needed action, because it would bring value directly to the food bank community. Finally raising food and money continued to be important because it was an ongoing challenge to keep the attention and interest of food manufacturers, knowing what they were looking for, and feeding their agenda in ways that were also consistent with Food Bank Canada's agenda. Fraser stated that Food Banks Canada needed to be seen as an effectively run national organization in order to appeal to the corporate audience.

Member Council Perspective

The Member Council representatives offered somewhat different perspectives on what Food Banks Canada's focus should be. One member who expressed serious concern for the future direction was Dianne Swinemar, Executive Director of Feed Nova Scotia. Swinemar led one of the strongest provincial bodies and she was of the belief that the role of those weak provincial bodies was in urgent need of strengthening.

Swinemar was hired in 1991 by what was then a metro-based food bank operating in and around Halifax. As such, its approach was similar to that of the much bigger Daily Bread Food Bank in Toronto, Ontario. In 2002, Nova Scotia food bank members met and restructured themselves around a strong provincial model, placing Feed Nova Scotia in the lead role and Swinemar as the CEO. They rebranded themselves, took on a 24/7 help line, and took on fund, food, and awareness raising for the province as a whole. As a result of these changes, the effectiveness of these services in Nova Scotia improved significantly. Swinemar believed this was because the communities, donors, and smaller food banks understood why these changes made sense.

Swinemar had played a leading role when Food Banks Canada restructured itself, chairing the transition team at the time. She felt progress had been made but she was also of the view that the current National Board and staff were still really struggling to have their actions match the vision identified at the time of Food Banks Canada's restructuring. Swinemar believed that the missing ingredient was strong provincial organizations to coordinate activities, and she did not believe Food Banks Canada could successfully provide service and support to 400–500 member agencies with such different levels of sophistication.

With the exception of Nova Scotia and Quebec, Swinemar believed the provincial organizations had not developed into the bodies envisioned at the time of the reorganization and that Food Banks Canada was not championing and supporting their evolution. It was her sense that politics might be getting in the way of them integrating their efforts in order to provide leadership and logistical support and other ingredients needed to enable local organizations and their volunteers to effectively deliver services.

She concluded that Food Banks Canada found it easier to send messages and work directly with the front line, rather than work with and build the capacity of the provincial bodies. As a result, many provincial bodies were weak and some had no staff and were barely on life support. Swinemar saw Canada as a mosaic and believed that it would always be an uphill struggle for Food Banks Canada to really become a vibrant national organization, if it did not possess strong provincial arms.

Wendi Campbell, head of Food Bank of Waterloo Region and a representative on the Member Council, was a trained and experienced manager. After graduating from university with a degree in English, she coordinated events for the Special Olympics program in south-west Ontario and from there found employment with the Food Bank of Waterloo Region in 1999. When the executive director of her organization ran for parliament in 2004, she met Schmidt who had been recruited as the new Executive Director. Campbell reported that she had enjoyed working with Schmidt and had learned a great deal from her. Both recognized that Campbell lacked accounting and finance skills and at the urging of Schmidt, Campbell enrolled in the Laurier MBA program, graduating in 2008.

When Schmidt left the Food Bank of Waterloo Region, Campbell was appointed the Executive Director. She saw her organization as a high performing one, in part due to the governance structure that had evolved over the years. It had an effective board that was very policy oriented and a culture that promoted innovation and risk taking. She noted that small food banks were challenged to find the capacity to do things and their structure and boards were often not up to the challenge. Campbell was concerned with how to develop the capacity in these small food banks.

Campbell believed the changes implemented in 2005–2006 had created a platform that had made the revival and revitalization of the national body possible. Campbell had been on the Board of Canadian Association of Food Banks when the decision was made to refocus on the strategy, restructure, and rebrand, and had been very supportive of Schmidt's appointment as Food Banks Canada's Executive Director.

Campbell saw several positive changes as a result of these decisions:

> As a local food bank, I am able to take Food Banks Canada's campaigns and use their messaging to help achieve my goals. There is a major halo effect I can use and rely on. I don't see them as competing for resources, though some food banks do. If Food Banks Canada gets funding from national organizations that had previously funded me, I see that as a corporate decision, not Food Banks Canada taking from me. Many food banks don't have the capacity to think that way. They lack the resources.

> As an example of what Food Banks Canada can do, I watched the last show of Oprah. Suddenly on the show was an ad from Food Banks Canada. Amazing! This was a new campaign, a new target market, and a move into prime time awareness, going after a new demographic. Food Banks Canada elevates the fight for food awareness to a new level.

Campbell was well aware of the issues and challenges between some of the provincial associations and Food Banks Canada. She believed that the challenges stemmed from the diversity of sophistication of the provincial associations and the varying ways that each province wanted Food Banks Canada to interact with its food banks. Nova Scotia had a strong provincially oriented governance structure and did not need Food Banks Canada to go directly to the local food banks. They believed that they should be the main contact and control point, and should not be bypassed. In contrast, Saskatchewan had a more loosely organized provincial association and a larger land base and were supportive of Food Banks Canada having direct interaction and support to their local food banks. However, when it came to service delivery, Campbell preferred a regional focus:

> There is some resistance now over what has happened with Food Banks Canada. It seems there is some pressure to return to a more provincially oriented model. Instead of this, we need to focus on increasing the capacity of local food banks by how they are linked with better resourced regional bodies.

Where to Next?

Schmidt pondered the strategic choices facing the organization. There were two main thrusts: providing access to more food (through food/fundraising) and engaging in research and advocacy. Should they continue to do what they were currently doing, focus more on one of the areas, or were there other things they should be doing?

Schmidt had been trying to position Food Banks Canada as an honest broker of information and she also wanted to position the organization as a solution provider. Schmidt noted that she believed that most poverty groups had not been influential on issues that mattered to them because they had taken a too aggressive activist approach to advocacy and had turned off both senior levels of government and the corporate sector. If Food Banks Canada was to push policy change in the wrong way, there was the risk that they would not get the ear of the federal and provincial governments. However, hunger and poverty were growing in Canada and becoming more pressing every day, suggesting that concerted action was needed. Should Food Banks Canada stay its current course in the advocacy area or should they approach it differently? Could Food Banks Canada develop a reasoned approach that others could and would buy into, which would help significantly with the problems of poverty?

Food Banks Canada had also been doing some capacity building with local food banks. Was this an area that deserved more of the national organization's energy? Some provincial bodies were struggling to show that they added value. How might Food Banks Canada work with them to find joint solutions?

Schmidt knew that the Board wanted to revisit and recalibrate where to focus the strategy going forward. Board members felt good about the progress that had been made, but there were important issues as well as resource constraints. What advice should she give them concerning the "where do we go next" question? What should be their focus as they looked to the next 3–5 years? And how could Schmidt recruit stakeholders (see Exhibit 6) to a single vision when they all had strong ideas about what the national organization should do?

Exhibit 1 Historical Overview of Food Banks Canada	
1986	First national food bank conference held in Edmonton
1987	Decision made to establish the Canadian Association of Food Banks and a steering committee was struck to develop a constitution and bylaws. A special effort was made to have founding members from each province.
November 17, 1989	First meeting held—43 food banks from nine provinces were accepted as members
	Main focus of the group was to create a common voice for food banks around public policy issues affecting food bank clients
	The association initially was set up with a sunset clause for three years which called for the wind-up of the organization which was subsequently eliminated since the need to feed hungry Canadians only increased.
1989	National Food Sharing System was adopted and an advisory committee from the industry was started to help with food, transportation, and fundraising.
1989	The first formal *HungerCount* was conducted and found that 378,000 people came to food banks for hampers
2005	Organization realized it was not as effective as it could be due to structure, leadership, and focus of the organization
2006	National conference Vancouver B to vote on new governance board, and membership structure
2007	New board formed and new strategy plan and mandate identified
	Later 2007 new ED, Katharine Schmidt hired
2008	Food Banks Canada rebrands itself as Food Banks Canada
2009	National conference as new organization
2012	Board beginning to revisit its strategy

Exhibit 2 Organizational Structure

Food Banks Canada is:

– governed by a community Board of Directors (16 members, including 2 Member Council representatives)
– guided by a Member Council, including representation from each of the 10 provincial food bank associations
– supported by an internal staff team

FOOD BANKS CANADA

- Supports Members by acquiring and distributing food and funds
- Initiates and implements national programs within selected structured and allocated resources
- Develops national partnerships
- Conducts research on hunger in Canada
- Provides key messaging on issues that impact the food bank community

MEMBERS

10 Provincial Food Banks Associations

- Work with Food Banks Canada to carry out programs and services including provincial NFSS hubs/ activities, National Hunger Count, Hunger Awareness Day, etc.
- Administer food bank memberships in Provincial Associations
- Act as the voice of affiliate members provincially
- Inform affiliate members of national programs, services, and resources
- Coordinate with Food Banks Canada on relationships to solicit food and funds on behalf of the network

AFFILIATE MEMBERS

450 Food Banks

- Provide direct service making a difference for the hungry
- Support Food Banks Canada Members (provincial associations) and Food Banks Canada
- Receive and invest/ disperse nationally, provincially, and locally secured funds and food
- Run local fund and food raising compaigns
- Provide Food Banks Canada with *Hunger Count Research* input
- Provide resources/best practices to provincial association and Food Banks Canada

Exhibit 2a Food Banks Canada National Structure

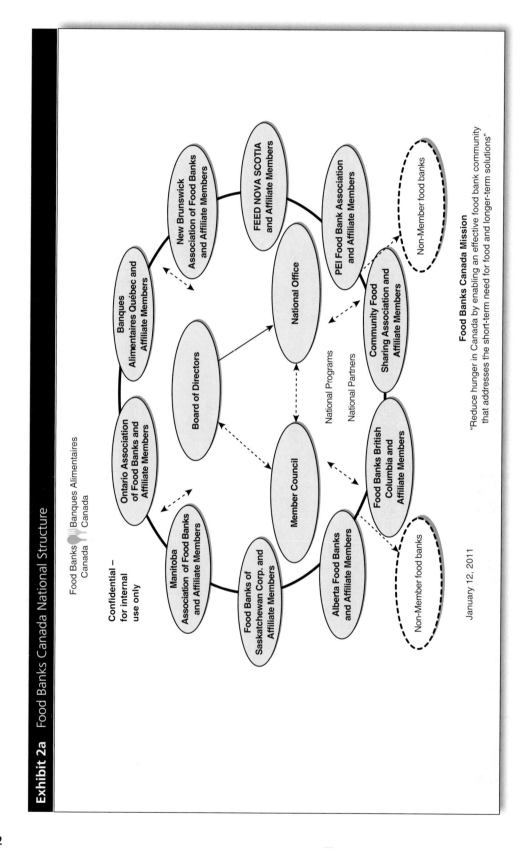

Food Banks Canada   Banques Alimentaires Canada

Confidential – for internal use only

Ontario Association of Food Banks and Affiliate Members

Banques Alimentaires Québec and Affiliate Members

New Brunswick Association of Food Banks and Affiliate Members

FEED NOVA SCOTIA and Affiliate Members

PEI Food Bank Association and Affiliate Members

Manitoba Association of Food Banks and Affiliate Members

Food Banks of Saskatchewan Corp. and Affiliate Members

Board of Directors

Member Council

National Office

National Programs

National Partners

Community Food Sharing Association and Affiliate Members

Non-Member food banks

Alberta Food Banks and Affiliate Members

Food Banks British Columbia and Affiliate Members

Non-Member food banks

January 12, 2011

Food Banks Canada Mission
"Reduce hunger in Canada by enabling an effective food bank community that addresses the short-term need for food and longer-term solutions"

Exhibit 2b Food Banks Canada National Structure: Member Council

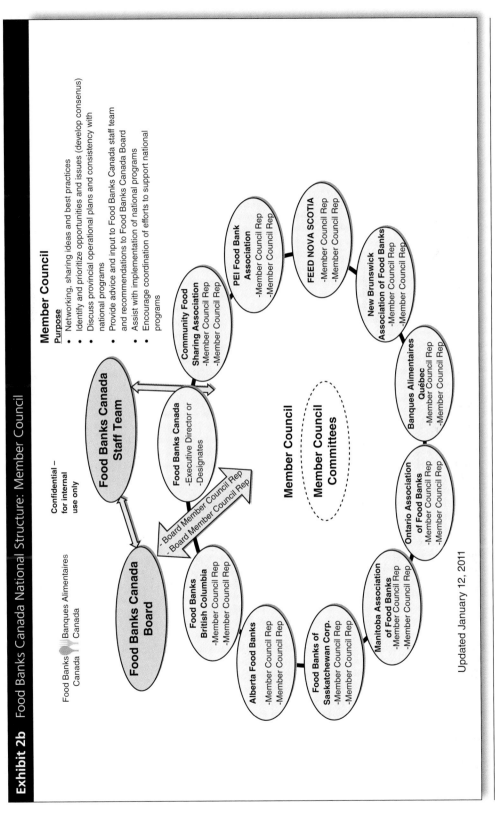

Food Banks Banques Alimentaires
Canada Canada

Confidential –
for internal
use only

Food Banks Canada Staff Team

Food Banks Canada Board

Food Banks Canada
- Executive Director or
- Designates

Member Council

Purpose
- Networking, sharing ideas and best practices
- Identify and prioritize opportunities and issues (develop consensus)
- Discuss provincial operational plans and consistency with national programs
- Provide advice and input to Food Banks Canada staff team and recommendations to Food Banks Canada Board
- Assist with implementation of national programs
- Encourage coordination of efforts to support national programs

Community Food Sharing Association
- Member Council Rep
- Member Council Rep

PEI Food Bank Association
- Member Council Rep
- Member Council Rep

FEED NOVA SCOTIA
- Member Council Rep
- Member Council Rep

New Brunswick Association of Food Banks
- Member Council Rep
- Member Council Rep

Banques Alimentaires Québec
- Member Council Rep
- Member Council Rep

Ontario Association of Food Banks
- Member Council Rep
- Member Council Rep

Manitoba Association of Food Banks
- Member Council Rep
- Member Council Rep

Food Banks of Saskatchewan Corp.
- Member Council Rep
- Member Council Rep

Alberta Food Banks
- Member Council Rep
- Member Council Rep

Food Banks British Columbia
- Member Council Rep
- Member Council Rep

- Board Member Council Rep
- Board Member Council Rep

Member Council Committees

Updated January 12, 2011

Note: Food Banks Canada provides secretarial support (clerical and administrative duties) for the Member Council and its committees, including drafting of minutes, maintaining records, maintaining intranet site, etc.

Exhibit 3 Food Banks Canada Organizational Structure

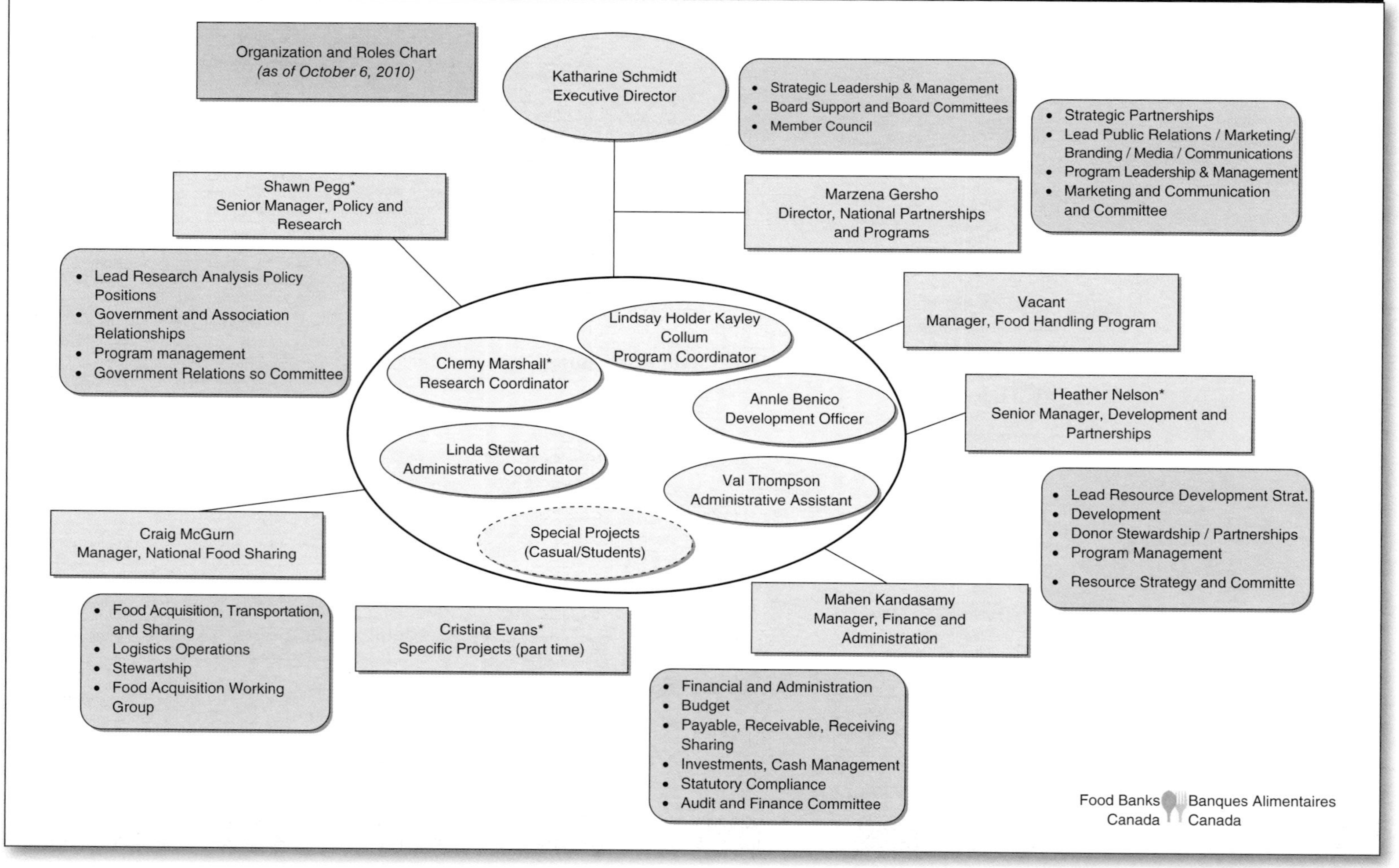

Organization and Roles Chart
(as of October 6, 2010)

Katharine Schmidt
Executive Director

Strategic Leadership & Management
Board Support and Board Committees
Member Council
-
-
-

Marzena Gersho
Director, National Partnerships
and Programs

Strategic Partnerships
Lead Public Relations / Marketing /
Branding / Media / Communications
Program Leadership & Management
Marketing and Communication
and Committee
-
-
-

Vacant
Manager, Food Handling Program

Heather Nelson*
Senior Manager, Development and
Partnerships

Lead Resource Development Strat.
Development
Donor Stewardship / Partnerships
Program Management
Resource Strategy and Committe
-
-
-
-

Lindsay Holder Kayley
Collum Program Coordinator

Annie Benico
Development Officer

Val Thompson
Administrative Assistant

Mahen Kandasamy
Manager, Finance and
Administration

Financial and Administration
Budget
Payable, Receivable, Receiving
Sharing
Investments, Cash Management
Statutory Compliance
Audit and Finance Committee
-
-
-
-
-

Chemy Marshall*
Research Coordinator

Linda Stewart
Administrative Coordinator

Special Projects
(Casual/Students)

Cristina Evans*
Specific Projects (part time)

Shawn Pegg*
Senior Manager, Policy and
Research

Lead Research Analysis Policy
Positions
Government and Association
Relationships
Program management
Government Relations so Committee
-
-
-
-

Craig McGurn
Manager, National Food Sharing

Food Acquisition, Transportation,
and Sharing
Logistics Operations
Stewartship
Food Acquisition Working
Group
-
-
-
-

Food Banks Banques Alimentaires
Canada   Canada

* French language skills

434

Exhibit 4 Food Banks Canada Summary Financial Information 2010 and 2011

Summarized Statement of Financial Position as of March 31, 2011

	2011	2010
Assets		
Current		
Cash	$ 338,261	$ 435,649
Investments	1,758,131	1,760,404
Accounts receivable	561,526	250,597
Prepaid expenses	22,017	16,685
	2,679,935	2,463,335
Capital assets	44,452	41,812
	2,724,387	2,505,147
Liabilities		
Current		
Accounts payable and accrued liabilities	618,804	129,121
Deferred contributions	10,004	146,868
	628,808	275,989
Net assets		
General fund		
Unrestricted	133,532	241,718
Invested in capital assets	44,452	41,812
Internally restricted funds	1,304,075	1,474,075
Externally restricted funds	613,520	471,553
	2,095,579	2,229,158
	$2,724,387	$2,505,147

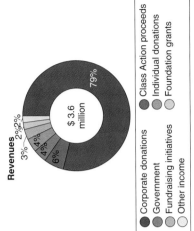

Revenues

$ 3.6 million

79% · 6% · 4% · 4% · 3% · 2% · 2%

- Corporate donations
- Government
- Fundraising initiatives
- Other income
- Class Action proceeds
- Individual donations
- Foundation grants

Expenses

$3.7 million

41% · 18% · 13% · 9% · 8% · 6% · 5%

- Distribution of funds to membership
- Food acquisition and sharing
- Administration
- Member services and support
- Public education and support
- Research and advocacy
- Fund development

Exhibit 5 Top Priorities Identified by the Food Bank Community

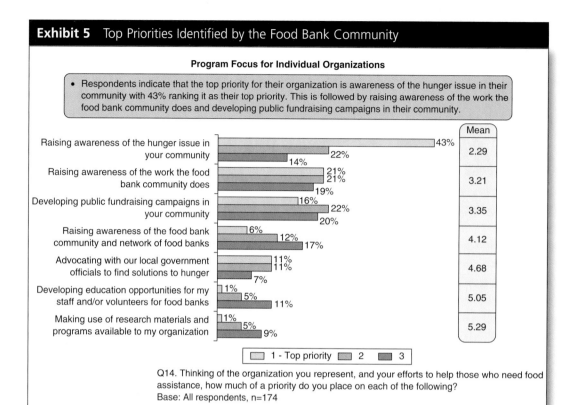

Program Focus for Individual Organizations

- Respondents indicate that the top priority for their organization is awareness of the hunger issue in their community with 43% ranking it as their top priority. This is followed by raising awareness of the work the food bank community does and developing public fundraising campaigns in their community.

	Mean
Raising awareness of the hunger issue in your community — 43% / 22% / 14%	2.29
Raising awareness of the work the food bank community does — 21% / 21% / 19%	3.21
Developing public fundraising campaigns in your community — 16% / 22% / 20%	3.35
Raising awareness of the food bank community and network of food banks — 6% / 12% / 17%	4.12
Advocating with our local government officials to find solutions to hunger — 11% / 11% / 7%	4.68
Developing education opportunities for my staff and/or volunteers for food banks — 1% / 5% / 11%	5.05
Making use of research materials and programs available to my organization — 1% / 5% / 9%	5.29

1 - Top priority   2   3

Q14. Thinking of the organization you represent, and your efforts to help those who need food assistance, how much of a priority do you place on each of the following?
Base: All respondents, n=174

Exhibit 6   Stakeholder Overview

	Definition	Role
Membership (provincial associations and affiliate member food banks)	10 provincial associations and 450 food banks	Made up our membership. Inform and provide input into the work we do
People assisted by food banks	Close to 900,000 Canadians -37% are children -Seniors, students, new Canadians	The primary reason for our mandate - to assist Canadians in need with goal of reducing hunger in Canada
Corporate donors	Financial donors: Across all sectors—however food and consumer manufacturers are highly influential	Our primary source of funding at this time. Several have high interest in participating in our work related to nutrition
Food only donors	Some retailers, farmers and producers, food manufacturers	Source of food for Food Banks Canada to share; source of food for our food banks
Government	Policies that impact Canadians living in poverty/ affect access to healthy foods	Develops and implements policy— has great impact on word of organizations like Food Banks Canada and low-income Canadians
Nongovernmental agencies and organizations	Organizations that are aligned with Food Banks from different areas of our success factors (e.g., FCPC, CFIG, CCPA, HSF . . .)	Many aligned with Food Banks Canada's mandate; many have very different mandates but have parallel areas that could overlap (e.g., FEPC/ Food Banks Canada re industry engagement)
Key opinion leaders	Academics, experts, influential media writers (e.g., Leslie Bank)	Individuals/groups that are active in areas that overlap with our work: poverty: nutrition
Media/Social network	Across all channels—daily print, broadcast, online	Helps to keep the issue in front of public—and hot!
Community	Local communities that support Canadians in need	Engaged in local food bank activities
Food Banks Canada staff (and board??)	The national organization that represents the food bank community	Works to bring together the other stakeholders; works to address priorities

Case Study 3

"Not an Option to Even Consider:" Contending With the Pressures to Compromise (A)[1]

Mary C. Gentile

Giving *Voice* to Values

A jith sighed as he hung up the phone. Once again, the health ministry had failed to move his registration application forward so that his company, Laurent Pharmaceuticals, could begin selling prescription medications in the Southeast Asian state of Kamaria. Though this new delay wasn't entirely unexpected, Ajith was still disappointed. A seasoned pharmaceutical executive, Ajith's primary goal, ever since arriving in Kamaria a year earlier to serve as Director of Operations and Chief Resident Representative overseeing Laurent's in-country businesses, had been to obtain these registrations. Laurent's existing businesses included personal care products and over-the-counter medications. Laurent hoped to enter the pharmaceutical and vaccine markets but without the registrations, Ajith knew that the firm could not enter the market, restricting the firm's ability to grow the small but promising Kamarian business.

His disappointment was not only due to the delays themselves, but also to the reasons for them. The products that Laurent Pharmaceuticals intended to introduce specifically addressed growing major health concerns in the country. Ajith suspected that if his application could get past the first gatekeeper and into the hands of the health ministry's review committees, he could make a compelling case for introducing Laurent's products into Kamaria and dramatically improving the health of its citizens. Yet other companies appeared to be getting priority over Laurent. "What was quite amazing to us at the time was that companies who came with files six months later or three months later, were getting registrations extremely quickly," Ajith recalled. How were his competitors achieving these results? "They were basically bribing the gatekeeper and their files quickly ended up in the review committees, and they then probably met up with the review committee people and starting doing the same," Ajith realized. "They were getting quite a few registrations, so what we finally saw was that all sorts of registrations were coming through for our competitors and none for us."

Every day, the pressures on Ajith increased. Both his commitment to uphold the official policy of the company, which stated that compromise was unacceptable, and his strong sense of personal integrity—a source of professional and personal pride for Ajith—were being tested. Externally, the competitive pressures were mounting as other companies' mangers compromised and obtained registrations. Internally, Ajith's Laurent managers were becoming impatient with the obstacles to progress and were beginning to think that policy or no policy, compromise was the only way forward. Ajith disagreed, but he knew that he needed to articulate a better way.

To make matters worse, further difficulties had arisen in the over-the-counter market that Ajith also oversaw in Kamaria. Laurent Pharmaceuticals produced a widely used over-the-counter painkiller under the brand name Theradil. At first, this product was quite successful in Kamaria, achieving over 50% market share by 2008. But Ajith had recently begun to notice that Theradil's market share was eroding. Cheap, locally-produced imitation products of inferior quality had begun to pop up in the pain relief market, decreasing Laurent's market share considerably. In investigating further, Ajith discovered that the factories producing the fake Theradil were run by former generals of the Kamarian army, who had been awarded these factories as rewards for their years of service and as spoils of war. Any attempt to shut them down could further impact Laurent Pharmaceuticals' ability to operate in Kamaria, and could potentially pose personal dangers for Ajith, due to the powerful nature of the individuals who ran these operations.

Ajith remained calm in the face of these challenges, reflecting that "these were standard issues that go with the terrain of operations in this part of the world, and especially the developing nations." Still, he acknowledged, "the situation after one year of operations in Kamaria was grim." How could he obtain registrations for the pharmaceutical products without compromising his integrity? And what strategies could he use to combat the growing problem of imitation Theradil without impacting Laurent's ability to do business in Kamaria?

Historical Context

Kamaria is a small, single-party state located in Southeast Asia. A former European colony, Kamaria suffered through decades of brutal civil war in the 20th century and finally achieved independence in 1987. Though it remained a closed market through the end of 1998, Kamaria began to open its markets to the outside world the following year, establishing a small private sector dominated by small- and medium-sized businesses and encouraging foreign-owned enterprises to set up local operations. By 2008, Kamaria was recognized as a fast-growing and export-driven emerging economy. The government of Kamaria was seeking to use their new status on the world stage to negotiate favorable trade agreements with the UK, the United States, and other developed nations to ensure the continued success of their exports. As in other developing countries, however, corruption was a problem that impaired Kamaria's ability to attract significant foreign direct investment, in spite of the attractiveness of its rapidly growing markets and manufacturing sector. Another issue facing Kamaria in trade agreements was the general lack of control they exerted over intellectual property, which was a concern to Western companies across a diverse set of industries, from entertainment and electronics to consumer goods and pharmaceuticals.

Laurent Pharmaceuticals was originally founded in the late 18th century as the first compounding pharmacies were beginning to appear throughout Europe. During the 19th century, Jean-Philippe Laurent inherited the firm and under his leadership, the company expanded into industrial manufacturing of chemical agents and early forms of pharmaceutical products. Though business suffered during the turbulent first half of the 20th century, Laurent recovered and became one of the first manufacturers of antibiotics, developing into one of the leading manufacturers of antibiotics and vaccines in the world by the 1970s. Today, they have evolved into a multinational, research-driven pharmaceutical and chemical company with operations in over 40 countries, including the United States, the UK, the EU, Australia, and dozens of emerging and developing nations. Producing and selling prescription medications for a variety of indications, as well as over-the-counter medications and personal care products, Laurent Pharmaceuticals is now one of the largest pharmaceutical companies in the world, earning $42 billion in revenues worldwide in 2008.

Growing a Business

In 1988 Ajith began his career in marketing, working for a large multinational firm in his home region of South Asia. After moving to Laurent Pharmaceuticals in 2000, he accepted several international posts, which took him to the Middle East and east Africa. Working in these challenging markets honed his talent for management of in-country operations in developing countries, attracting the attention of Laurent's regional management in Southeast Asia. In 2008, Ajith was recruited to serve as Director of Operations for Laurent's business in Kamaria.

Initially, Ajith managed Laurent's operations in Kamaria from Singapore, introducing over-the-counter medications and personal care products. In a short period of time, Laurent achieved a 50% market share in the lucrative pain relief market in Kamaria on the strength of its huge Theradil brand, an over-the-counter analgesic, creating a small but profitable (approximately $60,000 USD annually) operation. The next step in growing Laurent's Kamarian business was to enter the pharmaceutical market. To facilitate this new venture, Ajith was tasked with starting up a local office in Kamaria:

> Basically, when I went down to Kamaria, my first task, besides setting up the office, was to try and meet with the ministry of health officials and prepare all the registration files for all the vaccines that we needed to register and all the antibiotics we needed to register and accelerate the registration process.

> By about mid-2006, we had set up operations and we had started building a small team. We had probably about 15 to 20 medical delegates on board now, who were mostly qualified doctors—medical doctors—who were on the team as medical delegates. The pay that they were getting in government hospitals was pretty low, and I think that they saw this as an attractive option for them.

At the time, doctors in the state-run hospitals in Kamaria could expect to make approximately $30 USD per month. Ajith noted, "I think they were all finding it quite difficult to exist with that income." Doctors who became medical delegates to international pharmaceutical companies like Laurent could expect to start at $70-$100 USD per month, and could potentially earn as much as $200 a month if they were successful. "They had to make a call at that time," Ajith said, "and make a decision as to what they wanted to do." Doctors could not work for the hospitals and the pharmaceutical companies at the same time, "but they had the option of moving out anytime they wanted back into being doctors, and some of them saw this as a short-term measure to collect some cash."

By the time Laurent Pharmaceuticals entered the Kamarian market, there were already approximately 30 competitors operating in Kamaria, including companies based in the United States, Europe, South Korea, and

India, along with many local firms. "The Korean and Indian companies all had similar portfolios in terms of products to what we had. There were also Kamarian competitors, but very much in the lower-end product categories, like over-the-counter medicines, not in the high-end vaccine and antibiotics businesses." Though competition was healthy, the market was booming.

In part, this rapidly growing market was fueled by growing health concerns in Kamaria, as Ajith explains:

> There were two major health issues in Kamaria at the time. The first one was Hepatitis B. Hepatitis B in Kamaria has almost a 10% carrier rate, which means 1 in 10 Kamarians are prone to Hepatitis B. And the second big issue that was rising rapidly in Kamaria was resistance to antibiotics. Antibiotic resistance had now reached close to 18%, which meant that lots of frontline antibiotics were no longer effective amongst close to 20% of Kamaria's population. So most of the drugs that we were trying to register were high-end vaccines for Hepatitis B and also the better antibiotics that we had in our portfolio, because Laurent has always been a world leader in both vaccines and in antibiotics and continues that leadership today. So we knew the need was there, we knew the consumer problem was there, and we also knew that our products were significantly superior in delivering the remedial action compared to the drugs that were getting registered.

Pharmacists, Ajith noted, were a key population that Laurent needed to reach in order to make any progress against antibiotic resistance. "I don't think too many Kamarian pharmacists know what it is to deliver a prescription and not under-deliver a prescription, and also educate consumers of the need for giving the full antibiotic dose as opposed to under-dosing themselves."

It would not be possible for Ajith to undertake such a marketing campaign himself until he was able to convince the Kamarian government to issue registrations for Laurent Pharmaceuticals products:

> We were quite perturbed because it had taken close to one year that we'd been there, and we were struggling to get anywhere with registrations. It was becoming more and more clear that if we needed registrations that we had to be ready to compromise, and that the Korean companies were compromising, and the Indian companies were compromising, and some of the other European companies were compromising.

Compromising was not an acceptable solution for Ajith, however:

> It was extremely clear to me that that was not an option for us to even consider. That was a very clear integrated policy in the company and we practiced that in almost every market where we operated. However, I must mention that if left up to some of the managers, they would also compromise. Now for example, at the time I was running Kamaria for Laurent, the guy who was running [a major competitor] was compromising. So having an integrity principle is one thing, but deciding whether to practice it or not, depending on the pressure you are getting from the company, is another thing. I can tell you that I was getting quite a lot of pressure from my regional head and from the global operations people because they were seeing very little progress in growing the Kamaria business.

At the same time, problems were brewing in the previously robust over-the-counter business that Laurent Pharmaceuticals was operating in Kamaria.

> We realized that sales of our brand of pain reliever, Theradil, were beginning to crash down rapidly. We had probably about 50% of the market in Kamaria for pain relievers, and we were suddenly seeing a massive decline from a 50–55% share down to about a 30% share, and when we began to investigate this further, we found that there were close to 12 brands of fake imitation Theradil in our market.

Testing of samples of the fake Theradil products revealed that consumers who purchased these brands were being seriously underdosed—at best, the imitation pain relievers contained 72% of the minimum standard dose of the active ingredient, with the most inferior substitutes containing just 36% of the standard dose.

To address the imitation Theradil problem, Ajith hired a law firm to investigate these issues and made a disquieting discovery.

> Almost all the 11 fake Theradils that were available in different parts of Kamaria were manufactured by factories formerly owned by the Kamarian government which were run by the then-generals of the Kamarian army. These generals had been given a pharmaceutical factory each, as compensation or recognition of their great contribution to the success of the Kamarian war at the time. In different parts of Kamaria, each of these guys had their little companies and it doesn't cost much to get a printer and develop your own artwork ripping off the competition.

With their government connections, Ajith knew that it would be difficult to put pressure on these factory owners to shut down their operations, particularly since, as Ajith observes, they made no attempt to hide what they were doing.

Most of these companies were putting their factory addresses at the bottom of the pack. The detectives didn't have to do too much detection to figure out what was happening, because this was reasonably flagrant violation. Anyway, they probably knew that they were sort of above the law at the time and could get away with it, so they probably didn't worry too much about that.

By the time Ajith uncovered the extent of the Theradil problem, eight submissions of registration paperwork to the ministry of health for Laurent antibiotics and vaccines had now been missed. "We were now having a sales decline in our base business, and not having the opportunity to grow the potential business, and that was very much the situation we were in," Ajith recalled.

Developing Relationships

In the course of launching the office in Kamaria in 2008, Ajith had recruited a dedicated local management team. This team oversaw the staff of doctors and supervised all other aspects of day-to-day operations of Laurent in Kamaria. Ajith's commitment to accountability and transparency in his organization were inspirational to his staff. Determined to fit in with his staff, Ajith began learning the Kamarian language, and only stopped conducting meetings in Kamarian when his staff expressed their desire to practice their English with him instead. He also plied his team for their expertise on a wide range of issues involving local customs and traditions, gaining insight into the tightly knit culture of Kamaria. This expertise helped shape the vision Ajith was forming of what Laurent could offer the Kamarian consumer once the pharmaceutical registrations were approved.

At the same time, Ajith had been working closely with the French embassy in Kamaria as

Laurent's operations were ramping up. In recent discussions with embassy officials, Ajith observed that the upcoming trade negotiations were a frequent topic of speculation, with strong opinions on all sides of the debate. Some embassy officials felt that the government of Kamaria was simply too corrupt to be considered a good free trade partner. Others saw great potential in Kamaria, and supported Europe's participation in free trade agreements with Kamaria, but worried about the weak protections in Kamaria for intellectual property. Still others advocated for totally open trade, arguing that once Kamaria entered the global market, market forces would require the government to behave differently or risk losing their lucrative export position.

Taking Action

Ajith sat at his desk and pondered his options. He did not want to compromise, but unless he took some action, he knew that his management would give up on Kamaria and he would have to leave. In fact, some members of his legal team went so far as to suggest that it would be in his best interest to leave Kamaria, due to concerns about the reaction from the powerful factory owners about the investigations into the production of imitation Theradil. But Ajith was not willing to give up quite so easily. He knew that Laurent's products, particularly the vaccines and antibiotics, could make a real, long-term difference in addressing the growing health concerns for the people of Kamaria, and this motivated him to pursue a creative solution. Surely there was a path forward that did not involve either compromising or turning a blind eye to illegal competition, and Ajith felt that he was up to the challenge.

What resources could he use to motivate the Kamarian government to review his submissions and issue registrations? Who were the stakeholders that Ajith needed to involve? What levers could he use to address the growing problem with fake Theradil? And how could he address these issues without compromising his values and the values of his company?

Last Revision: 9/3/14

Note

1. This case was prepared by Heather Bodman under the supervision of Professor Cynthia Ingols of Simmons University School of Management. This case was inspired by interviews and observations of actual experiences but names and other situational details have been changed for confidentiality and teaching purposes.

Case Study 4

Diego Curtiz at Highland State University

Paul S. Myers

Director of Research & Consulting,
Digital Academicx and Adjunct Professor,
Simmons School of Management

W atching the mid-winter snow fall outside his office window, Diego Curtiz could not stop thinking about what his boss Lisa Tainer had just told him: "You have *got* to get Ken on board. If he continues to challenge the team at every turn, he could blow-up the SSA project." A high priority initiative for one of the U.S's largest public universities, the SSA project involved implementing a new campus-wide student advising system. The change included not only introducing a new technology but also new processes for delivering and managing student advising. Campus administrative and academic leaders expected the SSA system to reduce costs, increase tuition revenue, and improve student retention.

Curtiz had been the SSA project leader since its early planning stage began eighteen months earlier. Until now, he had many reasons to believe things had been progressing smoothly and that the necessary technical and behavioral changes would be implemented on schedule. He felt bewildered by what Tainer told him. Certainly, she could not expect him *to force* Ken

Cullen to accept the project plan. What was Curtiz supposed to do?

IT Projects at Highland State University

Curtiz was one of seven project managers in the Office of Information Technology's project office (PO) led by Associate Director Lisa Tainer (Exhibit 1). Their role at Highland State University (HSU) was to plan, coordinate, and control the process for building new IT services. Curtiz joined the group as a project analyst four years earlier after spending two years as a software developer in the private sector and then earning an MBA at HSU. Over time, Tainer gave him additional responsibilities that included overseeing smaller projects and supervising a PO assistant and two part-time student employees. He had recently earned project management certification, a highly valued credential and a prerequisite at HSU to lead larger projects. As a result, in April 2012 Curtiz received a promotion to project manager, a role referred to at

HSU as the "project lead." His duties now included negotiating task assignments, facilitating team work, and communicating with project stakeholders. Project leads managed up to six projects concurrently.

Tainer reported to Chad Simon, the director of the Enterprise Systems Group that had responsibility for all campus-wide administrative systems including PeopleSoft (for human resources management) and COGNOS (for financial reporting). Associate Director Stefan Flahive ran the Systems Engineering (SE) group with its twelve analysts and developers and reported to Simon. Each IT project paired a technical lead from Flahive's group with a project lead from Tainer's. While the project lead was accountable for keeping a project on time and within budget and scope, he or she depended on the technical lead for expertise and guidance on what needed to be done and the amount of resources required. Project leads typically had no formal authority over team members and relied instead on building trustful relationships.

Implementing the SSA System

The first of five projects assigned to Curtiz was "SSA", a new system to support student advising. Its capabilities included scheduling advising sessions, predicting when a student may be at risk for failing a course, and monitoring student progress toward a degree. SSA was to replace a hodgepodge of separate and much more limited tools used by each of HSU's eight schools and colleges. Almost all of HSU's peers among large state universities were using SSA to improve retention rates through early intervention to those needing academic or other assistance. A first-year student at HSU who failed to return for her sophomore year represented an average total loss of more than $60,000 in tuition and fees. Each percentage decrease in the dropout rate would net an estimated $3,000,000 annually. The university also expected that moving to a

centralized advising system would achieve cost savings by eliminating redundancies and creating efficiencies.

Curtiz had coordinated the year-long work of a planning committee comprised of faculty, student advising staff and senior academic administrators including associate and assistant deans. Committee members represented various stakeholders with different priorities and concerns given how they expected to use the new system to support their respective roles in the advising process. The SSA project's technical lead was Megan Jacobs, who with nearly three decades' experience at HSU was SE's most senior system analyst. She attended the SSA committee meetings to observe and provide expertise as needed. Ken Cullen, communication and training manager, also attended the meetings. His role included providing updates and other information about the new advising system to faculty, staff, and students. In addition to e-mail, Web posts and social media messages, Cullen met frequently with individuals and groups throughout the campus.

After lengthy and often heated discussions, the committee agreed on what the system should be able to do, how it would be used, and the implementation approach. The provost set a budget for the project accordingly and advised that no additional funds would be available. When asked for feedback on the planning process, committee member opinions were split; slightly more than half regarded it as one of the best group experiences of their careers, while the others found it far too contentious. Several comments specifically praised Jacob's contributions as constructive, respectful, objective, and jargon-free.

The committee established an aggressive timeline for the project and expected the system to be in operation by the start of the 2014–2015 academic year. With less than eighteen months to implement the system, Tainer asked Curtiz to apply leading-edge project management practices for rapid technology development and deployment. These included the use of cross-functional development teams, short-cycle iterations of work that incorporate customer feedback and daily in-person status update meetings, which were conducted standing up to keep them brief. Many of these techniques were new to HSU and required project team members to work in new ways both individually and as a group. Tainer and Flahive each led one two-hour meeting of their respective staff members to discuss the new rapid-development approach.

These adjustments notwithstanding, by the halfway point of the schedule the project had achieved every milestone and was on track to meet the deadline. With just under eight months to go, almost all of the technical pieces were in place. Importing the massive databases of student and course information remained, and the project team was working closely with the registrar's office to complete the associated tasks. The other significant deliverables yet to be finished included documentation on how to use the system and learning materials for workshops set to begin in mid-June. Cullen and his communication and training team had responsibility for this portion of the project. Although according to the project plan that work should already have been underway, Cullen insisted on waiting until Jacobs's group completed its tasks before starting to create any documentation or other materials.

The Project Team at Work

The SSA project launch went smoothly after Curtiz had developed the full project plan, assembled the team, and assigned tasks. All team members had attended training provided by SSA's vendor at the start of the project and were fully knowledgeable about its functionality and use. At regular project review meetings both Tainer and Flahive expressed support for how the project was proceeding and often noted Curtiz's careful attention to detail, timely communication, and decisiveness. Simon seemed pleased with the monthly briefings on SSA that Tainer and Flahive provided and left project-related decisions to them. At the end of one such update, though, he inquired whether they knew of any tension among project team members. He had recently received an anonymous note that said, in part:

> I don't know what you've been told about the SSA project, but someone needs to rein in Ken Cullen. He won't stop sticking his fingers into everything we do. He is supposed to inform the campus about the project status, but instead he's always questioning our decisions on everything. Last week, all of the sudden he starts ranting about how there should be fewer features and options and the user interface should be simpler. These decisions have already been made!! He thinks he's so charming, but half the time he doesn't know what he's talking about.

Tainer responded that Curtiz had mentioned disagreements at team meetings that seemed to make some attendees uncomfortable. She trusted his ability to work out any conflict and was not concerned given that to date the project was on time and on budget. Flahive said he thought Jacobs uncharacteristically had returned from some SSA meetings agitated, but had not spoken to her about it.

Immediately following that conversation, Tainer called Curtiz into her office to find out what was going on. He acknowledged some tension between Jacobs and Cullen, which he attributed to sincere differences about what was best for the project. Cullen also had challenged other members of the team occasionally and had even questioned Curtiz's decisions, once in front of the entire team. Cullen usually said he was just passing along suggestions and concerns he had heard from prospective SSA users. Still, Curtiz was taken aback to learn about the note Chad Simon had received:

It had to be Megan. I don't understand why someone would go behind my back and skip two levels to complain to the Director, let alone do so anonymously. No one is out of control; I think conflict and disagreements are normal and can lead to better decisions. If you're looking for something that needs attention, Stefan is the one always trying to micro-manage the project. One day it's "Do it this way, the deans want it". The next it's "No, Megan tells me it can't be done, so forget about it." Maybe you should talk to him.

Tainer knew Flahive typically provided his staff with much more direction than she gave to hers, but Simon seemed to favor Flahive and Simon's staff loved working for him. She said she would consider speaking to her peer, but for now thought it would be better for Curtiz to deal with Cullen: "You have *got* to get Ken on board. If he continues to challenge the team at every turn, he could blow-up the SSA project."

Curtiz walked back to his office and started to question his view of how the project was going. He rarely lacked confidence, but now felt uncertain about his abilities. Had he misinterpreted Cullen's behavior? Had he offended Jacobs somehow, perhaps by not giving her views enough weight? Was he misjudging how well the project was going? He slumped in his chair and watched the snow fall as he pondered his next steps.

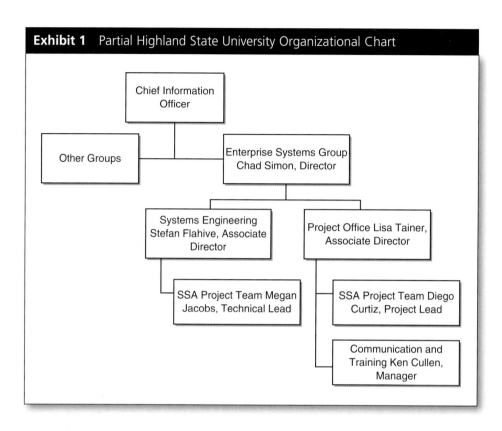

Exhibit 1 Partial Highland State University Organizational Chart

Case Study 5

Ellen Zane—Leading Change at Tufts/NEMC

Cynthia Ingols

Lisa Brem

Simmons College School of Management
Boston

It was a difficult decision to take this job. But there was something about the history of Tufts-NEMC and its importance to so many stakeholders that really grabbed me as the epitome of what one could do in one's career. I'd also learned not to be adverse to risks. You have to take risks, not stupid risks, but you have to take risks.

— Ellen Zane, CEO, Tufts-NEMC

Ellen Zane brought a cup of coffee into her home office. It was 4:30 a.m. and she was, as usual, starting the day early. She fired off a few e-mails to her senior staff and looked over the *Women's Business* magazine on her desk. Her photograph was on the cover, highlighting the article on the turnaround she was attempting to execute at Tufts-New England

Medical Center (Tufts-NEMC). It was the summer of 2006 and it had been an incredibly rough two-and-a-half years since she accepted the CEO position at the ailing Boston hospital. Since then the hospital had survived the worst of its financial troubles—they were meeting efficiency goals and for the first time in years, more doctors joined the hospital than left it. Tufts-NEMC posted an $18 million gain in 2005, after losing nearly $60 million since 2001 (see **Exhibit 1** for financial statements). People were smiling and thanking Zane in the corridors.

But that was a piece of the problem. This was the tricky part, she thought, in one of her rare moments of quiet as the predawn light slowly infused the room. Zane realized that she was still deeply worried about the future:

This place was just so fragile and I still consider it fragile. It's one month forward and one month back. This market is unforgiving and tough—I swim with the

Source: From Linda E. Swayne, W. Jack Duncan & Peter M. Ginter. *Strategic Management of Health Care Organizations.* Jossey-Bass. 2008.

449

sharks and nobody glad-hands us. I tell the staff all the time—not a minute do we take our foot off the gas.

Zane struggled with how to maintain the solidarity that the financial crisis had created among Tufts-NEMC's 5,000 employees.[1] She knew from her 30 years of experience in hospital management that sustaining change in Boston's cutthroat medical industry was the hardest part of any turnaround. She had been successful before with Quincy Hospital, but Quincy had been a much smaller player. Tufts-NEMC was a 450-bed Academic Medical Center (AMC) that was the primary teaching site for Tufts University School of Medicine, and conducted over $50 million in research each year. It had 17,000 admissions in 2005 and generated $600 million in revenue. Unfortunately, while Boston's other AMCs merged, built networks, and grew stronger, Tufts-NEMC had for years floundered directionless in Boston's rough seas. As Zane headed to her office overlooking Boston's Chinatown she wondered: How could she create and sustain true and lasting change for Tufts-NEMC?

The Health Care Industry in Boston

"Health care, together with education and computer technology, is what Massachusetts is known for throughout the world."[2]

Home to several high-profile Academic Medical Centers, the Boston area was a world-renowned destination for health care services. Massachusetts General Hospital (MGH), Brigham and Women's Hospital (BWH), and Beth Israel/Deaconess Medical Center were affiliated with Harvard Medical School, Boston University Medical Center with Boston University, and Tufts-New England Medical Center with Tufts. These large AMCs led the way in capturing $2.3 billion in National

Institutes of Health (NIH) research grant money, second only to California. Massachusetts hospitals employed 12.2% of the total labor pool, and accounted for a whopping 11.7% of the gross state product. Health care expenditures per capita were between 27% and 29% higher than the national average from 1990 to 2000 (see **Exhibits 2–9** for Massachusetts health care statistics). Consumers, health plans, and governing bodies tended to accept that heath care in Boston costs more in accordance with the high quality and cutting-edge services the region provided.

Nationally, however, years of underfunding by federal and state governments and rising enrollment left Medicare and Medicaid payments lagging behind surging medical costs. Hospitals in Massachusetts and the rest of the nation amassed significant debt in the 1970s and 1980s as they refurbished older facilities, expanded services, and purchased expensive new technologies. While reimbursements fell behind rising costs, hospital discharges declined sharply in the 1980s, as did the average length of stay. In Massachusetts, a decrease in hospital births and nonresident discharges[3] led to an overall decline of 24% in total hospital discharges from 1991 to 1996. The increase in outpatient surgeries also affected hospitalizations.[4]

Throughout the 1990s, Massachusetts health care insurance plans followed nationwide trends when they merged into three large competitors: Harvard Pilgrim Health Care, Blue Cross/Blue Shield of Massachusetts, and Tufts Health Plan. These "big three" plans wielded increasing power in the marketplace, and their movement to managed health (HMO) plans resulted in lower payments to providers[5] and more oversight on costs and medical services. All three expanded regionally, to entice large regional and national companies to offer their plans to employees. HMOs used capitated payments, meaning they reimbursed providers based on the number of "covered lives" in the provider system. Thus, providers of health care services such as hospitals and doctors believed volume and efficiency of services to be the most important factors in future financial success.

In 1991 Massachusetts deregulated hospitals for the first time in ten years. These conditions succeeded in making an impact—threatening the financial viability of hospitals and moving them toward more efficient and cost effective management practices. Boston's health care leaders struggled for a strategy to survive in the new environment. Mergers, closures, and conversions loomed.

The leaders of MGH and BWH made the first decisive move. Managers at both hospitals believed they needed additional leverage to hold their own in negotiations with the ever more powerful health insurance plans. They also envisioned building a network of community primary care and specialist providers who would refer tertiary[6] patients to the member hospitals, thus bolstering volume. In 1994, when the news of the merger of these two behemoths—forming Partner's Healthcare System, Inc. (Partner's)—became public, it was a seismic change in the landscape of the New England medical industry. Others quickly followed suit. From 1990 to 2000, there were 47 acquisitions and mergers and 19 acute care hospital closures, not including the formation of 10 major hospital systems in Massachusetts.[7]

Following the market consolidations in the 1990s, the turn of the twenty-first century years were difficult ones for Boston's hospitals and insurers. Both Harvard Pilgrim and Tufts Health Plans were hindered by regional over-expansion. In 1999, Harvard Pilgrim went into receivership after posting a $226 million loss, while Tufts Health Plan lost $42 million. Community hospitals also continued to struggle from high debt, inadequate reimbursements, high labor and pharmaceutical costs, and failed merger or network integration attempts. In Massachusetts particularly, consumers began to migrate to the more expensive AMCs from the smaller regional or community hospitals, seeking what they perceived to be higher quality of care. Cuts in payments from Medicaid, Medicare, and private insurance plans continued to plague many providers. To encourage more efficient management and cost containment practices among its providers, HMOs started to move away from capitated care and toward pay-for-performance plans.

Even some AMCs felt the pressure on their organizations. CareGroup—another Massachusetts-based hospital umbrella organization—posted a loss of $215 million over 1999 and 2000 and lost market share and network physicians. Partners, however, grew and remained strong, reaching 5,600 doctors in its Partner's Healthcare System, Inc. (PCHI) network. In a seminal flexing of its market strength, Partner's negotiated up to 30% increases from all three major health plans, at one point refusing to continue a contract with Tufts Health Plan until it agreed to higher payments.[8]

By 2005, the provider market was dominated by four major hospital systems: Partners, reporting a surplus of $30 million; Caritas Christi; CareGroup (which had decentralized most of its operations back to its member hospitals); and Boston Medical Center. See **Exhibit 10** for provider descriptions. When the dust settled on the consolidation activity, there were approximately 25 acute care, five psychiatric, and five rehabilitation hospitals in the metropolitan Boston area, with Partners leading in market share.[9] On the insurer's side, the major health plans recovered, with Blue Cross/Blue Shield of Massachusetts coming out on top, Harvard Pilgrim regaining strength, and Tufts maintaining a third position.

According to one survey of the Boston health care industry, trends through 2005 were:

- AMCs faced lack of capacity from years of merging and downsizing, while admissions moved to AMCs from community hospitals;
- pay-for-performance (quality incentive) programs were gaining in popularity, using measures such as cost, efficiency, IT capacity, admission rates, and patient satisfaction to bolster reimbursements;

- hospitals struggled to recruit new doctors and nurses, with AMCs poaching from each other;
- nationally, the growing number of uninsured and underinsured people increased the amount of bad debt hospitals carried. Although mitigated in Massachusetts by strong safety net programs, collections were still a rising concern.[10]

History of Tufts-NEMC[11]

New England Medical Center, originally the Boston Dispensary, was one of the oldest hospitals in the United States. Started in 1796 by the philanthropic activities of historical Boston figures Samuel Adams and Paul Revere, the Boston Dispensary was the first permanent medical facility in New England. First envisioned as a community medical service for the poor, the hospital quickly gained a reputation for innovation. It was the first U.S. hospital to assign nurses to patients, to form a visiting nurse association, and establish dental, rehabilitation, venereal disease, lung, food and nutrition, and evening pay clinics. It pioneered employer-paid clinic treatment, well-child services, and moving x-rays. The first modern test for syphilis, the first group psychotherapy experiment, the first human growth hormone, and immuno-suppression therapies were developed at the Boston Dispensary. In 1929 New England Medical Center was formed by the merger of the Dispensary and Tufts College Medical and Dental Schools. By 1965, it added the Floating Hospital and the Pratt Diagnostic Clinic–New England Center Hospital.[12]

In recent years, the tradition of innovation continued, with strong programs in cancer treatment, transplants, and neurosurgery. In 1992, with the addition of a maternity service, Tufts-NEMC became the first full-service, private teaching hospital in Boston. The Neely House, opened in 1997, was a unique bed and breakfast style home located within the hospital for cancer patients and their families. And in 2001, Tufts-NEMC opened a transplant exchange program, the first of its kind in the U.S. which allowed family members of transplant patients to donate kidneys to patients on the global waiting list, thus increasing the number of organs available for transplant.

Financially, however, Tufts-NEMC was struggling. Although in the 1990s the hospital had posted gains, it was largely due to a write-down in assets, and not improved efficiency or an enhanced revenue cycle. The hospital had fallen prey to the same negative market forces that had taken their toll on other non-affiliated hospitals in the 1990s. By 1996, it was $240 million in debt (up from $130 million in 1990) and was losing physicians, market share, and hospital acquisitions to Partners and CareGroup. Like many AMCs, Tufts-NEMC was slow to react to market pressures, and ineffective in improving processes and cash flow. In a particularly devastating blow to the hospital, Harvard Pilgrim Health Care discontinued coverage to Tufts-NEMC in 1995, citing high costs. As Zane explained:

> Harvard Pilgrim HC had taken Tufts-NEMC out of their network and it had almost killed the place. A doctor in Hyannis wants to send a patient to Boston. He or she has to ask "does this patient have Harvard Pilgrim?" The situation caused doctors to have to think too much about insurance. It was just easier to send everybody to the Brigham. So, for Tufts-NEMC, not being in that contract was incredibly hurtful.

The Lifespan Merger

In the mid-1990s, Tufts-NEMC began to actively look for a partner to remedy its fiscal dilemmas. It needed more clout against the health plans, more referrals from community hospitals, and a partner with deep enough pockets to help pay for growth to compete with Partners, Care-Group, and the other Boston systems. It was in talks with Columbia/HCA, a for-profit hospital chain from Tennessee that wanted to expand its presence in New England. If the merger went through, it would be the first AMC owned by a for-profit company in New England. This did not sit well with some of the board members, faculty, and community, who strongly wanted to preserve Tufts-NEMC's non-profit nature.

In late 1996, the hospital was treating a high-ranking official from the Lifespan Corporation, a regional non-profit hospital system formed in 1994 with a merger of the Miriam and Rhode Island hospitals.[13] One of Tufts-NEMC's physicians explained the hospital's dilemma and talks began between Lifespan and Tufts-NEMC to merge. Tufts-NEMC leadership saw benefits to joining with Lifespan, such as needed capital, a chance to gain back the Harvard Pilgrim Health Care contract, and the potential referrals from the Rhode Island system. On Lifespan's side, Tufts-NEMC was enticing for its status as an AMC, its base in Boston, and its expertise in high-level care. The merger would create, as one journal wrote, "a $1.5 billion, 14,500-employee health care giant with the ability to serve 70 percent of the entire New England market" and would rival the $1.8 billion Partners system and $1.1 billion CareGroup.[14] In January 1997, Tufts-NEMC and Lifespan officially announced the merger, which became effective in November of that year. Ed Schottland, Senior Vice President–System Integration at Lifespan and appointed COO at Tufts-NEMC at the time of the merger, explained:

> Lifespan was interested in Tufts-NEMC because it gave them instant access into Boston and made them the regional system they wanted to be. The plan was to create Lifespan of Rhode Island and Lifespan of Massachusetts—of which Tufts-NEMC would be the hub—both overseen by an overarching corporation.

Tufts-NEMC is a tertiary and quaternary[15] medical center, we do bone marrow, solid organ transplants, and we have a neonatal intensive care unit. They didn't do any of those things in Rhode Island. The only BMT[16] program allowed in Rhode Island was at Roger Williams Hospital. So Lifespan got instant access to highest levels of care. The merger filled out the service complement with a high class, well respected organization with great outcomes and great medical care. Everyone assumed that we would be able to direct our patients here from Rhode Island. We would have a system of care, just as Partners was trying to do with their North Shore hospitals.

The marriage was not a happy one however—the hoped-for synergies never materialized. Rhode Island regulators objected to large amounts of capital migrating to Boston and required Lifespan to reduce the amount Tufts-NEMC was to receive to $8.7 million a year for 10 years, down from 30 years as originally planned. Although Harvard Pilgrim did eventually re-contract with Tufts-NEMC, some in the industry believed that legislation or litigation would have forced that outcome regardless. The referrals also did not pan out. As Schottland explained:

> Physicians make their own decisions about where they refer. Physicians like to refer primarily based on personal and professional relationships. A secondary reason they didn't refer to Tufts-NEMC was they felt that if they started to support a program here they might never get approval within the Lifespan system to get that program down in Rhode Island.
>
> This was a unique system since there were two medical schools—Brown and Tufts. The Brown faculty wanted to have the

programs, like bone marrow transplants, in Rhode Island. So there was a certain reluctance to cooperate at times.

Another problem with the merger was the "brain drain". Lifespan took many of the administrative and support functions out of Tufts-NEMC and centralized them in Rhode Island. Tufts-NEMC lost their human resource, finance, purchasing/supply chain, and IT, an area where Tufts-NEMC had been groundbreaking in the past. The anticipated growth in acquisitions also failed to take place. Hospitals that had previously affiliated with Tufts-NEMC, such as Faulkner, another Tufts Medical School teaching site, joined Partners instead, while Tufts-NEMC was busy finalizing its merger with Lifespan. In 2000, Lifespan/Tufts-NEMC also lost Hallmark Health System in Malden. As one industry journal wrote:

> Every time a decision had to be made, Tufts-NEMC President and Chief Executive Officer Tom O'Donnell, M.D., traveled 55 miles across the state line to Providence, R.I. There he conferred with the 21-member board of his parent system, Lifespan Corp. He would return to meet with his own 21-member board, then respond to Hallmark. [...] The extra corporate layer proved to be too much. Hallmark, at the time a four-hospital system, walked away from the deal.[17]

Adding insult to injury, Quincy (Mass.) Medical Center and MetroWest Medical Center spurned Tufts-NEMC, citing that the "local hospitals did not think of Tufts-NEMC as a Massachusetts hospital."[18]

But perhaps the worst thing about the merger was that insurance contracting was done in Rhode Island. Lifespan did not understand the cost of doing business in the Boston market and therefore settled for reimbursement rates far below the average for an AMC

in Boston. Lifespan, struggling to keep control of five acute-care hospitals, suffered an operational loss of $34.1 million on total revenue of $1.3 billion ending fiscal year 2001. Zane explained her take on the Lifespan merger:

> When Partners came together it freaked out the whole market and everybody was looking for a partner. Long story short, Tufts-NEMC hooked up with the Lifespan system in Rhode Island. I could not understand why they did it. It was an ill fated, ill conceived, ill constructed, and ill-implemented merger and it had no meat on the bone. The health care market in Rhode Island might as well have been Siberia it was so different from eastern Mass.

In the summer of 2002, five years after they merged, both Lifespan and Tufts-NEMC agreed to separate at a cost of $30 million to Tufts-NEMC. Financial results for Tufts-NEMC for fiscal year 2002 were dismal—a loss of $12.3 million on revenue of $476 million; and 2003 was looking worse—a loss of $38.5 million on revenue of $582 million. The Massachusetts Attorney General's office stepped in to ensure that the hospital would meet bond covenants. O'Donnell and the chairman of Tufts-NEMC's board called Ed Schottland and enticed him to come back as COO. Schottland took the job and set about recreating the administrative departments lost in the merger. He also started initiatives to stem the millions of dollars that Tufts-NEMC was losing monthly. Schottland targeted improvements of $30 million in cost savings in the supply chain and human resources. He began a year of initiatives designed to improve the bottom line. In the first nine months of 2003, Tufts-NEMC reduced staffing levels by 200 FTEs through attrition and consolidation and made improvements in supplier contracts. The hospital also began to look at selling some of its 1.5 million square feet of prime real estate to gain needed capital. The Board, meanwhile, set about looking for a leader who could take Tufts-NEMC out of the shadow of Lifespan and orchestrate a true turnaround.

Ellen Zane

Ellen Zane was educated at Waltham Public Schools, and later graduated from George Washington University and Catholic University in Washington, DC with masters in both audiology and speech language pathology. She spent her entire career in health care, starting in 1975 as a speech language pathologist at Lawrence (Massachusetts) General Hospital. In 1979 she took a job as director of speech and language pathology and audiology at Morton Hospital in Taunton. Under the mentorship of the COO of Morton, Zane worked her way up to vice president of professional services until taking the COO job at Quincy (Mass.) Hospital in 1987. When Quincy's CEO left in 1990, both Quincy's board and the city's mayor convinced Zane to take on the task of turning around the hospital, which was on the brink of closure. Like many community hospitals, Quincy had taken out bonds to renovate its ailing facilities. When the Medicaid/Medicare and HMO reimbursement rates lowered drastically, Quincy found it almost impossible to meet payroll and other expenses. Hampered by years of nepotistic and political hiring practices and high competition in the surrounding area, the hospital was in danger of defaulting on its bonds. Zane recalled her decision to take the job at Quincy as the most difficult in her career:

> It was the hardest decision I ever had to make, since I really felt that failure was not an option. Closing a hospital as the result of my first CEO job would have been awful. However, at the same time, women weren't getting CEO jobs. I needed an underdog job to try to prove

myself, since it wasn't likely that a woman was going to get a job at what I called a "Bloomingdale hospital"—Mt. Auburn, Newton, Wellesley, Beverly, or South Shore. Those weren't coming to women in those days. But the main reason I took the job was that I could see the steps it would take to fix it. When I had a very quiet, private conversation with myself, I knew that if I could figure out the road map of what to do, then I would just need the grit to do it. And I *could* see the way. So I jumped off a cliff and took the job. It was the best decision I ever made.

> From a grass roots point of view the opportunity I got at Quincy was the bedrock foundation to my management prowess. And it was really hard. It taught me not only the value of risk, but it taught me that if you took a job that no one else wanted to do because it was too hard, then all the benefits accrue back to you. If you are successful at it, you are only better because it was harder. All these good old boys with the cushy jobs around me at richer hospitals, I believe, aren't as good at managing simply because they didn't have to be.

Quincy was unique in that it was managed by HCA, a for-profit hospital management chain that owned and managed hospitals across the U.S. In addition, Quincy had a strong union and civil service workforce. Working for HCA honed her business acumen and decision-making abilities. Working with unions helped Zane understand the need for clear, open, and honest communication and financial transparency. As Zane recalled:

> I sat down with stewards of all the unions and showed them the financial statements and highlighted all the things I wanted them to learn, like days cash on hand and cash reserves. I taught them the meanings

of those things and explained that we had no money and that I was worried about meeting payroll. One of the biggest joys of my career came when I left Quincy hospital and met with the stewards for the last time and one union steward said to me: "How many days cash on hand do we have?" The fact that they had learned that and appreciated it taught me the value of transparency, the value of admitting that I needed help and I couldn't do it alone.

She also learned the importance of reaching out to the community. As Zane explained:

I got in my car and drove out to community doctors who weren't referring many patients to us. I asked them: "What would it take for you to use Quincy Hospital?" They said simple things like parking. All the construction had closed the parking lots. It was not that intellectually complex. The doctors also complained that employee work ethic was dismal. The employees didn't smile or pick up a candy wrapper off the floor. They treated the hospital as though it existed solely for them and their paychecks. They didn't believe the day of reckoning was coming. Hearing that from the community doctors was incredibly valuable for me.

After a successful run at Quincy, she was tapped in late 1993 for a groundbreaking job with the nascent Partners organization. As Zane recalled:

I got a call from Dr. H. Richard Nessen. He was the CEO of the Brigham and Women's Hospital. He told me they had just gotten permission from the Attorney General to merge the General [MGH] and the Brigham [BWH]. This was huge, giant, gargantuan news. He told me they wanted to build a vast network of physicians

throughout eastern Massachusetts and that he wanted me to come run it.

I told him I had no idea how to do that job, but he said that no one did, it was completely new. He said he needed a leader. He told me that he had academic physicians who were lining up at his door to do this job, but that he didn't want to give it to any of them. He felt that academics wouldn't understand community doctors or community hospitals, and would turn them off. He was right about that.

Zane was successful at building what came to be called PCHI,[19] Partners Community Healthcare, Inc. At Partners, she gained expertise at negotiating affiliation agreements with physicians and contracts with health plans, and with building consensus with disparate groups. Zane recalled her time at PCHI:

I went from this incredibly resource poor environment at Quincy, where I was plugging holes and trying to meet payroll, to this environment that was so resource rich. There were so many smart people around, but there was no trust between the Brigham [BWH] and the General [MGH] people, they were fierce competitors for years. So each committee had to have counterparts from each organization. Trying to develop a strategy in that environment was a challenge. The committees were made up of type A personalities who wanted me to build a network overnight. I felt this intense need to get the strategy going very, very quickly. So we spent the summer of 1994 building the strategy. The most incredible thing for me is, when I go and talk to investment bankers or health plans now, PCHI is all they talk about. PCHI was the most formidable market transforming activity other than the [MGH/BWH] merger itself. PCHI is the 800-pound gorilla in this market. And I knew it and started it before it even had a name. It was very rewarding, and very hard.

As Partners grew, so did their clout in the marketplace. Zane was the lead negotiator in the famous clash between Partners and Tufts Health Plan, which culminated when Partners decided to no longer accept Tufts subscribers due to the plan's low reimbursement rates. Her bargaining skills and strategic planning won the day for Partners. In the end Tufts agreed to substantial rate increases. After that encounter, Zane's reputation as a tough and savvy negotiator became legendary.

Zane Moves to Tufts-NEMC

In late 2003, after 10 years with Partners, Zane was thinking of slowing down. Her husband had sold his successful business and had retired and Zane was hoping to do the same. She was getting ready to give her notice at Partners when she received a call from Lawrence Bacow, the President of Tufts University. Bacow was on the board of Tufts-NEMC, which had recently decided to dissolve the merger with Lifespan. He was looking for a new leader for Tufts-NEMC, and felt that Zane had the right mix of skills to build and implement a successful strategy for the hospital. Met by her initial reluctance, Bacow reminded Zane of the hospital's historical significance, its importance for its 5,000 employees, Tufts University, and Chinatown's economy. Zane recalled her reaction after the meeting with Bacow:

There were two enormous feelings that came over me. One was on the positive side: wow this could really be important. To help this ailing organization means to really help a lot of people in their careers, their lives, the economy, and the

University. The other feeling was: this is so daunting—I'm frozen. It was so scary.

In July 2003, O'Donnell announced his resignation, clearing the way for Zane, the first non-physician and female permanent CEO in Tufts-NEMC's history. Reaction from both industry pundits and employees at Tufts-NEMC was uniformly positive. As one expert wrote:

At this time and in this place, there is no one better for the top job than Ellen Zane. The first non-physician chief executive, she comes onboard at a time when tough decisions need to be made. Yes, she has the necessary management skills, but she also has demonstrated a passionate commitment to preserving the relationship that exists between physicians and patients and between this hospital and the community it serves.[20]

John Greenwood, VP of Finance, explained some of the things he felt Zane brought to Tufts-NEMC:

We lost our identity during the Lifespan merger. We also lost touch with the Mayor's office and Beacon Hill,[21] and making sure our concerns were being heard. So when Ellen came on board, for the first few months we spent a lot of time on Beacon Hill. She brought visibility and a very recognizable name in the market.

Accountability was also a big leadership trait that came on board with Ellen. She and the consultants she brought in assisted the leadership in diagnosing what the issues and root causes were, as well as prioritizing them. Then she held someone accountable for fixing it. We'd done a lot of diagnosis before, so we had an idea of what the problems were, but Ellen provided the leadership to drive the projects to completion.

She also provided unity to the physicians throughout the hospital. There used to be two autonomous physician corporations with faculty/staff physicians. Both groups were completely separate. The first year she came, Ellen pursued merging the two boards into one entity and eventually made it happen. So now there is input and a synergy between the faculty at the hospital. They speak with one voice.

Michael Burke, senior vice president and CFO added:

Ellen is so acutely aware of what's going on in the market—she's been in this market her whole life, she built PCHI. She knows all the players. She knows whom to call and she has the personal relationships so that people are willing to work with her.

Ellen is also the kind of person who takes action. She gets 80–90% of the information she needs and then she does something. Most academic medical centers have what I call "analysis paralysis." You can accept the status quo, but the reality is things never stay the same—they either get better or they get worse. And if you are not actively working to improve them, they will get worse. This place was constantly assessing what to do, but not doing anything. And things got worse, year after year after year. Now what we're doing is assessing the data, assessing the market, and acting, and doing, and getting things done.

Diagnosis: Critical (2004)

When Zane came on board, she brought in a consulting group called BDC Advisors, Inc. They gathered data to determine why Tufts-NEMC was losing an estimated $3 million a month. Zane sat down with Schottland who gave her the bad news: Tufts-NEMC was not

losing $3 million a month; since the split with Lifespan the number was closer to $6 million. Zane recalled how the new reality changed her priorities:

Although I had done a fair bit of due diligence before taking the job, I was still shocked to find out that we didn't have two years of cash on hand: we had 10 months. So it changed everything overnight. Because strategy was the last thing I could worry about—I had to worry about payroll. This place was hemorrhaging millions every month. It was incredibly important to begin to think about how to stabilize.

Zane and BDC conducted what she called a "rapid diagnostic" to quickly determine how to stem the losses. BDC concluded that, although Tufts-NEMC was on the right path with Schottland's initiatives, they were still behind industry benchmarks for many areas, such as days in accounts receivable, accounts payable, average length of stay, operating margin, and days cash on hand. There was also more savings to be had in the supply chain (see **Exhibit 11** for BDC analysis). After reviewing the managed care contracts, Zane also realized that Tufts-NEMC was woefully underpaid.

Another challenge for Tufts-NEMC was its size. In any other market, Tufts-NEMC would be considered one of the biggest players. But in Boston, it was dwarfed by Partners, CareGroup, and Caritas. Tufts-NEMC fundraised $10 million in 2005, up from $5 million the year before but impossibly behind the $200 million Partners raised. Tufts-NEMC was the smallest teaching hospital in the Boston area, but it was the primary teaching site for Tufts Medical School and was the 11th highest paid in NIH research funding. Underwriting that research cost Tufts-NEMC $15 million a year. Maintaining the level of services and research required for a major medical center was extremely difficult for an organization without the volume of cases or endowments enjoyed by its competitors. Zane realized early on that however difficult it may be, it was absolutely crucial for Tufts-NEMC to remain an AMC:

> We made a conscious decision to keep funding research because we are an AMC with a tripartite mission, which includes clinical excellence, research and teaching. If you take one of the legs off that stool we are no longer an AMC and I would venture to say that no fewer than 80% of the doctors who practice here would leave. They are here because they want to work in an AMC.

Treatment (2004–2006)

Zane set to work on building her management team and reopening the managed care contracts. Along with Schottland and BDC, she pushed hard on cost-cutting and efficiency initiatives to bring Tufts-NEMC in line with industry best practices. Zane continued plans to sell real estate in order to get the hospital on some solid financial footing while giving these initiatives time to take hold. She also felt the need to re-establish Tufts-NEMC's brand in the Boston marketplace, to set about rebuilding affiliations and networks, to reverse the trend of hospitals' poaching Tufts-NEMC's physicians, and to retain the talent it had.

Staff Changes

Once Zane assessed the mission, she set about evaluating the senior staff. She greatly appreciated the experience and expertise of people like Shottland and Deeb Salem, Tufts-NEMC's chief physician. But others she felt needed to be replaced. Within two weeks she replaced the senior vice president of strategy with Deborah Joelson, a network-building expert who Zane

recruited from Partners; and the vice president of fundraising and development with Deb Taft, who had been extremely successful at the Dana Farber/Jimmy Fund. In all, she replaced seven members—half of the senior management team. Zane shared her thoughts on the senior staff turnover:

> One of the people I fired was a favorite of one of the board members. I spent a lot of time listening to that board member telling me that I had no right to fire his guy. But in the end he supported me. There was no question that I had to do it.

> If you ask most people about me they will tell you I'm very good at picking people. I really do believe that is a skill I have—it's gut level for me. I'd like to get credit for picking good people, not for a brilliant turnaround, strategies, or anything like that. I'm only as good as the people around me, and I do pick great people. I have a sixth sense. I can tell when I go into the waiting room for interviews whether they have a shot. For most of these characters here I knew it wasn't going to happen. There were a couple of other positions in the administrative round that I changed pretty fast. The COO Ed Schottland was very solid. He was only here about 9 months. He came from Lifespan and I am very grateful to this day that he was here and that he stayed. I would be toast without him.

Schottland added:

> It was chaos here before. I think it's easy to disrupt the COO's role, especially in an organization this size. People used to go around the COO to the CEO—it doesn't take long before you are neutralized.

> Ellen has been very supportive of my role. She'll either say: "you really have to talk to Ed about that" or she'll just have me in the

room when they talk to her. Now, most people in the organization don't attempt to go around me. I appreciate that . . . that's important to me. Ellen's let me continue to run the operations in an appropriate way. We understand our roles and we know when to ask each other for help and advice.

Deb Taft, the new vice president for fundraising and development, talked about why she joined Tufts-NEMC:

If I could be a part of creating a fundraising department that was vibrant and strong, this would be a career moment for me. I had people stopping me in the street saying, "I can't believe you are taking this job". But what greater thing could there be than helping this place survive? It deserves to be here. Keeping this place alive was important enough for Ellen Zane not to retire. Ellen recognized that I had what she called fire in the belly. That was her number one criteria in bringing me in.

Communication and Outreach

Ellen is a remarkable communicator of good news and bad news. She was somehow able to be fully transparent about what was going on and have people appreciate that she was being honest with them about the situation. And no one felt that they had to bail out of here because the place was going down the tubes. I don't know how she did that. —**Deborah Joelson,** senior vice president for market development and planning

Very early on, Zane led a series of "town meetings" where she presented financial facts, specifics on new initiatives, and areas targeted for growth. Because the hospital worked around the clock, Zane scheduled a series of meetings at

various times throughout the day and night, to ensure that everyone had a chance to attend. The meetings worked so well to disseminate information that Zane continued to do them twice per year on all shifts. She also augmented them with regular e-mails updating the staff and physicians on finances and other topics. As Deeb Salem, Tufts-NEMC's chief physician explained:

The things that she and Ed do are quite remarkable. Periodically they have town meetings for the entire staff. They go out of their way to talk to everybody, even the housekeeping staff. They have sessions in the middle of the night so they can talk to the night shift.

Taft agreed:

Ellen does the town meetings in every shift, and she wants the senior staff and VPs there because every shift matters. I've been at employee parties and holiday parties helping her serve dessert from midnight to two a.m., and we've brought desserts to the emergency department when they are so busy they can't get there. Ellen greets people and introduces herself and says "thanks for coming." That is a big thing for an employee who's never met the CEO. So the staff starts to feel like she belongs to them. She laughs and says she gets more e-mails from the staff than anybody. But the fact is, she does.

Zane explained what she saw as the benefits of the town meeting format:

I did a lot of town meetings. I was new. I had to get to know employees and I had to tell them what was going on. I put up this chart, which turned out to be a wonderful chart. It had all the losses this place experienced during the Lifespan era. The $40 million loss in 96, the $20 million loss in 97. Loss after loss after loss after loss. That adds up to $250 million. I threw the chart up at my first board meeting. I threw it up at the Board. And I said a lot of people have got egg on their face. That's what I said to my Board. I used the same chart with the employees.

Then after those town meetings—to my utter shock—I would come back to my office and I would have 20 e-mails from employees who had been sitting in the audience and they were saying thank you. It was so incredible. People would say: "I want to help. I knew something was wrong but no one was ever honest enough." It was really encouraging. And that was the pearl I learned—that you *can* tell people bad news. But you have to do it in such a way that you are viewed as being honest, open, credible, and consistent.

Zane explained that the culture of Tufts-NEMC made it easier for her to effect change:

The one thing about this place that is so fabulous—that I can take no credit for—is that it has a different, better, unique culture. I had been used to the Harvard culture where there was all this bravado and testiness. This culture is much warmer, much more collegial, much more cooperative. And I call it an "Avis—we try harder culture." I tell them: "Guys, we have to go left," and they say "ok." At Partners you'd need a committee and two years to get a decision. Maybe it's because this place is smaller, I don't know.

I've never, ever worked in a place, where employees who've been there for decades, physicians who've been here a long time, will spontaneously, unsolicited, come up to me and say "I love this place. And I'm sorry to see what's happened." Even physicians who have left—and it hemorrhaged doctors in the tough days—felt that way. I

called up a lot of them and asked them to have a cup of coffee with me and tell me why they left. All of them—to a person said—I didn't want to leave.

Zane used a variety of mediums to get the word out and to manage the turnaround effort. She held weekly senior staff meetings with Schottland, the general counsel, the CFO, the vice president of external affairs, the vice president of development, and the senior vice president for market development and planning. The focus of the meetings was mostly external, with Schottland providing updates on internal operations from his weekly meetings with the operational vice presidents, the CIO, the vice presidents of clinical services, and the vice president of human resources. Zane also met regularly with the board of trustees.

She reached out to physicians in an attempt to both spread her message for change and to retain them in the face of active poaching from other AMCs. She worked hard on both retention and recruitment. In 2005 she convinced three neurosurgeons to move from Beth Israel Deaconess Medical Center to expand Tufts-NEMC's minimally invasive neurosurgery department. Schottland described the outreach that he and Zane conducted to physicians:

When Ellen came, she came with the reputation, credibility, and ability to deliver a hopeful message that prompted people to change and gave them more hope.

One thing we've done since she came here that I've never done anywhere else, is spend an incredible amount of time talking to physicians, both recruiting and retaining them. Ellen leads that charge, although I spend a lot of time with her on it. It's one of our challenges being in Boston—it's so hard to recruit from out of town—and everyone is stealing from everyone else.

The neurosurgery department was a great example of an Ellen coup. She led the negotiations on recruiting those new doctors. Our group, which was split between Beth Israel and Tufts-NEMC, announced that they wanted to consolidate to a single hospital. We gave them a better deal and they are doing a great job here. They are young and aggressive—great surgeons. Ellen is very good at recruitment and retention. She knows it's important. You can't run a hospital without physicians and they are very expensive to replace. A lot of hospitals have recruitment and retention programs, but most times the doctors don't get to talk to the CEO. This is a smaller and friendlier place in a lot of ways. It's not hard to get to Ellen or me. For physicians, that's a big deal. To have access to Ellen in particular is enticing for them, and she's very good at talking to them.

Not only did Zane work with physician groups, she began a monthly tour of different wards in the hospital to get in touch with patients and nurses. Salem explained:

Once a month Ellen and I tour a ward together and she speaks to patients. She'll ask them: "How's Tufts-NEMC treating you? Why did you come here? What can we do better?" The patients who understand it are shocked that the CEO is talking to them. She also learns from the patients and the floor nurses. They see that she really cares because she'll walk around their floor. When she's done touring, she'll talk to the head nurse and say, "You guys are doing a great job."

When you talk to the patients yourself, you get a whole new feel for things. We found that a lot of people liked the intimacy at Tufts-NEMC as opposed to one of the larger hospitals like Children's. We're thinking about how to use that fact in our

marketing. Another thing we learned was that a lot of people didn't like the food here. So now the food service is working to change the whole menu.

Agenda for Change

In 2004, Zane, Shottland, and BDC initiated a second round of cost-cutting and efficiency plans designed to improve Tufts-NEMC's processes. It was called the Agenda for Change. Along with improving the reimbursements, it included restructuring, and basic "blocking and tackling" as Zane called it:

Blocking and tackling means the day-to-day gritty operations. The eight areas we wanted to improve were: length of stay, managed care contracts, accounts receivable, FTEs, supply chain, real estate, ambulatory clinics, and research costs. We focused really hard on those things. I think a lot of people in my job like the limelight—they want to give speeches. But the fact is if your house isn't in order, the limelight is fleeting. My first year here I resigned from most of my boards, backed off from a lot of things. I had to stick to my knitting. At the very beginning, I really hunkered down, and then I slowly started to come up for air.

The latter half of 2004 Joelson and Schottland, along with the vice president of human resources, and the director of business planning, developed a restructuring plan. The plan created eight product lines that were essentially business lines: cardiac, cancer, surgery, general medicine, transplant, OB/GYN, pediatrics, psychiatry, and neurosciences. Every service in the hospital was included in one of these product lines. This was different from the past, when some services were left out of the product lines. As Schottland explained:

It's very hard to be all things to all people. That is one of our greatest challenges programmatically and financially. But, because we are committed to doing that, we really can't afford to have key constituents feeling they are unimportant. We can't deliver care in transplants, for example, without infectious disease or internal medicine. The product lines here give everyone an opportunity to have a forum to talk about their programs. It is also a way to drive decision making down to the physicians and give people who deliver the service control of that service.

The chief of cardiology was the clinical head of the cardiac product line, for example. He partnered with a clinical vice president—an administrator. Together, they were responsible for developing and implementing annual business plans, with goals, objectives, and budgets for the product line. The CFO and COO approved the budgets every year and reviewed the business plans monthly. The business plans were the venues by which decisions were made on investments in staff, facilities, infrastructure, and technology. The plans directed decisions regarding whether, and how much, to grow and how to accomplish that growth. Some of the areas Tufts-NEMC hoped to grow were core services, such as cardiac and cancer programs, pediatrics and maternal health, psychiatry, bariatric/obesity surgery, and organ and bone marrow transplants.

Support services such as pharmacy, nursing units, and radiology, however, were outside the management structure of product lines. Schottland explained why:

A lot of hospitals have tried product lines in different ways. One way is the matrix structure that we have and the other way is a purer structure. We weren't big enough to be pure. We can't have a free-standing heart hospital or cancer center. We can't afford to never put a medical patient on the cardiac unit. If we don't have a cardiac patient we need that bed to put someone else in. We have to have the flexibility. So that's why the product lines can't control the nursing units. The head of cardiac would want to keep those beds just for cardiac patients and we can't afford to do that.

Length of Stay

On the operations side, one of the most important cost-saving initiatives was to reduce length of stay (LOS). The consultants that Zane brought in identified that Tufts-NEMC was keeping patients a day and a half too long, compared to other AMCs. David Fairchild, Tufts-NEMC's new chief of general medicine, chaired the 30-person Care Management Committee, which was charged with reducing LOS. Fairchild and his committee set about educating the staff about the importance of reducing LOS, changing attitudes about patient care, and attacking and identifying procedural failures called "unnecessary delays" in various ways:

- The team set up a special internal e-mail address—LOS delays—where staff could send a complaint or description of an unnecessary delay that impacted length of stay. This delivered useful information directly to hospital leadership regarding causes of delays.
- The BDC consultants identified areas where Tufts-NEMC could improve, such as use of tracheotomies and blood transfusions.
- Use of data, which drilled down to individual physicians' LOS statistics year over year, and presenting that feedback to physicians frequently.

One major issue that the e-mail address identified was the use of "PICC lines". PICC lines were more durable IV lines that allowed patients to continue their medication at home. Specially trained nurses had to insert the PICC lines, and many times the doctor discharged the patient too late in the day, and these nurses were not available. Another problem with

PICC lines arose when the nurse was unable to insert the line and needed fluoroscopy to aid the insertion. In the old system, the nurse informed the doctor that the PICC line was unsuccessful, then the doctor arranged for the patient to go to the fluoroscopy suite. Doctors conducted teaching rounds between 10:30 a.m. and 1 p.m., so if the nurse was unable to insert the PICC line, the patient often had to wait until the next day for the fluoroscopy suite to become available.

Fairchild and his committee came up with new procedures to remedy the situation. They required doctors to make decisions on discharges before they went on teaching rounds and they gave the nurses who inserted PICC lines the authorization to send patients directly to fluoroscopy if the PICC line could not be inserted by the nurse. Within a year of raising awareness and using more efficient procedures, the committee was able to reduce LOS by a full day, saving Tufts-NEMC $2 million per year. Fairchild explained how Zane's leadership helped with the LOS project:

> Ellen brought a sense of urgency. She and the consultants identified a few key initiatives. One was the contracting initiative that she was heading, and another was reduction in length of stay for hospitalized patients. Ellen brought a compelling vision supported by compelling data for where we needed to go. One of the most compelling pieces of data was a graph showing our LOS compared to all our competitor hospitals. We were an outlier, above the line by a day and half! A one-day reduction in the average length of stay across our hospital is worth millions of dollars. I took that graph around to every department meeting I attended. After that it was just a matter of identifying what was causing the delays. There was almost no resistance to changing procedures, since everyone understood that length of stay was crucial to

financial turn-around, and that financial improvement was the first step toward fulfilling the vision for the future of NEMC. That is where good leadership came in.

Contract Negotiations

The hospital had just completed a round of contract negotiations with insurers when Zane joined Tufts-NEMC. She realized how critical it would be to immediately increase rates, so she went to the major health plans and asked them to reopen negotiations. Zane discussed her talks with the insurance companies:

> Because I went toe-to-toe with the insurance companies when I was at Partners, I was afraid they would think "it's payback time" since I no longer had the same leverage. To my utter delight none of them did that. They all had the attitude that it wasn't personal, it was a business decision. My argument to them about why Tufts-NEMC should get higher rates was simple. I said to them, "look if you guys want the strong to get stronger and the weak to get weaker, then don't open these contracts. But if you want competition in this market, you need to open these contracts." And they did. It wasn't a cakewalk, they didn't just write me a check. We fought about it. But the truth is they all stepped up to the plate and I will always be grateful to Blue Cross, Harvard Pilgrim, and Tufts.

The improvements in the contracts were absolutely critical to the financial bottom line. As Shottland explained:

> After Ellen arrived, we discovered that we were getting paid really poorly. We improved our reimbursement by $20–$25 million. That was the missing piece. That's what brought us from where we were,

which was a $10 million loss, to actually making some money last year. That was Ellen's guidance and leadership that did that.

Network Building

Zane went to work bringing back the affiliations and networks Tufts-NEMC had lost in the past. By October of 2004 the hospital announced plans to affiliate with Children's Hospital in order to augment the services of the Floating Hospital for Children, which was fragile and had lost sufficient scale over many years of neglect and poor management. Zane was able to move quickly on affiliation agreements, not allowing deals to get bogged down in red tape. Deborah Joelson, senior vice president for market development and planning, related one example of this:

> One of the first things I had on my desk when I arrived here was an affiliation agreement with a community hospital. I finished negotiating the deal and went to Ellen and said, "Ok we have an agreement." She said "Great, let's do it." I said, "What, just sign it? No committees? No … nothing?" At Partners, an agreement like that would take months, if not years, if it were ever to get done, because of all the internal constituencies that needed to approve everything. It was just a lot more complicated. So I always laugh when I think that she said "just do it, trust your instincts and just go ahead." With the sense of urgency and lack of resources that we have here, we don't have the time to spend noodling over every little decision.

A year later, Tufts-NEMC won a major coup when they affiliated with Primary Care, LLC (PCLLC)[22] one of the state's oldest and largest primary care independent networks. The new network became part of Tufts-NEMC and was called New England Quality Care Alliance (NEQCA). Zane recruited Jeffrey Lasker, the former chairman of the Partners physician network to run it. PCLLC had for nine years negotiated contracts (a large percentage of which were Medicare risk products, such as Secure Horizons) for its 164 physicians, which served 500,000 patients. The group felt that they needed to become affiliated with an AMC and sent out a proposal request to systems in the Boston area. Joelson recalled how Tufts-NEMC closed that deal, when every other hospital was vying for the practice:

> We had almost no network, and few people to manage the network we had. We didn't have the infrastructure here to deal with payer contracts. That had been done at Lifespan. The PCLLC physicians wanted a seat at the table—that was most important to them. We saw an opportunity to integrate PCLLCs infrastructure into Tufts-NEMC, and not only give them a place at the table, but *make* them a table. We created an organization, NEQCA, that they ran, that provided something to Tufts-NEMC that we didn't have.

> This is also an example of where Ellen is so good. If you need her at a meeting she goes. We literally met every week for two months with PCLLC and Ellen was there every week to meet with them. Quite frankly I don't think many CEOs would have sat down once a week to make this happen. She is willing to get her hands dirty, but she's a leader when she does. She doesn't micro manage the process, but she makes herself available and it's clear to everyone that this is important and that it matters to her.

Working With Tufts University

Zane cultivated a close working relationship with Bacow and Michael Rosenblatt, the new dean of Tufts Medical School. She recognized the importance of the hospital and the University to each other. She sat on the board of overseers for the medical school and worked to build joint initiatives in research and fundraising. As Zane described:

It is very famous in AMC cultures that Deans and hospital CEOs don't get along. There is usually a tremendous amount of tension. One of the things I'm proudest of—and I think the Dean would say this too—is that we get along extremely well. He started his job three weeks before I started mine, neither of us own a lot of the problems here or at the medical school so we started with a clean slate. The relationship is so strong between us. We have now developed a joint fundraising plan. We're better together than apart. That gives Larry Bacow a great deal of pleasure. He really is vested in Mike's success and mine.

Taft explained the disconnect that Tufts-NEMC had with Tufts University in the past:

Some years ago, Tufts-NEMC actually took the Tufts name off of its signs and logos. That was a big mistake. They were not building the Tufts name, or building that relationship. In a Harvard medical town, Tufts-NEMC was not leveraging one of the top trump cards they had: the terrific and growing reputation of Tufts University, their nutrition school, medical, dental, veterinary schools. So they had all of that at Tufts-NEMC, and it wasn't being leveraged.

In the real estate arena, Tufts-NEMC held many buildings on and around the Tufts University campus on Kneeland Street in Chinatown. When Tufts-NEMC decided to sell one building it made sense for the University to purchase it. In one local business journal, Zane explained her thinking:

If you drive down Huntington Avenue, you know when you're at Northeastern

University. When you're at Commonwealth Avenue, you know you're at Boston University. But if you drive down Kneeland Street into Chinatown, you don't know you're at Tufts. You don't get the feeling you're in an urban campus.[23]

The University and Tufts-NEMC were in the "preliminary stage of looking at how to make the area more like a traditional urban university campus. The university held 'town meetings' to discuss the issues and is hiring planners to develop possible scenarios" the magazine reported.[24]

Prognosis: Short- and Long-Term Outlook

Leadership is about what's next. A lot of initiatives were started before Ellen got here, but she added the extra "umph" to make it happen. Now it's about what is next. What is the strategy. We're still a small hospital, we're still challenged every day because of our size to meet the financial basics to succeed.

– Ed Schottland, COO

In 2006, with her leadership team established, the sale of a building to Tufts University for $28 million adding needed capital, cost savings initiatives in place and improved managed care contracts, Zane was starting to move to the next phase, building a strategy for the future. Zane and her team were working with the Board in a major strategic planning initiative. In addition, Joelson was doing marketing research, the first Tufts-NEMC had conducted in years. They were trying to answer questions such as:

- What scale should Tufts-NEMC be?
- How can we best market ourselves?
- How can we differentiate ourselves in the marketplace?

- What is the best way to work with community hospitals and physicians?

As Joelson explained:

We are trying to create an alternative. Our goal is to be big enough to have the scale we need to operate efficiently and to be able to provide sufficient sub- specialties to be an academic medical center— the principle teaching hospital of Tufts University School of Medicine. We don't want to be as big or expensive as Partners. We have 3% market share; Partners has 25% market share. We're at best a 400-bed hospital; Partners has 2,000 beds. We see ourselves as a network of some physicians and some community hospitals, and as a lower cost alternative in the market. We can be effective with the new pay for performance contracts. It is more efficient and less expensive to keep the care local, so our strategy is to try to move the care that can be moved to community hospitals where we have relationships.

On the marketing side, we are implementing what we call an anti-invisibility advertising campaign. Our market research determined we had no identity in the market. We also learned that we were a house of individual brands—the doctors—rather than a brand in itself. As a result, we are building a physician-to-physician marketing campaign, using NEQCA as the starting point. We also plan to grow NEQCA from 600 to 1,000 doctors by 2010.

Perhaps the biggest plan to come out of the strategic initiative was the partnership with New England Baptist Hospital, another Tufts Medical School affiliated teaching hospital, to build a new 190-bed hospital in the Boston suburbs. If the plan came to fruition, it would be the first hospital built in Massachusetts in 25 years.

Although the site had not yet been selected, Zane was quoted as saying that:

In the past, hospitals have asked people in the suburbs to come to them and pay more for parking than the co-pay on their health insurance. Our view is: Wouldn't it be a good idea to take sophisticated academic medicine and bring it to the people?[25]

This type of bold planning gave the employees at Tufts-NEMC confidence about the future. Deeb Salem gave his viewpoint on where the hospital stood in mid-2006:

I've never been more optimistic. There are still a lot of problems. But the main source of anxiety is what happens if Ellen decides to leave. That's the problem having somebody that good. We've seen how well she runs things. But with her in charge I do have a lot of hope.

Zane finally saw the light at the end of the tunnel she had entered in January 2004, but she knew that her work had only just begun. She needed to find a way to keep the staff on track for the turnaround. She needed improved efficiency and cash flows to keep wind in the sails in order to move the rudder in the right direction. She also knew that Tufts-NEMC was far from a safe harbor:

I have lots of friends at Partner's—but business is business—if they could steal my best bone marrow transplant surgeon they would. It's the way it is. That is the deal. I can't let down my guard for a minute.

I am able, now, to spend much more of my time on strategy, on the future, on where this place is going. That is, frankly, why I took the job. I didn't come here to pull down accounts receivable, I came here to do something to position this place for the future.

Exhibit 1 Tufts-NEMC Income and Expense for Fiscal Years 1989–2005 (in thousands)

	1989	1990	1991	1992	1993	1994	1995	1996
Revenue:								
Net patient services revenue	218,820	230,616	272,108	297,351	314,445	301,385	309,938	281,791
Direct expenditures on grants, contracts, and other activities	21,063	21,423	23,083	25,608	28,467	33,302	60,805	52,059
Recovery of indirect costs on grants and contracts	5,770	7,129	5,778	7,900	8,883	9,762		
Software including support and consulting			12,009	14,660	18,934	23,469	28,777	6,175
Other revenue	22,340	23,949	16,788	14,443	14,801	13,961	13,690	17,917
Endowment earnings contributed toward community benefit								
Net assets released from restrictions used for operations								
Net assets released from restrictions used for research								
Total Operating Revenue	267,993	283,117	329,766	359,962	385,530	381,879	413,210	357,942
Net Investment income	5,151	698						
Unrestricted gifts, grants, and awards/net assets released from restrictions	535	817					1,104	936
Adjustments to prior year estimates with third party payors						12,600	11,342	11,800
Total Revenue	273,679	284,632	329,766	359,962	385,530	394,479	425,656	370,678
Expenses:								
Salaries and wages	104,574	113,557	128,739	143,124	158,511	160,183	167,380	146,900
Employee benefits	15,591	18,920	21,163	23,407	26,004	26,787	31,130	24,581
Purchased services of physician groups	23,033	24,579	29,648	31,236	35,354	32,051	39,620	37,176

1997	1998	1999	2000	2001	2002	2003	2004	2005
287,076	299,930	318,145	341,894	371,273	397,212	473,012	452,786	495,005
55,205								
22,797	24,045	22,561	26,228	36,055	33,790	51,686	42,853	48,232
	9,229	10,647	16,512	7,949	1,596			
	3,435	2,272	3,037	3,020	4,753	4,526	17,259	2,924
	44,001	41,314	47,582	37,702	38,250	53,196	52,891	55,901
365,078	380,640	394,939	435,253	455,999	475,601	582,420	565,789	602,062
365,078	380,640	394,939	435,253	455,999	475,601	582,420	565,789	602,062
184,746	191,629	180,206	203,449	222,489	227,706	297,827	295,645	308,057
24,031	21,531	21,058	24,098	25,491	28,543	55,918	57,004	56,416
	34,021	35,875	36,416	40,201	43,075	49,461	40,303	47,627

(Continued)

Exhibit 1   (Continued)

	1989	1990	1991	1992	1993	1994	1995	1996
Supplies and expenses	63,924	68,740	77,499	87,684	96,660	102,688	132,843	119,242
Interest	8,266	8,561	8,048	8,165	9,194	8,996	12,115	14,230
Depreciation and amortization	15,687	15,382	18,914	19,188	22,548	26,065	32,033	32,996
Direct expenditures on grants, contracts, and other activities	21,063	21,423	23,083	25,608	28,467	33,302		
Uncompensated care/ provision for bad debts	16,433	7,911	12,171	18,878	14,087	12,796	16,187	17,175
Other expenses							(6,250)	
Total operating expenses	268,571	279,073	319,265	357,290	390,825	402,868	425,058	392,300
Income (loss) from operations	5,108	5,559	10,501	2,672	(5,295)	(8,389)	598	(21,622)
Nonoperating gains and losses:								
Net unrestricted investment income		8,611	9,748	6,090	5,242	2,995	805	5,461
Net realized gain on sale of investments	1,490	1,405	1,814	3,876	3,770	6,570	2,357	2,253
Gain on sale of TSI and other property								72,958
Other nonoperating losses								
Total nonoperating gains, net	1,490	10,016	11,562	9,966	9,012	9,565	3,162	80,672
Excess (deficit) of revenues over expenses	6,598	15,575	22,063	12,638	3,717	1,176	3,760	59,050
Total other capital items						(11,814)	4,765	13,455
Excess (deficit) of revenues over expenses	6,598	15,575	22,063	12,638	3,717	(10,638)	8,525	72,505

Source: Company Records

1997	1998	1999	2000	2001	2002	2003	2004	2005
115,950	95,124	109,120	119,730	135,132	140,891	158,501	141,793	140,371
14,164	13,983	13,775	13,576	13,350	13,193	12,561	12,044	11,607
32,646	14,525	15,168	16,034	18,076	18,959	21,410	23,976	23,307
18,853	18,344	19,492	21,309	17,099	15,747	15,934	21,184	12,541
(138,500)						14,638		
390,390	389,157	394,694	434,612	471,838	488,114	626,250	591,949	599,926
(163,812)	(8,517)	245	641	(15,839)	(12,513)	(43,830)	(26,160)	2,136
4,561	7,974	4,421	9,226	4,040	2,277	2,102	2,041	2,838
9,711	9,100	6,083	5,506	2,691	(2,150)	3,429	4,842	11,074
	(245)						19,698	2,075
50	(1,063)	(28)				(196)	188	234
14,272	16,829	10,476	14,732	6,731	127	5,335	26,769	16,221
(149,540)	8,312	10,721	15,373	(9,108)	(12,386)	(38,495)	609	18,357
(3,070)						18,041	5,888	2,636
(152,610)	8,312	10,721	15,373	(9,108)	(12,386)	(20,454)	6,497	20,993

Exhibit 2 Boston Comparative Demographic and Health Care Indicators

Demographics[a]

	Boston	Metropolitan Areas 200,000+ population
Population	4,579,137	
Persons Age 65 or Older	12.7%	10%
Median Family Income	$39,182	$31,301
Unemployment Rate	5.2%	6.0%
Persons Living in Poverty	9%	13%
Persons Without Health Insurance	5%	14%

Health System Characteristics

	Boston	Metropolitan Areas 200,000+ population
Staffed Hospital Beds per 1,000 Population (2002)	2.2	3.1
Physicians per 1,000 Population (2003)[b]	2.8	1.9
HMO Penetration (including Medicare/Medicaid)[c]	37%	29%
Medicare-Adjusted Average per Capita Cost Rate, 2005	$768	$718

Health Care Utilization[c]

	Boston	Metropolitan Areas 200,000+ population
Adjusted Inpatient Admissions per 1,000 Population	240	197
Persons with Any Emergency Room Visit in Past Year	20%	18%
Persons with Any Doctor Visit in Past Year	86%	78%
Persons Who Did Not Get Needed Medical Care During the Last 12 Months	3.6%	5.7%
Privately Insured People in Families with Annual Out-of-Pocket Costs of $500 or More	33%	44%

Source: Center for Studying Health System Change, Community Report Number 11 of 12, December 2005.

[a] Statistics for year ending 2003.

[b] Includes nonfederal, patient care physicians, except radiologists, pathologists, and anesthesiologists.

[c] Markets with population greater than 250,000.

Exhibit 3   Number of Acute Care Hospitals and Available Beds in Massachusetts (1990–2001)

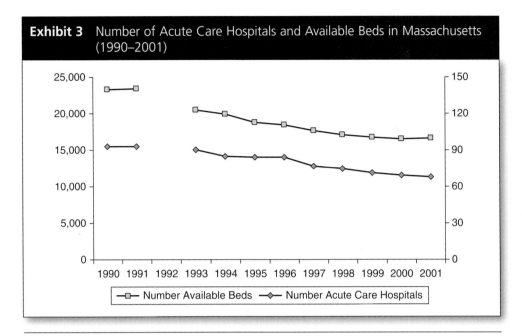

Source: Massachusetts Health Care Trends: 1990–2004

Exhibit 4   Total and Operating Margins for Acute Care Hospitals in Massachusetts (1990–2001)

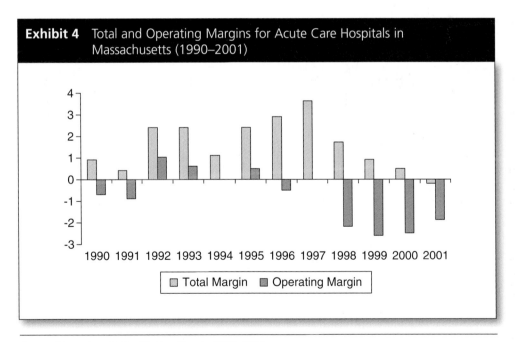

Source: Massachusetts Health Care Trends: 1990–2004

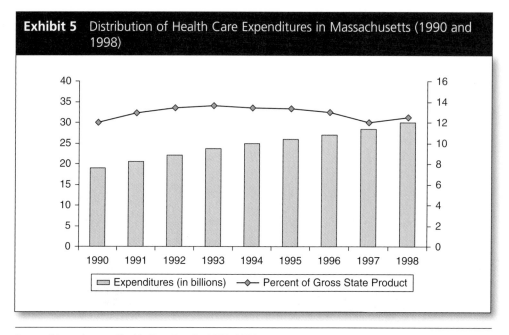

Exhibit 5 Distribution of Health Care Expenditures in Massachusetts (1990 and 1998)

Source: Massachusetts Health Care Trends: 1990–2004

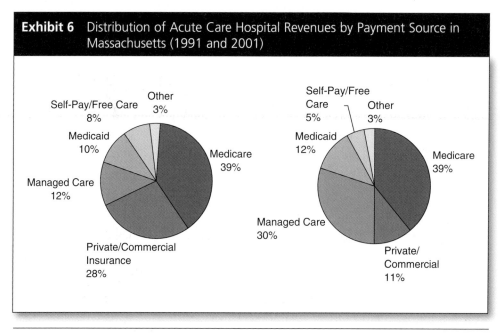

Exhibit 6 Distribution of Acute Care Hospital Revenues by Payment Source in Massachusetts (1991 and 2001)

Source: Massachusetts Health Care Trends: 1990–2004

Exhibit 7   Distribution of Patient Disposition at Discharge from an Acute Care Hospital in Massachusetts (1990 and 2001)

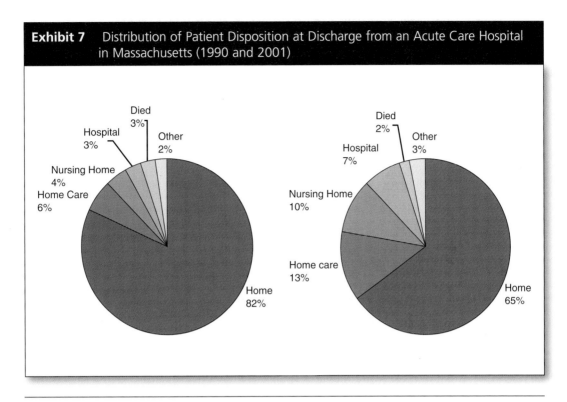

Source: Massachusetts Health Care Trends: 1990–2004

Exhibit 8   Inpatient Days and Discharges for Teaching versus Community Hospitals in Massachusetts (1990 and 2001)

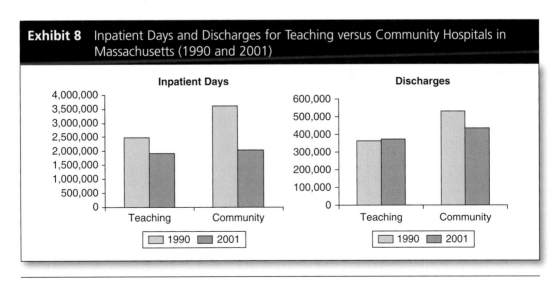

Source: Massachusetts Health Care Trends: 1990–2004

Exhibit 9 Acute Care Hospital Discharges per 1,000 Population and Average Length of Stay in Massachusetts (1990–2001)

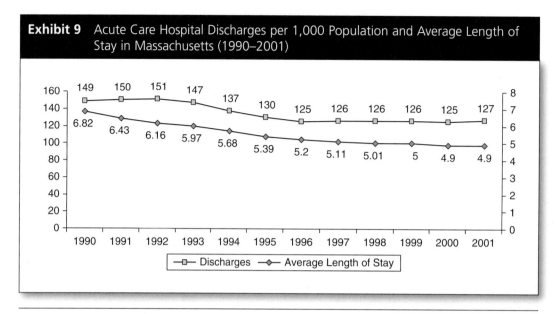

Source: Massachusetts Health Care Trends: 1990–2004

Exhibit 10 Major Provider Networks and Other Care Institutions in the Greater Boston Market

Name	Acute Care Hospitals	Physician Networks	Other Facilities	Medical School Affiliation	Employees (FTE)	Revenues/ Net Assets[26]	Admissions (2004)/ Discharge % (2003)
Partners Health Care System	MGH, BWH, Faulkner, Newton-Wellesley, North Shore Medical Center (NSMC), McLean (mental health)	PCHI	Spaulding Shaughnessy-Kaplan, RHCI, Partners Home Care, 2 Skilled Nursing homes	Harvard Tufts (Faulkner & NSMC)	35,300	$395 million $1.5 billion	87,616 20.8%
Boston Medical Center (BMC)		Boston HealthNet Quincy Medical Center		Boston University	4,429	$752 million $1.06 billion	28,173 6.0%
CareGroup	Beth Israel Deaconess, Mt. Auburn Hospital, New England Baptist, Beth Israel Deaconess-Needham	Community Care Alliance	Joslin Diabetes Center	Harvard Medical School	5,000 (Beth Isreal Deaconess)	$24 million $95 million	33,640 9.0%

(Continued)

Exhibit 10 (Continued)

Name	Acute Care Hospitals	Physician Networks	Other Facilities	Medical School Affiliation	Employees (FTE)	Revenues/ Net Assets[26]	Admissions (2004)/ Discharge % (2003)
Caritas Christi Healthcare	Caritas St.Elizabeth's St. Anne's Fall River, Holy Family Hospital and Medical Center, Caritas Norwood, Caritas Carney Hospital Dorchester, Caritas Good Samaritan Medical Center Brockton	Caritas Physician	St. Joseph Nursing Care Center, Neponset Valley Nursing Association, Good Samaritan Hospice, St. Mary's Women & Infants Center of Dorchester	Tufts Medical School	12,000	$90 million $20 million	15,781 11.6%
New England Medical Center	Tufts-NEMC Floating Hospital For Children	NEQCA		Tufts	3,000	$487 million $389 million	17,000 2.7%
Hallmark Health System	Lawrence Memorial, Melrose-Wakefield Hospitals	Ell Pond Medical Association	Malden Medical Center, other long term care, home health and diagnostic services	Tufts (family practice), Hallmark School of Nursing		$225 million $180 million	2.7%

Source: Massachusetts Health and Educational Facilities Authority. Accessed from: www.mehfa.org August 7, 2006. WebMD Quality Services. Accessed from: www.webmdqualityservices.com August 7, 2006.

Exhibit 11	Tufts-NEMC Operational Indicators Versus Industry Benchmarks			
	Industry Benchmark	**NEMC (FY 2006)**	**Translated Impact on Budget**	**Impact on Cash**
Days in Accounts Receivable	48.8	55.6	$ 775,416	$ 7,049,234
Accounts Payable Days	60.0	51.2	$ 1,203,061	$ 10,936,918
Average Length of Stay	5.5	5.79	$ 2,085,627	$ 2,085,627
Operating Margin	1.9%	0.4%	$ 10,169,579	$ 10,169,579
Days Cash on Hand	110.7	89.4	$ 609,468	$ 5,540,621
Commercial Insurance Contracts			$ 40,000,000	$ 40,000,000

Source: Company records

Notes

1. Tufts-NEMC employed roughly 5,000 people, who accounted for 3,000 full-time equivalent (FTE) positions in 2006.
2. Ferguson, Christine C. "Massachusetts Health Care Trends: 1990–2004," Massachusetts Division of Health Care Finance and Policy, March 2003, page 5. Accessed from: www.state .ma.us/dhcfp August 7, 2006.
3. Nonresident discharges refer to number of patients from out of state.
4. "Analysis in Brief—Massachusetts Inpatient Hospital Trends," Massachusetts Division of Health Care Finance and Policy, Number 6, April 2004, page 1. Accessed from: www.state.ma.us/ dhcfp August 7, 2006.
5. Provider refers to any hospital, AMC, or ancillary service that provided medical care.
6. Those patients who needed high levels of care, such as surgery.
7. Ferguson, Christine C. "Massachusetts health Care Trends: 1990–2001," appendix iii–vi.
8. Community Report—Boston, Massachusetts Third Visit 2000–2001. Center of Studying Health System Change, Report 11 of 12, summer 2001. www.hschange.org.
9. The Boston metropolitan area was generally described as being inside Interstate 495. Statistics provided by Massachusetts Health and Educational Facilities Authority, Revenue Bonds, Partners HealthCare System Issue, Series F (2005). Accessed from: www.mehfa.org August 7, 2006.
10. Community Report—Boston, Massachusetts Center of Studying Health System Change, Report 11 of 12, December 2005. www.hschange .org
11. Information in this section derived from www .nemc.org and www.bostonhistory.org/m_china .php accessed June 7, 2006.
12. The Boston Dispensary archived records. A summary available online at: simmons.edu/resources/ libraries//archives/char_coll/char_coll_027.htm accessed August 9, 2006.
13. The Miriam and Rhode Island hospitals were the two largest hospitals in Rhode Island and affiliated with Brown Medical School.
14. "NEMCs bold move," *Boston Business Journal*, January 17, 1997 and Van Voorhis, Scott. "NEMC discusses hospital network," *Boston Business Journal*, January 24, 1997. Accessed online at: http://boston.bixjournals.com July 21, 2006.
15. Quaternary refers to most advanced level of care, such as bone marrow and organ transplants.
16. Bone marrow transplant.
17. Duff, Susanna and Becker, Cinda, "Here we go again," *Modern Healthcare*, Chicago: September

9. 2002, pg. 8. Accessed online at: http://proquest.umi.com, July 20, 2006.

18. Ibid.

19. Pronounced "peachy."

20. Lutch Bender, Ellen., "A new chapter for the venerable Tufts-NEMC," *Boston Business Journal*, December 26, 2003. Accessed online at: http://boston.bizjournals.com July 21, 2006.

21. The Massachusetts legislature.

22. Pronounced "Pickle."

23. Hollmer, Mark, "Tufts-NEMC wants a more campus feel in Chinatown," *Boston Business Journal*, June 30, 2006. Accessed online at: http://boston.bizjournals.com July 21, 2006.

24. Ibid.

25. Rowland, Christopher and Bailey, Steve, "Tufts Affiliates Plan Hospital in Suburbs," *The Boston Globe*, September 8, 2006, page A1, Section: Metro/Region. Accessed online at: www.boston.com/news/bostonglobearchives September 13, 2006.

26. From IRS Form 990 fiscal year ending 2003. Available at: www.guidestar.org/findocuments/2004.

Case Study 6

Ellen Zane at Tufts Medical Center: Spring 2011

Cynthia Ingols

Lisa Brem

School of Management, Simmons College

As Ellen Zane weaved through the early evening traffic in mid-April 2011, she thought about how she would structure her speech that evening. She had been asked by the School of Management, Simmons College to talk to students and faculty about the goals she had reached and milestones she had witnessed in the last four years as CEO of Tufts Medical Center (TMC), an academic medical center (AMC) in Boston and the principle teaching hospital for Tufts University School of Medicine. Certainly, Tufts had come a long way from its earlier incarnation as Tufts-New England Medical Center (NEMC), an organization teetering on the brink of bankruptcy following a failed merger with Lifespan, a Rhode Island hospital system. She knew she should discuss her battles to keep the hospital adequately reimbursed from health insurers, to save the Floating Hospital for Children, and to rebrand the medical center using its close connection to Tufts University. Finally, she knew she should talk about the hospital's movement away from consolidation and mergers with other providers and towards a "Distributed Academic Medical Center" strategy.

However, Zane wasn't sure if she should discuss the one thing weighing most on her mind: the recent threat by the Tufts' nursing union of a one-day strike to take place on May 6. Tufts had been in negotiations with the nurses' union since September, but the two sides had been unable to agree on a new contract before the December 2010 deadline. The hospital and the union had agreed to a contract extension, but the last day of the extension was coming quickly—on April 25—and still no resolution was in sight. The most contentious issues focused on staffing levels: the union wanted mandatory staffing ratios, while Zane refused on the grounds that such mandatory ratios were too confining and had never been incorporated into Tufts' labor contracts thus far. Further, she knew the Medical Center's safety and quality of care were excellent (according to numerous independent agencies), and that the union's insistence on mandatory ratios would place an unwarranted financial burden on the Medical Center. From her point of view, the union's insistence on ratios served only to give it a platform from which to increase membership and dues.

When the union indicated it would strike, Zane hired a contract staffing firm to provide temporary nurses in the event of an actual work stoppage. But such a move would be costly: the contract firm required a minimum of five days of work for its nurses, with an all-in minimum cost of $4.2 million for the Medical Center.[1] Not to mention that this would be the first nurses' strike at a Boston hospital in 25 years, and Zane was obviously concerned about the firestorm of publicity and patient uncertainty that such an event would engender. Zane wondered how she could best prepare for what was sure to be a contentious and very public negotiation. What steps should she take to ensure that both parties arrived at the best outcome for the Medical Center? Zane had come out on top in difficult negotiations before, and had developed a reputation for taking risks and standing firm in showdowns with health care plans. How could she use the lessons learned from her long and successful career to find a solution to this stalemate?

Searching for an Identity: Rebranding as Tufts Medical Center

After taking over as CEO in 2004, Zane had been successful dealing with NEMC's immediate cash flow problems and by the end of 2006, she turned her focus to market research and strategic planning. One of her first orders of business was to conduct a study to determine how NEMC was viewed in Boston and in New England, what the sources of value were, and how to capitalize on them. What she found was that the "Tufts" brand added value, but the words "New England" did not. As Zane explained:

We wanted to determine where NEMC fit within the cosmos of health care in Boston. What I found was that "Tufts-New England Medical Center and the Floating Hospital for Children" was too long and not memorable. As a result, the marketing consultant we had hired recommended that we keep it simple and stick to what added value. Our affiliation with Tufts University School of Medicine brought the most brand value, so we changed the name to "Tufts Medical Center" and branded it exactly like the University. We changed our colors from crimson to blue, and asked the University to use their font, their logo, everything. I went to Larry Bacow, President, Tufts University and said: "I want to blur the lines between the University and the Medical Center because we want everyone to know that we are your principle teaching hospital. We want to benefit from your marketing and we want you to benefit from our marketing and we are going to raise all our boats together."

While President Bacow supported Zane's request, there were some University trustees that worried about liability and how any lapses at the hospital could affect Tufts University. In addition, the many logistical concerns of changing the name were daunting, including changing the name of the nearby subway stop from "New England Medical Center" to "Tufts Medical Center." Still Zane persevered and, with Bacow's help, eventually received the blessing of the trustees. As Zane recalled:

With Larry pushing the issue, the trustees recognized that although there was some risk, it was a risk they needed to take. The lesson I learned here was that in every important business decision there is an element of risk, but the question is: Is the risk worth it? In this case, the trusties realized it was. Larry had explained to his trustees that if this move was good for the Medical Center, then it was good for the School of Medicine. If it was good for the School of Medicine, then it was good for all of Tufts University. So in March 2008, we changed the name to Tufts Medical Center and kept the Floating Hospital for Children as a sub-brand under the Tufts Medical Center umbrella brand. We didn't want to abandon the Floating Hospital name, because the market research found that the Floating was a huge brand, particularly for pediatricians practicing in eastern Massachusetts, many of whom had trained there.

Keeping the Floating Hospital Afloat

Another major decision Zane needed to make was what to do with the Floating Hospital for Children. While it was clear that local physicians had a strong affinity for the brand, most agreed that the decades of mismanagement and neglect had taken its toll on the once-proud institution. When Zane took over the medical center in 2004, the Floating Hospital was losing $1 million per month, and the consensus among the pediatricians working there was that it was just a matter of time before Zane announced it would close. But Zane had other pressures to keep the hospital alive:

> The Dean of Tufts University School of Medicine rightly said to me, "I have to train all these doctors; you are the principle teaching hospital; you have to provide a pediatrics program for this mission. I cannot be at the behest of Harvard to graduate Tufts medical students from Tufts." And he was right. Also, for those of us who work for nonprofit institutions, it's not only about the money, it is ultimately about fulfilling the mission. So my job was

to find a way to continue to provide the Floating Hospital for the medical and educational academic mission, if nothing else. There was also the fact that I thought Boston needed the balance of another children's hospital. So I went to my board and we took $5 million dollars and used it to recruit more doctors. We recruited a wonderful chair for the Floating, and in the last few years, he has hired 35 new faculty in every area from hematology to neurology and pediatric surgery. It has been a tremendous turnaround, and we are incredibly proud of the Floating.

While the rebranding strategy proved extremely successful, with Tufts Medical Center's brand recognition climbing year after year and the Floating Hospital out of danger, Zane once again turned to planning for future growth. But before she could catch her breath, a new battle for the survival of the hospital forced Zane to make one of the riskiest moves in her career.

Seeking Solvency: The Showdown With Blue Cross Blue Shield

Although the big three health plans in Massachusetts (Harvard Pilgrim, Tufts, and Blue Cross Blue Shield) had initially cooperated in renegotiating their contracts with NEMC in 2006, the Blue Cross contract was up for renewal again in 2008. Zane struggled to gain rate increases from Blue Cross to cover cost of care in the hospital, but felt she was hitting a wall. Each month, as the negotiations wore on, Zane would extend the contract for another 30 days, hoping they would soon reach an agreement. After a year of this "dance," Zane was frustrated and ready to take drastic action. As she recalled:

> Our contracts with Blue Cross were truly ugly. Although I had been able to glean some rate increases from them when I first

arrived in 2004, we were still far from being paid a fair price for our services. What most insurance companies say to justify low rates is that "you cost too much" or "your care is not that great." But I knew that was not true. After about a year I finally had had enough. My team and I felt that we were not being dealt with in an above board manner. This happened at the end of 2008. The first week of January 2009, I called the CEO of Blue Cross and told him that I was not going to give him another extension. He immediately knew what that meant. When you are under extensions, you can keep the negotiations under the radar and hopefully get the job done, but once Blue Cross no longer had an extension, they were required, by law, to publicly announce that there might be a disruption in the Blue Cross provider network. I don't think he ever thought I would do that. Such a move clearly puts Blue Cross at a disadvantage to their competitor health plans who can offer a full non-disrupted network of providers.

Certainly it was very bold of our team and our board to support me on this. But we did it because our rates at Blue Cross were so low that we could not sustain services. My attitude was "you are going to kill me with these rates, so I'd rather you just kill me now." I would not roll over and play dead. We had a legitimate case: We have the highest acuity of all academic medical centers in Boston, which means that we see some of the sickest patients. But we also are a low cost provider, because the insurance companies have starved us all these years. In addition, our quality of care was very high (as noted by Blue Cross' own quality data). I believed our case was compelling enough that we should take the risk. So we were in meltdown for 12 days, while we worked to come to an agreement before the grace period on the

contract lapsed. But we were ready for it, and Blue Cross was not. Never underestimate how ready you have to be to do something difficult like this. Every person on my team, no matter what their day job was, had to be entirely focused on this.

While lawyers and negotiators worked around the clock to reach a settlement, Zane and her team went into crisis management mode. Within a half hour of Zane's announcement to the Blue Cross CEO, the hospital had posted a website and opened an 800 number to field consumer and business calls, and her team posted notices in all their affiliated physician offices.

Zane also took her case to the editorial board at the *Boston Globe*, which had been closely covering the dispute as soon as it was made public. As Zane explained:

> We laid it all out to them. We showed them that we were the solution to escalating health care costs, not the problem. We tried to get them to see that high quality/low cost providers, like us, should be fed, not starved. If we want to try to manage health care costs in the Commonwealth, we shouldn't be making the expensive guys more expensive and the low cost guys go out of business. And—it was wonderful—the *Globe* editorial board got it. In early 2009, in the middle of the global economic crisis, the *Boston Globe* wrote an editorial that advocated for our rate increases. It was extremely helpful when that happened.

Another turning point came when Bacow set up a meeting between Zane and the Blue Cross CEO in his office at Tufts University. Zane recalled how Bacow's support came at a crucial time:

> We met in Larry's quite august, presidential office. It was a management moment in my career when Larry opened the

meeting by saying: "You know, Tufts University graduates more primary care physicians than Harvard, BU, and UMass combined. And Tufts graduates more primary care physicians who stay and practice in eastern Massachusetts than Harvard, BU, and UMass combined. So this is far more than a dispute between a hospital and a health plan. If something happens to my hospital, it will affect the pipeline of physicians in Eastern Massachusetts forever." I wanted to jump across the table and hug him! It was just an unbelievable moment. Then our board chairman, who was the CEO of Sovereign Bank, said, "We know everyone on the Blue Cross board. And every day, we'll run into them at events in Boston and we will know and they will know that they tried to damage one of the best medical schools and one of the best hospitals in America." This was Friday morning and by 2:30 am on Saturday, we had a deal.

Eventually, Blue Cross offered Tufts a cutting-edge contract, called the "Alternative Quality Contract (AQC)." "It's very tricky," warned Zane. "You can't go into a contract like this without knowing what you are doing." The AQC is typically a three- to five-year agreement that Blue Cross Blue Shield developed to combine both capitated payments (i.e., lump sum payments) with performance incentives. To incent the hospitals and physicians to lower costs, the AQC paid them partially with a fixed "global budget," based on historical costs adjusted for inflation that covered all costs and services for a patient. These included inpatient, outpatient, pharmacy, rehabilitation center, etc. If the provider was able to lower costs below the budget, it could keep the savings. In addition, the provider could win bonus payments (up to 10% of the total fee) based on performance measures linked to clinical performance, such as in-hospital mortality and wound infection rates.[2] Tufts was the first academic medical center to

work under such a contract, and "we have performed stunningly on it," reported Zane. "I told the new CEO of Blue Cross that, even though we had a showdown, I truly believe that this type of contract is fair and incents us in the right way. In the end, I've been his best sales person for the AQC."

Affiliating for Care

With the disastrous effects of the Lifespan merger still fresh in Zane's mind, she and her leadership team sought alternate ways to expand the medical center's services and increase referrals from surrounding communities. Zane believed that creating a network of affiliates that agreed to provide reciprocal care was a better solution than costly mergers and acquisitions. As Zane explained:

Our strategy is to become a "Distributed Academic Medical Center." We assist community hospitals in stopping the "leakage" of care out of their communities (typically leaking to Boston) by sending our doctors to their hospitals to practice as requested. Community hospitals can provide routine, secondary care less expensively and more conveniently for community residents; while we provide the specialized high end services, like heart transplants and neonatal care, to the people who need it. This community-hospital-friendly strategy had a lot to do with the intense growth that we have seen in the last few years; it's truly been a success, and I'm very proud of it. Our aim is not to make the community care more expensive, but to bring the right type of quality care to the right location. The best thing is we are using affiliate agreements—not mergers involving millions of dollars—to accomplish this.

In October 2010, Tufts expanded its affiliation with MetroWest Medical Center in

Framingham/Natick (MWMC) adding adult health services to its year-long pediatric affiliation. In a press release, Tufts announced that "Tufts MC will work with MWMC to bring advanced specialty services to MWMC so residents do not have to travel to Boston for many services. When patients do need the highest level of care only available at an academic medical center, Tufts Medical Center will be MWMC's preferred referral partner."[3] Other affiliations and clinical partnerships included the Southcoast Physicians Network in New Bedford/Fall River and Highland Medical Associates in Winchester, which joined Tufts' physicians network (NEQCA), Morton Hospital of Taunton and Lawrence General Hospital for pediatric services, Quincy Medical Center, Signature Healthcare (including Brockton Hospital), Metrowest Medical Center and many of its physicians, and Jordan Hospital of Plymouth.

Validation

Zane's work and that of her team to rebuild Tufts Medical Center and the Floating Hospital did not go unnoticed. The University Health System Consortium (UHSC), an independent organization that measures quality and safety in academic medical centers in the United States, announced in November, 2010, that it named Tufts Medical Center 6th in the nation in its Quality and Accountability Study. Tufts was the only AMC in New England to be in the top ten. (See **Exhibit 1** for Press Release.) Tufts was also named Number 1 in the "equity" category, reflecting its excellence in delivering care to "all patients, regardless of race, gender or socioeconomic status."[4] "It was a wonderful validation of the great work that our nurses, doctors, and staff had done, by going down this very rocky road and meeting all these challenges," Zane recalled. "We knew we had the highest quality, the highest case mix, and did it all with the lowest cost, but receiving this external validation was just the cherry on the cake."

Nurse Staffing Levels and the Threat of a Strike

The dispute between Tufts and the Massachusetts Nurses Association (MNA) that erupted in earnest at the end of April 2011 began some months earlier, when Tufts instituted a change in its staffing model in recognition that professional nurses should not be spending their time doing menial tasks such as looking for wheelchairs or serving food trays. The Medical Center designed a new staffing plan to increase efficiency, distribute work responsibilities among the appropriate level of care giver, and reduce length of stay and staffing costs. Almost immediately, however, the nurses' union asserted and began to protest what it characterized as unsafe conditions, namely mandatory overtime, holes in minimum staffing schedules, expecting nurses to be responsible for up to seven patients per nurse on night shifts, and "floating" nurses to areas for which they were not adequately trained. Zane, however, disagreed strongly: "The union asserted all these things but most were untrue. We would never float a nurse, for example, to an area where he/she wasn't appropriately trained."

When the National Nurses Union (NNU) became involved, the intensity of the debate increased exponentially. What had been an in-house negotiation started to gain national attention. Zane felt that the NNU targeted the Medical Center for very specific reasons: "Part of it was chronological, since the nurses' contract was up for renewal. As an academic medical center, we were a high-profile target, and we were in a financial 'sweet spot' for the union. We weren't so poor that a strike would put us out of business, and we weren't so rich that we could afford to throw every penny at it." Zane also felt that the threat to strike was part of a strategy by the NNU to organize several strikes across the country (including Eastern Maine Medical Center in Bangor, Maine, and St. Vincent's Hospital in Worcester) on the same date.

Early in the contract negotiations, Zane offered to meet the union's request for a 3%

raise. "I offered them a 3% raise for one year, right off the bat." But she wouldn't bend on the staffing ratios. Nationally and in Massachusetts, nursing unions had fought for legislation to mandate ratios of nurses to patients, legislation that was strongly opposed by hospital coalitions. Tufts maintained that ratios would cost over $30 million per year to implement and would severely limit their ability to maintain flexible workforces to fit patient needs. Zane explained that "it would be irresponsible to our staff, patients and the people of Massachusetts to spend tens of millions of dollars each year on rigid staffing ratios that are not warranted in hospitals that have demonstrated high quality and safety and do nothing more than feather the bed of the union."[5]

The union turned down Zane's 3% offer, and held firm on their demand for staffing ratios. "I told them, if they decided to ignore this offer and go down the road toward a strike, then the offer was off the table, since I would have to use that money to hire temporary workers," Zane recalled. "People who know me know I don't bluff. But the union thought I wouldn't stand firm, and so they turned the offer down."

When it became clear that the union meant to strike, Zane began to plan her "strike preparedness" strategy. First, she knew that in the highly labor-friendly and politicized arena of Massachusetts, politicians often weighed in on the side of labor in such disputes. While Zane had no illusions that she would gain the support of the Democratic governor, the mayor, or congressional representatives, she did hope to convince them not to muddy the waters:

It is important, when you are trying to allay patients' fears, that you keep rhetoric and inflammatory statements out of the public debate as much as possible. So I met with each of our local and state politicians, and I told them about the situation. When they asked what I wanted from them, I said, "Nothing, just your silence." None of them ever did come out publically either for or

against us. It was a great help to keep the dispute from escalating in the political arena.

The second prong in her strategy was to communicate, clearly and continuously, to all the stakeholders of the hospital. Zane realized early on that messaging and communication was crucial in setting the tone of the dispute:

What I learned from this process is that you have to bring communications, public relations, and strategy people in the room from the very beginning. They have to weigh in and be aware of every decision and every part of the strategy when dealing with a situation like this. Communication and messaging is significant, particularly when your opponent is lying.

The nurses, most of them, had no idea about the lies that the union was telling, what was really happening at the bargaining table, or the nasty tactics the NNU engaged in," explained Zane. "At Christmas time, union people dressed up as elves and picketed a party we were having for the staff over at the Floating Hospital. They threatened to picket my home. And every week, the union had black balloons delivered to the Chief Nursing Officer. It was just mean and unprofessional. And I think most of our nurses would have been infuriated to know this was happening."

At the town meetings where Zane traditionally brought all of the Medical Center's employees up to speed on hospital business, she decided to take a strong stand against the Union's communications, particularly the accusations that the Medical Center had quality issues or unsafe staffing levels. "I told the hundreds of people assembled that I've had enough of calling it misinformation and misrepresentation. I'm going to call this what it is: these are plain lies that the union is telling." Zane showed slides of every union communication followed by a rebuttal slide to clarify the facts. "I was incredibly aggressive about it," she said. At one point, Zane became so infuriated about dealing with the Union's accusations that she complained to her husband. "I said, 'It's beneath me to have to respond to all this garbage talk.' But he said to me, 'Ellen, if President Obama has to respond to people like bin Laden, then you can respond to the Union.'"

Zane also took issue with the entire process that led to the strike vote. Numerous nurses told her they were intimidated because voters were not allowed to cast their votes privately, that nurses were given the impression that they would be able to vote again before the actual strike (which did not in fact happen), and that the Union told the nurses that the strike would last only one day. "I had to hire temporary workers on a minimum 5-day contract, so the Union lied about that too. If they decided to strike, their nurses would be out of work for a minimum of five days," Zane explained.

The third part of Zane's strategy was to consolidate the support of the physicians and nonunion workers in the hospital. "We have physicians with multiple degrees from prestigious institutions who have worked their entire professional career to assure the quality at this hospital," she said. "They were incensed that NNU representatives from outside the hospital co-opted the quality debate and set themselves up in the press as experts on quality at Tufts Medical Center."

The nonunion workers were largely against the strike as well. Because Zane had to be ready to bring in temporary workers, who could not meet the same staffing levels that the hospital currently employed, she needed to reduce the patient census. "At about T minus six days to the strike preparations, we reduced our census. That meant our nonunion employees knew we were at risk for having to cut back on employees other than nurses. Fewer patients meant fewer maintenance workers, security guards, and telephone operators. They were very unhappy about the Union's divisive behavior and decision to strike."

While mediators worked endless hours to bring both sides to a resolution, the deadline of May 6 grew ever closer. Finally, by the last day before the strike was to begin, only one issue remained: nurses wanted a guarantee that they would not be asked to care for more than five patients at a time, while Tufts continued to assert that it would need the flexibility to increase the number of patients to nurses in various circumstances.[6] Zane recalled her thinking on this point:

> In reality, our day-to-day practice hovered around a 5 to 1 ratio. But I was adamant that I would never put a rigid ratio in writing. What if changes in technology, pharmacology, and care practice made the 5 to 1 ratio obsolete? We would be saddled with an outdated ratio that costs us money, just because the union insisted on a number that truly wasn't relevant for high quality health care delivery.

Zane believed that the Union hadn't expected such lack of support for the strike. "They didn't bargain for the physicians being so passionate about defending the quality of their hospital. And they didn't bargain for how I dealt with the threat to strike. A lot of CEOs wring their hands and cave under the psychological pressure that the Union tries to inflict. They didn't expect me to be so dogged. But the more pressure they put on, the more dogged I became."

With both sides tantalizingly close, would Zane's team be able to avert the strike, or would the first nurses' strike in Boston in 25 years take place at Tufts Medical Center?

Exhibit 1   Tufts Medical Center Press Release November 10, 2010

**Tufts Medical Center Ranks #6 Among Nationally
Ranked Academic Medical Centers for Quality and Accountability**

BOSTON (Nov. 10, 2010) –Tufts Medical Center has gained the prestigious honor of being among the top 10 academic medical centers in the country when considering quality and safety measures, according to the University HealthSystem Consortium's 2010 Quality and Accountability Study. The study, which reviews quality and patient satisfaction data across a broad range of measures, compared scores from its 98 academic medical center members, representing nearly 90% of all AMCs in the United States. Tufts Medical Center, ranked 6th, was the only UHC member hospital in New England to rank in the top 10 in the study.

"Tufts Medical Center's performance in this study is a well-deserved acknowledgement of the work we have done around quality and patient satisfaction," said Tufts Medical Center President and CEO Ellen Zane. "We pride ourselves on offering patients the very highest quality while remaining a value provider in terms of our cost. This is further evidence of the tremendous quality patients can expect from our medical center."

The study, released annually, incorporates six areas identified by the Institutes of Medicine as key quality measures that are important to patient care: safety, timeliness, effectiveness, efficiency, equity, and patient centeredness. Specific measures include mortality rates for a variety of services including transplants, cardiology, neurology, and oncology among many others. The study also considered the hospital readmission rate within 30 days of discharge—a key indicator of how well patients are prepared to leave the hospital. Safety measures reviewed included the rate of pressure ulcers, central line infections, and postoperative respiratory failure, among others. The broad range of measures considered by the study provides a comprehensive look at how well a hospital meets quality standards. In the study, Tufts Medical Center was compared to academic medical centers throughout the country, including those in Boston and New England.

Tufts Medical Center achieved a #1 ranking in UHC's "equity" category, an indication that all patients, regardless of race, gender, or socioeconomic status, receive equal treatment at the Medical Center.

"Our commitment to patient outcomes shines through in our quality and safety performance," said Nancy Shendell-Falik, Senior Vice President of Patient Care Services and Chief Nursing Officer for Tufts MC. "We continue to build our model of care around achieving the highest standards of quality and patient satisfaction."

"Staff throughout Tufts Medical Center have worked extremely hard to measure the quality of care here and to achieve the highest standards," said David Fairchild, Chief Medical Officer for Tufts MC. "This is a reflection that our physicians, nurses, infection control staff, technicians and behind-the-scenes personnel are working tirelessly to ensure that our patients have the best possible experience in our hospital."

The University HealthSystem Consortium, formed in 1984, is an alliance that currently includes 111 academic medical centers and 255 of their affiliated hospitals, representing approximately 90 percent of the nation's nonprofit academic medical centers. UHC provides specific programs and services to improve clinical, operational, financial, and patient safety performance.

(Continued)

(Continued)

Tufts Medical Center is affiliated with a number of community hospitals throughout Eastern Massachusetts, including MetroWest Medical Center, Quincy Medical Center, Signature Healthcare Brockton Hospital, and Jordan hospital. Floating Hospital for Children at Tufts Medical Center has pediatric affiliations with Lawrence General Hospital, Lowell General Hospital, MetroWest Medical Center, and Morton Hospital. Tufts Medical Center serves as the preferred tertiary and quaternary referral center to its affiliates and helps them expand their capacity to care for patients in their communities.

Source: Tufts Medical Center, http://www.tuftsmedicalcenter.org/AboutUs/NewsReleases/2010NewsReleases/UHC_Ranking

Notes

1. "Tufts Medical Center Condemns MNA/NNU Call for Strike Vote," April 11, 2011, www.local-doctors.com, accessed June 2011.
2. BlueCross BlueShield of Massachusetts, "The Alternative Quality Contract," http://www.bluecrossma.com/visitor/pdf/alternative-quality-contract.pdf, accessed May 2011.
3. Tufts Medical Center, "MetroWest Medical Center and Tufts Medical Center Expand Clinical Partnership," press release, October 21, 2010, http://www.tuftsmedicalcenter.org/AboutUs/NewsReleases/2010NewsReleases/MWMC_Tufts_MC_NEQCA_Partnership, accessed May 2011.
4. Tufts Medical Center, "Tufts Medical Center Ranks #6 Among Nationally Ranked Academic Medical Centers for Quality and Accountability," press release, November 10, 2010, http://www.tuftsmedicalcenter.org/AboutUs/NewsReleases/2010NewsReleases/UHC_Ranking, accessed May 2011.
5. "Tufts Medical Center Condemns MNA/NNU Call for Strike Vote," April 11, 2011, www.local-doctors.com, accessed June 2011.
6. Robert Weisman, "Tufts, Union Talks Go Down to Wire," May 6, 2011, www.boston.com, accessed June 2011.

Notes

1. Strauss, M. (2014, February 25). Tim Hortons brewing "bold" changes. *Globe Investor*, Retrieved from http://www.globeinvestor.com/servlet/WireFeedRedirect?cf=GlobeInv estor/config&vg=BigAdVariableGenerator&date=20140225&archive=rtgam&slug=es cenic_17078297. Press releases from Tim Hortons' website, retrieved from http://www .timhortons.com/ca/en/about/news_archives.html; Dunkin' brands announces strong global growth in 2013. Corporate press release, January 13, 2014. Retrieved from http://investor.dunkinbrands.com/releasedetail.cfm?ReleaseID=818737.

2. A version of this quote can be found on p. 55 in Wheatley, M. J. (1994). *Leadership and the new science*. San Francisco: Berrett-Koehler.

3. Miles, R. H. (1997). *Leading corporate transformation*. San Francisco: Jossey-Bass.

4. Personal experience of the authors.

5. Appelbaum, S. H., Henson, D., & Knee, K. (1999). Downsizing failures: An examination of convergence/reorientation and antecedents—processes—outcomes. *Management Decision, 37*(6), 473–490.

6. Sourced from: http://www.ziglar.com/quotes/its-not-what-happens-you-matters.

7. The Conference Board of Canada. (2000, November). 2000 change management conference: Increasing change capability. See also Higgs, M., & Rowland, D. (2005). All changes great and small: Exploring approaches to change and its leadership. *Journal of Change Management, 5*(2), 121–151.

8. Moskowitz, M., & Levering, R. (2014, February 3). The 100 best companies to work for. *Fortune, 169*, 108.

9. Pfeffer, J., & Sutton, R. (1999). Knowing "what" to do is not enough: Turning knowledge into action. *California Management Review, 42*(1), 83–108.

10. Maynard, M. (2010, April 5). U.S. is seeking a fine of $16.4 million against Toyota. *New York Times*.

11. GM ignition switch recall lawsuits. (2014, April 1). *About Lawsuits.com*. Retrieved from http://www.aboutlawsuits.com/gm-recall/; GM seeks immunity for ignition lawsuits before 2009. (2014, April 22). Associated Press. Retrieved from http://www.cbc .ca/news/business/gm-seeks-immunity-for-ignition-lawsuits-before-2009-1.2617417.

12. How to play chicken and lose. (2009, January 22). *The Economist*.

13. Meltdown warnings ignored, analysis shows. (2008, December 1). *CBS News*. Retrieved from http://www.cbsnews.com/news/meltdown-warnings-ignored-analysis-shows/.

14. Demography: China's Achilles heel. (2012, April 12). *The Economist*; Germany's demographic challenge. (2013, May 28). *The Economist*; Demography, growth and inequality: Age invaders. (2014, April 26). *The Economist*; Japan's economy: The

incredible shrinking country. (2014, May 31). *The Economist*; Age invaders. (2014, April 26). *The Economist*.

15. Sovereign creditworthiness could be undermined by age-related spending trends. (2006, June 5). *Standard & Poor's*. Retrieved from www.standardandpoors.com.

16. Half a billion Americans? (2002, August 22). *The Economist*.

17. Mounting medical care spending could be harmful to the G-20's credit health. (2012, January 26). *Standard & Poor's*. Retrieved from http://www.standardandpoors.com/ratings/articles/en/eu/?articleType=HTML&assetID=1245328578642; Sovereign credit worthiness could be undermined by age-related spending trends. (2006, June 5). *Standard & Poor's*. Retrieved from www.standardandpoors.com.

18. Falling fertility. (2009, October 31). *The Economist*, pp. 29–32.

19. The gain before the pain: Mexico's demographic dividend will be short-loved. (2012, November 24). *The Economist*; China's concern over population aging and health. (2006, June). *Population Reference Bureau*. Retrieved from *http://www.prb.org/Publications/Articles/2006/ChinasConcernOverPopulationAgingandHealth.aspx*; Ranasinghe, D. (2013, September 22).The aging in Asia face a new decade like no other. *CNBC*. Retrieved from http://www.cnbc.com/id/101045746.

20. The dividend delayed: Hopes that Africa's dramatic population bulge may create prosperity seem to have been overdone. (2014, March 8). *The Economist*. Falling fertility. (2009, October 31). *The Economist*, pp. 29–32.

21. Davis, I., & Stephenson, E. (2006). Ten trends to watch in 2006. *McKinsey Quarterly; The Online Journal*. Retrieved from http://www.mckinseyquarterly.com/article_print.aspx?12=18&L3=30&ar=1734.

22. Supporting aging populations as demographics shift. (2011, June 10). *International Monetary Fund*. Retrieved from http://www.imf.org/external/pubs/ft/survey/so/2011/NEW061011A.htm; Davis, I., & Stephenson, E. (2006). Ten trends to watch in 2006. *McKinsey Quarterly; The Online Journal*. Retrieved from http://www.mckinseyquarterly.com/article_print.aspx?12=18&L3=30&ar=1734; Drouin, J., Hediger, V., & Henke, N. (2008, June). Health care costs: A market-based view. *McKinsey Quarterly*.

23. Revell, J. (2002). GM's slow leak. *Fortune, 146*(8), 105; Why GM's plan won't work—and the ugly road ahead. (2005, May 9). *Business Week Online*. Retrieved December 2010 from http://www.businessweek.com/magazine/content/05_19/b3932001_mz001.htm; Maynard, M. (2008, March 7). GM to freeze pension plan for salaried workers. *New York Times*. Retrieved from http://www.nytimes.com/2006/03/08/automobiles/08auto.html.

24. The silver tsunami. (2010, February 4). *The Economist*.

25. A billion shades of grey: An ageing economy will be a slower and more unequal one—unless policy starts changing now. (2014, April 26). *The Economist*.

26. Kelleher, J. B. (2013, June 21). Analysis: As boomers age, Harley hunts for younger riders. Reuters. Retrieved from http://www.reuters.com/article/2013/06/21/us-harley davidson-boomers-analysis-idUSBRE95K0GU20130621; Marketing to the old. (2002, August 8). *The Economist*.

27. Hannon, K. (2013, January 25). Why older workers can't be ignored. *Forbes*. Retrieved from http://www.forbes.com/sites/kerryhannon/2013/01/25/why-older-workers-cant-be-ignored/.

28. Sedensky, M. (2013, September 13). Some employers see perks in hiring older workers, *AP*. Retrieved from Yahoo! News: http://news.yahoo.com/employers-see-perks-hiring-older-workers-144536527—finance.html.

29. Ennis, S. R., Rios-Vargs, M., & Albert, N. G. (2011, May). The Hispanic population in 2010, 2010 census brief. *United States Census Bureau*, Publication C2010BR-04; Suro, R., & Singer, A. (2002). *Latino growth in metropolitan America*. Center on Urban & Metropolitan Policy and The Pew Hispanic Center, The Brookings Institution; Saenz, R. (2010, December). Population bulletin update: Latinos in the United States 2010. *Population Reference Bureau*, Update 2010.

30. Suro, R., & Singer, A. (2002). *Latino growth in metropolitan America* (Table 4, p. 9). Center on Urban & Metropolitan Policy and The Pew Hispanic Center, The Brookings Institution.

31. Erlanger, S. (2011, April 11). France enforces ban on full-face veils in public. *New York Times*; Seguin, R. (2014, January 21). Quebec Liberals stake out new position on PQ's secular charter. *Globe and Mail.*

32. Sam becomes first openly gay player to the drafted. (2014, May 10). *Reuters.* Retrieved from https://ca.news.yahoo.com/sam-becomes-leagues-first-openly-gay-player-ever-225731321—nfl.html?.tsrc=yahoo.

33. Florida, R. (2012, June 27). Race, gender, and the creative class. Retrieved from http://www.citylab.com/work/2012/06/race-gender-and-creative-class/2225/; Race, gender and careers: Why "stuffing the pipeline" is not enough. (2012, September 7). *Knowledge@Wharton.* Retrieved from http://business.time.com/2012/09/07/race-gender-and-careers-why-stuffing-the-pipeline-is-not-enough/.

34. Almasy, S. (2014, May 20). NBA charges Donald Sterling, schedules June 3 vote. *CNN U.S.* Retrieved from http://www.cnn.com/2014/05/19/us/donald-sterling-nba/index.html.

35. Rubin, C. (2010, November 8). Labor board backs workers' right to bad-mouth bosses online. *Inc.* Retrieved from http://www.inc.com/news/articles/2010/11/NLRB-backs-employees'-right-to-gripe-about-bosses-online.html; Bacon, J. (2013, December 5). Fast-food worker strike, protest for higher pay. *USA Today.* Retrieved from http://www.usatoday.com/story/money/business/2013/12/05/fast-food-strike-wages/3877023/.

36. Young, C. (2014, March 27). Food firm disgusted by employee's racist posting. *Bradford News.* Retrieved from http://m.thetelegraphandargus.co.uk/news/11107456.Police_probe_racist_Facebook_posting_after_mum_s_suicide_at_Shipley_super market/.

37. See TD's corporate responsibility section of their website: http://www.td.com/corporate-responsibility/diversity/diversity.jsp.

38. Thomas, D. A. (2004). Diversity as strategy. *Harvard Business Review, 82*(9), 98–109.

39. Mendoza, M. (2014, May 29). Google admits its work force is mostly white, male and must change. *Associated Press via the Globe and Mail.* Retrieved from http://www.theglobeandmail.com/report-on-business/international-business/us-business/google-says-work-force-must-diversify-as-tally-shows-most-are-white-male/article18903708/#dashboard/follows/.

40. Gabrielsson, M., & Manek Kirpalani, V. H. (2014). *Handbook of research on born globals.* Edward Elgar Pub.; Friedrich, J., Noam, A., & Ofek, E. (2014, May). Right up the middle: How Israeli firms go global. *Harvard Business Review.*

41. Savitz, A. W., & Weber, K. (2006). *The triple bottom line: How today's best-run companies are achieving economic, social and environmental success—and how you can too.* San Francisco: Jossey-Bass.

42. Kurucz, E., Colbert, B., & Wheeler, D. (2013). *Reconstructing value: Leadership skills for a sustainable world.* Rotman-Utp Publishing; Rea, M. H. (2013). *Review of sustainability reporting in South Africa 2013.* IRAS Integrated Reporting and Assurance Services; Deszca, G. (2014, May 2). Lessons from South Africa on sustainability, corporate social responsibility, and strategy. *LeadingIndicator.* Retrieved from http://www.leadingindicator.ca/article/478074/lessons-from-south-africa-on-sustainability-corporate-social-responsibility-and.

43. The data deluge. (2010, February 25). *The Economist*; Gantz, J., & Reinsel, D. (2012, December). The digital universe in 2020: Big data, bigger digital shadows, and biggest growth in the far east. *IDC IVEW.* Retrieved from http://www.emc.com/collateral/analyst-reports/idc-the-digital-universe-in-2020.pdf.

44. Tynan, D. (2012, March 19). How to get a hot job in big data. *InfoWorld.* Retrieved from http://www.infoworld.com/t/it-jobs/how-get-hot-job-in-big-data-188629?page=0,0.

45. The next disrupters. (2007, September). *Business 2.0.*

46. Manyika, J., Chui, M., Bughin, J., Dobbs, R., Bisson, P., & Marrs, A. (2013, May). Disruptive technologies: Advances that will transform life, business and the global economy. *McKinsey Global Institute.* Retrieved from http://www.mckinsey.com/insights/business_technology/disruptive_technologies.

47. Annual passenger totals approaches 3 billion according to ICAO 2012 air transport results. (2012, December 18). *International Civil Aviation Organization.* Retrieved from http://www.icao.int/Newsroom/Pages/annual-passenger-total-approaches-3-billion-according-to-ICAO-2012-air-transport-results.aspx.

48. Yergin, D., & Stanislaw, J. (2002). *The commanding heights: The battle for the world economy.* New York: Touchstone, 405.

49. List of countries by number of mobile phones in use. Retrieved from http://en.wikipedia.org/wiki/List_of_countries_by_number_of_mobile_phones_in_use.

50. Lomas, N. (2014, February 13). Gartner: Smartphones sales finally beat out dumb phone sales globally in 2013. *TC (TechCrunch).* Retrieved from http://techcrunch.com/2014/02/13/smartphones-outsell-dumb-phones-globally/.

51. Pagliery, J. (2014, May 28). Half of American adults hacked this year. *CNN Money.* Retrieved from http://money.cnn.com/2014/05/28/technology/security/hack-data-breach/index.html?hpt=hp_t3; Ponemon Institute releases 2014 cost of data breach: Global analysis (2014, May 5). Retrieved from http://www.ponemon.org/blog/ponemon-institute-releases-2014-cost-of-data-breach-global-analysis; Skimming off the top. (2014, February 15). *The Economist.* Retrieved from http://www.economist.com/news/finance-and-economics/21596547-why-america-has-such-high-rate-payment-card-fraud-skimming-top.

52. Finkle, J. (2014, May 22). Hackers raid eBay in historic breach, access 145 million records. *Reuters.* Retrieved from http://uk.reuters.com/article/2014/05/22/uk-ebay-password-idUKKBN0E10ZL20140522; Isadore, C. (2014, January 11). Target: Hacking hit up to 110 million customers. *CNNMoney.* Retrieved from http://money.cnn.com/2014/01/10/news/companies/target-hacking/index.html; Mullen, R. (2005, March 11). Security issues lurking beyond VOIP's cost saving promise. *Silicon Valley/San Jose Business Journal.* Retrieved from http://www.sanjose.bizjournals.com/sanjose/stories/2005/03/14/smallb3.html; Foster, P., & Moore, M. (2014, May 19). US charges Chinese officers with hacking and opens new front in cyber-espionage war. *The Telegraph.* Retrieved from http://www.telegraph.co.uk/news/worldnews/asia/china/10842484/US-charges-Chinese-officers-with-hacking-and-opens-new-front-in-cyber-espionage-war.html.

53. Violino, B. (2004, July). Fortifying supply chains. *Optimize,* pp. 73–75. Retrieved from http://www.optimizemag.com/article/showArticle.jhtml?articleID=22101759.

54. Daigle, K. (2011, October 6). India unveils $35 tablet computer for the rural poor. *The Sydney Morning Herald.* Retrieved from http://www.smh.com.au/digital-life/digital-life-news/india-unveils-35-tablet-computer-for-rural-poor-20111005-11aao.html.

55. Koebler, J. (2013, June 3). Study: A third of new marriages began with online meetings. *U.S. News.* Retrieved from http://www.usnews.com/news/articles/2013/06/03/study-a-third-of-new-marriages-began-with-online-meetings; Bindley, K. (2013, February 14). Sleep texting is on the rise, experts suggest. *Huffington Post.* Retrieved from http://www.huffingtonpost.com/2013/02/14/sleep-texting-on-the-rise_n_2677739.html.

56. Silcoff, S., McNish, J., & Ladurantaye, S. (2013, September 27). How BlackBerry blew it: The inside story. *Globe and Mail.* Retrieved from http://www.theglobeandmail.com/report-on-business/the-inside-story-of-why-blackberry-is-failing/article14563602/#dashboard/follows/.

57. Markoff, J. (2014, May 27). Google's next phase in driverless cars: No steering wheel or brake pedals. *New York Times.* Retrieved from http://www.nytimes.com/2014/05/28/technology/googles-next-phase-in-driverless-cars-no-brakes-or-steering-wheel.html?ref=technology&_r=0.

58. Others believe otherwise. Note the protests whenever the WTO meets, for example.

59. False heaven. (1999, July 29). *The Economist.*

60. Farrell, D., Khanna, T., Sinha, J., & Woetzel, J. R. (2004). China and India: The race to growth. *McKinsey Quarterly, Special Edition,* 110–119.

61. Speed is not everything. (2013, January 2). *The Economist.* Retrieved from http://www.economist.com/blogs/theworldin2013/2013/01/fastest-growing-economies-2013.

62. Transparency International Secretariat. (2002). Transparency international corruption perceptions index 2002. 10585 Berlin, Germany: Ott-Suhr-Allee, 97–99.

63. Transparency International Secretariat. (2002). Bribe payers' index. 10585 Berlin, Germany: Otto-Suhr-Allee 97–99; Wawro, L. (2014, March 31). Arms deals in the dark: Secret contracts in the defense sector. *Transparency International.* Retrieved from http://blog.transparency.org/2014/03/31/arms-deals-in-the-dark-secret-contracts-in-the-defence-sector/; Corruption perceptions index 2013. (2013, December 3). *Transparency International.* Retrieved from http://www.transparency.org/whatwedo/pub/cpi_2013.

64. Lawrence, A. (2007, Winter). Hewlett-Packard and a common supplier code of conduct. *Case Research Journal;* Siegle, L. (2013, October 6). How ethical are high-street clothes? *The Guardian.* Retrieved from http://www.theguardian.com/environment/2013/oct/06/ethical-high-street-clothes-supply-chain-bangladesh; Strauss, M. (2013, April 25). Loblaw moves to improve safety at Bangladeshi factories. *Globe and Mail.* Retrieved from http://www.theglobeandmail.com/report-on-business/loblaw-moves-to-improve-safety-at-bangladeshi-factories/article11563889/#dashboard/follows/.

65. Siemens sees green tech driving economic growth. (2009, August). *Industry Week.*

66. Senge, P., Smith, B., Kruschwitz, N., Laur, J., & Schley, S. (2010). *The necessary revolution: How individuals and organizations are working together to create a sustainable world.* New York: Crown (a division of Random House); Senge, P., & Carstedt, G. (2001). Innovating our way to the next industrial revolution. *Sloan Management Review, 42*(2), 24–38.

67. Where have all your savings gone? (2008, December 4). *The Economist.*

68. Personal communication with one author.

69. Sovereign debt: It isn't a debt crisis. (2012, April 12). *The Economist;* Stemming the tide. (2009, November 19). *The Economist.*

70. When giants slow down. (2013, July 27). *The Economist.* Retrieved from http://www.economist.com/news/briefing/21582257-most-dramatic-and-disruptive-period-emerging-market-growth-world-has-ever-seen; The hard slog ahead. The world in 2010. (2009, December). *The Economist.*

71. Not so fast. The world in 2010. (2009, December). *The Economist.*

72. Are Airbnb and Uber changing the world? (2014, July 5) *The Globe and Mail online.* Retrieved from http://www.theglobeandmail.com/globe-debate/are-airbnb-and-uber-changing-the-world/article19453855/?utm_source=Shared+Article+Sent+to+User&utm_medium=E-mail:+Newsletters+/+E-Blasts+/+etc.&utm_campaign=Shared+Web+Article+Links.

73. Barkema, H. G., Baum, J. A. C., & Mannix, E. A. (2002). Management challenges in a new time. *Academy of Management Journal, 45*(5), 916–930.

74. Weick, K. E., & Quinn, R. E. (1999). Organizational change and development. *Annual Review of Psychology, 50,* 361–386.

75. Thomas, D. (2008, September). The digital company 2013: Freedom to collaborate. *Economist Intelligence Unit, The Economist.* Retrieved from http://graphics.eiu.com/upload/portal/Digital_company_2013_WP2_WEB.pdf.

76. Savyas, A. (2005, March 8). Intel points to convergence. *Computer Weekly,* p. 12.

77. Lam, J. (2005, March 1). Continental sets tentative accords for cutting costs. *Wall Street Journal* (Eastern edition), p. A2.

78. Jick, T., & Peiperl, M. (2003). *Changing the culture at British Airways and British Airways Update, 1991–2000.* In T. Jick & M. Peiperl, *Managing change* (pp. 26–44). New York: McGraw-Hill Higher Education.

79. One strike and you're out: British Airways. (2003, August 2). *The Economist*, p. 64.

80. Flight plans: BA and Iberia take a step closer to becoming one of the world's biggest airlines. (2010, April 8). *The Economist online*. Retrieved from http://www.economist .com/node/15872745; and Maintaining altitude: BA's cabin staff appear to be fighting a losing battle. (2010, March 25). *The Economist*; BA united (2011, May 12). *The Economist*. Retrieved from http://www.economist.com/blogs/gulliver/2011/05/brit ish_airways; British Airways: One giant step for BA. (2013, July 5). *The Economist*. Retrieved from http://www.economist.com/blogs/gulliver/2013/07/british-airways?zid =303&ah=27090cf03414b8c5065d64ed0dad813d.

81. An interesting comparison of TQM and employee involvement is contained in Lawler, E. E. III. (1994). Total quality management and employee involvement: Are they compatible? *Academy of Management Executive, 8*(1), 68–76.

82. Drawn from Morgan, G. (1994, June 28). Quantum leaps, step by step. *Globe and Mail*, B22.

83. Kirton, M. J. (1984). Adaptors and innovators—Why new initiatives get blocked. *Long Range Planning, 17*(2), 137–143; Tushman, M. L., & O'Reilly, C. A. III. (1996). Ambidextrous organizations: Managing evolutionary and revolutionary change. *California Management Review, 38*(4), 8–30.

84. The life cycle of interventions is readily apparent in the management literature. First comes the concept, accompanied or followed closely by examples of successful implementation. Next are cautionary notes, examples of failure, and remedies. As the luster fades, new approaches emerge in the literature and the process recurs, hopefully building upon earlier learning. For example, see Miles, R. E., & Snow, C. C. (1992). Causes of failure in network organizations. *California Management Review, 34*(4), 53–72.

85. Helyar, J. (1998, August 10). Solo flight. *Wall Street Journal*. Quoted in T. Jick, *Managing change* (p. 503). New York: McGraw-Hill Higher Education.

86. Hamel, G., & Prahalad, D. K. (1994, October). Lean, mean and muddled. *Globe and Mail Report on Business Magazine*, 54–58.

87. Voelpel, S. C., Leibold, M., & Streb, C. (n.d.). The innovation meme: Managing innovation replicators for organizational fitness. *Journal of Change Management, 5*(1), 57–69.

88. Hamel, G., & Prahalad, D. K. (1994, October). Lean, mean and muddled. *Globe and Mail Report on Business Magazine*, 54–58.

89. McComb, W. L. (2014, April 1). Transformation is an era, not an event. *Harvard Business Review*; White, M. (2013, November 1). The reinvention imperative. *Harvard Business Review*.

90. An American revival: A Canadian manufacturer's quest to rebuild itself. (2014, July 7). *The Globe and Mail online*. Retrieved from http://www.theglobeandmail.com/report-on-business/an-american-revival-a-canadian-manufacturers-quest-to-rebuild-itself/ article19476053/?utm_source=Shared+Article+Sent+to+User&utm_medium=E-mail:+Newsletters+/+E-Blasts+/+etc.&utm_campaign=Shared+Web+Article+Links.

91. The future of jobs: The onrushing wave. (2014, January 18). *The Economist*. Retrieved from http://www.economist.com/news/briefing/21594264-previous-technological-innovation-has-always-delivered-more-long-run-employment-not-less; The New "New Economy." (2003, September 13). *The Economist*, p. 62.

92. Van Yperen, N. W. (1998). Informational support, equity and burnout: The moderating effect of self-efficacy. *Journal of Occupational and Organizational Psychology, 71*, 29–33.

93. Gordon, J. (1989, February 13). Employee alignment? Maybe just a brake job would do. *Wall Street Journal*. As reported in T. Jick. (1993). *Managing change*. Homewood, IL: Irwin.

94. Pfeffer, J. (1995). Managing with power: *Politics and influence* [video]. Executive Briefings. Stanford, CA: Stanford Videos.

95. Ricc, R., & Guerci, M. (2014, March 15). Diversity challenge: An integrated process to bridge the "implementation gap." *Business Horizons, 57*, 235–245.

96. Oshry, B. (1990). Finding and using a manager's power to improve productivity. *National Productivity Review, 10*(1), 19–33.

97. Russo, J. E., & Shoemaker, P. J. H. (1992). Managing overconfidence. *Sloan Management Review, 33*(2), 7–18.

98. Mishra, K. E., Spreitzer, G. M., & Mishra, A. K. (1998). Preserving employee morale during downsizing. *Sloan Management Review, 39*(2), 83–95.

99. Hamel, G. (2000). *Leading the revolution.* Boston: Harvard Business School Press.

100. CNNHEROES. Retrieved from http://www.cnn.com/SPECIALS/cnn.heroes/.

101. Vogelgesang, G., Clapp-Smith, R., & Sland, J. (2014, May). The relationship between positive psychological capital and global mindset in the context of global leadership. *Journal of Leadership and Organizational Studies, 21*(2); Caligiuri, P., & Tarique, I. (2012, October). *Journal of World Business, 47*(4), 612; Rajah, R., Song, Z., & Richard, D. (2011, December). Taking stock of the past decade of research. *Leadership Quarterly, 22*(6), 1107; Shapiro, E. C. (1996). *Fad surfing in the boardroom: Managing in the age of instant answers.* Cambridge, MA: Perseus.

102. Higgs, M., & Rowland, D. (2005). All changes great and small: Exploring approaches to change and its leadership. *Journal of Change Management, 5*(2), 121–151.

103. Zander, L., Mockaitis, A. I., & Butler, C. L. (2012, October). Leading global teams. *Journal of World Business, 47*(4), 572.

104. Holt, K., & Kyoko, S. (2012, June). Global leadership: A developmental shift for everyone. *Industrial and Organizational Psychology: Perspectives on Science and Practice, 5*(2), 196–215; Smith, W. K., & Lewis, M. W. (2012, June). Leadership skills for managing paradoxes. *Industrial and Organizational Psychology: Perspectives on Science and Practice, 5*(2), 227–231.

Chapter 2

1. Arnoff, M. (2009, September 14). The challenges for McDonald's top chef. *Business Week.*

2. McDonald's corporate social responsibility and sustainability report 2012–2013. Retrieved from http://www.aboutmcdonalds.com/content/dam/AboutMcDonalds/2.0/pdfs/2012_2013_csr_report.pdf; Schwartz, A. (2009, July 6). First "green" McDonald's to offer ChargePoint EV charging stations. *Fast Company*; California McDonald's adds electric vehicle fast charge station. (2013, April 24). *QSR Web.com.* Retrieved from http://www.qsrweb.com/news/california-mcdonalds-adds-electric-vehicle-fast-charge-station/

3. Retrieved from http://www.aboutmcdonalds.com/mcd/our_company/amazing_stories/food/catering_to_local_tastes.html.

4. Cullers, R. (2010, July 23). McDonald's goes local. *AdWeek.*

5. Schull, D. (1999). Why good companies go bad. *Harvard Business Review, 77*(4), 42–52.

6. Handy, C. (1994). *The age of paradox.* Boston: Harvard Business School Press.

7. Lewin, K. (1951). *Field theory in social science.* New York: Harper and Row.

8. A recent discussion of Lewin's contribution can be found in Rosch, E. (2002). Lewin's field theory as situated action in organizational change. *Organization Development Journal, 20*(2), 8–14.

9. Kotter, J. P. (1996). *Leading change.* Boston: Harvard Business School.

10. Gentile, M. C. (2010). *Giving voice to values: How to speak your mind when you know what's right.* New Haven, CT & London: Yale University Press. To receive the B case and the Faculty-Only Teaching Notes, please contact Mary Gentile at Mgentile3@babson.edu

11. Shapiro, M., Ingols, C., & Gentile, M. (2011). Helen Drinan: Giving voice to her values. *Case Research Journal, 31*(2).

12. Retrieved from http://www.babson.edu/academics/teaching-research/gvv/pages/curriculum.aspx.

13. Duck, J. D. (2001). *The change monster: The human forces that fuel or foil corporate transformation and change.* New York: Crown Business.

14. Beckhard, R., & Harris, R. T. (1987). *Organizational transitions: Managing complex change.* Reading, MA: Addison-Wesley.
15. Kotter, J. P. (1996). *Leading change.* Boston: Harvard Business School Press.
16. Duck, J. D. (2001). *The change monster: The human forces that fuel or foil corporate transformation and change.* New York: Crown Business.

Chapter 3

1. Seigworth, G. (n.d.). A brief history of bloodletting. Retrieved from http://www.pbs.org/wnet/redgold/basics/bloodlettinghistory.html
2. Bruch, H., & Gerber, P. (2005). Strategic change decisions: Doing the right change right. *Journal of Change Management, 5*(1), 99.
3. Bruch, H., & Gerber, P. (2005). Strategic change decisions: Doing the right change right. *Journal of Change Management, 5*(1), 98.
4. Stacey, R. D. (2003). *Strategic management of organisational dynamics: The challenge of complexity.* Englewood Cliffs, NJ: Prentice Hall.
5. See Holling, C. S. (1987). Simplifying the complex: The paradigms of ecological function and structure. *European Journal of Operations Research, 30,* 139–146; Hurst, D. K. (1995). *Crisis and renewal: Meeting the challenge of organizational change.* Boston: Harvard Business Review Press.
6. Schumpeter, J. (1942). *Capitalism, socialism and democracy.* New York: Harper & Row.
7. Nadler, D. A., & Tushman, M. L. (1977). A diagnostic model for organizational behavior. In J. R. Hackman, E. E. Lawler, & L. W. Porter (Eds.), *Perspectives in behavior in organizations* (pp. 85–100). New York: McGraw-Hill.
8. Nadler, D. (1987). The effective management of organizational change. In J. W. Lorsch (Ed.), *Handbook of organizational behavior* (pp. 358–369). Englewood Cliffs, NJ: Prentice Hall.
9. Nadler, D. A., & Tushman, M. L. (Summer, 1999). The organization of the future: Strategic imperatives and core competencies for the 21st century. *Organizational Dynamics, 28*(1), 45–60.
10. McManamy, R. (1995). Fourth quarterly cost report: South America—Hyperinflation dying off. *ENR, 235*(26), 43–45.
11. Nadler, D. A., & Tushman, M. L. (1980). A model for diagnosing organizational behavior. *Organizational Dynamics, 9*(12), *35–51.*
12. Peters, T., & Waterman, R. H. (1982). *In search of excellence.* New York: Harper & Row.
13. Material for the Dell story was drawn from Dell's do-over. (2009, October 26). *Business Week, 4152,* 36; and from Take two: Michael Dell pioneered a new business model at the firm that bears his name. Now he wants to overhaul it. (2008, May 1). *The Economist.* Retrieved February 2010 from the Dell website, http://content.dell.com/ca/en/corp/about-dell-investor-info.aspx.
14. Datamonitor. (2011, June). *Computer & Peripherals Industry Profile: Global,* p. 18.
15. Madway, G. (2009, October 15). Dell CEO forecasts "powerful" computer hardware refresh.
16. Guglielmo, C. (2013, November 18). You won't have Michael Dell to kick around anymore. *Forbes, 192*(7), p. 1.
17. Grant, R. M., Shani, R., & Krishnan, R. (1994). TQM's challenge to management theory and practice. *Sloan Management Review, 35*(2), 25–36.
18. Gates, R. (2003, September 3). How not to reform intelligence. *Wall Street Journal,* p. A16. See also Flynn, S., & Kirkpatrick, J. J. (2005). *The Department of Homeland Security: The way ahead after a rocky start.* Written testimony before a hearing of the Committee on Homeland Security and Governmental Affairs, U.S. Senate, Washington, DC.

19. Milstead, D. (2014, June 27). GM's bad news hangs over everything but its stock. *Globe and Mail*; GM fires 15 executives over deadly ignition switch. (2014, June 6). *ABC News.* Retrieved from www.abc.net.au/news/2014-06-06/general-motors-fires-15-exeutives -over-deadly-ignition-scandal/5504320.

20. Burke, W. W. (2002). *Organization change: Theory and practice* (p. 191). Thousand Oaks, CA: Sage.

21. Sterman, J. (2001). System dynamics modeling: Tools for learning in a complex world. *California Management Review, 43*(4), 8–25.

22. Adapted from Sterman, J. (2001). System dynamics modeling: Tools for learning in a complex world. *California Management Review, 43*(4), 13.

23. Argyris, C., & Schön, D. (1996). *Organizational learning II: Theory, method and practice.* Reading, MA: Addison-Wesley.

24. Senge, P. (1990). *The strategy.* London: Doubleday/Century Business.

25. Adapted from Gogoi, P., & Arndt, M. (2003, March 3). McDonald's hamburger hell. *Business Week.*

26. Rao, A. R., Bergen, M. E., & Davis, S. (2000). How to fight a price war. *Harvard Business Review, 78*(2), 107–116.

27. Boosting productivity on the shop floor. (2003, September 12). *The Economist,* p. 62.

28. Quinn, R. E. (1991). *Beyond rational management.* San Francisco: Jossey-Bass.

29. See Quinn, R. E., et al. (1990). *Becoming a master manager.* New York: Wiley.

30. For a detailed treatment of this topic, see Weick, K. (1999). Organizational change and development. *Annual Review of Psychology*; Romanelli, E., & Tushman, M. L. (1994). Organizational transformation as punctuated equilibrium: An empirical test. *Academy of Management Journal, 34,* 1141–1166; Gersick, C. G. G. (1991). Revolutionary change theories: A multilevel exploration of the punctuated equilibrium. *Academy of Management Review, 16,* 10–36.

31. Strebel, L. (1994, Winter). Choosing the right change path. *California Management Review,* 29–51.

32. Greiner, L. (1998, May–June). Evolution and revolution as organizations grow. *Harvard Business Review,* 55–67.

33. Beckhard, R., & Harris, R. T. (1987). *Organizational transitions: Managing complex change.* Reading, MA: Addisson-Wesley.

34. Mitleton-Kelly, E. (2003). The principles of complexity and enabling infrastructures. In E. Mitleton-Kelly, *Complex systems and evolutionary perspectives of organisations: The application of Stacey's Complexity Theory to organisations.* London: London School of Economics Complexity & Organisational Learning Research Programme, Elsevier.

35. Stacey, R. D. (1996). *Strategic management and organizational dynamics* (2nd ed.). London: Pittman.

36. Noori, H., Deszca, G., Munro, H., & McWilliams, B. (1999). Developing the right breakthrough product/service: An application of the umbrella methodology, Parts A & B. *International Journal of Technology Management, 17,* 544–579.

37. Letterman, E. (n.d.). Retrieved December 2010 from http://thinkexist.com/quotation/ luck_is_what_happens_when_preparation_meets/11990.html

Chapter 4

1. *Wall Street Journal* CEO council. (Producer). (2008). *Shaping the new agenda: Rahm Emanuel on the opportunities of crisis* [YouTube video]. Retrieved May 2010 from http:// www .youtube.com/watch?v=_mzcbXi1Tkk.

2. Ten people who predicted the financial meltdown. (2008, October 12). *Times Online, Money.* Retrieved May 2010 from http://timesbusiness.typepad.com/money_ weblog/2008/10/10-people-who-p/comments/page/2/

3. Schmitt, R. B. (2008, August 25). FBI saw threat of loan crisis: A top official warned of widening mortgage fraud in 2004, but the agency focused its resources elsewhere. *Los Angeles Times.*

4. The new role of risk management: Rebuilding the model. (2009, June 24). Knowledge@ Wharton. Retrieved from http://knowledge.wharton.upenn.edu/article/the-new-role-of-risk-management-rebuilding-the-model/; How to play chicken and lose. (2009, January 22). *The Economist.*

5. Critics say WHO overstated H1N1 threat. (2010, January 14). *China Daily Science and Health.*

6. Ebola virus disease, West Africa–update. (2014, May 30). *World Health Organization.* Retrieved from http://www.who.int/csr/don/2014_05_30_ebola/en/; WHO/MERS update from WHO. (2014, May 14). *Unifeed.* Retrieved from http://www.unmultimedia.org/tv/unifeed/2014/05/who-mers/.

7. Stoll, J. D., & Terlep, S. G. M. (2009, May 22). UAW reach crucial cost-cutting pact—agreement to modify work rules, trim cash obligation helps ease way for quick bankruptcy filing. *Wall Street Journal,* p. B1.

8. Lanes, W. J. III, & Logan, J. W. (2004, November). A technique for assessing an organization's ability to change. *IEEE Transactions in Engineering Management, 51*(4), 483.

9. Keeton, K. B., & Mengistu, B. (1992, Winter). The perception of organizational culture by management level: Implications for training and development. *Public Productivity & Management Review, 16*(2), 205–213.

10. Darley, J. M., & Latane, B. (1968). Bystander intervention in emergencies: Diffusion of responsibility. *Journal of Personality and Social Psychology, 8,* 377–383.

11. Senge, P. M. (1994). *The fifth discipline: The art and practice of the learning organization.* New York: Currency Doubleday.

12. Sull, D. N. (1999, July–August). Why good companies go bad. *Harvard Business Review,* 42–52; Charan, R., & Useem, J. (2002). Why companies fail. *Fortune, 145*(11), 50–62; Schreiber, E. (2002). Why do many otherwise smart CEOs mismanage the reputation asset of their company? *Journal of Communication Management, 6*(3), 209–219.

13. Hamel, G. (2002). *Leading the revolution.* New York: Penguin.

14. Kotter, J. P. (2002). *The heart of change.* Boston: Harvard Business School Press.

15. Mintzberg, H., & Westley, F. (1992). Cycles of organizational change. *Strategic Management Journal, 13,* 39–59.

16. Stapenhurst, T. (2009). *The benchmarking book: A how-to guide to best practice for managers and practitioners.* Oxford, UK: Elsevier.

17. Sull, D. N. (1999, July). Why good companies go bad. *Harvard Business Review,* 42–52.

18. Vakola, M. (2014). What's in there for me? Individual readiness to change and the perceived impact of organizational change. *Leadership and Organizational Development Journal, 35*(3), 195–209.

19. Weisbord, M., & Janoff, S. (2005). Faster, shorter, cheaper may be simple; it's never easy. *Journal of Applied Behavioral Science, 41*(1), 70–82.

20. Gene Deszca, personal communication.

21. Sirkin, H., Keenan, P., & Jackson, A. (2005, October). The hard side of change management. *Harvard Business Review,* 4.

22. T. Cawsey, personal communication.

23. Collins, J. (2001). *Good to great.* New York: HarperCollins; Jennings, J. (2005). *Think big, act small.* New York: Penguin.

24. Corner office—Tony Hsieh of Zappos.com. (2010, January 10). *New York Times.*

25. Collins, J., & Porras, J. I. (1994). *Built to last* (p. 94). New York: HarperCollins.

26. Confidence trumps accuracy in pundit popularity. (2013, May 28). *Washington State University News.* Retrieved from https://news.wsu.edu/2013/05/28/confidence-trumps-accuracy-in-pundit-popularity/#.U44wT2dOWUk; Ariely, D. (2008). *Predictable*

irrationality. New York: HarperCollins; Kahneman, D. (2011). *Thinking fast and slow*. New York: Farrar, Strauss and Giroux.

27. Kahneman, D., Lovallo, D., & Sibony, O. (2011, June). Before you make the big decision. *Harvard Business Review*, 51–60.

28. Barsh, J., & Lavoie, J. (2014, April). Lead at your best. *McKinsey Quarterly*; Anderson, D., & Ackerman Anderson, L. (2011, Fall). Conscious change leadership: Achieving breakthrough results. *Executive Forum*.

29. Anders, G. (2014, May 26). Nadella's bid to fix Microsoft: What Ballmer didn't dare. *Forbes*. Retrieved from http://www.forbes.com/sites/georgeanders/2014/05/07/nadel las-bid-to-fix-microsoft-what-ballmer-didnt-dare/; Metz, C. (2014, April 4). Why Microsoft got it right with new CEO Satya Nadella. *Wired*. Retrieved from http://www .wired.com/2014/02/microsoft-ceo-satya-nadella/.

30. Cited in Tunzelmann, A. V. (2007). *Indian summer* (p. 105). London: Simon and Schuster.

31. Beckhard, R., & Harris, R. T. (1987). *Organizational transitions: Managing complex change*. Reading, MA: Addison-Wesley.

32. Spector, B. (1993). From bogged down to fired up. In T. D. Jick (Ed.), *Managing change: Cases and concepts* (pp. 121–128). Boston: Irwin/McGraw-Hill.

33. Wallace, E. (2009, May 5). Why Chrysler failed. *Bloomberg Businessweek*. Retrieved May 2010 from http://www.businessweek.com/lifestyle/content/may2009/bw2009055 _922626.htm.

34. Target launch leaves retailers wary of coming to Canada. (2014, June 2). *CBC News*. Retrieved from http://www.cbc.ca/news/business/target-launch-leaves-retailers-wary-of-coming-to-canada-1.2662155; Lewis, K. (2003, November 10). Kmart's ten deadly sins. Book review in *Forbes.com*. Retrieved May 2010 from http://www.forbes .com/2003/10/10/1010kmartreview.html

35. Wessel, M. (2011, September 7). The failure of Yahoo's board. *Hbr Blog Network*. Retrieved from http://blogs.hbr.org/2011/09/failure-yahoo-board/; Silcoff, S., McNish, J., & Ladurantaye, S. (2013, September 27). How BlackBerry blew it: The inside story. *Globe and Mail*. Retrieved from http://www.theglobeandmail.com/report-on-business/ the-inside-story-of-why-blackberry-is-failing/article14563602/#dashboard/follows/

36. Thornhill, S., & Amit, R. (2003). *Learning from failure: Organizational mortality and the resource-based view*. Research Paper, Statistics Canada. Retrieved May 2010 from www.statcan.gc.ca/pub/11f0019m/11f0019m2003202-eng.pdf.

37. Verdú, A. J., & Gómez-Gras, J. M. (2009). Measuring the organizational responsiveness through managerial flexibility. *Journal of Organizational Change*, 22(6), 668–690; Santos, V., & García, T. (2007). The complexity of the organizational renewal decision: The managerial role. *Leadership and Organizational Development Journal*, 28(4), 336–355.

38. Trahant, B., & Burke, W. W. (1996). Creating a change reaction: How understanding organizational dynamics can ease reengineering. *National Productivity Review*, 15(4), 37–46; Lannes, W. J. III, & Logan, J. W. (2004). A technique for assessing an organization's ability to change. *IEEE Transactions in Engineering Management*, 51(4), 483.

39. Ratterty, A., & Simons, R. (2002). The influence of attitudes to change on adoption of an integrated IT system. *Organization Development Abstracts*, Academy of Management Proceedings; Mitchell, N., et al. Program commitment in the implementation of strategic change. *Organization Development Abstracts*, Academy of Management Proceedings.

40. Hyde, A., & Paterson, J. (2002). Leadership development as a vehicle for change during merger. *Journal of Change Management*, 2(3), 266–271.

41. Nevis, E. C., DiBella, A. J., & Gould, J. M. (1995). Understanding organizations as learning systems. *Sloan Management Review*, 36(2), 73–85.

42. Armenakis, A. A., Harris, S. G., & Field, H. S. (1999). Making change permanent: A model for institutionalizing change interventions. In W. Passmore & R. Woodman (Eds.), *Research in organizational change and development* (Vol. 12, pp. 289–319). Greenwich, CT: JAI Press.

43. Holt, D. (2002). Readiness for change: The development of a scale. *Organization Development Abstracts,* Academy of Management Proceedings.

44. Judge, W., & Douglas, T. (2009). Organizational change capacity: The systematic development of a scale. *Journal of Organizational Change Management, 22*(6), 635–649.

45. Stewart, T. A. (1994, February 7). Rate your readiness to change. *Fortune,* 106–110.

46. Castellano, J. F., Rosenzweig, K., & Roehm, H. A. (2004, Summer). How corporate culture impacts unethical distortion of financial numbers. *Management Accounting Quarterly;* Gellerman, S. W. (1989, Winter). Managing ethics from the top down. *Sloan Management Review.*

47. Lazaric, N., & Raybaut, A. (2014, January). Do incentive systems spur work motivation of inventors in high tech firms? A group based perspective. *Journal of Evolutionary Economics, 24*(1), 135–157; Proenca, E. J. (2007, December). Team dynamics and team empowerment in health care organizations. *Health Care Management Review;* Bartol, K. M., & Srivastava, A. (2002, Summer). Encouraging knowledge sharing: The role of organizational reward systems. *Journal of Leadership and Organizational Studies, 9*(1), 64–76.

48. Klarner, P., Probst, G., & Soparnot, R. (2005). Organizational change capacity in the public service: The case of the World Health Organization. *Journal of Change Management, 8*(1), 57–72.

49. Willey, D. (2008, February 28). Naples battles with rubbish mountain. *BBC News.* Retrieved May 2010 from http://news.bbc.co.uk/2/hi/europe/7266755.stm; Quattrone, A. M. (2009, November 20). Garbage crisis and organized crime. *Naples Politics.* Retrieved May 2010 from http://naplespolitics.com/2009/11/20/garbage-crisis-and-organized-crime/; Italy slammed by EU court over Naples garbage. (2010, March 4). *EUbusiness.* Retrieved May 2010 from http://www.eubusiness.com/news-eu/court-italy-waste.3h2/; Harrell, E. (2011, May 9). This stinks: Italy sends troops to handle trash crisis. *Time.* Retrieved from http://science.time.com/2011/05/09/this-stinks-italy-sends-troops-to-handle-trash-crisis/.

50. Mesco, M. (2013, November 25). Naples's garbage crisis piles up on city outskirts. *Wall Street Journal.* Retrieved from http://online.wsj.com/news/articles/SB10001424052702304465604579218014071052296.

51. Havman, H. A. (1992). Between a rock and a hard place: Organizational change and performance under conditions of fundamental environmental transformation. *Administrative Science Quarterly, 37*(1), 48–75.

52. Barnett, C. K., & Pratt, M. G. (2000). From threat-rigidity to flexibility: Toward a learning model of autogenic crisis in organizations. *Journal of Organizational Change Management, 13*(1), 74–88.

53. Simons, T. L. (1999). Behavioral integrity as a critical ingredient for transformational leadership. *Journal of Organizational Change Management, 12*(2), 89.

54. Hosmer, L. T., & Kiewitz, C. (2005). Organizational justice: A behavioral science concept with critical implications for business ethics and stakeholder theory. *Business Ethics Quarterly, 15*(1), 67.

55. Leadership tips, New York style: Lessons from the NYC MTA. (2012, November 14). *Forbes.* Retrieved from http://www.forbes.com/sites/johnkotter/2012/11/14/leadership-tips-new-york-style-lessons-from-the-nyc-mta/; Tucker, B. A., & Russell, R. F. (2004). The influence of the transformational leader. *Journal of Leadership and Organizational Studies, 10*(4), 103–111.

56. Lee, C. C., & Rodgers, R. A. (2009, Summer). Counselor advocacy: Affecting systemic change in the public arena. *Journal of Counseling and Development, 87*(3), 284–287.

57. Akgun, A. E., Lynn, G. S., & Bryne, J. C. (2006, January). Antecedents and consequences of unlearning in new product development teams. *The Journal of Product Innovation Management, 23*(1), 73–88.

58. Tucker, B. A., & Russell, R. F. (2004). The influence of the transformational leader. *Journal of Leadership and Organizational Studies, 10*(4), 103–111.

59. Naughton, K. (2002). The perk wars. *Newsweek, 140*(14), 44.

60. Mintzberg, H., Simons, R., & Basu, K. (2002, Fall). Beyond selfishness. *Sloan Management Review,* 67–74; Collins, J. (2001). *From good to great: Why some companies make the leap . . . and others don't.* New York: HarperBusiness; De Geus, A. (1997). The living company. *Harvard Business Review, 75*(2), 51–59.

61. Wall, S. J. (2005). The protean organization: Learning to love change. *Organizational Dynamics, 34*(1), 37.

62. Adapted from *Managing Change to Reduce Resistance.* Boston, Mass.: Harvard Business School Press, 2005, 143–150.

63. Enderle, R. (2014, March 5). Meg Whitman's amazing turnaround at HP. *IT Business Edge.* Retrieved from http://www.itbusinessedge.com/blogs/unfiltered-opinion/meg-whitmans-amazing-turnaround-of-hp.html; Hough, J. (2014, April 5). Meg Whitman's turnaround at HP. *Barron's.* Retrieved from http://online.barrons.com/news/articles/SB50001424053111903698104579473470353264720; Coyle, E. (2013, October 10). Meg Whitman's 6 steps to an HP turnaround. *Wall St, CheatSheet.* Retrieved from http://wallstcheatsheet.com/stocks/meg-whitmans-6-steps-to-an-hp-turnaround.html/?a=viewall; Canada's top 100 employers. (n.d.). Retrieved from http://www.canadastop100.com/national/.

64. Higgins, J. M., & McAllister, C. (2004). If you want strategic change, don't forget to change your culture artifacts. *Journal of Change Management, 4*(1), 63–73.

65. Helyar, J. (2004, October 4). Why is this man smiling? Continental's Gordon Bethune turned the airline around, guided it through 9/11, and became a great CEO. Now he's being forced out. How can this be? *Fortune.* Retrieved May 2010 from http://faculty.msb.edu/homak/homahelpsite/webhelp/Airlines_-_Why_s_Bethune_Smiling__Fortune_11-18-04.htm.

66. Higgins, J. M., & McAllister, C. (2004). If you want strategic change, don't forget to change your culture artifacts. *Journal of Change Management, 4*(1), 63–73.

67. World's most admired companies. (2009, March 16). *Fortune.* Retrieved from http://archive.fortune.com/magazines/fortune/mostadmired/2009/snapshots/2065.html; World Airline Awards for 2009. (2009). *World Airline Awards.* Retrieved from http://worldairlineawards.com/Awards_2009/AirlineYear-2009.htm.

68. The legacy that got left on the shelf—Unilever and emerging markets. (2008, February). *The Economist, 386*(8565), 76.

69. Unilever stock performance chart. Retrieved from http://ycharts.com/companies/UN.

70. Sull, D. N. (1999, July–August). Why good companies go bad. *Harvard Business Review.*

71. Finkelstein, S. (2003). *Why smart executives fail: And what you can learn from their mistakes.* New York: Penguin.

72. Eaton, J. (2001). Management communication: The threat of groupthink. *Corporate Communications, 6*(4), 183–192; Kahneman, D., Lovallo, D., & Sibony, O. (2011, June). Before you make the big decision. *Harvard Business Review,* 51–60.

73. Whyte, G. (1989). Groupthink reconsidered. *Academy of Management Review, 14,* 40–56; Neck, C. P., & Moorhead, G. (1992). Jury deliberations in the trial of *U.S. v. John DeLorean*: A case analysis of groupthink avoidance and enhanced framework. *Human Relations, 45*(10), 1077–1091.

74. Charan, R., & Useem, J. (2002, May 22). Why companies fail. *Fortune,* 50–62.

75. Cole, M. S., Harris, S. G., & Bernerth, J. B. (2006). Exploring the implications of vision, appropriateness, and execution of organizational change. *Leadership and Organizational Development Journal, 27*(5), 352–369.

76. Simons, G. F., et al. (1998). In S. Komives, J. Lucas, & T. R. McMahon, *Exploring leadership* (p. 54). San Francisco: Jossey-Bass.

77. Thornberry, N. (1997). A view about vision. *European Management Journal, 15*(1), 28–34.

78. Beach, L. R. (1993). *Making the right decision* (p. 50). Englewood Cliffs, NJ: Prentice Hall.

79. Nanus, B. (1992). *Visionary leadership.* San Francisco: Jossey-Bass; Kirkpatrick, S. A., & Locke, E. A. (1996). Direct and indirect effects of three core charismatic leadership components on performance and attitudes. *Journal of Applied Psychology, 81,* 36–51.

80. Baum, I. R., Locke, E. A., & Kirkpatrick, S. A. (1998). A longitudinal study of the relation of vision and vision communication to venture growth in entrepreneurial firms. *Journal of Applied Psychology, 83,* 43–54.

81. Jick, T. (2003). *Managing change* (pp. 98–100). Boston: Irwin.

82. Butterworth, C. (2013, November). Leading the way. *Occupational Health, 65,* 11.

83. Higgins, J. M., & McAllaster, C. (2004). If you want strategic change, don't forget to change your cultural artifacts. *Journal of Change Management, 4*(1), 63–73.

84. Jick, T. (1993). The vision thing (A). In T. Jick, *Managing change* (pp. 142–148). Homewood, IL: Irwin.

85. Langeler, G. H. (1992, March–April). The vision trap. *Harvard Business Review,* 46–55.

86. Deszca, G., & Cawsey, T. (2014). Information contained in this section was collected by the authors when developing the case: Food Banks Canada and Strategic Renewal (case is reprinted in this book). Further information on Food Banks Canada can be viewed on their website: http://www.foodbankscanada.ca/Learn-About-Hunger/About-Hunger-in-Canada.aspx.

87. Lipton, M. (1996, Summer). Demystifying the development of an organizational vision. *Sloan Management Review,* 86.

88. Lipton, M. (1996, Summer). Demystifying the development of an organizational vision. *Sloan Management Review,* 89–91.

89. Levin, I. M. (2000). Vision revisited. *Journal of Applied Behavioral Science, 36*(1), 91–107.

90. Kalogeridis, C. (2005). The Ford/Firestone fiasco: Coming to blows. *Radnor, 185*(1), 22–24.

91. Healey, J. R., & Irwin, J. (2014, June 18). GM recalls 3.16 million more cars for switches. *USA Today.* Retrieved from http://www.usatoday.com/story/money/cars/2014/06/16/gm-recall-key-switch/10629373/.

92. The National Business Hall of Fame. (1990, March 12). *Fortune, 121*(6), 42.

93. Serwer, A. (2001, September 17). P&G's covert operation. *Fortune, 144*(5), 42.

94. Searcey, D. (2010, April 19). Toyota agrees to $16.4 million fine. *Wall Street Journal Digital Network,* Auto Section. Retrieved May 2010 from http://online.wsj.com/article/SB10001424052748704508904575192873543926804.html.

95. World's most admired companies. *Fortune.* Retrieved May 2010 from http://money.cnn.com/magazines/fortune/mostadmired/2010/index.html.

96. Goss, T., Pascale, R., & Athos, A. (1993, November–December). The reinvention roller coaster: Risking the present for a powerful future. *Harvard Business Review,* 97–108.

97. McKinnon, N. (2008). We've never done it this way before: Prompting organizational change through stories. *Global Business and Organizational Excellence, 27*(2), 16–25.

98. Cranston, S., & Keller, S. (2013, January). Increasing the "meaning quotient" of work. *McKinsey Quarterly.*

99. Wheatley, M. (1994). *Leadership and the new sciences.* San Francisco: Berrett-Koehler.

100. Beach, L. R. (1993). *Making the right decision* (p. 58). Englewood Cliffs, NJ: Prentice Hall.

101. Jørgensen, H., Owen, L., & Nues, A. (2008). *Making change work.* IBM Global Services. Retrieved May 2010 from http://www-935.ibm.com/services/us/gbs/bus/pdf/gbe03100-usen-03-making-change-work.pdf; Lockwood, N. R. (2007). Leveraging employee engagement for competitive advantage: HR's strategic role. *Society for*

Human Resource Management Research Quarterly. Retrieved May 2010 from http://www.improvedexperience.com/doc/02_Leveraging_Employee_Engagement_for_Competitive_Advantage2.pdf; Morgan, D. E., & Zeffane, R. (2003). Employee involvement, organizational change and trust in management. *International Journal of Human Resource Management, 14*(1), 55–75.

102. How to create a powerful vision for change. *Forbes*. Retrieved from http://www.forbes.com/sites/johnkotter/2011/06/07/how-to-create-a-powerful-vision-for-change/.

103. Gross, A., & Minot, J. (2008, May). Meeting recruiting and retention challenges in India. *SHRM Global Forum*. Retrieved from Scribd: http://www.scribd.com/doc/10553235/Meeting-Recruiting-and-Retention-Challenges-in-India; Personal communication with G. Deszca, when visiting Infosys and Tata Consulting in March 2011.

104. Infosys to add 3,500 more employees. (2014, February 8). *The New Indian Express*. Retrieved from http://www.newindianexpress.com/cities/thiruvananthapuram/Infosys-to-Add-3500-More-Employees/2014/02/08/article2044683.ece.

105. Dr. Martin Luther King Jr.'s "I Have a Dream" Speech. *The Martin Luther King Jr. Papers Project* at Stanford University. Retrieved May 2010 from www.stanford.edu/group/King/publications/speeches/address_at_march_on_washington.pdf.

106. Sawhill, J. C., & Harmeling, S. S. (2000, March). National campaign to prevent teen pregnancy. *Harvard Business School Case Study*, 9–300–105.

107. Stohr, G. (2012, December 8). Gay marriage gets supreme court review for the first time. *Bloomberg*. Retrieved from www.bloomberg.com/news/.../gay-marriage-gets-supreme-court-review; Williams, P., & McClam, E. (2013, June 26). Supreme Court strikes down Defense of Marriage Act, paves way for gay marriage to resume in California. *NBC News*. Retrieved from http://nbcpolitics.nbcnews.com/_news/2013/06/26/19151971-supreme-court-strikes-down-defense-of-marriage-act-paves-way-for-gay-marriage-to-resume-in-california?lite.

108. Schneider, G. (2005, March 31). An unlikely meeting of the minds. *Washington Post*, p. E01.

109. Reed, B. (2010). How Google wants to change telecom: Google's foray into the telecom industry. *Network World*. Retrieved May 2010 from http://www.network world.com/news/2010/040110-google-telecom.html?page=3.

110. Retrieved from the Xerox website: http://www.xerox.ca/innovation/automated-work-flow/enca.html.

111. Retrieved May 2010 from http://www-03.ibm.com/employment/us/diverse/index.shtml.

112. Retrieved June 2014 from: http://www.rmhc.org/mission-and-vision.

113. Govindarajan, V. (2010). Vijay Govindarajan's Blog: Strategic innovation, industry transformation and global leadership. Tuck School of Business at Dartmouth. Retrieved May 2010 from http://www.vijaygovindarajan.com/2009/03/the_tata_nano_product_or_socia.htm; Vision for Nano achieved. (2012, March 10). *NDTV*. Retrieved from http://www.ndtv.com/video/player/ndtv-special-ndtv-profit/vision-for-nano-achieved-says-ratan-tata/225972.

114. Retrieved May 2010 from http://www.worldwildlife.org/what/communityaction/index.html.

115. The Millennium Development Goals Report 2013. *United Nations*. Retrieved from http://www.undp.org/content/dam/undp/library/MDG/english/mdg-report-2013-english.pdf.

116. Retrieved May 2010 from http://www.savethechildren.org/programs/health/child-survival/survive-to-5/?WT.mc_id=1109_hp_tab_s25.

117. Retrieved from http://www.globalgiving.org/pfil/2030/projdoc.pdf.

118. Retrieved from https://www.kickstarter.com/projects/readingrainbow/bring-reading-rainbow-back-for-every-child-everywh.

119. Latham, G. P., & Locke, E. P. (1987). How to set goals. In R. W. Beatty (Ed.), *The performance management sourcebook*. Amherst, MA: Human Resource Development Press.

120. Drawn from Jick, T. (1993). The vision thing (A). In T. Jick, *Managing change*. Homewood, IL: Irwin; Lipton, M. (1996, Summer). Demystifying the development of an organizational vision. *Sloan Management Review*, 83–92.

121. Lipton, M. (1996, Summer). Demystifying the development of an organizational vision. *Sloan Management Review*, 89–91.

Chapter 5

1. *New York Times*, November 3, 1986.

2. Retrieved from http://www.famousquotesandauthors.com/authors/winston_churchill_quotes.html.

3. Langton, N., Robbins, S. P., & Judge, T. A. (2010). *Organizational behaviour: Concepts, controversies, applications* (5th Canadian ed., p. 502). Toronto: Pearson Canada.

4. Daft, R. L. (2007). *Organization theory and design* (9th ed., p. 90). Cincinnati, OH: South-Western College.

5. Walmart. (2014). *Annual report*. Retrieved July 2014 from http://cdn.corporate.walmart.com/66/e5/9ff9a87445949173fde56316ac5f/2014-annual-report.pdf.

6. Team T. (2014, June 9). Wal-Mart expects 30% rise in e-commerce revenue this year. *Forbes*. Retrieved from http://www.forbes.com/sites/greatspeculations/2014/06/09/walmart-expects-30-rise-in-e-commerce-revenues-this-year/.

7. Competitive advantage lies in systems efficiencies. (2002). *Chain Store Age, 78*(8), 74.

8. Bolman, L., & Deal, T. (2008). *Reframing organizations: Artistry, choice, and leadership* (4th ed., pp. 45–116). San Francisco: Jossey-Bass.

9. Langton, N., Robbins, S. P., & Judge, T. A. (2010). *Organizational behaviour: Concepts, controversies, applications* (5th Canadian ed., pp. 500–527). Toronto: Pearson Canada.

10. For a detailed treatment of structural design dimensions, see Daft, R. L. (2007). *Organization theory and design* (9th ed.). Cincinnati, OH: South-Western College Publishing.

11. Thompson, J. D. (1967). *Organizations in action*. New York: McGraw-Hill.

12. Aragón-Correa, J. A., & Sharma, S. (2003). A contingent resource-based view of proactive corporate environmental strategy. *Academy of Management Review, 28*(1), 71–88; Moles, C., van der Gaag, A., & Fox, J. (2010). The practice of complexity: Review, change and service improvement in NHA department. *Journal of Health Organization and Management, 24*(2), 127–144; Davis, J. P., Eisenhardt, K. M., & Bingham, C. B. (2009). Optimal structure, market dynamism, and the strategy of simple rules. *Administrative Science Quarterly, 54,* 413–452.

13. Daft, R. L. (2007). *Organization theory and design* (9th ed., p. 152). Cincinnati, OH: South-Western College.

14. Martínez-León, I. M., & Martínez-García, J. A. (2011, 32.5/6). The influence of organizational structure on organizational learning. *International Journal of Manpower*, 537–566; Olden, P. C. (2012, October–December). Managing mechanistic and organic structure in health care. *The Health Care Manager*.

15. Tu, Q., Vonderembse, M. A., Ragu-Nathan, T. S., & Ragu-Nathan, B. (2004). Measuring modularity-based manufacturing practices and their impact on mass customization capability: A customer-driven perspective. *Decision Sciences, 35*(2), 147–168.

16. Galbraith, J. R. (1977). *Organization design*. Reading, MA: Addison-Wesley.

17. Daft, R. L. (2003). *Organization theory and design* (6th ed., pp. 204–211). Cincinnati, OH: South-Western College.

18. The 9–11 Commission. (2004). *9/11 Commission report: Final report of the National Commission on Terrorist Attacks upon the United States*. Washington, DC: Government Printing Office.

19. Keller, S., Meaney, M., & Pung, C. (2013, November). Organizing for change: McKinsey global survey results. *McKinsey and Company*; Cross, R. L., Parise, S., & Weiss, L. M. (2007, April). The role of networks in organizational change. *McKinsey Quarterly*.

20. Langton, N., Robbins, S. P., & Judge, T. A. (2010). *Organizational behaviour: Concepts, controversies, applications* (5th Canadian ed., p. 512). Toronto: Pearson Canada.

21. McGregor, J. (2008, January 28). Case study: To adapt, ITT lets go of unpopular ratings. *Business Week*, 4068, 46.

22. Survey: Partners in wealth. (2006, January 21). *The Economist, 378*(8461), 18.

23. Farrier, T. (2013, August 29). How do the challenges with Boeing's 787 Dreamliner compare to the introductions of other aircraft? *Forbes*. Retrieved from www.forbes.com./sites/quora/2013/08/29/how-do-the-challenges-with-boeings-787-dreamliner-compare-to-the-introductions-of-other-aircraft/; Kingsley-Jones, M. The Boeing 787 Dreamliner. *Flightglobal*. Retrieved July 3, 2014, from www.flightglobal.com/feature/787dreamlines/market/; Boeing's partnership for success strains supplier relationships. (2014, February 16). *Leeham News and Comment*. Retrieved from http://leehamnews.com.2014/02/16/boeing-partnership-for-success-strains-strains-supplier-relationship/; Boeing 787 Dreamliner. *Wikipedia*. Retrieved from http//en.wikipedia.org/wiki/Boeing_787_Dreamliner. Updated.

24. Boeing and the 787: Not so dreamy. (2009, June 24). *The Economist* online. Retrieved May 2010 from www.economist.com/businessfinance/displaystory.cfm?story_id=E1_TPRJQQDQ.

25. Wetzel, D. K., & Buch, K. (2009, Winter). Using a structural model to diagnose organizations and develop congruent interventions. *Organization Development Journal, 18*(4), 9–19.

26. Hill, D. (2004). The case for standards. *Health Management Technology, 25*(10), 48–50.

27. Yi, E. I., & Zhu, P. F. (2009, February 24). Faced with budget cuts, Harvard College Library consolidates. *Harvard Crimson*. Retrieved December 2010 from http://www.thecrimson.com/article/2009/2/24/faced-with-budget-cuts-harvard-college/.

28. Bolman, L., & Deal, T. (2008). *Reframing organizations: Artistry, choice, and leadership* (4th ed.). San Francisco: Jossey-Bass.

29. Bolman, L., & Deal, T. (2008). *Reframing organizations: Artistry, choice, and leadership* (4th ed., p. 73). San Francisco: Jossey-Bass.

30. Bolman, L., & Deal, T. (2008). *Reframing organizations: Artistry, choice, and leadership* (4th ed., p. 73). San Francisco: Jossey-Bass.

31. Bolman, L., & Deal, T. (2008). *Reframing organizations: Artistry, choice, and leadership* (4th ed., p. 74). San Francisco: Jossey-Bass.

32. Wischnevsky, J., & Damanpour, F. (2009). Radical strategic and structural change: Occurrence, antecedents and consequences. *International Journal of Technology Management, 44*(1/2), 53.

33. Masters, H., & Katrandjian, O. (2010, December 23). LifeSpring Hospitals: Bringing Maternity Care to Poor Mothers in India. *ABC News*. Retrieved from http://abcnews.go.com/Health/lifespring-hospitals-bring-maternity-care-to-poor-mothers-in-india/story?id=12459083; LifeSpring Maternity Hospital website. Retrieved from http://www.lifespring.in/; LifeSpring Hospitals. *Wikipedia*. Retrieved from http://en.wikipedia.org/wiki/LifeSpring_Hospitals; the Acumen Funds' website's description of LifeSpring was retrieved from http://acumen.org./investment/lifespring/.

34. Former ChevronTexaco executive tapped in special Labor Day board meeting. (2002, September 3). Retrieved May 2010 from money.cnn.com/2002/09/02/news/companies/ual/index.htm.

35. Air Canada seeking more labour concessions from unions. (2003, May 1). *CBC News*. Retrieved December 2010 from www.cbc.ca/money/story/2003/05/01/aircanada_030501.html.

36. Sackcloth and ashes: An entrenched dispute takes the shine off a proud airline. (2010, May 20). *The Economist*. Retrieved May 2010 from www.economist.com/node/16171321.

37. Roth, D. (2002, January 22). How to cut pay, lay off 8,000 people and still have workers who love you: It's easy: Just follow the Agilent way. *Fortune*. Retrieved December 2010 from http://www.danielroth.net/archive/2002/01/how_to_cut_pay_.html.

38. For information on awards, history, products, and financial performance see Agilent's corporate website. Retrieved from http://www.home.agilent.com/agilent/home.jspx?cc=CA&lc=eng. Information on stock performance retrieved from http://www.marketwatch.com/investing/stock/a and from http://www.investor.agilent.com/phoenix.zhtml?c=103274&p=irol-stockquotechart&control_javaupperindicator=&control_javauf=&control_javatype=&control_javascale=&control_javanumberperiods=&control_javamovingaverage=&control_javalowerindicator2=&control_javalowerindicator1=&control_javachartfunctions=&control_javaapplet=.

39. Nadler, D., Shaw, R. B., Walton, A. E., & Associates. (1994). *Discontinuous change: Leading organizational transformation*. San Francisco: Jossey-Bass.

40. Simons, R. (1995, March–April). Control in the age of empowerment. *Harvard Business Review*, 80–88; Simons, R. (1998, May–June). How risky is your company? *Harvard Business Review*, 85–94.

41. Howell, J., & Higgins, C. (1990). Champions of change: Identifying, understanding and supporting champions of technological innovations. *Organizational Dynamics, 19*(1), 40–55.

42. Tight, G. (1998). From experience: Securing sponsors and funding for new product development projects—the human side of enterprise. *Journal of Product Innovation Management, 15*(1), 75–81; Harrold, D. (1999). How to get control & automation projects approved. *Control Engineering, 46*(8), 34–37.

43. Harrold, D. (1999). How to get control & automation projects approved. *Control Engineering, 46*(8), 34–37.

44. Drew, S. A. W. (1996). Accelerating change: Financial industry experiences with BPR. *International Journal of Bank Marketing, 14*(6), 23–35.

45. Noori, H., Deszca, G., & Munro, H. (1997). Managing the P/SDI process: Best-in-class principles and leading practices. *International Journal of Technology Management*, 245–268.

46. Dillard, J., Hunter, J., & Burgoon, M. (1984). Sequential request persuasive strategies: Meta-analysis of foot-in-the-door and door-in-the-face. *Human Communication Research, 10*, 461–488.

47. Gladwell, M. (2000). *The tipping point: How little things can make a big difference*. New York: Little, Brown.

48. This example is drawn from Meyerson, D. E. (2001, October). Radical change, the quiet way. *Harvard Business Review*, 94–95.

49. Howell, J., & Higgins, C. (1990). Champions of change: Identifying, understanding and supporting champions of technological innovations. *Organizational Dynamics, 19*(1), 40–55.

50. Frost, P. J., & Egri, C. P. (1990). Influence of political action on innovation: Part II. *Leadership and Organizational Development Journal, 11*(2), 4–12.

51. Marshak, R. J. (2004). Morphing: The leading edge of organizational change in the twenty-first century. *Organizational Development Journal, 22*(3), 8–21.

52. Abrahamson, E. (2000, July–August). Change without pain. *Harvard Business Review*, 75–79.

53. The MASkargo website. Retrieved July 3, 2014, from http://www.maskargo.com/; Tomkins, N. (2014, June 6). MASkargo boss resigns. *Aircargo News*. Retrieved from http://www.aircargonews.net/news/single-view/news/maskargo-boss-resigns.html; Abdullah, M. (2003, March 24). *Business Times*, Kuala Lumpur, Malaysia.

54. 63% of CRM initiatives fail. (2013, July 17). *Direct Marketing News*. Retrieved from http://www.dmnews.com/63-of-crm-initiatives-fail/article/303470/; Choy, J. (2003, March 17). The Cold Truth about CRM. *Asia Computer Weekly*.

55. Prosci Benchmarking Report. (2002). *Best practices in change management*. Prosci 2000, 2.

56. Tsaparis. P. (2013, February 21). Why is common sense so uncommon? *Globe and Mail* Report on Business. Retrieved from http://m.theglobeandmail.com/report-on-business/careers-leadership/why-is-common-sense-so-uncommon/article8936634/?service=mobile; Paul Tsaparis: Executive profile and biography. *Bloomberg Businessweek*. Retrieved from http://investing.businessweek.com/research/stocks/people/person.asp?personid=7468530&ticker=HPQ; Canadian merger integration material drawn from Pitts, G. (2002, September 30). *Globe and Mail*, p. B3.

57. Waldersee, R., & Griffiths, A. (2004). Implementing change: Matching implementation methods and change type. *Leadership and Development Journal*, *25*(5), 424–434.

58. Mishra, K. E., Spreitzer, G. M., & Mishra, A. K. (1998, Winter). Preserving employee morale during downsizing. *Sloan Management Review*, 83–95.

59. Mishra, K. E., Spreitzer, G. M., & Mishra, A. K. (1998, Winter). Preserving employee morale during downsizing. *Sloan Management Review*, 83–95.

60. Nevis, E. C., DiBella, A. J., & Gould, J. M. (1995, Winter). Understanding organizations as learning systems. *Sloan Management Review, 36*(2), 73–85.

61. Beatty, R. W., & Ulrich, D. O. (1991, Summer). Re-energizing the mature organization. *Organizational Dynamics*, 16–31; Beer, M., & Nohria, N. (2000, May–June). Cracking the code of change. *Harvard Business Review*, 133–142.

62. Hoyte, D. S., & Greenwood, R. A. (2007). Journey to the North Face: A guide to business transformation. *Academy of Strategic Management Journal*, *6*, 91–104; Hoogervorst, J. A. P., Koopman, P. L., & van der Flier, H. (2005). Total quality management: The need for an employee-centred, coherent approach. *TQM Magazine*, *17*(1), 92–106.

63. Worley, C., & Lawler, E. (2009). Building a change capacity at Capital One Financial. *Organizational Dynamics*, *38*(4), 245–251.

64. Harris, M., Dopson, S., & Fitzpatrick, R. (2009). Strategic drift in international non-governmental development organizations—putting strategy in the background of organizational change. *Public Administration and Development*, *29*(5), 415–428.

65. Margonelli, L. (2002, October). How IKEA designs its sexy price tags. *Business 2.0*, 106.

66. Miles, R. E., & Snow, C. C. (1992, Summer). Causes of failure in network organizations. *California Management Review, 34*(4), 53–72.

67. Morgan, J. (2012). *The collaborate organization: A strategic guide to solving your internal business challenges using emerging social and collaborative tools*. New York: McGraw-Hill.

68. Ellard, C. (2012, November 25). Do collaborative workspaces work? *Psychology Today*. Retrieved from http://www.psychologytoday.com/blog/mind-wandering/201211/do-collaborative-workspaces-work.

69. The holes is holacracy. (2014, July 5). *The Economist*. Retrieved from http://www.economist.com/news/business/21606267-latest-big-idea-management-deserves-some-scepticism-holes-holacracy?frsc=dg%7Ce.

70. Chesbrough, H., & Brunswicker, S. (2013, May). *Managing open innovation in large firms: Survey report—Executive survey on open innovation 2013*. Stuttgart, Germany: Fraunhofer Institute for Industrial Engineering.

71. Keller, S., Meaney, M., & Pung, C. (2013, November). Organizing for change: McKinsey global survey results. *McKinsey and Company*.

72. Martínez-León, I. M., & Martínez-García, J. A. (2011, 32.5/6). The influence of organizational structure on organizational learning. *International Journal of Manpower*, 537–566.

73. Cross, R. L., Parise, S., & Weiss, L. M. (2007, April). The role of networks in organizational change. *McKinsey Quarterly*.

Chapter 6

1. Wheatley, M. J. (2006). *Leadership and the new science: Discovering order in a chaotic world*. San Francisco: Berrett-Koehler.
2. Naughton, K. (2000, December 11). A mess of a merger. *Newsweek*. Retrieved December 2010 from http://www.newsweek.com/2000/12/10/a-mess-of-a-merger.html.
3. Morosini, P., & Radler, G. (1999). DaimlerChrysler: The post-merger integration phase. *International Institute for Management Development, 121*.
4. Golden, B., & Nolan, N. (2002). *Crafting a vision at Daimler-Chrysler* (pp. 2–3). Richard Ivey School of Business, University of Western Ontario.
5. Golden, B., & Nolan, N. (2002). *Crafting a vision at Daimler-Chrysler* (p. 2). Richard Ivey School of Business, University of Western Ontario.
6. Edmondson, G. (2007, May 15). Why Daimler gave Chrysler to Cerberus: After ponying up billions, German automaker pays buyout firm to take over. *Bloomberg BusinessWeek*. Retrieved December 2010 from http://www.msnbc.msn.com/id/18680299/ns/business-bloomberg_businessweek/.
7. Eisenstein, P. (2000, December 13). Signs of discontent. *Professional Engineering*.
8. Daimler-Chrysler: Why the marriage failed. (2007, May 17). *Auto Observer*. Retrieved December 2010 from http://www.autoobserver.com/2007/05/daimler-chrysler-why-the-marriage-failed.html.
9. Useem, J. (2002, August 12). 3M + GE = ?: Jim McNerney thinks he can turn 3M from a good company into a great one—with a little help from his former employer, General Electric. *Fortune*. Retrieved December 2010 from http://money.cnn.com/magazines/fortune/fortune_archive/2002/08/12/327038/index.htm.
10. Piderit, S. K. (2000). Rethinking resistance and recognizing ambivalence: A multidimensional view of attitudes toward an organizational change. *Academy of Management Review, 4*(25), 783–794.
11. Robbins, S. P., Langton, N., & Judge, T. A. (2010). *Organizational behaviour* (5th Canadian ed., p. 300). Toronto: Pearson.
12. Bolman, L. G., & Deal, T. E. (2008). *Reframing organizations: Artistry, choice, and leadership*. San Francisco: Jossey-Bass.
13. Ringer, R. C., & Boss, R. M. (2000). Hospital professionals' use of upward tactics. *Journal of Management Issues, 12*(1), 92–108.
14. Treatment of these power-related concepts can be found in: Whetten, D. A., & Cameron, K. S. (2010). *Developing management skills* (8th ed.). Englewood Cliffs, NJ: Prentice Hall.
15. Hoffstead identified and referred to this cultural variable as power distance. See Hofstede, G. (1993, February). Cultural constraints in management theories. *Academy of Management Executive*, 81–94.
16. Hardy, C. (1994, Winter). Power and organizational development: A framework for organizational change. *Journal of General Management, 20*, 20–42.
17. Bolman, L. G. & Deal, T. E. (2008). *Reframing organizational: Artistry, choice, and leadership*. San Francisco, CA: Jossey-Bass.
18. Lewin, K., Lippitt, R., & White, R. K. (1939). Patterns of aggressive behavior in experimentally created "social climates." *Journal of Social Psychology, 10*, 271–299.
19. Deal, T. E., & Kennedy, A. A. (1982). *Corporate cultures: The rites and rituals of corporate life*. New York: Penguin Books; Kotter, J. P., & Heskett, J. L. (1992). *Corporate culture & performance*. New York: The Free Press; Schein, E. H. (1992). *Organization culture and leadership*. San Francisco: Jossey-Bass.
20. Retrieved from http://www.amazon.com/s/ref=nb_sb_ss_i_3_14?url=search-alias%3Dstripbooks&field-keywords=organization%20culture&sprefix=organization+c%2Cstripbooks%2C152.
21. Shani, A. B., Chandler, D., Coget, J.-F., & Lau, J. B. (2009). *Behavior in organizations: An experiential approach*. Boston: McGraw-Hill Irwin.

22. Lewin, K. (1951). *Field theory in social science*. New York: Harper and Row; Thomas, J. (1985). Force field analysis: A new way to evaluate your strategy. *Long Range Planning, 18*(6), 54–59.

23. Strebel, P. (1994, Winter). Choosing the right change path. *California Management Review*, 29–51.

24. More pain, waiting for the gain. (2006, February 11). *The Economist*, p. 58.

25. Savage, G. T., et al. (1991). Strategies for assessing and managing organizational stakeholders. *Academy of Management Executive, 5*(2), 61–75.

26. Cross, R., & Prusak, L. (2002, June). The people who make organizations go—or stop. *Harvard Business Review*, 5–12.

27. Luksha, P., personal communication to T. Cawsey.

28. Floyd, S., & Wooldridge, B. (1992). Managing the strategic consensus: The foundation of effective implementation. *Academy of Management Executive, 6*(4), 27–39.

Chapter 7

1. Howard; C., & Pierce, K. (eds.). (2014, May 28). The world's 100 most powerful women: #70 Ellen Johnson-Sirleaf. *Forbes*. Retrieved from http://www.forbes.com/power-women/; Ellen Johnson Sirleaf. *Wikipedia*. Retrieved from http://en.wikipedia.org/wiki/Ellen_Johnson_Sirleaf; Ellen Johnson Sirleaf—biographical. Nobel Peace Prize 2011. *Nobelprize.org*. Retrieved from http://www.nobelprize.org/nobel_prizes/peace/laureates/2011/johnson_sirleaf-bio.html .

2. Disney, A. (Producer), & Reticker, G. (Director). (2008). *Pray the devil back to hell* [Motion picture]. New York: Fork Films.

3. Frijda, N. H., & Mesquita, B. (2000). Beliefs through emotions. In N. H. Frijda, A. S. R. Manstead, & S. Bem (Eds.), *Emotions and beliefs: How feelings influence thoughts* (pp. 43–54). Paris: Oxford University Press.

4. Kunze, F., Boehm, S., & Bruch, H. (2013). Age, resistance to change, and job performance. *Journal of Managerial Psychology, 28*(7/8), 741–760.

5. Dent, E. B., & Goldberg, S. G. (1999). Challenging resistance to change. *Journal of Applied Behavioral Science, 35*(1), 25–41.

6. Withey, M. J., & Cooper, W. H. (1989). Predicting exit, voice, loyalty, and neglect. *Administrative Science Quarterly, 34*, 521–539.

7. Lines, R. (2004). Influence of participation in strategic change: Resistance, organizational commitment and change goal achievement. *Journal of Change Management, 4*(3), 193–215.

8. Nelson, J. (2013, Dec. 5). Desjardins Group's big tent approach. *Globe and Mail*.

9. Information in this example drawn from Kanter, R. M., & Malone, A. J. (2013). Monique Leroux: Leading change at Desjardins. Harvard Business School. Case 9-313-107; Nelson, J. (2012, October 5). Monique Leroux: A little bit of everything on her plate. *Globe and Mail*; Rockel, N. (2009, August 23). Monique Leroux mentors women as Desjardins chief. *Globe and Mail*.

10. 2013 Desjardins Group Annual Report. Retrieved from www.desjardins.com/ca/about-us/investor-relations/annual-quarterly-reports/desjardins-group/2013-annual-report/index.jsp.

11. Lines, R. (2004). Influence of participation in strategic change: Resistance, organizational commitment and change goal achievement. *Journal of Change Management, 4*(3), 193–215.

12. Piderit, S. K. (2000). Rethinking resistance and recognizing ambivalence: A multidimensional view of attitudes toward an organizational change. *Academy of Management Review, 25*(4), 783–794.

13. Piderit, S. K. (2000). Rethinking resistance and recognizing ambivalence: A multidimensional view of attitudes toward an organizational change. *Academy of Management Review, 25*(4), 783–794.

14. Smith, K. K. (1982). *Groups in conflict: Prisons in disguise.* Dubuque, IA: Kendall/Hunt; Spreitzer, G. M., & Quinn, R. E. (1996). Empowering middle managers to be transformational leaders. *Journal of Applied Behavioral Science, 32*(3), 237–261.

15. Piderit, S. K. (2000). Rethinking resistance and recognizing ambivalence: A multidimensional view of attitudes toward an organizational change. *Academy of Management Review, 25*(4), 783–794.

16. Avery, J. B., Wernsing, T. S., & Luthans, F. (2008). Can positive employees help positive organizational change? Impact of psychological capital and emotions on relevant attitudes and behaviors. *Journal of Applied Behavioral Science, 44*(1), 48–70; Tsirikas, A. N., Katsaros, K. K., & Nicolaidis, C. S. (2012). *Employee Relations, 34*(2), 344–359.

17. Much of the material on ambivalence and change management is drawn from two excellent articles: Lines, R. (2005). The structure and function of attitudes toward organizational change. *Human Resource Development Review, 4*(1), 8–32; and Piderit, S. K. (2000). Rethinking resistance and recognizing ambivalence: A multidimensional view of attitudes toward an organizational change. *Academy of Management Review, 25*(4), 783–794.

18. Lines, R. (2004). Influence of participation in strategic change: Resistance, organizational commitment and change goal achievement. *Journal of Change Management, 4*(3), 193–215.

19. Piderit, S. K. (2000). Rethinking resistance and recognizing ambivalence: A multidimensional view of attitudes toward an organizational change. *Academy of Management Review, 25*(4), 783–794.

20. Sull, D. N. (1999, July–August). Why good companies go bad. *Harvard Business Review,* 42–51.

21. Festinger, L. (1957). *A theory of cognitive dissonance.* Stanford, CA: Stanford University Press.

22. Hymes, R. W. (1986). Political attitudes as social categories: A new look at selective memory. *Journal of Personality and Social Psychology, 51,* 233–241.

23. Lines, R. (2004). Influence of participation in strategic change: Resistance, organizational commitment and change goal achievement. *Journal of Change Management, 4*(3), 193–215.

24. Simoes, P. M. M., & Esposito, M. (2014). Improving change management: How communication nature influences resistance to change. *Journal of Management Development, 33*(4), 324–341.

25. Barr, P. S., Stimpert, J. L., & Huff, A. S. (1992). Cognitive change, strategic action, and organizational renewal. *Strategic Management Journal, 13,* 15–36; Floyd, S. W., & Wooldridge, B. (1996). *The strategic middle manager.* San Francisco: Jossey-Bass.

26. Lines, R. (2004). Influence of participation in strategic change: Resistance, organizational commitment and change goal achievement. *Journal of Change Management, 4*(3), 193–215.

27. Peus, C., Frey, D., Gerkhardt, M., Fischer, P., & Traut-Mattausch, E. (2009). Leading and managing organizational change initiatives. *Management Review, 20*(2), 158–175; Giora, D. A., & Thomas, J. B. (1996). Identity, image, and issue interpretation: Sensemaking during strategic change in academia. *Administrative Science Quarterly, 41,* 370–403; Labianca, G., Gray, B., & Brass, D. J. (2000). A grounded model of organizational schema change during empowerment. *Organizational Science, 11*(2), 235–257; Lines, R. (2004). Influence of participation in strategic change: Resistance, organizational commitment and change goal achievement. *Journal of Change Management, 4*(3), 193–215; and Sagie, A., & Koslowsky, M. (1994). Organizational attitudes and behaviors as a function of participation in strategic and tactical decisions: An application of path–goal theory. *Journal of Organizational Behavior, 15*(1), 37–47.

28. Balogun, J., & Johnson, G. (2005). From intended strategies to unintended outcomes: The impact of change recipient sensemaking. *Organizational Studies, 26*(11), 1596.

29. Cullen, K. L., Edwards, B. D., Casper, W. C., & Gue, K. R. (2014, June). Employees' adaptability and perceptions of change-related uncertainty: Implications for perceived organizational support, job satisfaction, and performance. *Journal of Business and Psychology, 29*(2), 269–280; Paula Matos, M. S., & Esposito, M. (2014). Improving change management: How communication nature influences resistance to change. *Journal of Management Development, 33*(4), 324–341.

30. Hackman, J. R., & Oldham, G. R. (1980). *Work redesign.* Reading, MA: Addison-Wesley.

31. Gustafson, B. (2005). Plant closure "devastates" Newfoundland community. *National Fisherman, 85*(10), 11–12.

32. Gustafson, B. (2005). Plant closure "devastates" Newfoundland community. *National Fisherman, 85*(10), 11–12.

33. Gopinath, C., & Becker, T. E. (2000). Communication, procedural justice, and employee attitudes: Relationships under conditions of divestiture. *Journal of Management, 26*, 63–83.

34. Piderit, S. K. (2000). Rethinking resistance and recognizing ambivalence: A multidimensional view of attitudes toward an organizational change. *Academy of Management Review, 25*(4), 783–794.

35. Reicher, A. E., Wanous, J. P., & Austin, J. T. (1997). Understanding and managing cynicism about organizational change. *Academy of Management Executive, 11*(1), 48–60.

36. Lines, R. (2004). Influence of participation in strategic change: Resistance, organizational commitment and change goal achievement. *Journal of Change Management, 4*(3), 193–215.

37. Peus, C., Frey, D., Gerkhardt, M., Fischer, P., & Traut-Mattausch, E. (2009). Leading and managing organizational change initiatives. *Management Review, 20*(2), 158–175.

38. Kickul, J., Lester, S. W., & Finkl, J. (2002). Promise breaking during organizational change: Do justice interventions make a difference? *Journal of Organizational Behavior, 23*, 469–488.

39. Watson, T. J. (1982). Group ideologies and organizational change. *Journal of Management Studies, 19*, 259–275.

40. Kotter, J. P. (1995). Leading change: Why transformation efforts fail. *Harvard Business Review, 73*(2), 59–67.

41. Kerr, S. (1995). On the folly of rewarding A, while hoping for B. *Academy of Management Executive, 9*(1), 7–14.

42. Bareil, C. (2013, Fall). Two paradigms about resistance to change. *Organizational Development Journal, 31*(3).

43. Turnley, W. H., & Feldman, D. C. (1999). The impact of psychological contract violations on exit, voice, loyalty, and neglect. *Human Relations, 52*(7), 895–922; Rousseau, D. M. (1995). *Promises in action: Psychological contracts in organizations.* Thousand Oaks, CA: Sage.

44. Matthijs Bal, P., Chiaburu, D. S., & Jansen, P. G. W. (2010). Psychological contract breach and work performance; Is social exchange a buffer or an intensifier? *Journal of Managerial Psychology, 25*(3), 252–273; Richard, O. C., McMillan-Capehart, A., Bhuian, S. N., & Taylor, E. C. (2009). Antecedents and consequences of psychological contracts: Does organizational culture really matter? *Journal of Business Research, 62*(8), 818–825.

45. Deery, S. J., Iverson, R. D., & Walsh, J. T. (2006). Toward a better understanding of psychological contract breach: A study of customer service employees. *Journal of Applied Psychology, 91*(1), 13; Suazo, M. M., Turnley, W. H., & Mai-Dalton, R. R. (2005). The role of perceived violation in determining employees' reactions to psychological contract breach. *Journal of Leadership and Organizational Studies, 12*(1), 24–36.

46. Lee, J., and Taylor, M. S. (2014, March). Dual roles in psychological contracts: When managers take both agent and principal roles. *Human Resource Management Review, 24*(1).

47. Nesterkin, D. A. (2013). Organizational change and psychological reactance. *Journal of Organizational Change Management, 26*(3), 573–594.

48. Chi-jung, F., and Chin-I, C. (2014). Unfilled expectations and promises, and behavioral outcomes. *International Journal of Organizational Analysis, 22*(1), 61–75; Chambel, M. J. (2014). Does the fulfillment of supervisor psychological contract make a difference? Attitudes of in-house and temporary agency workers. *Leadership and Organizational Development Journal, 35*(1), 20–37.

49. Edmondson, A. C. (2003). Large-scale change at the WSSC. *Harvard Business School,* 9–603–056.

50. Edmondson, A. C. (2003). Large-scale change at the WSSC. *Harvard Business School,* 9–603–056. After leading the Washington Suburban Sanitary commission, John Griffen served as Secretary of Maryland's Department of Resources from 2007–2013 and was named Chief of Staff of Maryland's Governor O'Malley in 2013. See John Griffin named Governor O'Malley's new chief of staff (2013, April 18). *Baltimore News Journal.*

51. Kübler-Ross, E. (1969). *On death and dying.* New York: Macmillan.

52. Fink, S. L. (1967). Crisis and motivation: A theoretical model. *Archives of Physical Medicine and Rehabilitation, 48*(11), 592–597.

53. Jick, T. (2002). The recipients of change. In T. Jick & M. A. Peiperl, *Managing change: Cases and concepts* (2nd ed., pp. 299–311). New York: McGraw-Hill Higher Education.

54. Perlman, D., & Takacs, G. J. (1990). The ten stages of change. *Nursing Management, 21*(4), 33–38.

55. Piderit, S. K. (2000). Rethinking resistance and recognizing ambivalence: A multidimensional view of attitudes toward an organizational change. *Academy of Management Review, 25*(4), 783–794.

56. Kotter, J. P. (2007, January). Leading change: Why transformation efforts fail. *Harvard Business Review,* 96–103.

57. Doherty, N., Banks, J., & Vinnicombe, S. (1996). Managing survivors: The experience of survivors in British Telecom and the British financial services sector. *Journal of Managerial Psychology, 11*(7), 51–60.

58. Bedeian, A. G., & Armenakis, A. A. (1998, February). The cesspool syndrome: How dreck floats to the top of declining organizations. *Academy of Management Executive,* 58–67; Mishra, K. E., Spreitzer, G. M., & Mishra, A. K. (1998). Preserving employee morale during downsizing. *Sloan Management Review, 39*(2), 83–95.

59. For a detailed treatment of dealing with the survivor syndrome, see Noer, D. M. (1993). *Healing the wounds.* San Francisco: Jossey-Bass.

60. Jick, T., & Peiperl, M. A. (2002). *Managing change: Cases and concepts* (2nd ed.). New York: McGraw-Hill Higher Education.

61. Personal conversation with the author.

62. Rogers, E. M. (1995). *Diffusion of innovations* (4th ed.). New York: Free Press.

63. Deckop, J. R., Merriman, K. K., & Blau, G. (2004). Impact of variable risk preferences on the effectiveness of control of pay. *Journal of Occupational and Organizational Psychology, 77*(1), 63–80.

64. Oreg, S., Bayazıt, M., Vakola, M., Arciniega, L., Armenakis, A., Barkauskiene, R., . . . & van Dam, K. (2008). Dispositional resistance to change: Measurement equivalence and the link to personal values across 17 nations. *Journal of Applied Psychology, 93*(4), 935–944; Steenkamp, L. P., and Wessels, P. L. (2014). An analysis of the tolerance for ambiguity among accounting students. *International Business and Research Journal (Online), 13*(2).

65. Probst, T. M. (2003). Exploring employee outcomes of organizational restructuring: A Solomon four-group study. *Group & Organization Management, 28*(3), 416–439.
66. Tremblay, M., & Roger, A. (2004). Career plateauing reactions: The moderating role of job scope, role ambiguity and participation among Canadian managers. *International Journal of Human Resource Management, 15*(6), 996–1017.
67. Kass, S. J., Vodanovich, S. J., & Callender, A. (2001). State-trait boredom: Relationship to absenteeism, tenure, and job satisfaction. *Journal of Business and Psychology, 16*(2), 317–326.
68. Park, D., & Krishnan, H. A. (2003). Understanding the stability-change paradox: Insights for the evolutionary, adaptation, and institutional perspectives. *International Journal of Management, 20*(3), 265–270.
69. Barnett, W. P., & Sorenson, O. (2002). The Red Queen in organizational creation. *Industrial and Corporate Change, 11*(2), 289–325.
70. Kelly, P., & Amburgey, T. (1991). Organizational inertia and momentum: A dynamic model of strategic change. *Academy of Management Journal, 34*, 591–612; Huff, J., Huff, J., & Thomas, H. (1992). Strategic renewal and the interaction of cumulative stress and inertia. *Strategic Management Journal, 13*, 55–75.
71. Kovoor-Misra, S., & Nathan, M. (2000). Timing is everything: The optimal time to learn from crises. *Review of Business, 21*(3/4), 31–36.
72. Geller, E. S. (2002). Leadership to overcome resistance to change: It takes more than consequence control. *Journal of Organizational Behavior Management, 22*(3), 29; and Brown, J., & Quarter, J. (1994). Resistance to change: The influence of social networks on the conversion of a privately-owned unionized business to a worker cooperative. *Economic and Industrial Democracy, 15*(2), 259–283.
73. Loi, R., and Lai, J. Y. M., & Lam, L. W. (2012, June). Working under a committed boss: A test of the relationship between supervisors' and subordinates' affective commitment. *Leadership Quarterly, 23*(3), 466–475.
74. Kane-Frieder, R. E., Hochwarter, W. A., Hampton, H. L., & Ferris, G. R. (2014). Supervisor political support as a buffer to subordinates' reactions to politics perceptions: A three-sample investigation. *Career Development International, 19*(1), 27–48; Sales, M. (2002, July/August). Futures thinking by middle managers: A neglected necessity. *Systems Research and Behavioral Science, 19*(4), 367; Oshry, B. (1990). Finding and using a manager's power to improve productivity. *National Productivity Review, 10*(1), 19–33.
75. Bettenhausen, K. L. (1991). Five years of groups research: What we have learned and what needs to be addressed. *Journal of Management, 17*(2), 345–381.
76. Johnson, L. (2008). Helping employees cope with change in an anxious era. *Harvard Management Update, 13*(12), 1–5.
77. Brenneman, G. (1998). Right away and all at once: How we saved Continental. *Harvard Business Review, 76*(5), 162–173.
78. Tyler, T. R., & De Cremer, D. (2005). Process-based leadership: Fair procedures and reactions to organizational change. *Leadership Quarterly, 16*(4), 529–545.
79. Sherman, W. S., & Garland, G. E. (2007). Where to bury the survivors? Exploring possible ex post effects of resistance to change. *S. A. M. Advanced Management Journal, 72*(1), 52–63.
80. Arthur, C. (2013, November 4). BlackBerry fires CEO Thorsten Heins as $4.7bn Fairfax rescue bid collapses. *The Guardian*. Retrieved from http://www.theguardian.com/technology/2013/nov/04/blackberry-fires-ceo-thorsten-heins-fairfax-bid-collapses.
81. Reichers, A. E., Wanous, J. P., & Austin, J. T. (1997). Understanding and managing cynicism about organizational change. *Academy of Management Executive, 11*(1), 48–60.
82. Reichers, A. E., Wanous, J. P., & Austin, J. T. (1997). Understanding and managing cynicism about organizational change. *Academy of Management Executive, 11*(1), 50–51.

83. Munduate, L., & Bennebroek Gravenhorst, K. M. (2003). Power dynamics and organisational change: An introduction. *Applied Psychology: An International Review, 52*(1), 1–13; Weick, K. E., & Quinn, R. E. (1999). Organizational change and development. *Annual Review of Psychology, 50,* 361–386; Peus, C., Frey, D., Gerkhardt, M., Fischer, P., & Traut-Mattausch, E. (2009). Leading and managing organizational change initiatives. *Management Review, 20*(2), 158–175.

84. Brown, M., & Cregan, C. (2008). Organizational change cynicism: The role of employee involvement. *Human Resource Management, 47*(4), 667–686.

85. Personal communication, 2004.

86. Kramer, R. M. (2006). The great intimidators. *Harvard Business Review, 84*(2), 88–96.

87. Sherman, W. S., & Garland, G. E. (2007). Where to bury the survivors? Exploring possible ex post effects of resistance to change. *S. A. M. Advanced Management Journal, 72*(1), 52–63.

88. Source unknown.

89. Stimson, W. A. (2005). A Deming inspired management code of ethics. *Quality Progress, 38*(2), 67–75; Farson, R., & Keyes, R. (2002). The failure-tolerant leader. *Harvard Business Review, 80*(8), 64; Casio, J. (2002). Scare tactics. *Incentive, 176*(9), 56–62.

90. Collins, J. C. (2001). *From good to great: Why some companies make the leap . . . and others don't.* New York: Harper Business.

91. Werther, W. B., Jr. (1987). Loyalty: Cross-organizational comparisons and patterns. *Leadership and Organization Development Journal, 8*(2), 3–6.

92. Deming, W. E. (1986). *Drastic changes for western management.* Madison, WI: Center for Quality and Productivity Improvement.

93. Challagalla, G. N., & Shervgani, T. A. (1996). Dimensions and types of supervisory control: Effects on salesperson performance and satisfaction. *Journal of Marketing, 60,* 89–105.

94. Appelbaum, S. H., Bregman, M., & Moroz, P. (1998). Fear as a strategy: Effects and impact within the organization. *Journal of European Industrial Training, 22*(3), 113–127.

95. Collins, J. C., & Porras, J. I. (1994). *Built to last: Successful habits of visionary companies.* New York: HarperCollins.

96. Kolb, D. G. (2002). Continuity, not change: The next organizational challenge. *University of Auckland Business Review, 4*(2), 1–11.

97. Balogun, J., & Johnson, G. (2005). From intended strategies to unintended outcomes: The impact of change recipient sensemaking. *Organizational Studies, 26*(11), 1573–1601.

98. Cranston, S., and Keller, S. (2013, January). Increasing the meaning quotient at work. *McKinsey Quarterly.*

99. Evans, C., Hammersley, G. O., & Robertson, M. (2001). Assessing the role and efficacy of communication strategies in times of crisis. *Journal of European Industrial Training, 25*(6), 297–309; Ashkenas, R. N., DeMonaco, L. J., & Francis, S. C. (1998). Making the deal real: How GE Capital integrates acquisitions. *Harvard Business Review, 76*(1), 165–176.

100. Difonzo, N., & Bordia, P. (1998). A tale of two corporations: Managing uncertainty during organizational change. *Human Resource Management, 37*(3–4), 295–304.

101. Tersine, R., Harvey, M., & Buckley, M. (1997). Shifting organizational paradigms: Transitional management. *European Management Journal, 15*(1), 45–57.

102. Schneider, B., Brief, A. P., & Guzzo, R. A. (1996). Creating a climate and culture for sustainable organizational change. *Organizational Dynamics, 24*(4), 6–18.

103. Abrahamson, E. (2000, July–August). Change without pain. *Harvard Business Review,* 75–79.

104. Burke, R. J. (2002). The ripple effect. *Nursing Management, 33*(2), 41–43; Weakland, J. H. (2001). Human resources holistic approach to healing downsizing survivors.

Organizational Development Journal, *19*(2), 59–69; Mishra, K. E., Spreitzer, G. M., & Mishra, A. K. (1998). Preserving employee morale during downsizing. *Sloan Management Review*, *39*(2), 83–95.

105. McCann, J., Selsky, J., & Lee, J. (2009). Building agility, resilience and performance in turbulent environments. *People and Strategy*, *32*(3), 44–51.

106. Nadler, D. A., & Tushman, M. T. (1999). The organization of the future: Strategic imperatives and core competencies for the 21st century. *Organizational Dynamics*, *28*(1), 45–60.

107. Meyerson, D. E. (2001, October). Radical change, the quiet way. *Harvard Business Review*, 92–100.

108. Cohen, A. R., & Bradford, D. L. (1990). *Influence without authority*. New York: Wiley; Keys, B., & Case, T. (1990). How to become an influential manager. *Academy of Management Executive*, *4*, 38–49.

109. Reichers, A. E., Wanous, J. P., & Austin, J. T. (1997). Understanding and managing cynicism about organizational change. *Academy of Management Executive*, *11*(1), 53.

110. Adapted from Reicher, A. E., et al. (1997). Understanding and managing cynicism about organizational change. *Academy of Management Executive*, *11*(1), 53.

Chapter 8

1. Mead, M. Quote reported in *Webster's online dictionary—The Rosetta edition*, www .websters-online-dictionary.org.

2. Dover, P. A. (2003). Change agents at work: Lessons from Siemens Nixdorf. *Journal of Change Management*, *3*(3), 243–257.

3. Lattman, P. (2005). Rebound. *Forbes*, *175*(6), 58.

4. Jac the Knife new chairman of BHP. Retrieved May 2010 from http://www.smh.com.au/ business/jac-the-knife-new-chairman-of-bhp-20090804-e8mx.html.

5. Hamel, G. (2002). *Leading the revolution: How to thrive in turbulent times by making innovation a way of life*. Boston, MA: Harvard Business School Press.

6. Mass, J. (2000). Leading the revolution. *MIT Sloan Management Review*, *42*(1), 95.

7. Zaccaro, S. J., & Banks, D. (2004). Leader visioning and adaptability: Bridging the gap between research and practice on developing the ability to manage change. *Human Resource Management*, *43*(4), 367–380.

8. Huey, J. (1994). The new post-heroic leadership. *Fortune*, *129*(4), 42. Retrieved December 2010 from http://money.cnn.com/magazines/fortune/fortune_ archive/1994/02/21/78995/index.htm.

9. Jick, T., & Peiperl, M. (2003). *Managing change: Cases and concepts* (p. 362). New York: McGraw-Hill/Irwin.

10. Tandon, N. (2003). The young change agents. In T. Jick & M. Peiperl, *Managing change: Cases and concepts* (p. 428). New York: McGraw-Hill/Irwin.

11. Kanter, R. M. (2003). The enduring skills of change leaders. In T. Jick & M. Peiperl, *Managing change: Cases and concepts* (p. 429). New York: McGraw-Hill/Irwin.

12. Hammonds, K. (2001, November). Change agents: Michael J. Fox & Deborah Brooks. *Fast Company*, (52), 106.

13. Branson, C. M. (2009). Achieving organizational change through values alignment. *Journal of Educational Administration*, *46*(3), 376–395.

14. Frank, J. N. (2004). Newman's Own serves up a down-home public image. *PRweek*, *7*(5), 10.

15. Dickout, R. (1997). All I ever needed to know about change management I learned at engineering school. *McKinsey Quarterly*, *2*, 114–121.

16. Dickout, R. (1997). All I ever needed to know about change management I learned at engineering school. *McKinsey Quarterly*, *2*, 114–121.

17. Francis, H. (2003). Teamworking and change: Managing the contradictions. *Human Resource Management Journal, 13*(3), 71–90.

18. Chilton, S. (2004). Book review of *Creating leaderful organisations: How to bring out leadership in everyone. Journal of Organizational Change Management, 17*(1), 110.

19. Katzenbach, J. R. (1996). Real change. *McKinsey Quarterly, 1*, 148–163.

20. Doyle, M. (2003). From change novice to change expert. *Personnel Review, 31*(4), 465–481.

21. Appelbaum, S., Bethune, M., & Tannenbaum, R. (1999). Downsizing and the emergence of self-managed teams. *Participation and Empowerment: An International Journal, 7*(5), 109–130.

22. Kramer, R. M. (2006, February). The great intimidators. *Harvard Business Review*, 88–96.

23. Collins, J. (2001). *From good to great.* New York: HarperCollins.

24. Rubin, R., Dierdorff, E., Boomer, W., & Baldwin, T. (2009). Do leaders reap what they sow? Leader and employee outcomes of leader organizational cynicism about change. *Leadership Quarterly, 20*(5), 680–688.

25. McCall, M., & Lombardo, M. (1983). *Off the track: Why and how successful executives get derailed.* Greensboro, NC: Center for Creative Leadership.

26. Higgs, M. (2009). The good, the bad and the ugly: Leadership and narcissism. *Journal of Change Management, 9*(2), 165–178.

27. Francis, H. (2003). Teamworking and change: Managing the contradictions. *Human Resource Management Journal, 13*(3), 71–90.

28. Much of this is drawn from Jick, T., & Peiperl, M. (2003). *Managing change: Cases and concepts* (p. 362). New York: McGraw-Hill/Irwin.

29. Ilies, R., Gerhardt, M. W., & Le, H. (2004). Individual differences in leadership emergence: Integrating meta-analytic findings and behavioral genetics estimates. *International Journal of Selection and Assessment, 12*(3), 207.

30. Leban, W., & Zulauf, C. (2004). Linking emotional intelligence abilities and transformational leadership styles. *Leadership and Organization Development Journal, 25*(7/8), 554.

31. Caldwell, R. (2003). Change leaders and change managers: Different or complementary? *Leadership & Organization Development Journal, 24*(5), 285–293.

32. Higgs, M., & Rowland, D. (2005). All changes great and small: Exploring approaches to change and its leadership. *Journal of Change Management, 5*(2), 121–151.

33. Higgs, M., & Rowland, D. (2005). All changes great and small: Exploring approaches to change and its leadership. *Journal of Change Management, 5*(2), 147.

34. Kouzes, J. M., & Posner, B. Z. (2007). *The leadership challenge* (4th ed.). San Francisco: Jossey-Bass.

35. Retrieved May 2010 from http://www. ccl.org/leadership/index.aspx.

36. Criswell, C., & Martin, A. (2007). 10 trends: A study of senior executives' views on the future. Center for Creative Leadership. Retrieved December 10 from http://www.ccl.org/leadership/pdf/research/TenTrends.pdf.

37. Duck, J. D. (2001). *The change monster: The human forces that fuel or foil corporate transformation & change.* New York: Crown Business.

38. Bennis (1989), as reported in Komives, S., et al. (1998). *Exploring leadership* (p. 109). San Francisco: Jossey-Bass.

39. Cooperrider, D. L., & Whitney, D. (1998). *Collaborating for change: Appreciative Inquiry.* San Francisco: Berrett-Koehler Communications.

40. Miller, D. (2002). Successful change leaders: What makes them? What do they do that is different? *Journal of Change Management, 2*(4), 383.

41. Zaccaro, S. J., & Banks, D. (2004). Leader visioning and adaptability: Bridging the gap between research and practice on developing the ability to manage change. *Human Resource Management, 43*(4), 367–380.

42. Patton, J. R. (2003). Intuition in decisions. *Management Decision, 41*(10), 989–996.

43. Personal communication with the authors.

44. Nadler, D., & Tushman, M. (1989). Organizational frame bending. *Academy of Management Executive, 3*(3), 194–204.

45. Weick, K., & Quinn, R. (1999). Organizational change and development. *Annual Review of Psychology, 50*, 366.

46. McAdam, R., McLean, J., & Henderson, J. (2003). The strategic "pull" and operational "push" of total quality management in UK regional electricity service companies. *International Journal of Quality & Reliability Management, 20*(4/5), 436–457.

47. Kirton, M. J. (1984). Adaptors and innovators—Why new initiatives get blocked. *Long Range Planning, 17*(2), 137–143; Tushman, M. L., & O'Reilly, C. A. III. (1996). Ambidextrous organizations: Managing evolutionary and revolutionary change. *California Management Review, 38*(4), 8–30.

48. Saka, A. (2003). Internal change agents' view of the management of change problem. *Journal of Organizational Change Management, 16*(5), 480–497.

49. Hunsaker, P. (1982, September–October). Strategies for organizational change: The role of the inside change agent. *Personnel*, 18–28.

50. Wright, C. (2009). Inside out? Organizational membership, ambiguity and the ambivalent identity of the internal consultant. *British Journal of Management, 20*(3), 309–322.

51. Personal experience of the authors.

52. Saka, A. (2003). Internal change agents' view of the management of change problem. *Journal of Organizational Change Management, 16*(5), 489.

53. Personal experience of the authors.

54. Pitts, G. (2010, January 4). The fine art of managing change. *Globe and Mail.*

55. Jarrett, M. (2004). Tuning into the emotional drama of change: Extending the consultant's bandwidth. *Journal of Change Management, 4*(3), 247–258; Kilman, R. H. (1979, Spring). Problem defining and the consulting/intervention process. *California Management Review*, 26–33; Simon, A., & Kumar, V. (2001). Client's view on strategic capabilities which lead to management consulting success. *Management Decisions, 39*(5/6), 362–373.

56. Prosci Benchmarking Report. Best Practices in Change Management. (2000).

57. Adapted from Prosci Benchmarking Report. Best Practices in Change Management. (2000).

58. Worren, N., et al. (1999, September). From organizational development to change management: The emergence of a new profession. *Journal of Applied Behavioral Science*, 277.

59. Worren, N. et al. (1999, September). From organizational development to change management: The emergence of a new profession. *Journal of Applied Behavioral Science*, 277, Table 2.

60. Appelbaum, S., Bethune, M., & Tannenbaum, R. (1999). Downsizing and the emergence of self-managed teams. *Participation and Empowerment: An International Journal, 7*(5), 109–130.

61. Prosci Benchmarking Report. Best Practices in Change Management. (2000).

62. Kahn, W. A. (2004). Facilitating and undermining organizational change: A case study. *Journal of Applied Behavioral Science, 40*(1), 7–30.

63. Rooney, P. (2001, November 12). Bill Gates, chairman and chief software architect. Microsoft. *CNR.*

64. Retrieved May 2010 from http://www. newswire.ca/en/releases/archive/June2006/15/c4768. html.

65. H. Sheppard, personal communication with T. Cawsey.

66. Webber, A. M. (1999). Learning for change (an interview with Peter Senge). *Fast Company, 24*. Retrieved December 2010 from http://www.fastcompany.com/magazine/24/senge.html.

67. Senge, P. M. (1996). The leader's new work: Building learning organizations. In K. Starkey (Ed.), *How organisations learn* (pp. 288–315). London: International Thompson Business Press.

68. Gilley, A., McMillan, H., & Gilley, J. (2009). Organizational change and characteristics of leadership effectiveness. *Journal of Leadership and Organizational Studies, 16*(1), 38–47.

69. Banutu-Gomez, M. B., & Banutu-Gomez, S. M. T. (2007). Leadership and organizational change in a competitive environment. *Business Renaissance Quarterly, 2*(2), 69–90.

70. Wageman, R. (1997, Summer). Critical success factors for creating superb self-managing teams. *Organizational Dynamics*, 49–61.

71. Johnston Smith International (2000, November 22). 2000 Change Management Conference, The Change Institute, Toronto.

72. Gerstner, L. (2002). *Who says elephants can't dance?: Inside IBM's historic turnaround.* New York: HarperCollins.

73. Sheppard, P. (2003, February). Leading the Turnaround: Lou Gerstner of IBM. *Wharton Leadership Digest, 7*(5).

74. Lambert, T. (2006). Insight. *MENAFN.com.* Retrieved May 2010 from http://www.menafn.com/qn_print.asp?StroyID=129531&subl=true.

75. Katzenbach, J. (1996, July/August). From middle manager to real change leader. *Strategy and Leadership*, 34.

76. Oshry, B. (1993). Converting middle powerlessness to middle power: A systems approach. In T. Jick, *Managing change: Cases and concepts.* Homewood, IL: Irwin.

77. Howell, J., & Higgins, C. (1990, Summer). Champions of change. *Organizational Dynamics*, 40–55. Retrieved May 2010 from http://www.deloitte.com/view/en_US/us/Insights/Browse-by-Content-Type/Case-Studies/index.htm.

78. The sage of Quiznos: The skills of Greg Brenneman, a corporate-turnaround specialist, are in demand. (2008, August 28). *Economist,* Retrieved December 2010 from http://www.economist.com/node/12001911.

79. Shepard, H. (1975, November). Rules of thumb for change agents. *Organization Development Practitioner*, 1–5; Ransdell, E. (1997). Rules for Radicals. *Fast Company*, 11, 190–191; Hamel, G. (2000, July). How to start an insurrection. *Ideas@Work*, Harvard Business Review Press.

80. Prosci Benchmarking Report. Best Practices in Change Management. (2000).

Chapter 9

1. Retrieved July 2014 from http://www.brainyquote.com/quotes/keywords/action.html#zi4AZCg2W9R4mrj5.99.

2. Mattioli, D., & Maher, K. (2010, March 1). At 3M, innovation comes in tweaks and snips. *Wall Street Journal* (Digital Network). Retrieved May 2010 from http://online.wsj.com/article/SB10001424052748703787304575075590963046162.html.

3. Swanborg, R. (2010, April 30). Social networks in the enterprise: 3M's innovation process. *CIO.* Retrieved May 2010 from http://www.cio.com.au/article/344909/social_networks_enterprise_3m_innovation_process/; From Post-its to Face-bras: How 3M puts innovation into practice. (2010, April 1). *Knowledge@SMU.* Retrieved May 2010 from http://knowledge.smu.edu.sg/article.cfm?articleid=1281.

4. Retrieved May 2010 from http://en.wikiquote.org/wiki/Grace_Hopper; or www.ideafinder.com/history/inventors/hopper.htm; or www.inventors.about.com/library/inventors/bl_Grace_Hopper.htm.

5. Pfeffer, J., & Sutton, R. (1999). Knowing "what" to do is not enough: Turning knowledge into action. *California Management Review, 42*(1), 83–110.

6. O'Hara, S., Murphy, L., & Reeve, S. (2007). Action learning as leverage for strategic transformation: A case study reflection. *Strategic Change, 16*(4), 177–190.

7. Sayles, L. (1993, Spring). Doing things right: A new imperative for middle managers. *Organizational Dynamics*, 10.

8. Kahan, S. (2008, October 13). Personal empowerment in difficult times. *Fast Company*. Retrieved May 2010 from http://www.fastcompany.com/blog/seth-kahan/leading-change/personal-empowerment-difficult-times.

9. Mintzberg, H., & Westley, F. (2001). Decision making: It's not what you think. *Sloan Management Review, 42*, 89–93.

10. Nohria, N. (1993). Executing change: Three generic strategies. *Harvard Business School Press #9–494–039.*

11. Waldersee, R., & Griffiths, A. (2004). Implementing change: Matching implementation methods and change type. *Leadership and Organization Development Journal, 25*(5), 424–434.

12. Beer, M., Eisenstat, R., & Spector, B. (1990, November–December). Why change programs don't produce change. *Harvard Business Review*, 158–166.

13. Retrieved May 2010 from http://www.everyday-taichi.com/confucius-saying.html.

14. Beer, M., Eisenstat, R., & Spector, B. (1990, November–December). Why change programs don't produce change. *Harvard Business Review*, 158–166.

15. Rune, T. (2005). Organisational change management: A critical review. *Journal of Change Management, 5*(4), 375.

16. Source unknown.

17. Welbourne, T. M. (2009). Extreme strategy. *Leader to Leader, 2009*(2), 42–48.

18. Adapted from Mieszkowski, K. (1998). Change—Barbara Waugh. *Fast Company, 20*, 146.

19. Waldersee, R., & Griffiths, A. (2004). Implementing change: Matching implementation methods and change type. *Leadership and Organization Development Journal, 25*(5), 424–434.

20. Retrieved May 2010 from http://www.valuebasedmanagement.net/methods_scenario_planning.html.

21. Noori, H., Munro, H., Deszca, G., & McWilliams, B. (1999). Developing the right breakthrough product/service: An application of the umbrella methodology. Parts A & B. *International Journal of Technology Management, 17*, 544–579.

22. Wylie, I. (2002, July). There is no alternative to . . . *Fast Company*, 106–110.

23. Cummings, T. G., & Worley, C. G. (2009). *Organization development and change*. Mason, OH: South-Western.

24. Beckhard, R., & Harris, R. (1987). *Organizational transitions* (p. 95). Reading, MA: Addison-Wesley.

25. Personal communication with author.

26. Gladwell, M. (2002). *The tipping point*. New York: First Back Bay.

27. Burke, W. (2002). *Organization change: Theory and practice* (pp. 274–280). London: Sage.

28. Moore, G. (1999). *Crossing the chasm*. New York: HarperBusiness.

29. Lui, M. (2008, May 9). Clyburn sees "tipping point" to Obama. *New York Times*. Retrieved May 2010 from http://thecaucus.blogs.nytimes.com/2008/05/09/clyburn-sees-tipping-point-to-obama/; Balz, D. (2008, January 8). Obama's tipping point. *Washington Post*. Retrieved May 2010 from http://voices.washingtonpost.com/44/2008/01/obamas-tipping-point-1.html; Stanton, J. (2009, April 20). The man behind Obama's online election campaign. Web 2.0 Convergence Blogs. Retrieved May 2010 from http://www.digitalcommunitiesblogs.com/web_20_convergence/2009/04/the-man-behind-obamas-online-e.php.

30. Keller, S., Meaney, M., & Pung, C. (2013, November). Organizing for change through social technologies: McKinsey global survey results. *McKinsey & Company*.

31. Imai, M. (1986). *Kaizen: The key to Japan's competitive success* (p. 239). New York: Random House.

32. Rigby, D. (2001). Management tools and techniques: A survey. *California Management Review, 43*(2); Rigby, D., & Bilodeau, B. (2013, May 8). Management tools & trends 2013. *Bain and Company*. Retrieved August 2014 from http://www.bain.com/publications/articles/management-tools-and-trends-2013.aspx.

33. Argyris, C. (1991, May–June). Teaching smart people how to learn. *Harvard Business Review*, 104.

34. De Bono, E. (1984). *Tactics: The art and science of success* (p. 41). Toronto: Little, Brown.

35. Russo, J. E., & Schoemaker, P. J. H. (1992, Winter). Managing overconfidence. *Sloan Management Review*, 7–17.

36. Isern, J., & Pung, C. (2007). Harnessing energy to drive organizational change. *McKinsey Quarterly, 1*, 16–19.

37. Goodman, J., & Truss, C. (2004). The medium and the message: Communicating effectively during a major change initiative. *Journal of Change Management, 4*(3), 234.

38. Dutton, J., et al. (2001). Moves that matter: Issue selling and organizational change. *Academy of Management Journal, 44*(4), 716–736.

39. Kotter, J. P. (1995). Leading change: Why transformation efforts fail. *Harvard Business Review, 73*(2), 59–67.

40. Spector, B. (1989, Summer). From bogged down to fired up: Inspiring organizational change. *Sloan Management Review*, 29–34.

41. Klein, S. (1996). A management communication strategy for change. *Journal of Organizational Change Management, 9*(2), 37.

42. Klein, S. (1996). A management communication strategy for change. *Journal of Organizational Change Management, 9*(2), 37.

43. Welch, J., & Welch, S. (2007). How to really shake things up: Transforming a company requires total commitment and serious stamina. *Business Week, 4061*(84), 84.

44. Goodman, J., & Truss, C. (2004). The medium and the message: Communicating effectively during a major change initiative. *Journal of Change Management, 4*(3), 234; Nelissen, P., & van Selm, M. (2008). Surviving organizational change: How management communication helps balance mixed feelings. *Corporate Communications, 13*(3), 306–318.

45. Daft, D., & Lengel, R. H. (1984). Information richness: A new approach to managerial behavior and organizational design. In B. Staw & R. Cummings, *Research in organizational behavior* (Vol. 6, pp. 191–233). Greenwich, CT: JAI Press.

46. Daft, D., & Lengel, R. H. (1984). Information richness: A new approach to managerial behavior and organizational design. In B. Staw & R. Cummings, *Research in organizational behavior* (Vol. 6, pp. 191–233). Greenwich, CT: JAI Press.

47. Goodman, J., & Truss, C. (2004). The medium and the message: Communicating effectively during a major change initiative. *Journal of Change Management, 4*(3), 218.

48. Klein, S. (1996). A management communication strategy for change. *Journal of Organizational Change Management, 9*(2), 34.

49. Duck, J. D. (1993, November–December). Managing change: The art of balancing. *Harvard Business Review*, 4.

50. Cranston, S., & Keller, S. (2013, January). Increasing the meaning quotient at work. *McKinsey Quarterly*; Keller, S., Meaney, M., & Pung, C. (2013, November). Organizing for change through social technologies: McKinsey global survey results. *McKinsey & Company*.

51. Peus, C., Frey, D., Gerkhardt, M., Fishcher, P., & Traut-Mattausch, E. (2009). Leading and managing organizational change initiatives. *Management Review, 20*(2), 158–175.

52. Kotter, J. P. (1995). Leading change: Why transformation efforts fail. *Harvard Business Review, 73*(2), 59–67.

53. The first six highlighted points are drawn from Kotter, J., & Schlesinger, L. (1982). Choosing strategies for change. *Harvard Business Review, 57*(2), 106–114.

54. Geller, A. (2005, February 10). As union nears win, Wal-Mart closes store. *Associated Press*. Retrieved May 2010 from http://www.commondreams.org/headlines05/0210-13 .htm; Wal-Mart shutters Quebec auto shop after union win. (2008, October 16). *Montreal Gazette*. Retrieved from http://www.canada.com/finance/moneylibrary/story. html?id=01e454a4-b613-47d6-b0fa-ead56e06ec1d; Canadian Press. (2013, August 16).

Only Walmart union in Canada votes to decertify. *Huff-Post Canada.* Retrieved from http://www.huffingtonpost.ca/2013/08/16/walmart-canada-union-decertifies_n_3769807.html; Blackwell, R. (2014, June 22). Supreme Court rules Walmart broke Quebec labour codes by closing store. *Global News* (2014, June 27). Retrieved from http://globalnews.ca/news/1420291/supreme-court-rules-walmart-broke-quebec-labour-code-by-closing-store/.

55. Falbe, C., & Yukl, G. (1992). Consequences for managers of using single influence tactics and combinations of tactics. *Academy of Management Journal, 35*(3), 638–652.

56. Nutt, P. (1992). *Managing planned change* (p. 153). Toronto: Maxwell Macmillan Canada.

57. Source unknown.

58. Morris, K. F., & Raben, C. S. (1999). The fundamentals of change management. In D. Nadler et al., *Discontinuous change* (pp. 57–58). San Francisco: Jossey-Bass.

59. Duck, J. D. (1993, November–December). Managing change: The art of balancing. *Harvard Business Review,* 9.

60. Ackerman, L. (1982, Summer). Transition management: An in-depth look at managing complex change. *Organizational Dynamics,* 46–66.

61. Beckhard, R., & Harris, R. (1987). *Organizational transitions* (p. 95). Reading, MA: Addison-Wesley.

62. Personal correspondence with W. Allen, Ministry of Agriculture, Food and Rural Affairs, Ontario Government.

63. For information on how to conduct an After-Action Review, see *After-action review technical guidance.* (2006). Washington, DC: U.S. Agency for International Development, PN-ADF-360. Electronic version available at http://pdf.usaid.gov/pdf_docs/PNADF360.pdf.

Chapter 10

1. Beaty, R., Lipsey, R., & Elgie, S. (2014, July 9). The shocking truth about B.C.'s carbon tax: It works. *Globe and Mail.* Retrieved from http://www.theglobeandmail.com/globe-debate/the-insidious-truth-about-bcs-carbon-tax-it-works/article19512237/?utm_source=Shared+Article+Sent+to+User&utm_medium=E-mail:+Newsletters+/+E-Blasts+/+etc.&utm_campaign=Shared+Web+Article+Links.

2. Fred, E. (2004). Transition in the workplace. *Journal of Management Development, 23*(10), 962–964.

3. Ford, M. W., & Greer, B. M. (2005). The relationship between management control system usage and planner change achievement: An exploratory study. *Journal of Change Management, 5*(1), 29–46.

4. Ford, M. W., & Greer, B. M. (2005). The relationship between management control system usage and planner change achievement: An exploratory study. *Journal of Change Management, 5*(1), 29–46; Schreyogg, G., & Steinmann, H. (1987). Strategic control: A new perspective. *Academy of Management Review, 12*(1), 91–103; Preble, J. F. (1992). Towards a comprehensive system of strategic control. *Journal of Management Studies, 29*(4), 391–409.

5. Kotter, J. P., & Schlesinger, L. A. (2008). Choosing strategies for change. *Harvard Business Review, 86*(7–8), 130–139; Lorange, P. M., Morton, S., & Goshal, S. (1986). *Strategic control.* St. Paul, MN: West; Simons, R. (1995). Control in the age of empowerment. *Harvard Business Review, 73*(2), 80–88.

6. Kennerley, M., Neely, A., & Adams, C. (2003). Survival of the fittest: Measuring performance in a changing business environment. *Measuring Business Excellence, 7*(4), 37–43.

7. Brant, J. R. (2003). Dare to be different. *Chief Executive, 188,* 36.

8. RE/MAX shines in REAL Trends 500 study. (2012, May 15). Retrieved from: http://public.remax.net/public-news/Pages/2012REALTrends500.aspx#.T7eoet4sfcs.wordpress. See RE/MAX website sections that contain news releases and recount its history: http://www.remax.com.

9. Szamosi, L. T., & Duxbury, L. (2002). Development of a measure to assess organizational change. *Journal of Organizational Change Management, 15*(2), 184–201.

10. Harkins, P., & Hollihan, K. (2004). *Everybody wins: The story and lessons behind RE/MAX*. New York: Wiley.

11. Miller, D. (2002). Successful change leaders: What makes them? What do they do that is different? *Journal of Change Management, 2*(4), 356–368.

12. Grasso, L. P. (2006). Barriers to lean accounting. *Cost Management, 20*(2), 6–19.

13. Weber, P. S., & Weber, J. E. (2001). Changes in employee perceptions during organizational change. *Leadership and Organizational Development Journal, 22*(5/6), 291–300.

14. Nauta, A., & Sanders, K. (2001). Causes and consequences of perceived goal differences between departments within manufacturing organizations. *Journal of Occupational and Organizational Psychology, 74*(Pt. 3), 321–342; Cooke, J. A. (2003). Want real collaboration? Change your measures. *Logistics Management, 42*(1), 37–41.

15. Denton, D. K. (2002). Learning how to keep score. *Industrial Management, 44*(2), 28–33; Anonymous. (2002). Materials management benchmarks easy to find, but often measure wrong things. *Hospital Materials Management, 27*(3), 3–4.

16. Sellers, P. (1992). The dumbest marketing ploy. *Fortune, 126*(7), 88–92.

17. Kanter, R. M. (2003). Leadership and the psychology of turnarounds. *Harvard Business Review, 81*(6), 58–67.

18. Kim, W. C., & Mauborgne, R. (2003). Fair process: Management in the knowledge economy. *Harvard Business Review, 81*(1), 127–139.

19. Cawsey, T., & Deszca, G. Personal experience.

20. Kerr, S. (1995). On the folly of rewarding A, while hoping for B. *Academy of Management Executive, 9*(1), 7–14.

21. Higgins, J. M., & Currie, D. M. (2004). It's time to rebalance the scorecard. *Business and Society Review, 109*(3), 297–309.

22. Eisenhardt, K. M., & Sull, D. N. (2001). Strategy as simple rules. *Harvard Business Review, 79*(1), 106–116.

23. Stiglitz, J. E. (2000). The contributions of the economics of information to twentieth century economics. *Quarterly Journal of Economics, 115*(4), 1441–1478.

24. Lawson, E., & Price, C. (2003). The psychology of change management. *McKinsey Quarterly, Special Edition: Organization, 2003.*

25. Simons, R. (1995). Control in the age of empowerment. *Harvard Business Review, 73*(2), 80–88.

26. Hoque, Z., & Chia, M. (2012). Competitive forces and the levers of control framework in a manufacturing setting. *Qualitative Research in Accounting and Management, 9*(2), 123–145; Tero-Seppo, T. (2005, September). The interplay of different levers of control: A case study of introducing a new performance measurement system. *Management Accounting Research, 16*(3), 293–320.

27. Kaplan, R. S., & Norton, D. P. (2000). Having trouble with your strategy? Then map it. *Harvard Business Review, 78*(5), 167–176.

28. Kaplan, R. S., & Norton, D. P. (2004). The strategy map: Guide to aligning intangible assets. *Strategy and Leadership, 32*(5), 10–17.

29. Cheng, M. M., & Humphreys, K. A. (2012, May). The differential improvement effects of the strategy map and scorecard perspectives on managers' strategic judgments. *The Accounting Review, 87*(3), 899–924; González, J. J. H., Calderón, M. A., & González, J. (2012). The alignment of managers' mental models with the balanced scorecard strategy map. *Total Quality Management and Business Excellence, 23*(5–6), 613.

30. Kaplan, R. S., & Norton, D. P. (2000). Having trouble with your strategy? Then map it. *Harvard Business Review, 78*(5), 167–176.

31. Kaplan, R. S., & Norton, D. P. (1996). Using the balanced scorecard as a strategic management system. *Harvard Business Review, 74*(1), 75–85.
32. Simon, R. (1999). How risky is your company? *Harvard Business Review, 77*(3), 85–94.
33. Sirkin, H. L., Keenan, P., & Jackson, A. (2005, October). The hard side of change management. *Harvard Business Review, 91*(9), 108–118.

Chapter 11

1. Pustkowski, R., Scott, J., & Tesvic, J. (2014). Why implementation matters. *Insights & Publications.* Retrieved August 2014 from http://www.mckinsey.com/insights/operations/why_implementation_matters.
2. Neilson, G. L., Martin, K. L., & Powers, E. (2008, June). The secrets to successful strategy execution. *Harvard Business Review,* 61–70.
3. Barkema, H. G., et al. (2002). Management challenges in a new time. *Academy of Management Journal, 45*(5), 916.
4. Galbraith, J. R. (2005, August). *Organizing for the future: Designing the 21st-century organization. Strategy and structure. The process will continue.* Academy of Management Annual Meeting, Hawaii.
5. Malone, T. (2005, August). *Inventing organizations.* Academy of Management Annual Meeting, Hawaii.
6. Refer to Beckhard, R., & Harris, R. T. (1987). *Organizational transitions: Managing complex change* (p. 104). Reading, MA: Addison-Wesley, for a further discussion on responsibility charting.

Index

About the Authors

Tupper F. Cawsey is professor emeritus of Business, Wilfrid Laurier University. He served as editor, *Case Research Journal,* for the North American Case Research Association. He has served on several boards of directors and was chair, Lutherwood Board from 2003–2008. Tupper was recognized nationally in 2001 as one of Canada's top five business professors by receiving the Leaders in Management Education award, sponsored by PricewaterhouseCoopers and the National Post. He is also the 1994 recipient of the David Bradford Educator Award, presented by the Organizational Behavior Teaching Society, and the 1990 Wilfrid Laurier University "Outstanding Teacher Award."

Tupper created the Case Track for the Administrative Sciences Association of Canada, a peer review process for cases. He is author or coauthor of over six books and monographs including, *Toolkit for Organizational Change—1st Edition, Canadian Cases in Human Resource Management, Cases in Organizational Behaviour,* and several monographs including *Control Systems in Excellent Canadian Companies* and the *Career Management Guide.* Tupper has over 50 refereed journal and conference publications. In 2005, he received the Christiansen Award from the Kaufman Foundation and the North American Case Research Association (NACRA), and in 2007 his case, "Board Games at Lutherwood," won the Directors College Corporate Governance Award and the Bronze Case Award at the NACRA Conference. In 2009, his case, "NuComm International," won the Gold Case Award at the NACRA Conference.

Gene Deszca is professor of Business Administration, a former MBA director, and currently the associate MBA director in the School of Business and Economics at Wilfrid Laurier University. He has played a variety of leadership roles at Laurier, including the development and launch of the full-time, one-year MBA program, the executive MBA program, and the undergraduate international concentration. He was instrumental in the development of the post-university professional accreditation programs for one of Canada's major accounting bodies and was a member of their national board of directors for several years. He loves working with students and currently teaches fourth-year undergraduate, MBA, and executive courses in Organizational Behaviour, Leading Organizational Change, Integrated Strategic Thinking, and International Business. His consulting work follows similar themes and focuses on organizational change and the design and delivery of executive development programs to facilitate it.

Gene is the author or coauthor of over 100 journal, conference publications/presentations, books, monographs, cases, and technical papers. These include the books *Canadian Cases in Human Resource Management* and *Cases in Organizational Behaviour* and the articles *Driving Loyalty Through Time-to-Value* and *Managing the New Product Development Process: Best-in-Class Principles and Leading Practices.* He is an active case writer, and his current research focuses on organizational change and the development of high-performance enterprises.

Cynthia Ingols is a professor of Practice, School of Management (SOM), Simmons College, Boston. At the SOM, she directs the internship program for undergraduate and MBA students and teaches courses in organizational change, career management, and leadership. Cynthia works extensively in the SOM's executive education programs. She leads, for example, *Strategic Leadership for Women,* an executive education program with a global reach that strengthens the leadership skills and self-confidence of its international participants. In addition, she chairs the SOM's Assessment of Learning (AOL) Committee, a group that asks: Are our students learning what we say that they are learning? Because of the best practices that Cynthia and her colleagues follow in this area, she speaks and publishes on the topic of assessment of student learning.

Cynthia received her doctorate from the Harvard Graduate School of Education in Organization Behavior and a master's degree in Political Science from the University of Wisconsin–Madison. She taught Management Communication at the Harvard Business School (HBS), managed the 65-person Case Writing and Research staff at HBS, and taught qualitative methods courses at several Boston-area universities. She serves as an editorial member of the *Case Research Journal.* She has served on corporate boards for several organizations, including FOX RPM and Biosymposia.

Cynthia focuses her consulting work in three areas: conducting diagnostic work to promote change in organizations; developing interactive executive education programs, particularly using cases and simulations; and coaching executives to enhance their leadership capacity and careers. Cynthia's research and publications follow similar lines. Her research on executive education programs has been published in leading journals, such as *Harvard Business Review, Organizational Dynamics,* and *Training.* Her research work on creating innovative organizational structures and change was published in the *Design Management Journal.* She has published numerous articles about careers in journals such as the *Journal of Career Development* and *Human Resource Development Quarterly.* She coauthored two books on career management: *Take Charge of Your Career* (2005) and *A Smart, Easy Guide to Interviewing* (2003). Cynthia joined the Tupper and Gene team to publish the second edition of *Organizational Change: An Action-Oriented Toolkit* (2012).